Multifunctional Nanocomposites for Targeted Drug Delivery in Cancer Therapy

Multifunctional Nanocomposites for Targeted Drug Delivery in Cancer Therapy

Edited by

AWESH K. YADAV

Department of Pharmaceutics, National Institute of Pharmaceutical
Education and Research-Raebareli, Lucknow, Uttar Pradesh, India

RAHUL SHUKLA

Department of Pharmaceutics, National Institute of Pharmaceutical
Education and Research-Raebareli, Lucknow, Uttar Pradesh, India

REWATI RAMAN UJJWAL

Department of Orthopedics, University of Massachusetts Chan
Medical School, Worcester, MA, United States

ELSEVIER

ACADEMIC PRESS

An imprint of Elsevier

For Information on all Academic Press publications
visit our website at https://www.elsevier.com/books-and-journals

Publisher: Stacy Masucci
Acquisitions Editor: Linda Versteeg-Buschman
Editorial Project Manager: Matthew Mapes
Production Project Manager: Sajana Devasi P. K.
Cover Designer: Greg Harris

Typeset by MPS Limited, Chennai, India

Working together
to grow libraries in
developing countries

www.elsevier.com • www.bookaid.org

Dedication

I would like to dedicate this work to my father (Mr. Shiv Narayan Yadav) and my mother (Mrs. Maya Yadav) who motivate me. This book is also dedicated to my brother Anand, my sisters Rashmi and Reeta, my wife Archana, my daughter Doorva, and son Darsh for their constant support in completing this book.

—Dr. Awesh K. Yadav

Dedicated to my mother: Maa Sharda Shukla

—Dr. Rahul Shukla

To my mother and father, who never stopped believing in me

—Dr. Rewati Raman Ujjwal

Contents

3. Autophagy-targeted drug delivery system in the management of cancer   63

Surbhi Gupta, Preeti Bisht, Raja Babu, Yati Sharma and Debapriya Garabadu

6.   Multifunctional nanocomposites for targeted drug delivery in breast cancer therapy   139

Poornima Agrawal, Sakshi Soni, Shivangi Agarwal, Tanweer Haider, Arun K. Iyer, Vandana Soni and Sushil K. Kashaw

14. Nanocarrier-mediated delivery for targeting for prostate cancer   355

Sumel Ashique, Prathap Madeswara Guptha, Satish Shilpi, Saurabh Sharma,
Shubneesh Kumar, Mohammad A. Altamimi, Afzal Hussain, Sandhya Chouhan and
Neeraj Mishra

List of contributors

Mayur Aalhate
Department of Pharmaceutics, National Institute of Pharmaceutical Education and Research (NIPER), Hyderabad, Telangana, India

Shivangi Agarwal
Department of Pharmaceutical Sciences, Dr. Harisingh Gour University (A Central University), Sagar, Madhya Pradesh, India

Poornima Agrawal
Department of Pharmaceutical Sciences, Dr. Harisingh Gour University (A Central University), Sagar, Madhya Pradesh, India

Mohammad A. Altamimi
Department of Pharmaceutics, College of Pharmacy, King Saud University, Riyadh, Emirate of the Riyadh Province, Saudi Arabia

Meghna Singh Amrita
Department of Pharmaceutics, Delhi Pharmaceutical Science and Research University, New Delhi, Delhi, India

Sumel Ashique
Department of Pharmaceutics, Bharat Institute of Technology (BIT), School of Pharmacy, Meerut, Uttar Pradesh, India; Department of Pharmaceutics, Pandaveswar School of Pharmacy, Pandaveswar, West Bengal, India

Raja Babu
Department of Pharmacology, School of Health Sciences, Central University of Punjab, Bathinda, Punjab, India

Sumedh Bahadure
Department of Pharmaceutics, National Institute of Pharmaceutical Education and Research, Guwahati, Assam, India

Akansha Bhatt
Biocon Limited, Bengaluru, Karnataka, India

Preeti Bisht
Department of Pharmacology, School of Health Sciences, Central University of Punjab, Bathinda, Punjab, India

Mrunalini Boddu
Chemical Biology Unit, Institute of Nano Science and Technology, SAS Nagar, Punjab, India

Meenakshi Kanwar Chauhan
Department of Pharmaceutics, Delhi Institute of Pharmaceutical Sciences and Research, DPSR-University, New Delhi, India

Sudarshan Naidu Chilamakuri
Department of Pharmaceutics, National Institute of Pharmaceutical Education and Research, Guwahati, Assam, India

Subhasree Roy Choudhury
Chemical Biology Unit, Institute of Nano Science and Technology, SAS Nagar, Punjab, India

Sandhya Chouhan
Noida Institute of Engineering and Technology (Pharmacy Institute), Greater Noida, Uttar Pradesh, India

Adinath Dadhale
Department of Pharmaceutics, National Institute of Pharmaceutical Education and Research, Guwahati, Assam, India

Anish Dhuri
Department of Pharmaceutics, National Institute of Pharmaceutical Education and Research (NIPER), Hyderabad, Telangana, India

Mahesh Gaikwad
Department of Pharmaceutics, National Institute of Pharmaceutical Education and Research-Raebareli, Lucknow, Uttar Pradesh, India

Debapriya Garabadu
Department of Pharmacology, School of Health Sciences, Central University of Punjab, Bathinda, Punjab, India

Ashish Garg
Department of P.G. Studies and Research in Chemistry and Pharmacy, Rani Durgavati University, Jabalpur, Madhya Pradesh, India

Manish Kumar Goel
Department of Pharmacy, Madhav University, Pindwara, Rajasthan, India

Apurba Gouri
Chemical Biology Unit, Institute of Nano Science and Technology, SAS Nagar, Punjab, India

Arvind Gulbake
Department of Pharmaceutics, National Institute of Pharmaceutical Education and Research, Guwahati, Assam, India

Madhu Gupta
Department of Pharmaceutics, Delhi Pharmaceutical Science and Research University, New jjjjjDelhi, Delhi, India

Surbhi Gupta
Department of Pharmacology, School of Health Sciences, Central University of Punjab, Bathinda, Punjab, India

Ujala Gupta
Department of Pharmaceutics, National Institute of Pharmaceutical Education and Research (NIPER), Hyderabad, Telangana, India

Prathap Madeswara Guptha
Amity Institute of Pharmacy, Amity University Madhya Pradesh, Gwalior, Madhya Pradesh, India

Tanweer Haider
Department of Pharmaceutical Sciences, Dr. Harisingh Gour University (A Central University), Sagar, Madhya Pradesh, India

Afzal Hussain
Department of Pharmaceutics, College of Pharmacy, King Saud University, Riyadh, Emirate of the Riyadh Province, Saudi Arabia

Arun K. Iyer
Use-inspired Biomaterials & Integrated Nano Delivery (U–BiND) Systems Laboratory, Department of Pharmaceutical Sciences, Wayne State University, Detroit, MI, United States; Molecular Imaging Program, Karmanos Cancer Institute, Detroit, MI, United States

Sunil K. Jain
Department of Pharmacy, Guru Ghasidas Vishwavidyalaya (A Central University), Bilaspur, Chhattisgarh, India

Ramakant Joshi
School of Studies in Pharmaceutical Sciences, Jiwaji University, Gwalior, Madhya Pradesh, India

Surajit Karmakar
Chemical Biology Unit, Institute of Nano Science and Technology, SAS Nagar, Punjab, India

Sushil K. Kashaw
Department of Pharmaceutical Sciences, Dr. Harisingh Gour University (A Central University), Sagar, Madhya Pradesh, India

Monika Kaurav
KIET School of Pharmacy, KIET Group of Institutions Delhi-NCR, Ghaziabad, Uttar Pradesh, India

Kedar Khaparkhuntikar
Department of Pharmaceutics, National Institute of Pharmaceutical Education and Research (NIPER), Hyderabad, Telangana, India

Ankaj Kumar
Department of Pharmaceutics, National Institute of Pharmaceutical Education and Research, Guwahati, Assam, India

Ankit Kumar
Department of Pharmacology and Toxicology, National Institute of Pharmaceutical Education and Research (NIPER) – Guwahati, Kamrup, Assam, India

Shubneesh Kumar
Department of Pharmaceutics, Bharat Institute of Technology (BIT), School of Pharmacy, Meerut, Uttar Pradesh, India; Department of Life Sciences, School of Basic Sciences and Research, Sharda University, Greater Noida, Uttar Pradesh, India

Shweta Kumar
Department of General Medicine, All India Institute of Medical Sciences, Bhopal, Madhya Pradesh, India

Srushti Mahajan
Department of Pharmaceutics, National Institute of Pharmaceutical Education and Research (NIPER), Hyderabad, Telangana, India

J. Mahendran
Chemical Biology Unit, Institute of Nano Science and Technology, SAS Nagar, Punjab, India

Indrani Maji
Department of Pharmaceutics, National Institute of Pharmaceutical Education and Research (NIPER), Hyderabad, Telangana, India

Farhan Mazahir
Department of Pharmaceutics, National Institute of Pharmaceutical Education and Research-Raebareli, Lucknow, Uttar Pradesh, India

Sunita Minz
Department of Pharmacy, Indira Gandhi National Tribal University (A Central University), Amarkantak, Madhya Pradesh, India

Awanish Mishra
Department of Pharmacology and Toxicology, National Institute of Pharmaceutical Education and Research (NIPER) – Guwahati, Kamrup, Assam, India

Neeraj Mishra
Amity Institute of Pharmacy, Amity University Madhya Pradesh, Gwalior, Madhya Pradesh, India

Namitha Mohan C.
Department of Pharmaceutics, National Institute of Pharmaceutical Education and Research (NIPER), Hyderabad, Telangana, India

Soni Jignesh Mohanbhai
Chemical Biology Unit, Institute of Nano Science and Technology, SAS Nagar, Punjab, India

Mohd Aman Mohd Ateeq
Department of Pharmaceutics, National Institute of Pharmaceutical Education and Research (NIPER), Hyderabad, Telangana, India

Pooja Raj Mongia
Department of Pharmaceutics, DIPSAR, Delhi Institute of Pharmaceutical Science and Research, New Delhi, Delhi, India

Rajesh Singh Pawar
Truba Institute of Pharmacy, Bhopal, Madhya Pradesh, India

Sulakshana Pawar
Institute of Pharmacy, Bundelkhand University, Jhansi, Uttar Pradesh, India

Rakesh Raj
Department of Pharmacy, Delhi Skill and Entrepreneurship University, DSEU Maharani Bagh Campus, New Delhi, Delhi, India

Kuldeep Rajpoot
Department of Pharmacy, Guru Ghasidas Vishwavidyalaya (A Central University), Bilaspur, Chhattisgarh, India

Munindra Ruwali
Amity Institute of Biotechnology, Amity University Haryana, Gurgaon, Haryana, India

Kantrol Sahu
School of Pharmacy, Chouksey Engineering College, Bilaspur, Chhattisgarh, India

Mohammed Nadim Sardoiwala
Chemical Biology Unit, Institute of Nano Science and Technology, SAS Nagar, Punjab, India

Angela Sharma
Chemical Biology Unit, Institute of Nano Science and Technology, SAS Nagar, Punjab, India

Saurabh Sharma
School of Pharmaceutical Sciences, CT University, Sidhwan Khurd, Punjab, India; Chandigarh College of Pharmacy, Chandigarh Group of Colleges, Landran, Greater Mohali, Punjab, India

Yati Sharma
Institute of Pharmaceutical Research, GLA University, Mathura, Uttar Pradesh, India

Satish Shilpi
Amity Institute of Pharmacy, Amity University Madhya Pradesh, Gwalior, Madhya Pradesh, India; Department of Pharmacy, DIT University, Dehradun, Uttarakhand, India

Ajay Kumar Shukla
Institute of Pharmacy, Dr. Ram Manohar Lohia, Avadh University, Ayodhya, Uttar Pradesh, India

Rahul Shukla
Department of Pharmaceutics, National Institute of Pharmaceutical Education and Research-Raebareli, Lucknow, Uttar Pradesh, India

Shalini Shukla
Department of Pharmaceutics, National Institute of Pharmaceutical Education and Research-Raebareli, Lucknow, Uttar Pradesh, India

Pankaj Kumar Singh
Department of Pharmaceutics, National Institute of Pharmaceutical Education and Research (NIPER), Hyderabad, Telangana, India

Sandeep Kumar Singh
Institute of Pharmacy, Dr. Ram Manohar Lohia, Avadh University, Ayodhya, Uttar Pradesh, India

Shalu Singh
Department of Pharmaceutics, National Institute of Pharmaceutical Education and Research-Raebareli, Lucknow, Uttar Pradesh, India

Sakshi Soni
Department of Pharmaceutical Sciences, Dr. Harisingh Gour University (A Central University), Sagar, Madhya Pradesh, India

Vandana Soni
Department of Pharmaceutical Sciences, Dr. Harisingh Gour University (A Central University), Sagar, Madhya Pradesh, India

Saurabh Srivastava
Department of Pharmaceutics, National Institute of Pharmaceutical Education and Research (NIPER), Hyderabad, Telangana, India

Ajay Suryawanshi
Department of Pharmaceutics, National Institute of Pharmaceutical Education and Research-Raebareli, Lucknow, Uttar Pradesh, India

Monika Targhotra
Department of Pharmaceutics, Delhi Institute of Pharmaceutical Sciences and Research, DPSR-University, New Delhi, India

Awesh K. Yadav
Department of Pharmaceutics, National Institute of Pharmaceutical Education and Research-Raebareli, Lucknow, Uttar Pradesh, India

Krishna Yadav
Raipur Institute of Pharmaceutical Education and Research, Sarona, Raipur, Chhattisgarh, India

CHAPTER 1

Introduction: an overview of the multifunctional nanocomposites

Mahesh Gaikwad*, Ajay Suryawanshi*, Farhan Mazahir and Awesh K. Yadav
Department of Pharmaceutics, National Institute of Pharmaceutical Education and Research-Raebareli, Lucknow, Uttar Pradesh, India

1.1 Introduction

Nanotechnology is one of the most interesting and important areas for research since the last century. Numerous developments have been made since then in the area of nanotechnology (Marquis et al., 2011). A composite has defined as a material in which two or more different constituent materials each having their important characteristics like chemical or physical properties are combined simultaneously to form a new substance with excellent properties better than that of original materials in a particular structure. Some properties of composites are stiffness and specific strength, corrosion resistance, repairing damaged structures, and protection against fatigue (Sen, 2020). Composite systems involve three main matrix types, i.e., metal, ceramic, and polymer with different supplements in various forms such as laminar, fillers, fiber, particle, and flake (Zaferani and Chapter, 2018) (Fig. 1.1).

The nanocomposite (NC) term includes from a broad range of materials available from 3D metal matrix composites, two-dimensional (2D) lamellar composites, and single-dimensional nanowires to zero-dimensional core shells, which represent numerous varieties of nanomixed and layered materials. NC is defined as multiphase solid material that contains one or more phases of nanomaterials. This study is based on the straightforward premise that the use of components with measurements in the nano-size range enables the design and production of novel materials with extraordinary flexibility and enhances their physical properties (Jayalekshmi, 2018). Fullerenes, inorganic nanoclusters, metals, clays, oxides, semiconductors, various organic polymers, organic compounds, biological molecules, enzymes, and the sol-gel generated polymers can be combined to form NC (Sen, 2020). Refer to Fig. 1.2.

In the broadest sense, the goal of creating a NC is to combine one or more discontinuous nano-dimensional phases into a single continuous macrophase in order to produce

---

* Equal contribution.

Multifunctional Nanocomposites for Targeted Drug Delivery in Cancer Therapy
DOI: https://doi.org/10.1016/B978-0-323-95303-0.00011-3

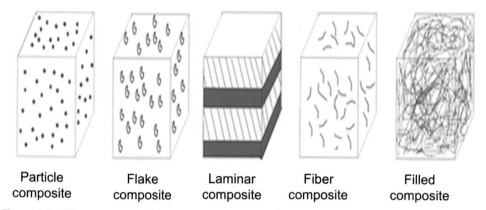

Particle	Flake	Laminar	Fiber	Filled
composite	composite	composite	composite	composite

Figure 1.1 Different common forms of composites.

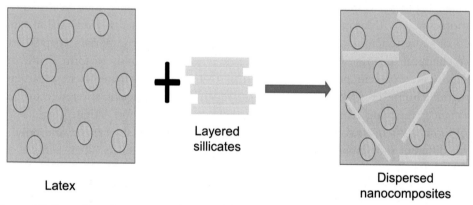

Figure 1.2 Formation of nanocomposite materials.

"synergistic properties," which refer to the physical and chemical characteristics of the combined entity being fundamentally distinct from individual component/material.

In this situation, one of the parts of the combined substance is usually significantly more concentrated and forms a continuous "matrix" encircling the others, which take on the function of a "nanofiller" or "reinforcement." Each of the various phases is structure and property-integrated to create hybrid materials with multifunctionalities in terms of both structures and material characteristics throughout the NC production process. The demand for higher-performance, more sustainable, and multifunctional nanomaterials in the latter half of the 20th century sparked an increase in research related to nanotechnology and nanocomposites. New materials and characterization tools in nanotechnology have made it possible for next-generation NCs to be simple to control and also have a variety of built-in engineering functions (Yan and Guo, 2018).

In terms of mechanics, NCs are different from conventional composite materials due to their unusually high surface-to-volume ratio of the reinforcing phase or their unusually high aspect ratio. The reinforcing material is formed from particles (e.g., minerals), sheets (e.g., exfoliated clay stacks), or fibers (e.g., carbon nanotubes [CNTs] or electrospun fibers). The area of interfaces between the matrix and reinforcement phase affects the matrix material properties of the NC (Schadler, 2003).

1.2 Structure and manufacturing processes for nanocomposite

NCs are mixed materials from a microscopic perspective, and their properties are primarily influenced by the composition, interfacial properties, and structure of their individual components. Typically, they have more complicated structures than microcomposites. (i.e., silicate nanoplatelets in polymer NC). In particular, for CNT-reinforced composite, nanofiller aggregation, and orientation play a critical role in influencing their structural characteristics. In more specific terms, aggregation predominates in NCs containing spherical nanoparticles. On the other hand, when it comes to nanofillers with various shape factors and a large interfacial area in relation to volume, the interfacial interactions are more significant. This is specifically relevant to how surface extension affects surface energy, which largely affects interactions in filler matrixes.

The final characteristics of the NCs can be significantly influenced by enhancing filler dispersion and homogeneity through careful processing mode selection. When creating a NC, the monomer and nano reinforcement are first combined. It is permitted for the monomer to intercalate between the layers.

According to the working principle that is influenced by chemical or physical (solvent or temperature) forces, NCs can be produced in a variety of ways, which can be categorized into three groups:

1.2.1 In situ polymerization

The monomer is polymerized once it has been intercalated. Any functionality responsible for catalyzing the process or some surface alteration at the silicate surface could be the cause of the polymerization (Alexandre and Dubois, 2000). Using virgin or sulfonated graphene oxides (SGOs) and a semiaromatic polyamide (PA), in situ interfacial polymerization was used to create NCs SGO or graphene oxide (GO), respectively. The interface between aqueous triethylenetetramine solutions containing various concentrations of disseminated SGO or GO nanosheets and an isophthaloyl dichloride nonaqueous solution led to the formation of the PA chains. The effects of pristine GO and SGO upon the structure, dynamic mechanical, and thermal stability properties of PA were examined through the use of X-ray diffractometry and Fourier transform infrared (FTIR) spectroscopy, and favorable interfacial interactions between SGO and PA were established. SGO thus markedly improved the heat stability of PA and char residues. Additionally, the addition of both pure and sulfonated GO nanosheets improved the PA's storage modulus and changed its glass transition temperature. Finally, PA displayed improvements in its conductance with dielectric constants of 10 and 3 times, respectively, by adding SGO content at 1.0 wt.% concentration (Yousefian-Arani et al., 2018).

1.2.2 Solvent-assisted methods

The chemical method may be one of the most useful methods for laboratory research, but this does not apply to large-scale production for the industrial market. With solvent-assisted methods, it is possible to use polymer, which is water-soluble, modulating the structure effect of the product. However, just a small magnitude of polymer matrices is compatible with this process, which is neither industrial nor economically feasible. A proper selection of the solvent in this case enables the complete dissolution of the polymer as well as the wide distribution of the layered nano reinforcement by assisting the movement of polymer chains, that in turn assists in the complexation of chains of the polymer along the tiered nano reinforcement (Jouault et al., 2014). These bare silica NPs and poly (2-vinyl pyridine) (PVP) NCs were made by casting them with two distinct solvents, methyl ethyl ketone (MEK) and the pyridine. The PVP dispersion in MEK strongly binds to the silica surface to form a layer of bound polymer that is temporally stable. Independent of the molecular weight of PVP, concentration, or NP loading, the resulting "hairy" particles were stabilized by a steric charge against agglomeration, resulting in excellent NP dispersion being always attained. PVP, on the other hand, did not adhere to the silica NPs in pyridine. Thus, a delicate balance between repulsion that is dependent on the electrostatic charge, polymer-induced depletion, and attraction, and the kinetic slowness of diffusion-limited NP aggregation controlled the phase behavior in this scenario.

1.2.3 Melt mixing methods

By managing material properties in relation to manufacturing time through a continuous, pressure, and temperature-controlled, rapid, and versatile operation for transforming raw materials into finished goods, melt extrusion techniques enable the manufacture of the final NCs. These techniques are "green" (solvent-free), industrially, and economically viable. Extruders or internal mixers are essentially employed. When polymer and nano reinforcement are combined in the extruder and vigorously mixed for a while, NC emerges from the die. The only source of polymer mobility in this approach is thermal energy (Whittington et al., 2013). There is no use of organic solvents, the approach is, therefore, environment friendly, but it could be intrusive when used with polymers that are susceptible to temperature breakdown (such as thermosets) (Abdelrazek et al., 2018). It is clear that the primary criteria to select the manufacturing process is not specific to the production of NC materials but may be influenced by particular product characteristics such as the necessary product geometry, the required performance, the cost, and the ease of manufacturing (Cubeddu et al., 2014).

Melt mixing methods are further subdivided into many types, which are described below.

1.2.3.1 Hydrothermal synthesis
This method is important for precipitating single or multiphase metal and semiconductor metal oxides obtained from their equivalent homogeneous or heterogeneous solution. It is preferred for forming many single or multiphase oxides and phosphates and which is a single-step process. Due to its purity and adaptability, this method is used to grow single crystals. This method could be utilized to form nanomaterial for use in environmental and energy applications differing from dye-sensitized solar cells to catalysis (Whittington et al., 2013).

1.2.3.2 Sol-gel synthesis
This synthesis method prepares a molecule from a metal or metalloid element and particular ligands by using a colloidal solution. From this synthesis, many types of nanocrystalline metal oxides, alloys, and composite metal or semiconductor metal oxides can be produced (Leventis et al., 2009).

1.2.3.3 Polymerized complex method (Pechini process)
A polymeric precursor is used in a wet chemical technique that depends on the Pechini process to form a large type of ceramic oxide. This process involves significant properties for processing ceramic powders with exact control of stoichiometry, at molecular scale uniform mixing of multicomponent and uniformity. This method is useful for the synthesis of high-temperature superconductors, fluorescent, dielectric, magnetic materials, and catalysts (Suresh Kumar et al., 2012).

1.2.3.4 Chemical vapor deposition
A chemical reaction in the vapor phase can result in chemical vapor deposition (CVD), which can form a coating of solid material on a heated surface. This flexible method can lead to nano/microstructured materials such as coatings, powders, fibers, metals, metal oxides, and other multiphase compounds as nonmetallic components like silicon and carbon. A benefit of CVD is its high throughput due to its fast rate of deposition and the creation of nanomaterials with one or more phases (Suresh Kumar et al., 2012).

1.2.3.5 Microwave synthesis

The use of microwave processing is widespread and includes everything from food processing to chemical and medical applications. Design of microwave equipment, creation of new materials, sintering, joining, and modeling of microwave material interaction are key areas of research in microwave processing. Microwave processing is being used to create carbon fibers and ceramics at low temperatures and short processing times because it provides homogeneous heating at a lower temperature.

Due to their synergy or improved qualities in comparison to their base counterparts, multifunctional NCs that combine the benefits of two or more basic constituents have drawn a lot of attention. Considerable focus has been placed on noble metal-based systems in the field of multifunctional nanomaterials, immobilizing noble metal onto various inorganic/organic substrates to produce the necessary functional NC (Sahay et al., 2012).

1.3 Properties of nanocomposites

NCs exhibit numerous characteristic properties that are made use of for their application in various fields of industry and research. Some of the most important properties are described below.

1.3.1 Electrical properties

The addition of CNTs to composites significantly improves the composite's electrical conductivity. The mechanical and thermal properties of composites are said to significantly improve with the inclusion of CNTs.

Thermal and electrical characteristics are considerably improved by multiscale reinforcement with CNTs. Traditional fillers like carbon and glass fibers offer a potential approach to the creation of composites with many uses (Choong et al., 2015).

Different nanoparticles, such as CNTs, can be added to clean thermoplastics and endless fiber-reinforced composites to significantly improve their properties. The polymer film and organic sheet now have better electrical conductivity because of the addition of carbon black and CNTs. Numerous variables, including the proportion of conductive fillers employed in the polymers, affect electrical conductivity. In comparison with amorphous polycarbonate (PC), semicrystalline PA has lower electrical conductivity. The aggregation of nanofibrils during the conversion of polymer films into organic sheets increases electrical conductivity (Hildebrandt and Mitschang, 2011).

An electric current can flow through conductive NCs, and an insulator like PC may be made conductive. It is a low-cost plastic with known mechanical and optical qualities that can be used in a more significant and advanced horizon in the future. Researchers changed the conductivity of PC, by adding CNTs, making the material into highly conductive NCs. A sufficient amount of CNTs can make plastic more electrically conductive. These cheap plastics are utilized to create optical disks, which are having use in high-tech military aircraft to shield them from developing electrical changes and failure-causing pulses. The conductivity of NCs also changes when the number of CNTs in PC is altered. Researchers changed the conductivity of PC, which was previously a poor conductor, by adding CNTs, making the material highly conductive NC. As the number of CNTs in plastic increases dramatically its conductivity. Such cheap plastic is utilized in the production of specialized military aircraft that employ optical disks to shield them from electrical changes in the structure. Conductivity of NCs is altered by changing the number of by CNTs in PC (Nogi and Yano, 2008).

According to the research, graphene, GO, and solar cells made of reduced GO are the best possible material for improving electrical conductivity owing to their excellent heat conductivity, high flexibility, mechanical, extraordinary durability, electrical, big particular surface area, and 2D organization. Electrochemical methods for enhancing chemical characteristics, and processability of their use. The mixture of graphene with nanoparticles will be beneficial for application in interfacial layers of electronic electrodes that are transparent (Díez-Pascual et al., 2018).

By using the melt mixing approach, flexible thermoelectric material can be produced. An electrical network is created by incorporating CNTs into the polypropylene matrix (Du et al., 2012).

1.3.2 Multifunctionality

Effective sensors that perform many functions can frequently be made with multifunctional NCs that can be used for co-oxidation, gas sensing, and Au (Pt) functionalized iron oxide (Fe_2O_3) applications. In a fixed poor stainless steel tubular reactor, catalytic activity was assessed while a gas sensing test was conducted by the gas sensing measuring equipment. In comparison to nonfunctionalized Fe_2O_3, they discovered that modified gold nanoparticles (AuNPs) have increased activity due to their functionality. The active AuNPs, which serve as a catalyst for sensing surface reactions and exhibited strong reactivity at low-temperature co-oxidation, are responsible for the improved results (Chen et al., 2011).

Due to the desirable characteristics and versatility of polymeric materials, they are getting a lot of attention. Most polymers are crucial for structural applications like marine, aerospace, automotive, etc. Very notably, high-strength thermoset polymers enable them to be compatible with metallic components and serve as replacements in a variety of settings. Because thermoset polymers are so simple to work with, they are highly used materials. NCs offer a number of advantages overconventional composite materials, including greater sustainability, lightness, and durability, thanks to recent advancements in nanotechnology (Garg et al., 2016). Due to their improved mechanical characteristics and higher durability, NCs have attracted a lot of interest. NCs made of thermoset materials are produced using a variety of materials. Carbon nanoparticles and nanoclays are the most often used materials (Wang and Irudayaraj, 2010).

The tensile and flexural strength of NCs that contain 10%−12% nanoclays is higher than that of nano calcium-based composites. Exfoliated and intercalated nanoparticles were found in nanoclay composites. This improves the mechanical and physical introduction of the fiber and matrix interface, which significantly aids in stress absorption and improves the mechanical properties of NCs (Siró and Plackett, 2010).

Liquid crystals that have been solidified have been employed in a variety of optical applications for security papers. Wood cellulose NCs are another source of the organic light-emitting diode that can be made for display substrates. Researchers succeeded in creating optically transparent wood cellulose NCs with low thermal expansion and extraordinary modulus. Additionally, they were able to successfully deposit electroluminescence on transparent, flexible wood cellulose NCs, which have a low thermal expansion coefficient.

Low concentrations of cellulose whiskers, such as those seen in low thickness polymer electrolytes used in lithium batteries, can also be employed to prevent dispersion ionic conductivity. Melamine-formaldehyde and micro-fibrillated cellulose can be used to create speaker membranes with low density and highly remarkable modulus. When utilized as an affinity membrane, electrospun cellulose nanofibers (CNFs) allow for the purification and clarification of molecules based on their biological roles or physical or chemical properties rather than their size or weight (Matsumura et al., 2000).

The production of sustainable materials with enhanced functionality and mechanical qualities benefits greatly from the use of NC. For sustainability and to reduce reliance on resins derived from petroleum, scientists are working to adapt thermoset NCs such that they use polyols and chemicals derived from vegetable oil rather than biobased resins. Recent studies claim that ecofriendly resins based on vegetable oils can also be used to create NC.

1.3.3 Mechanical properties

In the past, nanocellulose materials were combined with thermoplastic materials, which have the advantages of high fracture toughness and recyclable materials. Researchers addressed a few mechanical property findings for nanocellulose thermoset composites. Using nanocellulose in thermoplastic composites greatly improves the strength and stiffness of the material. Nanocellulose-based dispersed or particulate composites benefit from the comparatively high aspect ratio of the cellulose fibers or particles. It has also been documented how the amount of fiber affects the mechanical and thermal expansion characteristics of biocomposites based on CNFs. When phenolic resin was used along with CNFs, it was shown that fiber content might increase laminarly by up to 40%.

By adding CNF up to 2% weight, the mechanical characteristics of composites significantly increased, but further additions of CNF decreased mechanical and thermal properties due to agglomeration (Yu and Yan, 2017).

They discovered that by adding CNF, the fracture characteristics of the polylactic acid (PLA) matrix around bamboo fibers were improved, preventing the emergence of abrupt cracks. When CNF was added, it caused a 1% weight increase that doubled fracture energy. Researchers have looked into how properly processing CNF can result in lightweight composites with unique barrier and transparency properties that have several uses in electronics, energy storage devices, packaging, pharmaceuticals, and the production of automobiles. Barrier materials made of nanocellulose films are an option. Due to their hydrophobic properties, high-porosity aerogels can also be utilized to absorb moisture while still allowing the flow of gases (Jonoobi et al., 2010).

1.3.4 Biomedical properties

For use in biomedical applications, some novel materials are being created. Materials used in biomedical applications must exhibit certain structural, biological, physical, chemical, and mechanical properties, that is, they must be compatible with the tissues of their indirect hosts. Particularly important mechanical qualities are elastic modulus, load transfer, stiffness, and strength. The desired physical qualities can be specifically tailored using metals, polymers, and ceramic composites. The following list includes a few composites using polymer filler (Garmendia et al., 2010).

- Epoxide carbon fiber composite external fixators are used to repair bone fractures.
- Bone plates and screws.
- Joint replacements: A total hip replacement uses carbon fibers (PEEK).

1.3.5 Optical properties

NC nanosized aluminum oxide (Al_2O_3) distributed in the resin has a higher optical transmittance value in the near-infrared reflectance (NIR) after in situ sanitization and subsequent polymerization in comparison with untreated Al_2O_3. The addition of AuNPs to composites made up of polyethylene oxide and PVP (PEO/PVP) significantly increased the values of optical parameters such as reflectivity, reaction activation energy, and optical energy gap in a concentration-dependent manner (Abdelrazek et al., 2018).

1.3.6 Magnetic properties

One type of composite with metal nanoparticles and the other with ferrite nanoparticles exhibit magnetic characteristics. The majority of the nanoparticles lack hysteresis, which suggests a superparamagnetic substance. Fe_2O_3 content (2.8%) makes polymer

NC optically transparent and free of hysteresis at normal temperature. They also discovered that Y-Fe_2O_3 nanoparticle-containing NCs with electromagnetic polymer matrix were devoid of hysteresis (Makarchuk et al., 2016).

1.4 Classification of multifunctional nanocomposite

NCs are broadly classified into natural biopolymer-based, synthetic polymer-based, metal-based, and carbon-based NCs. Details of all these types of NCs are discussed here.

1.4.1 Biopolymer-based multifunctional nanocomposite

Biopolymers are obtained from plants, animals, and microbes. These are alternatives to synthetic polymers made from natural resources. Biopolymers are degraded by particular microbes and water through enzymatic activity. Several benefits of biopolymers include minimal extraction costs, environmental friendliness, biodegradability, biocompatibility, and the lack of environmental toxicity (Hassan et al., 2021). Consequently, biopolymers have been employed often in historical biological, pharmaceutical, food, and environmental industrial operations. Examples of biopolymers include protein separations (whey and gelatin), dietary fibers (pullulan and the chitosan [CS], alginates (Algs), and the derivatives of cellulose), lipids, and polysaccharides (honeybees wax and the fatty acids, which are unsaturated in nature). Additionally, polyvinyl alcohol (PVA) and polybutylene succinate, polyhydroxy butyrate, and polycaprolactone are a few examples of synthetic biopolymers and their mixtures (Basavegowda and Baek, 2021). Alg and CS are two natural polymers that have been promoted as being biocompatible, and mucoadhesive, that leading to a variety of pharmaceutical as well as biomedical uses, such as the creation of controlled release devices. Chitin, a component of crustacean exoskeletons, is deacetylated to produce cationic polysaccharides. The chemical characteristics of CS (α-[1−4] 2-amino 2-deoxy b-D glucan), a mucopolysaccharide nearly linked to cellulose, are defined by the molecular weight and the amount of deacetylation for viscosity. Rouget initially described it in 1859, but Hoppe-Seyler gave its official name in 1894. Mucoadhesive qualities of CS have been utilized for mucosal medication delivery. Additionally, by opening up tight intersections of the mucosal layer hindrances, the positive charge amino group at C-2 of CS connects well with the negatively charged surfaces of cells as well as tight junctions to enable paracellular pathway transport of wide-ranging hydrophilic compounds. Alg is an anionic polymer made up of varying lengths of β-D-mannuronic acid (M), α-L-guluronic acid (G), and alternate (MG) blocks that are 1,4-connected. Alg is a mucoadhesive, biocompatible, nonimmunogenic, nontoxic, and biodegradable polymer, making it a viable option for mucosal protein/antigen conveyance.

Some of the most important and highly useful biopolymers used for manufacturing NCs are described below.

1.4.1.1 Gelatin

It is widely known that gelatin is a naturally occurring, biodegradable protein that is obtained from the chemical and structural breakdown of collagen. It is a unique blend of single, multiple-stranded polypeptides that degrade in vivo into their constituent amino acids, primarily glycine, proline, and hydroxyproline. PEGylation of the particles enhances their endocytotic uptake into cells and fundamentally boosts their bloodstream circulation time. Gelatin nanoparticles modified with antibodies have been used to target lymphocyte uptake.

1.4.1.2 Polyanhydrides and polyphosphazenes

These are inorganic backbone compounds made up of phosphorous and nitrogen connected to one another directly by spinning single and double bonds, polyphosphazene are a unique family of degradable polymers. Two carbonyl groups connected by an ether link make up the class of surface-dissolving polymers known as polyanhydrides, which have only been researched for biological purposes.

1.4.1.3 Pullulan

Three a–1,4-linked glucose molecules are polymerized into three linear, water-soluble polysaccharides called pullulan by a–1,6 linkage on the terminal glucose molecule. Aureobasidium pullulans are a category of yeast that produces pullulan during fermentation (Kaur et al., 2018).

1.4.1.4 Chitosan-based nanocomposite

Glucosamine and N-acetylglucosamine residues with a 1,4-linkage make up the majority of CS. CS has exceptional biological characteristics that have facilitated the implementation of the technology in the pharmaceutical and medicinal fields, hydrogels, drug delivery systems, membranes, biomedicine, and others. A tissue engineering scaffold CS containing amine groups that have vast applications. However, other characteristics of chitin, such as its low solubility and its use for a particular application may be constrained by its toxicity in organic solvents or water. CS is solubilized via protonation of the $-NH_2$ functional group (Paquin et al., 2015). The chemical modifications of the chain, often by grafting the functional groups, without modifying the basic skeleton to retain the original capabilities, is a useful technique to enhance or impart new qualities to CS. The functionalization of the main amine group is typically accomplished by a hydroxyl group or quaternization by using an acidic polyelectrolyte (Li et al., 2018a).

Kartika et al. in the year 2020 developed a hybrid system that was highly biocompatible, water dispersible, fluorescent, and superparamagnetic, the multifunctional NC created by using the solvothermal approach. This hybrid had significant doxorubicin (DOX) anticancer drug loading capability of around 0.448 mg/mL. The release of

DOX could be magnetically regulated and pH-triggered. Particularly, folic acid (FA) surface modification of Fe_3O_4NPs led to enhanced cancer cell absorption. The nature of reduced graphene oxide (rGO)/Fe_3O_4/CS NC using A549 and HEK293 cells has been proved to be biocompatible during the toxicological investigation. The in vitro cellular imaging of A549 and MCF-7 cells rGO/ Fe_3O_4/CS/DOX/FA revealed significant localization in the cytoplasm (Karthika et al., 2020).

Liu et al. prepared NC hydrogel made up of CS-montmorillonite (MMT) in 2008, which was made to control the release of vitamin B12 during electrostimulation. The degree of crosslinking between CS and MMT significantly influenced the release of vitamin B12. Exfoliated silica nanosheets, which functioned as a crosslinking agent, determined the crosslinking density between CS and MMT as a crosslinker. When MMT concentration is low the kinetics of release are pseudo-first order. The release pattern during electrostimulation switched from diffusion to the swelling-regulated type. The diffusing exponent and the sensitivity of the nano hydrogel to electrostimulation were both reduced by further raising the MMT concentration. Additionally, a repeatedly performed "on" and "off" operation discloses as the electroresponsiveness of hydrogel was decreased along higher MMT concentrations, and its antifatigue behavior was noticeably increased. When compared to pure CS, the nano hydrogel containing 2 wt.% MMT demonstrated superior antifatigue performance and a pulsatile release profile that was mechanically dependable and practically desired (Liu et al., 2008).

A NC of magnetite (Fe_3O_4) and CS was developed by Arias et al. in the year 2012 for the intravenous administration of the anticancer nucleoside analog gemcitabine. By monitoring the hysteresis cycle while being subjected to a 1.1 Tesla (T) magnetic responsiveness was evaluated by a strong magnet. The loaded drug in the polymeric shell provided a delayed medication release and an increased drug loading profile. Consequently, a new delivery system was created that had magnetically focused, stimuli-sensitive, and high drug loading, delayed release, as well as the capacity to cause overheating, and the ability to treat cancer successfully. The delivery system could treat cancer successfully. Another study used a mesoporous magnetic NC made of silicon dioxide (SiO_2) and magnetite to regulate the DOX release. It was found that the release behavior was diffusion-regulated by using the Higuchi model (Arias et al., 2012).

1.4.1.5 Alginate-based nanocomposite

Brown seaweed (Phaeophyceae) contains natural polysaccharide polymers known as Algs. D-mannuronic acid and L-guluronic acid residues may be combined to form the linear polymer known as alginic acid (Porter et al., 2021). A weak alkaline solution is used to extract the seaweed, solubilizing the alginic acid in the process. After treatment, free alginic acid is produced. The resultant dense, viscous mass contains mineral acids. Afterward, the alginic acid may be changed into sodium Alg, the primary type of salt utilized. There are positioned residues inside the polymer chain blocks. These are symmetrical blocks (consisting of blocks either of acid residue or the acid residue alone composed of mannuronic acid or alternating components with guluronic acids, as well). According to previous reports, Algs were hydrolyzed during the protonation process, which is affected by time, temperature, and pH. Algs from various sources have varied ratios of blocks. Alginic acid is hydrated, which results owing to the creation of a very viscous "acid gel" intermolecular adhesion. The water has gelled after the physical entrapment of molecules inside the Alg matrix, yet they can still move around. Here is important in many applications (such as Alg gels for cell encapsulation or immobilization). The gel's ability to retain water results from vascular forces. Heat-stable gels can form at ambient temperature (Tønnesen and Karlsen, 2002).

Ibrahim et al. in 2020 developed tamoxifen containing NC using Alg and silver NP, and by embedding vitamin B9 in it. By comparing the folate-containing and blank formulations, the folate-containing formulation showed a 12-fold reduced IC_{50} value and a 12.5−14-fold more harmful index of cancer cells. These results explained the effectiveness and efficiency of NC as a potential breast cancer therapy in the future (Ibrahim et al., 2020).

Cattalini et al. in 2015 created new composite biomaterials for bone tissue engineering (BTE) using Alg and cross-linked bioactive glass nanoparticles (Nbg), that is, Alg-based bioactive glass nanoparticles of copper (AlgNbgCu), Alg-based bioactive glass NPs of calcium (AlgNbgCa). The NC biomaterials were synthesized on 2D scaffolds with desirable morphology, mechanical strength, bioactivity, and other properties of biodegradability, the potential for swelling, cross-linking cation release profile, and angiogenic qualities. It was discovered that Ca^{2+} and Cu^{2+} were both released in a controlled and sustained manner, and no burst discharge was observed. Finally, according to in vitro findings, both NC biomaterials were able to induce rat bone development through the release of bioactive ions in osteogenic lineage-directed mesenchymal stem cells from bone marrow. Additionally, human umbilical vein endothelial cells were shown to exhibit the normal endothelial cell trait i.e., forming tubes in matrigel when in contact. Hence, AlgNbgCu is one of the new biomaterials that showed their angiogenic characteristics. Thus, new NC biomaterials can be used for BTE (Cattalini et al., 2015).

Malagurski et al. in the year 2017 prepared NC by using Alg to facilitate biomineralization with the Zn-mineral phase, new bioactive and antimicrobial biomaterials were produced (Yu et al., 2013). The straightforward, economical synthesis process produced two distinct Algs that have been Zn mineralized, such as Zn-carbonate/Zn-Alg and Zn-phosphate/Zn-Alg. The Zn-mineral phase has significantly influenced the form, stability, total metallic loading, and release of the potential of NC-Zn (II) in a biological milieu stability, the total metallic loading, and the release pattern of NC-Zn (II) in a biological milieu have all been significantly influenced by the Zn-mineral phase. Both forms of Zn mineralized NCs displayed high antibacterial activity against

Bacillus staphylococcus and Candida albicans, Escherichia coli. These results showed that Alg biomineralization is a good process for producing biomaterials with a variety of functionalities as well as antimicrobial activity (Malagurski et al., 2017).

1.4.2 Synthetic polymer-based nanocomposite

Synthetic polymer-based NC mainly includes PLGA-based and polycaprolactone-based NCs.

1.4.2.1 Poly lactic-co-glycolic acid-based nanocomposites

Poly lactic-co-glycolic acid (PLGA) is synthetic in origin and is synthesized by randomly copolymerizing lactide and glycolide in a high vacuum environment using a catalyst like stannous octoate and maintaining the reaction temperature of 160°C and 190°C. Glycolides and lactides are dimers produced by drying lactic acid and glycolic acid. PLGA has an alternative ester or acid end group. PLGA with ester end groups has a slow hydrolytic breakdown. Commercially, PLGA has different PLGA grades based on molecular weight, intrinsic viscosity, and lactic acid to glycolic acid ratio (Yadav et al., 2010).

An NC was prepared by Maeda et al. in 2021 by altering the blend proportion of the polyethylene glycol (PEG)-b-PLGA diblock polymers utilizing various PLGA having molecular weights 800 g/mol and the 1600 g/mol: PEG-b-PLGA (1000−800, Diblock0.8k) and the PEG-b-PLGA (1000−800, Diblock0.9k), the gelation activity based on thermal condition and behavior of the NCs during degradation comprised of poly(ethylene glycol)-b-poly(lactic acid-co-glycolic acid) (PEG-b-PLGA) (1000−1600, Diblock1.6k) studied. When the PEG-b-PLGA concentration and laponite concentration was maintained at 3−4 wt.% and 1 wt.%, respectively, it showed that gelation temperature was present in the temperature range of 25°C−37°C. The Diblock1.6k/Diblock 0.8k blend ratio was shown to be an efficient way to control the degradation rate (Dr) at 37°C. In more detail, when the Dr was varied from the Dr = 0/100 to Dr = 100/0 after the 15 days of degradation studies, the weight loss was reduced by about 14%. Therefore, it was established that Dr was the crucial factor in determining how the laponite/blended PEG-b-PLGA NCs will degrade (Maeda et al., 2021).

Jose et al. produced in the year 2009 aligned nanofibrous scaffolds for BTE by electrospun of poly (D, L-lactide-co-glycolide) (PLGA), and the nano-hydroxyapatite (nano-HA). Using scanning electron microscopy for the morphological analysis, it was discovered that the addition of nano-HA in various concentrations 1%, 5%, 10%, and 20% by weight increased the average fiber diameter from 300 nm (neat PLGA) to 700 nm (20% nano-HA). Agglomeration of HA was seen at greater concentrations (P10%), and this was noticeable at 20% concentration where fiber breakage was caused by the presence of nano-HA. The thermal analysis demonstrated the quick processing of the electrospinning locked in the amorphous nature of PLGA and led to lower glass transition temperature of scaffolds. Furthermore, when the concentration of nano-HA was increased, a rise in the glass transition temperature was seen. The morphological finding showed that nano-HA served supportive in lower concentrations (1% and 5%) but was problematic at high concentrations that were reflected in the mechanical behavior of the scaffolds (10% and 20%). The value of the storage modulus of scaffolds was raised from 441 megapascal (MPa) for pure PLGA to about 724 MPa for 5% of nano-HA, while further boosting the concentration resulted in a reduction of storage modulus of 371 MPa for nano-HA at a 20% concentration. According to degradation characteristics, phosphate-buffered saline absorption and mass loss were affected by hydrophilic nano-HA. By the first week, the mechanical behavior had a sinusoidal pattern and a modest reduction in modulus. Due to the medium's plasticizing action, a rise in modulus brought on by shrinkage, and a subsequent decline by week 6 was observed that the result of degradation (Jose et al., 2009).

A biodegradable PLGA/silver NC with a controlled breakdown rate and antibacterial characteristics was produced by Rinaldi et al. in the year 2013. Solvent casting was used to create PLGA/silver NC films. At room temperature, the $CHCl_3$ was continuously stirred to dissolve the PLGA was dissolved. AgNPs (1−3 wt.%) were added to the PLGA/ $CHCl_3$ solutions with continuous stirring to prepare the NCs. The dispersion was placed in Teflon sheets and dried for 48 hours in a vacuum at 37°C after being air dried for 24 hours. Following the loss of mass and shape of the NC films with various stages of degradation, the influence of silver loading on the polymer matrix degradation was examined. To understand the kinetics of degradation, the diffusion model was used to investigate the release of Ag^+ during NC degradation. It was discovered that increased AgNPs loading lowered both the release rate and the Dr. Also, NC exhibited antibacterial properties (Rinaldi et al., 2013).

1.4.2.2 Poly-ε-caprolactone-based nanocomposite

Aliphatic polyester family member poly-ε-caprolactone (PCL) is a biodegradable polymer. PCL is created either through the polycondensation of 6-hydroxyhexanoic acid or the ring-opening polymerization (ROP) of caprolactone, a specific type of polycondensation. The method for producing polymers was called stepwise condensation. The melting point (Tm) of PCL is between 332K and 337K with a glass transition temperature of 213K. With other polymers, it blends well, and its comparatively low melting point makes the production process easier for drug delivery mechanisms and scaffolds. The heat from the fusion of crystalline PCL at 100% is 139.5 kJ/kg, which may be utilized to analyze the crystallinity of the PCL. The crystallinity of PCL depends on its molecular components such as the molecular weight. The crystallinity of PCL can modulate mechanical, chemical, and physical characteristics (Hasnain and Nayak, 2019). Additionally, PCL copolymerization impacts the crystallinity, solubility, and degradation of polymers. Depending on the ratios used, the pattern and permeability enable the development of custom polymers for medication delivery several polymers may be used to create PCL copolymers, poly (ethylene glycol), polyvinyl chloride, polystyrene, polyurethanes, substituted PCLs, and others, whether natural or synthetic starch, CS, poly(lactic acid), PLGA, and as well as PVA (Espinoza et al., 2020).

Asadi et al. in the year 2019 prepared a new NC hydrogel that was based on gelatin/ PCL/polyethylene glycol/tissue growth factor (gel/PCEC/TGF1), and using glutaraldehyde as a cross-linker. Briefly, gelatin was dissolved in distilled water at 40°C to create a 5% (w/v) gelatin aqueous solution. The gelatin solution was then supplemented with TGF-loaded PCEC nanoparticles (10 ng/mL of TGF1), and free TGF1 (10 ng/mL), and tested for the ability of human mesenchymal stem cells (hAD-MSCs), which were isolated from the adipose tissue to proliferate and differentiate into cartilage. The porosity of the scaffold was evaluated by scanning electron microscope. The 3-(4,5-dimethylthiazol-2-yl)-2,5-diphenyl-2H-tetrazolium bromide (MTT) assay was used for examining the cell viability, and a toluidine blue staining procedure was used to assess proteoglycan production. Collagen II and aggrecan gene expression were tracked using a real-time polymerase chain reaction (PCR) test. The information demonstrated that in contrast to the control group, scaffolds support cell proliferation. Toluidine blue staining in histological investigations revealed the accumulation of glycosaminoglycans. Reverse transcription-PCR study revealed that the hydrogels, particularly the NC hydrogel, could express collagen II and genes of aggrecan. Hence, gel/PCEC/TGF-1 NC hydrogels had the potential for expansion and a promising biomaterial for cartilage tissue engineering is h-AD-MSC differentiation as cartilage tissue has limited self-repair properties. The characteristics of an excellent substance for cartilage tissue engineering are hydrogels containing 3D hydrated polymers (Asadi et al., 2019).

In another study, a simple emulsion solvent evaporation approach was used to mix multiwalled carbon nanotubes (MWCNTs) along the PCL to create nonspherical NC, which had high aspect ratios by Niezabitowska in 2018. Various NPs morphologies and sizes were created based on the concentration of PCL, CNTs, and sodium dodecyl sulfate (SDS). PCL-CNT nanostructures containing 0.9 mg/mL of CNTs, 10 mg/mL of the SDS, and 1.5 mg/mL of SDS were produced with low polydispersity. According to AFM research, the moduli of the PCL and PCL-CNT NC were remarkably the same with 770 and 560 MPa respectively, demonstrating that at least 2 nm of PCL has been deposited onto every CNT. The PCL-CNT NC thermogravimetric measurement revealed that 9.6% of its mass was made up of CNTs. The asymmetric field flow fractionation showed that the PCL-CNT had hydrodynamic diameters that were greater than that of PCL. NC demonstrated comparable docetaxel entrapment efficiencies (89%) to that of CNTs alone about (95%) and the PCL merely nanoparticles (81%). It was simple to create nonspherical NC using this procedure by combining the high aspect ratio and modulus features of PCL and CNTs. These NC's high entrapment efficiency may have many uses in the delivery of biological molecules (Niezabitowska et al., 2018).

Ansari et al. conducted a study in 2020 in order to enhance the Ti_6Al_4V (90% titanium [Ti], 6% aluminum, 4% vanadium, and 0.25% [max] iron along with 0.2% [max] oxygen). Substrate behavior and in vitro bioactivity coatings made of different compositions of PCL, PCL/fluoride substituted-hydroxyapatite (PCL/fluoride substituted-hydroxyapatite [FHA]), and other nanomaterials are used (10, 20, and 30 wt.% of FHA). To demonstrate their prospective use for dental implants, the coatings' in vitro bioactivity, and corrosion behavior were also examined. The findings show that the in situ sol-gel technique was capable of creating coatings that are compact and devoid of cracks when FHA is evenly dispersed like a ceramic phase within the polymeric matrix. The hydrophilicity of NC, adhesive power, along surface roughness was all improved by increasing the FHA content. Furthermore, as an increase in the FHA concentration and the duration of incubation in the simulated body fluid, the in vitro bioactivity of the PCL/fluoride substituted-hydroxyapatite (FHA) NC coatings was enhanced. In comparison to pure PCL and the PCL/FHA coatings with 20 and 30 wt.% FHA, the corrosion resistance of the PCL/10 wt.% FHA coatings was significantly improved. Additionally, the PCL/20 wt.% FHA coating enhanced the proliferation and spread of MG-63 cells, and the MTT assay demonstrated that the coatings had no discernible cytotoxic effect. The PCL/FHA NC coating at the alkali-treated Ti_6Al_4V substrate was shown to be attractive candidate in dental implant applications (Ansari et al., 2020). Refer to the Table 1.1 for the illustration of various examples of nanomaterials used as fillers for the preparation of polymer-based composites.

1.4.3 Metal-based nanocomposite

Metal-based NCs are highly exploited for their industrial applications and some of their subtypes are mentioned below.

1.4.3.1 Metal/metal nanocomposite

Due to their enhanced catalytic high electrical and optical properties, bimetallic nanoparticles, whether in the form of alloys or core-shell structures, are currently the subject of extensive research. Their intriguing physicochemical characteristics are thought to be the outcome of the combination of two different metal types and their intricate architecture (Velempini et al., 2021).

1.4.3.2 Metal-ceramic nanocomposites

The electrical, magnetic, chemical, optical, and mechanical properties of both these types of composites combining phases Improvement in the performance results from component size reduction to the nanoscale of the aforementioned qualities and creates new applications. Such composites demonstrate a robust ceramic matrix that is chemically inert and rough (Choa et al., 2003).

Table 1.1 Nanomaterials that are used as fillers in polymer-based nanocomposites.

S. No.	Type of nanomaterial	Morphology	Method of production	Biomedical uses	References
1.	Fullerene	Buckyball-like sphere	Laser ablation, laser vaporization, thermal decomposition, thermal plasma pyrolysis	Act as optic sensor, temperature sensor, antimicrobial properties	Guarino et al. (2020)
2.	Carbon nanotubes (CNTs)	Less than 100 nm in diameter and less than 5 nm in thickness, forming a tube dimension of 0.66 nm (single-walled CNTs) 1.5–15 nm, and 2.5–50 nm for the outer diameter (multiwalled CNTs)	Depending on the processing method, different durations, and aspect ratios are possible. The most used method is chemical vapor deposition, which produces CNTs	Diagnostic CNT, Biosensor for biosensing made up of CNT, CNT in tissue engineering	Simon et al. (2019)
3.	Quantumdots	Quantum dots are a nanometer-sized spherical particles traditionally having a core-shell design. They typically have a diameter of 2–10 nm (10–50 atoms)	Colloidal synthesis uses the breakdown of precursors and the emergence of nanocrystals. Plasma technology allows for more precise control of the surface, size, shape, and composition of nanoparticles	Bioimaging, diagnosis, treatment, cell -tracking, ex vivo analyte detection, intracellular delivery	Wagner et al. (2019)
4.	Metallic nanocomposites	Metals that are nanoscale, defined as having length, breadth, or thickness measurements between 1 and 100 nm	Chemical techniques: The development of nanostructures is caused by the process of self-assembly. Chemical reduction ball milling, which causes a significant plastic deformation, is a physical strategy	Antibacterial properties, Antimicrobial textile, drug delivery	Zare and Shabani (2016)

In order to boost the antimicrobial properties of kaolinite surfaces Awad et al. in the year 2021 produced a silver Kaolonite NC (Ag-Kao-NC) agent having both antibacterial and antifungal activities. Silver nitrate was uniformly blended with pharmaceutical-grade kaolin powder samples in a ratio of 1:4 $AgNO_3$:Kao (weight-to-weight), and the mixture was sintered at 400°C for 30 minutes. Different levels of structural order and disorder were seen in the kao. The pyrofabricated NC was examined using X-ray diffraction/X-ray fluorescence, differential scanning calorimetry, FTIR spectroscopy, transmission electron microscopy/energy-dispersive X-ray, and zeta potential (mV) was determined within the pH of 2−12, and the BET method was used to determine their composition, microstructure, microtexture, and surface properties. Silver dissociation tests in the neutral and acidic pH and an Ag content assay using the inductively coupled plasma optical emission spectroscopy (ICP-OES) along with an Ag content assay by using ICP-OES were used to evaluating the physicochemical stability. With bulk silver varying concentrations from 9.29% to 13.32%, the resulting Ag-Kao-NC displayed outstanding physicochemical stability both in neutral, and acidic environments (Ag dissociation rate 0.5% in 5 days). The Ag nanocrystals were introduced and reinforced within the Kao Matrix, with particle sizes ranging from 5 to 30 nm. The size of the kaolinite platelet was controlled by the amount of structural order-disorder. The number of hydroxyls dangling from platelet edges, highly disordered state kaolinite (HI = 1) formed homogenous platelet basal that doped silver nanocrystals, whereas platelet edge-clustered silver nanocrystals were created by Hinckley Index (HI > 1) as a result of interplatelet silver diffusivity and the presence of certain basal hydroxyl groups that were exposed have leftover charges. The size of the silver nanocrystals had an impact on the extent of the positive surface charge at pH 2. The most favorable results were shown in NC with silver nanocrystals that were 5−10 nm in size. Bigger silver nanocrystals (up to 30 nm) suggested a higher zeta potential of (+15.2 mV to +17.0 mV), while the lower positive zeta potential values of (+9.5 mV to +3.6 mV) for small nanocrystals. During sintering (converting solid NPs in NC) proportionately and uniformly mixed kaolinite powders and silver nitrate in thermal nondehydroxylation conditions, dry pyro technique was employed using the Mueller-Hinton broth microdilution technique, the raw kaolin passed the tests under the same condition samples lacked any discernible antibacterial activity (Hackel et al., 2019). However, every Ag-Kao-NC made using pyro technology showed antimicrobial activity. The MIC range of the samples revealed strong antibacterial action at low dosages (0.1−0.0125 mg/mL). As a result, it was discovered that the pH and the size and microtexture of the silver nanocrystals were both highly correlated with the change of the kaolinite platelets' functional electrostatic surface charge when silver was thermally doped inside their basal planes and edges (mainly controlled by the order-disorder degree HI). The outcome of an improved synergistic biophysical antibacterial activity resulted from the modification of the nanostructure, which had physicochemical stability and effective surface features of the developed prefabricated NC (Awad et al., 2021).

The clinical effectiveness of coated implants in carrying out biological activities, such as long-term antibacterial activity without the need for antibiotics and sustained medication release, is crucial. To do this, Mishra et al. in the year 2017 prepared PVA nanocapsules with a core made of silver nanoparticles (AgNPs) and Ag-PVANC using the antiinflammatory medication naproxen contained in the CS matrix. The produced nanohybrids that were coated with (3-amino propyl) triethoxysilane Ti metal treated with (3-aminopropyl triethoxysilane [APTES]) displayed a dual role and good biofilm suppression drug formation and ongoing release. These two traits are primarily based on inherent antibacterial capability of AgNPs' and the many ways that drugs are entrapped in PVA polymeric AgNPs and CS matrix shells. As inorganic filler content and stress shielding on Ti metal were increased, the coatings also showed improved mechanical characteristics. The biocompatibility studies using osteoblast adhesion, proliferation, and differentiation showed effectiveness as a suitable coating material for orthopedic applications of Ag-PVA NCs incorporated CS matrix (Mishra et al., 2017).

1.4.4 Nanodiamond-based nanocomposite

One of the metastable allotropes of carbon is diamond, nanodiamond, or monocrystalline diamond with particles smaller than 100 nm, has been the subject of extensive research over the past few decades. Because of its remarkable mechanical and optical qualities, tunable surface structure, and recent advancements, nanodiamonds have gained attention (Garg et al., 2019).

Due to its large specific surface area, it has a variety of functional uses attributable to the distinctive core-shell structure and several functional groups on its own surface. Its optimum use as fillers in reinforcing polymer composites is made possible by its exceptional physical qualities, which produce materials with superior mechanical, thermal stability, thermal conductivity, and tribological properties. In addition to polymer composites, sensors, optical computing, and quantum computing all make extensive use of nanodiamonds and their composites. As nanoscale components, they are employed in bioapplications, wastewater treatment, and electrical energy storage. Nanodiamonds and their composites are becoming essential in biological applications because to their better biocompatibility and minimal cytotoxicity (Zhang et al., 2018).

1.4.5 Carbon material-based nanocomposite

These carbon-based NCs are recently being studied and researched a lot because of their unique characteristic properties and information regarding their subtypes is mentioned below.

1.4.5.1 Carbon nanotube morphologies and characteristics

The fullerene family of carbon allotropes includes CNTs. CNTs are hexagonal, cylinder-shaped molecules, and sp^2 arranged hybridized carbon atoms (C-C separation) of 1.4 Å. They are defined as fashioned into hollow cylinders by fusing sheets in single or multiple layers into smooth-bore cylinders. There are two of these cylindrical constructions. Single-walled carbon nanotubes (SWNTs) and MWCNT are two examples of CNTs with walls. SWNTs comprise one graphene layer, a single cylindrical layer, capped at both ends of a carbon hemispherical configuration network (Mohanta et al., 2019). The cylinder closes as a result of C-C structures with pentagonal and heptagonal faces during the growth process. MWNTs include several to tens of concentric graphitic shell cylinders, with each cylinder constituting an SWNT. Generally, MWNTs consist of a larger outer diameter (2.5−100 nm) compared with SWNTs have a smaller outer diameter (0.6−2.4 nm), and are made up of a variety of concentric SWNT layers with a 0.34 nm interlayer spacing, but SWNTs have a more clearly defined diameter. Because MWNTs are more prone to having structural flaws in an unsteady nanostructure. CNTs combine durability, high stiffness, and the reversible ability to budge and collapse. The strong C−C bond an axial force is produced by the hexagonal network's rigidity. Young's modulus, a measure of rigidity with about 1 terapascal (TPa), and 150 gigapascal (GPa), makes CNTs one of the strongest materials of the most available rigid materials, along with the capacity to change their shape elastically under compression (Kiran et al., 2020).

SWNTs come in a variety of shapes, just like there are numerous ways to roll a sheet of graphite into a seamless tube. This configuration can influence how SWNTs act as distinct semimetallic, semiconducting, or depending on the diameter and chirality, metallic structures. An SWNTs chiral vector C is used to determine its chirality. characterized by two integers derived from the position of the graphite hexagons about the Axis SWNTs. The couch arrangement with an armchair perpendicular to chiral vectors is what distinguishes the tube axis and the chair form, whereas the zigzag as conformation is represented by vectors and is of V-shaped, parallel to the axis of the tube (Monthioux et al., 2010).

Reddy et al. created an effective electrochemical sensor in 2017 that used a functionalized multiwall carbon nanotube-CS natural polymers (CS-fCNT-NC) electrode for the purpose of selectively detecting the neurotransmitter epinephrine (Epn). Nitric acid was used to functionalize MWCNTs, and confirmed by Raman spectrum data. The bioNC that formed by dispersing functionalized CNT in CS solution was employed to create the sensor surface using the drop-and-cast technique. For the purpose of detecting Epn in phosphate buffer, cyclic, differential pulse voltammetry (CV, DPV), and electrochemical impedance analysis were used for the understanding of the electrochemical properties of the manufactured sensor (pH 7.4). According to CV and impedance studies, the modified CS-CNT electrode improves the electrodic reaction of Epn and makes the transport of electrons easier than a bare electrode. In the determination range of 0.05–30 nM the lowest detection limit for Epn using DPV10 μM, and an analysis time of under 10 seconds was used. Reliable outcomes for the measurement of Epn were observed in the presence of biological electroactive interferents. The current biosensor has been successful in determining Epn directly from pharmaceutical samples urine samples and adrenaline preparations (Koteshwara Reddy et al., 2017).

Kilele et al. developed a NC in the year 2020 for the precise determination of theophylline (TPN). A NC made of zinc oxide NPs-MWCNTs-cytochrome c (ZnO NPs MWCNTs Cyt C) was used in this study. The alteration of cytochrome c, MWCNTs, and ZnO NPs was performed to develop an electrochemical sensor with great sensitivity for measuring TPN in pharmaceutical formulations. Using cyclic voltammetry, the electrocatalytic characteristics of ZnO NPs-MWCNTs-Cyt c-glass carbon electrode (GCE) in the direction of the TPN oxidation. Surprisingly, ZnONPs-MWCNTs-Cyt c-GCE showed better anodic currents than that of ZnONPs-MWCNTs-GCE. The established electrochemical biosensor had a detection limit of 0.0012 mM and a linear range of 0.4–15 mM ($R^2 = 0.9903$). Thus, could be suitable for the detection of TPN in the pharmaceutical formulation (Kilele et al., 2020).

1.4.5.2 Graphene-based nanocomposite

Graphene is a significant new material that has recently been added to the family of materials made of carbon materials. It is the first 2D carbon-based atomic material crystal that has attracted a lot of interest since its discovery in 2004 by Geim and colleagues (Karimzadeh et al., 2021). The composition of graphene represents a flat sheet of sp^2 that is one atom thick made up of carbon with bond atoms arranged in a honeycomb-like crystal lattice. These kinds of configurations in graphene present a strong carbon-to-carbon link and the existence of free π electrons in the plane and aromatic structure with confers mechanical, physicochemical, thermal, and surface reaction properties due to the existence of active surfaces for surface reactions and free electrons. There are a lot of materials that are composed of graphene having mechanical properties like strength and extremely high electrical and thermal conductivity, flexibility, and many others, which are superior as compared to other compounds. The most durable and powerful material is graphene (Deshmukh et al., 2020). The stretchable material is common. Its thermal conductivity is unprecedented. With extremely high intrinsic mobility, and being entirely impermeable, numerous characteristics of graphene make it potentially useful for biomedical applications. Its expensive surface, purity of the chemical, and potential for simple functionalization make it the perfect choice for the delivery of drugs. Also, its special mechanical characteristics offer possibilities for tissue engineering applications. Numerous characteristics of graphene make it potentially attractive for bioapplications. Chemically functionalized graphene is another compound that could find use in quick and sensitive measuring equipment that can identify various biological substances, including DNA, hemoglobin, glucose, and cholesterol. Graphene is also lipophilic, which could assist in addressing a different issue in Membrane barrier penetration in medication administration (Bai and Shen, 2012).

The GO has demonstrated potential biomedical uses in recent years because of its distinct chemical and physical features. Shen et al. developed a new, multifunctional GO-based NC in 2012 in which imaging with magnetic resonance (MRI) probe poly (diallyl dimethylammonium chloride)-diallyl diethylenetriamine-pentaacetic acid-gadolinium (Gd-DTPA-PDDA) was used to alter GO. To enhance its targeting ability to tumors, the efficiency of imaging and treatment of FA was added. The anticancer medication DOX hydrochloride was finally able to be loaded onto the NC through hydrophobic contact and stacking, with a loading capacity of 1.38 mg/mg. GO-PEG-FA/Gd/DOX had better tumor-targeting imaging efficiency than that of free Gd^{3+}, according to an MRI test. After the first 10 hours, the NC in vitro release of the DOX under tumor-relevant circumstances (pH 5.5) became slightly high. Additionally, through experimentation, it was found that the multifunctional NC had a strong cytotoxic effect on cancer cells. The aforementioned findings are encouraging for the following in vivo experiment and open up the possibility of being a prospective candidate for early cancer detection and targeted treatment (Shen et al., 2012).

Salahandish et al. in 2019 prepared a three-layer sandwich made of AgNPs, which contains functionalized graphene doped with nitrogen, and nanostructured polyaniline (PANI) NC. The modified Hummer process was used to create some layers of nitrogen dopped functionalized graphene (NFG) as a conductive substrate, and EDC/NHS was used to functionalize the NFG with the COOH functional group. N,N-Dimethylformamide and nitrogen-doped DI water were used to reduce the functionalized GO. By using these NC ascorbic acid (AA) can be detected in a stable and highly repeatable manner in the presence of dopamine, uric acid, and other interferences. Fluorine-doped tin oxide electrode coated with AgNPs-grafted NFGPANI enhanced the charge transfer conductivity of the electrode (the resistance decreased from 11,000 to 6), with a recovery rate of 98%, a good linear detection range of 10−11,460 M, and a low detection limit of 8 M. The outcomes prove that This NC is an option for the quick and accurate detection of AA in real-world clinical settings (Salahandish et al., 2019).

1.5 Applications of multifunctional nanocomposites

NCs exhibit numerous characteristic properties that are made use of for their application in various research areas and industrial development. Here, the use of NCs in the field of bioimaging, therapy, and management of neurodegenerative diseases and cancer are highlighted.

1.5.1 Bioimaging

In the year 2021, Du et al. developed (dibenzoyl methane) NC-based halloysite nano-tubes (HNTs) utilizing a basic one-step hydrothermal procedure, which exhibited high suspension stability and excellent photoluminescence behavior. Multiple approaches were used to describe the multifunctional Fe-HNT-Eu NC as it was pro-duced according to the results of the cell viability experiment, cell morphology obser-vation, and in vitro cytotoxicity assay, the produced Fe-HNT-Eu NC may be employed for bioimaging and biomedical applications in human hepatic carcinoma cells since it demonstrated over the investigated concentration range, high biocompati-bility. Effects of Fe-HNT-Eu NC on the survival of the human hepatic cell lines LO2 and HepG2, as well as the human hepatic adenocarcinoma cell line, respectively, were assessed using a CCK8 analysis. The Fe-HNT-Eu NC further demonstrated superpara-magnetic activity with strong saturation magnetization, which served as an MRI con-trast agent both in vitro and in vivo (Du et al., 2021).

Zhu et al. in the year 2018 developed a turn-on NIR fluorescence probe was developed using GO and transferrin (Tf)-functionalized gold NC (Tf-AuNC) as a technique for imaging small animals and cancer cells. Tf was used as the template for a biomineralization procedure that yielded TfAuNCs in a single step. It served as a func-tional ligand for the transferrin receptor as well as a stabilizer and reducer (TfR). Intense NIR fluorescence from the produced Tf-AuNCs allowed for the avoidance of biological medium interferences like tissue autofluorescence and light scattering. The superfluorescence quenching ability of GO allows the turn-on NIR fluorescent probe Tf-AuNCs/GO NC to have less background fluorescence, which was produced through the assembly of TfAuNCs and GO. The Tf AuNCs/GO NIR fluorescence due to the particular interaction between Tf and TfR and the competition between TfR and the GO for the Tf in the Tf-AuNCs/GO composite, NC was efficiently restored in the presence of TfR. The created turn-on NIR fluorescent probe had low cytotoxicity, high specificity to TfR, and high-water solubility, stability, and biocom-patibility. The probe had successfully turned on fluorescence bioimaging of tiny ani-mals and cancer cells (Zhu et al., 2018). In order to examine the cytotoxicity of an activatable NIR fluorescent probe, Wang et al. in 2013 incubated Hela, HepG-2, and 3T3 cell lines over 4 days with a higher concentration (80 M) of Tf-AuNCs/GO than that for bioimaging. The cell viability was examined every day. In spite of a relatively high concentration of 80 M Tf-AuNCs/GO over a 4-day incubation, neither primary cancer cells nor normal cells exhibited any cytotoxicity. Even though some studies indicated that GO was toxic GO nanosheets with Tf-AuNCs adsorbed on their sur-face may lessen GO's cytotoxicity in human cells (Wang et al., 2013).

Liang et al. developed in the year 2020 Core-shell-structured Ag NP-coated carbon quantum dot (CQD) NC (CQD@AgNCs,), and subsequent coating with silver NP, were developed for fluorescence imaging of intracellular superoxide anion (O2$^{\bullet-}$). By using of in situ chemical reduction, CQD@AgNC's were synthesized. CQD@AgNCs' morphology was examined using TEM, and their composition was determined using X-ray diffraction and X-ray photoelectron spectroscopy. CQDs emitted fluorescence of blue color along the excitation/emission peaks at 360/440 nm; in CQD@Ag NCs, Ag NPs suppress the fluorescence. Ag NPs were oxide-etched in the presence of O$_2^{\bullet-}$, and the fluorescence of CQDs was recovered. With a detection limit of 0.3 M, the comparative fluorescence intensity and O$_2\bullet$ solution concentration were found to be linearly related. They had low cytotoxicity, great sensitivity, and were extremely selective (Liang et al., 2020).

Rakhshaei et al. produced first-generation biodegradable and biocompatible hydrogels in the year 2019, which were the first generation of graphene quantum dots (GQDs), a novel and secure crosslinker with carboxymethyl cellulose (CMC). Several characterizations were performed, including mechanical testing analysis, scanning electron microscopy, gas permeability, and Fourier transform infrared spectroscopy, to determine the effects of the GQDs percentage on the physicochemical properties of the films. The CMC/GQDs showed higher tensile strength along with pH-sensitive swelling and breakdown. To evaluate the produced CMC/GQDs NC's potential for fluorescent bioimaging applications, fluorescence characteristics were also investigated. DOX was used as a model anticancer medication in the study of the CMC/GQDs' drug delivery (Rakhshaei et al., 2020).

Wang et al. in 2019 produced protein-sized aggregation-induced deep and powerful *in vivo* two-photon brain vasculature imaging is made possible by AIEgen-protein hybrid-fetal bovine serum (TPEPy-FBS) NC exhibiting strong far-red NIR emission, remarkable photostability, and low phototoxicity. Proteins from FBS form a compound with a small-molecule fluorogen called AIEgen. Just mixing TPEPy with an aqueous solution that included fetal bovine serum produced TPEPy-FBS NC and TPEPy mix to form TPEPy-FBS NC with "turn-on" fluorescence. The fluorescence of TPEPy was significantly boosted after complexation with FBS, and a 6-fold increase was seen when employing 10% FBS in an aqueous environment. After complexing with FBS, the phototoxicity of TPEPy was greatly diminished, and the resultant TPEPy-FBS had good physical stability in aqueous circumstances. Additionally, TPEPy-FBS exhibited strong 2 fluorescence within high-performance in vivo imaging using the far-red/NIR band and strong photostability after femtosecond laser activation (Wang et al., 2019).

To prevent the formation of a fibrous capsule and promote bone regeneration, biomaterials' controlled biomineralization activity is crucial. However, the majority of traditional biodegradable elastomeric biomaterials for bone regeneration lack inherent multifunctionality and biomineralization capacity (Wang et al., 2020). Li et al. in the year 2018 developed hybrid poly(citrate-siloxane) (PCS) elastomer based on bioactive glass (BG), along with the inherent biomineralization activity and luminescence characteristics for possible regeneration of bone tissue. Elastomeric behavior, biomineralization activity, photoluminescent capacity, and osteogenic cellular response were all controlled by monodispersed bioactive glass nanomaterials (BGNs). The PCS prepolymers were formulated earlier also. Based on prior research, monodispersed BGN was produced using a simple sol-gel template approach. Chemical crosslinking was used to create PCS-BGN NC in a moderate environment. The elastomeric modulus of BGNs was dramatically increased by 10 times (from 20 to 200 MPa), and the hydrophilicity was increased from 82 to 28 degrees in terms of water contact angle. BGNs were used to further customize the PCS elastomer's photoluminescent characteristics. By observing the fluorescence change in PCS-BGN NC, noninvasively the in vivo degradation of these materials could be easily followed. PCS-BGN NC improved the growth and differentiation of osteoblast (MC3T3-E1), while lowering in vivo inflammatory response. To formulate bioactive elastomeric biomaterials with multiple functions for bone regeneration purposes, this work offered unique design strategies (Li et al., 2018b).

In bioimaging, fluorescent gold nanoclusters with distinctive luminescence characteristics have received a lot of attention. Accurate fluorescence imaging might be performed by controlled multicolor fluorescence of gold nanoclusters. In a study by, Cong et al. in year 2021 regulated dual-color imaging under a single stimulation was reported to be possible with spiropyran ligands designed with gold nanoclusters (AuNC-SP). AuNC-SP exhibited reversibly dual-color fluorescence through the UV/VIS irradiation of the open-ring state merocyanine, which switched the Forster resonance energy transmission from the gold nanocluster segment. When AuNC-SP was combined with CS to form AuNC-SP@CS nanoparticles, the steric protection provided by CS significantly enhanced the oxidative stability of AuNC-SP. The AuNC-SP@CS could internalize cancer cells and release AuNC-SP as well, which was then transported into the nucleus. With this outstanding and reversible dual-color fluorescence, the AuNC-SP@CS could mark both the cytoplasm and the nucleus. AuNC-SP@CS may be suitable for light-controlled fluorescence imaging due to its good photochromic property and reversibility. Bright green fluorescence of the AuNC-SP@CS nanoparticles was seen from the MCF-7 cells after 6 hours of incubation, while there was no red fluorescence observed from the SH-MC. The combined image demonstrated that the MCF-7 cell had taken up AuNC-SP@CS. The cells were then exposed to UV light. The SH-MC in AuNC-SP@CS produced vivid red signals from the MCF-7 cells. According to the findings, the AuNC-SP@CS preserved internalization within the cell involving MC/SP photoisomerization. Then the toxicity of AuNC-SP@CS was thoroughly studied. More than 90% of the Cell lines were remained alive once the concentration of AuNC-SP@CS was increased from 0 to 1 mg/mL, indicating that the AuNC-SP@CS had good biocompatibility (Cong et al., 2021).

Zang et al. developed biocompatible and photostable quantum dots (QDs) for biomedical optical imaging in 2017, which explains the creation of biocompatible, environmentally friendly, and photostable AgInZnS-graphene oxide (AIZS-GO) NC with controllable emissions via a mini-emulsion technique. Even after phase transfer by utilizing GO, the hydrophilic AIZS-GO NC continued to exhibit strong and stable photoluminescence (PL). In addition, the PL emission could be strictly controlled in the range of 530–680 nm by controlling the composition of Zn. AIZS-GO NC may also be administered intratumorally for the imaging of SK-BR-3 breast cancer cells. Due to the absence of highly poisonous cadmium, the results of the MTT assay showed that these NC had comparably low cytotoxicity. The generated red-emitted AIZS-GO NC might be employed for the labeling of cancer cells and organs in mice during in vivo imaging tests, suggesting possible uses in phototherapy, imaging, and allied domains, including bioimaging (Zang et al., 2017).

Menezes et al. in the year 2021 explained the magneto-optical and biophysical characteristics of the produced europium-based carbon NC (EuCQD). The produced EuCQD was just 5 nm or smaller, extremely water dispersible, and primarily made of carbon, europium, and oxygen. Additionally, the produced NC has strong NMR relaxivities and Eu/CQD hybrid luminous characteristics. On the basis of cytotoxicity experiments and interactions between plasma proteins, the effect on biological media was also examined. The findings showed that Van der Waals contact and hydrogen bonding are the primary mechanisms by which EuCQDs securely bind (Ka = 104–105 M1) to the examined plasma proteins (BSA and HTF). Furthermore, the NC exhibited very low toxicity against HBMEC, A549, and HTC116 cells, and protein CD spectra showed that both proteins undergo structural modifications during EuCQD contact (Menezes et al., 2021).

According to Gu et al., Specific biomarkers are raised or altered in bodily fluids or tissues at the beginning of cancer. The survival rate can be significantly increased or effective treatment with various modalities can be facilitated by early detection of these biomarkers. Due to their extremely high selectivity and sensitivity, potential nanomaterial-based biosensing and bioimaging are the principal approaches in nano diagnostics. The discipline of biosensing and bioimaging is becoming increasingly explored in developing graphene, including graphene hybrids (GHs) nanostructures, three-dimensional (3D) graphene architectures, and 2D graphene films. Graphene-based nanomaterials are viable options as flexible platforms for early-stage cancer biomarker detection because of their exceptional optical, electrical, and thermal capabilities, chemical stability, large surface area, and strong biocompatibility. Additionally, significant advancements in the detection of cancer have been made possible by graphene-based biosensing and bioimaging (Gu et al., 2019).

1.5.2 Application in the management of cancer

Apurinic/apyrimidinic endonuclease 1 (APE1), a necessary DNA repair enzyme, has been found as cancer predictive and diagnostic indicator for cancer risk assessment, diagnosis, prognosis, and prediction of therapy success (Tell et al., 2010). It is overexpressed in the majority of human malignancies. Despite this biomarker's significance in cancer, it is still difficult to detect abundant change and keep track of its enzymatic activity in living cells today. Zang et al. described the development of biocompatible multifunctional NC that combines minutely crafted unimolecular DNA with tiny graphene QDs. Although using graphene sheets as the starting material, a redesigned acidic oxidation process was used to create graphene QDs. Simply a limited amount of cellular APE1 can cause a huge amount of fluorescence in living tissue when these NC are used as diagnostic probes through repetitive rounds of enzymatic catalysis. The ability of this graphene QD-based NC to sense the cancer biomarker APE1 in identical cell types under various cell environments and to utilize it in diverse tumor cells in extremely sensitive and accurate methods is crucial and is made possible by delicate structural designs. This study established a broad basis for creating diagnostic probes that target multiple physiological biomarkers in living cells in addition to novel techniques for cytology-based cancer screening (Li et al., 2019).

1.5.3 Management of neurodegenerative diseases

Throughout the population, the prevalence of Parkinson's disease (PD) is dramatically increased. The second most common neurodegenerative condition, PD, is caused by death of dopamine neural cells in the substantia nigra compacta (SNpc), α-synuclein deposition. There is presently no cure for PD, despite substantial research to understand the mechanism of the disease (Balestrino and Schapira, 2020). A natural substance called puerarin (Pue) has exceptional anti-PD effects. Its application in the treatment of Parkinson's disease (PD) is constrained, by its poor pharmacological properties, which include poor water solubility, insufficient bioavailability, and partial permeability of the blood-brain barrier (BBB). Xiong et al., employed GO nanosheets GO loaded with pue, which showed superior biocompatibility, excellent drug loading capacity, and adjustable surface, functional groups. As the intended ligand, lactoferrin (Lf) would attach to vascular endothelial receptors on the BBB. Pue was then carried across the BBB and into the brain. According to both in vivo and in vitro data, this delivery system (Lf-GO Pue) had been a multipurpose efficient and secure treatment for Parkinson's disease (Xiong et al., 2021).

Alzheimer's disease (AD) is a progressive neurodegenerative disorder having no cure. Recent research has shown that amyloid-β (Aβ) plays a crucial part in AD. However, there is no solid proof that the current therapeutic approaches had any impact on concurrently reducing A-induced neurotoxicity and eliminating Aβ aggregates in vivo. Here, Zhao et al. created a new NC that can reduce Aβ -induced neurotoxicity in AD mice and remove harmful aggregates. Small particles with Aβ-binding peptides (KLVFF) were incorporated on the surface of NC. A protein molecule was wrapped in a layer of KLVFF-containing polymer that has been in situ polymerized and was cross-linked into

NC. The existence of NC significantly altered the shape of Aβ aggregates, causing a NC assembled nanoclusters to form in place of oligomers. The NC reduced the harm caused by disease. Oligomers restored the ability of endocranial microglia to phagocyte and finally shielded hippocampus neurons against apoptosis. As a result, we believe that the small-sized NC may provide a workable approach for the creation of novel AD treatments (Zhao et al., 2018).

1.6 Conclusion

To fulfill the need of desirable biomaterial, extensive research is being conducted by scientists. The NCs being an extraordinary material possess extraordinary properties, which are not present in their parent materials. The NCs demonstrate remarkable bioimaging and electrical magnetic properties that can be utilized in the field of biomedicine/nanomedicine. As novel drug delivery materials, they may modulate the release of the drug, biomineralization, may act as scaffolds for tissue engineering, and as sensors for the detection of disease and other agents.

Acknowledgment

The authors are thankful to the National Institute of Pharmaceutical Education and Research-Raebareli (NIPER-R), Department of Pharmaceuticals, Ministry of Chemicals and Fertilizers, Govt. of INDIA, for kind support. NIPER Raebareli communication number for the book chapter is 371.

Conflict of interest

The authors declare no conflict of interest.

Consent for publication

The authors have given their consent.

References

Abdelrazek, E.M., Abdelghany, A.M., Badr, S.I., Morsi, M.A., 2018. Structural, optical, morphological and thermal properties of PEO/PVP blend containing different concentrations of biosynthesized Au nanoparticles. J. Mater. Res. Technol. 7 (4), 419–431. Available from: https://doi.org/10.1016/j.jmrt.2017.06.009.

Alexandre, M., Dubois, P., 2000. Polymer-layered silicate nanocomposites: preparation, properties and uses of a new class of materials. Mater. Sci. Eng.: R: Rep. 28 (1–2), 1–63. Available from: https://doi.org/10.1016/s0927-796x(00)00012-7.

Ansari, Z., Kalantar, M., Kharaziha, M., Ambrosio, L., Raucci, M.G., 2020. Polycaprolactone/fluoride substituted-hydroxyapatite (PCL/FHA) nanocomposite coatings prepared by in-situ sol-gel process for dental implant applications. Prog. Org. Coat. 147, 105873.

Arias, J.L., Reddy, L.H., Couvreur, P., 2012. Fe$_3$O$_4$/chitosan nanocomposite for magnetic drug targeting to cancer. J. Mater. Chem. 22, 7622–7632.

Asadi, N., Alizadeh, E., Rahmani Del Bakhshayesh, A., Mostafavi, E., Akbarzadeh, A., Davaran, S., 2019. Fabrication and in vitro evaluation of nanocomposite hydrogel scaffolds based on gelatin/PCL-PEG-PCL for cartilage tissue engineering. ACS Omega 4, 449–457.

Awad, M.E., López-Galindo, A., Medarević, D., Milenković, M., Ibrić, S., El-Rahmany, M.M., et al., 2021. Enhanced antimicrobial activity and physicochemical stability of rapid pyro-fabricated silver-kaolinite nanocomposite. Int. J. Pharm. 598, 120372.

Bai, S., Shen, X., 2012. Graphene-inorganic nanocomposites. RSC Adv. 2, 64–98.

Balestrino, R., Schapira, A.H., 2020. Parkinson disease. Eur. J. Neurol. 27 (1), 27–42.

Basavegowda, N., Baek, K.-H., 2021. Advances in functional biopolymer-based nanocomposites for active food packaging applications. Polymers 13 (23). Available from: https://doi.org/10.3390/polym13234198.

Cattalini, J.P., Hoppe, A., Pishbin, F., Roether, J., Boccaccini, A.R., Lucangioli, S., et al., 2015. Novel nanocomposite biomaterials with controlled copper/calcium release capability for bone tissue engineering multifunctional scaffolds. J. R. Soc. Interface 12.

Chen, F., Chen, Q., Fang, S., Sun, Y., Chen, Z., Xie, G., et al., 2011. Multifunctional nanocomposites constructed from Fe$_3$O$_4$-Au nanoparticle cores and a porous silica shell in the solution phase. Dalton Trans. 40 (41), 10857–10864. Available from: https://doi.org/10.1039/c1dt10374a.

Choa, Y.H., Yang, J.K., Kim, B.H., Jeong, Y.K., Lee, J.S., Nakayama, T., et al., 2003. Preparation and characterization of metal/ceramic nanoporous nanocomposite powders. J. Magn. Magn. Mater. 266 (1–2), 12–19.

Choong, G.Y.H., Lew, C.Y., De Focatiis, D.S.A., 2015. Role of processing history on the mechanical and electrical behavior of melt-compounded polycarbonate-multiwalled carbon nanotube nanocomposites. J. Appl. Polym. Sci. 132 (28). Available from: https://doi.org/10.1002/app.42277.

Cong, Y., Wang, X., Zhu, S., Liu, L., Li, L., 2021. Spiropyran-functionalized gold nanoclusters with photochromic ability for light-controlled fluorescence bioimaging. ACS Appl. Bio Mater. 4 (3), 2790–2797.

Cubeddu, A., Rauh, C., Delgado, A., 2014. 3D thermo-fluid dynamic simulations of high-speed-extruded starch based products. Open. J. Fluid Dyn. 04 (01), 103–114. Available from: https://doi.org/10.4236/ojfd.2014.41008.

Deshmukh, M.A., Jeon, J.Y., Ha, T.J., 2020. Carbon nanotubes: an effective platform for biomedical electronics. Biosens. Bioelectron. 150, 111919.

Du, Y., Shen, S.Z., Cai, K., Casey, P.S., 2012. Research progress on polymer-inorganic thermoelectric nanocomposite materials. Prog. Polym. Sci. 37 (6), 820–841. Available from: https://doi.org/10.1016/j.progpolymsci.2011.11.003.

Du, W., Zhou, L., Zhang, Q., Liu, X., Wei, X., Li, Y., 2021. Inorganic nanomaterial for biomedical imaging of brain diseases. Molecules 26 (23), 7340.

Díez-Pascual, A.M., Sánchez, J.A.L., Capilla, R.P., Díaz, P.G., 2018. Recent developments in graphene/polymer nanocomposites for application in polymer solar cells. Polymers 10 (2). Available from: https://doi.org/10.3390/polym10020217.

Espinoza, S.M., Patil, H.I., San Martin Martinez, E., Casañas Pimentel, R., Ige, P.P., 2020. Poly-ε-caprolactone (PCL), a promising polymer for pharmaceutical and biomedical applications: focus on nanomedicine in cancer. Int. J. Polym. Mater. Polym. Biomater. 69 (2), 85–126.

Garg, S., Garg, A., Sahu, N.K., Yadav, A.K., 2019. Synthesis and characterization of nanodiamond-anticancer drug conjugates for tumor targeting. Diam. Relat. Mater. 94, 172–185.

Garg, A., Rai, G., Lodhi, S., Jain, A.P., Yadav, A.K., 2016. Hyaluronic acid embedded cellulose acetate phthlate core/shell nanoparticulate carrier of 5-fluorouracil. Int. J. Biol. Macromol. 87, 449–459. Available from: https://doi.org/10.1016/j.ijbiomac.2015.11.094.

Garmendia, N., Santacruz, I., Moreno, R., Obieta, I., 2010. Zirconia-MWCNT nanocomposites for biomedical applications obtained by colloidal processing. J. Mater. Sci.: Mater. Med. 21 (5), 1445–1451. Available from: https://doi.org/10.1007/s10856-010-4023-7.

Guarino, V., Focarete, M.L., Pisignano, D., 2020. From nanocomposites to nanostructured materials. Advances in Nanostructured Materials and Nanopatterning Technologies: Applications for Healthcare, Environmental and Energy. Elsevier, pp. 3–39. Available from: https://doi.org/10.1016/B978-0-12-816865-3.00001-9.

Gu, H., Tang, H., Xiong, P., Zhou, Z., 2019. Biomarkers-based biosensing and bioimaging with graphene for cancer diagnosis. Nanomaterials 9 (1), 130.

Hackel, M.A., Tsuji, M., Yamano, Y., Echols, R., Karlowsky, J.A., Sahm, D.F., 2019. Reproducibility of broth microdilution MICs for the novel siderophore cephalosporin, cefiderocol, determined using iron-depleted cation-adjusted Mueller-Hinton broth. Diagn. Microbiol. Infect. Dis. 94 (4), 321–325.

Hasnain, M.S., Nayak, A.K., 2019. Nanocomposites for improved orthopedic and bone tissue engineering applications, Applications of Nanocomposite Materials in Orthopedics, 1. Woodhead Publishing, pp. 145–177.

Hassan, T., Salam, A., Khan, A., Khan, S.U., Khanzada, H., Wasim, M., et al., 2021. Functional nanocomposites and their potential applications: a review. J. Polym. Res. 28 (2). Available from: https://doi.org/10.1007/s10965-021-02408-1.

Hildebrandt, K., Mitschang, P., 2011. Effect of incorporating nanoparticles in thermoplastic fiber-reinforced composites on the electrical conductivity. In: ICCM International Conferences on Composite Materials. http://www.iccm-central.org/Conferences.html.

Ibrahim, O.M., El-Deeb, N.M., Abbas, H., Elmasry, S.M., El-Aassar, M.R., 2020. Alginate based tamoxifen/metal dual core-folate decorated shell: nanocomposite targeted therapy for breast cancer via ROS-driven NF-κB pathway modulation. Int. J. Biol. Macromol. 146, 119–131.

Jayalekshmi, A.C., 2018. Nanocomposites used for drug delivery application. Drug Delivery Nanosystems for Biomedical Applications. Elsevier, pp. 181–199. Available from: https://doi.org/10.1016/B978-0-323-50922-0.00009-2.

Jonoobi, M., Harun, J., Mathew, A.P., Oksman, K., 2010. Mechanical properties of cellulose nanofiber (CNF) reinforced polylactic acid (PLA) prepared by twin screw extrusion. Compos. Sci. Technol. 70 (12), 1742–1747. Available from: https://doi.org/10.1016/j.compscitech.2010.07.005.

Jose, M.V., Thomas, V., Johnson, K.T., Dean, D.R., Nyairo, E., 2009. Aligned PLGA/HA nanofibrous nanocomposite scaffolds for bone tissue engineering. Acta Biomater. 5 (1), 305–315.

Jouault, N., Zhao, D., Kumar, S.K., 2014. Role of casting solvent on nanoparticle dispersion in polymer nanocomposites. Macromolecules 47 (15), 5246–5255. Available from: https://doi.org/10.1021/ma500619g.

Karimzadeh, S., Safaei, B., Jen, T.C., 2021. Prediction effect of ethanol molecules on doxorubicin drug delivery using single-walled carbon nanotube carrier through POPC cell membrane. J. Mol. Liq. 330, 115698.

Karthika, V., AlSalhi, M.S., Devanesan, S., Gopinath, K., Arumugam, A., Govindarajan, M., 2020. Chitosan overlaid Fe₃O₄/rGO nanocomposite for targeted drug delivery, imaging, and biomedical applications. Sci. Rep. 10, 1–17.

Kaur, L., Sharma, A., Yadav, A.K., Mishra, N., 2018. Recent advances on biodegradable polymeric carrier-based mucosal immunization: an overview. Artif. Cells Nanomed. Biotechnol. 46, 452–464.

Kilele, J.C., Chokkareddy, R., Rono, N., Redhi, G.G., 2020. A novel electrochemical sensor for selective determination of theophylline in pharmaceutical formulations. J. Taiwan Inst. Chem. Eng. 111, 228–238.

Kiran, A.R., Kumari, G.K., Krishnamurthy, P.T., 2020. Carbon nanotubes in drug delivery: focus on anticancer therapies. J. Drug Deliv. Sci. Technol. 59, 101892.

Koteshwara Reddy, K., Satyanarayana, M., Yugender Goud, K., Vengatajalabathy Gobi, K., Kim, H., 2017. Carbon nanotube ensembled hybrid nanocomposite electrode for direct electrochemical detection of epinephrine in pharmaceutical tablets and urine. Mater. Sci. Eng. C 79, 93–99.

Leventis, N., Chandrasekaran, N., Sadekar, A.G., Sotiriou-Leventis, C., Lu, H., 2009. One-pot synthesis of interpenetrating inorganic/organic networks of CuO/ resorcinol-formaldehyde aerogels: nanostructured energetic materials. J. Am. Chem. Soc. 131 (13), 4576–4577. Available from: https://doi.org/10.1021/ja809746t.

Liang, H., Liu, H., Tian, B., Ma, R., Wang, Y., 2020. Carbon quantum Dot@ Silver nanocomposite—based fluorescent imaging of intracellular superoxide anion. Microchim. Acta 187, 1–9.

Liu, K.H., Liu, T.Y., Chen, S.Y., Liu, D.M., 2008. Drug release behavior of chitosan-montmorillonite nanocomposite hydrogels following electrostimulation. Acta Biomater. 4, 1038–1045.

Li, J., Cai, C., Li, J., Li, J., Li, J., Sun, T., et al., 2018a. Chitosan-based nanomaterials for drug delivery. Molecules 23, 1−26.

Li, Y., Guo, Y., Niu, W., Chen, M., Xue, Y., Ge, J., et al., 2018b. Biodegradable multifunctional bioactive glass-based nanocomposite elastomers with controlled biomineralization activity, real-time bioimaging tracking, and decreased inflammatory response. ACS Appl. Mater. Interfaces 10 (21), 17722−17731.

Li, X., Xiong, M., Huang, Y., Zhang, L., Zhao, S., 2019. Simple label-free fluorescence detection of apurinic/apyrimidinic endonuclease 1 activity and its inhibitor using the abasic site-binding fluorophore. Anal. Methods 11, 739−743.

Maeda, T., Kitagawa, M., Hotta, A., 2021. Degradation of thermoresponsive laponite/PEG-b-PLGA nanocomposite hydrogels controlled by blending PEG-b-PLGA diblock copolymers with different PLGA molecular weights. Polym. Degrad. Stab. 187, 109535.

Makarchuk, O.V., Dontsova, T.A., Astrelin, I.M., 2016. Magnetic nanocomposites as efficient sorption materials for removing dyes from aqueous solutions. Nanoscale Res. Lett. 11 (1). Available from: https://doi.org/10.1186/s11671-016-1364-2.

Malagurski, I., Levic, S., Pantic, M., Matijasevic, D., Mitric, M., Pavlovic, V., et al., 2017. Synthesis and antimicrobial properties of Zn-mineralized alginate nanocomposites. Carbohydr. Polym. 165, 313−321.

Marquis, D.M., Guillaume, E., Chivas-Joly, C., 2011. Properties of nanofillers in polymer. Nanocomposites and Polymers with Analytical Methods. IntechOpen (Original work published 2011).

Matsumura, H., Sugiyama, J., Glasser, W.G., 2000. Cellulosic nanocomposites. I. Thermally deformable cellulose hexanoates from heterogeneous reaction. J. Appl. Polym. Sci. 78 (13), 2242−2253. Available from: https://doi.org/10.1002/1097-4628(20001220)78:13 < 2242::AID-APP20 > 3.0.CO;2-5.

Menezes, T.M., Garcia, Y.S., de Assis, C.R., Ventura, G.T., de Queiroz, R.M., Dias, W.B., et al., 2021. Evaluation of europium-based carbon nanocomposites as bioimaging probes: preparation, NMR relaxivities, binding effects over plasma proteins and cytotoxic aspects. Colloids Surf. A: Physicochem. Eng. Asp. 628, 127250.

Mishra, S.K., Teotia, A.K., Kumar, A., Kannan, S., 2017. Mechanically tuned nanocomposite coating on titanium metal with integrated properties of biofilm inhibition, cell proliferation, and sustained drug delivery. Nanomed.: Nanotechnol. Biol. Med. 13 (1), 23−35.

Mohanta, D., Patnaik, S., Sood, S., Das, N., 2019. Carbon nanotubes: evaluation of toxicity at biointerfaces. J. Pharm. Anal. 9 (5), 293−300.

Monthioux, M., Serp, P., Flahaut, E., Razafinimanana, M., Laurent, C., Peigney, A., et al., 2010. Introduction to carbon nanotubes. Springer Handbook of Nanotechnology. Springer, pp. 47−118.

Niezabitowska, E., Smith, J., Prestly, M.R., Akhtar, R., Von Aulock, F.W., Lavallée, Y., et al., 2018. Facile production of nanocomposites of carbon nanotubes and polycaprolactone with high aspect ratios with potential applications in drug delivery. RSC Adv. 8, 16444−16454.

Nogi, M., Yano, H., 2008. Transparent nanocomposites based on cellulose produced by bacteria offer potential innovation in the electronics device industry. Adv. Mater. 20 (10), 1849−1852. Available from: https://doi.org/10.1002/adma.200702559.

Paquin, F., Rivnay, J., Salleo, A., Stingelin, N., Silva, C., 2015. Multi-phase semicrystalline microstructures drive exciton dissociation in neat plastic semiconductors. J. Mater. Chem. C 3, 10715−10722.

Porter, G.C., Schwass, D.R., Tompkins, G.R., Bobbala, S.K.R., Medlicott, N.J., Meledandri, C.J., 2021. AgNP/Alginate nanocomposite hydrogel for antimicrobial and antibiofilm applications. Carbohydr. Polym. 251, 117017.

Rakhshaei, R., Namazi, H., Hamishehkar, H., Rahimi, M., 2020. Graphene quantum dot cross-linked carboxymethyl cellulose nanocomposite hydrogel for pH-sensitive oral anticancer drug delivery with potential bioimaging properties. Int. J. Biol. Macromol. 150, 1121−1129.

Rinaldi, S., Fortunati, E., Taddei, M., Kenny, J.M., Armentano, I., Latterini, L., 2013. Integrated PLGA-Ag nanocomposite systems to control the degradation rate and antibacterial properties. J. Appl. Polym. Sci. 130, 1185−1193.

Sahay, R., Sundaramurthy, J., Suresh Kumar, P., Thavasi, V., Mhaisalkar, S.G., Ramakrishna, S., 2012. Synthesis and characterization of CuO nanofibers, and investigation for its suitability as blocking layer in ZnO NPs based dye sensitized solar cell and as photocatalyst in organic dye degradation. J. Solid State Chem. 186, 261−267. Available from: https://doi.org/10.1016/j.jssc.2011.12.013.

Salahandish, R., Ghaffarinejad, A., Naghib, S.M., Niyazi, A., Majidzadeh-A, K., Janmaleki, M., et al., 2019. Sandwich-structured nanoparticles-grafted functionalized graphene based 3D nanocomposites for high-performance biosensors to detect ascorbic acid biomolecule. Sci. Rep. 9 (1), 1226.

Schadler, L.S., 2003. Polymer-based and polymer-filled nanocomposites. Nanocomposite Sci. Technol. 26, 77–153 (Original work published 2003).

Sen, 2020. European Heart Journal—Case Reports, 1–2. (Original work published 2020).

Shen, A.J., Li, D.L., Cai, X.J., Dong, C.Y., Dong, H.Q., Wen, H.Y., et al., 2012. Multifunctional nanocomposite based on graphene oxide for in vitro hepatocarcinoma diagnosis and treatment. J. Biomed. Mater. Res. Part A 100 (9), 2499–2506.

Simon, J., Flahaut, E., Golzio, M., 2019. Overview of carbon nanotubes for biomedical applications. Materials 12 (4). Available from: https://doi.org/10.3390/ma12040624.

Siró, I., Plackett, D., 2010. Microfibrillated cellulose and new nanocomposite materials: a review. Cellulose 17 (3), 459–494. Available from: https://doi.org/10.1007/s10570-010-9405-y.

Suresh Kumar, P., Sahay, R., Aravindan, V., Sundaramurthy, J., Ling, W.C., Thavasi, V., et al., 2012. Free-standing electrospun carbon nanofibres—a high performance anode material for lithium-ion batteries. J. Phys. D: Appl. Phys. 45 (26). Available from: https://doi.org/10.1088/0022-3727/45/26/265302.

Tell, G., Fantini, D., Quadrifoglio, F., 2010. Understanding different functions of mammalian AP endo-nuclease (APE1) as a promising tool for cancer treatment. Cell. Mol. Life Sci. 67, 3589–3608.

Tønnesen, H.H., Karlsen, J., 2002. Alginate in drug delivery systems. Drug Dev. Ind. Pharm. 28, 621–630.

Velempini, T., Prabakaran, E., Pillay, K., 2021. Recent developments in the use of metal oxides for photocatalytic degradation of pharmaceutical pollutants in water—a review. Mater. Today Chem. 19, 100380.

Wagner, A.M., Knipe, J.M., Orive, G., Peppas, N.A., 2019. Quantum dots in biomedical applications. Acta Biomater. 94, 44–63. Available from: https://doi.org/10.1016/j.actbio.2019.05.022.

Wang, Y., Chen, J.T., Yan, X.P., 2013. Fabrication of transferrin functionalized gold nanoclusters/graphene oxide nanocomposite for turn-on near-infrared fluorescent bioimaging of cancer cells and small animals. Anal. Chem. 85 (4), 2529–2535.

Wang, S., Hu, F., Pan, Y., Ng, L.G., Liu, B., 2019. Bright AIEgen—protein hybrid nanocomposite for deep and high-resolution in vivo two-photon brain imaging. Adv. Funct. Mater. 29 (29), 1902717.

Wang, C., Irudayaraj, J., 2010. Multifunctional magnetic-optical nanoparticle probes for simultaneous detection, separation, and thermal ablation of multiple pathogens. Small 6 (2), 283–289. Available from: https://doi.org/10.1002/smll.200901596.

Wang, W., Liu, X., Zheng, X., Jin, H.J., Li, X., 2020. Biomineralization: an opportunity and challenge of nanoparticle drug delivery systems for cancer therapy. Adv. Healthc. Mater. 9 (22), 2001117.

Whittington, A.M., Brouse, S.M., Malusis, M.A., Wakabayashi, K., 2013. Efficient fabrication of polymer nanocomposites with effective exfoliation and dispersion by solid-state/melt extrusion. Adv. Polym. Technol. 32 (1). Available from: https://doi.org/10.1002/adv.21334.

Xiong, S., Luo, J., Wang, Q., Li, Z., Li, J., Liu, Q., et al., 2021. Targeted graphene oxide for drug delivery as a therapeutic nanoplatform against Parkinson's disease. Biomater. Sci. 9 (5), 1705–1715.

Yadav, A.K., Agarwal, A., Jain, S., Mishra, A.K., Bid, H., Rai, G., et al., 2010. Chondroitin sulphate decorated nanoparticulate carriers of 5-fluorouracil: development and in vitro characterization. J. Biomed. Nanotechnol. 6, 340–350.

Yan, X., Guo, Z., 2018. Chapter 1: Introduction to nanocomposites, Multifunctional Nanocomposites for Energy and Environmental Applications, first ed. Wiley (Original work published 2018).

Yousefian-Arani, M., Sharif, A., Bahramian, A.R., 2018. Semi-aromatic polyamide-based nanocomposites: I. in-situ polymerization in the presence of graphene oxide. Polym. Bull. 75 (12), 5387–5402. Available from: https://doi.org/10.1007/s00289-018-2331-0.

Yu, C., Yang, K., Xie, Y., Fan, Q., Yu, J.C., Shu, Q., et al., 2013. Novel hollow Pt-ZnO nanocomposite microspheres with hierarchical structure and enhanced photocatalytic activity and stability. Nanoscale 5, 2142–2151.

Yu, H.-Y., Yan, C.-F., 2017. Mechanical Properties of Cellulose Nanofibril (CNF)- and Cellulose Nanocrystal (CNC)-Based Nanocomposites. Wiley, pp. 393–443. Available from: https://doi.org/10.1002/9783527689972.ch12.

Zaferani, S.H., Chapter, 2018. Introduction of polymer-based nanocomposites, Polymer-Based Nanocomposites for Energy and Environmental Applications, first ed. Woodhead Publishing (Original work published 2018).

Zang, Z., Zeng, X., Wang, M., Hu, W., Liu, C., Tang, X., 2017. Tunable photoluminescence of water-soluble AgInZnS−graphene oxide (GO) nanocomposites and their application in-vivo bioimaging. Sens. Actuators B: Chem. 252, 1179−1186.

Zare, Y., Shabani, I., 2016. Polymer/metal nanocomposites for biomedical applications. Mater. Sci. Eng.: C 60, 195−203. Available from: https://doi.org/10.1016/j.msec.2015.11.023.

Zhang, Y., Rhee, K.Y., Hui, D., Park, S.J., 2018. A critical review of nanodiamond based nanocomposites: synthesis, properties, and applications. Compos. Part B: Eng. 143, 19−27.

Zhao, Y., Cai, J., Liu, Z., Li, Y., Zheng, C., Zheng, Y., et al., 2018. Nanocomposites inhibit the formation, mitigate the neurotoxicity, and facilitate the removal of β-amyloid aggregates in Alzheimer's disease mice. Nano Lett. 19 (2), 674−683.

Zhu, S., Yung, B.C., Chandra, S., Niu, G., Antaris, A.L., Chen, X., 2018. Near-infrared-II (NIR-II) bioimaging via off-peak NIR-I fluorescence emission. Theranostics 8 (15), 4141.

CHAPTER 2

Multifunctional nanocarrier-mediated approaches and conventional therapies for effective treatment of cancer

Ajay Kumar Shukla[1], Sandeep Kumar Singh[1], Manish Kumar Goel[2], Ashish Garg[3], Kuldeep Rajpoot[4] and Sunil K. Jain[4]

[1]Institute of Pharmacy, Dr. Ram Manohar Lohia, Avadh University, Ayodhya, Uttar Pradesh, India
[2]Department of Pharmacy, Madhav University, Pindwara, Rajasthan, India
[3]Department of P.G. Studies and Research in Chemistry and Pharmacy, Rani Durgavati University, Jabalpur, Madhya Pradesh, India
[4]Department of Pharmacy, Guru Ghasidas Vishwavidyalaya (A Central University), Bilaspur, Chhattisgarh, India

2.1 Introduction

Presently employed pharmaceutical multifunctional nanocomposite (MNC) carriers include liposomes (Guimaraes et al., 2021), solid lipid nanoparticles (NPs) (Rajpoot and Jain, 2019, 2020a, 2020b), micelles (Ghosh and Biswas, 2021), nanoemulsions (Rajpoot, 2017), polymeric NPs (Pandey et al., 2021, 2020a; Jain et al., 2016a, 2016b, 2021), microspheres (Patrey et al., 2016; Nayak et al., 2020; Jain et al., 2019), etc. (Rajpoot and Jain, 2020a, 2020b; Rajpoot, 2017). These MNC carriers have handy characteristics like long life in the blood circulation. It is permitting for collection in the pathological regions with compromised vasculature. It also offers to reach at a definite targeting location in definite illnesses using different targeting tactics (Rajpoot, 2020a, 2020b; Rajpoot and Jain, 2018, 2021). These MNC carriers strike the definite targeted site because targeting ligand moieties are close to the surface of the NPs. It improved intracellular diffusion rate with the aid of surface-attached cell-penetrating molecules. These dissimilarity properties of MNC carriers are used in many areas for in vivo investigation, stimuli sensitivity (Jain et al., 2020), drug discharge effect through the carrier systems under specific physiological environments, and many others (Rajpoot, 2019).

Numerous pharmaceutical nanocarriers have previously developed their way into clinics; however, others are still under preclinical advancement stages. Moreover, MNC carriers are the pharmaceutical formulations usually combining numerous capabilities, for instance, long-circulating ability (Wang et al., 2021; Liu et al., 2021), efficient prolonged residence in the blood, and specific target identification (Jurczyk et al., 2021). It exhibits various other worthwhile properties and therefore can drastically improve the efficacy of numerous therapeutic as well as diagnostic protocols (Bevilacqua et al., 2021; Sharma et al., 2021). This chapter covered the earlier reported and recent status and promising upcoming prospects in the developing area of multifunctional nanocarriers, with prime

Multifunctional Nanocomposites for Targeted Drug Delivery in Cancer Therapy
DOI: https://doi.org/10.1016/B978-0-323-95303-0.00005-8

attention on the mixture of such properties as durability, target-ability, intracellular dissemination, contrast loading, etc. (Valencia et al., 2011).

The current advancement in nanodrug delivery has played a key role in the development of multifunctional nanomaterials; therefore, it is known as MNC carriers. MNC carriers show a paradigm shift from single materials to multiple objectives (Shahbazi et al., 2021; Tabassum et al., 2021). MNC carriers have been projected to enable concurrent target site imaging and release of therapeutic compounds at a specific site. This technology is useful for potent drugs like chemotherapeutics. MNC carriers discreetly deliver drugs and interact with cells/tissues only locally (Tabassum et al., 2021; Rajpoot, 2017). These two advanced properties of imaging and precisely controlled and localized delivery make it very special. These MNC carriers are very essential in cancer therapy as well as their application in theragnostic exhibits promise to minimize adverse effects and enhance the therapeutic potential of therapy (Shao et al., 2021).

Cancer therapy required long treatment that enhanced the probability of adverse responses of the drug agents. The side effects as well as drug resistance can be reduced by using the drug in a low dose, specific site, and controlled manner (Zhang et al., 2021; Gavas et al., 2021). The nonselective/nontargeted drug delivery in tumor therapy is very less used now due to unsought side responses in healthy cells, and inadequate dose sizes do not destroy cancer tissues. In modern times, intelligent technology is used like multifunctional targeted nanocomposites-based medicines. In these systems, diverse nanocarriers for example dendrimers (Rajani et al., 2020; Patel et al., 2020), quantum dots (QDs) (Zhu et al., 2021), carbon-based nanoformulations (Luo et al., 2021; Ravi Kiran et al., 2021), self-emulsifying lipidic systems (Rajpoot et al., 2020; Rajpoot and Tekade, 2019), carbon nanotubes (CNTs) (Ravi Kiran et al., 2021), etc.

They have been investigated tremendously in the therapy of cancer. Further, cancer disease is one of the most causes of human death worldwide. There has been a boost in developing nanocomposite carrier-based therapies. MNC carriers' techniques are used for treating cancer or other critical diseases. One of the main advantages of nanocomposite carriers is the small size range from 1−1000 nm. Therefore, it is easy to reach the targeted site of tumors, and thus more amounts of drugs collect at tumor sites through the enhanced permeability and retention (EPR) effect (Fakhri et al., 2021).

Multifunctional nanocarriers merge as a valuable tactic to overcome these restrictions as well as increase the therapeutic action of anticancer agents. Several amalgamation treatment approaches for multiple drugs with diverse mechanisms can overcome drug resistance and improve safety as well as efficacy of drugs (Persano et al., 2021; Alhajamee et al., 2021). Therefore, it may become a hopeful approach in cancer treatment. Though, the difference in physicochemical and pharmacokinetic properties of the collective drugs could result into suboptimal uptake and biodistribution of two drugs at the tumor sites (Tambe et al., 2021a,b; Rajpoot et al., 2021a,b; Polaka et al., 2021; Anup et al., 2021).

Firstly, particular targetability that diminishes toxicity enhances therapeutic efficacy. Secondly, intracellular penetration enhances the biodistribution of drugs as well as the pharmacokinetic efficacy of bioactive(s). The third is the bioimaging property, which offers real-time supervision of the progress of biological performances and NP distribution in vivo. Fourth, biocompatibility and stability of formulation increase therapeutic performance. Fifth, extending residence time in systemic circulation as well as sustaining therapeutic plasma levels in the body also enhance patient efficacy. Innovation in nanotechnology has opened a novel paradigm in the pharmaceutical field (Rajpoot, 2020a). These novel fields have various challenges and require more research work to improve safety in clinical applications. In contrast, MNCs can combine different functionalities in the inner core or at the tumor surface to synergistically attain maximumanti-cancer effect (Fig. 2.1). For instance, folate-anchored MNCs can easily track folate receptors, which are present on the surface of tumor cells, and thus offer targeted drug delivery. Therefore, this tactic can be used in the therapy of cancer (Rajpoot and Jain, 2018).

2.1.1 Nanocomposites employed in the fabrication of multifunctional nanoparticles

Several organic as well as inorganic substances have been used in the formulation of multifunctional NPs with their distinguishing architecture and linked functionalities. MNCs are found very efficient in targeted drug delivery for the treatment of tumors (Nazir et al., 2014). MNC carriers are made up of various inorganic and organic materials. They are employed in the fabrication of MNC particles. They are classified into two forms, i.e., organic (micelles, liposomes, nanogels, dendrimers, etc.) and inorganic (super paramagnetic iron oxide, QDs, lanthanide ions, gold, etc.) (Fig. 2.2) (Pandey et al., 2020b). Examples of organic or polymeric MNC formulations include dendrimers, liposomes, and nanogels (Rajpoot, 2017; Li et al., 2021; Dalir Abdolahinia et al., 2022).

Figure 2.1 Multifunctional nanocomposites can be used in three ways in the treatment of cancer.

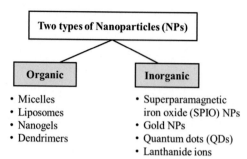

Figure 2.2 Multifunctional nanocomposites based on types of materials employed.

Moreover, these are appealing building blocks for multifunctional owing to their multipurpose surface and core chemistry. Furthermore, they show a high biodegradability, high drug loading capacity, and enhanced endocytosis via the target cell (Jia et al., 2013; Bansal et al., 2020).

2.1.2 Types of multifunctional nanocomposites

These MNCs can be proteins, peptides, lipids, polymers, metals, and oxides. They can be used in different therapeutic fields, for instance, in the formulation of dendrimers (Devadas et al., 2021), micelles (Ghosh and Biswas, 2021), liposomes (Guimaraes et al., 2021), CNTs (Nurazzi et al., 2021), QDs (Zhu et al., 2021), iron oxide NPs (Li and Tang, 2022), gold NPs (AuNPs) (Pandey et al., 2020b), and silica NPs (Kalyane et al., 2021). The modern research on nanocomposites depends on the development of multifunctional nanocarriers. These nanocarriers are made up of lipid-, thiol-, polyethylene glycol (PEG)-modified polymeric materials, and these are decorated for therapeutic, targeting, and imaging purpose (Akbari et al., 2021; Zhen et al., 2021). In this segment, these polymeric carrier classes are summarized in Fig. 2.3.

MNCs have smaller sizes and larger surface areas. These properties are making special of it. The MNCs particles very easily reach the target site and interact with cell membranes, reducing NP size may lead to an improvement in mobility. Consequently, these MNC particles are used for better cellular uptake of NPs (Ha et al., 2015). MNCs are having a small size. These NPs are not recognized as foreign agents. Sometimes these particles do not enter macrophages through membrane pores (Choi et al., 2009; Donkor and Tang, 2014). In a succeeding investigation, researchers advocated that comparatively smaller diameters (i.e., 2–6 nm) of the core of AuNPs were satisfactory for increasing dramatic alterations in NP penetration effectiveness and mechanism (Doane and Burda, 2012; Jiang et al., 2015).

The shape size of MNC particles is affected by the membrane energies of the site of the targeted tumor. It is identified by the free energy analysis method. The ideal size of MNC particles is mandatory for successful target drug delivery. The spherical

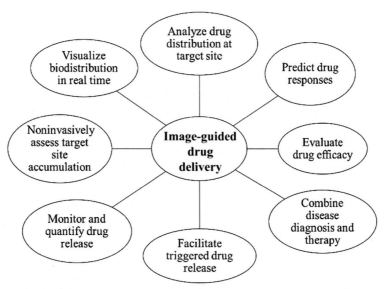

Figure 2.3 Applications of image-guided drug delivery systems.

MNC particles thus showed high targetability at the site (Li et al., 2015). The formation of aggregates of MNCs represented characters like size and types of shape (Verma and Stellacci, 2010).

2.1.3 Surface chemistry

Surface characteristics of MNCs' play a vital role in communication with the cell. The hydrophilic surface of MNCs is protected from macrophage capture (Moghimi and Szebeni, 2003). These all MNC particles are usually developed by coating surface of NPs using hydrophilic polymer like PEG. The PEG has approved intrinsic physicochemical properties of MNC particles. It is biocompatible and shows high flexibility. It is having low toxicity and immunogenicity nature also. Therefore, MNC particles are fabricated by using copolymers with hydrophilic and hydrophobic parts (Adams et al., 2003; Harris et al., 2001).

The MNC particles that accumulate in off-target organs like the liver and spleen are reduced by surface modification techniques, including PEG. It was found to reduce the size of MNC particles. PEG-coated NPs have various therapeutic advantages, such as high solubility in several solvents, decreased adsorption of circulated proteins, and prolonged circulation half-life over non-PEGylated NPs (Sperling and Parak, 2010; Svenson and Prud'homme, 2012; Ulusoy et al., 2016). The MNCs decrease aggregation at the site of targeted tumors site. PEG chains have functional groups of alcohols, carboxylic acids amines, and thiols. These functional groups help to conjugate tiny materials or target ligands. Scientists reported that the tumor-targeting potential of hyaluronic acid NPs was increased after the chemical conjugation of amine-functionalized PEG. It also helps to escape the unintended accumulation in the liver (Yoon et al., 2012).

2.2 Pitfalls associated with traditional cancer therapy

The nonspecific nature of cancers cells creates problems. It cannot be easily traced by the patient, and it is not easy to confirm this disease. In some cases, the patient does not have any symptoms of cancer. Therefore, the beginning stage of cancer is not traceable and is ignored by the patient. This phase provides time for the cancer cells to spread throughout the body. Proper diagnosis of cancer disease is in the primary stage is essential. It is a surety of successfully curing of a disease. Identification and confirmation of cancer in the early stage is the first step toward the treatment of cancer disease. If the cancer cell spread out to other organs of the body that stage is called the secondary stage of cancer disease. It is not easy to cure, and that stage becomes out of reach, as does clinical treatment (Tomasello et al., 2022; Sinicrope et al., 2013). Some common examples of diagnosis difficulties are discussed below related to cancer diseases.

2.2.1 Diagnosis difficulties associated with cancers

2.2.1.1 Esophageal cancer

The esophageal cancer (OC) results in majority of death globally. This disease is very critical to treat due to a lack of symptoms. Moreover, OC disease's early symptoms are not simply to overcome. In this disease, earlier symptoms are not easy to identify because the primary stage of cancer disease has smaller tumors and sometimes causes few or no symptoms. OC cells are transmitted to the diverse regions of the body, including stomach, liver, lungs, lymph nodes, etc. The last phase of cancer is known as a metastasized stage in this stage tumor is incurable. The majority of cancer cases for the treatment come at a final stage where patients emphasis on prolonging their life by relieving the symptoms (Schlansky et al., 2006; Jamel et al., 2019; Jeene et al., 2018).

2.2.1.2 Prostate cancer

The most common second cancer disease is prostate cancer. The problems associated with prostate cancer are not easy to diagnose. It typically occurs in elderly patients who are over 50. Additionally, it is a common cancer in older males. It is related to the sex organ of males; therefore, it does not display any signs in the primary stage. In most of the cases, it has been seen that prostate cancer progress slowly. It does not have detectable indications of metastasizing from the prostate into diverse regions of the body, particularly in the bones and lymph nodes. Prostate cancer disease is easy to detect through the prostate-specific antigen method or biopsy (Downing et al., 2019; Ilic et al., 2018; Melegh and Oltean, 2019).

2.2.1.3 Pancreatic cancer

The third cancer disease is pancreatic cancer. It is a silent cancer disease that comes into the body very silently and does not often show early symptoms. The symptoms depend on the location of the cancer disease (Hanahan and Weinberg, 2000).

2.2.2 Absence of efficient biomarkers for the identification of cancer

Biomarkers are widely used in the identification of cancer types. In the majority of cases, the cancer remains undiagnosed due to the unavailability of the best biomarkers. Biomarkers are widely used not only for cancer diagnosis but also to give an idea of their prognostic value. Researchers are still searching for suitable new biomarkers that will be best for the diagnosis of certain types of cancer. Biomarkers were found suitable for identifying the primary stage of cancer. However, several technical problems are faced during using proteomic profiling of patients as a diagnostic tool. Hence, research should be validated to get high standard results (Raaijmakers et al., 2005).

2.2.3 Drawbacks of traditional chemotherapeutic drugs

Available chemotherapeutic drugs are used for the treatment of cancer. These all produce side effects due to their toxic nature. These all–chemotherapy agents kill cancer cells and normal cells in the body. When patients take these chemotherapy agents, they cause various toxicity or adverse effects. Sometimes these chemotherapy agents also produce more toxicity and death in patients. Therefore, there is a need for suitable targeted therapy and the selection of proper chemotherapy agents in cancer treatment (Knezevic and Clarke, 2020).

2.2.4 Metastasis phase of cancer

Different factors in metastasis phase of cancer-induced difficulties in diagnosis. For instance, during the metastasis phase, no indications for occurring of cancer are highlighted. A cancer patient does not feel any changes in their body, and cancers cells are spread from one body part to another very slowly, and during this phase, the cancer becomes so critical. Therefore, the metastasis phase is also called the asymptomatic phase. The metastasis stage of cancer disease is not diagnosed with symptoms and permits cancer to spread to distinctive parts of the body devoid of any medical interference. This phase of cancer is also known as the "primary cancer site" while the dissemination of cancer through the original locations in other parts of the body is called the "secondary or metastatic site" (Ganesh and Massague, 2021; Caswell-Jin et al., 2018; Schau et al., 2020).

In the secondary or metastasis phase of cancer disease, the cancer cells collect in one place and form colonies of cells and create small tumors (Schau et al., 2020). The formation of this small tumor is the main problem of the disease. Small tumors, later on, change into big size under the metastasis phase. In the metastasis phase, small tumors are spread out from one organ to another organ through blood circulation as well as the lymphatic system. In most of the cases, cancers cells discharged some specific proteins that are called marker proteins (e.g., circular RNA) (Tian et al., 2020; Su et al., 2018). The marker proteins have been used for diagnosis and confirmation of cancer disease, but many cancer cells do not discharge this protein. Consequently, we need some other specific techniques. Researchers are still searching for any other suitable, simple, economic, and convenient alternative.

2.2.5 Traditional cancer therapy

During the therapy of cancer, some conventional methods were using chemotherapy, radiation, and surgery. This therapy produces many problems such as side effects, toxicity, drug resistance, etc. These problems are associated with the following reasons found during research by researchers.

2.2.5.1 Identification and targeting of cancer stem cells

Targeted cancer therapy is related to stem cells of cancer, where it needs detection of specific stem cells that are responsible for causing cancer. Traditional treatment approaches do not follow this technique, which is the primary cause for unsuccessful cancer treatment. Researchers are still searching for discovering a suitable method for the identification of specific stem cells that are liable for cancer disease (Afify and Seno, 2019; Yang et al., 2020).

2.2.5.2 Drug resistance of chemotherapy agents

Stem cells possess self-renewal properties. These stem cells are grown through the unique mechanism. In this manner, they can shield themselves from several destructive anticancer agents. For instance, adenosine 5′-triphosphate (ATP)-binding cassette transporter proteins are expressed at extreme amount in the stem cells. In addition, these transporter proteins may employ energy through ATP. Thus, ATP energy is freed through ATP after hydrolysis. It facilitates an energy-dependent process through the substrate efflux. In this manner, it helps stem cells to flush out the toxic substances through the intracellular cytoplasm in the extracellular regions against the concentration gradient. In addition, the CSCs uphold this property, however, genetic instability has been observed in cancer in various clinical studies (Raaijmakers et al., 2005; Copland et al., 2005).

2.2.5.3 Requirement of specificity and cancer epigenetic profiling of epi-drugs

Earlier, the principle behind the treatment of cancer was the detection and identification of disease. The general cause of cancer disease is due to changes in cells' DNA, including mutational or any other chromosomal aberration actions. Moreover, genetic mutations are detected in the many cancer's patients. However, genetic mutations have not been seen in some cancer cases. Moreover, no huge genetic deviations are seen. Ultimately types of cancer come under the malignant phenotype of cancer, which proves that some missing links are still present to determine the exact cause for cancer disease. The epigenetic mechanisms have been represented as the growth and initiation of tumorigenesis. Furthermore, it may permit the persistence of the malignant phenotype in the cancer tissues (Chen et al., 2004; Laird et al., 1995).

2.3 Targeting mechanisms employed in cancer therapy

Medications used to combat cancer are found useless if they don't reach their target within a suitable amount and timeframe, which may hurt patient health. Once the medicine is supplied in the appropriate dose and exhibits maximum potency in cancerous cells, only then will chemotherapeutic drug therapy be efficacious. This means that to reduce the risk of toxic effects on healthy cells, nanostructures used to target cancer cells must be able to increase the local concentration of medications, mostly around tumors (Du and Elemento, 2015; Han et al., 2007). It is possible to classify the effective transport of NPs to target cells as active or passive, as will be detailed below.

2.3.1 Passive targeting

Intravenous injection is the most frequent mode of delivery for NP-based antitumor medicines. This method avoids the intestinal epithelial absorption necessary following oral delivery (Zhao and Castranova, 2011). The circulatory wall is compromised at tumor locations, allowing nanocomposites to aggregate in malignant cells as shown in (Maeda et al., 2013). Based on the cancer type, location, and microenvironment, the spacing between vascular endothelium in the tumor tissues might vary from 200 to 2000 nm. Furthermore, the nanomaterials are not immediately removed and concentrated in the tumor interstitium owing to poor lymphatic activity (Jain and Stylianopoulos, 2010; Hobbs et al., 1998).

Physical and chemical factors, for instance, size, shape (morphology), surface charge, and surface chemistry are important in the aggregation of nanomaterials (Bertrand et al., 2014). The size of nanomaterials affects the extent and kinetics of their deposition in the target tissue. The NPs must be smaller than the proportional cutoff in the neovasculature, with the size of the vehicle having a significant impact on extravasation to the tumor. Furthermore, blood circulation, passive interactions with macromolecules, and immunologic elimination mechanisms, such as phagocytosis, also impact the biodistribution of nanomaterial-based pharmaceutical formulations (Rosenblum et al., 2018).

Numerous studies have reported on the effective use of passive carcinoma cell targeting and the implementation of these findings into clinical therapies.

The first Food and Drug Administration (FDA)-approved nanodrug is a PEGylated liposome entrapped doxorubicin-based treatment for human immunodeficiency virus (HIV)-related Kaposi sarcoma tumor and ovarian cancer. Encapsulated doxorubicin within a lipid substance resulted in a significant decrease in the drug's intracellular and systemic cytotoxicity, as well as enhanced pharmacokinetics, regulated bioavailability, and release (Shi et al., 2017).

For the therapy of acute myeloid leukemia, recently FDA authorized a nanoformulation consisting of "liposomal entrapped cytarabine-daunorubicin combination (CPX-351 Vyxeos)." After 9.6 months investigation, results showed survival of patient's comparison to free drug after 6 months (Lancet et al., 2016). In the passive targeting phenomenon, the nanomaterials penetrate through the porous membranes and aggregate at the tumor location due to the EPR effect of passive targeting. Specialized ligands that attach to the receptors over cancer cells may be used to accomplish active targeting. Many of these compositions have received FDA approval (Shi et al., 2017), paving the way for novel cancer therapies. To increase biodistribution and reduce immune clearance, these nanoformulations may be given an extra level of targeting capabilities. The variety of EPR effects that have been reported previously and across different cancers limits the therapeutic effectiveness of passive tailored methods. Variable endothelium gaps caused by aggressive tumorous cell proliferation may lead to nonuniform nanomaterial extravasation into the target region (Chauhan and Jain, 2013).

Although it seems obvious that NP penetration should be greater in the hypoxic center of cancer than in the peripheral, little research contradicts this finding (Lee et al., 2010). Passive targeting becomes much more complicated as a result of this variability. Furthermore, extravasation has been demonstrated to be affected not just by permeability but also by the rate of blood flow near the tumor tissues. Passive targeting is even more difficult because there is a lot of "spatial and temporal" variation inside and across cancerous cells (Ernsting et al., 2013).

Furthermore, the interstitial cancer matrix blocks deeper penetration of nanostructures that can traverse the vascular. The size and shape characteristics of the material will play a vital role in enhancing matrix penetration there. According to Wong and colleagues, they've developed a nanosystem that changes size as it reaches distinct tumor regions. Destruction by tumor-associated metalloproteinases causes the gelatin particles to shrink from 100 to 10 nm in diameter after extravasation. Consequently, the lack of human solid tumor specimens that can be used to study the impacts of EPR has hindered our capacity to fully comprehend these consequences. A few subcutaneous "tumor xenograft models" that divide rapidly, characterized by extremely large EPR effects, are the foundation of our present understanding. It's possible that the information gained from these models might provide a misleading impression regarding the effectiveness of passive targeted NPs (Bogart et al., 2014).

Also, fewer studies exist on patients describing the EPR effect, which is critical to note. Consequently, more research into cancer pathogenesis and EPR effects on tumor types are required. Such a thorough understanding of nanomaterials will be important in the development of tailored cancer therapy, which will lead to even greater therapeutic effects.

2.3.2 Active targeting

Active targeting, "commonly referred to as the ligand-mediated" targeted method, is characterized by affinity-based identification, persistence, and enhanced uptake by the target tissue (Bertrand et al., 2014). Biochemical affinities for targeted delivery are dependent on many molecular interactions, such as "receptor-ligand interactions, charge-based interactions, and facilitated motif-based interactions with substrate molecules" (Byrne et al., 2008; Varki, 2007). A ligand may be any of a variety of macromolecules, including carbohydrates, peptides, nucleic acid, proteins, antibodies, and small chemical compounds like micronutrients (i.e., vitamins) (Verma and Stellacci, 2010; Mout et al., 2012; Weissleder et al., 2005). Surface chemicals produced by cancer cells, proteins, carbohydrates, or lipids already present inside the body, compounds released by tumor in the vicinity of damaged cells, or even the physicochemical environment in their proximity may all be targeted substrates (Peer et al., 2007).

A NP-based smart, targeted technique takes advantage of the bifunctional characteristic of ligand-target antigen interactions. The avidity of nanomaterials for their corresponding targets increases when multiple ligand compounds are deposited onto the nanostructures (Weissleder et al., 2005). Furthermore, via cooperativity impacts, the interaction of one compound often helps the attachment of successive molecules, thus improving the binding efficiencies and subsequent activities. The active targeting strategy has been used to enhance medication delivery effectiveness by enhancing NP uptake by target cells. Antihuman epidermal growth factor receptor (anti-HER2) targeting ligand components functionalized on the NP surface improve cellular absorption of nanomaterials in HER2-expressing tumor cells. Contrary to this, the use of non-HER2 targeting molecules and/or nontargeted liposome NPs lead in the increased deposition of NPs in the tumor site's perivascular and stromal spaces. These accumulating NPs were swiftly caught and removed by macrophages, leading to tumor cell internalization (Kirpotin et al., 2006).

In some other work, scientists produced insulin-like growth factor 1 (IGF1) and then they attached it with the iron oxide NPs with doxorubicin as a therapeutic component (Zhou et al., 2015). The tumor targeting and penetration were extraordinary after intravenous delivery of nanomaterials into a patient-derived xenograft (PDX) prototype of pancreatic cancer. Theragnostic IGF1-iron oxide NPs-doxorubicin treatment greatly slowed the development of pancreatic PDX tumors, indicating that it has the potential to enhance therapeutic results (Kumar and Mohammad, 2011; Sigismund et al., 2018; Ohno et al., 2013; Messersmith and Ahnen, 2008).

The variation in the NP's attraction toward normal and cancer cells would ordinarily not be adequate for high precision and effective distribution to the specified location needed for broad functionality in biomedical applications due to the complexity of nanomaterial routes of administration and unpleasant interrelations with nonspecific substances within the organisms. Recent techniques have looked at simultaneously targeting numerous receptors present on the cell using singular NP structures coupled with various ligands (Li et al., 2011).

Bhattacharyya et al. used AuNPs to build and study dual ligand-receptor nanomaterials. They utilized monoclonal antibodies targeting EGFR and folate receptor, which are abundantly expressed in ovarian cancer, as the dual ligands for AuNPs targeting (Bhattacharyya et al., 2011) and discovered that this dual-targeting approach is more effective in transporting AuNPs to cancerous cells than the single ligand method (Bhattacharyya et al., 2011). Multiple parameters, therefore, must be tuned for active-targeted cancer treatments to be successful. The degree of avidity toward the substrate is determined by the density of ligands on the surface of NPs; hence, the methods utilized to conjugate ligands over the outer region of NPs are key components of the targeted systems. Normally, covalent coupling techniques are being employed by scientists, although affinity complexes with physical absorption may also be used efficiently (Gao et al., 2010).

There are many ways to keep conjugated ligands stable in the hostile environment of the human body, and each has its own advantages and disadvantages (Bertrand et al., 2014). According to the "more-ligand-more-targeting" idea, there have been certain occurrences where enhancing ligand density to improve overall affinity did not necessarily have a linear relationship with ligand density. Molecular saturation, the incorrect orientation of ligands and ligand bond restrictions, and steric limitations from surrounding molecules have been cited as possible explanations for this phenomenon (Elias et al., 2013).

Even while NPs with a significant level of hydrophobicity accumulated on them, they were more susceptible to macrophage absorption and did not give a substantial benefit in terms of quick target cell internalization (Valencia et al., 2011). Some of this research raises questions regarding the importance of targeted moieties, conjugation methods, and densities in the expected results of therapeutic nanosystems based on these findings. To maximize the effectiveness and viability of NP-based active target devices in vivo, their targeting precision and payload transport capability must be optimized. To measure uniqueness, researchers look at how well the ligand-conjugated NPs interact with their target molecules, taking into account any off-target impacts that may have occurred before the NPs reached their targets. Biodistribution interactions have a major role in determining this level of specificity. NPs' approach to their target locations might be hindered by some smaller interactions offered by varied complex biomolecules based on simple "Van-der Waals interactions." Additionally, in vivo environment, a phenomenon known as Vroman's effect occurs when a large number of smaller proteins and intrinsic biomolecules attach nonspecifically to the surfaces of NPs, changing the overall nanosystem's "identity" (Vroman, 1962).

This change may cause nanomaterials to lose their affinity, resulting in less-than-ideal localization in desirable areas or cellular targets. Active clearance mechanisms offered by different immune cells, as well as blood flow/renal filtration rate, have a significant impact on the improved pharmacokinetic characteristics. The higher affinity depends on ligands may not reimburse the clearance procedures since tumor blood circulation is minimal in comparison to other organs and tissue (Bertrand et al., 2014). As a result, actively targeted nanostructures with long blood circulation durations and biocompatible profiles, as well as neutral coating to avoid widespread nonspecific binding of blood molecules, must be created. The majority of cognate substrates for NP-bound ligands are found outside of the epithelial lining of blood vessels in the extravascular area of malignancies. To reach the target, active targeting heavily depends on endoplasmic retention effects. As a result, it's critical to think about how we may use endoplasmic retention effects to accomplish active targeting. Further, endoplasmic retention potential can differ by tumor type, and certain malignancies have large epithelial fenestrations, allowing for the usage of NPs with a wider size range (Bansal et al., 2020).

In certain tumor situations, the size of NPs should be adjusted to match the size of the vascular lining gap (Hobbs et al., 1998). One of the processes characterizing tumor biology is endoplasmic retention. A variety of additional variables, such as less blood circulation in the tumor vasculature, tumor site macrophages, and the extracellular matrix milieu surrounding tumor cells, might provide obstacles for nanotherapeutics. These variables have a big impact on how targeted NPs discover their substrate and distribute their content. A comprehensive grasp of these parameters will lead to crucial synthesis techniques for active and passive targeting of tailored NPs treatment.

2.4 Multifunctional nanoparticles in therapeutics

Currently, the MNC particle technique is more important for development as well as biomedical applications. Moreover, MNC particles are synthesized using nanocrystalline method, advanced polymer processing, and fictionalization approaches. The MNC particle technology plays a key role in the following significant areas: (1) as a contrast agent, (2) for targeted delivery of drug/gene, and (3) in the thermal therapies. These MNC particles showed immense offers that are developing biomedical areas, for example, multimodal imaging, theranostics, image-directed therapies, etc. The other importance of multifunctional NPs is discussed below.

2.4.1 As a contrast agent

In cancer therapy, proper diagnosis of cancer disease is an earlier stage of metastasis. It is the key step for effective treatment. If cancer disease is not diagnosed at the primary stage of metastasis, then it is transferred to other parts of the body and comes under the second phase. The multifunctional NPs have been used for early diagnosis as well as efficient therapy of dangerous ailments like cancer. These MNC particles are continually enhancing the pressure for the advancement of well-organized and trustworthy techniques. The current application of multifunctional NPs in the biomedical fields in medical imaging continues to increase for optimizing and obtaining a good quality image and minimizing radiation dose. Therefore, these MNC particles are used for getting a better diagnosis of pathologies and patient safety (Manson et al., 2020).

Novel multifunctional NPs are attracting diagnostic technology. In this technology, MNC particles consist of fluorescent semiconductor nanocrystals (i.e., QDs) and magnetic NPs. In addition, this novel technology has been proven its excellent properties for the diagnosis of in vivo imaging. These imaging techniques play a key role in the medical diagnosis of the metastasis phase of cancer, and improved research in imaging can be helpful for the earlier diagnosis, effective treatment, and management of dangerous diseases such as cancer. Multifunctional NP medical imaging techniques are using numerous different imaging tactics like radiography, ultrasound, magnetic resonance imaging (MRI), nuclear medicine, emission tomography, computed tomography, and numerous optical imaging methods (Llinás et al., 2005), etc. The importance of multifunctional NPs in medical imaging techniques is shown below (Fig. 2.4).

MNC particles have been used for obtaining a medical image of cancer cells. MNC particles have also been used in nanoforms of nanocomposite materials like liposomes, proteins, dendrimers, and micelles for obtaining confirmation of cancers cell. The MNC particles are used to deliver anticancer drugs to pathologic sites. Nowadays, the most commonly used NPs of therapeutic agents are Doxil, Ambisome, Abraxane, etc. (Kiessling et al., 2014).

2.4.2 Targeted delivery of drug/gene

Multilayered nanocomposite particles have been used as nanomedical carriers for cancer targeted therapy. The MNC particles technology becomes more popular due to the following reasons such as low toxicity, low dose of drug requires, and fixed target of the site make effective treatment. The correct site and definite cancers cell-targeted therapy keep away from enzymatic destruction within the endosomes of the normal cell. Since the multilayered NPs system is only about one-millionth the volume of a human cell. MNC particles are used to deliver that drug or gene to a suitable site within the living normal cell. In addition, portions of the multilayered NPs system may be protected from premature degradation or mistargeting to normal cells. All of

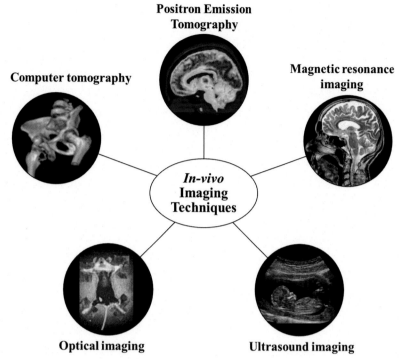

Figure 2.4 Main in vivo imaging techniques employed using multifunctional nanoparticles.

these problems were removed by using a multilayered NPs system. These multilayered nanocomposite carriers successful target cancer. Further, these drug delivery systems induce minimum deleterious effects to the patient (Pham et al., 2018; Men et al., 2020; Jafari et al., 2019).

Multilayered nanocomposite particle systems have been used to achieve efficient cancer drug delivery. The multilayered nanocomposite particles were required to identify interactions of cancer cells with nanomaterials environment, stem cell targeting, stability of drugs, cell-surface receptors study, anticancer drug discharge, molecular transmissions of cell signaling concerned with pathobiology of illness, etc. Numerous multilayered nanocomposite particles were developed using anticancer drugs, such as paclitaxel, doxorubicin, 5-fluorouracil, and dexamethasone, for the therapy of cancer disease. The others formulated forms of multilayered NPs are QDs, chitosan, polylactic/glycolic acid (PLGA), and PLGA-derived NPs have been employed in the RNAi delivery (in vitro), respectively. In brain cancer, diagnosis and targeting of drug using multilayered NPs technology were very challenging tasks, but they were significantly resolved with multilayered NPs technique. Brain diagnosis and treatment became easy with the multilayered NPs technique. Through this technique, we can obtain easily image and deliver therapeutic agents to the brain. The anticancer drugs are loperamide and doxorubicin. The multilayered NPs of loperamide and doxorubicin not only cross the blood-brain barrier but also discharge drugs at the desired therapeutic level in the brain domain successfully (Stylios et al., 2005).

2.4.3 Thermal therapies

Nanotechnology provides offers for the development of numerous choices for anticancer tactics like thermal therapies. These thermal therapies significantly destruct normal cells. Present limitations related to cancer treatment are associated with the identification of cancer cells without producing any side effects. The image-guided technique is useful to detect metastasis or initial phase of cancer. In thermal therapies, one heating source is used for heat-induced therapies. These have been used for the identification of surface plasmon resonance (SPR) in the near-infrared region as well as alternating magnetic fields (AMFs). A wide range of inorganic multifunctional composite NPs are SPR and AMFs. It is based on thermal therapies and medical imaging techniques. The prospects of photothermal therapy (PTT) can be combined with immunotherapy (PTTi). PTTi can be employed as immunoadjuvants in amalgamation to PTT agents (Wang et al., 2013; Zheng et al., 2011).

Further, it not only gives a synergistic antitumor result but also shows a wonderful possibility in thermal-induced therapies as well as in the inorganic NPs research. It should solve several types of problems, photostability, physiological stability, as well as clearance, prior advancing into clinical trials. Over traditional therapy approaches, the stability of inorganic NPs is having various benefits and removes long-term adverse responses. Some inorganic MNC particles have been utilized in clinical diagnosis in the form of iron oxide in the MRI technique for clinically relevant problems, for instance, systemic toxicity and drug clearance. However, it should be resolve prior employing thermal therapies for clinical application. In addition, these inorganic MNC particles have confirmed their tremendous potential as a theranostic tool as well as exposed a novel era in the cancer therapy (Wang et al., 2013; Zheng et al., 2011).

2.4.4 Other significant roles of multifunctional nanoparticles

MNC particles have been applied for diverse purposes like nutraceutical delivery, cancer therapy, diagnosis, HIV/acquired immunodeficiency syndrome therapy, etc. (Resch-Genger et al., 2008; Doria et al., 2012).

2.5 Challenges and limitations of targeted cancer therapies

Ideal properties of different nanocomposite materials are preferred in current targeted drug delivery system, especially in the cancer therapy. The targeted cancer drug delivery field has exposed various challenges and limitations in the treatment and management of cancer (Fig. 2.5).

Based on a clinical report, it is expected that the nanocomposite materials will develop a complete health care system. The targeted cancer drug delivery sector is based on the remarkable developments in targeted cancer drugs over the past many years. Moreover, the purpose, plan, design, and development of efficient cancer nanocomposite particles are still immensely challenging tasks because very few nanocomposite particle formulations have entered in clinical trials process. The physical, chemical, and development factors of nanocomposite particles contribute an important role related to biocompatibility and toxicity (Daima et al., 2014, 2013).

Consequently, synthesis as well as evaluation of the nanocomposite particles for cancer-targeted drug delivery are used to reduce the major unwanted toxicity of anticancer drug nanocomposite particles. The MNC nanocarriers deliver the anticancer drug. Additionally, since these nanocomposite particle carriers come into contact with biomolecular substances such as lipids, proteins, and amino acids, they tend to aggregate and then form a protein corona. It is disturbing the regular function of nanocomposite particle formulations, which lead to failure in controlling cancer cell growth (Shi et al., 2017). Therefore, physical characteristics are key factors for formulation success. The storage and stability of nanocomposite particle formulations are

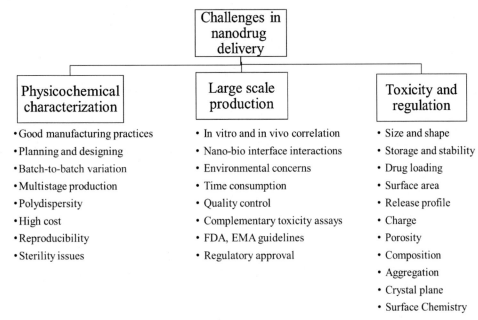

Figure 2.5 Diagrammatic representation of various challenges seen in the delivery of cancer nanotherapeutics.

related to their physical and chemical nature. The nanocomposite particles' storage and instability also affect their pharmacological performance (Ruozi et al., 2015; Ma et al., 2016). The major issue of targeted cancer drug delivery is human safety, and it is associated with MNC material (Wang et al., 2015).

Several clinical studies have seen the unfavorable properties of MNC particle carriers that are toxic. Consequently, "nanotoxicology," a branch of nanocomposite particle therapy that has evolved as an important domain of research and shown a way for the evaluation of the toxicity of nanocomposite particles. In addition, the manufacturing of nanocomposite particle products for commercialization, the big scale-production, is also difficult. Normally, only small quantities of nanocomposite particles are employed for preclinical and clinical trial reports. In the large-scale manufacturing of nanocomposite particles formulations, the variation of their physical and chemical properties from batch to batch is a major problem. Moreover, the high cost of raw materials for multistage production of nanocomposite particle formulation also makes this nanotherapeutics a costly option (Coradeghini et al., 2013; Ji et al., 2012).

The success of any formulation of targeted drug delivery systems is based on well-planned manufacturing tactics. These are vital for clinical use. The main challenges behind the formulation success of MNC particles are regulatory approval because the FDA does not release specific guidelines for nanomaterial products (Santos et al., 2019; Foulkes et al., 2020; Halamoda-Kenzaoui et al., 2019).

The development of a successful novel targeted cancer drug delivery formulation depends upon the removal of all challenges and limitations related to the following parameters: nanocomposite-particle interactions with cancers and normal cells, an environment of nanocomposite particles, drug and carrier, and pharmacokinetics study. There is a need for development of more effective, acceptable, potential nanocomposite particles for effective cancer therapy. In addition, it required a thorough study of all types of targeted drug delivery formulation cases, their limitations, and a comprehensive set of rules by the regulatory authorities to accelerate the evaluation and approval of cancer-targeted cancer nanocomposite therapeutics.

2.6 Limitations of targeted cancer therapies

The limitation of targeted cancer drug therapy is that only some cancer cells show a single genetic mutation. These types of genetic mutation flexibility as well as cellular heterogeneity cause failure of antagonist. In fact, if it is possible to develop targeted cancer drug therapy for individual mutations, the detection and prediction of mutations within one single tumor cell are very difficult. In some of cancer therapy where only a single mutation may be targeted, the malignant cells ultimately avoid drug action as well as become resistant (Salomoni and Calabretta, 2009; Mahoney et al., 2015; Negrier et al., 2017; Xiao et al., 2015).

An example of cancer therapeutic combinations is the combination of two targeted agents like sorafenib and bevacizumab (Azad et al., 2008; Sosman and Puzanov, 2009). In the clinical trial of Parasol, the toxicity report of combined bevacizumab and pazopanib chemotherapy overshadowed the insignificant effectiveness (22% patients) (Negrier et al., 2017; Bitting et al., 2014; Postow et al., 2015), and in clinical trials of combined EGFR- and vascular endothelial growth factor anticancer drug targeting agents in nonsmall cell lung cancer patients (Ma et al., 2016). Many anticancer drug combinations are used for clinical studies (Lucchini et al., 2014). These drugs should not only target EGFR-expressing tumor cells but also target cells inside GI and oral mucosae (Lucchini et al., 2014; Sandoo et al., 2015).

Another example has been seen with immunosuppressants (monoclonal antibodies) drugs such as ipilimumab, pembrolizumab, atezolizumab, and nivolumab. They were used as excellent anticancer agents (De Velasco et al., 2017; Luo et al., 2018). As per the literature survey, various challenges and limitations have been reported by researchers, which are associated with formulation, targeted drug delivery, an environment of target and drug, side effects related to targeted drug therapy, and regulatory authority regulation law. These all factors should be considered to rectify the problems and carry out more research based on a clinical trial database to develop more successful nanocomposite particles therapy (Simchowitz et al., 2010).

2.7 Conclusion

The prevailing world has exploited nanoscale-based multifunctional drug delivery systems not only to decrease in vivo toxic effects but also to increase the efficiency of numerous therapeutic molecules. Moreover, recently clinically employed nanocomposites have revealed a great response, especially in the alleviation of drug-associated toxicity. Further, the expansion of "multifunctional" NPs with extraordinary topographies like targetability and tomography by employing some contrast agents in the NPs have boosted their applicability in cancer therapy. Though the addition of more functionality results in an increase in development costs as well as effort, more intricate in vivo performance, and regulatory-related difficulties.

Abbreviations

AIDS	acquired immunodeficiency syndrome
AMFs	alternating magnetic fields
Anti-HER2	antihuman epidermal growth factor receptor
ATP	adenosine 5′-triphosphate
AuNPs	gold NPs
CNTs	carbon nanotubes
CSCs	cancer stem cells

EGFR	epidermal growth factor receptor
EPR	enhanced permeability and retention
FDA	Food and Drug Administration
HER2	human epidermal growth factor receptor
HIV	human immunodeficiency virus
IGF1	insulin-like growth factor 1
MNCs	multifunctional nanocomposites
MRI	magnetic resonance imaging
NPs	nanoparticles
OC	esophageal cancer
PDX	patient-derived xenograft
PEG	polyethylene glycol
PLGA	polylactic/glycolic acid
PTT	photothermal therapy
PTTi	PTT combined immunotherapy
QDs	quantum dots
SPIO	superparamagnetic iron oxide
SPR	surface plasmon resonance
VEGF	vascular endothelial growth factor

References

Adams, M.L., Lavasanifar, A., Kwon, G.S., 2003. Amphiphilic block copolymers for drug delivery. J. Pharm. Sci. 92, 1343—1355.

Afify, S.M., Seno, M., 2019. Conversion of stem cells to cancer stem cells: undercurrent of cancer initiation, Cancers (Basel), 11. p. 345.

Akbari, E., Mousazadeh, H., Sabet, Z., Fattahi, T., Dehnad, A., Akbarzadeh, A., et al., 2021. Dual drug delivery of trapoxin A and methotrexate from biocompatible PLGA-PEG polymeric nanoparticles enhanced antitumor activity in breast cancer cell line. J. Drug. Deliv. Sci. Technol. 61, 102294.

Alhajamee, M., Marai, K., Al Abbas, S.M.N., Homayouni Tabrizi, M., 2021. Co-encapsulation of curcumin and tamoxifen in lipid-chitosan hybrid nanoparticles for cancer therapy, Mater. Technol., 37. pp. 1183—1194.

Anup, N., Rajpoot, K., Tekade, R.K., 2021. Overview of biopharmaceutics and pharmacokinetics. In: Tekade, R.K. (Ed.), Biopharmaceutics and Pharmacokinetics Considerations. Elsevier, Academic Press, pp. 1—16.

Azad, N.S., Posadas, E.M., Kwitkowski, V.E., Steinberg, S.M., Jain, L., Annunziata, C.M., et al., 2008. Combination targeted therapy with sorafenib and bevacizumab results in enhanced toxicity and antitumor activity. J. Clin. Oncol. 26, 3709—3714.

Bansal, S.K., Rajpoot, K., Sreeharsha, N., Youngren-Ortiz, S.R., Anup, N., Tekade, R.K., 2020. Endosomal escape tendency of drug delivery systems to mediate cytosolic delivery of therapeutics. In: Tekade, R.K. (Ed.), The Future of Pharmaceutical Product Development and Research. Academic Press, pp. 227—258.

Bertrand, N., Wu, J., Xu, X., Kamaly, N., Farokhzad, O.C., 2014. Cancer nanotechnology: the impact of passive and active targeting in the era of modern cancer biology. Adv. Drug. Deliv. Rev. 66, 2—25.

Bevilacqua, P., Nuzzo, S., Torino, E., Condorelli, G., Salvatore, M., Grimaldi, A.M., 2021. Antifouling strategies of nanoparticles for diagnostic and therapeutic application: a systematic review of the literature, Nanomaterials (Basel), 11. p. 780.

Bhattacharyya, S., Khan, J.A., Curran, G.L., Robertson, J.D., Bhattacharya, R., Mukherjee, P., 2011. Efficient delivery of gold nanoparticles by dual receptor targeting. Adv. Mater. 23, 5034—5038.

Bitting, R.L., Healy, P., Creel, P.A., Turnbull, J., Morris, K., Wood, S.Y., et al., 2014. A phase Ib study of combined VEGFR and mTOR inhibition with vatalanib and everolimus in patients with advanced renal cell carcinoma. Clin. Genitourin. Cancer 12, 241−250.

Bogart, L.K., Pourroy, G., Murphy, C.J., Puntes, V., Pellegrino, T., Rosenblum, D., et al., 2014. Nanoparticles for imaging, sensing, and therapeutic intervention. ACS Nano 8, 3107−3122.

Byrne, J.D., Betancourt, T., Brannon-Peppas, L., 2008. Active targeting schemes for nanoparticle systems in cancer therapeutics. Adv. Drug. Deliv. Rev. 60, 1615−1626.

Caswell-Jin, J.L., Plevritis, S.K., Tian, L., Cadham, C.J., Xu, C., Stout, N.K., et al., 2018. Change in survival in metastatic breast cancer with treatment advances: meta-analysis and systematic review. JNCI Cancer Spectr. 2, pky062.

Chauhan, V.P., Jain, R.K., 2013. Strategies for advancing cancer nanomedicine. Nat. Mater. 12, 958−962.

Chen, W., Cooper, T.K., Zahnow, C.A., Overholtzer, M., Zhao, Z., Ladanyi, M., et al., 2004. Epigenetic and genetic loss of Hic1 function accentuates the role of p53 in tumorigenesis. Cancer Cell 6, 387−398.

Choi, J., Zhang, Q., Reipa, V., Wang, N.S., Stratmeyer, M.E., Hitchins, V.M., et al., 2009. Comparison of cytotoxic and inflammatory responses of photoluminescent silicon nanoparticles with silicon micron-sized particles in RAW 264.7 macrophages. J. Appl. Toxicol. 29, 52−60.

Copland, M., Jorgensen, H.G., Holyoake, T.L., 2005. Evolving molecular therapy for chronic myeloid leukaemia—are we on target? Hematology 10, 349−359.

Coradeghini, R., Gioria, S., Garcia, C.P., Nativo, P., Franchini, F., Gilliland, D., et al., 2013. Size-dependent toxicity and cell interaction mechanisms of gold nanoparticles on mouse fibroblasts. Toxicol. Lett. 217, 205−216.

Daima, H.K., Selvakannan, P.R., Shukla, R., Bhargava, S.K., Bansal, V., 2013. Fine-tuning the antimicrobial profile of biocompatible gold nanoparticles by sequential surface functionalization using polyoxometalates and lysine. PLoS One 8, e79676.

Daima, H.K., Selvakannan, P.R., Kandjani, A.E., Shukla, R., Bhargava, S.K., Bansal, V., 2014. Synergistic influence of polyoxometalate surface corona towards enhancing the antibacterial performance of tyrosine-capped Ag nanoparticles. Nanoscale 6, 758−765.

Dalir Abdolahinia, E., Barati, G., Ranjbar-Navazi, Z., Kadkhoda, J., Islami, M., Hashemzadeh, N., et al., 2022. Application of nanogels as drug delivery systems in multicellular spheroid tumor model. J. Drug. Deliv. Sci. Technol. 68, 103109.

De Velasco, G., Je, Y., Bosse, D., Awad, M.M., Ott, P.A., Moreira, R.B., et al., 2017. Comprehensive meta-analysis of key immune-related adverse events from CTLA-4 and PD-1/PD-L1 inhibitors in cancer patients. Cancer Immunol. Res. 5, 312−318.

Devadas, B., Periasamy, A.P., Bouzek, K., 2021. A review on poly(amidoamine) dendrimer encapsulated nanoparticles synthesis and usage in energy conversion and storage applications. Coord. Chem. Rev. 444, 214062.

Doane, T.L., Burda, C., 2012. The unique role of nanoparticles in nanomedicine: imaging, drug delivery and therapy. Chem. Soc. Rev. 41, 2885−2911.

Donkor, D.A., Tang, X.S., 2014. Tube length and cell type-dependent cellular responses to ultra-short single-walled carbon nanotube. Biomaterials 35, 3121−3131.

Doria, G., Conde, J., Veigas, B., Giestas, L., Almeida, C., Assuncao, M., et al., 2012. Noble metal nanoparticles for biosensing applications, Sensors (Basel), 12. pp. 1657−1687.

Downing, A., Wright, P., Hounsome, L., Selby, P., Wilding, S., Watson, E., et al., 2019. Quality of life in men living with advanced and localised prostate cancer in the UK: a population-based study. Lancet Oncol. 20, 436−447.

Du, W., Elemento, O., 2015. Cancer systems biology: embracing complexity to develop better anticancer therapeutic strategies. Oncogene 34, 3215−3225.

Elias, D.R., Poloukhtine, A., Popik, V., Tsourkas, A., 2013. Effect of ligand density, receptor density, and nanoparticle size on cell targeting. Nanomedicine 9, 194−201.

Ernsting, M.J., Murakami, M., Roy, A., Li, S.D., 2013. Factors controlling the pharmacokinetics, biodistribution and intratumoral penetration of nanoparticles. J. Control. Rel. 172, 782−794.

Fakhri, K.U., Sultan, A., Mushtaque, M., Hasan, M.R., Nafees, S., Hafeez, Z.B., et al., 2021. Obstructions in nanoparticles conveyance, nano-drug retention, and EPR effect in cancer therapies. In: Kumar, S., Rizvi, M.A., Verma, S. (Eds.), Handbook of Research on Advancements in Cancer Therapeutics. IGI Global, Hershey, PA, pp. 669–704.

Foulkes, R., Man, E., Thind, J., Yeung, S., Joy, A., Hoskins, C., 2020. The regulation of nanomaterials and nanomedicines for clinical application: current and future perspectives. Biomater. Sci. 8, 4653–4664.

Ganesh, K., Massague, J., 2021. Targeting metastatic cancer. Nat. Med. 27, 34–44.

Gao, J., Feng, S.S., Guo, Y., 2010. Antibody engineering promotes nanomedicine for cancer treatment. Nanomedicine (London, Engl.) 5, 1141–1145.

Gavas, S., Quazi, S., Karpinski, T.M., 2021. Nanoparticles for cancer therapy: current progress and challenges. Nanoscale Res. Lett. 16, 173.

Ghosh, B., Biswas, S., 2021. Polymeric micelles in cancer therapy: state of the art. J. Control. Rel. 332, 127–147.

Guimaraes, D., Cavaco-Paulo, A., Nogueira, E., 2021. Design of liposomes as drug delivery system for therapeutic applications. Int. J. Pharm. 601, 120571.

Ha, H.K., Kim, J.W., Lee, M.R., Jun, W., Lee, W.J., 2015. Cellular uptake and cytotoxicity of beta-lactoglobulin nanoparticles: the effects of particle size and surface charge. Asian-Australas. J. Anim. Sci. 28, 420–427.

Halamoda-Kenzaoui, B., Holzwarth, U., Roebben, G., Bogni, A., Bremer-Hoffmann, S., 2019. Mapping of the available standards against the regulatory needs for nanomedicines. Wiley Interdiscip. Rev. Nanomed. Nanobiotechnol. 11, e1531.

Han, G., Ghosh, P., De, M., Rotello, V.M., 2007. Drug and gene delivery using gold nanoparticles. J. NanoBiotechnol 3, 40–45.

Hanahan, D., Weinberg, R.A., 2000. The hallmarks of cancer. Cell 100, 57–70.

Harris, J.M., Martin, N.E., Modi, M., 2001. Pegylation: a novel process for modifying pharmacokinetics. Clin. Pharmacokinet. 40, 539–551.

Hobbs, S.K., Monsky, W.L., Yuan, F., Roberts, W.G., Griffith, L., Torchilin, V.P., et al., 1998. Regulation of transport pathways in tumor vessels: role of tumor type and microenvironment. Proc. Natl. Acad. Sci. USA. 95, 4607–4612.

Ilic, D., Djulbegovic, M., Jung, J.H., Hwang, E.C., Zhou, Q., Cleves, A., et al., 2018. Prostate cancer screening with prostate-specific antigen (PSA) test: a systematic review and meta-analysis. BMJ 362, k3519.

Jafari, A., Sun, H., Sun, B., Mohamed, M.A., Cui, H., Cheng, C., 2019. Layer-by-layer preparation of polyelectrolyte multilayer nanocapsules via crystallized miniemulsions. Chem. Commun. (Camb.) 55, 1267–1270.

Jain, R.K., Stylianopoulos, T., 2010. Delivering nanomedicine to solid tumors. Nat. Rev. Clin. Oncol. 7, 653–664.

Jain, S.K., Prajapati, N., Rajpoot, K., Kumar, A., 2016a. A novel sustained release drug-resin complex-based microbeads of ciprofloxacin HCl. Artif. Cell Nanomed. Biotechnol. 44, 1891–1900.

Jain, S.K., Kumar, A., Kumar, A., Pandey, A.N., Rajpoot, K., 2016b. Development and in vitro characterization of a multiparticulate delivery system for acyclovir-resinate complex. Artif. Cell Nanomed. Biotechnol. 44, 1266–1275.

Jain, S.K., Patel, K., Rajpoot, K., Jain, A., 2019. Development of a berberine loaded multifunctional design for the treatment of helicobacter pylori induced gastric ulcer. Drug Deliv. Lett. 9, 50–57.

Jain, S.K., Jain, A.K., Rajpoot, K., 2020. Expedition of Eudragit® polymers in the development of novel drug delivery systems. Curr. Drug. Deliv. 17, 448–469.

Jain, S.K., Dubey, V., Rajpoot, K., 2021. D-mannose-decorated chitosan nanoparticles for enhanced targeting of 5-fluorouracil in the therapy of colon cancer. IJPSN 14, 5315–5322.

Jamel, S., Tukanova, K., Markar, S., 2019. Detection and management of oligometastatic disease in oesophageal cancer and identification of prognostic factors: a systematic review. World J. Gastrointest. Oncol. 11, 741–749.

Jeene, P.M., van Laarhoven, H.W.M., Hulshof, M., 2018. The role of definitive chemoradiation in patients with non-metastatic oesophageal cancer. Best. Pract. Res. Clin. Gastroenterol., 36– 37, 53–59.

Ji, Z., Wang, X., Zhang, H., Lin, S., Meng, H., Sun, B., et al., 2012. Designed synthesis of CeO2 nanorods and nanowires for studying toxicological effects of high aspect ratio nanomaterials. ACS Nano 6, 5366−5380.

Jia, F., Liu, X., Li, L., Mallapragada, S., Narasimhan, B., Wang, Q., 2013. Multifunctional nanoparticles for targeted delivery of immune activating and cancer therapeutic agents. J. Control. Rel. 172, 1020−1034.

Jiang, Y., Huo, S., Mizuhara, T., Das, R., Lee, Y.W., Hou, S., et al., 2015. The interplay of size and surface functionality on the cellular uptake of sub-10 nm gold nanoparticles. ACS Nano 9, 9986−9993.

Jurczyk, M., Jelonek, K., Musial-Kulik, M., Beberok, A., Wrzesniok, D., Kasperczyk, J., 2021. Single- versus dual-targeted nanoparticles with folic acid and biotin for anticancer drug delivery. Pharmaceutics 13, 326.

Kalyane, D., Kumar, N., Anup, N., Rajpoot, K., Maheshwari, R., Sengupta, P., et al., 2021. Recent advancements and future submissions of silica core-shell nanoparticles. Int. J. Pharm. 609, 121173.

Kiessling, F., Mertens, M.E., Grimm, J., Lammers, T., 2014. Nanoparticles for imaging: top or flop? Radiology 273, 10−28.

Kirpotin, D.B., Drummond, D.C., Shao, Y., Shalaby, M.R., Hong, K., Nielsen, U.B., et al., 2006. Antibody targeting of long-circulating lipidic nanoparticles does not increase tumor localization but does increase internalization in animal models. Cancer Res. 66, 6732−6740.

Knezevic, C.E., Clarke, W., 2020. Cancer chemotherapy: the case for therapeutic drug monitoring. Ther. Drug. Monit. 42, 6−19.

Kumar, C.S., Mohammad, F., 2011. Magnetic nanomaterials for hyperthermia-based therapy and controlled drug delivery. Adv. Drug. Deliv. Rev. 63, 789−808.

Laird, P.W., Jackson-Grusby, L., Fazeli, A., Dickinson, S.L., Jung, W.E., Li, E., et al., 1995. Suppression of intestinal neoplasia by DNA hypomethylation. Cell 81, 197−205.

Lancet, J.E., Uy, G.L., Cortes, J.E., Newell, L.F., Lin, T.L., Ritchie, E.K., et al., 2016. Final results of a phase III randomized trial of CPX-351 versus 7 + 3 in older patients with newly diagnosed high risk (secondary) AML. J. Clin. Oncol. 34, 7000. -7000.

Lee, H., Hoang, B., Fonge, H., Reilly, R.M., Allen, C., 2010. In vivo distribution of polymeric nanoparticles at the whole-body, tumor, and cellular levels. Pharm. Res. 27, 2343−2355.

Li, D., Tang, M.-L., 2022. The effects of superparamagnetic iron oxide nanoparticle exposure on gene expression patterns in the neural stem cells under magnetic field. STEMedicine 3, e117.

Li, X., Zhou, H., Yang, L., Du, G., Pai-Panandiker, A.S., Huang, X., et al., 2011. Enhancement of cell recognition in vitro by dual-ligand cancer targeting gold nanoparticles. Biomaterials 32, 2540−2545.

Li, Y., Kroger, M., Liu, W.K., 2015. Shape effect in cellular uptake of PEGylated nanoparticles: comparison between sphere, rod, cube and disk. Nanoscale 7, 16631−16646.

Li, Z., Huang, J., Wu, J., 2021. pH-Sensitive nanogels for drug delivery in cancer therapy. Biomater. Sci. 9, 574−589.

Liu, S., Chiu-Lam, A., Rivera-Rodriguez, A., DeGroff, R., Savliwala, S., Sarna, N., et al., 2021. Long circulating tracer tailored for magnetic particle imaging. Nanotheranostics 5, 348−361.

Llinás, R.R., Walton, K.D., Nakao, M., Hunter, I., Anquetil, P.A., 2005. Neuro-vascular central nervous recording/stimulating system: using nanotechnology probes. J. Nanopart. Res. 7, 111−127.

Lucchini, E., Pilotto, S., Spada, E., Melisi, D., Bria, E., Tortora, G., 2014. Targeting the epidermal growth factor receptor in solid tumors: focus on safety. Expert. Opin. Drug. Saf. 13, 535−549.

Luo, W., Wang, Z., Tian, P., Li, W., 2018. Safety and tolerability of PD-1/PD-L1 inhibitors in the treatment of non-small cell lung cancer: a meta-analysis of randomized controlled trials. J. Cancer Res. Clin. Oncol. 144, 1851−1859.

Luo, X., Wang, H., Ji, D., 2021. Carbon nanotubes (CNT)-loaded ginsenosides Rb3 suppresses the PD-1/PD-L1 pathway in triple-negative breast cancer. Aging (Albany NY.) 13, 17177−17189.

Ma, S., Zhou, J., Zhang, Y., He, Y., Jiang, Q., Yue, D., et al., 2016. Highly stable fluorinated nanocarriers with iRGD for overcoming the stability dilemma and enhancing tumor penetration in an orthotopic breast cancer. ACS Appl. Mater. Interfaces 8, 28468−28479.

Maeda, H., Nakamura, H., Fang, J., 2013. The EPR effect for macromolecular drug delivery to solid tumors: improvement of tumor uptake, lowering of systemic toxicity, and distinct tumor imaging in vivo. Adv. Drug. Deliv. Rev. 65, 71–79.

Mahoney, K.M., Freeman, G.J., McDermott, D.F., 2015. The next immune-checkpoint inhibitors: PD-1/PD-L1 blockade in melanoma. Clin. Ther. 37, 764–782.

Manson, E.N., Hasford, F., Inkoom, S., Gedel, A.M., 2020. Integrating image fusion with nanoparticle contrast agents for diagnosis: a review. Egypt. J. Radiol. Nucl. Med. 51, 208.

Melegh, Z., Oltean, S., 2019. Targeting angiogenesis in prostate cancer. Int. J. Mol. Sci. 20, 2676.

Men, W., Zhu, P., Dong, S., Liu, W., Zhou, K., Bai, Y., et al., 2020. Layer-by-layer pH-sensitive nanoparticles for drug delivery and controlled release with improved therapeutic efficacy in vivo. Drug. Deliv. 27, 180–190.

Messersmith, W.A., Ahnen, D.J., 2008. Targeting EGFR in colorectal cancer. N. Engl. J. Med. 359, 1834–1836.

Moghimi, S.M., Szebeni, J., 2003. Stealth liposomes and long circulating nanoparticles: critical issues in pharmacokinetics, opsonization and protein-binding properties. Prog. Lipid Res. 42, 463–478.

Mout, R., Moyano, D.F., Rana, S., Rotello, V.M., 2012. Surface functionalization of nanoparticles for nanomedicine. Chem. Soc. Rev. 41, 2539–2544.

Nayak, D., Rajpoot, K., Jain, S.K., 2020. Development and evaluation of cholestyramine-amoxicillin tri-hydrate-loaded gastro-retentive microspheres for attaining extended therapeutic effect against *H. Pylori* infection. Biomed. J. Sci. Tech. Res. 29, 22728–22738.

Nazir, S., Hussain, T., Ayub, A., Rashid, U., MacRobert, A.J., 2014. Nanomaterials in combating cancer: therapeutic applications and developments. Nanomedicine 10, 19–34.

Negrier, S., Perol, D., Bahleda, R., Hollebecque, A., Chatelut, E., Boyle, H., et al., 2017. Phase I dose-escalation study of pazopanib combined with bevacizumab in patients with metastatic renal cell carcinoma or other advanced tumors. BMC Cancer 17, 547.

Nurazzi, N.M., Sabaruddin, F.A., Harussani, M.M., Kamarudin, S.H., Rayung, M., Asyraf, M.R.M., et al., 2021. Mechanical performance and applications of CNTs reinforced polymer composites-a review, Nanomaterials (Basel), 11. p. 2186.

Ohno, S., Takanashi, M., Sudo, K., Ueda, S., Ishikawa, A., Matsuyama, N., et al., 2013. Systemically injected exosomes targeted to EGFR deliver antitumor microRNA to breast cancer cells. Mol. Ther. 21, 185–191.

Pandey, A.N., Rajpoot, K., Jain, S.K., 2020a. Using 5-fluorouracil-encored PLGA nanoparticles for the treatment of colorectal cancer: the in-vitro characterization and cytotoxicity studies. Nanomed. J. 7, 211–224.

Pandey, A.N., Rajpoot, K., Jain, S.K., 2021. 5-Fluorouracil loaded orally administered wga-decorated poly(lacticco- glycolic acid) nanoparticles for treatment of colorectal cancer: in vivo evaluation. Curr. Nanomed. 11, 51–60.

Pandey, V., Ganeshpurkar, A., Thakur, A., Sharma, M., Rajpoot, K., Tekade, M., et al., 2020b. Gold nanoparticles: an advanced drug delivery and diagnostic tool. In: Tekade, R.K. (Ed.), The Future of Pharmaceutical Product Development and Research. Academic Press, pp. 609–669.

Patel, V., Rajani, C., Paul, D., Borisa, P., Rajpoot, K., Youngren-Ortiz, S.R., et al., 2020. Dendrimers as novel drug-delivery system and its applications. In: Tekade, R.K. (Ed.), Drug Delivery Systems. Academic Press, pp. 333–392.

Patrey, N.K., Rajpoot, K., Jain, A.K., Jain, S.K., 2016. Diltiazem loaded floating microspheres of Ethylcellulose and Eudragit for gastric delivery: in vitro evaluation. AJBR 2, 71–77.

Peer, D., Karp, J.M., Hong, S., Farokhzad, O.C., Margalit, R., Langer, R., 2007. Nanocarriers as an emerging platform for cancer therapy. Nat. Nanotechnol. 2, 751–760.

Persano, F., Gigli, G., Leporatti, S., 2021. Lipid-polymer hybrid nanoparticles in cancer therapy: current overview and future directions. Nano Express 2, 012006.

Pham, T.T., Nguyen, T.T., Pathak, S., Regmi, S., Nguyen, H.T., Tran, T.H., et al., 2018. Tissue adhesive FK506-loaded polymeric nanoparticles for multi-layered nano-shielding of pancreatic islets to enhance xenograft survival in a diabetic mouse model. Biomaterials 154, 182–196.

Polaka, S., Desai, N., Kshirsagar, B., Rajpoot, K., Tekade, R.K., 2021. Revamping the pharmacokinetics of poorly soluble drugs using different formulations. In: Tekade, R.K. (Ed.), Biopharmaceutics and Pharmacokinetics Considerations. Elsevier, pp. 387–413.

Postow, M.A., Chesney, J., Pavlick, A.C., Robert, C., Grossmann, K., McDermott, D., et al., 2015. Nivolumab and ipilimumab versus ipilimumab in untreated melanoma. N. Engl. J. Med. 372, 2006—2017.

Raaijmakers, M.H., de Grouw, E.P., Heuver, L.H., van der Reijden, B.A., Jansen, J.H., Scheper, R.J., et al., 2005. Breast cancer resistance protein in drug resistance of primitive CD34 + 38- cells in acute myeloid leukemia. Clin. Cancer Res. 11, 2436—2444.

Rajani, C., Borisa, P., Karanwad, T., Borade, Y., Patel, V., Rajpoot, K., et al., 2020. Cancer-targeted chemotherapy: emerging role of the folate anchored dendrimer as drug delivery nanocarrier. In: Chauhan, A., Kulhari, H. (Eds.), Pharmaceutical Applications of Dendrimers, Eds. Elsevier, pp. 151—198.

Rajpoot, K., 2017. Acyclovir-loaded sorbitan esters-based organogel: development and rheological characterization. Artif. Cell Nanomed. Biotechnol. 45, 551—559.

Rajpoot, K., 2017. Recent advances and applications of biosensors in novel technology. Biosens. J. 06, 145.

Rajpoot, K., 2019. Solid lipid nanoparticles: a promising nanomaterial in drug delivery. Curr. Pharm. Des. 25, 3943—3959.

Rajpoot, K., 2020a. Nanotechnology-based targeting of neurodegenerative disorders: a promising tool for efficient delivery of neuromedicines. Curr. Drug. Targets 21, 819—836.

Rajpoot, K., 2020b. Lipid-based nanoplatforms in cancer therapy: recent advances and applications. Curr. Cancer Drug. Targets 20, 271—287.

Rajpoot, K., Tekade, R.K., 2019. Microemulsion as drug and gene delivery vehicle: an inside story. In: Tekade, R.K. (Ed.), Drug Delivery Systems. Academic Press, pp. 455—520.

Rajpoot, K., Jain, S.K., 2021. The role of nanoparticles in the treatment of gastric cancer. In: Yadav, A. K., Gupta, U., Sharma, R. (Eds.), Nano Drug Delivery Strategies for the Treatment of Cancers. Academic Press, pp. 165—189.

Rajpoot, K., Jain, S.K., 2018. Colorectal cancer-targeted delivery of oxaliplatin via folic acid-grafted solid lipid nanoparticles: preparation, optimization, and in vitro evaluation. Artif. Cell Nanomed. Biotechnol. 46, 1236—1247.

Rajpoot, K., Jain, S.K., 2019. Irinotecan hydrochloride trihydrate loaded folic acid-tailored solid lipid nanoparticles for targeting colorectal cancer: development, characterization, and in vitro cytotoxicity study using HT-29 cells. J. Microencapsul. 36, 659—676.

Rajpoot, K., Jain, S.K., 2020a. (99m)Tc-labelled and pH-awakened microbeads entrapping surface-modified lipid nanoparticles for the augmented effect of oxaliplatin in the therapy of colorectal cancer. J. Microencapsul. 37, 609—623.

Rajpoot, K., Jain, S.K., 2020b. Oral delivery of pH-responsive alginate microbeads incorporating folic acid-grafted solid lipid nanoparticles exhibits enhanced targeting effect against colorectal cancer: a dual-targeted approach. Int. J. Biol. Macromol. 151, 830—844.

Rajpoot, K., Tekade, M., Pandey, V., Nagaraja, S., Youngren-Ortiz, S.R., Tekade, R.K., 2020. Self-microemulsifying drug–delivery system: ongoing challenges and future ahead. In: Tekade, R.K. (Ed.), Drug Delivery Systems. Academic Press, pp. 393—454.

Rajpoot, K., Tekade, R.K., Sharma, M.C., Tekade, M., 2021a. Pharmacokinetics and biopharmaceutics: a leader or attendant. In: Tekade, R.K. (Ed.), Biopharmaceutics and Pharmacokinetics Considerations. Elsevier, Academic Press, pp. 17—27.

Rajpoot, K., Tekade, R.K., Sharma, M.C., Safavi, M., Tekade, M., 2021b. Pharmacokinetics modeling in drug delivery. In: Tekade, R.K. (Ed.), Biopharmaceutics and Pharmacokinetics Considerations. Elsevier, Academic Press, pp. 279—334.

Ravi Kiran, A.V.V.V., Kusuma Kumari, G., Krishnamurthy, P.T., Chintamaneni, P.K., Pindiprolu, S.K. S.S., 2021. Carbon nanotubes in cancer therapy. In: Abraham, J., Thomas, S., Kalarikkal, N. (Eds.), Handbook of Carbon Nanotubes. Springer International Publishing, Cham, pp. 1—33.

Resch-Genger, U., Grabolle, M., Cavaliere-Jaricot, S., Nitschke, R., Nann, T., 2008. Quantum dots versus organic dyes as fluorescent labels. Nat. Methods 5, 763—775.

Rosenblum, D., Joshi, N., Tao, W., Karp, J.M., Peer, D., 2018. Progress and challenges towards targeted delivery of cancer therapeutics. Nat. Commun. 9, 1410.

Ruozi, B., Belletti, D., Sharma, H.S., Sharma, A., Muresanu, D.F., Mossler, H., et al., 2015. Loaded cerebrolysin: studies on their preparation and investigation of the effect of storage and serum stability with reference to traumatic brain injury. Mol. Neurobiol. 52, 899—912.

Salomoni, P., Calabretta, B., 2009. Targeted therapies and autophagy: new insights from chronic myeloid leukemia. Autophagy 5, 1050–1051.

Sandoo, A., Kitas, G.D., Carmichael, A.R., 2015. Breast cancer therapy and cardiovascular risk: focus on trastuzumab. Vasc. Health Risk Manag. 11, 223–228.

Santos, A.C., Morais, F., Simoes, A., Pereira, I., Sequeira, J.A.D., Pereira-Silva, M., et al., 2019. Nanotechnology for the development of new cosmetic formulations. Expert. Opin. Drug. Deliv. 16, 313–330.

Schau, G.F., Burlingame, E.A., Thibault, G., Anekpuritanang, T., Wang, Y., Gray, J.W., et al., 2020. Predicting primary site of secondary liver cancer with a neural estimator of metastatic origin. J. Med. Imaging (Bellingham) 7, 012706.

Schlansky, B., Dimarino Jr., A.J., Loren, D., Infantolino, A., Kowalski, T., Cohen, S., 2006. A survey of oesophageal cancer: pathology, stage and clinical presentation. Aliment. Pharmacol. Ther. 23, 587–593.

Shahbazi, N., Zare-Dorabei, R., Naghib, S.M., 2021. Multifunctional nanoparticles as optical biosensing probe for breast cancer detection: a review. Mater. Sci. Eng. C. Mater. Biol. Appl. 127, 112249.

Shao, J., Liang, R., Ding, D., Zheng, X., Zhu, X., Hu, S., et al., 2021. Multifunctional nanoparticle for enhanced near-infrared image-guided photothermal therapy against gastric cancer. Int. J. Nanomed. 16, 2897–2915.

Sharma, S., Lamichhane, N., Parul, T., et al., 2021. Iron oxide nanoparticles conjugated with organic optical probes for in vivo diagnostic and therapeutic applications. Nanomedicine. (London, Engl.) 16, 943–962.

Shi, J., Kantoff, P.W., Wooster, R., Farokhzad, O.C., 2017. Cancer nanomedicine: progress, challenges and opportunities. Nat. Rev. Cancer 17, 20–37.

Sigismund, S., Avanzato, D., Lanzetti, L., 2018. Emerging functions of the EGFR in cancer. Mol. Oncol. 12, 3–20.

Simchowitz, B., Shiman, L., Spencer, J., Brouillard, D., Gross, A., Connor, M., et al., 2010. Perceptions and experiences of patients receiving oral chemotherapy. Clin. J. Oncol. Nurs. 14, 447–453.

Sinicrope, F.A., Mahoney, M.R., Smyrk, T.C., Thibodeau, S.N., Warren, R.S., Bertagnolli, M.M., et al., 2013. Prognostic impact of deficient DNA mismatch repair in patients with stage III colon cancer from a randomized trial of FOLFOX-based adjuvant chemotherapy. J. Clin. Oncol. 31, 3664–3672.

Sosman, J., Puzanov, I., 2009. Combination targeted therapy in advanced renal cell carcinoma. Cancer 115, 2368–2375.

Sperling, R.A., Parak, W.J., 2010. Surface modification, functionalization and bioconjugation of colloidal inorganic nanoparticles. Philos. Trans. A Math. Phys. Eng. Sci. 368, 1333–1383.

Stylios, G.K., Giannoudis, P.V., Wan, T., 2005. Applications of nanotechnologies in medical practice. Injury 36 (Suppl 4), S6–S13.

Su, Y., Zhong, G., Jiang, N., Huang, M., Lin, T., 2018. Circular RNA, a novel marker for cancer determination (Review). Int. J. Mol. Med. 42, 1786–1798.

Svenson, S., Prud'homme, R.K., 2012. Multifunctional nanoparticles for drug delivery applications. Nanostructure Science and Technology. Springer, US, p. 344.

Tabassum, N., Kumar, D., Verma, D., Bohara, R.A., Singh, M.P., 2021. Zirconium oxide (ZrO2) nanoparticles from antibacterial activity to cytotoxicity: a next-generation of multifunctional nanoparticles. Mater. Today Commun. 26, 102156.

Tambe, V., Shukla, H., Rajpoot, K., Pandey, M.M., Tekade, R.K., 2021a. Pharmacokinetics aspects of biotechnological products. In: Tekade, R.K. (Ed.), Biopharmaceutics and Pharmacokinetics Considerations. Elsevier, Academic Press, pp. 539–565.

Tambe, V., Ditani, A., Rajpoot, K., Tekade, R.K., 2021b. Pharmacokinetics aspects of structural modifications in drug design and therapy. In: Tekade, R.K. (Ed.), Biopharmaceutics and Pharmacokinetics Considerations. Elsevier, Academic Press, pp. 83–108.

Tian, C., Ohlund, D., Rickelt, S., Lidstrom, T., Huang, Y., Hao, L., et al., 2020. Cancer cell-derived matrisome proteins promote metastasis in pancreatic ductal adenocarcinoma. Cancer Res. 80, 1461–1474.

Tomasello, G., Ghidini, M., Galassi, B., Grossi, F., Luciani, A., Petrelli, F., 2022. Survival benefit with adjuvant chemotherapy in stage III microsatellite-high/deficient mismatch repair colon cancer: a systematic review and meta-analysis. Sci. Rep. 12, 1055.

Ulusoy, M., Jonczyk, R., Walter, J.G., Springer, S., Lavrentieva, A., Stahl, F., et al., 2016. Aqueous synthesis of PEGylated quantum dots with increased colloidal stability and reduced cytotoxicity. Bioconjug Chem. 27, 414−426.

Valencia, P.M., Hanewich-Hollatz, M.H., Gao, W., Karim, F., Langer, R., Karnik, R., et al., 2011. Effects of ligands with different water solubilities on self-assembly and properties of targeted nanoparticles. Biomaterials 32, 6226−6233.

Varki, A., 2007. Glycan-based interactions involving vertebrate sialic-acid-recognizing proteins. Nature 446, 1023−1029.

Verma, A., Stellacci, F., 2010. Effect of surface properties on nanoparticle-cell interactions. Small 6, 12−21.

Vroman, L., 1962. Effect of absorbed proteins on the wettability of hydrophilic and hydrophobic solids. Nature 196, 476−477.

Wang, C., Xu, H., Liang, C., Liu, Y., Li, Z., Yang, G., et al., 2013. Iron oxide @ polypyrrole nanoparticles as a multifunctional drug carrier for remotely controlled cancer therapy with synergistic antitumor effect. ACS Nano 7, 6782−6795.

Wang, R., Zhang, Z., Liu, B., Xue, J., Liu, F., Tang, T., et al., 2021. Strategies for the design of nanoparticles: starting with long-circulating nanoparticles, from lab to clinic. Biomater. Sci. 9, 3621−3637.

Wang, Y., Santos, A., Evdokiou, A., Losic, D., 2015. An overview of nanotoxicity and nanomedicine research: principles, progress and implications for cancer therapy. J. Mater. Chem. B 3, 7153−7172.

Weissleder, R., Kelly, K., Sun, E.Y., Shtatland, T., Josephson, L., 2005. Cell-specific targeting of nanoparticles by multivalent attachment of small molecules. Nat. Biotechnol. 23, 1418−1423.

Xiao, B.K., Yang, J.Y., Dong, J.X., Ji, Z.S., Si, H.Y., Wang, W.L., et al., 2015. Meta-analysis of seven randomized control trials to assess the efficacy and toxicity of combining EGFR-TKI with chemotherapy for patients with advanced NSCLC who failed first-line treatment. Asian Pac. J. Cancer Prev. 16, 2915−2921.

Yang, L., Shi, P., Zhao, G., Xu, J., Peng, W., Zhang, J., et al., 2020. Targeting cancer stem cell pathways for cancer therapy. Signal. Transduct. Target. Ther. 5, 8.

Yoon, H.Y., Koo, H., Choi, K.Y., Lee, S.J., Kim, K., Kwon, I.C., et al., 2012. Tumor-targeting hyaluronic acid nanoparticles for photodynamic imaging and therapy. Biomaterials 33, 3980−3989.

Zhang, Y., Hai, Y., Miao, Y., Qi, X., Xue, W., Luo, Y., et al., 2021. The toxicity mechanism of different sized iron nanoparticles on human breast cancer (MCF7) cells. Food Chem. 341, 128263.

Zhao, J., Castranova, V., 2011. Toxicology of nanomaterials used in nanomedicine. J. Toxicol. Environ. Health. B. Crit. Rev. 14, 593−632.

Zhen, X., Pu, K., Jiang, X., 2021. Photoacoustic imaging and photothermal therapy of semiconducting polymer nanoparticles: signal amplification and second near-infrared construction. Small 17, e2004723.

Zheng, X., Xing, D., Zhou, F., Wu, B., Chen, W.R., 2011. Indocyanine green-containing nanostructure as near infrared dual-functional targeting probes for optical imaging and photothermal therapy. Mol. Pharm. 8, 447−456.

Zhou, H., Qian, W., Uckun, F.M., Wang, L., Wang, Y.A., Chen, H., et al., 2015. IGF1 receptor targeted theranostic nanoparticles for targeted and image-guided therapy of pancreatic cancer. ACS Nano 9, 7976−7991.

Zhu, Y.D., Kang, Y., Gu, Z.G., Zhang, J., 2021. Step by step bisacrificial templates growth of bimetallic sulfide QDs-attached MOF nanosheets for nonlinear optical limiting. Adv. Opt. Mater. 9, 2002072.

CHAPTER 3

Autophagy-targeted drug delivery system in the management of cancer

Surbhi Gupta[1], Preeti Bisht[1], Raja Babu[1], Yati Sharma[2] and Debapriya Garabadu[1]
[1]Department of Pharmacology, School of Health Sciences, Central University of Punjab, Bathinda, Punjab, India
[2]Institute of Pharmaceutical Research, GLA University, Mathura, Uttar Pradesh, India

3.1 Introduction

Cancer can be defined as a series of genomic alterations or mutations that provide pro-apoptotic signals along with growth-inhibitory signals to a cell to divide endlessly (Nowell, 1974). Malignant diseases enforce a dramatic clinical burden, disturb social standards, and reduce economic resources, and thus can be considered the first and foremost public healthcare issue across the globe. Due to expensive drugs and new drug development projects, it is imperative to develop alternative drug delivery methods in the pharmacotherapy of cancer (Mattiuzzi and Lippi, 2019).

3.2 Autophagy and its role in the pathogenesis of cancer

Autophagy is considered one of the dynamic physiological events that exist in most types of eukaryotic cells. It involves the transportation of misfolded proteins, damaged, injured, or useless organelles, or other components of cytoplasm to the lysosome for degradation and re-cycled (Klionsky, 2007; Mizushima and Komatsu, 2011). Cytosolic materials are transported to lysosomes where they degrade and recover through autophagy. Autophagy reestablishes the cellular energy balance inside the cell during the period of varying nutrient availability. Eventually, autophagy provides energy and molecular substrates for cellular homeostasis and renewal (Green and Levine, 2014). The lysosome and autophagosome can fuse under controlled conditions that are regulated by the autophagosome itself. In certain cell stress-related conditions, autophagy can trigger pro-death or pro-survival processes. Autophagy may induce pro-survival or pro-death processes in various stress-related conditions of cells (Kimmelman and White, 2017; Amaravadi et al., 2016; Buszczak and Krämer, 2019). It also includes instability of the genome, including micronuclei (Bartsch et al., 2017) endogenous retrotransposons (Guo et al., 2014) and chromatin fragments containing damaged deoxyribonucleic acid (DNA) (Ivanov et al., 2013). The autophagy process is illustrated in Fig. 3.1.

Autophagy is well-established in the pathophysiology of cancer (Shintani and Klionsky, 2004). Autophagy plays a significant role in tumorigenesis, stages of neoplasia along with the cellular and metabolic context of the cells (Kondo et al., 2005).

Multifunctional Nanocomposites for Targeted Drug Delivery in Cancer Therapy
DOI: https://doi.org/10.1016/B978-0-323-95303-0.00002-2

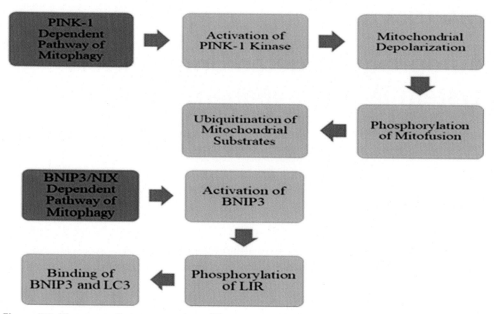

Figure 3.1 Diagrammatic representation of the process of autophagy.

Reports suggest that autophagy constitutively protects tumors by removing damaged/injured organelles or by recycling misfolded macromolecules (Singh et al., 2018). Moreover, autophagy fulfills the metabolic needs of the dividing tumor cells during nutrient deficiency, hypoxia, oxidative stress, or in response to therapy (Fiorini et al., 2013). Genetic and pharmacological inhibition of autophagy suppresses tumors in genetic mouse models and pancreatic cancer xenografts (Yang et al., 2011). Thus, autophagy in tumor cells is a pro-survival mechanism that involves an increase in stress tolerance and provides an alternate source of nutrients to cancerous cells. However, cancerous cells with unrestrained autophagy can go through cell death due to massive deprivation of cellular organelles and constituents that are needed for cellular homeostasis. Therefore, in cancer cells, autophagy is thought to be a process that suppresses tumor growth (White, 2012). Defects in autophagy can cause mitochondrial dysfunction, which subsequently leads to genomic instability, and thus can initiate and progress cancer (Kumari et al., 2018). Dysfunction in autophagy can activate DNA damage, vary DNA copy number, and destabilize genetics, which terminates into genomic mutations and tumorigenesis (Mathew et al., 2007). The long-lasting tissue injury induces the production of cytokines and chemokines that can stimulate tumor growth (White, 2012). Therefore, mutagenesis may lead to tumor promotion conferred by autophagy abnormalities. Mice with monoallelic deleted autophagy-related gene beclin1 spontaneously develop tumors. Loss of the beclin1 allele has been reported in 40%—75% of ovarian, breast, and prostate cancers (Shen et al., 2008).

Moreover, an enhanced level of the autophagy adaptor protein, p62/SQSTM1 is also accountable for tumorigenesis by multiple mechanisms (Moscat and Diaz-Meco, 2009). Thus, autophagy has a substantial impact on the initiation and progression of different types of cancer. Strategies to terminate the process of autophagy gain critical attention in the management of cancer.

3.3 Pharmacodynamic targets for autophagy-mediated cancer management

Several pharmacodynamic targets have been explored in the management of autophagy dysfunction. The autophagy-related protein 8 (Atg8) and microtubule-associated protein 1A/1B light chain (LC3) interact with autophagy receptors along with cargo molecules. It is documented that a membrane translocation domain is absent in soluble autophagy receptors, but the later possesses the ubiquitin–binding domain (Johansen and Lamark, 2011; Williams and Ding, 2018). Furthermore, autophagy receptors such as a family with sequence similarity 134, member B, SEC62, reticulon 3, cell cycle progression 1, atlastin GTPase 3, and testis expressed 264 (TEX264) that are anchored to the endoplasmic reticulum. These receptors have been reported to also act as specific ER-phagy receptors by directly interacting with LC3 (Grumati et al., 2018; Ma et al., 2018; Wilkinson, 2020). The summary of the pharmacodynamic targets of autophagy is depicted in Fig. 3.2.

3.4 Mammalian target of rapamycin-mediated signaling pathway in autophagy

Importantly, adenosine monophosphate (AMP)-activated protein kinase (AMPK) regulates the process of autophagy. The mammalian target of rapamycin (mTOR) is a serine/threonine protein kinase that belongs to the family of phosphatidylinositol

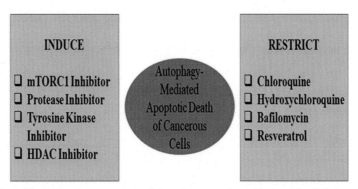

Figure 3.2 The schematic representation of the pharmacodynamic targets of the autophagy. *PINK*, PTEN-induced kinase.

kinase-related kinase. It has been suggested that mTOR is a potent suppressor of autophagy (Noda and Ohsumi, 1998). mTOR is comprised of mammalian target of rapamycin complex 1 (mTORC1) and mammalian target of rapamycin complex 2 (mTORC2) subunits. In response to cellular energy signals, it phosphorylates TSC2 and Raptor, which reduces mTORC1 activity (Gwinn et al., 2008; Inoki et al., 2006). The unc-51-like kinase 1 (ULK1) complex induces autophagy by initiating numerous processes, including actin-associated motor protein myosin II and ATG9 during energetic stress conditions (Kim et al., 2011). The phosphorylation of ULK1, which is AMPK-dependent, is a requisite step in the initial stage of the autophagic process (Kim et al., 2011). Unlike mTORC2, mTORC1 is rapamycin-sensitive, directly controlled by cellular nutrients, such as amino acids and growth factors, and also plays crucial roles in the management of autophagy and translation of protein (Wullschleger et al., 2006). The mTORC2 participates in chaperone-mediated autophagy and can trigger autophagy through FoxO3 activity (Wullschleger et al., 2006; Mammucari et al., 2007). Studies in both biochemistry and genetics show that mTOR's suppression of ULK1 is a key mechanism in the attenuation of autophagy (Crighton et al., 2007; Mizushima 2010; Kim et al., 2011). Interaction between AMPK and wtp53 is an established mechanism that is engaged in the suppression of tumors (Jones et al., 2005; Feng et al., 2007; Budanov and Karin 2008; Okoshi et al., 2008; He et al., 2014). Thus, the mTOR-mediated signaling pathway significantly influences the pathophysiology of autophagy-related cancer.

3.5 Mitophagy: a special case of autophagy

The attenuated mitochondria are selectively targeted by autophagosomes during mitophagy. Subsequently, they are transported to the lysosomes for degradation and recycling. The integrity and functionality of mitochondrial activity are thus guaranteed by mitophagy, which is considered to be a crucial quality control mechanism. Mitophagy permits selective targeting of the injured mitochondria into the nascent autophagosome without disrupting the overall mitochondrial network (Ashrafi and Schwarz, 2013; Eiyama and Okamoto, 2015). The diagrammatic representation of mitophagy is well explained in Fig. 3.3.

3.6 Roles of lncRNAs and miRNAs in regulating autophagy

The gene-mediated mechanism is also established in the pathophysiology of autophagy. The microribonucleic acid (miRNA) interacts with target gene transcriptional sequences and regulates autophagy-related diseases, including cancer (Bartel, 2004).

Starvation-triggered autophagy is restored by Beclin1 (ATG6) in yeast strains and in human breast cancer cells with defective ATG6 (Wirawan et al., 2012). In medulloblastoma

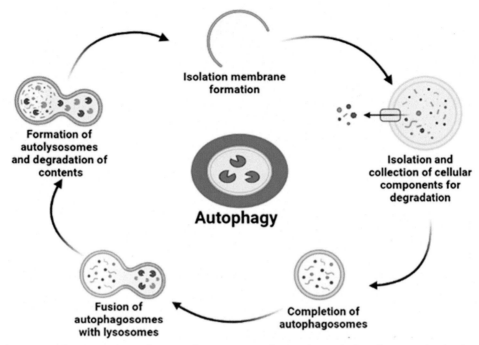

Figure 3.3 Illustrates the inducer and suppressor of autophagy-mediated apoptotic death of cancerous cells. *mTORC1*, mammalian target of rapamycin complex 1; *HDAC*, histone deacetylase.

cell lines, the miR-30a suppresses autophagy by downregulating the expression of Beclin1 (Singh et al., 2017). The anti-miR-21 increases autophagy-related proteins. such as Beclin-1, LC3-II, and Vps34. which ultimately leads to a rise in autophagy flux in chronic myeloid leukemia (Seca et al., 2013). Upregulation of miR-301a/b induced by hypoxia increases autophagy of cells and survival of prostate cancerous cells through N-myc downstream regulatory gene 2 that results in an increase in LC3-II (Bai et al., 2015; Guo et al., 2016; Yu et al., 2017).

The myotubularin-related protein 3 (MTMR3) decreases phosphatidylinositol-3phosphate and also the extent of autophagy through LC3-II- and ATG5-dependent mechanism in the macrophages (Taguchi-Atarashi et al., 2010). In human gastric cancer tissues and cell lines, miR-181a is markedly increased, whereas MTMR3 is downregulated (Lin et al., 2012). Additionally, miR-181a overexpression or MTMR3 deletion attenuates the autophagy triggered by starvation in adenogastric sarcoma cells, which ultimately promotes proliferation of the cell, colony formation, migration, invasion, and apoptosis suppression (Lin et al., 2017).

Sirtuin 1 (Sirt1) deacetylates endogenous LC3 and promotes autophagy (Li et al., 2016; Huang et al., 2015). Deacetylated LC3 binds with nuclear protein DOR and translocates into the cytoplasm. Subsequently, the complex binds to cytosolic ATG7 and promotes the formation of autophagosomes. By raising the levels of Sirt1 and dea-cetylated LC3, the miR-152 and miR-24 activate autophagy, which inhibits the growth of uterine sarcoma (Tong et al., 2018). It has been reported that the increased levels of LC3-II and Beclin1 encourage autophagy in lung cancer cell lines, A549 and H460 (Chen et al., 2015).

Smad2, the principal downstream element of the TGF-β signaling pathway plays a significant role in the initiation of cancer, invasion, metastasis, and self-renewal of CRC stem cells (Gong et al., 2014). Since Smad2 can be directly targeted by MiR-140−5p, its overexpression lowers Smad2 expression levels, which in turn limits cell invasion and proliferation. In cancer stem cells (CSCs) ectopic expression of miR-140−5p inhibits the growth of CSC and the formation of the sphere in vitro by inhi-biting autophagy through the suppression of ATG12 (Zhai et al., 2015). Recently, autophagy has been suggested to prevent cervical cancer (Fang et al., 2016).

X-linked inhibitor of apoptosis (XIAP) encourages cell survival and inhibits autophagy through the XIAP-Mdm2-p53 pathway (Huang et al., 2013). miR-23a overexpression significantly decreases XIAP expression and promotes autophagy, whereas its downregulation increases the expression of XIAP and suppresses autophagy in breast cancer cells (Chen et al., 2013; Gallagher et al., 2016; Guo et al., 2017). Additionally, it has been found that in nonsmall-cell lung cancer, the AMPK-mTOR signaling pathway controls cell autophagy. Ye et al. (2017) suggest that miR-138 overexpression can inhibit the autophagy of lung cancer cells possibly through the AMPK-mTOR signaling pathway and consequently suppresses the proliferation of cells, invasion, and migration. The upregulation of miR-18a facilitates autophagy through the inhibition of the mTOR signaling pathway in paclitaxel-resistant triple-negative breast cancer (TNBC) cells (Fan et al., 2016). In PCa cells, hypoxia enhances the expression of miR-96, which promotes autophagy through the inhibition of mTOR (Ma et al., 2014). The list of long non-coding ribonucleic acid (lncRNA)/miRNA is depicted in Table 3.1.

3.7 Autophagy-targeted drugs/agents in the management of cancer

There are several drugs that are used to inhibit the process of autophagy and are used in the management of cancer. The list of the drugs is reported in Table 3.2.

3.8 Autophagy targeted drug delivery system

3.8.1 Nanotechnology-based drug delivery system

Nanotechnology offers several tools and techniques to fight against cancer with the novel, tailored, and effective therapeutic agents while overcoming obstacles or disad-vantages typically associated with conventional medications (Conde et al., 2012). The

Table 3.1 The list of LncRNA/miRNA that are used in different cancers.

Sl. No.	LncRNA/miRNA	Expression level target	Promote/ suppress	Cancer type	References
1.	miR–18a	↑ mTOR	Promote	TNBC	Fan et al. (2016)
2.	miR–24–3p	↑ DEDD/p62	Promote	Bladder cancer	Yu et al. (2017)
3.	miR–152/miR–24	↑ Sirt1	Promote	Uterine sarcoma	Tong et al. (2018)
4.	miR–21	↑ Beclin1/ Vps34/LC3II	Suppress	CML	Seca et al. (2013)
5.	miR–138	↓ AMPK/ mTOR	Suppress	Lung cancer	Ye et al. (2017)
6.	miR–30d	↓ ATG5/PI3K/ Beclin1	Suppress	Colon cancer	Zhang et al. (2017)
7.	HOTAIR	↑ ATG3/ATG7	Promote	HCC	Yang et al. (2016)
8.	HOTAIR	↑ ULK1	Promote	NSCLC	Yang et al. (2018)
9.	MEG3	↓ p53	Suppress	Bladder cancer	Ying et al. (2013)
10.	LINC00470	↑ AKT	Suppress	Glioblastoma	Liu et al. (2018)

AMPK, adenosine monophosphate-activated protein kinase; *CML*, chronic myelogenous leukemia; *mTOR*, mammalian target of rapamycin; *NSCLC*, nonsmall-cell lung cancer; *TNBC*, triple-negative breast cancer; *ULK1*, unc-51-like kinase 1; ↑, upregulation; ↓, downregulation.

nanomaterials have unique physicochemical properties that enable them an efficient therapeutic tool in cancer management. Based on the above facts, nanomaterials can be classified into several types such as carbon based, liposomes, metals and metals oxide, polymers, and ceramics (Sun et al., 2014).

3.9 Silver-based nanoparticles

The silver nanoparticles (Ag-NPs) encapsulated in a particular exopolysaccharide (EPS) have a lethal effect on several cancer cell lines. The NPs induce autophagy and apoptosis in these cancer cell lines. It is further confirmed Ag-NPs−EPS exposure induces autophagy in SKBR3 cells through fluorescence microscopy and western blot technique (Buttacavoli et al., 2018). In another study, Ag-NPs exhibit significant toxicity in PANC-1 cancer cells. Additionally, it has been noted that when PANC-1 cells are treated with Ag-NPs, the protein level of the autophagy marker LC3-II increases significantly, suggesting that adenocarcinoma pancreatic cancer cells are experiencing apoptotic and necroptotic cell death in conjunction with autophagy (Zielinska et al., 2018). In another study, cisplatin along with a reduced graphene oxide−Ag-NPs nanocomposite (rGO−Ag-NPs) promotes autophagy in HeLa cancer cells (Yuan and Gurunathan, 2017). In another study, the combination of salymicin and Ag-NPs exerts significant

Table 3.2 The list of drugs that are used to inhibit autophagy.

S. No.	Drugs	Targets	Effect on autophagy	References
1.	Chloroquine	Lysosomes	Inhibitory	Sui et al. (2013)
2.	Hydroxychloroquine	Lysosomes	Inhibitory	Sui et al. (2013)
3.	Hydroxychloroquine + erlotinib	Lysosomes, EGFR	Inhibitory	Goldberg et al. (2012)
4.	Hydroxychloroquine + temsirolimus	Lysosomes, mTOR pathway	Inhibitory	Lee et al. (2015)
5.	Hydroxychloroquine + tamoxifen	Lysosomes, estrogen receptor-α (ERα)	Inhibitory	Cook et al. (2014)
6.	Temozolomide, dasatinib	Alkylating agents, tyrosine kinase inhibitors	Induction	Milano et al. (2009)
7.	Histone deacetylase inhibitors	Histone deacetylase	Induction	Liu et al. (2010)
8.	Bortezomib	Proteasome	Induction	Zhu et al. (2010)
9.	Temsirolimus + vorinostat	mTOR pathway, histone deacetylase	Induction	Yazbeck et al. (2008)
10.	Everolimus + vincristin	mTOR pathway, tubulin	Induction	Crazzolara et al. (2009)
11.	Rapamycin, everolimus	mTOR pathway	Induction	Guba et al. (2002)
12.	Everolimus	mTOR pathway	Induction	Motzer et al. (2008)
13.	Hydroxychloroquine + temsirolimus	mTOR pathway	Induction	Xie et al. (2013)

synergistic cytotoxicity in A2780 ovarian cancer cells by encouraging autophagy (Zhang et al., 2016). Moreover, Ag-NPs and radiation together considerably promote cytotoxicity in glioblastoma cells and in an animal model of brain tumor. This shows that altering the autophagic mechanism may enhance the effectiveness of treatment for glioblastoma (Liu et al., 2016). Recently, it was demonstrated that Ag-NPs decreased TFEB expression and induces autophagy in cancerous cells of the lung (Miyayama et al., 2018). Hence, Ag-NPs could be also a viable therapeutic choice in the management of cancer.

3.10 Gold-based nanoparticles

The polymeric NPs with gold(I) that are pH-sensitive cause the autophagy-dependent death of MCF7 breast cancer cells (Lin et al., 2015). A gold-based NP, SMI#9-tethered Au-NPs, increases apoptotic and autophagy markers in the SUM1315 TNBC cells and thus allows the survival of cancer cells (Koken et al., 1991; Koken et al., 1992; Haynes et al., 2016). In another study, human leukemic U937 and K562 cell lines are used to examine gold NPs conjugated to snake venom protein toxin NKCT1 (Au-NPs—NKCT1). It has been suggested that Au-GNPs—NKCT1 treatment exhibits cytotoxicity through caspase 3-dependent apoptosis and AKT/mTOR signaling-dependent autophagic cell death. Hence, combining gold nanoparticles (Au-NPs) with NKCT1 establishes a promising approach for creating medicines from natural resources, such as snake venoms (Bhowmik and Gomes, 2016). Furthermore, Au-NPs and tumor necrosis factor-related apoptosis-inducing ligand together encourage Drp1-mediated mitochondria dysfunction-dependent apoptosis and autophagy. It is also observed that markers of the mitophagy PINK1 and Parkin are employed in mitochondrial fractions in Calu-1 cells after the combined treatment (Ke et al., 2017). Hence, gold-based NPs could be a potential therapeutic strategy in the management of cancer.

3.11 Metal oxide-based nanoparticles

The zinc oxide nanoparticles (ZnO-NPs) in SKOV3 ovarian cancer cells can be made to undergo substantial cytotoxicity, apoptosis, and autophagy by increasing intracellular ROS and oxidative stress (Bai et al., 2017). ZnO-NPs also encourage cytotoxicity in oral cancerous cell lines through PINK1/Parkin-mediated mitophagy (Wang et al., 2018). Further, the ZnO-NPs conjugation and meso-tetra (4-carboxyphenyl) porphyrin increases the cytotoxicity and the extent of autophagy in MCF-7 and breast cancerous cells of MDA-MB-468 (Mozdoori et al., 2017).

According to reports, iron oxide nanoparticles can increase autophagy through a number of different pathways, including lysosome dysfunction, mitochondrial damage, and ER stress (Zhang et al., 2016). The conjugation of IO/Au-NPs with anti-EGFR reduces the growth of tumors in the lung by facilitating the process of autophagy in both in vitro and in vivo studies (Kuroda et al., 2014).

3.12 Silicabased nanoparticles

Amorphous silica nanoparticles accumulate in cervix carcinoma cells in humans and are considered one of the major causes of lysosomal dysfunctions and autophagy defects that eventually lead to a reduction in the metabolic activity of cancerous cells (Schütz et al., 2016). Recently, it has been demonstrated that genistein—PEGylated silica hybrid nanomaterials (Gen—PEG—SiHNM) possess significant antiproliferative effects by inducing autophagy in human colon cancerous cells. Thus, Gen—PEG—SiHNM is considered as a potential substitute treatment against colorectal cancer in the near future (Pool et al., 2018).

3.13 Gene-targeted drug delivery system

The amalgamation of lncRNA and miRNA regulates the progress of several diseases, including cancer (Salmena et al., 2011; Guttman and Rinn, 2012; Tay et al., 2014). Guide, decoy, and scaffold functions of lncRNAs are also recognized. Due to the guiding function of lncRNAs, chromatin-modifying enzymes are recruited to genes of interest. lncRNAs affect the polymeric form of protein and regulate protein activity (Weidle et al., 2017). lncRNA also acts as a competing endogenous RNA by combining the miRNA with other RNA transcripts to abolish the functionality of the target gene mRNA. Thus, lncRNAs are also considered effective modulators of pre-mRNA splicing, mRNA decay, and translation (Yoon et al., 2013). Thus, by interacting with several sites and targets, lncRNA and miRNA can facilitate the development of cancer. They can also control these interactions by adjusting their relative abundance in the pathophysiology of cancer.

3.14 Liposome-based drug delivery system

The potency of regular chemotherapy is evidently hampered by multidrug resistance and severe toxicity. However, the toxicity has been suppressed by the administration of drug liposomes. Various types of liposomes based drug delivery systems are illustrated in Table 3.3.

Table 3.3 List of lipososme-based drug delivery system against autophagy.

Sl. No.	Product name	Enclosed drug	Forms of liposomes	References
1.	Alocrest	Vinorelbine	Optisomes	Semple et al. (2005), Cattaneo et al. (2010)
2.	Aroplatin	Analog of cisplatin	MLVs	Lu et al. (2005), Dragovich et al. (2006)
3.	ATI-1123	Docetaxel	Protein stabilized liposomes	Mahalingam et al. (2014)
4.	Brakiva (TLI)	Topotecan	Optisomes	Tardi et al. (2000)
5.	NanoVNB	Vinorelbine	PEGylated liposomes	Yang et al. (2012), Lin et al. (2013)
6.	MCC-465	Doxorubicin	Antibody conjugated PEGylated liposomes	Hamaguchi et al. (2004), Matsumura et al. (2004)

(Continued)

Table 3.3 (Continued)

Sl. No.	Product name	Enclosed drug	Forms of liposomes	References
7.	SGT-53	p53 DNA plasmid	Anti-TfR conjugated cationic liposomes	Xu et al. (2001), Camp et al. (2013), Kim et al. (2015)
8.	TKM-080301 (TKM-PLK1)	PLK1 siRNA	Cationic PEGylated liposomes	Leung et al. (2014)
9.	CPX-351	Cytarabine and daunorubicin (5:1)	Bilamellar liposomes	Feldman et al. (2011), Cortes et al. (2015)
10.	Lipoplatin	Cisplatin	PEGylated liposomes	Boulikas (2009), Stathopoulos et al. (2010)
11.	MM-398 (PEP02)	Irinotecan	PEGylated liposomes	Drummond et al. (2006), Kang et al. (2015), Roy et al. (2013), Saif (2014)
12.	Thermodox	Doxorubicin	Lyso-lipid temperature sensitive liposomes	May and Li (2013)

3.15 Conclusion and future prospects

Autophagy contributes to the cellular function that degrades the unnecessary components of cells in the lysosomal system. Autophagy is reported in the pathophysiology of breast, ovarian, and prostate cancer. It has been well suggested that autophagy and apoptosis are well associated with the pathophysiology of cancer. Mitochondrial dysfunction is also well established along with the activation of autophagy in the pathophysiology of neurodegenerative disorders. The interrelation between mitochondrial dysfunction and excitotoxicity is well documented in the pathophysiology of neurodegenerative disorders. Several studies have demonstrated mTOR signaling pathway is a crucial mechanism involved in autophagy repression. Moreover, the interaction between AMPK and wild type53 protein is well described in the pathophysiology of cancer. Mitophagy and apoptosis are also well established along with autophagy in the pathophysiology of cancer. Indeed, there have been several drugs available for the management of cancer, but due to expensive drugs and new drug development projects, it is imperative to develop alternative drug delivery systems in the pharmacotherapy of cancer. Thus, this review aims to incline attention toward autophagy-targeted formulations in the therapeutic and diagnostic applications in cancer.

References

Amaravadi, R., Kimmelman, A.C., White, E., 2016. Recent insights into the function of autophagy in cancer. Genes. Dev. 30 (17), 1913—1930.

Ashrafi, G., Schwarz, T.L., 2013. The pathways of mitophagy for quality control and clearance of mitochondria. Cell Death Differ. 20 (1), 31—42.

Bai, D.P., Zhang, X.F., Zhang, G.L., Huang, Y.F., Gurunathan, S., 2017. Zinc oxide nanoparticles induce apoptosis and autophagy in human ovarian cancer cells. Int. J. Nanomed. 12, 6521.

Bai, R., Zhao, A.Q., Zhao, Z.Q., Liu, W.L., Jian, D.M., 2015. MicroRNA-195 induced apoptosis in hypoxic chondrocytes by targeting hypoxia-inducible factor 1 alpha. Eur. Rev. Med. Pharmacol. Sci. 19 (4), 545—551. PMID: 25753868.

Bartel, D.P., 2004. MicroRNAs: genomics, biogenesis, mechanism, and function. Cell. 116 (2), 281—297.

Bartsch, K., Knittler, K., Borowski, C., Rudnik, S., Damme, M., Aden, K., et al., 2017. Absence of RNase H2 triggers generation of immunogenic micronuclei removed by autophagy. Hum. Mol. Genet. 26 (20), 3960—3972.

Bhowmik, T., Gomes, A., 2016. NKCT1 (purified Najakaouthia protein toxin) conjugated gold nanoparticles induced Akt/mTOR inactivation mediated autophagic and caspase 3 activated apoptotic cell death in leukemic cell. Toxicon. 121, 86—97. Oct 1.

Boulikas, T., 2009. Clinical overview on Lipoplatin™: a successful liposomal formulation of cisplatin. Expert. Opin. investig. Drugs 18 (8), 1197—1218.

Budanov, A.V., Karin, M., 2008. p53 target genes sestrin1 and sestrin2 connect genotoxic stress and mTOR signaling. Cell. 134 (3), 451—460.

Buszczak, M., Krämer, H., 2019. Autophagy keeps the balance in tissue homeostasis. Dev. Cell 49 (4), 499—500.

Buttacavoli, M., Albanese, N.N., Di Cara, G., Alduina, R., Faleri, C., Gallo, M., et al., 2018. Anticancer activity of biogenerated silver nanoparticles: an integrated proteomic investigation. Oncotarget. 9 (11), 9685.

Camp, E.R., Wang, C., Little, E.C., Watson, P.M., Pirollo, K.F., Rait, A., et al., 2013. Transferrin receptor targeting nanomedicine delivering wild-type p53 gene sensitizes pancreatic cancer to gemcitabine therapy. Cancer Gene Ther. 20 (4), 222—228.

Cattaneo, A.G., Gornati, R., Sabbioni, E., Chiriva-Internati, M., Cobos, E., Jenkins, M.R., et al., 2010. Nanotechnology and human health: risks and benefits. J. Appl. Toxicol. 30 (8), 730—744.

Chen, S., Li, P., Li, J., Wang, Y., Du, Y., Chen, X., et al., 2015. MiR-144 inhibits proliferation and induces apoptosis and autophagy in lung cancer cells by targeting TIGAR. Cell. Physiol. Biochem. 35 (3), 997—1007.

Chen, Y., Sun, J., Lu, Y., Tao, C., Huang, J., Zhang, H., et al., 2013. Complexes containing cationic and anionic pH-sensitive liposomes: comparative study of factors influencing plasmid DNA gene delivery to tumors. Int. J. Nanomed. 8, 1573.

Conde, J., Doria, G., Baptista, P., 2012. Noble metal nanoparticles applications in cancer. J. Drug Deliv 2012, 751075.

Cook, K.L., Wärri, A., Soto-Pantoja, D.R., Clarke, P.A., Cruz, M.I., Zwart, A., et al., 2014. Chloroquine inhibits autophagy to potentiate antiestrogen responsiveness in ER + breast cancer. Clin. Cancer Res. 20 (12), 3222—3232.

Cortes, J.E., Goldberg, S.L., Feldman, E.J., Rizzeri, D.A., Hogge, D.E., Larson, M., et al., 2015. Phase II, multicenter, randomized trial of CPX-351 (cytarabine: daunorubicin) liposome injection versus intensive salvage therapy in adults with first relapse AML. Cancer. 121 (2), 234—242.

Crazzolara, R., Cisterne, A., Thien, M., Hewson, J., Baraz, R., Bradstock, K.F., et al., 2009. Potentiating effects of RAD001 (Everolimus) on vincristine therapy in childhood acute lymphoblastic leukemia. Blood. 113 (14), 3297—3306.

Crighton, D., Wilkinson, S., Ryan, K.M., 2007. DRAM links autophagy to p53 and programmed cell death. Autophagy. 3 (1), 72—74.

Dragovich, T., Mendelson, D., Kurtin, S., Richardson, K., Von Hoff, D., Hoos, A., 2006. A Phase 2 trial of the liposomal DACH platinum L-NDDP in patients with therapy-refractory advanced colorectal cancer. Cancer Chemother. Pharmacol 58 (6), 759–764.

Drummond, D.C., Noble, C.O., Guo, Z., Hong, K., Park, J.W., Kirpotin, D.B., 2006. Development of a highly active nanoliposomal irinotecan using a novel intraliposomal stabilization strategy. Cancer Res. 66 (6), 3271–3277.

Eiyama, A., Okamoto, K., 2015. PINK1/Parkin-mediated mitophagy in mammalian cells. Curr. Opin. Cell Biol. 33, 95–101.

Fan, Y.X., Dai, Y.Z., Wang, X.L., Ren, Y.Q., Han, J.J., Zhang, H., 2016. MiR-18a upregulation enhances autophagy in triple negative cancer cells via inhibiting mTOR signaling pathway. Eur. Rev. Med. Pharmacol. Sci. 20 (11), 2194–2200.

Fang, W., Shu, S., Yongmei, L., Endong, Z., Lirong, Y., Bei, S., 2016. miR-224-3p inhibits autophagy in cervical cancer cells by targeting FIP200. Sci. Rep. 6, 33229.

Feldman, E.J., Lancet, J.E., Kolitz, J.E., Ritchie, E.K., Roboz, G.J., List, A.F., et al., 2011. First-in-man study of CPX-351: a liposomal carrier containing cytarabine and daunorubicin in a fixed 5: 1 molar ratio for the treatment of relapsed and refractory acute myeloid leukemia. J. Clin. Oncol. 29 (8), 979.

Feng, Z., Hu, W., De Stanchina, E., Teresky, A.K., Jin, S., Lowe, S., et al., 2007. The regulation of AMPK β1, TSC2, and PTEN expression by p53: stress, cell and tissue specificity, and the role of these gene products in modulating the IGF-1-AKT-mTOR pathways. Cancer Res. 67 (7), 3043–3053.

Fiorini, C., Menegazzi, M., Padroni, C., Dando, I., DallaPozza, E., Gregorelli, A., et al., 2013. Autophagy induced by p53-reactivating molecules protects pancreatic cancer cells from apoptosis. Apoptosis. 18 (3), 337–346.

Gallagher, L.E., Williamson, L.E., Chan, E.Y., 2016. Advances in autophagy regulatory mechanisms. Cells. 5 (2), 24.

Goldberg, S.B., Supko, J.G., Neal, J.W., Muzikansky, A., Digumarthy, S., Fidias, P., et al., 2012. A phase I study of erlotinib and hydroxychloroquine in advanced non–small-cell lung cancer. J. Thorac. Oncol. 7 (10), 1602–1608.

Gong, Y., Guo, Y., Hai, Y., Yang, H., Liu, Y., Yang, S., et al., 2014. Nodal promotes the self-renewal of human colon cancer stem cells via an autocrine manner through Smad2/3 signaling pathway. BioMed. Res. Inte. 2014, 364134. Jan 1;2014.

Green, D.R., Levine, B., 2014. To be or not to be? How selective autophagy and cell death govern cell fate. Cell. 157 (1), 65–75.

Grumati, P., Dikic, I., Stolz, A., 2018. ER-phagy at a glance. J. Cell Sci. 131 (17), jcs217364.

Guba, M., von Breitenbuch, P., Steinbauer, M., Koehl, G., Flegel, S., Hornung, M., et al., 2002. Rapamycin inhibits primary and metastatic tumor growth by antiangiogenesis: involvement of vascular endothelial growth factor. Nat. Med. 8 (2), 128–135.

Guo, H., Chitiprolu, M., Gagnon, D., Meng, L., Perez-Iratxeta, C., Lagace, D., et al., 2014. Autophagy supports genomic stability by degrading retrotransposon RNA. Nat. Commun. 5 (1), 1.

Guo, W., Wang, H., Yang, Y., Guo, S., Zhang, W., Liu, Y., et al., 2017. Down-regulated miR-23a contributes to the metastasis of cutaneous melanoma by promoting autophagy. Theranostics. 7 (8), 2231.

Guo, Y.J., Liu, J.X., Guan, Y.W., 2016. Hypoxia induced upregulation of miR-301a/b contributes to increased cell autophagy and viability of prostate cancer cells by targeting NDRG2. Eur. Rev. Med. Pharmacol. Sci. 20 (1), 101–108.

Guttman, M., Rinn, J.L., 2012. Modular regulatory principles of large non-coding RNAs. Nature. 482 (7385), 339–346.

Gwinn, D.M., Shackelford, D.B., Egan, D.F., Mihaylova, M.M., Mery, A., Vasquez, D.S., et al., 2008. AMPK phosphorylation of raptor mediates a metabolic checkpoint. Mol. Cell 30 (2), 214–226.

Hamaguchi, T., Matsumura, Y., Nakanishi, Y., Muro, K., Yamada, Y., Shimada, Y., et al., 2004. Antitumor effect of MCC-465, pegylated liposomal doxorubicin tagged with newly developed monoclonal antibody GAH, in colorectal cancer xenografts. Cancer Sci. 95 (7), 608–613.

Haynes, B., Zhang, Y., Liu, F., Li, J., Petit, S., Kothayer, H., et al., 2016. Gold nanoparticle conjugated Rad6 inhibitor induces cell death in triple negative breast cancer cells by inducing mitochondrial dysfunction and PARP-1 hyperactivation: synthesis and characterization. Nanomed. Nanotechnol. Biol. Med. 12 (3), 745−757.

He, G., Zhang, Y.W., Lee, J.H., Zeng, S.X., Wang, Y.V., Luo, Z., et al., 2014. AMP-activated protein kinase induces p53 by phosphorylating MDMX and inhibiting its activity. Mol. Cell. Biol. 34 (2), 148−157.

Huang, R., Xu, Y., Wan, W., Shou, X., Qian, J., You, Z., et al., 2015. Deacetylation of nuclear LC3 drives autophagy initiation under starvation. Mol. Cell 57 (3), 456−466.

Huang, X., Wu, Z., Mei, Y., Wu, M., 2013. XIAP inhibits autophagy via XIAP-Mdm2-p53 signalling. EMBO J. 32 (16), 2204−2216.

Inoki, K., Ouyang, H., Zhu, T., Lindvall, C., Wang, Y., Zhang, X., et al., 2006. TSC2 integrates Wnt and energy signals via a coordinated phosphorylation by AMPK and GSK3 to regulate cell growth. Cell. 126 (5), 955−968.

Ivanov, A., Pawlikowski, J., Manoharan, I., van Tuyn, J., Nelson, D.M., Rai, T.S., et al., 2013. Lysosome-mediated processing of chromatin in senescence. J. Cell Biol. 202 (1), 129−143.

Johansen, T., Lamark, T., 2011. Selective autophagy mediated by autophagic adapter proteins. Autophagy. 7 (3), 279−296.

Jones, R.G., Plas, D.R., Kubek, S., Buzzai, M., Mu, J., Xu, Y., et al., 2005. AMP-activated protein kinase induces a p53-dependent metabolic checkpoint. Mol. Cell 18 (3), 283−293.

Kang, M.H., Wang, J., Makena, M.R., Lee, J.S., Paz, N., Hall, C., et al., 2015. Activity of MM-398, nanoliposomal irinotecan (nal-IRI), in Ewing's family tumor xenografts is associated with high exposure of tumor to drug and high SLFN11 expression. Clin. Cancer Res. 21 (5), 1139−1150.

Ke, S., Zhou, T., Yang, P., Wang, Y., Zhang, P., Chen, K., et al., 2017. Gold nanoparticles enhance TRAIL sensitivity through Drp1-mediated apoptotic and autophagic mitochondrial fission in NSCLC cells. Int. J. Nanomed. 12, 2531.

Kim, J., Kundu, M., Viollet, B., Guan, K.L., 2011. AMPK and mTOR regulate autophagy through direct phosphorylation of Ulk1. Nat. Cell Biol. 13 (2), 132−141.

Kim, S.S., Rait, A., Kim, E., Pirollo, K.F., Chang, E.H., 2015. A tumor-targeting p53 nanodelivery system limits chemoresistance to temozolomide prolonging survival in a mouse model of glioblastoma multiforme. Nanomed. Nanotechnol. Biol. Med. 11 (2), 301−311.

Kimmelman, A.C., White, E., 2017. Autophagy and tumor metabolism. Cell Metab. 25 (5), 1037−1043.

Klionsky, D.J., 2007. Autophagy: from phenomenology to molecular understanding in less than a decade. Nat. Rev. Mol. Cell Biol. 8 (11), 931−937.

Koken, M.H., Reynolds, P., Jaspers-Dekker, I., Prakash, L.O., Prakash, S., Bootsma, D., et al., 1991. Structural and functional conservation of two human homologs of the yeast DNA repair gene RAD6. Proc. Natl Acad. Sci. 88 (20), 8865−8869.

Koken, M.H., Smit, E.M., Jaspers-Dekker, I., Oostra, B.A., Hagemeuer, A., Bootsma, D., et al., 1992. Localization of two human homologs, HHR6A and HHR6B, of the yeast DNA repair gene RAD6 to chromosomes Xq24−q25 and 5q23−. Genomics 12 (3), 447−453.

Kondo, Y., Kanzawa, T., Sawaya, R., Kondo, S., 2005. The role of autophagy in cancer development and response to therapy. Nat. Rev. Cancer 5 (9), 726.

Kumari, S., Badana, A.K., Malla, R., 2018. Reactive oxygen species: a key constituent in cancer survival. Biomark. insights 13, 1177271918755391.

Kuroda, S., Tam, J., Roth, J.A., Sokolov, K., Ramesh, R., 2014. EGFR-targeted plasmonic magnetic nanoparticles suppress lung tumor growth by abrogating G2/M cell-cycle arrest and inducing DNA damage. Int. J. Nanomed. 9, 3825.

Lee, H.O., Mustafa, A., Hudes, G.R., Kruger, W.D., 2015. Hydroxychloroquine destabilizes phospho-S6 in human renal carcinoma cells. PLoS One 10 (7), e0131464.

Leung, A.K., Tam, Y.Y., Cullis, P.R., 2014. Lipid nanoparticles for short interfering RNA delivery, In Advances in Genetics, 88. Academic Press, pp. 71−110, Jan 1.

Li, X., Wang, Y., Xiong, Y., Wu, J., Ding, H., Chen, X., et al., 2016. Galangin induces autophagy via deacetylation of LC3 by SIRT1 in HepG2 cells. Sci. Rep. 6, 30496. Jul 27.

Lin, Y., Nie, Y., Zhao, J., Chen, X., Ye, M., Li, Y., et al., 2012. Genetic polymorphism at miR-181a binding site contributes to gastric cancer susceptibility. Carcinogenesis. 33 (12), 2377—2383.

Lin, Y., Zhao, J., Wang, H., Cao, J., Nie, Y., 2017. miR-181a modulates proliferation, migration and autophagy in AGS gastric cancer cells and downregulates MTMR3. Mol. Med. Rep. 15 (5), 2451—2456.

Lin, Y.X., Gao, Y.J., Wang, Y., Qiao, Z.Y., Fan, G., Qiao, S.L., et al., 2015. pH-sensitive polymeric nanoparticles with gold (I) compound payloads synergistically induce cancer cell death through modulation of autophagy. Mol. Pharm 12 (8), 2869—2878.

Lin, Y.Y., Kao, H.W., Li, J.J., Hwang, J.J., Tseng, Y.L., Lin, W.J., et al., 2013. Tumor burden talks in cancer treatment with PEGylated liposomal drugs. PLoS One 8 (5), e63078.

Liu, C., Zhang, Y., She, X., Fan, L., Li, P., Feng, J., et al., 2018. A cytoplasmic long noncoding RNA LINC00470 as a new AKT activator to mediate glioblastoma cell autophagy. J. Hematol. Oncol. 11 (1), 77.

Liu, P., Jin, H., Guo, Z., Ma, J., Zhao, J., Li, D., et al., 2016. Silver nanoparticles outperform gold nanoparticles in radiosensitizing U251 cells in vitro and in an intracranial mouse model of glioma. Int. J. Nanomed. 11, 5003.

Liu, Y.L., Yang, P.M., Shun, C.T., Wu, M.S., Weng, J.R., Chen, C.C., 2010. Autophagy potentiates the anti-cancer effects of the histone deacetylase inhibitors in hepatocellular carcinoma. Autophagy. 6 (8), 1057—1065.

Lu, C., Perez-Soler, R., Piperdi, B., Walsh, G.L., Swisher, S.G., Smythe, W.R., et al., 2005. Phase II study of a liposome-entrapped cisplatin analog (L-NDDP) administered intrapleurally and pathologic response rates in patients with malignant pleural mesothelioma. J. Clin. Oncol 23 (15), 3495—3501.

Ma, X., Parson, C., Ding, W.X., 2018. Regulation of the homeostasis of hepatic endoplasmic reticulum and cytochrome P450 enzymes by autophagy. Liver Res. 2 (3), 138—145.

Ma, Y., Yang, H.Z., Dong, B.J., Zou, H.B., Zhou, Y., Kong, X.M., et al., 2014. Biphasic regulation of autophagy by miR-96 in prostate cancer cells under hypoxia. Oncotarget. 5 (19), 9169.

Mahalingam, D., Nemunaitis, J.J., Malik, L., Sarantopoulos, J., Weitman, S., Sankhala, K., et al., 2014. Phase I study of intravenously administered ATI-1123, a liposomal docetaxel formulation in patients with advanced solid tumors. Cancer Chemother. Pharmacol 74 (6), 1241—1250.

Mammucari, C., Milan, G., Romanello, V., Masiero, E., Rudolf, R., Del Piccolo, P., et al., 2007. FoxO3 controls autophagy in skeletal muscle in vivo. Cell Metab. 6 (6), 458—471.

Mathew, R., Kongara, S., Beaudoin, B., Karp, C.M., Bray, K., Degenhardt, K., et al., 2007. Autophagy suppresses tumor progression by limiting chromosomal instability. Genes. Dev. 21 (11), 1367—1381.

Matsumura, Y., Gotoh, M., Muro, K., Yamada, Y., Shirao, K., Shimada, Y., et al., 2004. Phase 1 and pharmacokinetic study of MCC-465, a doxorubicin (DXR) encapsulated in PEG immunoliposome, in patients with metastatic stomach cancer. Ann. Oncol. 15 (3), 517—525.

Mattiuzzi, C., Lippi, G., 2019. Current cancer epidemiology. J. Epidemiol. Glob. Health 9 (4), 217—222.

May, J.P., Li, S.D., 2013. Hyperthermia-induced drug targeting. Expert. Opin. Drug Deliv 10 (4), 511—527.

Milano, V., Piao, Y., LaFortune, T., de Groot, J., 2009. Dasatinib-induced autophagy is enhanced in combination with temozolomide in glioma. Mol. Cancer Ther 8 (2), 394—406.

Miyayama, T., Fujiki, K., Matsuoka, M., 2018. Silver nanoparticles induce lysosomal-autophagic defects and decreased expression of transcription factor EB in A549 human lung adenocarcinoma cells. Toxicol. Vitro 46, 148—154. Feb 1.

Mizushima, N., Komatsu, M., 2011. Autophagy: renovation of cells and tissues. Cell. 147 (4), 728—741.

Mizushima, N., 2010. The role of the Atg1/ULK1 complex in autophagy regulation. Curr. Opin. Cell Biol. 22 (2), 132—139.

Moscat, J., Diaz-Meco, M.T., 2009. p62 at the crossroads of autophagy, apoptosis, and cancer. Cell 137 (6), 1001—1004.

Motzer, R.J., Escudier, B., Oudard, S., Hutson, T.E., Porta, C., Bracarda, S., et al., 2008. Efficacy of everolimus in advanced renal cell carcinoma: a double-blind, randomised, placebo-controlled phase III trial. Lancet 372 (9637), 449—456.

Mozdoori, N., Safarian, S., Sheibani, N., 2017. Augmentation of the cytotoxic effects of zinc oxide nanoparticles by MTCP conjugation: non-canonical apoptosis and autophagy induction in human adenocarcinoma breast cancer cell lines. Mater. Sci. Eng. C. 78, 949—959. Sep 1.

Noda, T., Ohsumi, Y.T., 1998. A phosphatidylinositol kinase homologue, controls autophagy in yeast. J. Biol. Chem. 273 (7), 3963−3966.

Nowell, P.C., 1974. Diagnostic and prognostic value of chromosome studies in cancer. Ann. Clin. Lab. Sci. 4 (4), 234−240.

Okoshi, R., Ozaki, T., Yamamoto, H., Ando, K., Koida, N., Ono, S., et al., 2008. Activation of AMP-activated protein kinase induces p53-dependent apoptotic cell death in response to energetic stress. J. Biol. Chem. 283 (7), 3979−3987.

Pool, H., Campos-Vega, R., Herrera-Hernández, M.G., García-Solis, P., García-Gasca, T., Sánchez, I. C., et al., 2018. Development of genistein-PEGylated silica hybrid nanomaterials with enhanced anti-oxidant and antiproliferative properties on HT29 human colon cancer cells. Am. J. Transl. Res. 10 (8), 2306.

Roy, A.C., Park, S.R., Cunningham, D., Kang, Y.K., Chao, Y., Chen, L.T., et al., 2013. A randomized phase II study of PEP02 (MM-398), irinotecan or docetaxel as a second-line therapy in patients with locally advanced or metastatic gastric or gastro-oesophageal junction adenocarcinoma. Ann. Oncol. 24 (6), 1567−1573.

Saif, M.W., 2014. MM-398 achieves primary endpoint of overall survival in phase III study in patients with gemcitabine refractory metastatic pancreatic cancer. J. Pancreas 15 (3), 278−279.

Salmena, L., Poliseno, L., Tay, Y., Kats, L., Pandolfi, P.P., 2011. A ceRNA hypothesis: the Rosetta Stone of a hidden RNA language? Cell. 146 (3), 353−358.

Schütz, I., Lopez-Hernandez, T., Gao, Q., Puchkov, D., Jabs, S., Nordmeyer, D., et al., 2016. Lysosomal dysfunction caused by cellular accumulation of silica nanoparticles. J. Biol. Chem. 291 (27), 14170−14184.

Seca, H., Lima, R.T., Lopes-Rodrigues, V., Guimaraes, J.E., Gabriela, G.M., Vasconcelos, M.H., et al., 2013. Targeting miR-21 induces autophagy and chemosensitivity of leukemia cells. Curr. Drug Targets 14 (10), 1135−1143.

Semple, S.C., Leone, R., Wang, J., Leng, E.C., Klimuk, S.K., Eisenhardt, M.L., et al., 2005. Optimization and characterization of a sphingomyelin/cholesterol liposome formulation of vinorelbine with promising antitumor activity. J. Pharm. Sci. 94 (5), 1024−1038.

Shen, Y., Li, D.D., Wang, L.L., Deng, R., Zhu, X.F., 2008. Decreased expression of autophagy-related proteins in malignant epithelial ovarian cancer. Autophagy. 4 (8), 1067−1068.

Shintani, T., Klionsky, D.J., 2004. Autophagy in health and disease: a double-edged sword. Science. 306 (5698), 990−995.

Singh, S.S., Vats, S., Chia, A.Y., Tan, T.Z., Deng, S., Ong, M.S., et al., 2018. Dual role of autophagy in hallmarks of cancer. Oncogene. 37 (9), 1142−1158.

Singh, S.V., Dakhole, A.N., Deogharkar, A., Kazi, S., Kshirsagar, R., Goel, A., et al., 2017. Restoration of miR-30a expression inhibits growth, tumorigenicity of medulloblastoma cells accompanied by autophagy inhibition. Biochem. Biophys. Res. Commun. 491 (4), 946−952.

Stathopoulos, G.P., Antoniou, D., Dimitroulis, J., Michalopoulou, P., Bastas, A., Marosis, K., et al., 2010. Liposomal cisplatin combined with paclitaxel versus cisplatin and paclitaxel in non-small-cell lung cancer: a randomized phase III multicenter trial. Ann. Oncol. 21 (11), 2227−2232.

Sui, X., Chen, R., Wang, Z., Huang, Z., Kong, N., Zhang, M., et al., 2013. Autophagy and chemotherapy resistance: a promising therapeutic target for cancer treatment. Cell Death Dis. 4 (10), e838.

Sun, T., Zhang, Y.S., Pang, B., Hyun, D.C., Yang, M., Xia, Y., 2014. Engineered nanoparticles for drug delivery in cancer therapy. Angew. Chem. Int. Ed. 53 (46), 12320−12364.

Taguchi-Atarashi, N., Hamasaki, M., Matsunaga, K., Omori, H., Ktistakis, N.T., Yoshimori, T., et al., 2010. Modulation of local PtdIns3P levels by the PI phosphatase MTMR3 regulates constitutive autophagy. Traffic. 11 (4), 468−478.

Tardi, P., Choice, E., Masin, D., Redelmeier, T., Bally, M., Madden, T.D., 2000. Liposomal encapsulation of topotecan enhances anticancer efficacy in murine and human xenograft models. Cancer Res. 60 (13), 3389−3393.

Tay, Y., Rinn, J., Pandolfi, P.P., 2014. The multilayered complexity of ceRNA crosstalk and competition. Nature. 505 (7483), 344−352.

Tong, X., Wang, X., Wang, C., Li, L., 2018. Elevated levels of serum MiR-152 and miR-24 in uterine sarcoma: potential for inducing autophagy via SIRT1 and deacetylated LC3. Br. J. Biomed. Sci. 75 (1), 7−12.

Wang, J., Gao, S., Wang, S., Xu, Z., Wei, L., 2018. Zinc oxide nanoparticles induce toxicity in CAL 27 oral cancer cell lines by activating PINK1/Parkin-mediated mitophagy. Int. J. Nanomed. 13, 3441.

Weidle, U.H., Birzele, F., Kollmorgen, G., Rueger, R., 2017. Long non-coding RNAs and their role in metastasis. Cancer Genom. Proteom 14 (3), 143−160.

White, E., 2012. Deconvoluting the context-dependent role for autophagy in cancer. Nat. Rev. Cancer 12 (6), 401−410.

Wilkinson, S., 2020. Emerging principles of selective ER autophagy. J. Mol. Biol. 432 (1), 185−205.

Williams, J.A., Ding, W.X., 2018. Mechanisms, pathophysiological roles and methods for analyzing mitophagy−recent insights. Biol. Chem. 399 (2), 147−178.

Wirawan, E., Lippens, S., VandenBerghe, T., Romagnoli, A., Fimia, G.M., Piacentini, M., et al., 2012. Beclin1: a role in membrane dynamics and beyond. Autophagy. 8 (1), 6−17.

Wullschleger, S., Loewith, R., Hall, M.N., 2006. TOR signaling in growth and metabolism. Cell. 124 (3), 471−484.

Xie, X., White, E.P., Mehnert, J.M., 2013. Coordinate autophagy and mTOR pathway inhibition enhances cell death in melanoma. PLoS One 8 (1), e55096. Available from: https://doi.org/10.1371/journal.pone.0055096. Epub 2013 Jan 30. PMID: 23383069; PMCID: PMC3559441.

Xu, L., Tang, W.H., Huang, C.C., Alexander, W., Xiang, L.M., Pirollo, K.F., et al., 2001. Systemic p53 gene therapy of cancer with immunolipoplexes targeted by anti-transferrin receptor scFv. Mol. Med. 7 (10), 723−734.

Yang, L., Zhang, X., Li, H., Liu, J., 2016. The long noncoding RNA HOTAIR activates autophagy by upregulating ATG3 and ATG7 in hepatocellular carcinoma. Mol. Biosyst. 12 (8), 2605−2612.

Yang, S.H., Lin, C.C., Lin, Z.Z., Tseng, Y.L., Hong, R.L., 2012. A phase I and pharmacokinetic study of liposomal vinorelbine in patients with advanced solid tumor. Invest. New Drugs 30 (1), 282−289.

Yang, Y., Jiang, C., Yang, Y., Guo, L., Huang, J., Liu, X., et al., 2018. Silencing of LncRNA-HOTAIR decreases drug resistance of non-small cell lung cancer cells by inactivating autophagy via suppressing the phosphorylation of ULK1. Biochem. Biophys. Res. Commun. 497 (4), 1003−1010.

Yang, Z.J., Chee, C.E., Huang, S., Sinicrope, F.A., 2011. The role of autophagy in cancer: therapeutic implications. Mol. Cancer Ther 10 (9), 1533−1541.

Yazbeck, V.Y., Buglio, D., Georgakis, G.V., Li, Y., Iwado, E., Romaguera, J.E., et al., 2008. Temsirolimus downregulates p21 without altering cyclin D1 expression and induces autophagy and synergizes with vorinostat in mantle cell lymphoma. Exp. Hematol. 36 (4), 443−450.

Ye, Z., Fang, B., Pan, J., Zhang, N., Huang, J., Xie, C., et al., 2017. miR-138 suppresses the proliferation, metastasis and autophagy of non-small cell lung cancer by targeting Sirt1. Oncol. Rep. 37 (6), 3244−3252.

Ying, L., Huang, Y., Chen, H., Wang, Y., Xia, L., Chen, Y., et al., 2013. Downregulated MEG3 activates autophagy and increases cell proliferation in bladder cancer. Mol. Biosyst. 9 (3), 407−411.

Yoon, J.H., Abdelmohsen, K., Gorospe, M., 2013. Posttranscriptional gene regulation by long noncoding RNA. J. Mol. Biol. 425 (19), 3723−3730.

Yu, G., Jia, Z., Dou, Z., 2017. miR-24-3p regulates bladder cancer cell proliferation, migration, invasion and autophagy by targeting DEDD. Oncol. Rep. 37 (2), 1123−1131.

Yuan, Y.G., Gurunathan, S., 2017. Combination of graphene oxide−silver nanoparticle nanocomposites and cisplatin enhances apoptosis and autophagy in human cervical cancer cells. Int. J. Nanomed. 12, 6537.

Zhai, H., Fesler, A., Ba, Y., Wu, S., Ju, J., 2015. Inhibition of colorectal cancer stem cell survival and invasive potential by hsa-miR-140-5p mediated suppression of Smad2 and autophagy. Oncotarget 6 (23), 19735.

Zhang, R., Xu, J., Zhao, J., Bai, J., 2017. Mir-30d suppresses cell proliferation of colon cancer cells by inhibiting cell autophagy and promoting cell apoptosis. Tumor Biol. 39 (6), 1010428317703984.

Zhang, X., Zhang, H., Liang, X., Zhang, J., Tao, W., Zhu, X., et al., 2016. Iron oxide nanoparticles induce autophagosome accumulation through multiple mechanisms: lysosome impairment, mitochondrial damage, and ER stress. Mol. Pharm 13 (7), 2578–2587.

Zhu, K., Dunner, K., McConkey, D.J., 2010. Proteasome inhibitors activate autophagy as a cytoprotective response in human prostate cancer cells. Oncogene. 29 (3), 451–462.

Zielinska, E., Zauszkiewicz-Pawlak, A., Wojcik, M., Inkielewicz-Stepniak, I., 2018. Silver nanoparticles of different sizes induce a mixed type of programmed cell death in human pancreatic ductal adenocarcinoma. Oncotarget. 9 (4), 4675.

CHAPTER 4

Multifunctional nanocarrier-mediated codelivery for targeting and treatment of prostate cancer

Ankaj Kumar, Sumedh Bahadure, Sudarshan Naidu Chilamakuri, Adinath Dadhale and Arvind Gulbake
Department of Pharmaceutics, National Institute of Pharmaceutical Education and Research, Guwahati, Assam, India

4.1 Introduction

Prostate cancer (PC) ranks fourth among all cancers in terms of human mortality (Thakur, 2021). Prostate is a walnut-shaped gland that helps in the transportation of nutrients and secretion of seminal fluid in males. The gland offer useful components of zinc and citrate for the maintenance of the man's reproductive system. The occurrence of PC is generally associated with a reduction in zinc and citrate levels in prostatic fluid (Abrams, 2018). In men, PC is the second most frequent malignancy (Tas and Keklikcioglu Cakmak, 2021). It begins in early adulthood but is clinically diagnosed in men beyond the age of 60, and it is uncommon in the late 40 s. Men having BRCA-2 gene mutation and a history of urinary tract infection are more likely to develop PC (Sarath Chandran et al., 2021). After the successful diagnosis of cancer, the U.S. National Cancer Institute divides the PC into four different levels/stages. Stage one consists of the presence of small cell proliferations and is limited to the prostate gland. Stage two of PC is associated with an increase in cancer size but is still limited to the prostate gland. There is a slight advancement in the transmission of cancer to nearby cells in the prostate gland, mainly seminal vesicles, which are signs of stage three. The last stage, that is, stage four, is also known as advanced PC since cancer spreads toward vital or different organs. It infects the rectum, lymph nodes, lungs, bones, etc. The occurrence of a deadly stage or progression or higher proliferation comes under the advanced stage of PC (Barve et al., 2014; Trump, 2004).

The overall treatment of PC is mostly determined by the patient's prostate-specific antigens (PSAs) level, clinical stage of disease progression, and Gleason scores, as well as the functionality of the urinary system at a basic level, comorbidities, and age (Karpisheh et al., 2021). There are various treatment options for PC, including hormonal therapy, chemotherapy, radiation therapy, and surgery. The researchers found it

Multifunctional Nanocomposites for Targeted Drug Delivery in Cancer Therapy
DOI: https://doi.org/10.1016/B978-0-323-95303-0.00007-1

easy to deal with level one and level two PC owing to limited proliferation (Chung et al., 2020).However, it becomes difficult when cancer reaches stages three and four. Thus, there are high-risk factors in the treatment of such advanced PC. Among all approaches, chemotherapy-based approaches are mostly studied by researchers. Although chemotherapy through conventional carrier systems provides a toxicological impression to the healthy cells (de Araújo et al., 2021). Thus, it requires a targeted drug delivery system that can specifically bind with the target site and release therapeutics in a controlled fashion.

This chapter highlights the key challenges associated with the current PC therapies and the finding of potential targets to way out of such problems. In addition, the chapter also highlights the rationale of the codelivery approach through the use of different drug-nanocarrier. Finally, clinical data and patented products demonstrate the achievement of such a multifunctional codelivery system in gaining marketed potential in the future.

4.2 Pathophysiology of prostate cancer

In connection with the pathophysiology of PC, the steroid hormone i.e. androgen plays an important evaluative role, which is responsible for the beginning and sustentation of manful characters (Mitobe et al., 2018). The robust risk factor in PC is men's age. Initially, testosterone has a role to regulate the nitric oxide—cyclic guanosine monophosphate pathway, and its level declines with aging (age > 40 years). The decreased level results in endothelial dysfunction due to the inadequacy of testosterone and thereby ultimately resulting in prostatic hyperplasia carcinogenesis (Phua, 2021). Some other factors associated with PC prognosis are obesity, hypercholesterolemia, diabetes, and hyperinsulinemia (Rhee et al., 2016). The androgen signaling pathway is mostly involved in the pathophysiology of PC (El Badri et al., 2019). Fig. 4.1 illustrates the key factors involved in the progression of PC.

The pathogenesis of PC is complicated due to interactions between intrinsic vulnerability, acquired somatic gene alterations, and micro and macroenvironmental variables. Multiple foci accommodate various genetic alterations with an independent capacity for metastatic seeding and inherent treatment resistance. The matured human prostate is intrinsically split into three different parts central, transition, and peripheral region. The utmost prostate tumor origin lies in the outermost peripheral region. The PC stem cells may be either basal or luminal prostate epithelial cells, both have the potential to produce high-grade lesions that mimic adenocarcinomas when genetically manipulated. The primary reasons for the progression of PC are oxidative stress, which is the production of reactive oxygen species that incite DNA damage, chronic inflammation, and urinary infection due to microbes speeding up the mutation of cells (Sandhu et al., 2021). The autopsy study proved that bone is the most common site

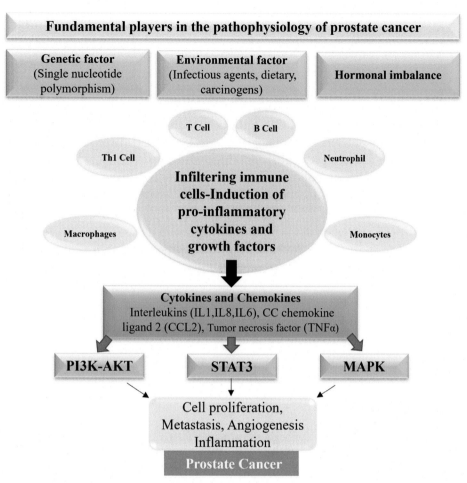

Figure 4.1 Pathophysiological factors associated with prostate cancer-induced production of proinflammatory cytokines that trigger the cell proliferation, angiogenesis, and metastasis by phosphatidylinositol 3-kinase —protein kinase (PI3K-AKT), signal transducer and activator of transcription (STAT3), and mitogen-activated protein kinase (MAPK) pathways.

for metastasis; unfortunately, to date, the exact mechanism for bone metastasis is unclear. It is revealed that the bone microenvironment is a notable mediator of PC bone tropism (El Badri et al., 2019).

Immunohistochemistry study helps in the diagnosis of PC by use of basal cell–specific immunohistochemical stains (KER 903, p63, CK5/6) for malignant diagnosis. Histological findings like infiltrative growth pattern, absence of basal cells as well as nuclear atypia about nuclear enlargement and prominent nucleoli conclude PC. Nevertheless, any single major diagnostic marker can't diagnose malignancy by itself, but nuclear atypia is considered a crucial diagnostic parameter for PC (Magi-Galluzzi, 2018).

Overexpression of glycoproteins containing LacdiNAc and sialic acid moieties contained by PC cells is confirmed by lectin histochemical staining analysis. For the screening as well as diagnosis of PC, serum PSA is considered ideal (Haga et al., 2019).

4.3 Treatment options for prostate cancer

The hormonal therapy to treat PC is known as androgen deprivation therapy (ADT) in which a class of antiandrogenic agents competes with circulating or locally derived androgens to the androgen receptor. The other treatment techniques for localized PC are focal irreversible electroporation (FIE), photodynamic therapy, high-intensity focused ultrasound therapy, focal laser ablation (FLA), and focal cryotherapy.

ADT: ADT is the most common and primary treatment for PC. ADT suppresses PSA, stabilizes disease, alleviates symptoms of advanced disease, and thereby prolongs survival (Collier et al., 2012). Antiandrogens such as flutamide, nilutamide, etc., have the potential to inhibit androgen receptors and play a distinctive role in the treatment of PC. Antiandrogen drugs function by blocking androgen receptor activation, reducing the nuclear translocation process, inhibiting DNA binding, and also preventing the androgen receptor-mediated transcription (Crawford et al., 2018).

FIE: It is the arising treatment for clinically significant localized PC. It is done by a single urologist using an irreversible electroporation device and 18-gage electrodes (van den Bos et al., 2018). FIE is known for its safer action with lower morbidity. Various research articles demonstrate the role of electroporation therapy in PC to overcome the reoccurrence for up to 1 or 2 years.

Photodynamic therapy: It is the most studied therapy among the other well-studied focal therapies and is usually done with the help of photosensitizer drugs. It works by systemic administration of moderately biologically inert drug moiety, which will be activated by exposed light to release cytotoxic substances (Ahdoot et al., 2019).

High-intensity focused ultrasound therapy (HIFU): It is a hybrid type of therapy and works by two different physical mechanisms, such as thermal and mechanical, which account for the treatment effect. HIFU is characterized as a noninvasive approach to the treatment by sending high-intensity ultrasound to achieve tumor necrosis and changes in the biological structures of targeted cells free from radiation or surgical excision (Chaussy and Thüroff, 2017).

FLA: It is a type of photothermal treatment in which thermal destruction of tissue is achieved by laser. The diffusing laser is inserted in a transperineal way like a schematic midline sagittal section of the prostate, bladder, urethra, and striated sphincter. The absorption of radiant energy by tissue-receptive chromophores incites heat energy, which results from irreversible destruction. The amount of heat energy delivered and the depth of light distribution affect the thermal effect, and the wavelength of the laser also matters for ineffective treatments such as deeper tissue penetration (Colin et al., 2012).

Focal cryotherapy: It was used for whole gland ablation, but later on, it was reused for the treatment of focal prostate lesions. The frequent freeze and thaw cycles of cryotherapy result in irreversible cell rupture and apoptosis. The limitation of cryotherapy is elevated rates of erectile dysfunction and fistula interconnected with entire gland cryoablation (Ahdoot et al., 2019).

Chemotherapy: The therapy associated with the use of bioactive chemical or phytochemicals are known to prolong the life of PC patients. However, as per the safety issues and drug resistance such therapy needs to be developed through various drug carriers' systems. There are some effective and commonly used drugs (Docetaxel, Doxorubicin [DOX], Mitoxantrone, Carbazetaxel, etc.) in PC treatments that are found to be beneficial through drug delivery systems or a combination of two drug approaches.

Each therapy has its advantages and disadvantages that make it useful for effective treatment options for PCs. There are a few hurdles or challenges that must be encountered through the drug delivery system. The challenges may be associated with the pathophysiology of cancer, physicochemical characteristics of the drugs, etc. Below is an explanation of some of the challenges that must be kept in mind before designing any drug carrier's systems.

4.4 Challenges in the treatment of prostate cancer

From the 1940s, it was considered that orchiectomy can avoid PC as it leads to the depletion of androgens. The main treatment associated with PC is the reduction in androgen level, but cancer can develop into castration-resistant prostate cancer (CRPC). CRPC is the result of androgen receptors that get sensitized in smaller quantities of androgens. The mutation causes these receptors to activate even in the absence of androgens also. In CRPC, growth factors can also induce cascades by keratinocyte insulin-like growth factor-1 that can be curable with novel treatments (Lauer et al., 2015). Surgical removal of tumors and then treating them with radiation therapy can be an effective treatment, but this procedure cannot be done for cancer that has already spread to other parts of the body. Radiation therapy is not target-specific and may kill normal cells also. The use of chemotherapeutic agents with conventional drug delivery systems is also deprived of specificity as they are ineffective to deliver drugs intracellularly. There is a lack of precision for the target and an inability to discriminate between healthy and tumor cells, thus conventional drug delivery systems possess serious side effects (Hema et al., 2018). The drugs with poor bioavailability need to administer at higher concentrations and frequent delivery of such agents can lead to dose-dependent side effects. Even drugs with a low solubility profile, when administered through the intravenous (IV) route, can lead to embolization. Apart from this, it becomes difficult for acid-sensitive drugs to deliver in PC due to the highly acidic physiology of the cells (Edis et al., 2021). The mentioned challenges can be encountered through multifunctional nanocarrier (MNC) systems.

4.5 Mechanism of drug targeting

The main mechanism associated to achieve passive targeting is diffusion and convection. Passive diffusion occurs due to concentration difference and lipophilicity of the drug as it has been observed that low molecular weight can easily attain passive diffusion. In the case of the convection process, it is driven by the apertures of the endothelium. As tumors don't have a good drainage system of lymph, an accumulation of drugs is occurring which is known as the enhanced permeation and retention (EPR) effect. The other main mechanism of drug targeting is active targeting, which helps to increase the targeting and uptake of drugs to cancerous cells. Active targeting is done by attaching drug carriers with ligands like folate, galactosamine, and transferrin moieties. Sometimes carrier system is loaded with biological moieties like antibodies or aptamers to increase its target specificity. Active targeting helps to transport drugs to the subcellular level (Kumaraswamy et al., 2021; Garg et al., 2021). The study conducted to investigate active targeting, nanoparticles of resveratrol and docetaxel were coupled with folate moiety resulting in a better cytotoxic effect. The effect of such a system was found to be 28 times more efficient compared with free drugs. Through such study, authors found nanoparticles helped to increase the intracellular accumulation of drugs with more specificity and selectivity to the cancerous cells with the advantage of increased stability. Thus, through the receptor-mediated endocytosis process, the nanosystem was able to tackle the multiple drug resistance developed at the tumor site (Singh et al., 2018). Through these mechanisms, we can target the drugs toward a specific site. Generally, it requires a brief understanding of the target biomarkers for designing the drug delivery aspects in a well efficient manner. As shown in Fig. 4.2 which demonstrates the receptors mediated endocytosis by clathrin or caveolin types that help in the release of the drug from the drug carrier system.

4.6 Potential targets of multifunctional nanocarriers in codelivery of drugs

It requires specific target sites for the drug carriers to attach and release their active content. The delivery of drugs toward specific target sites can be achieved through the modification of carriers with ligands, proteins, peptides, and polymers. The modifications depend on the pathophysiological conditions of the diseases as some biomarkers are expressed in disease sites only (Kumaraswamy et al., 2021; Adamaki and Zoumpourlis, 2021). The expressed biomarkers may be receptors, antigens, and proteins. Thus, these components become the potential sites to target the disease with specificity. The approach toward such specificity is not only to attain targeted drug delivery but also to reduce the toxic effects associated with normal cells (Alberts et al., 2021). Numerous different types of potential targets are expressed in PC, which offers targeting opportunities for drug carriers.

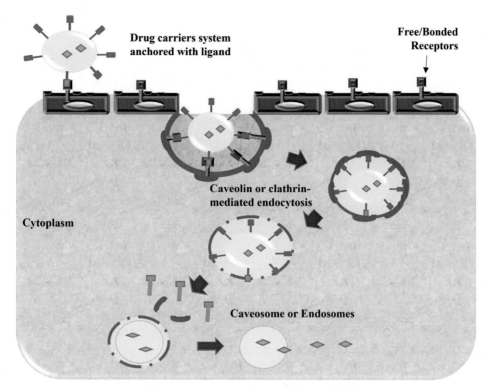

Figure 4.2 Illustration of the active drug targeting through overexpressed receptors.

4.6.1 Prostate-specific membrane antigens

It is the prominent potential target for PC treatment as antigens are highly overexpressed on the epithelium of the prostate gland, kidney, or other cancer-caused tissues. The expression of such antigens varies from cell to cell as in normal cells cytoplasmic splices are seen compared with fully surface attained proteins in cancerous cells (Weber et al., 2021). There is a binary enzymatic function of prostate-specific membrane antigen (PSMA) as glutamate carboxypeptidase and folate hydrolase that can break the amide bond of glutamates and also help in folic acid uptake. These antigens can become a promising strategic approach through antibodies, ligands, aptamers, and folate receptors as shown in Fig. 4.3 (Sheehan et al., 2021; Nauseef et al., 2021).

4.6.1.1 Antibodies

The antibodies have gained more potential to bind with prostate antigens due to their immunogenicity and high affinity. There are several types of antibodies through which we can modify the nanocarriers to attain a high affinity toward specific prostate antigens (Loo and Mather, 2008). To investigate such affinity, CD133 antibodies were

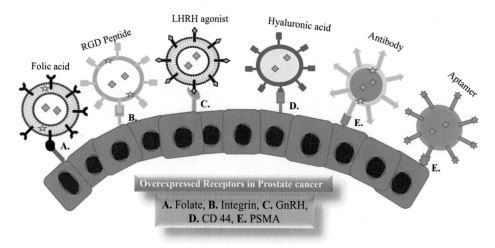

Figure 4.3 Targeting approaches of MNCs toward overexpressed receptors.

fabricated on the nanosystem containing coloaded IR820 and docetaxel. The authors conducted an in-vivo examination through IV administration of different groups of nanosystems (fabricated CD133 nanosystem and antibody-free nanosystem). It was found that under NIR-light irradiation, CD133-containing nanosystems were safer and were able to reduce the size of the tumor compared with other nanosystems through a targeted approach (Tan et al., 2020).

4.6.1.2 Aptamers

Aptamers are oligonucleotides consisting of different nucleic acids either DNAs or RNAs containing approximately 50 nucleotides sequences. These sequences offer wide applications of aptamers in the diagnosis and treatment of PC. It helps the drug to recognize the affinity toward specific receptors and behaves to work as a molecular probe. These are biomarkers that are more prominently utilized through such aptamers-based carriers' systems (Campos-Fernández et al., 2021). In one such study, authors investigated the targeting efficiency of the aptamer functionalized codelivery of anticancer drugs. The aptamer's functionalization helped the carrier's systems to accumulate at the tumor site and depicted an enhanced tumor inhibition effect. It was found that aptamers containing carriers showed synergistic activity with two different drugs compared with an aptamer-free system (Chen et al., 2020). Despite the targeting, aptamers are also useful in the identification of disease biomarkers as investigated by Miranda et al. The expression of nucleolin was evaluated and confirmed by the modified AS1411-N5 aptamers system. The examined aptameric system was able to bind with high affinity to expressed nucleolin biomarkers as confirmed through ELISA, confocal microscopy, and fluorescence (Miranda et al., 2021).

4.6.1.3 Folates

Folic acid receptors are also studied under prostate-specific membrane target sites for nanocarrier systems. It requires three-to-fourfold enhancements in overexpression of each receptor for site-specificity in cancerous cells than normal cells to reduce the toxicity toward normal tissues (Rana and Bhatnagar, 2021). Folate receptors are highly overexpressed in PC to meet the requirement of folic acid and can become the potential target through folic acid ligands. These natural, nonimmunological ligands achieve site-specificity through receptor-mediated endocytosis (Decarlo et al., 2021). To explain the targeting specificity through folate receptors, Baig et al. conducted the study by taking bleomycin-loaded DNA-nanotubes fabricated with folate receptors antibodies. Modified nanotubes were evaluated for the targeting efficiency through the CWR22R and were found to be highly adventurous confirmed through MTT assay and flow cytometry (Baig et al., 2020). Another study by Nassir et al. developed folate-modified nanoliposomes to check the anticancer potential of the oleuropein-loaded lipidic system. Through the study, it was found that surface functionalization with folate helps the nanocarrier system to bind with the negatively charged cell surface to achieve a mechanism of targeting (active or passive targeting) through receptor-mediated endocytosis (Nassir et al., 2019).

4.6.1.4 Small molecules

Glu, Urea, Lys, ACUPA, and LIG are some small molecules that also show affinity toward PSMA. These small molecules have higher diffusibility toward solid tumors and multiple ligands protein binding interactions to produce affinity effects (Kwon et al., 2019). To investigate such interactions, small molecules containing Glu-NH-CO-NH-Lys (f [18 F] 16) were studied for the specificity of PSMA. Through LNCap cell lines owing to express the high amount of PSMA were used to check affinity of f [18 F] 16 toward PSMA. It was confirmed that 95% of Glu-NH-CO-NH-Lys are bound with prostate antigens (Zha et al., 2018). Another study by Wang Z et al. examined the cascade targeting through a dual targeting system consisting of PLA-PEG-ACUPA/TPP. The use of such a system is to target the mitochondria and PSMA. The system was able to produce antitumor inhibition and synergistic effect (Wang et al., 2022).

4.6.2 Prostate stem cell antigens

Prostate stem cell antigen (PSCA) are the surface proteins that are upregulated in PC. The antigens are expressed in cancerous cells and are a potential therapeutic target for the drug delivery system toward cancerous cells (Raff et al., 2009; Fujimoto and Kanno, 2016). For such a study, Wu et al. developed a conjugated system containing multi-walled carbon nanotubes (WCNTs) to investigate such targets. The PSCA-specific antibody (mAb) was conjugated with dye and polyethyleneimine to examine the targeting potential of the WCNT. It was confirmed that a multifunctional system containing antibodies was targeted to deliver the drug toward the expressed stem cell antigens (Wu et al., 2014). Another study by Xin et al. explain the targeting role of stem cell antigens. The multifunctional nanoparticles were fabricated with PSCAs and other polymeric systems to achieve the targeted delivery. Through in-vivo evaluation, it was found that PSCA Ab effectively targets the tumor and enhances the antitumor efficacy confirmed through MRI contrast enhancement (Gao et al., 2012).

4.6.3 Gastrin-releasing peptide receptors

The receptors are associated with the bombesin family, consisting of 14-amino acid peptides. These receptors play an ambient role in the stimulation of the growth of androgen-dependent PC cells through G-protein coupled receptors. A high level of overexpression was found in the cancerous cell of PC when compared with normal prostate cells (Baratto et al., 2018). Such targeting was achieved by Dubuc et al. in their study by taking sulfonated aluminum phthalocyanines (AIPcS) for gastrin-releasing peptide receptors. The conjugated system was evaluated through mass spectroscopy and found to be highly efficacious to bind with gastrin receptors (Dubuc et al., 2008).

4.6.4 Miscellaneous potential targets

Apart from the above-discussed targets, there are some other potential targets through which we can target the cancerous cell or reduce the toxicity toward normal cells. Integrins are the cell surface receptors that are useful in adhesion and interactions between cells. The presence of α and β subunits are associated with cancer metastasis. PC progenesis is associated with overexpression of such types of integrins as found in many studies (Drivalos et al., 2021, 2016). Another important target is sigma 1 and sigma 2, which are the membrane-binding proteins having an affinity toward neuroleptics. The expression of such types of proteins are found in PC and studied through various nanocarrier systems for targeting purposes (van Waarde et al., 2015). In addition, $CD44^+$ is known for its multifunctional role in showing greater clonogenicity and metastasis (Costa et al., 2019). These markers are also studied to attain the target disease through hyaluronic acid (Ashrafizadeh et al., 2021). Table 4.1 shows the potential biomarkers that are overexpressed and can be potential target sites for carrier systems along with their ligands or polymers to effectively target PC.

4.7 Multifunctional nanocarriers in codelivery of anticancer drugs to target prostate cancer

As discussed above there are several potential targets through which we can achieve the targeted drug delivery. The loading of a single chemotherapeutic agent in a drug carriers system offers great advantages as easy to load, no drug interactions, easy to check the cellular uptake study. Apart from the offered benefits, it also develops drug

Table 4.1 Potential targets in prostate cancer.

Potential target	Ligand	Drug	Nanocarriers system	Brief	References
1. Prostate-specific membrane antigens	Aptamers	Doxorubicin	Micelles	The micellar aptamer conjugated system enhances the cellular uptake, which ultimately increases the cytotoxicity of prostate cancer cell lines	Xu et al. (2013)
	Folic acid	Iron oxide	Nanoparticles	The overexpressed folate receptors are targeted through conjugated iron oxide nanoparticles for high potential of imaging and treatment by hyperthermia	Bonvin et al. (2017)
	CD44 antibodies	Salinomycin	Lipid-PLGA nanoparticles	The lipid polymer system efficiently bonded with overexpressed CD44 antigens and showed a better antitumor effect	Wei et al. (2019)
2. Sigma-2 receptors	3-(4-cyclohexylpiperazine-1-yl) propyl amine (CPPA)	Telmisartan	Nanostructured lipid particles (NLPs)	The ligand anchored NLPs reduce the IC-50 value significantly compared with normal NLPs. Through receptors, mediated endocytosis CPPA anchored NLPs able to give higher cytotoxicity by targeting sigma 2 receptors specifically	Puri et al. (2016)

(Continued)

Table 4.1 (Continued)

Potential target	Ligand	Drug	Nanocarriers system	Brief	References
3. Sigma–1 and Sigma 2	[3 H] (+)-pentazocine and [3 H]1,3-di-o-tolylguanidine	Dextrallorphan	Drug–ligand conjugated system	It was found that ligand conjugated drug was able to bind with sigma receptors with high affinity leading to higher uptake and retention in prostate cancer cell lines	John et al. (1999)
4. CD 44 + +	Hyaluronic acid	Cabazitaxel prodrug and orlistat	Polymer lipid hybrid nanoparticles	The drug conjugated hyaluronic acid nanosystem was able to provide the enhanced in vivo and in vitro antitumor effect when compared with single drug-loaded polymer lipid hybrid nanoparticles through CD + 44 targeting	Qu et al. (2021)
5. Gastrin releasing peptide receptors	Bombesin peptide	—	Conjugated system	The peptide conjugated system showed a higher affinity toward gastrin–releasing peptide receptors and enhanced the cellular internalization	Alshehri et al. (2020)

resistance to the tumor, and at higher concentrations produces toxic effects (McCrea et al., 2016). Thus, it requires the loading of two drugs having different molecular mechanisms of targeting that can reduce the developed resistance and side effects (Jonnalagadda et al., 2020). It generally requires advancement in formulation perspective to load dual drugs in the carrier system and reduces the challenges associated with the codelivery of the agents. The challenges associated with dual drug loading are the different physicochemical properties of both drugs, there may be chances of drug–drug interactions, and sometimes it becomes difficult to achieve the dual drug loading and cellular uptake study (Upadhyay et al., 2021).

To overcome the pharmacokinetic and pharmacodynamics-limitations of the drugs various nanocarrier systems have emerged which provide multifunctional roles towards codelivery of the anticancer agents. These are lipids, polysaccharides, and proteins that offer prominent functions to the drug delivery systems and make them MNCs systems (Ang et al., 2021). Fig. 4.4 demonstrates the prostate-specific ligands-modified nanocarriers that prominently overcome the hurdles associated with conventional drug delivery systems.

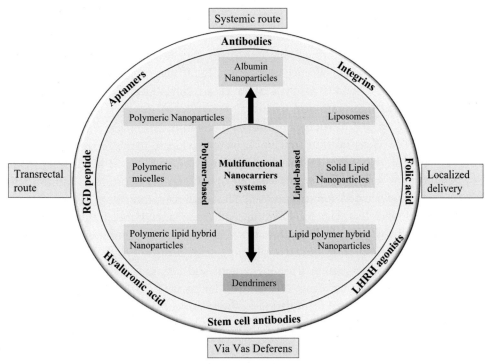

Figure 4.4 Ligand fabricated MFNs through various routes of the administration against prostate cancer.

4.7.1 Multifunctional lipid-based nanotherapeutics

As discussed above, there are expressions of several types of proteins that can be an effective codelivery targets in PC treatment. Various studies have demonstrated the targeted role of multifunctional lipid-based nanocarriers in PC targeting. One such study revealed the targeted approach through the conjugated system for the expression of PSAs. Dual drug-loaded folate-targeted liposomes were developed and studied for cellular uptake and binding affinity of folate ligands toward PSA receptors. The co-entrapment involves mito-mycin C prodrug(MCP) and DOX which were tested for cytotoxic activity. Drugs coloaded folate modified liposomes (FT-MCP-DOX-Lipo) and unmodified liposomes (MCP-DOX-Lipo) were physically characterized. It was found that unmodified and modified liposomes have a particle size in the nanometric range (90−105, 105−120 nm), good PDI (0.065−0.085), and zeta potential in the range of −10 to −15 mV which was optimum for in-vitro evaluation. The study was conducted on LNCaP cells to evaluate the cellular activity of the conjugated system. Results revealed 8−10 times more enhancements in cellular uptake for both the drugs (DOX and MCP) through modified formulation (FT-MCP-DOX-Lipo) than the unmodified system. Although it was also found that there was a 10-fold decrease in IC-50 concentration through folate-decorated liposomal formula-tion than unmodified liposome indicating higher cellular toxicity in a lower concentration. This enhancement activity of FT-MCP-DOX-Lipo was due to the higher binding affinity of the folate toward PSA receptors which specifically bind and enhance the cytotoxicity activity of the system. Thus through this study, the author revealed the multifunctional role of a lipid-based system in the effective treatment of PC (Patil et al., 2018).

In another study conducted by Mahira et al., developed hyaluronic acid (HA) modified coloaded liposomes and evaluated for anticancer activity. Liposomes were co-loaded with drugs Cabazitaxel (CBX) and silibinin (SIL). The HA-coated lipo-somes with 90% encapsulation efficiency were having a particle size range below 100 nm and PDI below 0.3. Further study through SEM-EDS, TEM, and ^{1}H NMR was conducted which confirmed the coating of the HA on liposomes. The modified liposomes were evaluated for in-vitro cell line studies by use of PC-3 and DU-15 cells. It was found that HA-modified liposomes enhanced the antitumor efficacy, intracellular delivery of both drugs and arrest G2/M cell cycle more prominently than the unmodified system. The coated hyaluronic acid along with nano-sized liposomes enhances the anticancer potential of the system and acts as a multifunctional carrier system for co-delivering the drugs efficiently (Mahira et al., 2019). Table 4.2 demon-strates the role of lipid-based formulation in the treatment of prostatic cancer.

4.7.2 Multifunctional polysaccharide-based nanotherapeutics

The use of the naturally occurring biopolymers from different sources [animals (hyaluronic acid, gelatin, chitosan, etc.), plants (pectin, cellulose, and starch), and

Table 4.2 Lipid-based nanocarriers in the treatment of prostate cancer.

Multifunctional nanocarrier	Drugs	Lipids used	Characterization	Outcomes	References
Liposomes	Genistein and Plumbagin	1−α−phosphatidylcholine	50−130 nm particle size, −30.0 to −36.0 mV zeta potential, and loading efficiency of Genistein and plumbagin drugs was 89.20 & 71.50% in liposomes	The developed formulation was checked for antitumor activities using PC-3 cells and results revealed the decrease in reactive oxygen species, reduction in cell viability, nontoxicity to normal cells. Although through an in-vivo study, there is a synergistic effect produced through both drugs within the liposome	Song et al. (2020)
Herceptin decorated Liposomes	Doxorubicin (DOX) and Simvastatin (SIM)	Phosphatidylcholine	Encapsulation efficiency of H-Lipo for (DOX 84.32%) and (SIM-81.7%), 134 ± 5 nm particle size, and 0.08 ± 0.01 PDI	The authors formulated the Herceptin (HCN) decorated liposomes loaded with DOX and SIM to effectively treat prostate cancer. Results from the study revealed an increase in the inhibition rate of tumor volumes by approximately 80.36% for HCN-decorated liposomes when compared with nondecorated liposomes	Li et al. (2019)

(Continued)

Table 4.2 (Continued)

Multifunctional nanocarrier	Drugs	Lipids used	Characterization	Outcomes	References
Nanoliposomes	AKT3 siRNA and PTEN plasmid (tumor suppressor gene)	Egg phosphatidylcholine	The liposomes were having a size below 150 nm, + 26.76 ± 0.73 zeta potential, and 100% PTEN encapsulation efficiency	The multifunctional liposomes were able to deliver the PTEN and siRNA more efficiently and reduced PC's proliferation and metastatic potential	Bhagat and Singh (2020)
Niosomes	miRNA-15a and miRNA-16−1	1,2-Distearoyl-phosphatidylethanolamine	Niosomes having particle size 118.9 nm, −3.52 mV zeta potential, and 0.30 PDI	The cationic niosomes were evaluated for MTT assay and cellular uptake assay. The results showed higher toxicity, higher cellular uptakes confirmed through higher peak intensities of the lipidic formulation than free drugs. In addition, the lipidic formulation has significantly enhanced the rate of cell death (34.4%)	Ghaffari et al. (2021)
Lipidic hybrid nanoparticles	Docetaxel and pDNA	Compritol and soya lecithin	The particle size of the lipid hybrid nanoparticles was 216 ± 21.7 nm, 0.23 PDI with encapsulation efficiency 92.3% ± 1.6%	The cytotoxicity and antitumor activity of the nanoparticles were evaluated, and it was found that at lower concentrations the tumor growth inhibition occurred with the antitumor effect	Dong et al. (2016)

microorganisms (dextran, pullulan, and xanthan gum)] also find its therapeutic applications in the design and development of the drug delivery system toward PC. These are the properties that make polymers emerging biomaterials as polymers are biodegradable, stabilizer, and flexible for the nanocarriers formulations (Raval et al., 2021). These materials also provide the site of attachments for loading two different types of drugs (hydrophilic and hydrophobic). Some examples illustrate the role of polymer in the codelivery of two different drugs and act as MNCs in the treatment of PC.

Recently Shitole et al. developed the dual drug-loaded (DTX and QU) nanocapsules system consisting of copolymer PEGylated-PLGA and LHRH conjugated-PEGylated -PLGA for effective drugs targeting towards PC. The adopted PEGylation was to increase the circulation of the carrier's system in the blood. The tumor targeting was achieved through LHRH to reduce the toxicity and delivery of the drug at a site-specific location within tumors. To achieve the EPR effect in the tumor site, nanosized vesicles were formulated having particle size range <200 nm, 0.171 PDI, -36.5 Zeta potential, and (87.52 ± 2.26 75, 78 ± 2.87) encapsulation efficiency for both drugs (DTX and QU simultaneously). A study was conducted on the PC cell lines (LNCaP and PC-3) to assess the in-vitro activity of the PPL-DTX: QU. The outcomes from the study showed higher uptake of the nanocapsules containing PPL-DTX: QU when compared with PP-DTX: QU and DTX: QU. It was observed that there is a decrease in the IC_{50} value of the LHRH conjugated system (PPL-DTX: QU) when compared with free drugs and PP-DTX: QU. This reduction in the value was due to the affinity-based targeted action of the ligand toward the receptor. Further to confirm the targeting ability of the nanocapsules the in-vivo study was conducted using PC-3 tumor-bearing mice. Results from the study revealed higher caspase-3 activity by the LHRH formulation than others (no targeted). It becomes necessary to find the distribution of the drug at an active site or other organs. The localization of the formulation was examined in various organs of BalB/c nude mice. After 24 hours of incubation, it was found that there was a higher increase in accumulation and localization in tumors which may be attributed due to the targeting affinity of LHRH. Finally, the PPL-DTX: QU was able to produce the antitumor activity with the sustained-release effect which enhances the tumor-targeting activity and efficacy of the formulation (Shitole et al., 2020).

The polymeric micelles were also found to be effective in the treatment of PC. Through micelles, we can deliver both types of drugs (hydrophilic and hydrophobic) due to both types of structural properties. Thus it improves the loading and encapsulation efficiency of the formulations to co-deliversizes the drugs (Hu and Xu, 2021). Apart from all these examples Table 4.3 demonstrates the role of polymers in making carriers' systems cost-effective and suitable for antiprostatic therapy.

Table 4.3 Polysaccharides based nanocarriers in the treatment of prostate cancer.

Multifunctional nanocarrier system	Drugs	Polymer used	Characterization	Outcomes	References
Nanoparticles	SN38 and Snail specific siRNA	Chitosan	Particle size 169 ± 6 nm. 11.8 ± 0.5 mV zeta potential, 0.3 PDI with EE of siRNA 86% and SN38 79%	PC-3 was taken as an in-vitro model to study the cytotoxicity and it was found through nanosystem that there was the highest reduction of cell viability	Afkham et al. (2018)
Polymeric Micelles	Docetaxel and retinoic acid	Polyethylene glycol	The characterization study was conducted through ^{1}H NMR and FTIR which confirmed successful conjugation with their characteristic peaks. The final formulation containing PEG and both drugs were having particle size 130.4 nm and 3.74 mV zeta potential.	The well-designed and formulated micelles were studied for cellular uptake by prostate cancer cell lines C4−2 and 22Rv1. The formulated polymeric micelles exhibited enhanced cellular uptake and cytotoxicity in dose-dependent manners	Hu and Xu (2021)
Polymeric micelles	Doxorubicin and microRNA	Poly(L−arginine)−poly (L−histidine)−stearoyl copolymer	TEM image illustrated the spherical shape, dynamic light scattering provided 169.8 ± 2 nm particle size, 0.202 ± 0.01 PDI, and +30 ± 1.31 mV zeta potential. The encapsulation efficiency was found to be 91.25%	In-vitro evaluation confirmed the higher cellular uptake and cytotoxicity at lower concentrations confirmed through DU145 and PC3 cell lines. In-vivo, a study through xenografts tumor-bearing mice found to be effective and safe compared with free drugs and without mRNA	Yao et al. (2016)

Type	Drugs	Polymer	Characterization	Outcome	Reference
Polymeric nanoparticles	Docetaxel and curcumin	Polyethylene glycol	The characteristics peaks defined through NMR confirmed the synthesis of the conjugated system. The particle size was 166.7 nm, PDI- 0.213, zeta potential- −37.5 mV with entrapment efficiency of drugs, DTX 91% and cur 87.5%	The cytotoxicity was found to be in a dose-dependent manner and higher at a lower concentration. In-vivo evaluation through prostate cancer mice model for antitumor effect was found to be highly efficacious other than final formulation (GE11-DTX-CUR NPS)	Yan et al. (2017)
Polymeric nanoparticles	Hesperetin and bicalutamide	Chitosan and polycaprolactones	Characterization study revealed formulation has particle size 355 ± 21.4 nm, zeta potential 12.80 ± 3.06 mV with EE of drug BCT 91.52% ± 3.41% and HSP 89.24% ± 4.07%	In-vitro cytotoxicity examination revealed that the formulated polymeric nanoparticles significantly showed higher toxicity to cells in lower concentrations. The safety, efficacy, and distribution were further confirmed when compared with plain drugs	Arya et al. (2016)
Nanoparticles	Dimethyl curcumin (DMC) and Docetaxel (DTX)	HP-β-CD, PEG	^{1}H NMR confirmed the conjugation system. Dynamic light scattering analysis revealed nanoparticles having particle size range 170–190 nm, PDI 0.2, zeta potential 3.93 ± 0.35, and encapsulation efficiency of drugs were 86.4% for DMC and 78.4% for DTX	The nanoparticles were able to produce the synergistic effect with a combination of the drugs (DMC and DTX). In addition, it was found that the NPs showed programmed drug release for co-loaded drugs	Hu et al. (2020)

4.7.3 Other multifunctional nanocarriers systems

Numerous research studies explain the role of the lipid and polymeric nanocarriers system in the co-delivery of anticancer drugs. Apart from these nanocarriers, some advance in nanotechnology has occurred which has driven the MNCs to overcome the issues related to conventional formulations. This advancement involves protein-based formulations (Albumin Nanoparticles), self-nano emulsifying drug delivery systems (SNEDDS), and modified dendrimers. The co-delivery of two different drugs through these systems has provided the flexibility to co-load the drugs with high efficiency. As shown in Table 4.4 various MFN systems are useful in the treatment of prostate cancer therapy.

4.8 Ideal characteristics of multifunctional nanocarriers

The MNCs are known for their excellent characteristics in terms of their physico-chemical properties. The carrier's system acquires nano-sized drug particles, that can increase the bioavailability of BCS class 2 or BCS class 4 drugs by enhancing the solubility or permeability, ultimately outweighing the disadvantages of traditional bulk pharmaceutical systems (Jabr-Milane et al., 2008). In addition, smaller molecules with a diameter of less than 200 nm have the advantage of penetrating the leaking vasculature of tumors, resulting in the EPR effect (Kang et al., 2020). MNCs are the types of polymeric nanoparticles, micelles, emulsions, lipid nanoparticles (liposomes, solid lipid nanoparticles, and nanostructured lipid carriers), dendrimers, carbon nanotubes, gold nanoparticles, and so on, all of which have the advantage of changing surface properties, solubility, and optical activity, resulting in numerous advantages (Torchilin, 2012). Nanoparticles' flexibility and superior surface chemistry make them useful as carrier platforms in the treatment of PC (Moghimi et al., 2005). It is possible to obtain multiple effects through such a single delivery system, which includes targeting specific diseased parts, diagnostic, imaging, and delivery of multiple drugs, resulting in compound effects (Salvador-Morales et al., 2009). Low immunogenic nanoparticles can be utilized as medical devices and can also act as carriers for medication, making them helpful for both diagnostic and therapeutic purposes. For the optimum design of multifunctional nanoparticles to treat PC, it is vital to understand the architecture and physiology of prostate glands and tumors, as well as the drug's physicochemical qualities. Surface modifications in MNCs can be easily incorporated by changing surface properties by coupling with targeting moieties like small peptides, antibodies, aptamers, fluorescent dyes, genes, and medicines with high selectivity for receptors on a specific part of the tumor through which drugs can reach the desired site to achieve the desired effect of simultaneous imaging/diagnosis, targeting, and drug delivery at the targeted site (Torchilin, 2012). MNCs have the property of combining high

Table 4.4 Miscellaneous nanocarriers system in the treatment of prostate cancer.

Multifunctional nanocarriers	Drugs	Polymer/lipid used	Characterization parameters	Outcomes	References
Conjugated Albumin Nanoparticles	Docetaxel and p44/42	Bovine serum albumin and polyethyleneimine	The conjugated system was confirmed through zeta sizer, TEM, and FTIR. The data from the characterization study revealed the confirmatory formation of layer by layer with bPEI nanoparticles. The zeta potential and particle size were found to be -30.5 ± 3.6 mV, and 170.9 ± 10.7 nm with characteristic peaks of amides	The fabricated system was able to induce cell death by targeting PSMA as a potential target to enhance the targeting efficiency of the nanosystem. The cell viability assay found that the conjugated system successfully targets the overexpressed α-tubulin, MAPK–ERK1/2 in prostate cancer cells	Pang et al. (2017)
Surface Modified Nanoparticles	Doxorubicin and siRNA	Porous silicon, Polyethylene glycol, polyamidoamine (PAMAM) dendrimer	The porous silicon nanoparticles for effective size (180 ± 5), and surface area (489 m^2/g^{-1}) were confirmed by TEM and BET. Further to confirm the conjugation of PAMAM and PEG zeta potential and FTIR studies were carried out	The nanobodies moieties were able to target the endothelial growth receptors and prostate-specific membrane antigens. The conjugated system successfully delivers the drug and RNA with an increase in cytotoxicity with dose-dependent manners to cancerous cells. NB-pSiNPs were found to be effective dual drug delivery therapy for prostate cancer	Tieu et al. (2021)
Self-nano emulsifying drug delivery system	Hesperitin and bicalutamide	Castor oil, kolliphor EL and triton X-100	The self-nano emulsifying drug delivery system was optimized through surface response methodology on central composite design	The results from the in-vivo evaluation showed enhancement in plasma level profile when compared with drug-containing suspension. It was found that the formulated system was able to reduce the toxicity and increase the therapeutic efficacy of the anticancer drug	Arya et al. (2017)

loadings of numerous drugs and genes, allowing for the best benefits of cancer-targeting which also protects siRNA chains and extends their half-life in the blood. It has been postulated that co-delivering pharmaceuticals and siRNA using the nanocarrier system would be significantly more effective in tackling cancer cell resistance than either siRNA or drug treatments alone (Creixell and Peppas, 2012). Apart from all these characteristics MNCs also offer modulation in drug pharmacokinetic parameters by increasing the solubility, absorption, distribution, and drug penetrability at targeted tumor sites (Arya et al., 2019).

4.9 Patents and clinical trials

A patent is a legal mechanism that grants an inventor market exclusivity over an invention/formulation/ medication. Market exclusivity can result in enormous economic gains for the patent holder because it grants the creator a monopoly over the invention for the entire 20-year patent period. During the life of the patent, this allows the inventor to restrict others from financially exploiting ideas or innovations without the author's permission (Himanshu et al., 2010). As shown Table 4.5 explains the list of some patents with their patent no and type of nanocarriers toward PC treatment.

4.10 Clinical trials and marketed products

Several research groups have established the in-vitro and preclinical utility of MNCs for screening and treatment by active and passive targeting, but only a few approaches have been successfully converted into clinical trials. All clinical trials concurred that pegylated liposomes outperformed hormone-refractory PC (Arya et al., 2019). Many research groups have reported on the in vitro synergistic effect of DOX and docetaxel. Keeping this in mind, a phase I clinical trial of weekly liposomal DOX treatment was co-administered with non-liposomal docetaxel, although the in-vitro results did not match the in vivo findings. Although codelivery resulted in a greater than 50% decrease in PSA levels in 50% of the patients, docetaxel alone is capable of decreasing PSA in 45%—48% of the patients (Hori et al., 2019). BIND-014 was a polymeric nanoparticle containing PEG-PLGA polymers loaded with docetaxel that was studied in 30 cancer patients for safety, tolerability, acceptable dose, and pharmacokinetics. BIND-014 is the first controlled release and targeted NPs system that uses active targeting techniques to target PSMA-expressing cancer cells. Apart from the clinical trials, some products have passed all the clinical examinations and gained market potential in the treatment of PC which are shown in Table 4.6.

Table 4.5 Patented list of some nanocarriers systems.

Sr. no.	Patent no	Year of filing	Title	Description of patent	Status	References
1.	US 1110359B2 U S1110359B2	2018	Nanocarriers for prostate cancer cell-targeted therapy and/or diagnosis thereof	The researchers patented for making a novel micelle consisting of phosphate as surfactant loaded with ermustin and also consists of fluorescent material for targeting prostate cancer	Granted	US11103599B2
2.	EP 3402484A1	2017	Peptide conjugated nanoparticles for targeting, imaging, and treatment of prostate cancer	Here the researchers synthesize a peptide ligand (SP204) displayed on prostate cancer cells that acts as a targeting agent and that ligand was attached to liposomes containing a sulforhodamine B and doxorubicin so that the drug increases at the target site	Granted	EP3402484A1
3.	US 20120015023A1	2011	Treatment of tumors prostate with arsonoliposomes	The inventors demonstrated that arsonoliposomes containing arsonolipids, where the arsonolipids are 2,3-diacyloxypropylarsonic acids, are extremely selective and efficient in-vitro and in-vivo in targeting and inhibiting the growth of prostate tumor cells	Granted	US20120015023A1

(Continued)

Table 4.5 (Continued)

Sr. no.	Patent no	Year of filing	Title	Description of patent	Status	References
4.	CA2648099C	2012	Systems for targeted delivery of therapeutic agents	Prostate-specific membrane antigens are targeted through polymer conjugated nanocarriers systems to increase cell internalization and cell specificity	Granted	CA2648099C
5.	CA2646329C	2018	Engineered anti-prostate stem cell antigen (PSCA) antibodies for prostate cancer targeting	The overexpressed prostate antigens are targeted through such inventions for prostate cancer	Granted	CA2646329C
6.	US9527919B2	2016	High-affinity anti-prostate stem cell antigen (PSCA) antibodies for cancer targeting and detection	The invention bind with PSCA with a high affinity for effective track of treatment, diagnosis, and visualization	Granted	US9527919B2
7.	US7582736B2	2009	Prostate cancer-specific internalizing human antibodies	The invention internalize the human antibodies that help in the reduction of proliferation of prostate cancer cells	Granted	US7582736B2

Table 4.6 Clinical trials status of carrier in the treatment of prostate cancer.

Sr. no.	Agent delivering	Materials	Translational status	Details of the study	References
1.	Docetaxel	PEG-PLGA (polymeric nanoparticles)	Phase II clinical trials	PSMA (prostate-specific membrane antigen), a protein found on the surface of prostate cancer, is targeted by these polymeric nanoparticles, which release the medicine at the target spot	Hrkach et al. (2012)
2.	Doxorubicin	Non-pegylated liposomes	Phase II clinical trials	In-vitro, nonpegylated liposomal doxorubicin (NPLD) showed much better activity than pegylated liposomal doxorubicin in castration-resistant prostate cancer (CRPC) and docetaxel-resistant prostate cancer cells. Its activity appears to be attributable to a high intracellular drug concentration and Golgi-dependent apoptotic induction. Based on these findings, a clinical trial was developed to evaluate the efficacy of NPLD and low-dose prednisone as second-line therapy	Montanari et al. (2012)
3.	Leuprolide acetate	Polymer-based	Phase 4	The drug with 22.5 mg can produce its effects when given through the subcutaneous route	NCT03035032
4.	Iron oxide and aminosilane	Metal-based therapy	Phase 4	The nanoparticles are placed on prostate cancer lesions and a magnetic field ablates the prostate cancer lesions	NCT05010759

4.11 Conclusion and future perspectives

PC is known for higher mortality and morbidity in men. The knowledge of the presence of various stages of PC and their diagnostic markers are critical aspects of the drug delivery system. The nanocarrier acquires prominent characteristics that make them multifunctional for diagnosing, imaging, and effective drug targeting toward PC. It became necessary to understand the pathophysiological changes related to PC, which can be utilized through MNCs to smartly deliver therapeutic agents. The presence of various types of biomarkers in PC, including PSAs, stem cells, CD44 + , sigma 1 and sigma 2, folic receptors, and integrins helps researchers to modify the carriers accordingly. It does not only target the disease specifically but also reduces the toxicity toward normal cells thus reducing the frequency of dosing. The MNCs provide a suitable environment for the co-loading of two different natures (hydrophilic and hydrophobic) of drugs. MNCs for the co-delivery of anticancer drugs provide a higher potency for PC treatment and overcome the drug resistance issue. It is possible to gain synergistic effects with two different drugs that vary with the distinct biological mechanism of action.

Finding new biomarkers and combining the therapies are new ways to improve the current PC treatment. In addition, personalized nanomedicines are also beneficial and are areas of concern in the future that can be made into modulative formulations. Such formulation can be tailored to engage well-defined targets and barriers associated with PC. Apart from this, it can be a potential treatment option in targeting aspects of PC when conjugating the surface functionalization and pH trigger release system in a single entity to gain much more cell specificity. The use of MNCs in co-delivering of anticancer drugs is an effective approach towards PC treatment and in overcoming the resistance produced by conventional formulations. Thus, it serves an important role as a targeted delivery mechanism, as detailed in this book chapter.

References

Abrams, D.I., 2018. An integrative approach to prostate cancer. J. Altern. Complement. Med. 24 (9−10), 872−880.

Adamaki, M., Zoumpourlis, V., 2021. Prostate cancer biomarkers: from diagnosis to prognosis and precision-guided therapeutics, Pharmacology and Therapeutics, 228. Elsevier Inc.

Afkham, A., Aghebati-Maleki, L., Siahmansouri, H., Sadreddini, S., Ahmadi, M., Dolati, S., et al., 2018. Chitosan (CMD)-mediated co-delivery of SN38 and Snail-specific siRNA as a useful anticancer approach against prostate cancer. Pharmacol. Rep. 70 (3), 418−425.

Ahdoot, M., Lebastchi, A.H., Turkbey, B., Wood, B., Pinto, P.A., 2019. Contemporary treatments in prostate cancer focal therapy, Current Opinion in Oncology, 31. Lippincott Williams and Wilkins, pp. 200−206.

Alberts, I.L., Seifert, R., Rahbar, K., Afshar-Oromieh, A., 2021. Prostate cancer theranostics: from target description to imaging, PET Clinics, 16. W.B. Saunders, pp. 383−390.

Alshehri, S., Fan, W., Zhang, W., Garrison, J.C., 2020. In vitro evaluation and biodistribution studies of HPMA copolymers targeting the gastrin releasing peptide receptor in prostate cancer. Pharm. Res. 37 (11).

Ang, M.J.Y., Chan, S.Y., Goh, Y.Y., Luo, Z., Lau, J.W., Liu, X., 2021. Emerging strategies in developing multifunctional nanomaterials for cancer nanotheranostics. Adv. Drug Deliv. Rev Elsevier B.V.

Arya, A., Khandelwal, K., Ahmad, H., Laxman, T.S., Sharma, K., Mittapelly, N., et al., 2016. Co-delivery of hesperetin enhanced bicalutamide induced apoptosis by exploiting mitochondrial membrane potential via polymeric nanoparticles in a PC-3 cell line. RSC Adv. 6 (7), 5925–5935.

Arya, A., Ahmad, H., Tulsankar, S., Agrawal, S., Mittapelly, N., Boda, R., et al., 2017. Bioflavonoid hesperetin overcome bicalutamide induced toxicity by co-delivery in novel SNEDDS formulations: optimization, in vivo evaluation and uptake mechanism. Mater. Sci. Eng. C. 71, 954–964. Feb 1.

Arya, A., Ahmad, H., Khandelwal, K., Agrawal, S., Dwivedi, A.K., 2019. Novel multifunctional nanocarrier-mediated codelivery for targeting and treatment of prostate cancer. Nanomaterials for Drug Delivery and Therapy,. William Andrew, pp. 185–224, Jan 1.

Ashrafizadeh, M., Mirzaei, S., Gholami, M.H., Hashemi, F., Zabolian, A., Raei, M., et al., 2021. Hyaluronic acid-based nanoplatforms for Doxorubicin: a review of stimuli-responsive carriers, co-delivery and resistance suppression. Carbohydr. Polym. 272, 118491. Nov 15.

Baig, M.M.F.A., Lai, W.F., Akhtar, M.F., Saleem, A., Mikrani, R., Farooq, M.A., et al., 2020. Targeting folate receptors (α1) to internalize the bleomycin loaded DNA-nanotubes into prostate cancer xenograft CWR22R cells. J. Mol. Liq. 316 (10). Available from: https://doi.org/10.1016/j.molliq.2020.113785.

Baratto, L., Jadvar, H., Iagaru, A., 2018. Prostate cancer theranostics targeting gastrin-releasing peptide receptors, Molecular Imaging and Biology, 20. Springer New York LLC, pp. 501–509.

Barve, A., Jin, W., Cheng, K., 2014. Prostate cancer relevant antigens and enzymes for targeted drug delivery. J. Control. Release 118–132.

Bhagat, S., Singh, S., 2020. Co-delivery of AKT3 siRNA and PTEN plasmid by antioxidant nanoliposomes for enhanced antiproliferation of prostate cancer cells. ACS Appl. Bio Mater. 3 (7), 3999–4011.

Bonvin, D., Bastiaansen, J.A.M., Stuber, M., Hofmann, H., Mionić Ebersold, M., 2017. Folic acid on iron oxide nanoparticles: platform with high potential for simultaneous targeting, MRI detection and hyperthermia treatment of lymph node metastases of prostate cancer. Dalton Trans. 46 (37), 12692–12704.

CA2646329C. Engineered anti-prostate stem cell antigen (psca) antibodies for cancer targeting - Google Patents.

CA2648099C. System for targeted delivery of therapeutic agents - Google Patents.

Campos-Fernández, E., Oliveira Alqualo, N., Moura Garcia, L.C., Coutinho Horácio Alves, C., Ferreira Arantes Vieira, T.D., Caixeta Moreira, D., et al., 2021. The use of aptamers in prostate cancer: a systematic review of theranostic applications, Clinical Biochemistry, 93. Elsevier Inc, pp. 9–25.

Chaussy, C.G., Thüroff, S., 2017. High-intensity focused ultrasound for the treatment of prostate cancer: a review. J. Endourol. 31, S30–S37. Apr 1.

Chen, Y., Deng, Y., Zhu, C., Xiang, C., 2020. Anti prostate cancer therapy: aptamer-functionalized, curcumin and cabazitaxel co-delivered, tumor targeted lipid-polymer hybrid nanoparticles. Biomed. Pharmacother. 127, Jul 1.

Chung, J.S., Morgan, T.M., Hong, S.K., 2020. Clinical implications of genomic evaluations for prostate cancer risk stratification, screening, and treatment: a narrative review. Prostate Int. 8 (3), 99–106.

Colin,, P., Mordon,, S., Nevoux,, P., Marqa,, M.F., Ouzzane,, A., Puech,, P., et al., 2012. Focal laser ablation of prostate cancer: definition, needs, and future. Adv. Urol 2012, 589160.

Collier, A., Ghosh, S., McGlynn, B., Hollins, G., 2012. Prostate cancer, androgen deprivation therapy, obesity, the metabolic syndrome, type 2 diabetes, and cardiovascular disease: a review. Am. J. Clin. Oncol.: Cancer Clin. Trials 504–509.

Costa, C.D., Justo, A.A., Kobayashi, P.E., Story, M.M., Palmieri, C., Laufer Amorim, R., et al., 2019. Characterization of OCT3/4, Nestin, NANOG, CD44 and CD24 as stem cell markers in canine prostate cancer. Int. J. Biochem Cell Biol. 108, 21–28. Mar 1.

Crawford, E.D., Schellhammer, P.F., McLeod, D.G., Moul, J.W., Higano, C.S., Shore, N., et al., 2018. Androgen receptor targeted treatments of prostate cancer: 35 years of progress with antiandrogens. J. Urol. 956–966.

Creixell, M., Peppas, N.A., 2012. Co-delivery of siRNA and therapeutic agents using nanocarriers to overcome cancer resistance. Nano Today 367–379.

de Araújo, J.T.C., Tavares Junior, A.G., di Filippo, L.D., Duarte, J.L., Ribeiro, T., de, C., et al., 2021. Overview of chitosan-based nanosystems for prostate cancer therapy. Eur. Polym. J. 160, 110812. Nov 5.

Decarlo, A., Malardier-Jugroot, C., Szewczuk, M.R., 2021. Folic acid-functionalized nanomedicine: folic acid conjugated copolymer and folate receptor interactions disrupt receptor functionality resulting in dual therapeutic anti-cancer potential in breast and prostate cancer. Bioconjugate Chem. 32 (3), 512–522.

Dong, S., Zhou, X., Yang, J., 2016. TAT modified and lipid — PEI hybrid nanoparticles for co-delivery of docetaxel and pDNA. Biomed. Pharmacother 84, 954–961. Dec 1.

Drivalos, A., Chrisofos, M., Efstathiou, E., Kapranou, A., Kollaitis, G., Koutlis, G., et al., 2016. Expression of α5-integrin, α7-integrin, E-cadherin, and N-cadherin in localized prostate cancer. Urol. Oncol.: Semin. Orig. Investig 34 (4), 165.e11–165.e18.

Drivalos, A., Emmanouil, G., Gavriatopoulou, M., Terpos, E., Sergentanis, T.N., Psaltopoulou, T., 2021. Integrin expression in correlation to clinicopathological features and prognosis of prostate cancer: a systematic review and meta-analysis, Urol. Oncol.: Semin. Orig. Investig, 39. pp. 221–232.

Dubuc, C., Langlois, R., Bénard, F., Cauchon, N., Klarskov, K., Tone, P., et al., 2008. Targeting gastrin-releasing peptide receptors of prostate cancer cells for photodynamic therapy with a phthalocyanine-bombesin conjugate. Bioorganic Med. Chem. Lett. 18 (7), 2424–2427.

Edis, Z., Wang, J., Waqas, M.K., Ijaz, M., Ijaz, M., 2021. Nanocarriers-mediated drug delivery systems for anticancer agents: an overview and perspectives. Int. J. Nanomed. 16, 1313–1330.

El Badri, A.M., Salawu, S., Brown, A., Bone, J.E., 2019. Health in men with prostate cancer: review article, Current Osteoporosis Reports, 17. Springer, pp. 527–537.

EP3402484A1. Peptide-conjugated nanoparticles for targeting, imaging, and treatment of prostate cancer - Google Patents.

Fujimoto, N., Kanno, J., 2016. Increase in prostate stem cell antigen expression in prostatic hyperplasia induced by testosterone and 17β-estradiol in C57BL mice. J. Steroid Biochem. Mol. Biol. 158, 56–62. Apr 1.

Gao, X., Luo, Y., Wang, Y., Pang, J., Liao, C., Lu, H., et al., 2012. Prostate stem cell antigen-targeted nanoparticles with dual functional properties: in vivo imaging and cancer chemotherapy. Int. J. Nanomed. 7, 4037–4051.

Garg, A., Garg, S., Swarnakar, N.K., 2021. Nanoparticles and prostate cancer. Nano Drug Delivery Strategies for the Treatment of Cancers. Elsevier, pp. 275–318.

Ghaffari, M., Kalantar, S.M., Hemati, M., Dehghani Firoozabadi, A., Asri, A., Shams, A., et al., 2021. Co-delivery of miRNA-15a and miRNA-16–1 using cationic PEGylated niosomes downregulates Bcl-2 and induces apoptosis in prostate cancer cells. Biotechnol. Lett. 43 (5), 981–994.

Himanshu, G., Suresh, K., Saroj Kumar, R., Gaud, R.S., 2010. Patent protection strategies. J. Pharm. Bioallied Sci. 2 (1), 125–132.

Haga, Y., Uemura, M., Baba, S., Inamura, K., Takeuchi, K., Nonomura, N., et al., 2019. Identification of multisialylated LacdiNAc structures as highly prostate cancer specific glycan signatures on PSA. Anal. Chem. 91 (3), 2247–2254.

Hema, S., Thambiraj, S., Shankaran, D.R., 2018. Nanoformulations for targeted drug delivery to prostate cancer: an overview. J. Nanosci. Nanotechnol. 18 (8), 5171–5191.

Hori, K., Ito, K., Kuritani, K., Kuji, S., Furukawa, N., Tsubamoto, H., et al., 2019. Phase I study on pegylated liposomal doxorubicin in combination with docetaxel for patients with platinum-resistant or partially platinum-sensitive epithelial ovarian cancer: The Kansai Clinical Oncology Group study. J. Cancer Res. Ther 15 (6), 1201–1206.

Hrkach, J., von Hoff, D., Ali, M.M., Andrianova, E., Auer, J., Campbell, T., et al., 2012. Preclinical development and clinical translation of a PSMA-targeted docetaxel nanoparticle with a differentiated pharmacological profile. Sci. Transl. Med. 4 (128).

Hu, H., Xu, D., 2021. Co-delivery of docetaxel and retinoic acid by poly (ethylene glycol)-retinoic acid conjugates based micelles for synergistic prostate cancer therapy. Micro Nano Lett. 16 (6), 336–343.

Hu, H., Wang, C., Zhang, R., Xiao, C., Lai, C., Li, Z., et al., 2020. Branched worm-like nanoparticles featured with programmed drug release for synergistic castration-resistant prostate cancer therapy. J. Mater. Sci. 55 (16), 6992–7008.

Jabr-Milane, L.S., van Vlerken, L.E., Yadav, S., Amiji, M.M., 2008. Multi-functional nanocarriers to overcome tumor drug resistance. Cancer Treat. Rev. 592–602.

John C., Vilner B., Geyer B., Moody T., research W.B.-C., Targeting sigma receptor-binding benzamides as in vivo diagnostic and therapeutic agents for human prostate tumors. Cancer Res. 1999; 59:4578–4583.

Jonnalagadda, B., Arockiasamy, S., Krishnamoorthy, S., 2020. Cellular growth factors as prospective therapeutic targets for combination therapy in androgen independent prostate cancer (AIPC), Life Sciences, 259. Elsevier Inc.

Kang, H., Rho, S., Stiles, W.R., Hu, S., Baek, Y., Hwang, D.W., et al., 2020. Size-dependent EPR effect of polymeric nanoparticles on tumor targeting. Adv. Healthc. Mater. 9 (1).

Karpisheh, V., Mousavi, S.M., Naghavi Sheykholeslami, P., Fathi, M., Mohammadpour Saray, M., Aghebati-Maleki, L., et al., 2021. The role of regulatory T cells in the pathogenesis and treatment of prostate cancer, Life Sciences, 284. Elsevier Inc.

Kumaraswamy, A., Welker Leng, K.R., Westbrook, T.C., Yates, J.A., Zhao, S.G., Evans, C.P., et al., 2021. Recent advances in epigenetic biomarkers and epigenetic targeting in prostate cancer. Eur. Urol 71–81.

Kwon, H., Son, S.H., Byun, Y., 2019. Prostate-specific membrane antigen (PSMA)-targeted radionuclide probes for imaging and therapy of prostate cancer. Asian J. Org. Chemistry. 1588–1600.

Lauer, R.C., Friend, S.C., Rietz, C., Pasqualini, R., Arap, W., 2015. Drug design strategies for the treatment of prostate cancer. Expert. Opin. Drug Discov. 81–90.

Li, N., Xie, X., Hu, Y., He, H., Fu, X., Fang, T., et al., 2019. Herceptin-conjugated liposomes co-loaded with doxorubicin and simvastatin in targeted prostate cancer therapy [Internet]. Am. J. Transl. Res.

Loo, D.T., Mather, J.P., 2008. Antibody-based identification of cell surface antigens: targets for cancer therapy. Curr. Opin. Pharmacol 627–631.

Magi-Galluzzi, C., 2018. Prostate cancer: diagnostic criteria and role of immunohistochemistry. Mod. Pathol. 31, 12–21. Jan 1.

Mahira, S., Kommineni, N., Husain, G.M., Khan, W., 2019. Cabazitaxel and silibinin co-encapsulated cationic liposomes for CD44 targeted delivery: a new insight into nanomedicine based combinational chemotherapy for prostate cancer. Biomed. Pharmacother 110, 803–817. Feb 1.

McCrea, E., Sissung, T.M., Price, D.K., Chau, C.H., Figg, W.D., 2016. Androgen receptor variation affects prostate cancer progression and drug resistance. Pharmacol. Res 152–162.

Miranda, A., Santos, T., Carvalho, J., Alexandre, D., Jardim, A., Caneira, C.R.F., et al., 2021. Aptamer-based approaches to detect nucleolin in prostate cancer. Talanta. 226, May 1.

Mitobe, Y., Takayama, K.I., Horie-Inoue, K., Inoue, S., 2018. Prostate cancer-associated lncRNAs. Cancer Lett 159–166.

Moghimi, S.M., Hunter, A.C., Murray, J.C., 2005. Nanomedicine: current status and future prospects. FASEB J. 19 (3), 311–330.

Montanari, M., Fabbri, F., Rondini, E., Frassineti, G.L., Mattioli, R., Carloni, S., et al., 2012. Phase II trial of non-pegylated liposomal doxorubicin and low-dose prednisone in second-line chemotherapy for hormone-refractory prostate cancer. Tumori. 98 (6), 696–701.

Nassir, A.M., Ibrahim, I.A.A., Md, S., Waris, M., Tanuja, Ain, M.R., et al., 2019. Surface functionalized folate targeted oleuropein nano-liposomes for prostate tumor targeting: in vitro and in vivo activity. Life Sci. 220, 136–146. Mar 1.

Nauseef, J.T., Bander, N.H., Tagawa, S.T., 2021. Emerging prostate-specific membrane antigen-based therapeutics: small molecules, antibodies, and beyond. Eur. Urol. Focus. 7 (2), 254–257.

NCT03035032. A Study of ELIGARD® in Hormone-dependent Prostate Cancer Patients - Full Text View - ClinicalTrials.gov.

NCT05010759. Study of Focal Ablation of the Prostate with NanoTherm® Therapy System for Intermediate-Risk Prostate Cancer - Full-Text View - ClinicalTrials.gov.

Pang, S.T., Lin, F.W., Chuang, C.K., Yang, H.W., 2017. Co-delivery of docetaxel and p44/42 MAPK siRNA using PSMA antibody-conjugated BSA-PEI layer-by-layer nanoparticles for prostate cancer target therapy. Macromol. Biosci. 17 (5).

Patil, Y., Shmeeda, H., Amitay, Y., Ohana, P., Kumar, S., Gabizon, A., 2018. Targeting of folate-conjugated liposomes with co-entrapped drugs to prostate cancer cells via prostate-specific membrane antigen (PSMA). Nanomed.: Nanotechnol. Biol. Med. 14 (4), 1407−1416.

Phua, T.J., 2021. The etiology and pathophysiology genesis of benign prostatic hyperplasia and prostate cancer: a new perspective. Medicines. 8 (6), 30.

Puri, R., Kaur Bhatia, R., Shankar Pandey, R., Kumar Jain, U., Katare, O.P., Madan, J., 2016. Sigma-2 receptor ligand anchored telmisartan loaded nanostructured lipid particles augmented drug delivery, cytotoxicity, apoptosis and cellular uptake in prostate cancer cells. Drug Dev. Ind. Pharm. 42 (12), 2020−2030.

Qu, Z., Ren, Y., Shen, H., Wang, H., Shi, L., Tong, D., 2021. Combination therapy of metastatic castration-recurrent prostate cancer: hyaluronic acid decorated, cabazitaxel-prodrug and orlistat co-loaded nano-system. Drug Design, Dev. Ther. 15, 3605−3616.

Raff, A.B., Gray, A., Kast, W.M., 2009. Prostate stem cell antigen: a prospective therapeutic and diagnostic target. Cancer Lett 126−132.

Rana, A., Bhatnagar, S., 2021. Advancements in folate receptor targeting for anti-cancer therapy: a small molecule-drug conjugate approach. Bioorg. Chem .

Raval, N., Maheshwari, R., Shukla, H., Kalia, K., Torchilin, V.P., Tekade, R.K., 2021. Multifunctional polymeric micellar nanomedicine in the diagnosis and treatment of cancer. Mater. Sci. Eng. C.

Rhee, H., Vela, I., Chung, E., 2016. Metabolic syndrome and prostate cancer: a review of complex interplay amongst various endocrine factors in the pathophysiology and progression of prostate cancer. Horm. Cancer 75−83.

Salvador-Morales, C., Gao, W., Ghatalia, P., Murshed, F., Aizu, W., Langer, R., et al., 2009. Multifunctional nanoparticles for prostate cancer therapy. Expert. Rev. Anticancer. Ther. 211−221.

Sandhu, S., Moore, C.M., Chiong, E., Beltran, H., Bristow, R.G., Williams, S.G., 2021. Prostate cancer. The Lancet 1075−1090.

Sarath Chandran, C., Raj, A., Shahin, Muhammed, T.K., 2021. Advanced drug delivery systems in prostate cancer. Advanced Drug Delivery Systems in the Management of Cancer,. Academic Press, pp. 197−206.

Sheehan, B., Guo, C., Neeb, A., Paschalis, A., Sandhu, S., de Bono, J.S., 2021. Prostate-specific membrane antigen biology in lethal prostate cancer and its therapeutic implications. Eur. Urol. Focus 8.

Shitole, A.A., Sharma, N., Giram, P., Khandwekar, A., Baruah, M., Garnaik, B., et al., 2020. LHRH-conjugated, PEGylated, poly-lactide-co-glycolide nanocapsules for targeted delivery of combinational chemotherapeutic drugs Docetaxel and Quercetin for prostate cancer. Mater. Sci. Eng. C 114, Sep 1.

Singh, S.K., Lillard, J.W., Singh, R., 2018. Reversal of drug resistance by planetary ball milled (PBM) nanoparticle loaded with resveratrol and docetaxel in prostate cancer. Cancer Lett. 427, 49−62. Jul 28.

Song, Y.Y., Yuan, Y., Shi, X., Che, Y.Y., 2020. Improved drug delivery and anti-tumor efficacy of combinatorial liposomal formulation of genistein and plumbagin by targeting Glut1 and Akt3 proteins in mice bearing prostate tumor. Colloids Surf. B: Biointerfaces 190, Jun 1.

Tan, H., Hou, N., Liu, Y., Liu, B., Cao, W., Zheng, D., et al., 2020. CD133 antibody targeted delivery of gold nanostars loading IR820 and docetaxel for multimodal imaging and near-infrared photodynamic/photothermal/chemotherapy against castration resistant prostate cancer. Nanomed.: Nanotechnol. Biol. Med. 27, Jul 1.

Tas, A., Keklikcioglu Cakmak, N., 2021. Synthesis of PEGylated nanographene oxide as a nanocarrier for docetaxel drugs and anticancer activity on prostate cancer cell lines. Hum. Exp. Toxicol. 40 (1), 172−182.

Thakur, A., 2021. Nano therapeutic approaches to combat progression of metastatic prostate cancer. Adv. Cancer Biol. - Metastasis 2, 100009. Oct.

Tieu, T., Wojnilowicz, M., Huda, P., Thurecht, K.J., Thissen, H., Voelcker, N.H., et al., 2021. Nanobody-displaying porous silicon nanoparticles for the co-delivery of siRNA and doxorubicin. Biomater. Sci. 9 (1), 133−147.

Torchilin, V.P., 2012. Multifunctional nanocarriers. Adv. Drug Deliv. Rev. 64 (SUPPL), 302−315. Dec 1.

Trump, D.L. 2004. Early versus delayed hormonal therapy for prostate specific antigen only recurrence of prostate cancer after radical prostatectomy. Moul JW, Wu H, Sun L, McLeod DG, Amling C, Donahue T, Kusuda L, Sexton W, O'Reilly K, Hernandez J, Chung A, Soderdahl D, Department of Surgery, Uniformed Services University of the Health Sciences, National Naval Medical Center, Bethesda, MD.: J Urol 2004;171:1141−7. Urologic Oncology: Seminars and Original Investigations. 2004 Sep 1;22(5):434.

Upadhyay N., Tilekar K., Hess J.D., Pokrovsky V.S., Aguilera R.J.. Benefits and pitfalls: epigenetic modulators in prostate cancer intervention. Curr. Res. Chem. Biol. 2021; 1:100006.

US11103599B2. Nanocarriers for prostate cancer cell targeted therapy and/or diagnosis thereof - Google Patents.

US20120015023A1. Treatment of tumors prostate with arsonoliposomes - Google Patents.

US7582736B2. Prostate cancer specific internalizing human antibodies - Google Patents.

US9527919B2. High affinity anti-prostate stem cell antigen (PSCA) antibodies for cancer targeting and detection - Google Patents.

van den Bos, W., Scheltema, M.J., Siriwardana, A.R., Kalsbeek, A.M.F., Thompson, J.E., Ting, F., et al., 2018. Focal irreversible electroporation as primary treatment for localized prostate cancer. BJU Int. 121 (5), 716−724.

van Waarde, A., Rybczynska, A.A., Ramakrishnan, N.K., Ishiwata, K., Elsinga, P.H., Dierckx, R.A.J.O., 2015. Potential applications for sigma receptor ligands in cancer diagnosis and therapy. Biochim. Biophys. Acta 2703−2714.

Wang, Z., Sun, C., Wu, H., Xie, J., Zhang, T., Li, Y., et al., 2022. Cascade targeting codelivery of ingenol-3-angelate and doxorubicin for enhancing cancer chemoimmunotherapy through synergistic effects in prostate cancer. Mater. Today Bio 13, Jan 1.

Weber, M., Hadaschik, B., Ferdinandus, J., Rahbar, K., Bögemann, M., Herrmann, K., et al., 2021. Prostate-specific membrane antigen−based imaging of castration-resistant prostate cancer. Eur. Urol. Focus. 7 (2), 279−287.

Wei, J., Sun, J., Liu, Y., 2019. Enhanced targeting of prostate cancer-initiating cells by salinomycin-encapsulated lipid-PLGA nanoparticles linked with CD44 antibodies. Oncol. Lett. 17 (4), 4024−4033.

Wu, H., Shi, H., Zhang, H., Wang, X., Yang, Y., Yu, C., et al., 2014. Prostate stem cell antigen antibody-conjugated multiwalled carbon nanotubes for targeted ultrasound imaging and drug delivery. Biomaterials. 35 (20), 5369−5380.

Xu, W., Siddiqui, I.A., Nihal, M., Pilla, S., Rosenthal, K., Mukhtar, H., et al., 2013. Aptamer-conjugated and doxorubicin-loaded unimolecular micelles for targeted therapy of prostate cancer. Biomaterials 34 (21), 5244−5253.

Yan, J., Wang, Y., Jia, Y., Liu, S., Tian, C., Pan, W., et al., 2017. Co-delivery of docetaxel and curcumin prodrug via dual-targeted nanoparticles with synergistic antitumor activity against prostate cancer. Biomed. Pharmacother 88, 374−383. Apr 1.

Yao, C., Liu, J., Wu, X., Tai, Z., Gao, Y., Zhu, Q., et al., 2016. Reducible self-assembling cationic polypeptide-based micelles mediate co-delivery of doxorubicin and microRNA-34a for androgen-independent prostate cancer therapy. J. Control. Release 232, 203−214. Jun 28.

Zha, Z., Ploessl, K., Choi, S.R., Wu, Z., Zhu, L., Kung, H.F., 2018. Synthesis and evaluation of a novel urea-based ^{68}Ga-complex for imaging PSMA binding in tumor. Nucl. Med. Biol. 59, 36−47. Available from: https://doi.org/10.1016/j.nucmedbio.2017.12.007.

CHAPTER 5

Multifunctional nanocarrier-mediated delivery for targeting and treating skin cancer

Pooja Raj Mongia[1], Meghna Singh Amrita[2], Kantrol Sahu[3], Krishna Yadav[4], Ramakant Joshi[5], Monika Kaurav[6], Sunita Minz[7], Rakesh Raj[8] and Madhu Gupta[2]

[1]Department of Pharmaceutics, DIPSAR, Delhi Institute of Pharmaceutical Science and Research, New Delhi, Delhi, India
[2]Department of Pharmaceutics, Delhi Pharmaceutical Science and Research University, New Delhi, Delhi, India
[3]School of Pharmacy, Chouksey Engineering College, Bilaspur, Chhattisgarh, India
[4]Raipur Institute of Pharmaceutical Education and Research, Sarona, Raipur, Chhattisgarh, India
[5]School of Studies in Pharmaceutical Sciences, Jiwaji University, Gwalior, Madhya Pradesh, India
[6]KIET School of Pharmacy, KIET Group of Institutions Delhi-NCR, Ghaziabad, Uttar Pradesh, India
[7]Department of Pharmacy, Indira Gandhi National Tribal University (A Central University), Amarkantak, Madhya Pradesh, India
[8]Department of Pharmacy, Delhi Skill and Entrepreneurship University, DSEU Maharani Bagh Campus, New Delhi, Delhi, India

5.1 Introduction

In current scenario, skin cancer is one of the most prevalent forms of cancer, and mortality and morbidity rates are still continuously rising in many other countries.

Skin cancer is classified into two types: melanoma skin cancer and nonmelanoma skin cancer. Further, nonmelanoma skin cancer is subdivided into basal cell carcinoma and squamous cell carcinoma. Occurrence of the skin cancer is due to many reasons, and UV radiation is one of the major contributors. So majority of approaches are now a days designed to reduce exposure of UV radiations. Excision is still a gold standard treatment for localized skin cancer. But in very rare cases, cancerous cells spread to regional lymph nodes (LNs) as well as to distant sites (Lalan et al., 2021; Kaur and Kesarwani, 2021; Borgheti-Cardoso et al., 2020).

For the treatment of metastasized skin cancers, nanocarriers are one of the effective drug delivery systems, which allow anticancer drugs to reach exactly to the cancer site and, thus, enhance therapeutic efficacy.

It is a revolutionary approach that includes designing, preparation, evaluation, and application by controlling shape and size at the nanoscale. These biomimetic features of nanocarriers and the possibility of modifying their properties raised the interest in its theranostic applications.

Targeted nanomedicine enhances permeability in cancerous cells, thus allowing the delivery of drugs to cancer cells specifically. Moreover, specific binding of nanocarriers to cancer cells improves the efficiency of the treatment of cancerous cells, without effecting healthy cells (Singh and Lillard, 2009; Sanvicens and Marco, 2008; Dianzani et al., 2014).

In the current chapter, we illustrated the need for nanoparticles (NPs) for systemic and transdermal drug delivery of therapeutics in skin cancer cells and the specific drug nanocarriers that have been reported with improved therapeutic effectiveness for treating melanoma and nonmelanoma skin cancer.

5.2 Physiological barriers in skin cancer targeting

The skin is the outermost biological barrier in which the primarily responsible horny layer is stratum corneum (SC), as seen in Fig. 5.1. This thin and semipermeable layer ranges between 5 and 8 μm, but occasionally could be 20 μm (Pirot et al., 1998). The anatomical barrier is made up of intracutaneous degradation of molecules, effivium by blood or lymph capillaries in the dermis, and the peripheral immune system (Steinstraesser and Merkle, 1995; Boderke et al., 2000), all of which are located below the epidermis and above the epidermal/dermal junction.

Biological, chemical, and mechanical protective characteristics enhance the barrier's effectiveness. Corneocytes accounted up to 90% of the cells in the SC. Corneocytes are precisely flat, terminally distinguished, and closely filled in vertical heaps at the skin's surface. A few partially detached cell layers at the surface of the skin, where corneocyte arrangement is not more compact and surrounding cells of the stratum granulosum are prominent exceptions. Corneocyte thickness in mammals ranges from 0.22 to 0.4 μm (Schatzlein and Cevc et al., 1998), but thickness greater than 0.7 μm has been documented (Johnson et al., 1997). This value does not include the width of interconeocyte space, which fluctuates substantially along the skin surface and weakly with skin depth or across skin layers. The gap between

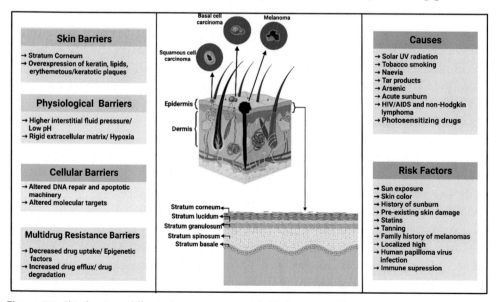

Figure 5.1 Skin barriers, different layers, causes, and risk factor for skin cancer.

corneocyte in air dried is not more than 0.1 μm wide and nearly 75 nm wide. In the stratum corneum, there are approximately 15 corneocyte layers.

The corneocytes width is four times lesser in the in the epidermis than SC proper. The area covered by surface corneocyte is around 1100−1200 μm^2 (Hajime, 1994). The fundamental permeation resistance unit in the SC is formed by clusters of dozen corneocyte columns. Corneocytes are combined individually along with desmosomes and closely packed by specific intercellular lipids linked to the cell envelope. The skin barrier perfection depends on the quality and crystallinity of the lipids, as well as their overall quantity in the SC (15 wt.%). The epidermal diffusion and skin fine structure may differ between species, gender, and body site (pigs and humans having higher levels than rodents).

5.2.1 The skin as penetration barrier

The size of the molecule, lipid solubility, and capability to intermingle with molecules via hydrogen bonding are the main characteristics to facilitate molecular penetration via SC of the skin (Potts and Guy, 1992; Moss et al., 2002; Forslind, 2000; Schaefer et al., 2002; Barratt, 1995). The following correlation was proposed by Cronin et al. between the octanol-water partition coefficient (Ko/w), molecular weight (MW) of permeate, and partition coefficient (Kp).

$$LogK_p = logP\text{-}log(D/d_{sc})$$

$$LogK_p = 0.77logK_{o/w}\text{-}0.013\,MW\text{-}2.33$$

The equation shows that higher MW compounds diffuse at a rate below a μgh^{-1}cm^2. While low MW compound with balanced hydrophilic-lipophilic partitioning can permeate easily. The water content of the skin also affects penetrability, which depends on relative humidity.

From the permeant view, it can be said that the skin barriers represent a lipoidal layer along which each molecule moves by diffusion. The diffusion primarily directed aqueous solubility of permeant, hydrogen binding capacity, and MW of drugs. Hence, extremely polar drugs and/or molecules bigger than a few hundred dalton cannot move via SC through diffusion. Such phenomena also apply to tiny water molecules, which are accountable for skin surface dryness. Except through transport shunts, much bigger colloidal molecules and classic colloids do not penetrate into the SC in considerable proportion.

5.3 The semipermeable, nonporous nature of skin

As discussed above, skin acts as a nonporous blockade pierced by a large number of gaps or quasi-semicircular routes from a penetrant's perspective. On average, published reports for diffusion distance across skin ranging from 0.4 to 36 nm is estimated by Cevc. To present, there is no comprehensive data on the allocation of hydrophilic transcutaneous path width in the skin is exactly known. Generally, opening is asymmetrical with maxima about 20 nm and a steeper drop on the lower site (Cevc, 1997).

A larger number of crossings across the blockade for water soluble molecules are reported by water flux and transcutaneous electrical current (iotophoresis) measurement. The mean opening of the most abundant transepidermal hydrophilic route, according to Cevc et al., is on the order of 10 nm. Many areas have also reported very narrow (around 0.4 nm pathways for water evaporation) along with very wide (inter-corneocyte cluster, 100 nm) pathways. On the basis of the known cell perimeter in the SC researcher reported that the total porosity in the skin is 0.25% because one path is equal to two cells in contact. This shunt-like pathway structure minimizes the effect of such a geometric factor close to the skin surface. They widen to 50–100 μm in width and become deeper below the SC for several days during depilation. Electrically opened shunts, such as those used in iontophoresis, stay open for at least one day. There may be relatively long-lasting pores created in the SC after application of a certain lipid detergent mixture (Cevc, 1997; Schatzlein and Cevc, 1998; Kontturi and Murtomaeki, 1996; Van-den Bergh et al., 1999).

5.4 Hydrophilic routes through the skin barrier: their location and nature

Reports on similar quality but quantitatively dissimilar hydrophilic permeation path via SC, when it had been treated with highly deformable peameanants, were documented using confocal laser scanning microscopy. Due to its position among the adjacent corneocyte enevelopes and the intercellular lamellae, the inter-corneocyte opening has comparatively more diffusion resistance. Under intermediate magnification view of parallel skin surface, the inter-corneocyte route appears as a crisscross because of overlapping of lateral cell (Schatzlein and Cevc 1998). Several parallel hydrophilic pathways, i.e., a group of parallel stripes with cell border, pass across the SC in some areas. The average hydrophilic path width and width distribution may vary by body place and/or animal type. Skin blockade properties are spatially nonuniform due to lateral skin heterogenicity. Within each cluster of cells, the hydration and stress-dependent pathway has a rather more penetration resistance and often seems among the proximal coneocyte envelope and intercellular lipid lamellae. The hydrophilic routes between corneocyte clusters in the SC, on the other hand, are less resistant and sparser. Such a hydrophilic pathway between clusters of skin cells can operate as a shunt pathway, which is often more broader than 30 nm and almost unfasten. Transepidermal shunts involve a wide range of distances, from inter-cluster opening (around 5 μm) to a hair follicle (more than 50 μm).

5.5 Dermis

Dermis is a 250-μm thick layer of connective tissue that contains blood arteries, lymph vessels, and nerves. The cutaneous blood supply plays an important role in body temperature regulation. As a result, the blood supply keeps the drug's dermal concentration low, and the ensuing concentration gradient across the epidermis provides the necessary gradient for transdermal penetration.

5.6 Hypodermis

The dermis and epidermis are supported by subcutaneous fat tissue or hypodermis. This fat storage compartment aids in temperature regulation, nutritional support, and mechanical strength. It may contain sensory pressure organ and carries main nerves and blood vessels to the skin. On average, the human skin surface has 10−70 hair follicles and around 200−250 sweat ducts per centimeter square area of the skin.

Skin anatomy explains why, despite topical delivery of drug has significant achievements over the last 35 years, the route of administration is confined to a relatively minor subject of highly potent, low MW, moderately lipophilic drug. The skin delivery enhancements through the use of several excipients and combinations, only a minor increase in flux can be accomplished in practice. In present scenario, various approaches are used to enhance skin delivery of drug.

5.7 Need and employment of nanocarriers-based formulations in skin cancer treatment

5.7.1 Nanoparticles

NPs have been used for skin cancer from years ago based on its *in-vivo* and *in-vitro* application. These NPs put forward new prospect for cure of skin diseases. Use of these NPs is primarily based on their ability of improving penetration of bioactive molecules in skin cancer. NPs are suitable for the delivery of newer antioxidants also such as diindolylmethane derivative. It increases its skin penetration and deposition by forming ultraflexible nanovesicles (ultraFLEX Nano) with high elasticity having a mean size of 110.50 ± 0.71 nm and zeta potential of $+16.02 \pm 0.86$ mV. These NPs provide the chemoprevention of UV-induced skin cancers in mice (Boakye et al., 2016).

Some vehicles such as hydroxypropyl methylcellulose and dimethyl sulfoxide (DMSO) also enhance the skin penetration of active constituents. Menezes et al. explained that by using DMSO, the skin penetration of 1-(1-naphthyl) piperazine (1-NPZ), a serotonergic derivative of quipazine is significantly improved. DMSO being as polar aprotic solvent helps in reducing the barrier of stratum corneum of skin and potentiates NPs to traverse easily that fights skin cancer (Menezes et al., 2016). Cationic gold NPs incorporated with plasmid DNA and conjugated with HIV-1 twinarginine translocation peptides (TAT) potentially targets the cutaneous melanoma (Niu et al., 2017).

5.7.2 Polymeric micelles

In 1990s, polymeric micelles were the most widely used carrier system while publication related to its promising delivery for drugs and nucleic acid speeds up since year 2000 (Yokoyama, 2014). Basically, polymeric micelles are spherically shaped amphiphilic NPs with an inner core of hydrophobic blocks and an outer shell of hydrophilic blocks in an aqueous medium (Miyata et al., 2011; Kwon and Okano, 1996).

Polymeric micelles support the delivery of various hydrophobic anticancer drugs by increasing their aqueous solubility. It facilitates the intravenous administration of anticancer agents, which show poor water solubility. Drug solubilization is enhanced by the mechanism of intermolecular interaction between drug and core-forming block (Lavasanifar et al., 2002). This ultimately leads to better drug distribution and tumor accumulation. Polymeric micelles are so designed that it easily functionalizes itself with ligands such as peptides, carbohydrates, antibodies, aptamers, and other micromolecules. It enters the skin by accumulating at the site of hair follicles, i.e., via follicular infiltration pathway (Fang et al., 2014). This fact is confirmed by the work of Bachhav et al. who explored the deposition of antifungal agents carrying polymeric micelles over skin (Bachhav et al., 2011).

5.7.3 Nanotubes

Carbon nanotubes (CNTs) have attracted researchers and companies from all over the world to do research in the field of cancer diagnosis and therapy. It has wonderful strength to the weight ratio from any other known material (Liang et al., 2009; Favila et al., 2007). It is compatible with human body and has shown variable function, which is the main reason for its explored research. It has interestingly high degree of the structure purity with uniform atomic structure, which makes it available for perfect computer modeling. It is rising nowadays as one of the alternative and competent tools for transportation and translocation of active constituents (Tserpesa and Papanikos, 2005). It is well known and widely accepted for its excellent transport and bioavailability of drugs, which ultimately enhance distribution, selectivity, and affectivity of drug (Kostarelos et al., 2007; Bottini et al., 2006).

Huang et al. proposed the use of single-wall carbon nanotubes (SWNTs) for skin cancer treatment. SWNTs are a special type of nanotubes that absorb radiation at 785 nm near infrared (IR) laser light. This property of absorbing radiation by SWNTs leads to significant increase in temperature ($>10°C$) at the tumor site of administration. The local hyperthermia so created resulted in the destruction of skin cancer cells in a murine model (Huang et al., 2010). Another such study was done by Gulla et al. to study the effect of titanium dioxide nanotubes (TNTs) for delivery of quercetin in the treatment of skin cancer. They showed that TNTs have large surface area that profoundly reduces tumor growth by inhibiting squamous cell carcinoma without affecting the skin color. Thus, TNTs can be a better option for delivery of active constituent like quercetin for skin cancer treatment (Gulla et al., 2022).

5.7.4 Solid lipid nanoparticles

Solid lipid nanoparticles (SLNPs) are one of the most successful new generation delivery system comprising of spherical and nanometric size range. SLNPs are the colloidal system with the size range of 50–1000 nm (Muller et al., 2011). It is composed of solid lipids, water, and emulsifiers with the high-pressure blend of homogenization. Commonly used solid lipids are glycerides, triglycerides, fatty acids, and waxes (Mukherjee et al., 2009). It has a tendency for controlled release of encapsulated active constituents and their enhanced absorption by forming a thin film over the skin (Lai et al., 2007; Souto et al., 2007). It also has capability to protect the active ingredient from chemical damage and thus possess more stability (Ibsen et al., 2010). Anticancer agents containing SLNPs are most promising and widely investigated in this field (Rostami et al., 2014).

SLNPs are generally nontoxic as they are composed of nontoxic materials and approved for safe application in humans (Liu et al., 2007; Pardeshi et al., 2012). While, sometimes improper drug encapsulation and drug leakage are problem associated with the stability of SLNPs (Muller et al., 2002).

5.7.5 Dendrimers

Dendrimers are nanosized structures with a central core, homogenous, unimolecular, and monodispersed morphologies and radially symmetric with well-defined branching resembling to tree. Dendrimers have the capacity to accommodate and transport nucleic acids, diagnostic agents, and medications that are hydrophilic and hydrophobic in nature (Khodabandehloo et al., 2016; Tripathi et al., 2019). They are multivalent since all the branches may have varied terminal groupings and the existence of multiple cavities. Dendrimer's potential to promote ligand-specific targeting and tumor killing is supported by a large number of literature sources. Some examples of these molecules include polysaccharides, polyunsaturated fatty acids, oligopeptides, and antigens specific to tumor cells. Dendrimer-associated medications have a released in a regulated manner. Synthesis or conjugation of the medication to a dendrimer, which may regulate its release, is one method of including a degradable link (Tong and Cheng, 2007; Xie et al., 2022). Dendrimers have been shown to be effective in the treatment of squamous cell carcinoma and melanoma by the use of therapeutic interventions, as immunotherapeutic, as well as for radioimmunotherapy in animal models. They also have various applications in cancer cell diagnostic imaging, such as magnetic resonance imaging (MRI). The use of gadolinium-conjugated dendrimers has made it possible to target and imaging cancers in a more targeted and accurate way (Gorbet and Ranjan, 2020; Rawding et al., 2022).

For melanoma, a group of researchers developed temozolomide (TMZ) dendritic NPs. They examined TMZ-loaded polyamide amine (PAMAM) dendrimers for their capacity to target human melanoma (A375) cells in an in-vitro investigation and found that they were promising as intended (Jiang et al., 2017). Dendrimers have been shown to be useful in the treatment of metastatic melanoma. Dendrimer nanocomplexes are also being created for the delivery of genetic materials in skin cancer via iontophoresis (Venuganti et al., 2015). Furthermore, peptide-based dendrimers are being studied for a variety of skin-related disorders. These advancements in medication delivery and material science will undoubtedly result in improved skin cancer care in the future (Tornesello et al., 2020).

5.7.6 Liposomes

Liposomes are micro to nanosized vesicles with a phospholipid bilayer around the aqueous core, measuring 50–100 nm in diameter (Bhia et al., 2021; Yadav et al., 2021). It has the appearance of a biological membrane and can encapsulate both hydrophilic and lipophilic molecules (Yadav et al., 2020). Through PEGylation, it can be structurally modified to evade the RES during intravenous administration, resulting in stealth liposomes with longer circulation duration and lower clearance. It may also be modified by combining ligands and polymers to make it more particular for targeting. Aside from that, liposomes have intrinsic qualities such as improved penetration, exceptional diffusion, and extended circulation. Liposomes remained inside the tumor interstitial fluid near tumor vasculature, according to the findings (Vu et al., 2020; Yadav et al., 2020).

Woźniak and a colleague produced a liposomal formulation containing curcumin and tested it against melanoma MUGMel2, normal keratinocyte HaCaT, and squamous cell carcinoma SCC-25 for photosensitizing effectiveness (Woźniak et al., 2021). The formulation was shown to be efficacious and capable of demonstrating superior stability and bioavailability, proving them to be potent against both the above described cell line and healthy skin keratinocytes of HaCaT cells with less phototoxicity. Finally, the findings support the use of liposomal formulations of poorly soluble bioactives in skin cancer treatment to increase photosensitizing action (Woźniak et al., 2021). Several liposomal formulations are currently available in clinical practices for the treatment of skin cancer (Akhtar and Khan, 2016).

5.7.7 Gold nanoparticles

Traditional cancer therapies, including surgical resection, radiation, and chemotherapy, have made considerable advances in cancer treatment. However, traditional medicines still have significant drawbacks (such as hazardous unwanted effects), which drives research into new theranostics pathways (Yadav et al., 2022). Gold NPs (AuNPs and GNPs) have been created to act as targeted delivery vehicles, sensors, molecular probes, and other applications due to their unique features, ease of surface modification, and excellent biocompatibility (Zhang, 2015; Khodabandehloo et al., 2016). They may extravagate and enter the tumor microenvironment (TME) because of their tiny size and surface features, which is a viable approach for achieving extremely effective therapies. Furthermore, the stimuli-responsive features (response to hypoxia and acidic pH) of NPs to TME allow for unequaled control of therapeutic cargo delivery (Bagheri et al., 2018).

Because of their simplicity of synthesis, high surface-to-volume ratio, and diverse surface functions, GNPs might be effective conjugating platforms for a variety of medicinal drugs (Bagheri et al., 2018). Furthermore, GNPs are typically nontoxic, nonimmunogenic, and extremely stable, according to reports. As a result, Au NPs are perfect for integrating hydrophobic or extremely toxic pharmacological compounds, as well as anticancer peptides, to increase bioavailability. Preet and coinvestigators recently revealed that using Nisin as an adjuvant to doxorubicin in the treatment of mouse skin cancer considerably increased the anticancer efficacy of drug (Nirmala et al., 2017). The antitumor activity of both nisin and doxorubicin integrated to gold NPs was tested further in the same cancer model. In vivo skin cancer treatment with Nisin-, doxorubicin-, and nisin-Dox-conjugated GNPs was found to be more effective (Preet et al., 2019). The use of numerous chemotherapeutics that work through diverse pathways may lessen the likelihood of drug-resistant cancerous cells developing. However, more research into the specific mechanism of anticancer activity of GNPs, nisin-GNPs, doxorubicin-GNPs, and nisin-dox-GNPs is needed in order to create successful anticancer therapy techniques (Preet et al., 2019).

5.7.8 Silver nanoparticles

Silver NPs (Ag NPs) have unique chemical, physical, and biological characteristics, as well as a broad range of biomedical uses in the prevention, treatment, and management of a variety of diseases (Vlăsceanu et al., 2016; Miranda et al., 2022). The effective delivery of medicines specifically to the infectious cell or place while limiting harm to normal cells is one of the fundamental problems of NPs in treatment. Currently, authorized therapeutic drugs for the treatment of malignant skin malignancies may produce substantial side effects, necessitating the development of novel therapeutic agents that are more effective and have fewer negative side effects (Vlăsceanu et al., 2016; Miranda et al., 2022). The effectiveness of metallic NPs, particularly silver NPs, as medication carriers or antibacterial compounds in the treatment of different malignancies and skin problems has been established in several recent studies (Ferdous and Nemmar, 2020).

In a research, Kim and a coinvestigator created bovine serum albumin-coated Ag NPs (BSA-AgNPs) and evaluated them for in vitro therapeutic actions for skin cancer therapy (Kim et al., 2021). The cytocidal impacts of the produced BSA-AgNPs on

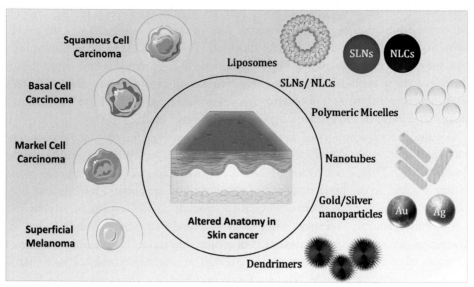

Figure 5.2 Potential of various nanocarrier approaches in skin cancer therapy.

specialized B16F10 melanoma cells were likely induced by oxidative stress. BSA-AgNPs also inhibited cell proliferation, mobility, and tube formation of human umbilical vein endothelial cells (HUVEC) (Kim et al., 2021). Furthermore, BSA-AgNPs demonstrated a high rate of light-to-heat transformation, indicating that they might be used as photothermal agents. The data show that BSA-AgNPs are suitable choice for skin cancer multilevel treatment (Kim et al., 2021). Furthermore, a group of researchers (Valenzuela-Salas et al., 2019) tested AgNPs for their antiproliferative and antitumor effects on skin cancer. After 6 hours of exposure to AgNPs or cisplatin, these NPs were discovered to be capable of causing cell apoptosis, necrosis, and ROS in B16-F10 cells. Despite the fact that AgNPs and cisplatin had equal antiproliferative activity and ROS generation, they activated drastically distinct cell death pathways (Valenzuela-Salas et al., 2019). Cisplatin promotes both apoptosis and necrosis at the same time, whereas AgNPs exclusively induce apoptosis. In this way, the AgNPs were proved to be effective against skin cancer cell (Valenzuela-Salas et al., 2019) (Fig. 5.2).

5.8 Strategies involved in multifunctional nanocarriers targeting skin cancer

Skin cancer is the most frequent cancer, affecting a large percentage of the people and feat epidemic proportions in standings of morbidity. Chemotherapy drug delivery, messenger ribonucleic acid (mRNA) vaccine therapy, nanocarriers targeted for immunotherapy, and nanocarriers employed in combination therapy for skin cancer are now the focus of therapeutic techniques. Despite considerable improvements in cancer genomes, biology, and proteomics in recent decades, cancer treatment has remained unsatisfying, and for several people with cancer, overall survival rates have remained low. Skin cancer may, however, be treated in a variety of methods. Chemotherapy is still one of the most often used techniques in modern skin cancer treatments. Chemotherapeutic agents are harmful drugs that are often injected into the body. Notwithstanding this, chemotherapeutic treatments frequently have limitations such as limited solubility and bioavailability, improper pharmacokinetics, and quasi-biodistribution, all of which can complicate clinical usage, resulting in disagreeable adverse effects (Khan et al., 2021). Aside from that, in terms of manufacturing and application, mRNA, as the technical foundation for therapeutics and vaccines, is extremely versatile. Because any protein may be transcribed and generated by mRNA, it is potentially conceivable to develop prophylactic and therapeutic immunizations for illnesses as diverse as infections and cancer and also protein substitute therapies (Schlake et al., 2012). Melanoma immunotherapy has emerged as the next therapeutic option in recent years. Cancer immunotherapy stimulates or strengthens the host immune system, which subsequently boosts antitumor immune reactions, opening up a novel way to fight cancer (Zuo et al., 2021). On the nanomedicine platform, combination treatment was recently created. Traditional chemotherapy and photodynamic treatment (PDT) were combined to create multimodality NPs. PDT is particularly beneficial for the identification and treatment of various stages of melanoma, particularly metastasized melanoma, as well as the diagnosis and destruction of cancer stem cells. It depends upon the wavelengths at which a photosensitizer is excited (Liu et al., 2018).

5.9 Nanocarriers involve in chemotherapy drug delivery for skin cancer

Cancer patients undergoing chemotherapy are put in a dangerous condition by conventional chemotherapeutic drugs. The reason for this is that they have a nonspecific distribution, low absorption, and, most significantly, strong adverse effects, which cause many patients to stop taking the medication. An evolutionary basis for the interpretation of therapeutic reactions to malignant locations has arisen from a progressive line of attack to nanocarrier-based delivery systems for chemotherapeutic drugs (Kaur and Kesarwani, 2021). There are a variety of anticancer drugs for treating skin cancers, including 5-fluorouracil, Imiquimod, Ingenol mebutate, sinecatechins, epigallocatechin-3-gallate, and betulinic acid, all of which have shown to be effective in curing various malignancies (Thomas and Zalcberg, 1998; Schön and Schön, 2007; Ramsay et al., 2011; Stockfleth and Meyer, 2014; Lu et al., 2002; Zuco et al., 2002). All of these approaches to skin cancer treatment are still being refined to address the obstacles that patients and target sites face. Nanoscale drug delivery technologies have shown their potential in investigations, administration of drugs, and therapies, particularly in cancer care, to overcome the existing flaws, and challenges with skin therapy, as well as other limitations. Nanomaterials have shown potential in enhancing drug absorption, lengthening circulation duration, regulating drug release, and tumor targeting, in contrast to typical drug delivery approaches. In accumulation to these essential roles, nanocarriers may be able to do additional tasks or functions as a result of newly developed materials and technologies for cancer identification and therapy (Tang et al., 2017; Ye et al., 2019).

Because of their ability to increase the diffusion of bioactive compounds into tumor cells, NP-based systems have been extensively studied for topical therapy of skin malignancies. Nanomaterials promote medications to stay in the tumor and on the skin, resulting in better patient compliance, lower poisonousness, and decreased doses (Krishnan and Mitragotri, 2020). The most often used nanocarriers include organic nanocarriers like polymeric micelles, liposomes, and dendrimers along with inorganic nanocarriers like gold NPs, quantum dots (QDs), magnetic NPs, silica NPs, and CNTs. Polymeric structures provide several biological and physicochemical benefits above all other forms of nanomaterials, including simple shapes, ease of manufacturing, drug solubility, improved bioactivity, and enhanced pharmacokinetics and biodistribution. Furthermore, these have the potential for advanced engineering and can be fruitfully used to plan stimuli-responsive drug delivery systems, such as magnetic-field responsive, multiresponsive, temperature-responsive, pH-responsive, redox-responsive, enzyme-responsive, light-responsive, and ultrasound-responsive for tumor discerning distribution of drug and genes to preclude the emergence of multidrug-resistant melanomas (Mir et al., 2017; Zhou et al., 2018; Kesharwani et al., 2019).

Liposomes are double-layered phospholipid vesicles with a small diameter and an internal hydrophilic core, made up of environmentally benign phospholipids and cholesterol (Samad et al., 2007). Their substantial usage as a replacement for carrying the drug component to the target position has been utilized to broaden the therapeutic side view and reduce the occurrence of adverse events accompanying anticancer medicines (Olusanya et al., 2018). The lipid layer has been labeled as an excellent carrier of bioactive chemicals into the skin due to its hydrophobic nature. Biocompatibility, permeability, diffusivity, shielding effect, increased half-life, lower immunostimulatory reaction, enhanced systemic circulation, and better effectiveness and protection are all factors contributing to the growing demand for liposomal options (Li et al., 2019a). Because of the target-specific release, researchers were able to achieve optimal cytotoxic activity and a reduction in side events by integrating numerous medicines onto the surface of liposomes (Millet et al., 2017).

Nanofibers (NFs) are fascinating solid fibers with submicrometer diameters, great porosity, and a vast surface area (Thakkar and Misra, 2017). High surface-to-volume ratio, large permeability of NF matrix, the decreased obstacle for mass transference, malleable management, varied morphological structures, and improved mechanical strength are some of the appealing characteristics that make NFs excellent possibilities for biomedical use (Venugopal et al., 2008). NFs have previously been shown to act as scaffolds with anticarcinogenic drug encapsulation capability, as well as controlled release qualities for diagnostic applications, such as medication delivery and cancer treatment (Chen et al., 2018).

Dendrimers are highly branching, distinct three-dimensional polymeric nanostructures with homogeneous form and dimension, biocompatible, polyvalence, and MW precision (Tomalia, 2005). Tomalia first investigated these macromolecules in 1985, and the phrase is derived from a mixture of Greek terms, specifically "dendron" (tree-like) and "meros" (part of) (Jang et al., 2009). Antitumor drug dendrimeric complexes have shown the capacity to circumvent efflux transporters for intracellular drug delivery and to improve the bioavailability of molecular medicines (Singh et al., 2016).

5.10 Strategies for messenger ribonucleic acid vaccine therapy for skin cancer treatment

Cancer vaccines, unlike vaccinations for infectious illnesses, are designed to treat the disease rather than prevent it. The goal of therapeutic cancer vaccines is to stimulate the patient's immune system specifically with tumor antigens, resulting in an antitumor reaction and tumor elimination. Cancer vaccines come in a variety of forms categorized on a various basis like whole-cell vaccines; mRNA or DNA basis; heat shock proteins, peptides, and gangliosides basis; recombinant virus basis, and dendritic cells (DCs) basis (Thomas and Prendergast, 2016). Spontaneous point mutations in the tumor that start or govern the neoplastic process might be a target for cancer vaccines. Melanoma, being a malignant tumor with one of the greatest mutation rates, namely a high tumor mutation load, is a good target for tumor mutation burden (Alexandrov et al., 2013).

mRNA-based vaccinations are now generating a lot of buzz in the scientific and medical worlds. The creation of mRNA-based vaccines is one of the most advancing and successful solutions. The only benefit of mRNA-based vaccines is their capacity to generate equal humoral and cellular immunity, especially overstimulation of the CD^{8+} T cell response, which is critical in combating contrary to malignancies (Kramps and Elbers, 2017). mRNA vaccinations, on the other hand, do not have the same significant side effects as vaccines, such as incorporation into the patient's genome. Gene interruption, insertional mutagenesis, cell death, and even tumorigenesis might all be negative consequences of integration (Desfarges and Ciuffi, 2012). Furthermore, mRNA acts in the cytoplasm and does not reach the target cell's nucleus, making distribution easier. Finally, mRNA vaccines have the benefit of being quick and affordable to create, allowing for high quantities of the required products to be generated in vitro. Vaccines are classified into two types: nonreplicating mRNA vaccines that simply encode the antigen of interest, and self-amplifying mRNA (saRNA) vaccines that encode the viral replication mechanism and are created from single-stranded viruses. Previous reviews have gone through the mechanism of action of saRNA vaccines in great depth (Iavarone et al., 2017). Nonreplicating mRNA has five organizational components: cap structures, a 50-, an open reading frame (ORF) containing antigens of attention, a 30-, and a polyadenine (poly[A]) tail. Because of its simpler arrangement and the existence of only one ORF, regular mRNA is smaller than siRNA. siRNA contains not only an antigen-encoding gene but also a viral replication gene (Lundstrom, 2020). Because the template is amplified in the target cells, saRNA expresses large amounts of the gene of attention. saRNA can be classified as plasmid-based saRNA, a virus-like constituent part delivery saRNA, or in vitro transcribed saRNA, depending on the method of synthesis (Deering et al., 2014).

As mRNA is an unstable, big, negatively-charged molecule that has trouble traversing the membrane organization, getting mRNA vaccines over the membrane and into the cells is another hurdle. RNA-based medications are mainly taken up through endocytosis since mRNA cannot move across the membrane by passive diffusion. Even though naked mRNA vaccines may be administered directly into cells like dendritic cells (DCs), transport vehicles are needed to achieve substantial rates of expression and inhibition (Diken et al., 2011). Contrasting carrier-based mRNA vaccines, naked mRNA administration is generally accomplished by injecting the mRNA solution directly into the patient. For immunization, naked mRNA is frequently dissolved in Ringer's solution or lactated Ringer's solution (Ringer, 1882). Ca^{2+} is included in these two solutions since it has been shown to increase mRNA uptake in an ion-dependent way (Probst et al., 2007). Anticancer clinical studies have already used naked mRNA dissolved in Ringer's solution. In research by Sahin et al., naked mRNA was diluted in Ringer's solution to a concentration of 1.0 mg/mL and injected into 13 melanoma patients' inguinal LNs (Sahin et al., 2017). The patients were well-tolerated, and the clinical experiment yielded encouraging findings. Viral or nonviral vectors can be used in delivery systems. Modified viruses are employed to transmit the antigen's genetic information to target cells in vaccines based on viral vectors. These vaccines act in the same way as natural infections produced by viruses, which release enormous amounts of antigens after infecting cells, triggering an immune response (Wadhwa et al., 2020). Adenoviruses have high transduction efficiency, thus there's a lot of attention to designing them as vectors for transporting genes/mRNA, albeit this would need the incidence of specialized internalization receptors. Nucleic acids can be delivered via a variety of synthetic and natural lipids (Midoux and Pichon, 2015). Lipids in the form of liposomes or lipid NPs are utilized to deliver mRNA vaccines (LNPs). Because of their beneficial features, such as ease of manufacture and minimal toxicity, liposomes have long been employed as drug transporters (Torchilin, 2005). Liposomes have been created and tested for the delivery of mRNA vaccines, and they have shown promise in the treatment of illnesses, including cancer (Kranz et al., 2016). Polymer-based carriers have been utilized in clinical studies less frequently than lipid-based carriers, yet they offer tremendous possibilities for nucleic acid delivery. Polymers can have both cationic and anionic structures; nevertheless, cationic polymers are better for carrying nucleic acids. Electrostatic interactions allow cationic polymers to form compounds with anionic mRNA (Kowalski et al., 2019).

Polyplex NPs and micelleplex NPs are the product of such interactions, and they differ and are similar (Gary et al., 2011). The most extensively utilized cationic polymer is polyethyleneimine, which is also the most regularly used nucleic acid transfection agent (Lungwitz et al., 2005). Several different chemicals may be used as carrier systems for delivering mRNA vaccines. Lipopolyplexes and cationic nanoemulsions are examples of hybrid carriers. A lipopolyplex is made up of an inner core, a complex containing nucleic acid and a polycationic component (cationic polymer or cationic peptide), and an outside lipid shell (Rezaee et al., 2016). These hybrid carriers combine the benefits of a lipoplex with a polyplex, and they outperform nonhybrid systems (Guan and Rosenecker, 2017). As of their relative stability, minimal immunogenicity, and low toxicity, peptides can be employed as nonviral mRNA delivery vehicles (Hoyer and Neundorf, 2012). Because of the positive charge originating from the amino groups in their amino acids, cationic peptides simply bind with negatively-charged mRNA (Qiu et al., 2019). Cationic peptides such as protamine's and cell-penetrating peptides can be utilized to transfer mRNA to cells. The ability of protamine to shield mRNA against destruction by serum nucleases is a desired trait (Hoerr et al., 2000). The use of protamine—mRNA complexes alone, however, stops the translation procedure and lowers the efficiency of a vaccine owing to the extraordinarily tight interaction between protamine and mRNA. This can be mitigated by employing RNActive tools, in which the mRNA—protamine combination works as an immune system stimulant rather than being involved in the expression mechanism (Schlake et al., 2012). DCs are the most powerful antigen-presentation cells in the immune system, capable of internalizing, processing, and presenting antigens to CD^{8+} or CD^{4+} T cells via major histocompatibility complexes (MHCs), such as MHC class I and MHC class II. DCs are a potential vaccine target for cancer prevention due to their important biological properties that are connected with the development of the adaptive immune response. Furthermore, DCs release a variety of cytokines and chemokines that are required for T-cell proliferation, stimulation, and enlistment (Del Prete et al., 2020). As a result, multiple preclinical and clinical experiments evaluating DC-based mRNA vaccines have been launched in prior decades.

5.11 Nanocarriers targeting immunotherapy

The majority of cancer immunotherapies are now founded on T cell-mediated cellular immunity, which has been characterized by Chen and Mellman as the famous cancer-immunity cycle, which contains seven steps, i.e., cancer cell antigen release, cancer antigen presentation, T cell priming and activation, T cell trafficking to tumors, T cell penetration into tumors, T cell detection of cancer cells, and T cell death of cancer cells. These seven phases may be separated mad into dual phases: the preparation stage (T cells reacting) (cancer cell antigen release, cancer antigen presentation, and T cell priming and activation), which occurs mostly in LNs, and the effector stage (T cells killing), which occurs primarily in the TME (T cell trafficking to tumors, T cell penetration into tumors, T cell detection of cancer cells, and T cell death of cancer cells). In most cancers, one or more of these phases in the cancer-immunity cycle are obstructed, resulting in suppressed anticancer immune responses and tumor immune discharge (Chen and Mellman, 2013).

In the arena of anticancer therapy, nanodrug delivery methods ought to be situated extensively employed (Yang et al., 2020). NPs can improve medication stability and protect them from being digested in the bloodstream, allowing for lower dosage administration and the avoidance of elevated dose-related poisonousness. Furthermore, NPs can boost therapeutic drug accumulation in tumor tissue and LNs, resulting in improved therapeutic efficacy and fewer adverse effects (Luo et al., 2014). Tumors and LNs are well-known targets of immunotherapy (Sautès-Fridman et al., 2019; Li et al., 2019b). The enhanced permeability and retention effect describes how NPs can passively travel into tumor tissue over and done with juvenile tumor vasculature and accumulate owing to impaired lymphatic drainage (Ding et al., 2020). After surface ligand modification, NPs can also actively target tumor cells. NPs can also build up in LNs and transmit cancer vaccines to antigen-presenting cells, triggering an immune response. Furthermore, NPs offer specific benefits for combined drug delivery, allowing several immunotherapy mechanisms to work together to improve the overall immune response (Ding et al., 2020).

However the above nanoimmunotherapies ought to show efficacy in preclinical tests, they can only help a small percentage of patients. Most of these therapies fail because they only target one phase of the cancer-immunity sequence, which is inadequate when the sequence is influenced by several variables. One path ahead is to use a combination of immunotherapies. NPs have appeared as a viable carrier for multiple agent delivery. Through physical adsorption, hydrogen bonding, or chemical bonding, innovative nanocarriers can codeliver several medicines with distinct physicochemical features. In addition to this benefit, LN/tumor-targeted NPs can restrict medication acquaintance to ordinary tissues, boosting therapeutic effectiveness while lowering systemic toxicity. Multiple drugs with distinct qualities can be delivered by NPs, resulting in efficient synergetic treatment. Because of their unfavorable pharmacokinetic profiles and tumor accumulation, indoleamine 2,3-dioxygenase (IDO) inhibitors like NLG-8189 have low clinical effectiveness. Because IDO inhibitors are ineffective when used alone, they must be combined with other treatments. As a result, NPs have been employed to increase IDO inhibitor bioactivity and achieve successful codelivery. NPs can minimize immunotherapeutic drug dispersion in ordinary tissues and let them collect precisely in target tissues, which is important for lowering systemic toxicity (Zuo et al., 2021).

5.12 Nanocarriers used in combination therapy for targeting skin cancer

Specific inhibitors of the proto-oncogene protein B-raf (BRAF) and mitogen-activated protein kinase have appeared employing unique existence advantages in the research of novel targeted therapeutics. The concept of cancer-targeted therapy centers on the targets that malignant cells must be sure of for advancement, existence, and propagation. Because cancer growth is more reliant on hyperactivated pathways than normal cells, they provide a therapeutic possibility. As sensibly intended drugs may bind selectively to active sites and possibly intercede a therapeutic impact, kinases, phosphatases, and proteases are viable tools deserving of clinical exploration (Bennasroune et al., 2004; McConnell and Wadzinski, 2009). Neuroblastoma (NRAS) and BRAF mutations are not present at the same time and are not thought to cause pathogenesis in metastatic melanoma via the same route (Ekedahl et al., 2013). When studied in conjunction with carboplatin and paclitaxel, sorafenib, a broad-spectrum kinase inhibitor that targets both CRAF and BRAF, showed a moderate response of around 30%; however, monotherapy results were poor (Flaherty et al., 2004). The early clinical success of BRAF (V600E) inhibitors vemurafenib and dabrafenib, with response rates of 50%, was a most important advance in the management of metastatic skin cancer (Chapman et al., 2011).

However, the initial joy was quickly overtaken by regret when the majority of patients relapsed, and molecular investigations indicated various paths of acquired resistance, mostly through compensatory mechanisms (Sullivan and Flaherty, 2013). Overall, targeted treatments have been clinically effective in the treatment of melanoma; however, they have the disadvantage of developing resistance after an initial response or failing to translate target inhibition into disease control. The effective transformation of understanding of molecular mechanisms of resistance into clinically relevant treatment combinations is critical for the forthcoming targeted medicines in melanoma care (Liu et al., 2018).

5.13 Patents on nanocarriers targeting skin cancer

Various patents have been implemented to protect scientific activities in the field of nanolipoidal systems. Some of the patents mention responsive liposomes for precise targeting, nanocarriers for chemotherapeutics, nucleic acids, and photosensitizer's delivery or codelivery. There are also more current patents on innovative delivery techniques available, which are listed below (Table 5.1).

Table 5.1 Representation of patents on nanocarriers targeting skin cancer.

S/No.	Application no.	Publication	Title	Inventors	Specifications	References
1.	201831034495	20 March 2020	Bionanoengineered ethosomal formulation of silk sericin proteins and uses thereof for treatment of skin cancer	Dr. Bismita Nayak Dr. Debasis Nayak	The developed ethosomal formulation has nontoxic, nonimmunogenic, biodegradable, and hemocompatible properties. It also showed excellent antimicrobial activity, highly cytocompatibility, and effective drug release property with longer bioavailability of the drug	Nayak and Nayak (2020)
2.	202141018014	30 April 2021	Monoolein-based self-assembled resveratrol and piperine-loaded cubosome for the management of melanoma using transdermal cubogel	Mr. Bhaskar Kurangi Dr. Sunil Jalalpure Mr. Satveer Jagwani	The formulation enhances the activity and efficacy of resveratrol and piperine. The thermodynamic stable cumbersome formulation discloses its prophylactic and therapeutic antimelanoma activity	Kurangi et al. (2021)
3.	201821017563	25 May 2018	A low-cost novel method for synthesis of green tea extract nanogel	Prashant Sahu Sushil K Kashaw	It exhibits a biodegradable and biocompatible character with a less toxic nature	Sahu and Kashaw (2018)

No.	Application/Patent number	Date	Title	Inventors	Description	Reference
4.	WO/2021/226033	11 November 2021	Hyaluronic acid drug conjugates	Mitragotri, Samir Krishnan, Vinu	Polymer-drug conjugates in combinations with hyaluronic acid, doxorubicin, and camptothecin, which targeted skin cancer, blood cancer, and intestinal cancer	Mitragotri and Krishnan (2021)
5.	201721011564	12 May 2017	Topical biodegradable chitosan nanogel Of temozolomide in treatment of melanoma	Prashant Sahu Sushil K Kashaw	Biodegradable nanogel effective against lethal cancers	Sahu and Kashaw (2017)
6.	WO/2016/102613	30 June 2016	Nanoparticles and their use in cancer therapy	Golding Jon, Williams Phillip, Roskamp Meike	Reveals the treatment of nanoparticles alone or in combination with radiotherapy	Jon et al. (2016)
7.	EP3753549	23 December 2020	Liposomal doxorubicin formulation, method for producing a liposomal doxorubicin formulation, and use of a liposomal doxorubicin formulation as a medicament	Halbherr Stéfan Jonathan, Halbherr Pascal, Mathieu Christoph, Buschor Patrick	Particular formulation targeting, cancer, uterine leiomyosarcoma, and adnexal skin cancer	Jonathan et al. (2020)
8.	EP3600563	05 February 2020	Pharmaceutical compositions	Albarano Teo	This composition showed a synergistic effect of vitamin D3 or its derivative on hyaluronic acid. Targeting skin cancers	Albarano (2020)

5.14 Conclusion

Nanotechnology has given a new approach to the treatment of various diseases. Emerging nanotechnological approaches play a major role in powerful anticarcinogenic effects, with the advantages of administering drugs only to tumor sites, which enhance therapeutic effectiveness, reduce toxicity, and prevent the spreading of tumors.

Careful choice of suitable nanocarriers for loading appropriate chemotherapeutic agents has shown promising results by reducing the dosage, when compared to conventional therapy. Moreover, a newer approach of nanotechnology may be used for diagnostic purposes and also improves the survival rate of patients suffering from skin cancer, thus reducing the health burden on medical facilities.

References

Akhtar, N., Khan, R.A., 2016. Liposomal systems as viable drug delivery technology for skin cancer sites with an outlook on lipid-based delivery vehicles and diagnostic imaging inputs for skin conditions. Prog. Lipid Res 64, 192–230.

Albarano, T., 2020. Pharmaceutical Compositions, EP3600563, 05 February 2020.

Alexandrov, L.B., Nik-Zainal, S., Wedge, D.C., Aparicio, S.A., Behjati, S., Biankin, A.V., et al., 2013. Erratum: signatures of mutational processes in human cancer. Nature 500, 415–421.

Bachhav, Y.G., Mondon, K., Kalia, Y.N., Gurny, R., Moller, M., 2011. Novel micelle formulations to increase cutaneous bioavailability of azole antifungals. J. Control. Rel. 153, 126–132.

Bagheri, V., Memar, B., Momtazi, A.A., Sahebkar, A., Gholamin, M., Abbaszadegan, M.R., 2018. Cytokine networks and their association with *Helicobacter pylori* infection in gastric carcinoma. J. Cell. Physiol 233, 2791–2803. Available from: https://doi.org/10.1002/jcp.25822.

Barratt, M.D., 1995. Quantitative structure-activity relationships for skin permeability. Toxicol. Vitro 9, 27–37.

Bennasroune, A., Gardin, A., Aunis, D., Crémel, G., Hubert, P., 2004. Tyrosine kinase receptors as attractive targets of cancer therapy. Crit. Rev. Oncol. Hematol. 50 (1), 23–38.

Bhia, M., Motallebi, M., Abadi, B., Zarepour, A., Pereira-Silva, M., Saremnejad, F., et al., 2021. Naringenin nano-delivery systems and their therapeutic applications. Pharmaceutics 13, 291. Available from: https://doi.org/10.3390/pharmaceutics13020291.

Boakye, C.H.A., Patel, K., Doddapaneni, R., Bagde, A., Behl, G., Chowdhury, N., et al., 2016. Ultra-flexible nanocarriers for enhanced topical delivery of a highly lipophilic antioxidative molecule for skin cancer chemoprevention. Colloids Surf. B: Biointerfaces 143, 156–167.

Boderke, P., Schittkowski, K., Wolf, M., Merkle, H.P., 2000. Modeling of diffusion and concurrent metabolism in cutaneous tissue. J. Theor. Biol. 204, 393–407.

Borgheti-Cardoso, L.N., Viegas, J.S.R., Silvestrini, A.V.P., Caron, A.L., Praça, F.G., Kravicz, M., Bentley, M.V.L.B., 2020. Nanotechnology approaches in the current therapy of skin cancer. Adv. Drug. Delivery Rev. 153, 109–136.

Bottini, M., Cerignoli, F., Dawson, M.I., Magrini, A., Rosato, N., Mustelin, T., 2006. Noncovalentlysilylated carbon nanotubes decorated with quantum dots. Biomacromolecules 7, 2259–2263.

Cevc, G., Gebauer, D., Stieber, J., Schatzlein, A., Blume, G., 1998. Ultraflexible vesicles, transfersomes, have an extremely low pore penetration resistance and transport therapeutic amounts of insulin across the intact mammalian skin. Biochem. Biophys. Acta 1368, 201–215.

Cevc, G., 1997. Drug delivery across the skin. Exp. Opin. Invest. Drugs 6, 1887–1937.

Chapman, P.B., Hauschild, A., Robert, C., Haanen, J.B., Ascierto, P., Larkin, J., et al., 2011. Improved survival with vemurafenib in melanoma with BRAF V600E mutation. N. Engl. J. Med. 364 (26), 2507–2516.

Chen, D.S., Mellman, I., 2013. Oncology meets immunology: the cancer-immunity cycle. Immunity 39 (1), 1–10.

Chen, S., Boda, S.K., Batra, S.K., Li, X., Xie, J., 2018. Emerging roles of electrospun nanofibers in cancer research. Adv. Healthc. Mater. 7 (6), 1701024.

Deering, R.P., Kommareddy, S., Ulmer, J.B., Brito, L.A., Geall, A.J., 2014. Nucleic acid vaccines: prospects for non-viral delivery of mRNA vaccines. Expert. Opin. Drug Deliv. 11 (6), 885–899.

Del Prete, A., Sozio, F., Barbazza, I., Salvi, V., Tiberio, L., Laffranchi, M., et al., 2020. Functional role of dendritic cell subsets in cancer progression and clinical implications. Int. J. Mol. Sci. 21 (11), 3930.

Desfarges, S., Ciuffi, A., 2012. Viral integration and consequences on host gene expression. Viruses: Essential Agents of Life. Springer, Dordrecht, pp. 147–175.

Dianzani, C., Zara, G.P., Maina, G., Pettazzoni, P., Pizzimenti, S., Rossi, F., et al., 2014. Drug delivery nanoparticles in skin cancers. BioMed. Res. Int. 13, 1–13.

Diken, M., Kreiter, S., Selmi, A., Britten, C.M., Huber, C., Türeci, Ö., et al., 2011. Selective uptake of naked vaccine RNA by dendritic cells is driven by macropinocytosis and abrogated upon DC maturation. Gene Ther. 18 (7), 702–708.

Ding, Y., Xu, Y., Yang, W., Niu, P., Li, X., Chen, Y., et al., 2020. Investigating the EPR effect of nanomedicines in human renal tumors via ex vivo perfusion strategy. Nano Today 35, 100970.

Ekedahl, H., Cirenajwis, H., Harbst, K., Carneiro, A., Nielsen, K., Olsson, H., et al., 2013. The clinical significance of BRAF and NRAS mutations in a clinic-based metastatic melanoma cohort. Br. J. Dermatol. 169 (5), 1049–1055.

Fang, C.L., Aljuffali, I.A., Li, Y.C., Fang, J.Y., 2014. Delivery and targeting of nanoparticles into hair follicles. Ther. Deliv. 5, 991–1006.

Favila, A., Gallo, M., Glossman-Mitnik, D., 2007. DFT studies of functionalized carbon nanotubes and fullerenes as nanovectors for drug delivery of antitubercular compounds. J. Mol. Mod. 13, 505.

Ferdous, Z., Nemmar, A., 2020. Health impact of silver nanoparticles: a review of the biodistribution and toxicity following various routes of exposure. Int. J. Mol. Sci 21, 2375. Available from: https://doi.org/10.3390/ijms21072375.

Flaherty, K.T., Brose, M., Schuchter, L., Tuveson, D., Lee, R., Schwartz, B., et al., 2004. Phase I/II trial of BAY 43–9006, carboplatin (C) and paclitaxel (P) demonstrate preliminary antitumor activity in the expansion cohort of patients with metastatic melanoma. J. Clin. Oncol. 22 (14_suppl), 7507.

Forslind, B., 2000. The skin barrier: analysis of physiologically important elements and trace elements. Acta Derm. Suppl. (Stockh.) 208, 46–52.

Gary, D.J., Lee, H., Sharma, R., Lee, J.S., Kim, Y., Cui, Z.Y., et al., 2011. Influence of nano-carrier architecture on in vitro siRNA delivery performance and in vivo biodistribution: polyplexes vs micelleplexes. ACS Nano 5 (5), 3493–3505.

Gorbet, M.J., Ranjan, A., 2020. Cancer immunotherapy with immunoadjuvants, nanoparticles, and checkpoint inhibitors: recent progress and challenges in treatment and tracking response to immunotherapy. Pharmacol. Ther 207, 107456. Available from: https://doi.org/10.1016/j.pharmthera.2019.107456. Epub 2019 Dec 19. PMID: 31863820; PMCID: PMC7039751.

Guan, S., Rosenecker, J., 2017. Nanotechnologies in delivery of mRNA therapeutics using nonviral vector-based delivery systems. Gene Ther. 24 (3), 133–143.

Gulla, S., Reddy, V.C., Araveti, P.B., Lomada, D., Srivastava, A., Reddy, M.C., et al., 2022. Synthesis of titanium dioxide nanotubes (TNT) conjugated with quercetin and its in vivo antitumor activity against skin cancer. J. Mol. Struct. 1249, 131556.

Hajime, I., 1994. Epidermal turnover time. J. Dermatol. Sci. 8, 215–217.

Hoerr, I., Obst, R., Rammensee, H.G., Jung, G., 2000. In vivo application of RNA leads to the induction of specific cytotoxic T lymphocytes and antibodies. Eur. J. Immunol. 30 (1), 1–7.

Hoyer, J.A.N., Neundorf, I., 2012. Peptide vectors for the nonviral delivery of nucleic acids. Acc. Chem. Res. 45 (7), 1048–1056.

Huang, N., Wang, H., Zhao, J., Lui, H., Korbelik, M., Zeng, H., 2010. Single-wall carbon nanotubes assisted photothermal cancer therapy: animal study with a murine model of squamous cell carcinoma. Lasers Surg. Med. 42, 638–648.

Iavarone, C., O'hagan, D.T., Yu, D., Delahaye, N.F., Ulmer, J.B., 2017. Mechanism of action of mRNA-based vaccines. Expert. Rev. Vaccines 16 (9), 871−881.

Ibsen, S., Zahavy, E., Wrasdilo, W., Berns, M., Chan, M., Esener, S., 2010. A novel doxorubicin prodrug with controllable photolysis activation for cancer chemotherapy. Pharm. Res. 27, 1848−1860.

Jang, W.D., Selim, K.K., Lee, C.H., Kang, I.K., 2009. Bioinspired application of dendrimers: from biomimicry to biomedical applications. Prog. Polym. Sci. 34 (1), 1−23.

Jiang, G., Li, R., Tang, J., Ma, Y., Hou, X., Yang, C., et al., 2017. Formulation of temozolomide-loaded nanoparticles and their targeting potential to melanoma cells. Oncol Rep 37 (2), 995−1001. Available from: https://doi.org/10.3892/or.2016.5342. Epub 2016 Dec 29. PMID: 28035395.

Johnson, M., Blankschtein, D., Langer, R., 1997. Evaluation of solute permeation through the stratum corneum: lateral bilayer diffusion as the primary transport mechanism. J. Pharm. Sci. 86, 1162−1172.

Jon G., Phillip W., Meike R., 2016. Nanoparticles and their Use in Cancer Therapy, WO/2016/ 102613, 30 June 2016.

Jonathan, H.S., Pascal, H., Christoph, M., Patrick, B., 2020. Liposomal Doxorubicin Formulation, Method For Producing A Liposomal Doxorubicin Formulation and Use Of A Liposomal Doxorubicin Formulation as Aa Medicament, EP3753549, 23 Dec 2020.

Kaur, H., Kesarwani, P., 2021. Advanced nanomedicine approaches applied for the treatment of skin carcinoma. J. Control. Rel. 337, 589−611.

Kesharwani, S.S., Kaur, S., Tummala, H., Sangamwar, A.T., 2019. Multifunctional approaches utilizing polymeric micelles to circumvent multidrug-resistant tumors. Colloids Surf. B: Biointerfaces 173, 581−590.

Kim, D., Amatya, R., Hwang, S., Lee, S., Min, K.A., Shin, M.C., 2021. BSA-silver nanoparticles: a potential multimodal therapeutics for conventional and photothermal treatment of skin cancer. Pharmaceutics 13, 575. Available from: https://doi.org/10.3390/pharmaceutics13040575.

Khan, N.H., Mir, M., Qian, L., Baloch, M., Khan, M.F.A., Ngowi, E.E., et al., 2021. Skin cancer biology and barriers to treatment: recent applications of polymeric micro/nanostructures. J. Adv. Res. 36, 223−247.

Khodabandehloo, H., Zahednasab, H., Ashrafi Hafez, A., 2016. Nanocarriers Usage for Drug Delivery in Cancer Therapy. Iran. J. Cancer Prev 9 (2), e3966. Available from: https://doi.org/10.17795/ijcp-3966. PMID: 27482328; PMCID: PMC4951761.

Kontturi, K., Murtomaeki, L., 1996. Mechanistic model for transdermal transport including iontophoresis. J. Control. Rel. 41, 177−185.

Kostarelos, K., Bianco, A., Prato, M., 2007. Promises, facts, and challenges for carbon nanotubes in imaging and therapeutic. Nature 2, 108.

Kowalski, P.S., Rudra, A., Miao, L., Anderson, D.G., 2019. Delivering the messenger: advances in technologies for therapeutic mRNA delivery. Mol. Ther. 27 (4), 710−728.

Kramps, T., Elbers, K., 2017. Introduction to RNA vaccines. Methods Mol. Biol. 1499, 1−11.

Kranz, L.M., Diken, M., Haas, H., Kreiter, S., Loquai, C., Reuter, K.C., et al., 2016. Systemic RNA delivery to dendritic cells exploits antiviral defence for cancer immunotherapy. Nature 534 (7607), 396−401.

Krishnan, V., Mitragotri, S., 2020. Nanoparticles for topical drug delivery: potential for skin cancer treatment. Adv. Drug. Deliv. Rev. 153, 87−108.

Kurangi, B., Jalalpure, S., Jagwani, S., 2021. Monoolein Based Self Assembled Resveratrol and Piperine Loaded Cubosome for the Management of Melanoma using Transdermal Cubogel, 202141018014, 30 April 2021.

Kwon, G.S., Okano, T., 1996. Polymeric micelles as new drug carriers. Adv. Drug. Deliv. Rev. 71, 227−234.

Lai, F., Sinico, C., De Logu, A., 2007. SLN as a topical delivery system for Artemisia arborescens essential oil: in vitro antiviral activity and skin permeation study2007 Int. J. Nanomed. 2, 419−425.

Lalan, M., Shah, P., Barve, K., Parekh, K., Mehta, T., Patel, P., 2021. Skin cancer therapeutics: nanodrug delivery vectors—present and beyond. Futur. J. Pharm. Sci. 7, 179.

Lavasanifar, A., Samuel, J., Kwon, G.S., 2002. Poly(ethylene oxide)-block poly (L-amino acid) micelles for drug delivery. Adv. Drug. Deliv. Rev. 54, 169−190.

Li, M., Du, C., Guo, N., Teng, Y., Meng, X., Sun, H., et al., 2019a. Composition design and medical application of liposomes. Eur. J. Med. Chem. 164, 640−653.

Li, Y., Ayala-Orozco, C., Rauta, P.R., Krishnan, S., 2019b. The application of nanotechnology in enhancing immunotherapy for cancer treatment: current effects and perspective. Nanoscale 11 (37), 17157−17178.

Liang, Z.J., Yuan, Q., Chao, W.F., Pu, Z.Y., 2009. A comparative study of Young's modulus of single-walled carbon nanotube. Comput. Mater. Sci. 46, 621−625.

Liu, J., Hu, W., Chen, H., Ni, Q., Xu, H., Yang, X., 2007. Isotretinoin-loaded solid lipid nanoparticles with skin targeting for topical delivery. Int. J. Pharm. 328, 191−195.

Liu, Q., Das, M., Liu, Y., Huang, L., 2018. Targeted drug delivery to melanoma. Adv. Drug. Deliv. Rev. 127, 208−221.

Lu, Y.P., Lou, Y.R., Xie, J.G., Peng, Q.Y., Liao, J., Yang, C.S., et al., 2002. Topical applications of caffeine or (−)-epigallocatechin gallate (EGCG) inhibit carcinogenesis and selectively increase apoptosis in UVB-induced skin tumors in mice. Proc. Natl Acad. Sci. 99 (19), 12455−12460.

Lundstrom, K., 2020. Self-amplifying RNA viruses as RNA vaccines. Int. J. Mol. Sci. 21 (14), 5130.

Lungwitz, U., Breunig, M., Blunk, T., Göpferich, A., 2005. Polyethylenimine-based non-viral gene delivery systems. Eur. J. Pharm. Biopharm. 60 (2), 247−266.

Luo, C., Sun, J., Sun, B., He, Z., 2014. Prodrug-based nanoparticulate drug delivery strategies for cancer therapy. Trends Pharmacol. Sci. 35 (11), 556−566.

McConnell, J.L., Wadzinski, B.E., 2009. Targeting protein serine/threonine phosphatases for drug development. Mol. Pharmacol. 75 (6), 1249−1261.

Menezes, A.C., Campos, P.M., Euleterio, C., Simoes, S., Praca, F.S., Bentley, M.V., et al., 2016. Development and characterization of novel 1-(1-Naphthyl)piperazine-loaded lipid vesicles for prevention of UV-induced skin inflammation. Eur. J. Pharma. Biopharm. 104, 101−109.

Midoux, P., Pichon, C., 2015. Lipid-based mRNA vaccine delivery systems. Expert. Rev. Vaccines 14 (2), 221−234.

Millet, A., Martin, A.R., Ronco, C., Rocchi, S., Benhida, R., 2017. Metastatic melanoma: insights into the evolution of the treatments and future challenges. Med. Res. Rev. 37 (1), 98−148.

Mir, M., Ahmed, N., Ur Rehman, A., 2017. Recent applications of PLGA-based nanostructures in drug delivery. Colloids Surf. B: Biointerfaces 159, 217−231.

Mitragotri, S., Krishnan, V., 2021. Hyaluronic Acid Drug Conjugates, WO/2021/226033, 11 November 2021.

Miranda, R.R., Sampaio, I., Zucolotto, V., 2022. Exploring silver nanoparticles for cancer therapy and diagnosis. Colloids Surf. B Biointerfaces 210, 112254.

Miyata, K., Christie, R.J., Kataoka, K., 2011. Polymeric micelles for nanoscale drug delivery. React. Funct. Polym. 71, 227−234.

Moss, G.P., Dearden, J.C., Patel, H., Cronin, M.T.D., 2002. Quantitative structure-permeability relationships (QSPRs) for percutaneous absorption. Toxicol. Vitro 16, 299−317.

Mukherjee, S., Ray, S., Thakur, R.S., 2009. Solid lipid nanoparticles: a modern formulation approach in drug delivery system. Indian. J. Pharm. Sci. 71, 349−358.

Muller, R., Radtke, M., Wissing, S., 2002. Nanostructured lipid matrices for improved microencapsulation of drugs. Int. J. Pharm. 242, 121−128.

Muller, R.H., Shegokar, R., Keck, C.M., 2011. 20 years of lipid nanoparticles (SLN and NLC): present state of development and industrial applications. Curr. Drug. Discov. Technol. 8, 207−227.

Nayak, B., Nayak, D., 2020. Bio-Nanoengineered Ethosomal Formulation of Silk Sericin Proteins and uses thereof for Treatment of Skin Cancer, 201831034495, 20 March 2020.

Nirmala, J.G., Akila, S., Narendhirakannan, R.T., Chatterjee, S., 2017. Vitis vinifera peel polyphenols stabilized gold nanoparticles induce cytotoxicity and apoptotic cell death in A431 skin cancer cell lines. Adv. Powder Technol. 28, 1170−1184.

Niu, J., Chu, Y., Huang, Y.F., Chong, Y.S., Jiang, Z.H., Mao, Z.W., et al., 2017. Transdermal gene delivery by functional peptide-conjugated cationic gold nanoparticle reverses the progression and metastasis of cutaneous melanoma. ACS Appl. Mater. Interfaces 9, 9388−9401.

Olusanya, T.O., Haj Ahmad, R.R., Ibegbu, D.M., Smith, J.R., Elkordy, A.A., 2018. Liposomal drug delivery systems and anticancer drugs. Molecules 23 (4), 907.

Pardeshi, C., Rajput, P., Belgamwar, V., Tekade, A., Patil, G., Chaudhary, K., et al., 2012. Solid lipid-based nanocarriers: an overview/nanonosaci na bazi cvrstih lipida: pregled. Acta Pharm. 62, 433−472.

Pirot, F., Kalia, Y.N., Berardesca, E., Singh, M., Maibach, H.I., Guy, R.H., 1998. Stratum corneum thickness and apparent water diffusivity: facile and noninvasive quantitation in vivo. Pharm. Res. 15, 490−492.

Preet, S., Pandey, S.K., Kaur, K., Chauhan, S., Saini, A., 2019. Gold nanoparticles assisted co-delivery of nisin and doxorubicin against murine skin cancer. J. Drug Deliv. Sci. Technol. 53, 101147.

Potts, R.O., Guy, R.H., 1992. Predicting skin permeability. Pharm. Res. 9, 663−669.

Probst, J., Weide, B., Scheel, B., Pichler, B.J., Hoerr, I., Rammensee, H.G., et al., 2007. Spontaneous cellular uptake of exogenous messenger RNA in vivo is nucleic acid-specific, saturable, and ion dependent. Gene Ther. 14 (15), 1175−1180.

Qiu, Y., Man, R.C., Liao, Q., Kung, K.L., Chow, M.Y., Lam, J.K., 2019. Effective mRNA pulmonary delivery by dry powder formulation of PEGylated synthetic KL4 peptide. J. Control. Rel. 314, 102−115.

Ramsay, J.R., Suhrbier, A., Aylward, J.H., Ogbourne, S., Cozzi, S.J., Poulsen, M.G., et al., 2011. The sap from Euphorbia peplus is effective against human nonmelanoma skin cancers. Br. J. Dermatol. 164 (3), 633−636.

Rawding, P.A., Bu, J., Wang, J., Kim, D.W., Drelich, A.J., Kim, Y., Hong, S., 2022. Dendrimers for cancer immunotherapy: Avidity-based drug delivery vehicles for effective anti-tumor immune response. Wiley Interdisc. Rev. Nanomed. Nanobiotechnol 14 (2), e1752. Available from: https://doi.org/10.1002/wnan.1752.

Rezaee, M., Oskuee, R.K., Nassirli, H., Malaekeh-Nikouei, B., 2016. Progress in the development of lipopolyplexes as efficient non-viral gene delivery systems. J. Control. Rel. 236, 1−14.

Ringer, S., 1882. Regarding the action of the hydrate of soda, hydrate of ammonia, and hydrate of potash on the ventricle of the frog's heart. J. Physiol. 3 (3−4), 195.

Rostami, E., Kashanian, S., Azandaryani, A.H., Faramarzi, H., Dolatabadi, J.E.N., Omidfar, K., 2014. Drug targeting using solid lipid nanoparticles. Chem. Phys. Lipids 181, 56−61.

Sahin, U., Derhovanessian, E., Miller, M., Kloke, B.P., Simon, P., Löwer, M., et al., 2017. Personalized RNA mutanome vaccines mobilize poly-specific therapeutic immunity against cancer. Nature 547 (7662), 222−226.

Sahu, P., Kashaw, S.K., 2018. A Low Cost Novel Method For Synthesis of Green Tea Extract Nanogel, 201821017563, 25 May 2018.

Sahu, P., Kashaw, S.K., 2017. Topical Biodegradable Chitosan Nanogel of Temozolomide In Treatment of Melanoma, 201721011564, 12 May 2017.

Samad, A., Sultana, Y., Aqil, M., 2007. Liposomal drug delivery systems: an updated review. Curr. Drug Delivry 4 (4), 297−305.

Sanvicens, N., Marco, M.P., 2008. Multifunctional nanoparticles—properties, and prospects for their use in human medicine. Trends Biotechnol. 26 (8), 425−433.

Sautès-Fridman, C., Petitprez, F., Calderaro, J., Fridman, W.H., 2019. Tertiary lymphoid structures in the era of cancer immunotherapy. Nat. Rev. Cancer 19 (6), 307−325.

Schaefer, P., Bewick-Sonntag, C., Capri, M.G., Berardesca, E., 2002. Physiological changes in skin barrier function in relation to occlusion level, exposure time, and climatic conditions. Skin. Pharmacol. Appl. Skin Physiol. 15, 7−19.

Schatzlein, A., Cevc, G., 1998. Non-uniform cellular packing of the stratum corneum and permeability barrier function of intact skin: a high-resolution confocal laser scanning microscopy study using highly deformable vesicles (Transfersomes). Br. J. Dermatol. 138, 583−592.

Schlake, T., Thess, A., Fotin-Mleczek, M., Kallen, K.J., 2012. Developing mRNA-vaccine technologies. RNA Biol. 9 (11), 1319−1330.

Schön, M.P., Schön, M., 2007. Imiquimod: mode of action. Br. J. Dermatol. 157, 8−13.

Singh, R., Lillard Jr., J.W., 2009. Nanoparticle-based targeted drug delivery. Exp. Mol. Pathol. 86 (3), 215−223.

Singh, J., Jain, K., Mehra, N.K., Jain, N.K., 2016. Dendrimers in anticancer drug delivery: mechanism of interaction of drug and dendrimers. Artif. Cells Nanomed. Biotechnol. 44 (7), 1626−1634.

Souto, E.B., Almeida, A.J., Muller, R.H., 2007. Lipid nanoparticles (SLN®, NLC®) for cutaneous drug delivery: structure, protection and skin effects. J. Biomed. Nanotechnol. 3, 317−331.

Steinstraesser, I., Merkle, H.P., 1995. Dermal metabolism of topically applied drugs: pathways and models reconsidered. Pharm. Acta Helv. 70, 3–24.

Stockfleth, E., Meyer, T., 2014. Sinecatechins (Polyphenon E) ointment for the treatment of external genital warts and possible future indications. Expert. Opin. Biol. Ther. 14 (7), 1033–1043.

Sullivan, R.J., Flaherty, K.T., 2013. Resistance to BRAF-targeted therapy in melanoma. Eur. J. Cancer 49 (6), 1297–1304.

Tang, J.Q., Hou, X.Y., Yang, C.S., Li, Y.X., Xin, Y., Guo, W.W., et al., 2017. Recent developments in nanomedicine for melanoma treatment. Int. J. Cancer 141 (4), 646–653.

Thakkar, S., Misra, M., 2017. Electrospun polymeric nanofibers: new horizons in drug delivery. Eur. J. Pharm. Sci. 107, 148–167.

Thomas, D.M., Zalcberg, J.R., 1998. 5-Fluorouracil: a pharmacological paradigm in the use of cytotoxics. Clin. Exp. Pharmacol. Physiol. 25 (11), 887–895.

Thomas, S., Prendergast, G.C., 2016. Cancer vaccines: a brief overview. Methods Mol. Biol. 1403, 755–761.

Tomalia, D.A., 2005. Birth of a new macromolecular architecture: dendrimers as quantized building blocks for nanoscale synthetic polymer chemistry. Prog. Polym. Sci. 30 (3–4), 294–324.

Tong, R., Cheng, J., 2007. Anticancer polymeric nanomedicines. Polym. Rev 47 (3), 345–381. Available from: https://doi.org/10.1080/15583720701455079.

Torchilin, V.P., 2005. Recent advances with liposomes as pharmaceutical carriers. Nat. Rev. Drug Discov. 4 (2), 145–160.

Tornesello, A.L., Tagliamonte, M., Tornesello, M.L., Buonaguro, F.M., Buonaguro, L., 2020. Nanoparticles to improve the efficacy of peptide-based cancer vaccines. Cancers 12, 1049.

Tripathi, P.K., Gorain, B., Choudhury, H., Srivastava, A., Kesharwani, P., 2019. Dendrimer entrapped microsponge gel of dithranol for effective topical treatment. Heliyon 5, e01343.

Tserpesa, K.I., Papanikos, P., 2005. Finite element modeling of single-walled carbon nanotubes. Compos. B 36, 468–477.

Van-den Bergh, B.A.I., Vroom, J., Gerritsen, H., Junginger, H.E., Bouwstra, J.A., 1999. Interactions of elastic and rigid vesicles with human skin in vitro: electron microscopy. Biochim. Biophys. Acta 1461, 155–173.

Valenzuela-Salas, L.M., Girón-Vázquez, N.G., García-Ramos, J.C., Torres-Bugarín, O., Gómez, C., Pestryakov, A., et al., 2019. Antiproliferative and antitumour effect of nongenotoxic silver nanoparticles on melanoma models. Oxid. Med. Cell. Longev 2019, 4528241.

Venugopal, J., Prabhakaran, M.P., Low, S., Choon, A.T., Zhang, Y.Z., Deepika, G., et al., 2008. Nanotechnology for nanomedicine and delivery of drugs. Curr. Pharm. Des. 14 (22), 2184–2200.

Venuganti, V.V.K., Saraswathy, M., Dwivedi, C., Kaushik, R.S., Perumal, O.P., 2015. Topical gene silencing by iontophoretic delivery of an antisense oligonucleotide–dendrimer nanocomplex: the proof of concept in a skin cancer mouse model. Nanoscale 7, 3903–3914.

Vlăsceanu, G.M., Marin, Ş., Ţiplea, R.E., Bucur, I.R., Lemnaru, M., Marin, M.M., et al., 2016. Chapter 2-silver nanoparticles in cancer therapy. In: Grumezescu, A.M. (Ed.), Nanobiomaterials in Cancer Therapy. William Andrew Publishing, pp. 29–56.

Vu, M.T., Le, N.T.T., Pham, T.L.-B., Nguyen, N.H., Nguyen, D.H., 2020. Development and characterization of soy lecithin liposome as potential drug carrier systems for codelivery of letrozole and paclitaxel. J. Nanomater 8896455. Available from: https://doi.org/10.1155/2020/8896455.

Wadhwa, A., Aljabbari, A., Lokras, A., Foged, C., Thakur, A., 2020. Opportunities and challenges in the delivery of mRNA-based vaccines. Pharmaceutics 12 (2), 102.

Woźniak, M., Nowak, M., Lazebna, A., Więcek, K., Jabłońska, I., Szpadel, K., et al., 2021. The comparison of in vitro photosensitizing efficacy of curcumin-loaded liposomes following photodynamic therapy on melanoma MUG-Mel2, squamous cell carcinoma SCC-25, and normal keratinocyte HaCaT cells. Pharmaceuticals 14, 374. Available from: https://doi.org/10.3390/ph14040374.

Xie, F., Li, R., Shu, W., Zhao, L., Wan, J., 2022. Self-assembly of Peptide dendrimers and their bio-applications in theranostics. Mater. Today Bio 14, 100239. Available from: https://doi.org/10.1016/j.mtbio.2022.100239.

Yang, Z., Ma, Y., Zhao, H., Yuan, Y., Kim, B.Y., 2020. Nanotechnology platforms for cancer immunotherapy. Wiley Interdiscip. Reviews: Nanomed. Nanobiotechnol. 12 (2), e1590.

Yadav, S., Sharma, A.K., Kumar, P., 2020. Nanoscale self-assembly for therapeutic delivery. Front. Bioeng. Biotechnol 8. Available from: https://doi.org/10.3389/fbioe.2020.00127.

Yadav, K., Singh, D., Singh, M.R., 2021. Nanovesicles delivery approach for targeting steroid mediated mechanism of antipsoriatic therapeutics. J. Drug Deliv. Sci. Technol 65, 102688ISSN 1773-2247. Available from: https://doi.org/10.1016/j.jddst.2021.102688.

Yadav, P., Mimansa, Munawara, R., Kapoor, K., Chaturvedi, S., Kailasam, K., et al., 2022. Nontoxic in vivo clearable nanoparticle clusters for theranostic applications. ACS Biomater. Sci. Eng 8, 2053−2065.

Ye, Y., Wang, J., Sun, W., Bomba, H.N., Gu, Z., 2019. Topical and transdermal nanomedicines for cancer therapy. Nanotheranostics for Cancer Applications. Springer, Cham, pp. 231−251.

Yokoyama, M., 2014. Polymeric micelles as drug carriers: their lights and shadows. J. Drug. Target. 22, 576−583. Available from: https://doi.org/10.3109/1061186X.2014.934688.

Zhang, X., 2015. Gold nanoparticles: recent advances in the biomedical applications. Cell Biochem. Biophys 72, 771−775.

Zhou, Q., Zhang, L., Yang, T., Wu, H., 2018. Stimuli-responsive polymeric micelles for drug delivery and cancer therapy. Int. J. Nanomed. 13, 2921.

Zuco, V., Supino, R., Righetti, S.C., Cleris, L., Marchesi, E., Gambacorti-Passerini, C., et al., 2002. Selective cytotoxicity of betulinic acid on tumor cell lines, but not on normal cells. Cancer Lett. 175 (1), 17−25.

Zuo, S., Song, J., Zhang, J., He, Z., Sun, B., Sun, J., 2021. Nano-immunotherapy for each stage of cancer cellular immunity: which, why, and what? Theranostics 11 (15), 7471.

Multifunctional nanocomposites for targeted drug delivery in breast cancer therapy

Poornima Agrawal[1],*, **Sakshi Soni[1],***, **Shivangi Agarwal[1]**, **Tanweer Haider[1]**, **Arun K. Iyer[2,3]**, **Vandana Soni[1]** and **Sushil K. Kashaw[1]**

[1]Department of Pharmaceutical Sciences, Dr. Harisingh Gour University (A Central University), Sagar, Madhya Pradesh, India
[2]Use-inspired Biomaterials & Integrated Nano Delivery (U-BiND) Systems Laboratory, Department of Pharmaceutical Sciences, Wayne State University, Detroit, MI, United States
[3]Molecular Imaging Program, Karmanos Cancer Institute, Detroit, MI, United States

6.1 Introduction

In 2020, there were approximately 10.0 million deaths and 19.3 million new cases recorded of cancer worldwide, and being one of the deadliest diseases, it will affect 29.5 million new people and cause 16.3 million deaths by 2040 (Sung et al., 2021). Detection of cancer has significantly impaired a patient's ability to lead a normal life and in addition to pain, suffering, had called for lengthy stays in hospitals and unofficial care. These obligations do not leave without impacting one's financial and social strings as well. Since the first half of the 20th century, when surgery, radiation, and chemotherapy were combined, there have been significant advancements in the treatment of cancer, increasing the life expectancy of those who are affected by it. One of the most commonly faced difficulties in chemotherapy is development of resistance of cancer cells towards the drugs administered. For which recent attention has been focused on simultaneous delivery of two or more therapeutic agents because it may result in more effective anticancer outcomes. Along with regimen of therapy, its early detection has been the most crucial part for its successful treatment, but current detection techniques have also posed sensitivity limitations. Numerous conventional anticancer drug therapies have begun showing low efficacy and high morbidity (Feldman, 2019). Keeping all these scenarios in mind nanoscale materials' distinctive physical properties can be used to create new and efficient cancer diagnostic tools, tumor imaging tools, and cancer therapeutics. Engineering responsive and multifunctional composite systems is made possible by functionalizing inorganic nanoparticles with biocompatible polymers and naturally occurring or artificially created biomolecules

---

* Authors with equal contribution.

(Dash et al., 2021). Even though only a few of these developments have reached human clinical trials to date, nanocomposite materials based on functionalized metal and semiconductor nanoparticles have the potential to completely alter how cancer is detected and treated. Drug delivery to the targeted tissue, cell, or organs (subcellular targeting) is more precise and effective with targeted nanocomposites, and the risk of side effects is reduced. With less drug removal from the system, these nanosystems deliver drugs to tumor areas in passive and active modes (Raj et al., 2021). The biodistribution of chemotherapy drugs in the body as well as the effectiveness of nanocarriers are significantly influenced by the size and surface properties of nanoparticles. Numerous types of nanocarriers, including polymers, dendrimers, liposome-based, and carbon-based ones, are being extensively researched in the treatment of cancer. Although the FDA has only approved a small number of nanotechnology-based cancer therapies, numerous studies are being conducted to create novel nanocarriers for effective cancer treatment (Alexiou et al., 2006). This chapter will help in refreshing about various types of nanocomposites designed, materials improvised and catering the requirements of delivery, along with various strategies adopted for effective delivery of developed systems on cancerous sites.

6.2 Types of nanoparticles in cancer therapy

6.2.1 Liposomes and polymeric micelles

With discovery of liposomes since 1960 (Bangham et al., 1965), they have been utilized by frame in delivery as multifunctional carrier systems for target specific cells by adding specialized components like antibodies, proteins, or suitable compounds that target certain receptor sites. Their suitability in terms of mimicking the cellular components and further modifications catered with time have led to its receptivity as leading carrier to deliver therapeutics on site. Their adaptability to carry drugs in combinational form specially in case of cancer have welcomed their use even more along with their crucial concentrating property on location (Noble et al., 2004). The way HER2-positive breast cancer is treated and is constantly changing. The creation of monoclonal antibody-based therapeutics was one of the interesting developments in the treatment of breast cancer. Antibody therapeutics have revolutionized the treatment of cancer over the past few decades. Antibodies as antibody–drug conjugates (ADCs) have been in trend recently but their high molecular weight have hindered their journey further to a limit. In certain ways, immunoliposomes offer an ADC-complimentary—and even superior—drug delivery approach. Elamir et al. created monoclonal antibody Trastuzumab-functionalized TRA immunoliposomes loaded with calcein and doxorubicin along with readily exposing it to low-frequency ultrasound (LFUS), power densitizing the drug released, allowing greater cellular uptake in shorter period of time through both membrane fusion and receptor-mediated endocytosis pathways traversed by TRA-liposomes (Di et al., 2020). Further extrapolating the use of liposomes as carrier, Avanzo et al. studied the effect of targeting gC1q receptor (gC1qR)/p32 proteins overexpressed in breast cancer cells and checking the combined effect of Doxorubicin (DOX) and sorafenib (SRF) loaded in liposomes in both 2D and 3D breast cancer cell models. It was also seen that primary M2 macrophages partially adsorbed LinTT1-functionalized liposomes as well as they along with cancer associated fibroblasts also expressed p32 protein, which further concentrated the dual drug concentration in the core of tumor of cells (d'Avanzo et al., 2021). Dealing further with the complexity of anticancer drugs, polymeric micelles are investigated as potential carriers solving problems related to solubility and bioavailability of drugs (Majumder et al., 2020). Micelles are of different types depending on changes made in composition as well as environment for achieving desired therapeutic action like RNA based micelles (Shu et al., 2018), photothermal/photodynamic responsive micelles (Xing et al., 2019), and physical stimuli responsive micelles (Rapoport, 2007), including enzyme responsive (Yan et al., 2020), pH sensitive (Guo et al., 2019), dual targeted biodegradable micelles (Jelonek et al., 2019), respectively. Micelles are colloidal suspensions made up of phospholipids, fatty acids, fatty acid salts (soap), or other like substances of amphiphilic nature that self-assemble into a structure with both hydrophobic and hydrophilic regions in aqueous solution ranging in the range of 5—100 nm (Hanafy et al., 2018). A novel formulation was prepared by Zhang et al. containing a new photosensitizer (BIIB021) that targets the mitochondria that is based on IR780 iodide and a heat shock protein 90 inhibitor to accumulate passively following NIR radiation and achieved high level of biocompatibility and biological stability, with encapsulation effectiveness of roughly 84% (Zhang et al., 2021).

6.2.2 Dendrimers

Dendrimers, reported for the very first time by Dr. Donald Tomalia in 1985, are three-dimensional polymeric structure influenced by a tree's branches whose basic architectural design decides the amount and type of drug being loaded. Different dendritic platforms have been created and investigated as drug delivery systems, including polyamidoamine (PAMAM), poly (propylene imine) (PPI), poly-L-lysine, melamine, poly (ether hydroxylamine) (PEHAM), poly (ester amine) (PEA), and polyglycerol (Madaan et al., 2014). Targeted administration is made possible by the fusion of nanocarriers with antibodies that bind to certain membrane receptors overexpressing in cancer cells. Human epidermal growth factor receptor-2 is overexpressed in more than 20% of breast tumors (HER-2). To precisely target SKBR-3 HER-2 positive cells, in breast cancer trastuzumab was employed by Marcinkowska et al., in the current trial as a PAMAM-drug-trastuzumab combination containing paclitaxel (ptx) or docetaxel (doc). Improved cellular uptake and efficacious targeting was achieved (Marcinkowska et al., 2019).

Adding on to improving the triple negative breast cancer (TNBC) therapy, and making use of the accelerated metabolism and high glucose requirements of cancer cells over-express a series of GLUT transporters which were targeted by glycosylated MTX-loaded one step PAMAM dendrimers were prepared by Torres et al., and were found to be substantially more potent than free MTX decreasing the cell viability by up to 20%, primarily in MDA-MB-231 cells (Torres-Pérez et al., 2020). Cai et al., explored siRNA administration, using bio-reducible fluorinated peptide dendrimers (BFPD) for delivery (Cai et al., 2017). In cancer therapy dendrimers have been used for diagnostic applications as well (Rai et al., 2020).

6.2.3 Mesoporous silica nanoparticles

Mesoporous silicas discovered first by Kuroda and coworkers of Japan and Mobil Oil USA researchers in 1990 are surfactant molecules that self-assembled provided as templates for condensation of the precursors of silica encompassing them, which served as excellent source of surface functionalization manifesting greater pore volume and surface area. These properties of working other than zeolites were explored for development of drug delivery matrices (Manzano and Vallet-Regí, 2020). Increasing the mono-dispersibility and reproducibility of MSNs, Lohiya et al., developed chitosan coated MSN which helped in imparting a pH responsive character to the system achieving EGF receptor-mediated targeting by doxorubicin-loaded, aptamer-coated mesoporous silica nanoparticle (MSN) bioconjugates concentrating on breast cancer cells (EGFR/HER2) achieving desired drug release kinetics (Lohiya and Katti, 2022). Delivering of antibody was mediated through creating a conjugate between MSN surface and Transtuzumab and Mozafarinia et al., predicted the impact of pH on the interaction of doxorubicin with these amine NH_2 modified MSNs, making the use of quantum chemical modeling. Formulation was able to achieve specific targeting and appropriate size and volume (Mozafarinia et al., 2021). MSNs have garnered a lot of scholarly attention and publications, but the Food and Drug Administration (FDA) has not yet given the technology its seal of approval for use in medical procedures. In order to do that, it is crucial to consider the potential biodistribution, clearance pathways, and ultimate destiny of these nanoparticles within the body. They being able to incorporate both inorganic and organic molecules in their surface can be used to alter the dissolution rates of MSNs depending upon the property imparted by them (Li et al., 2012).

6.2.4 Quantum dots

Ekimov and Onushenko initially described quantum dots (QDs), as nanoscale size from 2 to 10 nm semiconductor inorganic fluorophoric crystals with modifiable optical characteristics often made up of elements from the periodic table's groups II—VI, III—IV, and IV—VI (such as Cd, Pb, and Hg). The ternary I-III-VI QDs (where I is

Cu or Ag, III is Ga or In, and VI is S or Se) have been created more recently by researchers. By having a control over their size, scientists have been able to play with their quantum yield, controllable light emission, and excellent chemical and photostability (Jamieson et al., 2007). The workable narrow range of excitation spectrum, along with the width of the emission spectrum has been responsible for their diversified use in bioimaging (Lim et al., 2015). The suitability and selectivity of carbon quantum dots CQDs for tumor-specific imaging and medication administration due to their flexible functionalization was seen in anticancer therapy via designing of large amino acid mimicking LAAM CQDs that include paired -carboxyl and amino groups on their edges and checking their multivalent interactions with Large amino acid transporters LAT overexpressed in tumors. Li et al. discovered that LAAM TC-CQDs, a subclass of LAAM CQDs made from 1,4,5,8-tetraminoanthraquinone (TAAQ) and citric acid (CA), are able to scan and distribute chemotherapeutic medications to tumors, including brain tumors, as well as perform near-infrared (NIR) fluorescence and photoacoustic (PA) imaging. Unlike conventional CQDs, LAAM CQDs can scan and deliver therapeutic chemicals to tumors with precision (Li et al., 2020). Diseases like acute kidney injury, a result of excess reactive oxygen species (ROS) generation in the kidneys, pectized as major cause of hospital mortalities due to renal failure were tried to be mitigated by CQDs and graphene quantum dots GQDs. Antioxidants currently on the market for the treatment of AKI frequently fall short of the necessary antioxidative effectiveness or renal accumulation rate. Wang et al., proposed, phenol-like group functionalized graphene quantum dots (h-GQDs) with excellent ROS scavenging effectiveness and renal specificity for AKI antioxidative treatment, inspired by the structure of natural phenolic antioxidant. And reported that the clinical antioxidant N-acetylcysteine (NAC) can successfully protect the kidneys from oxidative damage with only a one-sixteenth dose of h-GQDs, and there is no sign of toxicity (Wang et al., 2020). Fatima et al., reported the HER2 receptor, Herceptin (trastuzumab) conjugation with quantum dots for efficient targeting, bioimaging, and localized treatment of breast cancer via intravenous delivery where killing of cancer cells was through release of free radicals as major cause (Fatima et al., 2021).

6.2.5 Gold nanoparticles

A great deal of technological interest has been shown in Au NPs because of their easy to synthesize procedures, distinctive optical characteristics, biomedical, cancer therapy applications, acting as a contrast agent, dose enhancer in kilovoltage cone-beam computed tomography, radiotherapy guided nanoparticle-enhanced therapy and effective radiosensitizers in medical applications such as drug delivery and cancer therapy (Kong et al., 2017). With advancement in therapeutic deliveries to subcellular compartment for achieving desired localized efficacy Mitoxantrone was delivered by Jafarizad et al., in gold Au nanoparticles modified for pH sensitive drug delivery along with thiolates and disulfides in MCF cell lines of breast cancer. They proved efficacy for passive targeting (Jafarizad et al., 2017). Their image and pathway illumination properties have led to development of nanotags based on the 3D surface enhanced Raman spectroscopy (SERS) where Kapara et al., in MCF-7 ER-positive human breast cancer cells, studied the effect of SERS to monitor cellular uptake and localization of AuNPs functionalized with an anti-ER (estrogen receptor alpha) antibody under various conditions, such as temperature and dynamin inhibition. The data obtained was interpreted using Fiji image processing package by accounting for the cell area following SERS mapping and the nanotag pixel counts. Instead of quantifying the overall amount of nanotags in the cells, an estimation of the SERS response for each individual cell was made. This method, succored we were able to locate the nanotags, estimate the SERS signal per cell area, quantify the pixels that matched to this signal, and enabled comparisons across several samples (Jafarizad et al., 2017).

6.2.6 Silver nanoparticles

Due to their diverse commercial uses in many different fields, such as functionalization, bioimaging, targeting, noble metal nanostructures of silver owing to their distinct photothermal, chemical, and optical properties, nanometer size, they put forth various workable combinations of large surface-to-volume ratios, chemically as well as physical reactive surfaces of nanostructures for naive functionalization with various biological stabilizing agents, biomolecules, and chemotherapeutic agents. Their amazing optical capabilities derived from a singular one on one interaction with light causes a localized surface plasmon resonance (LSPR), or collective coherent oscillation of their free conduction band electrons. Silver nanoparticles (AgNPs), which have unique surface plasmon resonance and surface functionalization, are regarded as the most useful modern material (Ivanova, 2018). Giving importance to nontoxic eco-friendly procedures of synthesis Gomathi et al., reported the anabolic property of fruit shell of Tamarindus indica tree extract to produce silver nanoparticles for breast cancer treatment (Gomathi, 2020). Use of herbal extracts for preparation of silver nanoparticles was seen with Cuminum (Dinparvar et al., 2020), anabaena flos aquae (Ebrahimzadeh et al., 2020), chitosan (Gounden et al., 2021), acacia Luciana flower extract (Sargazi et al., 2020) also for breast cancer therapy. For promising hybrid therapies Ponsanti et al., created mesoporous silica nanoparticles-silver nanoparticles (MSNs-AgNPs) for detection of HER2-positive breast cancer cells using colorimetric methods in which sensors for the detection of breast cancer depended on using 3Dporous MSNs structure as base platform for loading of AgNPs' redox activity to trigger a colorimetric response. Through antigen/antibody recognition, site-specific targeting of breast cancer cells was made possible by the surface functionalization of MSNs with anti-HER2 antibodies, increasing sensitivity and amplifying colorimetric responses (Ponsanti et al., 2022).

6.2.7 Carbon nanotubes

It was during the fullerene synthesis that, Iijima and associates discovered carbon nanotubes as descendant of this reaction in 1990s (Dresselhaus, 2000). With further performing of experimentation using electric arc discharge, laser ablation, and chemical vapor deposition (CVD) (methods of synthesis) and recording observations making use of high-resolution TEM, scanning tunneling microscopy (STM), conductance, and Raman scattering a recognizable rolled-up seamless cylinders of graphene sheets with sp2 linked carbon atoms arranged into a honeycomb shape as a flat graphene sheet were identified as single-walled carbon nanotubes. It was due of their size ranging between 0.4 to 100 nm, while their length reaching maximum to few micrometers, biocompatibility, stability, extremely appreciated ultra-high aspect ratio, high cargo loading, intracellular bioavailability, and high solubility raised their acceptance quotient when compared to other nanocarriers based on carbon like (fullerenes, carbon nanotubes, graphene, cones) (Kiran et al., 2020). Because CNTs are lipophilic, which causes cellular buildup and toxicity, they have been functionalized (f-CNT) to overcome this intrinsic drawback. CNT functionalization is of various types: those with covalent and noncovalent modifications (Jampilek and Kralova, 2021). CNTs depending on their size and loading capacity are divided into two groups: single-walled multiwalled CNTs with single graphene cylinders they are smaller, both versatile and helpful for imaging, and multiwalled CNTs (MWCNTs) are a complex cylinder nesting in graphene, with improved surface area expansion and endohedral filling (Venkataraman et al., 2019). The challenge of breast cancer cell recognition was addressed by Ozgen et al., via simultaneously enabled dual-targeting therapy thanks to the synergistic benefits of either noncovalent or covalent functionalized CNTs with biocompatible glycoblock copolymers that promote effective stimuli drug release.

In order to create a successful nanocarrier system for a targeted drug delivery method, a unique combination of Dox-conjugated glycoblock copolymers with CNTs was presented, where using one-step noncovalent or covalent functionalization technique either the alkynyl group-decorated CNT surface was functionalized with poly(1-O-methacryloyl—D-fructopyranose-b-(2-methacryloxyethoxy)benzaldehyde)-N3/Dox via a copper catalyzed azide alkyne click reaction (CuAAC) or the carboxylic acid-modified CNT surface was functionalized with poly(1-O). Enhancing the interactions between glycoblocks, water solubility, and biocompatibility as main objective in breast cancer cell lines (Ozgen et al., 2020).

6.2.8 Super para-magnetic iron oxide nanoparticles

Often the things that have the most value or quality are little/small, science is no exception when talked in terms of drug delivery systems being welcomed with each passing day. The reasons of complications emerging in our biosystem when recognized at molecular level pave pathways for coining out therapies at molecular size and level at the same time. Metal oxides nanoparticles which could be synthesized by both biological or chemical method and especially those composed of iron oxide (an element being part of human biome as the chelator of hemoglobin comprised of Fe(II) atoms) possess an antique character due to its superparamagnetic nature (Dulińska-Litewka et al., 2019). Additionally, superparamagnetic iron oxide nanoparticles (SPIONs) mostly magnetite (Fe_3O_4), maghemite (γ-Fe_2O_3), and ferrites are usually crystalline in nature which demonstrate excellent magnetic resonance imaging and are relatively harmless when compared to nanoparticles containing manganese and gadolinium. When subjected to an alternating magnetic field (AMF), they exhibit photothermal and magnetic heating capabilities as well as strong biocompatibility. These qualities make them desirable candidates for potential application in thermotherapy, MRI contrast, and drug delivery systems Superparamagnetic Iron Oxide Nanoparticles (SPIONs) mostly magnetite (Fe_3O_4), maghemite (γ-Fe_2O_3) and ferrites are usually crystalline in nature (Zhi et al., 2020). Exploring their theranostic potential Khaniabadi et al., designed a single integrated nanoprobe, of Fe_3O_4 nanoparticles (IONs) for the detection and treatment of cancer. And in order to create the trastuzumab TZ-conjugated SPION-porphyrin [ION-PP-TZ], oleylamin-coated IONs (ION-Ol) were manufactured and the surface of the IONs were changed using protoporphyrin (PP) and (TZ). After exposing MCF 7 cells to different Fe concentrations of nanoparticles and theranostic drugs, no cytotoxicity was seen (Khaniabadi et al., 2020). Further improvising the therapeutic potential of (SPIONs) Panda et al., prepared improved poly (D,L-lactide-co-glycolic acid)-based superparamagnetic nano-size carrier ideally in the lower nano-size range (200 nm) to accomplish effective cancer cell penetration and smart RES escape. To attain the requisite physicochemical properties, several crucial growth parameters were standardised and transport of DTX to breast cancer cells specifically was achieved (Panda et al., 2019).

6.3 Nanomaterials used for cancer

When molecular diagnosis of diseases took our vision from surface of biosystem to subcellular organelles, intrinsic as well as extrinsic pathways, de novo mechanisms of microenvironment as well as cellular physiology, their came an evolution of simultaneous exploration of materials that could be exploited for deliverance of more than one means. The parallel experiment runned by scientists for deducing functionalization, therapeutic potential, localization, transformation of moieties for better loading capacities, drug release studies were conducted. Various nanomaterials used and developed for drug loading, bioimaging, biosensing shall be discussed in the table below (Table 6.1).

6.4 Strategies for targeting of nanoparticles at requisite site

Nanoparticles (NPs) are atomic clusters of crystalline or amorphous structure that possess unique physical and chemical properties associated with a size range of between 1 and 100 nm. Their nano-sized dimensions, which are in the same range as those of vital biomolecules, such as antibodies, membrane receptors, nucleic acids, and proteins, allow them to interact with different structures within living organisms. Because of these features, numerous nanoparticles are used in medicine as delivery agents for biomolecules. However, off-target drug delivery can cause serious side effects to normal tissues and organs. Considering this issue, it is essential to develop bioengineering strategies to significantly reduce systemic toxicity and improve therapeutic effect. The conventional approach to cancer therapy resulted in minimal anticancer drug accumulation at the required tumor location, as well as off-target consequences. As a result, numerous ways for targeting and delivering anticancer drugs at the required region have been developed and used to get the best possible response in cancer therapy employing nanoparticles (Lila and Ishida, 2017). The major tactics for delivering anticancer medicines to the tumor site are passive targeting (with improved permeability and retention effect) and active targeting (Deshpande et al., 2013; L Arias, 2011; Lila and Ishida, 2017; Piktel et al., 2016; Sawant and Torchilin, 2012). In contrast to passive delivery, nanosystems enable to obtain enhanced therapeutic efficacy, decrease the possibility of drug resistance, and reduce side effects of "conventional" therapy in cancers.

6.4.1 Enhanced permeability and retention effect

The enhanced permeability and retention (EPR) effect refers to the capacity of tiny nanoparticles and macromolecular medicines to accumulate in tumors more than in normal tissues. The EPR effect is caused by greater hole sizes in neo-vasculatures and poor lymphatic clearance in tumors, and it is greatly impacted by the size of tiny molecules, such as nanoparticles. The EPR effect has been proposed as an alternate delivery strategy for traditional anticancer medications, and a good bio-distribution of cancer therapeutic nanoparticles in blood would be regarded to obtain a high degree of accumulation in solid tumors (Yhee et al., 2013). In cancer therapy, conventional delivery techniques have a major interaction with the reticuloendothelial system (RES). The creation of a delivery system or nanocarriers that may escape being eliminated by bodily defense systems, such as phagocytosis, is referred to as passive targeting. Preparing PEGylated liposomes is one technique to extend circulation time,

Table 6.1 Nanomaterials and their functionalization for effective drug/sensor delivery.

Nanomaterial	Nanocarrier	Drug/imaging dye/sensor	Functionalization/surface modification/processing	Strategy	References
Carbon Allotropes based	Active Carbon	Fluorescent carbon dots	Banana Peel	One-step hydrothermal process	Strong, bright-blue photoluminescence (average diameter: 3–6 nm) was produced by the dispersion of carbon dots, applied for biosensing, electronics, and catalysis.	Nguyen et al. (2020)
	Carbon-based nanomaterials	Carbon Nanotubes	Doxorubicin	Doxorubicin, was conjugated with poly(1-O-methacryloyl-β-D-fructopyranose-b-(2-methacryloxyethoxy)) benzaldehyde glycoblock copolymers, by reversible addition−fragmentation chain transfer (RAFT) polymerization	Folic acid (FA) and the synthetic drug-conjugated glycoblock copolymers were independently coated on CNTs to create an effective drug delivery platform for simultaneously targeting the folic acid receptors (FR) and the glucose transporter protein (GLUT5) in breast cancer	Ozgen et al. (2020)
		CNT	Ginsenoside Rg3 is a component of puffed ginseng	–	Effect of CNTs-loaded Rg3 (Rg3-CNT) on the PD-1/PD-L1 signaling and the development of triple–negative breast cancer (TNBC) was checked	Luo et al. (2021)

Nanomaterial	Carrier	Drug	Description	Reference
Graphene and Graphene oxide	GO–PCH–g–HPG nanocarrier, and are encapsulated into pullulan nanofibers using electrospinning	Paclitaxel (PTX) and curcumin (Cur)	Hydroxyl groups at the edges of GO are grafted by poly (epichlorohydrin) (PCH) to form GO–PCH. Then, the hydroxyl end groups of PCH are grafted (g) with hyperbranched polyglycerol (HPG) leading to formation of oxygen-rich nanocarrier (GO–PCH–g–HPG)	For local anticancer applications, a co-drug-loaded graphene oxide-based nanocarrier is included in an electro spun composite	Asgari et al. (2021)
	Magnetic Nanoparticles	Camptothecin	4-hydroxycoumarin was cross-linked with reduced graphene oxide *via* an allylamine (AA) linker	CPT and 4-HC loaded carriers show higher toxicity effect against the human breast cancer cell line (MCF-7) compared with the normal fibroblast cell line (WS-1)	Vinothini et al. (2020)
Nanodiamonds	Polymer/ nanodiamond hybrids	Amonafide	Poly(1–O–methacryloyl-2,3:4,5–di–O–isopropylidene-β-d-fructopyranose)–b-poly (3-vinylbenzaldehyde-*co*-methyl methacrylate), is prepared by RAFT polymerization	Amonafide-conjugated to glycopolymers onto the surface of nanodiamonds via oxime ligation, which is acid degradable linkage used in breast cancer therapy	Zhao et al. (2018)
Fullerene	C_{60}–PEI Fullerenes cage	Doxorubicin	DOX was covalently conjugated onto C_{60}–PEI by the pH-sensitive hydrazone linkage	Combined chemotherapy and photodynamic therapy in one system	Shi et al. (2014)

(Continued)

Table 6.1 (Continued)

Nanomaterial	Nanocarrier	Drug/imaging dye/ sensor	Functionalization/surface modification/processing	Strategy	References
C_{60} Fullerenes	Nanoconstruct	Docetaxel	C_{60}-fullerenes were carboxylated, acylated and conjugated with the drug	Enhanced cancer cell cytotoxicity and better pharmacokinetic profile	Raza et al. (2015)
Carbon-based nanomaterials	Single-walled carbon nano-horns (SWNH)	Hypericin	–	Remarkable tumor cell death as well as tumor growth inhibition was proved via photothermal therapy and PDT of SWNH-Hypericin	Gao et al. (2019)
Nanoscale carrier material	Soporous Carbons	Doxorubicin DOX	Graphene oxide−polyethylene glycol GO-PEG-DOX complex	The GO-PEG-DOX combination has assisting effects on DOX-induced tumor cell death and can boost the water solubility and targeting sensitivity of DOX	Yan et al. (2018)
Carbon dots	Nanomicelle	Doxorubicin	Carbodiimide coupling agent was used to create the amphiphile stearic acid-g-polyethyleneimine functionalized with folic acid carbon dots	Reduction in dose	Sarkar et al. (2021)

Metal organic frameworks	Zn-based MOF	Microspheres	5-fluorouracil	Chitosan coated zinc-based metal-organic framework Zn-MOF with graphene oxide (CS/Zn-MOF@GO) microspheres as an anticancer drug carrier	pH-sensitive and sustained release pattern achieved	Pooresmaeil et al. (2021)
	Zr-based MOF	Zirconium-based porphyrinic (MOFs) (PCN-222)	Piperlongumine	Polyethylene glycol (PEG)-coated PCN-222 (PEG-PCN)	Sonodynamic therapy, which uses ultrasound (US) to create harmful reactive oxygen species (ROS) given along with nanosensitizers	Hoang (2022)
	Fe– based MOF	Nanoscale MOF	Doxorubicin Cisplatin	–	MOF based on Fe2 + to deliver Fe2 + to cancer cells to start the Fenton reaction and generate too much ROS	Xu et al. (2020)
Polysaccharide based	Chitosan	Nanoparticles	Doxorubicin	Modified with cell penetrating peptide (CPP)	Thermosensitive poly(N-vinylcaprolactam) (PNVCL)–chitosan (CS) nanoparticles	Niu et al. (2019)
	Dextran	Nanoparticles	Paclitaxel (PTX) and Docosahexanoic acid (DHA)	PTXand DHA were covalently coupled with dextran CMD to generate CMD-DHA-PTX with different linkers camino acids Gly-Gly or Lys-Gly-Gly	Dextran was combined with paclitaxel and DHA in order to create dual drug conjugates	Wang et al. (2022)

method known as passive targeting. The permeability, or leakiness, of cancer cells is increased. Furthermore, clogged lymphatic outflow leads to a build-up of macromolecules. The increased permeability and retention (EPR) effect is another term for the targeted technique (Barenholz, 2012; Zylberberg and Matosevic, 2016). By carefully considering the particle size of liposomes, the EPR effect may be maximized. Extravasation was shown to be greater in liposomes with particle sizes ranging from 40 to 200 nm. Recently, recommendations were made to strengthen the EPR effect in order to improve anticancer drug delivery to tumor locations. The major proposals are to employ an external or internal stimulation to promote cancer cell permeability (Maeda et al., 2013). Sang et al. (2020) developed the tumor-targeted redox controlled self-assembled nano-system with magnetic increased EPR effects (mPEG-HA/CSO-SS-Hex/SPION/GA) to increase the anticancer effectiveness of gambogic acid (GA). Three layers make up the nanosystem: the outer layer is made of mono-aminated poly (ethylene glycol) grafted hyaluronic acid (mPEG-HA), which can target the CD44 receptor in breast cancer cells; the middle layer is made of disulfide linked hexadecanol (Hex) and chitosan oligosaccharide (CSO), which can control the release of drugs by triggering a reduction response; and the inner On triple-negative breast cancer, the mPEG-HA/CSO-SS-Hex/SPION/GA nanosystem may aggregate at tumor locations and have good therapeutic benefits (TNBC).

6.4.2 Surface active targeting nanoparticles that have been functionalized with targeting ligands

Anticancer therapies, that is, drugs, are currently focused at the diseased tissue site, that is, tumor tissues, with less deposition in nontargeted tissues or with fewer off-target effects. (Maeda et al., 2013). This method, known as active targeting or ligand-based targeting, resulted in direct payload targeting at the required location. This entails attaching a targeting ligand to the surface of nanoparticles, which, when given to cancer-bearing mice, tracks and targets the diseased cells' receptors. Known as ligand targeted nanoparticles or targeted nanoparticles, these nanoparticles are used to target ligands (Torchilin, 2010). Active targeting ligands have been added to lipids directly or at the distal end of PEG chains (Patel et al., 2007). By using a postinsertion approach, the ligand-lipid-PEG conjugate micelles can be incorporated into nanoparticles that have already been prepared. In this process, stealth nanoparticles with PEG on the surface are incubated with micelles resulting in the creation of targeted nanoparticles. The ligand, i.e. the lipid-PEG-ligand combination, is incorporated, into the nanoparticles formation process is another extensively used technique based on standard liposome formulation methods (Saul et al., 2003; Torchilin, 2006). In three approaches, the cell penetrating peptide (CPP) has been proposed to help deliver anticancer medicines via nanocarriers such liposomes: (1) drug molecule covalent conjugation with a

CPP; (2) drug encapsulation in CPP-attached nanocarriers, such as liposomes; and (3) physical adsorption of medicines with CPPs by electrostatic complexation (Ye et al., 2016). Optimization of ligand density on the liposomes surface utilizing applicable surface engineering techniques is a crucial part of customizing a targeted liposomal system. Increased ligand density above an acceptable level might cause problems such aggregation (Feng and Mumper, 2013). Furthermore, targeting ligands improves liposome internalization in cancer cells (Benhabbour et al., 2012). Active targeting has another benefit, viz less nonspecific distribution to undesirable tissues (Fathi and Oyelere, 2016). Li et al. (2017) describes novel active targeting based on the large amino acid transporter 1 (LAT1), which is overexpressed in a number of malignancies. For PLGA nanoparticles that target LAT1, glutamate was coupled to polyoxyethylene stearate as a targeting ligand. The tumor accumulation and anticancer effects of the LAT1 targeting nanoparticles were better.

6.4.2.1 On the surface of cancer cells, overexpressed receptors are targeted

In cancer cells, many receptors are overexpressed as compared to normal cells. Overexpressed receptors must be targeted because they provide the foundation of active targeting, which results in greater anticancer drug absorption and accumulation in cancer cells at the tumor site (Bertrand et al., 2014). Fig. 6.1 depicts external and intracellular sites for active anticancer drug targeting in cancer treatment. EGFR, also known as HER1, is a protein that is overexpressed in various solid tumors, colorectal

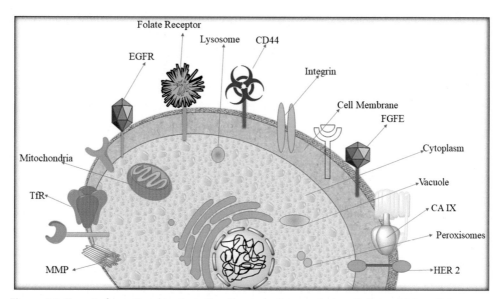

Figure 6.1 Targets for active drug targeting in cancer therapy (extracellular and intracellular receptors or overexpressed proteins). Organelles, such as lysosomes and mitochondria etc.

cancer (CRC), nonsmall cell lung cancer (NSCLC), breast, ovary, and prostate cancer are among the most common cancers. EGFR (HER1), HER2 (HER3), and HER4 (HER4) are the four receptors in the EGFR family (Iqbal and Iqbal, 2014; Krasinskas, 2011). Fibroblast Growth Factor Receptors (FGFRs) are transmembrane tyrosine kinases that are targeted. There are four members of the FGFR family: FGFR 1, FGFR 2, FGFR 3, and FGFR 4. When these receptors bind to fibroblast growth factors (FGFs), intracellular signaling is activated. Many malignancies, including prostate, bladder, and lung tumors, have high levels of all four FGFRs (Haugsten et al., 2010; Lin et al., 2015).

Folate Receptors are surface receptors that are overexpressed in a variety of cancer cells, including lung, breast, and prostate cancer (Low et al., 2008). Transferrin (Tf) is a carrier protein for serum iron ($Fe3+$) with a molecular weight of around 80 kDa. TfRs (TfR1 and TfR2 or CD77) are transferrin (Tf) receptors that are found on the cell surface. Endocytosis is used to internalize the Tf-TfR complex (Heath et al., 2013). Transferrin receptors are overexpressed in malignancies due to increased iron requirement by cancer cells. The therapeutic effect of TfR-targeted doxorubicin liposomes against liver cancer was enhanced (Li et al., 2009).

6.4.2.2 Over-expressed receptors in the cytoplasm and nucleus directly target the desired organelle

Anticancer drugs should be delivered specifically to the intended organelle inside the cytoplasm rather than to the organelles in general. Drugs that target lysosomes and mitochondria is studies here. The transfer of drug load to mitochondria is successful using nanocomposites containing triphenylphosphonium (TPP) a ligand molecule. Paclitaxel liposomes with TPP or rhodamine 123 targeting ligand displayed mitochondrial targeting and increased cytotoxicity when compared to nontargeted liposomes. Dual-functional paclitaxel nanocomposites with pH responsiveness and mitochondrial targeting have recently been discovered (Jiang et al., 2015). Ceramides cause permeability in the lysosome membrane when they are targeted towards the lysosome. Ceramide administration to lysosomes utilizing transferrin modified liposomes resulted in enhanced cancer cell killing (Koshkaryev et al., 2012). Overexpressed receptors in the cell cytoplasm and nucleus include Cyclooxygenase-2 (COX-2) in the cytosol and Peroxisome Proliferator Activated Receptor- (PPAR-) in the nucleus. Peroxisome proliferator-activated receptor (PPAR-) is a nuclear receptor protein that may be targeted. A significant amount of PPAR-mRNA was observed in CRC cancer tissues (Sarraf et al., 1998). The enzyme prostaglandin H2 synthase, also known as cyclooxygenase (COX), catalyzes the conversion of arachidonic acid (AA) to prostaglandin H2 (PG). Inflammation is aided by PGs (Pablos et al., 1999). COX-2 is overexpressed in a variety of malignancies, including prostate, colorectal, and lung tumors (Gupta et al., 2000). Inhibition of a cancer's route might be used as a treatment or preventative technique. Several transient receptors potential Melastatin (TRPM2, TRPM4, TRPM7, TRPM8) and GPCRs in triple-negative breast cancer (TNBC) are essential for the development, survival, and metastasis of breast cancer cells, and individuals with breast cancer often have somatic mutations that impair TRPM6 (Wong and Hussain, 2020; Feigin et al., 2014). The growth and metastasis of cancers are influenced by a variety of growth factors and their receptors. A family of receptors called receptor tyrosine kinases (RTKs) is crucial for the development of cancer (Butti et al., 2018). The nuclear receptor superfamily of transcription factors, which includes the estrogen receptors (ER), plays a major role in mediating the effects of estrogen. Complex processes, including extensive alternative splicing of ER, transcription factors, epigenetic control of ER expression, and post-transcriptional regulation of ER expression, underlie the abnormal expression of ER in breast cancer and other kinds of human malignancies (Hua et al., 2018).

6.4.2.3 Tumor microenvironments targeting

Overexpressed receptors in the tumor microenvironment/tumor vasculature/endothelium of tumur neovasculature, such as tumor blood vessels, are being targeted. The creation of new blood vessels is required to give blood to tumors in order for them to grow. The breakdown of a tumor's vasculature (the arrangement of blood vessels in an organ) slows cancer cell proliferation. In the tumor microenvironment, several receptors are overexpressed, and they can be targeted for efficient anticancer drug delivery to the desired location (Linton et al., 2016). VEGFR, VCAMs (e.g., vascular cell-adhesion molecule 1 (VCAM 1)), MMPs (e.g., membrane type-1-MMP (MT1-MMP)), and integrins are examples of such targets. Fig. 6.2 depicts active medication targeting targets in the tumor microenvironment or vasculature in cancer treatment.

VCAMs (Vascular Cell-Adhesion Molecules) are involved in the inflammatory process and can be targeted. VCAM 1 is an antigen that has been found to be overexpressed in NSCLC cells and cancer vasculature (Fotis et al., 2012; Zylberberg and Matosevic, 2016). VCAM 1 targeted liposomes accumulated in tumor blood arteries in mice with tumor xenograft, according to one research (Gosk et al., 2008). Integrins are transmembrane glycoproteins that are overexpressed in tumor cells with neovascular epithelial cells. RGD (Arg-Gly-Asp) is a tripeptide with a high affinity for integrins. To target integrins, liposomes were combined with RGD. The drug concentration in tumor cells was higher in RGD liposomes with encapsulated paclitaxel than in nontargeted paclitaxel liposomes (Meng et al., 2011). MMPs (matrix-metalloproteases) are a type of enzyme (protein) that may breakdown extracellular matrix (ECM) and help the body make new blood cells (angiogenesis) (Handsley and Edwards, 2005). On tumor tissues, Many MMPs are expressed, including MT1-MMP. In HT 1080 cancer cells, anti-MT1-MMP Fab liposomes encapsulated with doxorubicin demonstrated a greater cellular uptake than nontargeted liposomes (with overexpressed MT1-MMP)

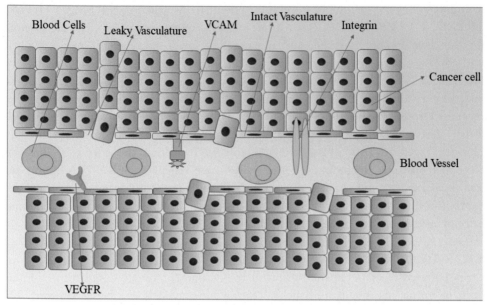

Figure 6.2 Active medication targeting in cancer therapy: targets in the tumor microenvironment or vasculature (receptors or overexpressed proteins).

(Cathcart et al., 2015). CD44 (Cluster-of-Difference 44) is a receptor protein (transmembrane adhesion molecule). It is overexpressed in a variety of cancers, including the colon, breast, and others. Because CD44 is a hyaluronic acid-specific receptor, doxorubicin-loaded hyaluronic acid-modified mesoporous silica nanoparticles were created to target it. Cancer cells showed more cytotoxicity than nontarget silica particles (Ye et al., 2016). Cellular, soluble, and physical components makeup the TME in breast cancer. Local (intratumoral), regional (breast), and metastatic compartments can be found within the cellular components. The term "local compartment" describes the biological characteristics of the tumor cells as well as the inflammatory cells that have infiltrated the tumor, such as lymphocytes, plasma cells, dendritic cells, macrophages, and neutrophils. The term "regional compartment" refers to the interaction between tumor cells and surrounding stromal cells, especially at the infiltrating edge, involving stromal fibroblasts, myoepithelial cells, adipocytes, endothelium and vascular/lymphatic endothelial cells. The host cells in lymph nodes and other distant organs are referred to be metastatic sites by the metastatic compartment when they produce new TME. The progression of tumors in the breast and at other places is also influenced by a number of soluble and physical variables, such as enzymes, cytokines, and growth factors (Li et al., 2021).

6.5 Stimuli-responsive functionalized nanocomposites

Stimuli cause nanocomposites to become unstable, allowing trapped material to escape. The primary stimuli utilized for improved delivery of anticancer drugs to the required place utilizing nanocomposites are listed below (Fig. 6.3).

6.5.1 Temperature responsive drug delivery materials

Thermo-responsive nanocomposites, or intelligent materials, are based on the use of temperature as a simple stimulus. They maintain a constant temperature of 37°C, which is body temperature. There is a variation in hydrogen bonding inside the matrix of a thermo-responsive polymer (Zangabad et al., 2018). A hydrogel is a kind of thermo-responsive polymer that undergoes a transition from the hydrolyzed to the precipitated phase in response to a temperature change, which is accompanied by a considerable volume shift. The polymer switches phases when the temperature decreases, and the transition temperature (which includes poly(acrylamide) and poly (acrylic acid) copolymers) is known as the upper critical solution temperature (UCST). Nanoconstructs constructed of dipalmitoylphosphatidylcholine (DPPC) and cholesterol released over 80% of the encapsulated methotrexate within 0.5 hours. Temperature sensitive liposomes are used in Thermodox, a commercial anticancer liposomal product (Celsion, Lawrenceville, NJ, USA). MSPC (1-myristoyl-2-stearoyl-sn-glycero-3-phosphocholine), which has a 40°C transition temperature, is one of the components. These intelligent polymeric systems' temperature-sensitive characteristics cause a phase

Figure 6.3 Various stimuli-responsive nanocomposites.

change that happens above or below a certain temperature. Thermoresponsive polymers are classified into two groups based on how they react to temperature changes: the first has a lower critical solution temperature (LCST), while the second has a higher critical solution temperature (UCST) (Fig. 6.4). Temperature responsive DDSs (Pippa et al., 2015) include properties like as tunability, design flexibility, and site-specific phase transition. PNIPAAm is the best researched temperature sensitive polymer, having a well-known and consistent LCST behavior (Gao et al., 2013). Depending on the solvent and chain modifications (Yoo et al., 2000), the LCST of PNIPAAm may range from 30°C to 35°C. Below the transition temperature of the LCST, polymers with transitional behavior are soluble and polymeric medium is swollen because of hydrogen bonds formed between molecules of water and the functional groups of incorporated polymer, making them ready to be loaded with drug molecules. When the temperature is increased beyond the LCST, a hydrophilic hydrophobic transition occurs accompanied by a change in morphology from coil-to-globule. During this transition, the hydrogen bonds and the network collapses, and the polymer becomes insoluble, leading to volumetric shrinkage and squeezing-out of internal water molecules. This transition results in release of the encapsulated cargo from the medium (Lue et al., 2011).

Shrinkage of a loaded polymer is shown in Fig. 6.1 as a result of LCST transition. As it is obvious, the shrinkage is accompanied with release of loaded drug (Cheng et al., 2015). Although this scheme refers to a cross-linked PNIPAAm hydrogel network, but same scenario is applicable in the case of polymeric micelles and so on (Bastakoti et al., 2015). Originally, LCST transition is related to the nature of polymer. Regardless of carrier state, that is, polymeric hydrogel or micelle and so on, below the LCST temperature, the polymeric medium is hydrophilic in nature, while above the LCST, it became hydrophobic. Increasing temperature beyond transitional temperature decrease solubility and volumetric features of carrier medium, leading to release

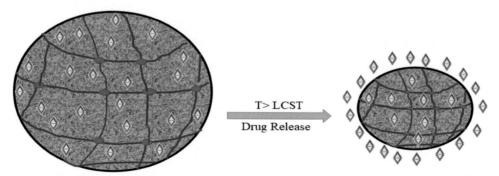

T> LCST

Drug Release

Figure 6.4 Shrinkage of a loaded hydrogel and release of drug during LCST behavior. *LCST*, lower critical solution temperature.

of loaded drug (Pennadam et al., 2004). On the other hand an increase in the polymer solubility can occur when the temperature rises above the UCST, resulting in the swelling of the carrier medium (Schmaljohann, 2006; Ward and Georgiou, 2011). It is worth noting that the volumetric change is reversible and it is termed "swelling-shrinkage" behavior (Cha et al., 2012).

6.5.1.1 Core-shell structures

Besides temperature-sensitive polymers such as hydrogels and micelles, core-shell nanostructures and even films have been also designed. Fig. 6.5 illustrates a commonly employed core-shell structure. The main polymer network which has been of particular interest is formed from poly(N-isopropyl acrylamide) (PNIPAAm). This polymeric network can undergo a volumetric phase transition after temperature elevation or by solvent uptake at low temperatures followed by swelling. After that phase transition, the swollen network then expels water and shrinks. Another common structure that has been used in drug carriers, is that of thermo-responsive star block copolymers that can encapsulate the drug between their branches. Xiaojie Li and his group (Li et al., 2011) developed a star-shaped block copolymer H40-PCL-b-P(OEGMA-co-AzPMA). The polymer micelle showed satisfactory drug-release properties, with controlled release at temperatures higher than the LCST temperature.

As a potential targeted method against breast cancer, temperature-sensitive liposomes filled with the dual drugs tamoxifen and imatinib are being developed.

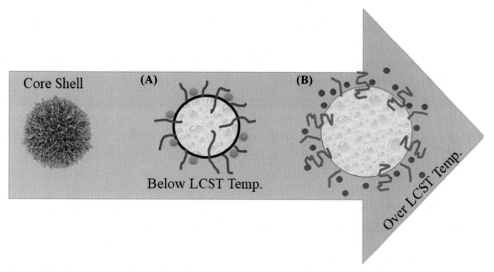

Figure 6.5 Schematic of drug release from a temperature responsive core-shell nanocarrier: (A) Below LCST temperature and (B) Over LCST temperature. *LCST*, lower critical solution temperature.

Liposomes were created utilizing the surface-active compounds monopalmitoyl-2-hydroxy-sn-glycero-3-phosphocholine (MPPC), 1,2-dipalmitoyl-sn-glycero-3-phosphocholine (DPPC), and others. Tamoxifen and imatinib co-encapsulated in temperature-sensitive liposomes exhibit synergistic efficacy against MCF-7 and MDA-MB-231 breast cancer cells. The liposomal nanoparticles demonstrated >70% encapsulation efficiency for tamoxifen and imatinib and a transition temperature of 39.4°C. As a prospective breast cancer targeting technique, codelivery of tamoxifen and imatinib utilizing temperature-sensitive liposomes can be produced.

6.5.2 Magnetic-field responsive liposomes

Due to their chemical instability, metallic nanoparticles MNPs consisting of iron, cobalt, or nickel are frequently disregarded for biological applications. These metallic MNPs are often covered by coatings, such as gold or silica, to form a core—shell structure, as they readily form oxides in the presence of water and oxygen. Despite the difficulty of the production process, research on metallic nanoparticles continues due to the distinct benefits that certain of these MNPs may provide. In comparison to their oxide counterparts, iron nanoparticles have a comparatively strong magnetization and may sustain superparamagnetism at greater particle sizes (Huber, 2005). Peng et al. demonstrated that crystalline Fe_3O_4 shells may provide a durable protective covering for iron nanoparticles, but amorphous coatings cannot shield the metallic core from severe oxidation (Peng et al., 2006). The oxide coating was generated and its thickness was regulated by controlled oxidation using an oxygen transferring agent in this work, which started with a thermal degradation procedure to make iron nanoparticles. Fe/Fe_3O_4 nanoparticles with a core radius of 4 nm and an oxide thickness of 2.5 nm were created. The particles were superparamagnetic, with a Ms of 102.6 emu/g Fe, as determined by magnetic characterization. Alternatively, Qiang et al. recently described employing a nanocluster deposition technology to produce stable Fe/Fe_3O_4 nanoparticles. Controlling growth conditions allowed the group to adjust core diameters from 2 to 100 nm and shell thicknesses from 2.5 to 5 nm. The Ms of nanoparticles shorter than 10 nm created by this technique was around 80 emu/g Fe (Qiang et al., 2006). All MNP platforms for biomedical applications have polymeric coatings as a standard feature. Nanoparticles have a strong tendency to agglomerate despite not being magnetically attracted owing to their superparamagnetic features. This is due to their high surface energy. Because of the presence of salts or other electrolytes that may neutralize this charge, colloidal electrostatic stabilization resulting from repulsion of surface charges on nanoparticles is often insufficient to avoid aggregation in biological fluids. Furthermore, MNPs' surfaces are prone to opsonization, or the adsorption of plasma protein, as the initial stage in their clearance by the RES, following intravenous administration. Many MNP uses in medicine have a big problem in avoiding RES absorption and maintaining a lengthy plasma half-life (Berry and Curtis, 2003). Polymeric coatings act as a steric barrier between nanoparticles and the environment, preventing agglomeration and opsonization. Furthermore, these coatings allow MNPs' surface features, such as surface charge and chemical activity, to be tailored. The chemical structure of the polymer (e.g., hydrophilicity/hydrophobicity, biodegradation characteristics), the length or molecular weight of the polymer, the manner in which the polymer is anchored or attached (e.g., electrostatic or covalent bonding), the conformation of the polymer, and the degree of particle surface coverage are some critical aspects of polymeric coatings that may affect the performance of an MNP system. Various monomeric species, such as bisphosphonates, dimercaptosuccinic acid (DMSA) (Portet et al., 2001; Fauconnier et al., 1997; Zhang et al., 2007), and alkoxysilanes, have been tested as anchors to help polymer coatings adhere to MNPs. As a drug carrier, curcumin—a representative hydrophobic substance—was loaded into PEGylated magnetic liposomes. Superparamagnetic drug carriers distribute uniformly in aqueous solution, and they may induce magnetic heating in the presence of an external high-frequency magnetic field (HFMF). At 37°C, drug carriers showed no discernible release, but at 45°C, they showed fast releasing. In contrast to that at 45°C without HFMF exposure, it would exhibit huge (three times more) curcumin release under the HFMF exposure. Alongside rising curcumin concentrations, curcumin-loaded PEGylated magnetic liposomes may effectively kill MCF-7 cells. The use of new hydrophobic drug-loaded PEGylated magnetic liposomes with inductive magnetic heating in conjunction with chemotherapy and thermotherapy for the treatment of breast cancer appears promising (Hardiansyah et al., 2017).

6.5.3 Ultrasound responsive

Acoustic waves having frequencies more than 20 kHz, which is higher beyond the audible range of human hearing, can be simply defined as US (Chen et al., 2010). Imaging, tissue ablation, kidney stone breakup, physiotherapy, and other medical uses of US are frequent (Leighton, 2007). However, the concept of utilizing US to transport drugs dates back to the age when biochemists used it to tear biological cell membranes and extract the contents before purification (Schroeder et al., 2009).

US-responsive liposomal DDSs have centered on developing "sonosensitive" materials for use in liposomes. Evjen et al. obtained encouraging results using liposomes made of 1,2 distearoyl-sn-glycero-3-phosphatidylethanolamine (DSPE) and dioleoyl-phosphatidylethanolamine (DOPE) (Yu et al., 2016). DSPE released roughly 70% of DOX within 6 minutes after US exposure, a sevenfold improvement over typical PEGylated liposomal DOX. DOPE produced significantly greater results in vitro, releasing 95% of DOX from liposomes in 6 minutes of 40-kHz US exposure, a 35% improvement over DSPE and a ninefold increase over conventional PEGylated liposomes (Unger et al., 2014). In addition to utilizing sonosensitive compounds to change the phospholipid bilayer, bile salts (BS) can be used to create vesicles that are more sensitive to a US stimulation. The structure of the phospholipid bilayer has been shown to be destabilized by BSs. Mujoo et al. recently sought to enhance US-sensitive phospholipid bilayers with BSs (e.g., cholate, chenodeoxycholate, urso-deoxycholate, glycocholate, and taurocholate). They also found that low-frequency US elicited significant responses, but high-frequency US elicited nonsignificant responses. Liposomes containing taurocholate and DOPE were similarly shown to be less sensitive to high-frequency US than liposomes containing only DOPE. This was thought to be due to a preferred form in the phospholipid bilayer resulting from the combination of taurocholate and DOPE (Evjen et al., 2010). Breast cancer treatment using ultrasound and innovative, alginate-stabilized perfluorohexane nanodroplets. The development of Doxorubicin (Dox)-loaded multifunctional nanodroplets (Dox-NDs). Dox-NDs coupled with sonication for tumor treatment (Dox-ND-US) These multifunctional nanodroplets' potent therapeutic effects in combination with their ultrasonic contrast ability demonstrated that this drug delivery technology has a lot of potential for effective cancer treatment (Baghbani et al., 2017).

6.5.4 Redox-responsive drug delivery systems

The reducing environment of tumors acts as a unique internal signal, allowing redox-responsive nanocarriers to breakdown and release loaded payloads in tumor cells. Redox-responsive nanocarriers have three key benefits. For starters, they are frequently stable in normal tissues, which reduces biological toxicity and side effects in both carriers and payloads (Guo et al., 2018). Second, they demonstrate a rapid reaction to increased GSH levels in tumor cells by releasing payloads (usually a few minutes to hours). Finally, when compared to other possible cargo release locations, cytoplasmic cargo release is frequently considered to have higher therapeutic benefits. The reduction and oxidation states of NADPH/NADP + and glutathione (GSH, GSH/GSSG), both of which have different reduction potentials and capabilities, are tightly regulated and largely governed by the reducing environment of tumor cells (Wu et al., 2004). When the concentration of GSH is higher than that of NADPH in a reducing environment, GSH plays a key function in microenvironment control. GSH regulates the cellular reducing environment primarily through the creation and fragmentation of disulfide bonds, as well as the interaction with excess ROS at the molecular level (Aon et al., 2010; Such et al., 2015). Because the Se—Se and C—Se bonds have lower bond energies than S—S bonds (Se—Se 172 kJ/mol; C—Se 244 kJ/mol; S—S 268 kJ/mol), diselenide bonds can be used to provide a more sensitive redox-responsive delivery mechanism in tumor treatment (Cheng et al., 2012; Ji et al., 2014; Zhai et al., 2017). To make the polycationic carrier OEI800-SeSex, Gang

Cheng et al. introduced the active ester containing diselenide linkages to the branched oligo-ethyleneimine 800 Da (OEI800). The findings revealed that OEI800-SeSex and OEI800-SSx had comparable redox-responsive degradation characteristics and were much less hazardous than PEI25k. Aside from that, OEI800-SeSex and OEI800-SSx had much greater transfection efficiency than OEI800 (De La Rica et al., 2012). Podophyllotoxin (PPT), a toxic polyphenol derived from Podophyllum species roots. PPT was covalently linked to T7-peptide (Pep) modified polyethylene glycol (PEG) or methoxy-polyethylene glycol (mPEG) through a disulfide bond to produce the final polymer in a redox/pH double-sensitive and tumor active targeted drug delivery system (Pep-PEG-SS-PPT or PEG-SS-PPT). Compared to paclitaxel (PTX) or docetaxel, the mixed micelles (Pep-SS-NPs) produced by combining Pep-PEG-SS-PPT and PEG-SS-PPT exhibit various drug-resistant cancer cell lines (DTX). Pep-SS-NPs exhibits a strong anticancer activity against MCF-7/ADR xenograft tumors, which suggests that mixed micelles could work well as a nanomedicine for MDR breast cancer treatment (Li et al., 2019).

6.5.5 Enzyme responsive drug delivery materials

Hydrolases, which include proteases, lipases, and glycosidases, are the most commonly employed enzymes for drug administration, owing to their simple design, which involves attaching bioactive moieties to the carrier via enzyme cleavable units, as illustrated schematically in Fig. 6.6A, B, and C. When inorganic nanoparticles are formed by biomolecules exhibiting cleavable components, a hydrolase can also cause their dispersion. While several hydrolase-responsive nanomaterials are already in clinical trials, oxidoreductases are still at the proof-of-concept stage, and some cutting-edge instances of their use for drug delivery and diagnostics are discussed here. Other enzymes, like as kinases (Gupta et al., 2010, 2011), which are linked to cancer, and acetyltransferases (George et al., 2011), which are important in epigenetics, have only been studied for biosensing purposes. An enzyme-responsive drug delivery system using nanoparticles based on dendrimer-doxorubicin (dendrimer-DOX) conjugates. An enzyme-responsive tetra-peptide linker Gly-Phe-Leu-Gly is used to attach the medication DOX to the dendrimer's edge (GFLG). Potential nanoscale drug delivery technology for the treatment of breast cancer may be found in the mPEGylated peptide dendrimer-DOX conjugate-based nanoparticle (Table 6.2).

6.5.6 Photoresponsive drug delivery systems

Through the spatiotemporal regulation of light, light responsive nano vehicles using various light sources, such as ultraviolet, visible, and NIR light, demonstrate more controlled drug release (Yuan et al., 2015). The light intensity, emission wavelength, pulse duration, and exposure period can all influence the reaction process in a

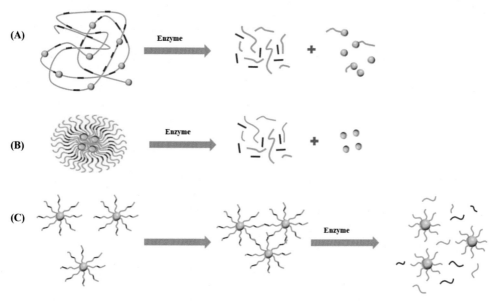

Figure 6.6 Enzyme-responsive nanomaterials for drug delivery and diagnostics.
(A) Polymer-based nanoparticles can be covalently modified with drugs through an enzymecleava-
ble linker so that the enzyme activity triggers drug delivery in the tissue of interest; (1) proteases can trigger drug delivery when the drug is linked to the carrier by a peptide; (2)
glycosidases can trigger drug delivery when the carrier is a polysaccharide;
(B) Polymer stabilized liposomes can be loaded with drugs, whose degradation can be programmed to be triggered by an enzyme; (1) proteases can trigger drug delivery when the stabilizing polymer is linked to the unstable liposome via peptide connections; (2) lipases can
trigger drug delivery when they hydrolyze the phospholipid building blocks;
(C) Inorganic nanoparticles can be used for diagnostics when the activity of the target hydrolase
controls the assembly or disassembly of the nanoparticles, which in turn changes the physical
properties of the nanoparticle solution.

nanovesicle (Viger et al., 2013). Two types of light induced chemical transformation
and a light generated intermediate reaction are shown by the photo responsiveness.
The chemical structure of photo responsive molecules, for example, can be altered by
events such as photoisomerization and photocleavage when specific wavelengths of
light are absorbed. Photosensitive agents (PSAs) such as metal nanoparticles, carbon
nanotubes, and organic dyes are used in the second group of photo responsive nano
vehicles to generate intermediate molecules. Photo responsive nano vehicles have
been used in the prevention and treatment of malignancies for optical imaging, photo–
therapy, and theragnosis. Breast cancer cells overexpress the mucin 1 (MUC1) protein.
For the purpose of selectively targeting MUC1–positive tumor cells, the sequence of a
MUC1 aptamer was coupled to a DNA tetrahedron to create MUC1-TDNs.

Table 6.2 Key examples of enzyme-responsive nanomaterials classified by the type of effector biomolecule.

Class	Subclass	Enzyme	Nanomaterial	Applications	References
Hydrolases	Proteases	Cathepsin B	Polymeric nanoparticles (HPMA)	Intracellular drug delivery	Vicent et al. (2005)
			Polymer-stabilized liposomes	Extracellular drug delivery	Satchi et al. (2001)
		CAPs	Semiconductor nanoparticles (quantum dots)	Targeted drug delivery	Basel et al. (2011)
		Caspase 1 thrombin collagenase chymotrypsin		Biosensing via FRET	Medintz et al. (2006)
		PSA	Gold nanoparticles	Prostate cancer diagnosis	Laromaine et al. (2007)
	Lipases	PLA2	Polymer-stabilized	Synergistic drug delivery	Andresen et al. (2004)
	Glycosidases	α-amilase	Liposomes	Phospholipase sensor	Aili (2011)
			Polymeric nanoparticles (dextran)	Targeted drug delivery	Ferguson and Duncan (2009)
	Others	Urease	Gold nanoparticles	ELISA	De La Rica and Velders (2011)
Oxidoreductases	enzymes	Glucose oxidase	Liposomes	Drug delivery triggered by glucose	Napoli et al. (2004)
		Peroxidase	Gold nanoparticles	ELISA	De La Rica and Velders (2011)

CAPs are cancer associated proteases, PSA is prostate specific antigen, FRET is Förster resonant energy transfer.

TMPyP4 strong affinity for DNA allowed it to be loaded into MUC1-TDNs together with the photosensitizer. This technique made it possible to distribute TMPyP4 to cancer cells that were MUC1-positive alone. Additionally, MTT increased cytotoxicity and the formation of reactive oxygen species in MUC1-positive cells while having less of an impact on MUC1-negative cells. Photo responsive nano vehicles are summarized in Fig. 6.7 and Table 6.3.

6.5.7 Responsive to multiple stimuli drug delivery systems

The majority of multi-stimuli-responsive DDSs are made of polymers with unique sensitivity. Wang's group, for example, used graft copolymer assembly to create a triple-stimuli responsive DDS. The graft copolymer was made out of a backbone made of thermo-responsive tetraethylene glycolyl poly (trimethylene carbonate) and a side chain made of light-sensitive poly (2-nitrobenzyl methacrylate) joined by a disulfide bond. The polymer can self-assemble into micelle loading medicines in aqueous solution. Also, the drug's release could be affected by temperature, a lowering agent, or light. Similarly, Cao et al. (2016) demonstrated a multi-stimulus-responsive nanogel enabling spatiotemporally regulated release of simultaneously encapsulated hydrophobic and hydrophilic cargos. The nanogel was made up of a hydrophilic poly(2-(dimethylamino)ethyl methacrylate) and a hydrophobic photo-cleavable o-nitrobenzyl linkage that was pH and temperature responsive. The

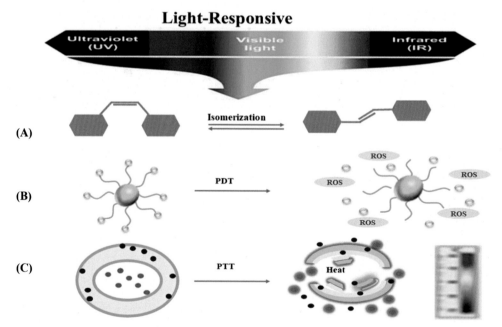

Figure 6.7 Light responsive drug delivery systems (DDSs): (A) Photo-isomerization, (B) Photodynamic responsive DDSs, and (C) Photothermal-responsive DDSs.

Table 6.3 Classification of photoresponsive nano vehicles.

Classification	DDS	Photosensitive material	Wave-length	Tumor model	References
Photo-induced chemical transformation					
Photoisomerization	Photo-responsive cationic vesicle	Azobenzene	350, 434 nm	MDA–MB-231	Seidel et al. (2020)
	Micelle based on SP- (PDMAEMA-block– PMMA), SP-(PMMA-block–PDMAEMA) blocks	Spiropyran	365 nm	HeLa	Razavi et al. (2020)
Photo-induced Cleavage	MCP/DOC/shRNA LIP–DT–COU–MTX	Coumarinyl ester Coumarin	405, 365 nm 800 nm	HepG2/ADR HeLa, A549	Wu et al. (2018) Chen et al. (2018)
Photo-mediated materials					
Photothermal therapy (PTT)	GNRs/SiO2/GO-PEG DOX@PCNFs	Graphene oxide Carbon nanotubes	808 nm 808 nm	MCF-7 Mg-63	Qi et al. (2019) Dai (2020)
	DOX/MSN–Au	Au	808 nm	A549	Yang et al. (2017)
	CuS@MPS-DOX	Cupric sulfide	808 nm	U87MG	Peng et al. (2017)
	PBNP	Prussian blue	808 nm	Neuro2a	Cano–Mejia et al. (2017)
	FM	Indocyanine green	808 nm	KB	Yan and Qiu (2015)

hydrophobic cargos were chemically connected to the nanogel precursor polymer poly (2-(dimethylamino) ethyl methacrylate) through a redox-cleavable disulfide junction, while the hydrophilic cargos were noncovalently encapsulated into the lipophilic interiors of the nanogels. The hydrophobic cargos can be released in response to temperature, pH, and UV light, while the hydrophilic cargos can be released in response to the redox reagent in these dual-loaded nanogels. Li et al. (2017) used a distillation precipitation polymerization technique to create a pH, temperature, and reduction multi-stimuli responsive polymeric microsphere with or without a hollow layer between their pH and reduction responsive poly(methacrylic acid) (PMAA) cores and temperature sensitive poly(N-isopropylacrylamide) (PNIPAM) shells. The PMAA/PNIPAM yolk/shell microspheres had a larger drug loading capacity and improved tumor microenvironment responsive controlled release performance due to the middle hollow layer between their pH and reduction responsive PMAA cores and temperature sensitive PNIPAM shells. Liu et al. (2017) recently developed PEG-S-S-SN$_{38}$, a multiple stimuli-responsive SN$_{38}$ prodrug, by conjugating PEG (MW: 2000) and SN$_{38}$ with disulfide bonds and carbonic ester linkages as linkers for efficient SN$_{38}$ delivery. The amphiphilic PEG-S S-SN$_{38}$ could self-assemble into nanoparticles with a high SN$_{38}$ loading content, and the release of SN$_{38}$ was very sluggish at physiological pH, but very fast in the presence of glutathione (GSH), esterase, and H$_2$O$_2$, all of which are plentiful in the cytoplasm of cancer cells (Wen and Sun, 2017).

6.5.8 pH-responsive drug delivery systems

pH-responsive drug delivery systems utilize the variations in pH levels in different biological environments as triggers for controlled drug release. These systems are designed to remain stable during systemic circulation at normal physiological pH (around 7.4) but release the drug in response to the acidic pH found in specific target sites, such as tumor tissues, inflammatory regions, or intracellular compartments. There are various types of pH-responsive drug delivery materials, including organic-materials-based systems, inorganic-nanostructured materials-based systems, inorganic/inorganic nanocomposites-based systems, and inorganic/organic composite systems.

6.5.8.1 pH-responsive hydrogel drug delivery systems

Hydrogels are three-dimensional cross-linked polymer networks that can absorb large amounts of water or fluids. pH-responsive hydrogel drug delivery systems have gained significant attention for targeted cancer therapy and peptide drug delivery. These hydrogels can be modified to exhibit pH-sensitive properties, allowing them to release drugs in response to changes in pH, such as the acidic conditions found in tumor tissues. pH-sensitive liposomes are an example of pH-responsive hydrogel drug delivery systems that can release drugs due to bilayer instability at lower pH levels (Elsherif et al., 2019; Hardiansyah et al., 2017) (Fig. 6.8).

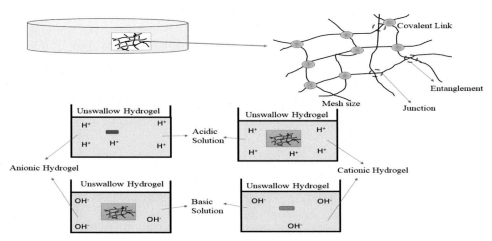

Figure 6.8 pH responsive hydrogel drug delivery systems.

6.5.8.2 pH and temperature-responsive release of bioactive agents

Nanoparticles, such as those integrated into chitosan-based hydrogels, can be tailored to target cancer cells effectively. These nanoparticles may be responsive to external stimuli like an external magnetic field or infrared irradiation, enabling targeted drug delivery and improved retention. Additionally, redox-responsive drug carriers, created by crosslinking chitosan-based composites with disulfide connections, can release drugs in response to the specific pH and redox state of the target cells.

Overall, pH-responsive drug delivery systems, including hydrogels and various nanoparticles, offer promising applications for targeted drug administration and controlled release in different biological environments. These systems hold potential for enhancing drug efficacy and reducing side effects, making them valuable tools in modern medicine and cancer therapy (Xu et al., 2020).

References

Aili, D., 2011. Hybrid nanoparticle − liposome detection of phospholipase activity. Nano. Lett. 11 (4), 1401−1405.

Alexiou, C., Schmid, R.J., Jurgons, R., Kremer, M., Wanner, G., Bergemann, C., et al., 2006. Targeting cancer cells: magnetic nanoparticles as drug carriers. Eur. Biophys. J. 35 (5), 446−450.

Andresen, T.L., Davidsen, J., Begtrup, M., Mouritsen, O.G., Jørgensen, K., 2004. Enzymatic release of antitumor ether lipids by specific phospholipase A2 activation of liposome-forming prodrugs. J. Med. Chem. 47 (7), 1694−1703.

Aon, M.A., Cortassa, S., O'rourke, B., 2010. Redox-optimized ROS balance: a unifying hypothesis. Biochim. Biophys. Acta - Bioenerg. 1797 (6−7), 865−877.

Asgari, S., Pourjavadi, A., Setayeshmehr, M., Boisen, A., Ajalloueian, F., 2021. Encapsulation of drug-loaded graphene oxide-based nanocarrier into electrospun pullulan nanofibers for potential local chemotherapy of breast cancer. Macromol. Chem. Phys. 222 (15), 2100096.

Baghbani, F., Chegeni, M., Moztarzadeh, F., Mohandesi, J.A., Mokhtari-Dizaji, M., 2017. Ultrasonic nanotherapy of breast cancer using novel ultrasound-responsive alginate-shelled perfluorohexane nanodroplets: in vitro and in vivo evaluation. Mater. Sci. Eng. C: Mater. Biol. Appl. 77, 698—707. Available from: https://doi.org/10.1016/j.msec.2017.02.017.

Bangham, A.D., Standish, M.M., Watkins, J.C., 1965. Diffusion of univalent ions across the lamellae of swollen phospholipids. J. Mol. Biol. 13 (1), 238—IN27.

Barenholz, Y.C., 2012. Doxil®—the first FDA-approved nano-drug: lessons learned. J. Control. Release 160 (2), 117—134.

Basel, M.T., Shrestha, T.B., Troyer, D.L., Bossmann, S.H., 2011. Protease-sensitive, polymer-caged liposomes: a method for making highly targeted liposomes using triggered release. ACS Nano. 5 (3), 2162—2175.

Bastakoti, B.P., Guragain, S., Nakashima, K., Yamauchi, Y., 2015. Stimuli-induced core—corona inversion of micelle of poly (acrylic acid)-block-poly (N-isopropylacrylamide) and its application in drug delivery. Macromol. Chem. Phys. 216 (3), 287—291.

Benhabbour, S.R., Luft, J.C., Kim, D., Jain, A., Wadhwa, S., Parrott, M.C., et al., 2012. In vitro and in vivo assessment of targeting lipid-based nanoparticles to the epidermal growth factor-receptor (EGFR) using a novel Heptameric ZEGFR domain. J. Control. Release 158 (1), 63—71.

Berry, C.C., Curtis, A.S., 2003. Functionalisation of magnetic nanoparticles for applications in biomedicine. J. Phys. D: Appl. Phys. 36 (13), R198.

Bertrand, N., Wu, J., Xu, X., Kamaly, N., Farokhzad, O.C., 2014. Cancer nanotechnology: the impact of passive and active targeting in the era of modern cancer biology. Adv. Drug Deliv. Rev. 66, 2—25.

Butti, R., Das, S., Gunasekaran, V.P., Yadav, A.S., Kumar, D., Kundu, G.C., 2018. Receptor tyrosine kinases (RTKs) in breast cancer: signaling, therapeutic implications and challenges. Mol. Cancer, 17 (1), 1—8.

Cai, X., Zhu, H., Zhang, Y., Gu, Z., 2017. Highly efficient and safe delivery of VEGF siRNA by bioreducible fluorinated peptide dendrimers for cancer therapy. ACS Appl. Mater. Interfaces 9 (11), 9402—9415.

Cano-Mejia, J., Burga, R.A., Sweeney, E.E., Fisher, J.P., Bollard, C.M., Sandler, A.D., 2017. Prussian blue nanoparticle-based photothermal therapy combined with checkpoint inhibition for photothermal immunotherapy of neuroblastoma. Nanomed.: Nanotechnol. Biol. Med. 13 (2), 771—781.

Cao, Z., Zhou, X., Wang, G., 2016. Selective release of hydrophobic and hydrophilic cargos from multistimuli-responsive nanogels. ACS Appl. Mater. Interfaces 8 (42), 28888—28896.

Cathcart, J., Pulkoski-Gross, A., Cao, J., 2015. Targeting matrix metalloproteinases in cancer: bringing new life to old ideas. Genes Dis. 2 (1), 26—34.

Cha, R., He, Z., Ni, Y., 2012. Preparation and characterization of thermal/pH-sensitive hydrogel from carboxylated nanocrystalline cellulose. Carbohydr. Polym. 88 (2), 713—718.

Chen, D., Jiang, X., Huang, Y., Zhang, C., Ping, Q., 2010. pH-sensitive mPEG-Hz-cholesterol conjugates as a liposome delivery system. J. Bioact. Compat. Polym. 25 (5), 527—542.

Chen, Z., Li, B., Xie, X., Zeng, F., Wu, S., 2018. A sequential enzyme-activated and light-triggered pro-prodrug nanosystem for cancer detection and therapy. J. Mater. Chem. B. 6 (17), 2547—2556.

Cheng, G., He, Y., Xie, L., Nie, Y., He, B., Zhang, Z., et al., 2012. Development of a reduction-sensitive diselenide-conjugated oligoethylenimine nanoparticulate system as a gene carrier. Int. J. Nanomed. 7, 3991—4006.

Cheng, X., Jin, Y., Sun, T., Qi, R., Fan, B., Li, H., 2015. Oxidation-and thermo-responsive poly (N-isopropylacrylamide-co-2-hydroxyethyl acrylate) hydrogels cross-linked via diselenides for controlled drug delivery. RSC Adv. 5 (6), 4162—4170.

Dai, J., Luo, Y., Nie, D., Jin, J., Yang, S., Li, G., et al., 2020. pH/photothermal dual-responsive drug delivery and synergistic chemo-photothermal therapy by novel porous carbon nanofibers. Chem. Eng. J. 397, 125402.

d'Avanzo, N., Torrieri, G., Figueiredo, P., Celia, C., Paolino, D., Correia, A., et al., 2021. LinTT1 peptide-functionalized liposomes for targeted breast cancer therapy. Int. J. Pharm. 597, 120346.

Dash, B.S., Das, S., Chen, J.-P.J.I., 2021. Photosensitizer-functionalized nanocomposites for light-activated cancer theranostics. Int. J. Mol. Sci. 22 (13), 6658.

De La Rica, R., Aili, D., Stevens, M.M., 2012. Enzyme-responsive nanoparticles for drug release and diagnostics. Adv. Drug Deliv. Rev. 64 (11), 967–978.

De La Rica, R., Velders, A.H., 2011. Supramolecular Au nanoparticle assemblies as optical probes for enzyme-linked immunoassays. Small 7 (1), 66–69.

Deshpande, P.P., Biswas, S., Torchilin, V.P., 2013. Current trends in the use of liposomes for tumor targeting. Nanomed.: Nanotechnol. Biol. Med. 8 (9), 1509–1528.

Di, J., Xie, F., Xu, Y., 2020. When liposomes met antibodies: drug delivery and beyond. Adv. Drug Deliv. Rev. 154, 151–162.

Dinparvar, S., Bagirova, M., Allahverdiyev, A.M., Abamor, E.S., Safarov, T., Aydogdu, M., et al., 2020. A nanotechnology-based new approach in the treatment of breast cancer: biosynthesized silver nanoparticles using Cuminum cyminum L. seed extract. J. Photochem. Photobiol. B, Biol. 208, 111902.

Dresselhaus, M.S., Dresselhaus, G., Eklund, P., Rao, A., 2000. The physics of fullerene-based and fullerene-related materials. Phys. Chem. Mater. Low-Dimens. Struct. 23, 331–379.

Dulińska-Litewka, J., Łazarczyk, A., Hałubiec, P., Szafrański, O., Karnas, K., Karewicz, A., 2019. Superparamagnetic iron oxide nanoparticles—Current and prospective medical applications. Materials 12 (4), 617.

Ebrahimzadeh, Z., Salehzadeh, A., Naeemi, A.S., Jalali, A., 2020. Silver nanoparticles biosynthesized by Anabaena flos-aquae enhance the apoptosis in breast cancer cell line. J. Mater. Sci. 43 (1), 1–7.

Elsherif, M., Hassan, M.U., Yetisen, A.K., Butt, H., 2019. Hydrogel optical fibers for continuous glucose monitoring. Biosens. Bioelectron. 137, 25–32.

Evjen, T.J., Nilssen, E.A., Rögnvaldsson, S., Brandl, M., Fossheim, S.L., 2010. Distearoylphosphatidylethanolamine-based liposomes for ultrasound-mediated drug delivery. Eur. J. Pharm. Biopharm. 75 (3), 327–333.

Fathi, S., Oyelere, A.K., 2016. Liposomal drug delivery systems for targeted cancer therapy: is active targeting the best choice? Future Med. Chem. 8 (17), 2091–2112.

Fatima, I., Rahdar, A., Sargazi, S., Barani, M., Hassanisaadi, M., Thakur, V.K., 2021. Quantum dots: synthesis, antibody conjugation, and HER2-receptor targeting for breast cancer therapy. J. Funct. Biomater. 12 (4), 75.

Fauconnier, N., Pons, J., Roger, J., Bee, A., 1997. Thiolation of maghemite nanoparticles by dimercaptosuccinic acid. J. Colloid Interface Sci. 194 (2), 427–433.

Feigin, M.E., Xue, B., Hammell, M.C., Muthuswamy, S.K., 2014. G-protein–coupled receptor GPR161 is overexpressed in breast cancer and is a promoter of cell proliferation and invasion. Proc. Natl. Acad. Sci. 111 (11), 4191–4196.

Feldman, D., 2019. Polymers and polymer nanocomposites for cancer therapy. Appl. Sci. 9 (18), 3899.

Feng, L., Mumper, R.J., 2013. A critical review of lipid-based nanoparticles for taxane delivery. Cancer Lett. 334 (2), 157–175.

Ferguson, E.L., Duncan, R., 2009. Dextrin – phospholipase A2: synthesis and evaluation as a bioresponsive anticancer conjugate. Biomacromolecules 10 (6), 1358–1364.

Fotis, L., Agrogiannis, G., Vlachos, I.S., Pantopoulou, A., Margoni, A., Kostaki, M., et al., 2012. Intercellular adhesion molecule (ICAM)-1 and vascular cell adhesion molecule (VCAM)-1 at the early stages of atherosclerosis in a rat model. In Vivo (Athens, Greece) 26 (2), 243–250.

Gao, X., Cao, Y., Song, X., Zhang, Z., Xiao, C., He, C., et al., 2013. pH-and thermo-responsive poly (N-isopropylacrylamide-co-acrylic acid derivative) copolymers and hydrogels with LCST dependent on pH and alkyl side groups. J. Mater. Chem. B 1 (41), 5578–5587.

Gomathi, A., 2020. Anticancer activity of silver nanoparticles synthesized using aqueous fruit shell extract of Tamarindus indica on MCF-7 human breast cancer cell line. J. Drug Deliv. Sci. Technol. 55, 101376

Gao, C., Jian, J., Lin, Z., Yu, Y.-X., Jiang, B.-P., Chen, H., et al., 2019. Hypericin-loaded carbon nanohorn hybrid for combined photodynamic and photothermal therapy in vivo. Langmuir 35 (25), 8228–8237.

George, S., Xia, T., Rallo, R., Zhao, Y., Ji, Z., Lin, S., Wang, X., et al., 2011. Use of a high-throughput screening approach coupled with in vivo zebrafish embryo screening to develop hazard ranking for engineered nanomaterials. ACS Nano 5 (3), 1805–1817.

Gosk, S., Moos, T., Gottstein, C., Bendas, G., 2008. VCAM-1 directed immunoliposomes selectively target tumor vasculature in vivo. Biochim. Biophys. Acta (BBA)-Biomembr. 1778 (4), 854–863.

Gounden, S., Daniels, A., Singh, M., 2021. Chitosan-modified silver nanoparticles enhance cisplatin activity in breast cancer cells. Biointerface Res. Appl. Chem. 11, 10572–10584.

Guo, X., Cheng, Y., Zhao, X., Luo, Y., Chen, J., Wei-En Yuan, W.-E., 2018. Advances in redox-responsive drug delivery systems of tumor microenvironment. J. Nanobiotechnology 16 (1), 1–10.

Guo, Z., Zhao, K., Liu, R., Guo, X., He, B., Yan, J., et al., 2019. pH-sensitive polymeric micelles assembled by stereocomplexation between PLLA-b-PLys and PDLA-b-mPEG for drug delivery. J. Mater. Chem. B 7 (2), 334–345.

Gupta, S., Andresen, H., Ghadiali, J.E., Stevens, M.M., 2010. Kinase-actuated immunoaggregation of peptide-conjugated gold nanoparticles. Small 6 (14), 1509–1513.

Gupta, S., Andresen, H., Stevens, M.M., 2011. Single-step kinase inhibitor screening using a peptide-modified gold nanoparticle platform. ChemComm 47 (8), 2249–2251.

Gupta, S., Srivastava, M., Ahmad, N., Bostwick, D.G., Mukhtar, H., 2000. Over-expression of cyclooxygenase-2 in human prostate adenocarcinoma. The Prostate 42 (1), 73–78.

Hanafy, N.A.N., El-Kemary, M., Leporatti, S., 2018. Micelles structure development as a strategy to improve smart cancer therapy. Cancers 10 (7), 238.

Handsley, M.M., Edwards, D.R., 2005. Metalloproteinases and their inhibitors in tumor angiogenesis. Int. J. Cancer 115 (6), 849–860.

Hardiansyah, A., Yang, M.C., Liu, T.Y., Kuo, C.Y., Huang, L.Y., Chan, T.Y., 2017. Hydrophobic drug-loaded PEGylated magnetic liposomes for drug-controlled release. Nanoscale Res. Lett. 12 (1).

Haugsten, E.M., Wiedlocha, A., Olsnes, S., Wesche, J., 2010. Roles of fibroblast growth factor receptors in carcinogenesis. Mol. Cancer Res. 8 (11), 1439–1452.

Heath, J.L., Weiss, J.M., Lavau, C.P., Wechsler, D.S., 2013. Iron deprivation in cancer—potential therapeutic implications. Nutrients 5 (8), 2836–2859.

Hoang, Q.T., Kim, M., Kim, B.C., Lee, C.Y., Shim, M.S., 2022. Pro-oxidant drug-loaded porphyrinic zirconium metal-organic-frameworks for cancer-specific sonodynamic therapy. Colloids Surf. B 209, 112189.

Hua, H., Zhang, H., Kong, Q., Jiang, Y., 2018. Mechanisms for estrogen receptor expression in human cancer. Exp. Hematol. Oncol. 7 (1).

Huber, D.L., 2005. Synthesis, properties, and applications of iron nanoparticles. Small (Weinheim an der Bergstrasse, Germany) 1 (5), 482–501.

Iqbal, N., Iqbal, N., 2014. Human epidermal growth factor receptor 2 (HER2) in cancers: overexpression and therapeutic implications. Mol. Biol. Int. 2014.

Ivanova, N., 2018. Silver nanoparticles as multi-functional drug delivery systems. IntechOpen, London, UK.

Ji, S., Cao, W., Yu, Y., Xu, H., 2014. Dynamic diselenide bonds: exchange reaction induced by visible light without catalysis. Angew. Chem. Int. Ed. 53 (26), 6781–6785.

Jafarizad, A., Aghanejad, A., Sevim, M., Metin, Ö., Barar, J., Omidi, Y., et al., 2017. Gold nanoparticles and reduced graphene oxide-gold nanoparticle composite materials as covalent drug delivery systems for breast cancer treatment. ChemistrySelect 2 (23), 6663–6672.

Jamieson, T., Bakhshi, R., Petrova, D., Pocock, R., Imani, M., Seifalian, A.M., 2007. Biological applications of quantum dots. Biomaterials 28 (31), 4717–4732.

Jampilek, J., Kralova, K., 2021. Advances in drug delivery nanosystems using graphene-based materials and carbon nanotubes. Materials 14 (5), 1059.

Jelonek, K., Zajdel, A., Wilczok, A., Latocha, M., Musiał-Kulik, M., Foryś, A., et al., 2019. Dual-targeted biodegradable micelles for anticancer drug delivery. Mater. Lett. 241, 187–189.

Jiang, L., Li, L., He, X., Yi, Q., He, B., Cao, J., et al., 2015. Overcoming drug-resistant lung cancer by paclitaxel loaded dual-functional liposomes with mitochondria targeting and pH-response. Biomaterials 52, 126–139.

Khaniabadi, P.M., Shahbazi-Gahrouei, D., Aziz, A.A., Dheyab, M.A., Khaniabadi, B.M., Mehrdel, B., et al., 2020. Trastuzumab conjugated porphyrin-superparamagnetic iron oxide nanoparticle: a potential PTT-MRI bimodal agent for herceptin positive breast cancer. Photodiagnosis Photodyn. Ther. 31, 101896.

Kiran, A.V.V.V.R., Kusuma Kumari, G., Krishnamurthy, P.T., 2020. Carbon nanotubes in drug delivery: focus on anticancer therapies. J. Drug Deliv. Sci. Technol. 59, 101892.

Kong, F.-Y., Zhang, J-W., Li, R.-F., Wang, Z.-X., Wang, W.-J., Wang, W., 2017. Unique roles of gold nanoparticles in drug delivery, targeting and imaging applications. Molecules 22 (9), 1445.

Koshkaryev, A., Piroyan, A., Torchilin, V.P., 2012. Increased apoptosis in cancer cells in vitro and in vivo by ceramides in transferrin-modified liposomes. Cancer Biol. Ther. 13 (1), 50−60.

Krasinskas, A.M., 2011. EGFR signaling in colorectal carcinoma. Pathol. Res. Int. 2011.

L Arias, J., 2011. Drug targeting strategies in cancer treatment: an overview. Mini-Rev. Med. Chem. 11 (1), 1−17.

Laromaine, A., Koh, L., Murugesan, M., Ulijn, R.V., Stevens, M.M., 2007. Protease-triggered dispersion of nanoparticle assemblies. J. Am. Chem. Soc. 129 (14), 4156−4157.

Leighton, T.G., 2007. What is ultrasound? Prog. Biophys. Mol. Biol. 93 (1−3), 3−83.

Li, X., Ding, L., Xu, Y., Wang, Y., Ping, Q., 2009. Targeted delivery of doxorubicin using stealth liposomes modified with transferrin. Int. J. Pharm. 373 (1−2), 116−123.

Li, X., Qian, Y., Liu, T., Hu, X., Zhang, G., You, Y., et al., 2011. Amphiphilic multiarm star block copolymer-based multifunctional unimolecular micelles for cancer targeted drug delivery and MR imaging. Biomaterials 32 (27), 6595−6605.

Li, L., Di, X., Wu, M., Sun, Z., Zhong, L., Wang, Y., et al., 2017. Targeting tumor highly-expressed LAT1 transporter with amino acid-modified nanoparticles: toward a novel active targeting strategy in breast cancer therapy. Nanomed. Nanotechnol. Biol. Med. 13 (3), 987−998.

Li, Y., Chen, M., Yao, B., Lu, X., Zhang, X., He, P., et al., 2019. Transferrin receptor-targeted redox/pH-sensitive podophyllotoxin prodrug micelles for multidrug-resistant breast cancer therapy. J. Mater. Chem. B. 7 (38), 5814−5824.

Li, S., Su, W., Wu, H., Yuan, T., Yuan, C., Liu, J., et al., 2020. Targeted tumour theranostics in mice via carbon quantum dots structurally mimicking large amino acids. Nat. Biomed. Eng. 4 (7), 704−716.

Li, J.J., Tsang, J.Y., Tse, G.M., 2021. Tumor microenvironment in breast cancer—Updates on therapeutic implications and pathologic assessment. Cancers. 13 (16), 4233.

Li, L.L., Yin, Q., Cheng, J., Yi Lu, Y., 2012. Polyvalent mesoporous silica nanoparticle-aptamer bioconjugates target breast cancer cells. Adv. Healthc. Mater. 1 (5), 567−572.

Li, J., Zeng, J., Jia, X., Liu, L., Zhou, T., Liu, P., 2017. pH, temperature and reduction multi-responsive polymeric microspheres as drug delivery system for anti-tumor drug: effect of middle hollow layer between pH and reduction dual-responsive cores and temperature sensitive shells. J. Taiwan Inst. Chem. Eng. 74, 238−245.

Lila, A.S.A., Ishida, T., 2017. Liposomal delivery systems: design optimization and current applications. Biol. Pharm. Bull. 40 (1), 1−10.

Lim, S.Y., Shen, W., Gao, Z., 2015. Carbon quantum dots and their applications. Chem. Soc. Rev. 44 (1), 362−381.

Lin, C., Ng, H.L.H., Pan, W., Chen, H., Zhang, G., Bian, Z., et al., 2015. Exploring different strategies for efficient delivery of colorectal cancer therapy. Int. J. Mol. Sci. 16 (11), 26936−26952.

Linton, S.S., Sherwood, S.G., Drews, K.C., Kester, M., 2016. Targeting cancer cells in the tumor microenvironment: opportunities and challenges in combinatorial nanomedicine. Wiley Interdiscip. Rev. Nanomed. Nanobiotechnol. 8 (2), 208−222.

Liu, X., Huang, Q., Yang, C., Zhang, Q., Chen, W., Shen, Y., et al., 2017. A multi-stimuli responsive nanoparticulate SN38 prodrug for cancer chemotherapy. J. Mater. Chem. B 5 (4), 661−670

Lohiya, G., Katti, D.S., 2022. Carboxylated chitosan-mediated improved efficacy of mesoporous silica nanoparticle-based targeted drug delivery system for breast cancer therapy. Carbohydr. Polym. 277, 118822.

Low, P.S., Henne, W.A., Doorneweerd, D.D., 2008. Discovery and development of folic-acid-based receptor targeting for imaging and therapy of cancer and inflammatory diseases. Acc. Chem. Res. 41 (1), 120–129.

Lue, S.J., Chen, C.-H., Shih, C.-M., 2011. Tuning of lower critical solution temperature (LCST) of poly (N-isopropylacrylamide-co-acrylic acid) hydrogels. J. Macromol. Sci. B 50 (3), 563–579.

Luo, X., Wang, H., Ji, D, 2021. Carbon nanotubes (CNT)-loaded ginsenosides Rb3 suppresses the PD-1/PD-L1 pathway in triple-negative breast cancer. Aging (Albany NY) 13 (13), 17177.

Madaan, K., Kumar, S., Poonia, N., Lather, V., Pandita, D., 2014. Dendrimers in drug delivery and targeting: drug-dendrimer interactions and toxicity issues. J. Pharm. Bioallied Sci. 6 (3), 139.

Maeda, H., Nakamura, H., Fang, J., 2013. The EPR effect for macromolecular drug delivery to solid tumors: improvement of tumor uptake, lowering of systemic toxicity, and distinct tumor imaging in vivo. Adv. Drug Deliv. Rev. 65 (1), 71–79.

Majumder, N., Das, N.G., Das, S.K., 2020. Polymeric micelles for anticancer drug delivery. Ther. Deliv. 11 (10), 613–635.

Marcinkowska, M., Stanczyk, M., Janaszewska, A., Sobierajska, E., Chworos, A., Klajnert-Maculewicz, B., 2019. Multicomponent conjugates of anticancer drugs and monoclonal antibody with PAMAM dendrimers to increase efficacy of HER-2 positive breast cancer therapy. Pharm. Res. 36 (11), 1–17.

Medintz, I.L., Clapp, A.R., Brunel, F.M., Tiefenbrunn, T., Uyeda, H.T., Chang, E.L., et al., 2006. Proteolytic activity monitored by fluorescence resonance energy transfer through quantum-dot–peptide conjugates. Nat. Mater. 5 (7), 581–589.

Manzano, M., Vallet-Regí, M.J., 2020. Mesoporous silica nanoparticles for drug delivery. Adv. Funct. Mater. 30 (2), 1902634.

Meng, S., Su, B., Li, W., Ding, Y., Tang, L., Zhou, W., et al., 2011. Integrin-targeted paclitaxel nanoliposomes for tumor therapy. Med. Oncol. 28 (4), 1180–1187.

Mozafarinia, M., Karimi, S., Farrokhnia, M., Esfandiari, J., 2021. In vitro breast cancer targeting using Trastuzumab-conjugated mesoporous silica nanoparticles: towards the new strategy for decreasing size and high drug loading capacity for drug delivery purposes in MSN synthesis. Microporous Mesoporous Mater 316, 110950.

Napoli, A., Boerakker, M.J., Tirelli, N., Nolte, R.J.M., Sommerdijk, N.A.J.M., Hubbell, J.A., 2004. Glucose-oxidase based self-destructing polymeric vesicles. Langmuir 20 (9), 3487–3491.

Nguyen, T.N., Le, P.A., Phung, V.B.T., 2020. Facile green synthesis of carbon quantum dots and biomass-derived activated carbon from banana peels: synthesis and investigation. Biomass Convers. Biorefin. 1–10.

Niu, S., Williams, G.R., Wu, J., Wu, J., Zhang, X., Chen, X., et al., 2019. A chitosan-based cascade-responsive drug delivery system for triple-negative breast cancer therapy. J. Nanobiotechnology 17 (1), 1–18.

Noble, C.O., Kirpotin, D.B., Hayes, M.E, Mamot, C., Hong, K., Park, J.W., et al., 2004. Development of ligand-targeted liposomes for cancer therapy. Expert Opin. Ther. Targets. 8 (4), 335–353.

Ozgen, P.S.O., Atasoy, S., Kurt, B.Z., Durmus, Z., Yigit, G., Dag, A., 2020. Glycopolymer decorated multiwalled carbon nanotubes for dual targeted breast cancer therapy. J. Mater. Chem. B 8 (15), 3123–3137.

Pablos, J., Santiago, B., Carreira, P., Galindo, M., Gomez-Reino, J., 1999. Cyclooxygenase-1 and-2 are expressed by human T cells. Clin. Exp. Immunol. 115 (1), 86–90.

Panda, J., Satapathy, B.S., Majumder, S., Sarkar, R., Mukherjee, B., Tudu, B., 2019. Engineered polymeric iron oxide nanoparticles as potential drug carrier for targeted delivery of docetaxel to breast cancer cells. J. Magn. Magn. Mater. 485, 165–173.

Patel, J.D., O'Carra, R., Jones, J., Woodward, J.G., Mumper, R.J., 2007. Preparation and characterization of nickel nanoparticles for binding to his-tag proteins and antigens. Pharm. Res. 24 (2), 343–352.

Peng, S., He, Y., Er, M., Sheng, Y., Gu, Y., Chen, H., 2017. Biocompatible CuS-based nanoplatforms for efficient photothermal therapy and chemotherapy in vivo. Biomater. Sci. 5 (3), 475–484.

Peng, S., Wang, C., Xie, J., Sun, S., 2006. Synthesis and stabilization of monodisperse Fe nanoparticles. J. Am. Chem. Soc. 128 (33), 10676–10677.

Pennadam, S.S., Firman, K., Alexander, C., Górecki, D.C., 2004. Protein-polymer nano-machines. Towards synthetic control of biological processes. J. Nanobiotechnol. 2 (1), 1—7.

Piktel, E., Niemirowicz, K., Wątek, M., Wollny, T., Deptuła, P., Bucki, R., 2016. Recent insights in nanotechnology-based drugs and formulations designed for effective anti-cancer therapy. J. Nanobiotechnol. 14 (1), 1—23.

Pippa, N., Meristoudi, A., Pispas, S., Demetzos, C., 2015. Temperature-dependent drug release from DPPC: C12H25-PNIPAM-COOH liposomes: control of the drug loading/release by modulation of the nanocarriers' components. Int. J. Pharm. 485 (1—2), 374—382.

Ponsanti, K., Tangnorawich, B., Ngernyuang, N., Pechyen, C., 2022. Synthesis of mesoporous silica nanoparticles (MSNs)/silver nanoparticles (AgNPs): promising hybrid materials for detection of breast cancer cells. J. Mater. Sci.: Mater. Electron. 33 (10), 7515—7527.

Pooresmaeil, M., Asl, E.A., Namazi, H., 2021. A new pH-sensitive CS/Zn-MOF@ GO ternary hybrid compound as a biofriendly and implantable platform for prolonged 5-Fluorouracil delivery to human breast cancer cells. J. Alloys Compd. 885, 160992.

Portet, D., Denizot, B., Rump, E., Lejeune, J.-J., Jallet, P., 2001. Nonpolymeric coatings of iron oxide colloids for biological use as magnetic resonance imaging contrast agents. J. Colloid Interface Sci. 238 (1), 37—42.

Qi, Z., Shi, J., Zhang, Z., Cao, Y., Li, J., Cao, S., 2019. PEGylated graphene oxide-capped gold nanorods/silica nanoparticles as multifunctional drug delivery platform with enhanced near-infrared responsiveness. Mater. Sci. Eng. C 104, 109889.

Qiang, Y., Antony, J., Sharma, A., Nutting, J., Sikes, D., Meyer, D., 2006. Iron/iron oxide core-shell nanoclusters for biomedical applications. J. Nanopart. Res. 8 (3), 489—496.

Rai, D.B., Gupta, N., Pooja, D., Kulhari, H., 2020. Dendrimers for diagnostic applications. In Pharmaceutical Applications of Dendrimers. Elsevier, pp. 291—324.

Raj, S., Khurana, S., Choudhari, R., Kesari, K.K., Kamal, M.A., Garg, N., et al., 2021. Specific targeting cancer cells with nanoparticles and drug delivery in cancer therapy, In Seminars in Cancer Biology, 69. Academic Press, pp. 166—177.

Rapoport, N., 2007. Physical stimuli-responsive polymeric micelles for anti-cancer drug delivery. Prog. Polym. Sci. 32 (8—9), 962—990.

Raza, K., Thotakura, N., Kumar, P., Joshi, M., Bhushan, S., Bhatia, A., et al., 2015. C60-fullerenes for delivery of docetaxel to breast cancer cells: a promising approach for enhanced efficacy and better pharmacokinetic profile. Int. J. Pharm. 495 (1), 551—559.

Razavi, B., Abdollahi, A., Roghani-Mamaqani, H., Salami-Kalajahi, M., 2020. Light-, temperature-, and pH-responsive micellar assemblies of spiropyran-initiated amphiphilic block copolymers: kinetics of photochromism, responsiveness, and smart drug delivery. Mater. Sci. Eng. C 109, 110524.

Sang, M., Han, L., Luo, R., Qu, W., Zheng, F., Zhang, K., et al., 2020. CD44 targeted redox-triggered self-assembly with magnetic enhanced EPR effects for effective amplification of gambogic acid to treat triple-negative breast cancer. Biomater. Sci. 8 (1), 212—223.

Sargazi, A., Barani, A., Heidari Majd, M., 2020. Synthesis and apoptotic efficacy of biosynthesized silver nanoparticles using acacia luciana flower extract in MCF-7 breast cancer cells: activation of bak1 and bclx for cancer therapy. BioNanoScience 10 (3), 683—689.

Sarkar, P., Ghosh, S., Sarkar, K., 2021. Folic acid based carbon dot functionalized stearic acid-g-polyethyleneimine amphiphilic nanomicelle: targeted drug delivery and imaging for triple negative breast cancer. Colloids Surf. B 197, 111382.

Sarraf, P., Mueller, E., Jones, D., King, F.J., DeAngelo, D.J., Partridge, J.B., et al., 1998. Differentiation and reversal of malignant changes in colon cancer through PPARγ. Nat. Med. 4 (9), 1046—1052.

Satchi, R., Connors, T.A., Duncan, R., 2001. PDEPT: polymer-directed enzyme prodrug therapy. Br. J. Cancer 85 (7), 1070—1076.

Saul, J.M., Annapragada, A., Natarajan, J.V., Bellamkonda, R.V., 2003. Controlled targeting of liposomal doxorubicin via the folate receptor in vitro. J. Control. Release 92 (1—2), 49—67.

Sawant, R.R., Torchilin, V.P., 2012. Challenges in development of targeted liposomal therapeutics. AAPS J. 14 (2), 303—315.

Schmaljohann, D., 2006. Thermo-and pH-responsive polymers in drug delivery. Adv. Drug Deliv. Rev. 58 (15), 1655–1670.

Schroeder, A., Kost, J., Barenholz, Y., 2009. Ultrasound, liposomes, and drug delivery: principles for using ultrasound to control the release of drugs from liposomes. Chem. Phys. Lipids 162 (1–2), 1–16.

Sung, H., Ferlay, J., Rebecca L. Siegel, R.L., Laversanne, M., Soerjomataram, I., Jemal, A., 2021. Global cancer statistics 2020: GLOBOCAN estimates of incidence and mortality worldwide for 36 cancers in 185 countries. CA Cancer J. Clin. 71 (3), 209–249.

Seidel, Z.P., Zhang, X., MacMullan, M.A., Graham, N.A., Wang, P., Ted Lee Jr., C., 2020. Photo-triggered delivery of sirna and paclitaxel into breast cancer cells using catanionic vesicles. ACS Appl. Bio Mater. 3 (11), 7388–7398.

Shi, J., Liu, Y., Wang, L., Gao, J., Zhang, J., Yu, X., et al., 2014. A tumoral acidic pH-responsive drug delivery system based on a novel photosensitizer (fullerene) for in vitro and in vivo chemo-photodynamic therapy. Acta Biomater 10 (3), 1280–1291.

Shu, Y., Yin, H., Rajabi, M., Li, H., Vieweger, M., Guoet, S., et al., 2018. RNA-based micelles: a novel platform for paclitaxel loading and delivery. J. Control. Release 276, 17–29.

Such, G.K., Yan, Y., Johnston, A.P.R., Gunawan, S.T., Caruso, F., 2015. Interfacing materials science and biology for drug carrier design. Adv. Mater. 27 (14), 2278–2297.

Torchilin, V.P., 2006. Recent approaches to intracellular delivery of drugs and DNA and organelle targeting. Annu. Rev. Biomed. Eng. 8, 343–375.

Torchilin, V.P., 2010. Passive and active drug targeting: drug delivery to tumors as an example. Drug Deliv. 3–53.

Torres-Pérez, S.A., Andrés, S., María del Pilar Ramos-Godínez, M.d.P., Ramón-Gallegos, E., 2020. Glycosylated one-step PAMAM dendrimers loaded with methotrexate for target therapy in breast cancer cells MDA-MB-231. J. Drug Deliv. Sci. Technol. 58, 101769.

Unger, E., Porter, T., Lindner, J., Grayburn, P., 2014. Cardiovascular drug delivery with ultrasound and microbubbles. Adv. Drug Deliv. Rev. 72, 110–126.

Venkataraman, A., Amadi, E.V. Chen, Y., Papadopoulos, C., 2019. Carbon nanotube assembly and integration for applications. Nanoscale Res. Lett. 14 (1), 1–47.

Vicent, M.J., Greco, F., Nicholson, R.I., Paul, A., Griffiths, P.C., Duncan, R., 2005. Polymer therapeutics designed for a combination therapy of hormone-dependent cancer. Angew. Chem. 117 (26), 4129–4134.

Viger, M.L., Grossman, M., Fomina, N., Almutairi, A., 2013. Low power upconverted near-ir light for efficient polymeric nanoparticle degradation and cargo release. Adv. Mater. 25 (27), 3733–3738.

Vinothini, K., Rajendran, N.K., Rajan, M., Ramu, A., Marraiki, N., Elgorban, A.E., 2020. A magnetic nanoparticle functionalized reduced graphene oxide-based drug carrier system for a chemo-photodynamic cancer therapy. New J. Chem. 44 (14), 5265–5277.

Wang, S., Liu, J., Lv, H., Huang, X., Dong, P., Wang, Q., et al., 2022. Complete regression of xeno-grafted breast tumors by dextran-based dual drug conjugates containing paclitaxel and docosahexae-noic acid. Eur. J. Med. Chem. 114567.

Wang, H., Yu, D., Fang, J., Zhou, Y., Li, D., Zhen Liu, L., et al., 2020. Phenol-like group functiona-lized graphene quantum dots structurally mimicking natural antioxidants for highly efficient acute kidney injury treatment. Chem. Sci. 11 (47), 12721–12730.

Ward, M.A., Georgiou, T.K., 2011. Thermoresponsive polymers for biomedical applications. Polymers 3 (3), 1215–1242.

Wen, J., Sun, S., 2017. Recent advances of multi-stimuli-responsive drug delivery systems for cancer therapy. Curr. Trends Biomed. Eng. Biosci. 3 (2), 5555607.

Wong, K.K., Hussain, F.A., 2020. TRPM4 is overexpressed in breast cancer associated with estrogen response and epithelial-mesenchymal transition gene sets. PLoS One 15 (6), e0233884.

Wu, G., Fang, Y.-Z., Yang, S., Lupton, J.R., Turner, N.D., 2004. Glutathione metabolism and its impli-cations for health. J. Nutr. 134 (3), 489–492.

Wu, M., Lin, X., Tan, X., Li, J., Wei, Z., Zhang, D., et al., 2018. Photoresponsive nanovehicle for two independent wavelength light-triggered sequential release of P-gp shRNA and doxorubicin to optimize and enhance synergistic therapy of multidrug-resistant cancer. ACS Appl. Mater. Interfaces 10 (23), 19416−19427.

Xing, Y., Ding, T., Wang, Z., Wang, L., Guan, H., Tang, J., et al., 2019. Temporally controlled photo-thermal/photodynamic and combined therapy for overcoming multidrug resistance of cancer by polydopamine nanoclustered micelles. ACS Appl. Mater. Interfaces 11 (15), 13945−13953.

Xu, X., Chen, Y., Zhang, Y., Yao, Y., Ji, P., 2020. Highly stable and biocompatible hyaluronic acid-rehabilitated nanoscale MOF-Fe 2 + induced ferroptosis in breast cancer cells. J. Mater. Chem. B 8 (39), 9129−9138.

Yan, L., Qiu, L., 2015. Indocyanine green targeted micelles with improved stability for near-infrared image-guided photothermal tumor therapy. Nanomed 10 (3), 361−373.

Yan, J., Song, B., Hu, W., Meng, Y., Niu, F., Han, X., et al., 2018. Antitumor effect of GO-PEG-DOX complex on EMT-6 mouse breast cancer cells. Cancer Biother. Radiopharm. 33 (4), 125−130.

Yan, K., Zhang, S., Zhang, K., Miao, Y., Qiu, Y., Zhang, P., et al., 2020. Enzyme-responsive polymeric micelles with fluorescence fabricated through aggregation-induced copolymer self-assembly for anti-cancer drug delivery. Polym. Chem. 11 (48), 7704−7713.

Yang, Y., Lin, Y., Di, D., Zhang, X., Wang, D., Zhao, Q., et al., 2017. Gold nanoparticle-gated meso-porous silica as redox-triggered drug delivery for chemo-photothermal synergistic therapy. J. Colloid Interface Sci. 508, 323−331.

Ye, J., Liu, E., Yu, Z., Pei, X., Chen, S., Zhang, P., et al., 2016. CPP-assisted intracellular drug delivery, what is next? Int. J. Mol. Sci. 17 (11), 1892.

Yhee, J.Y., Son, S., Son, S., Joo, M.K., Kwon, I.C., 2013. The EPR effect in cancer therapy. In Cancer Targeted Drug Delivery. Springer, New York, pp. 621−632.

Yoo, M., Sung, Y., Lee, Y., Cho, C., 2000. Effect of polyelectrolyte on the lower critical solution tem-perature of poly (N-isopropyl acrylamide) in the poly (NIPAAm-co-acrylic acid) hydrogel. Polymer 41 (15), 5713−5719.

Yu, F.T., Chen, X., Wang, J., Qin, B., Villanueva, F.S., 2016. Low intensity ultrasound mediated lipo-somal doxorubicin delivery using polymer microbubbles. Mol. Pharm. 13 (1), 55−64.

Yuan, Y., Wang, Z., Cai, P., Liu, J., Liao, L.-D., Hong, M., et al., 2015. Conjugated polymer and drug co-encapsulated nanoparticles for chemo-and photo-thermal combination therapy with two-photon regulated fast drug release. Nanoscale 7 (7), 3067−3076.

Zangabad, P.S., Mirkiani, S., Shahsavari, S., Masoudi, B., Masroor, M., Hamed, H., et al., 2018. Stimulus-responsive liposomes as smart nanoplatforms for drug delivery applications. Nanotechnol. Rev. 7 (1), 95−122.

Zhai, S., Hu, X., Hu, Y., Wu, B., Xing, D., 2017. Visible light-induced crosslinking and physiological stabilization of diselenide-rich nanoparticles for redox-responsive drug release and combination che-motherapy. Biomaterials 121, 41−54.

Zhang, C., Wängler, B., Morgenstern, B., Zentgraf, H., Eisenhut, M., Untenecker, H., et al., 2007. Silica-and alkoxysilane-coated ultrasmall superparamagnetic iron oxide particles: a promising tool to label cells for magnetic resonance imaging. Langmuir 23 (3), 1427−1434.

Zhang, T., Wu, B., Akakuru, O.U., Yao, C., Sun, S., Chen, L., 2021. Hsp90 inhibitor-loaded IR780 micelles for mitochondria-targeted mild-temperature photothermal therapy in xenograft models of human breast cancer. Cancer Lett 500, 41−50.

Zhao, J., Lu, M., Lai, H., Lu, H., Lalevée, J., Barner-Kowollik, C., et al., 2018. Delivery of amonafide from fructose-coated nanodiamonds by oxime ligation for the treatment of human breast cancer. Biomacromolecules 19 (2), 481−489.

Zhi, D., Yang, T., Yang, J., Fu, S., Zhang, S., 2020. Targeting strategies for superparamagnetic iron oxide nanoparticles in cancer therapy. Acta Biomater 102, 13−34.

Zylberberg, C., Matosevic, S., 2016. Pharmaceutical liposomal drug delivery: a review of new delivery systems and a look at the regulatory landscape. Drug Deliv. 23 (9), 3319−3329.

CHAPTER 7

Recent advancement of hybrid nanoparticles synthesis and applications in lung cancer management

Apurba Gouri, Angela Sharma, Mrunalini Boddu, J. Mahendran, Soni Jignesh Mohanbhai, Mohammed Nadim Sardoiwala, Subhasree Roy Choudhury and Surajit Karmakar
Chemical Biology Unit, Institute of Nano Science and Technology, SAS Nagar, Punjab, India

7.1 Introduction

Scientists still face great challenges in the fight against cancer, a disease that arises from normal cells and affects nearly every tissue lineage in the human body due to divergent genetic mutations (Zhai et al., 2022). According to the American Cancer Society, Cancer is a disorder of uncontrolled growth of cells in the body that can develop anywhere in the human body (Danese et al., 2021). The process of cell division in humans allows cells to divide for the regeneration of new cells. Normal cells die when they become aged or damaged, and a new one replaces them (Ullah et al., 2021). This orderly process can sometimes break down, resulting in abnormal or damaged cells multiplying when they shouldn't. These abnormal cells will eventually form tumors, which are lumps of tissue. A tumor can be cancerous or noncancerous. Cancerous tumors can invade, spread into nearby tissues, and move to distant places in the body to form new tumors that are called metastasis (Zhang et al., 2021) and the tumor is called as malignant. A proto-oncogene plays a role in normal cellular growth and division, but when it is altered in certain ways or is more active than normal, it may become a cancer-causing gene called as oncogene allowing cells to grow and survive when it should not (Malebary et al., 2021). Additionally, tumor suppressor genes control cell growth and division. Cell division can be uncontrolled when tumor suppressor genes are altered (Martin et al., 2021).

Cancer has more than 100 types (Elshahat et al., 2021). Almost all cancers are named after the organs and tissues where they develop. On the other hand, lung cancer starts in the lung, while brain cancer starts in the brain (Li et al., 2021a). The type of cell that caused cancer can also be described, such as epithelial cells or squamous cells (Pourrahmat et al., 2021).

Multifunctional Nanocomposites for Targeted Drug Delivery in Cancer Therapy
DOI: https://doi.org/10.1016/B978-0-323-95303-0.00010-1

In the United States, lung cancer is the second most common form of cancer (Larsen and Minna, 2011). There are over 200,000 lung cancer cases every year in the United States and an estimated 2.3 million cases worldwide (Nguyen et al., 2004). Lung cancer is most commonly caused by cigarette smoking, but it can affect anyone. Histologically, lung tumors can be divided into two groups (Tan et al., 2012). The majority of lung cancers are caused by non-small cell lung cancer (NSCLC) and only 15% by small cell lung cancer (SCLC). Furthermore, NSCLCs can be classified into three subtypes based on their histological characteristics: large cell carcinoma, squamous-cell carcinoma, and adenocarcinoma (Tan et al., 2012). Lung cancer has a low survival rate because it can be difficult to detect and treat. Approximately, 16% of cases are discovered before malignancy and most are discovered in locally advanced or metastatic stages (Ruiz-Ceja and Chirino, 2017). For this reason, the Food and Drug Administration (FDA) has approved several biomarkers and drugs to detect lung cancer. The protein biomarker carcinoembryonic antigen (CEA) has been approved for lung cancer diagnosis since 2019; however, it is a poor diagnostic marker and should be combined with other markers, such as cytokeratin fragment-21 (Ruiz-Ceja and Chirino, 2017). A prognosis of more than one biomarker is necessary to detect lung cancer in the early stages. Additional biomarkers used in conjunction with CEA for lung cancer diagnosis include tumor-infiltrating lymphocytes (TILs), C4d complement split product, autoantibodies, circulating tumor cells (Krebs et al., 2014), cell-free deoxyribonucleic acid, and microribonucleic acid (Gao et al., 2021). Lung cancers can also be detected with X-ray, computed tomography (CT), positron emission tomography (PET), magnetic resonance imaging (MRI) (Bębas et al., 2021), and bone scan, as well as other imaging technologies (Zeng et al., 2016). Moreover, the primary treatment option for lung cancer is surgery, which is not suitable for metastatic and end-stage lung cancer, and most patients with high malignancy relapse after surgery (Sachs et al., 2021). Radiation and chemotherapy are generally administered after surgery. Lung cancer has been treated with a variety of chemotherapeutics (Abera et al., 2020) approved by the FDA. The three most effective drugs used to treat lung adenocarcinoma are Crizotinib, Gefitinib (Liu et al., 2021), and Atezolimuzab, which inhibit the anaplastic lymphoma kinase (ALK), epidermal growth factor receptor (EGFR), and programmed death-ligand 1 (PDL1), respectively. Lung adenocarcinoma is usually treated with this therapeutics as a second line of treatment. The first-line and second-line treatments of squamous cell carcinoma of the lung are using Gefitinib and Erlotinib to inhibit the overexpression of the EGFR receptor (Yamamoto et al., 2021; Nakagawa et al., 2021).

Despite the advances in diagnostic and therapeutic tools for lung cancer, the drawbacks of the existing systems, such as their invasiveness and low sensitivity, call for the development of new methods with fewer side effects and greater detection and treatment efficiencies (Cryer and Thorley, 2019). It has been proven that nanotechnology can assist the basic and clinical research on pulmonary cancer. For the detection of lung tumors, a variety of nanoparticle imaging tools are clinically used, including semiconductor nanocrystals and metallic and inorganic nanoparticles (Huang et al., 2009). Polystyrene nanoparticles doped with quantum dots (QDs) have been used to detect CEA and CYFRA21−1 in the serum of lung cancer patients (Chen et al., 2017). As well, nanoparticle systems can be used to treat lung cancer (Yang et al., 2009). Different nanoparticulate drug delivery systems using metals, semiconductors, and polymers have shown promising results for lung cancer therapy both in vitro and in vivo. The FDA-approved nano-drug Abraxane (Celgene) is a paclitaxel-bound albumin NP that is used to treat NSCLC. Examination proved it is more soluble in the bloodstream as well as it was more likely to penetrate cancerous cells by passive targeting (Thangavel et al., 2022). Opaxio is a second nano drug-containing polyglutamic acid conjugated paclitaxel used in lung cancer treatment that failed to exhibit acceptable therapeutic effects in an early clinical trial (Verschraegen et al., 2009). Nanoplatin (NC-6004, micellar form of cisplatin) and Genexol-PM (a micellar form of paclitaxel composed of a block of MPEG and D, L-PLA) are also approved for the treatment of patients with NSCLC in phase I and II clinical trials (Ventola, 2017). Thus, the development of more complex nanocarriers with improved diagnostic and therapeutic efficacy are required to overcome the limitations of existing treatments or conventional nanoparticle-mediated delivery. Hybrid nanoparticles (NPs) gain attention in response to current nanoparticle systems' structural and functional weaknesses (Rizvi et al., 2022).

To achieve this, hybrid nanoparticles, which contain both inorganic and organic structural moieties with the ability to deliver drugs to the lung, which have been introduced as a new generation of nanoparticles (Vengurlekar and Chaturvedi, 2021). The field of nanomedicine and nanotherapeutics is constantly developing new drug delivery systems to address immediate infirmities, and nanotherapeutics are proving to be very effective in the diagnosis and treatment of lung cancer (Li et al., 2021b). Biomedicine and therapeutics are becoming more focused on nanotechnology. There are many advantages to nanotherapeutic approaches, including their less toxicity, biocompatibility, and ability to solubilize and deliver an effective amount of drug molecules to a specific site in a disease (Gholizadeh et al., 2021). Nanocarriers have the advantages of being able to cross physical barriers as well as their nanoscale size, making them a major advantage for developing new and noninvasive treatments for lung cancer (Gholizadeh et al., 2021). Nanocarriers are molecules that have a size between 10 and 100 nanometers, which makes them efficient at carrying drugs to sites inside the lung tissue (Tao et al., 2021). They can transport poorly soluble, potent drugs to specific sites within the body in a cell-specific manner. It is known that nanocarriers, like protein nanoparticles or organic/inorganic nanomaterials, can bind to specific receptors and therefore uptake themselves within disease-associated cells or tumors (Ahmad et al., 2021). It is possible to deliver more than one potent drug simultaneously with help of nanocarriers in the development of therapy. Nanocarriers having higher drug encapsulation efficiency, good biodistribution, and drug release capability are useful for nanotherapeutic approaches in the treatment of diseases (He and Lin, 2015). Nanomaterials exhibiting nontoxic, cost-efficient, biodegradable, biocompatible, noninflammatory, higher bioavailability, and being able to penetrate in tumor sites are a good choice for the development of hybrid nanoparticles (Khan et al., 2019). To address the problem of lung cancer with the help of hybrid nanoparticles, two therapeutic targets should be focused on which EGFR and ALK fused products play a major role in lung cancer progression. Cancer cells proliferate and survive using both EGFR and ALK-mediated signaling pathways. The inhibitions of these molecular markers or the blocking of their mediated pathways pave the way for lung cancer therapy. In the development of hybrid nanoparticles-mediated lung cancer treatment, several hybrid nanoparticles have been developed for in vitro diagnostics of lung cancer, including hybrid magnetic silica nanoparticles (Pfaff et al., 2011), hybrid super magnetic iron oxide nanoparticles (SPIONs), and multifunctional gold nanoparticles. In addition, hybrid SPIONs (Pfaff et al., 2011), lipid-coated polymers (Thevenot et al., 2007), and hybrid NPs coupled with genes (Pfaff et al., 2011) have been used both in vitro and in vivo for the treatment of lung cancer. In a single hybrid nanoparticle, multiple components are combined to allow for the customization of structural and functional properties. Many articles have been written on the use of hybrid nanoparticles for the detection and treatment of lung cancer, but there is a comprehensive literature that discusses the potential for hybrid nanoparticles to deliver contrast agents or chemotherapy for optimal imaging and treatment of lung cancer (Ihde, 1992). Indeed, hybrid nanoparticles have been shown to extend the residence time and bioavailability of anticancer drugs with improved intracellular internalization in lung tumorigenic cells (Shepard et al., 2021). In the selection of therapeutic agents for hybrid nanoparticle-mediated lung cancer therapy, one should understand the molecular mechanism of the lung cancer and its therapeutic target molecules.

7.1.1 Molecular mechanism and lung cancer therapeutic targets

Several genetic and epigenetic factors influence the molecular mechanisms of lung cancer. DNA damage stimulates the conversion of lung epithelial cells into tumorigenic cells (Liu et al., 2012). As such, it is challenging to pinpoint which mutations cause lung cancer. The next-generation sequencing provided insight into the molecular alterations that occur in lung cancer and identified some of the genetic changes in the cancer cells. There are over 727 mutations found in 31 cases with NSCLC that have not previously been found in the COSMIC database (Liu et al., 2012). According to genomic studies, lung cancer is due to mutations in specific biomolecules, including EGFR, ALK, Kirsten rat sarcoma viral oncogene homolog (KRAS), human epidermal growth factor receptor-2 (HER2), murine sarcoma viral oncogene homolog B (BRAF), tyrosine-protein kinase, mitogen-activated protein kinase kinase (MEK-1), phosphatidylinositol-3-kinase/protein kinase B/

mammalian target of rapamycin (PI3K/AKT/mTOR), ROS proto-oncogene 1 (ROS1), RET proto-oncogene (RET), P53 proto-oncogene, decoding domain receptor tyrosine kinase-2 (DDR2), serine/threonine kinase 11 (LKB-1), and phosphatase and tensin homolog (PTEN) gene. Among them, EGFR mutations as well as rearrangements of ALK are the most clinically relevant mutations that cause lung cancer with different levels of prevalence in patients (Cooper et al., 2013). Signaling pathways triggered by overexpression of EGFR, ALK, and echinoderm microtubule-associated protein-like 4 (EML4) lead to cancer cell proliferation are illustrated schematically in Fig. 7.1. The therapeutic option might be paved effective way by inhibiting activated signaling pathways. The EGFR transmembrane protein transfers signaling molecules from the extracellular matrix into the cell. It is overexpressed in >70%–80% of NSCLCs, making it an important therapeutic target of lung tumors. Several inhibitors are available for various mutations of the EGFR kinase domain. In a recent study, it was shown that a combination of Gefitinib and EGFR small interfering RNA (siRNA) could be effective for treating lung tumors since it inhibits the activation of AKT and STAT pathways and limits the overexpression of EGFR (Sordella et al., 2004). In another study, by targeting single-chain variable fragment EGFR antibodies with Heparin-cisplatin NPs (ScFvEGFR), it has been demonstrated that cisplatin and Pt-DNA are much more likely to penetrate tissues through EGFR-mediated

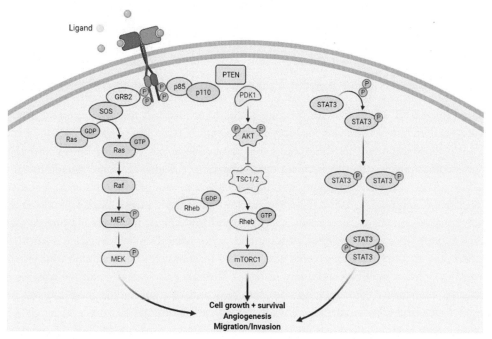

Figure 7.1 Schematic representation of molecular mechanism pathway involved in lung cancer progression and pathogenesis.

endocytosis and enhanced the antitumor activity of heparin/cisplatin NPs (Peng et al., 2011). The combination of an EGFR antibody (C225) and plasmonic magnetic nanoparticles could also be used to treat NSCLC. In the enhanced therapeutic, elevated apoptosis and autophagy have been found with C225 hybrid NPs while they treated NSCLCs compared to free C225 and plasmonic magnetic NPs conjugated C225 (Yokoyama et al., 2011). Most lung cancers are caused by rearrangements of the ALK gene rather than EGFR mutations, caused by the fusion of the ALK gene with the EML4 gene, which encodes an abnormal tyrosine kinase (Cooper et al., 2013). There is evidence that ALK mutations are found in >5% of patients with NSCLCs. Tyrosine kinase inhibitors, such as crizotinib, are common therapies used to treat lung cancers with ALK mutations (Cirne et al., 2021). Moreover, since the lung cancer genome is diverse and heterogeneous, it makes detection and treatment much harder. Therefore, it is essential to understand how lung epithelial and cancerous cells look histologically rather than the molecular pathways involved. It would be possible to improve clinical outcomes by understanding the highly complex molecular mechanisms and histopathological appearances of lung cancers.

7.1.2 Current methods for diagnosis and treatment of lung cancer

It is usually detected by abnormalities in the chest radiograph or symptoms like cough, wheezing, blood in the sputum, weight loss, and difficulty swallowing. Lung cancer is diagnosed based on the type of cancer (SCLCs, NSCLCs), the location of the primary tumor, its size and location of metastases, as well as the clinical grade of the patient (Rivera et al., 2013). The diagnosis of lung cancer involves a physical exam, a medical history, routine blood work, urine testing, X-rays of internal organs and bones, bronchoscopy, biopsy, CT scan, MRI, PET scan, and combined PET-CT scans. Combining PET-CT scan with imaging of the lung tumor is the gold standard procedure for detecting its size and location (Rivera et al., 2013; Gould et al., 2013).

It is more important for the optimal treatment of lung cancers to perform appropriate therapeutic strategies than to perform early lung cancer diagnosis. Surgery, radiotherapy, radiosurgery, chemotherapy, and immunotherapy are routinely used for lung cancer treatment (Collins et al., 2007). The best method for treating lung cancer depends on the functional assessment of the patient, the stage, and the type of histologically proven cancer. Surgery is usually preferred for patients who have NSCLC in stage I to IIIA. Chemotherapeutics are administered after surgery to eliminate the remaining cancer cells, but they are also used before surgery to shrink the cancer cells and make them easier to remove. In patients who undergo complete resection of tumorigenic lung and did not receive primary chemotherapy, adjuvant therapy is an option (Kozower et al., 2013). Preoperative chemotherapy has been found to increase survival rates in NSCLC patients. For cases where lung tumors cannot be removed because of diffusion in the surrounding area or when surgery isn't needed, the most effective treatment would be a combination of radiotherapy and chemotherapy. Avastin or Bevacizumab targeted therapies are also useful for targeting the anticancer and drug delivery to the tumor microenvironment. Furthermore, palliative care can help reduce side effects and symptoms of disease and improve a patient's survival rate (Collins et al., 2007).

It is imperative to find effective methods of treating lung cancer at an early stage. Lung cancer detection and treatment methods are still in their infancy. In recent years, nanoparticulate systems with appropriate biocompatibility, biodegradability, and structural and biological properties have gained more attention for use in this field (He and Lin, 2015). By combining different functional groups and targeting agents with nanoparticulate systems, drugs are better distributed and directed into the tumor microenvironment through active or passive targeting, increasing the therapeutic efficiency and diagnostic capability (Brannon-Peppas and Blanchette, 2004). Nonspecific toxicity is reduced by these systems, and also the permeation and retention (EPR) effect is enhanced, resulting in better drug internalization (Parvanian et al., 2017). Various nanoparticulate systems have been studied to deliver imaging and therapeutic agents into lung cancer cells based on lipids, natural, synthetic, organic, inorganic, and viral nanoparticles (Babu et al., 2013). Synthetic and natural polymeric nanoparticles have been shown to improve the efficacy of anticancer drugs and the diagnostic capability of lung tumors. They can highly control drug release rates, deliver imaging agents directly into the target site, and can be administered orally, intravenously, and inhalational. The structure of several novel nanoparticulate formulations used to treat lung cancer has been briefly illustrated in Fig. 7.2.

Classes of Nanoparticles

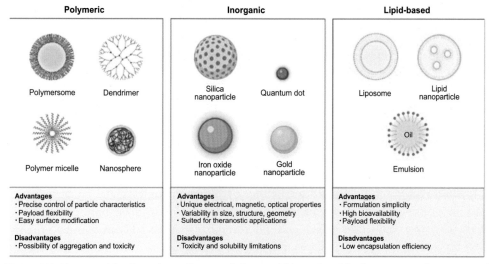

Figure 7.2 Nanoparticles have been illustrated that could be utilized for lung cancer diagnosis and therapy.

7.2 Hybrid nanoparticles—synthesis strategy

Hybrid nanomaterials are the chemical conjugates of organic and/or inorganic materials, which are mixtures of:

- Two or more than two inorganic constituents.
- Two or more than two organic constituents.
- A minimum of one of both types of constituents.

The resulting material is a synergistic material, instead of being a simple mixture of its components. This bestows them with properties and performance to develop applications with unique properties, which are determined by the interface of the constituents at the molecular or supramolecular level. Improvement in the physicochemical properties of the nanoparticles is associated with enhanced functionality. By the optimization largely of electronic, optical, magnetic, and thermal properties or an amalgamation of them, electrochemical or biochemical properties can be altered. The astonishing properties of hybrid materials are further expanded by the inclusion of nanosized materials owing to the task of having greater options for multifunctional materials. These innovative materials are suitable for a huge range of applications comprising optics, electronics, sensors, ionics, energy conversion and storage, mechanics, membranes, protective coatings, catalysis, etc. The unique adaptability of these materials permits the design of materials with tunable properties as well as improved performance and properties compared to their age-old counterparts in the market. Gómez-Romero, 2006 #1378.

7.2.1 Preparation methods for hybrid nanoparticles

Broadly, hybrid nanoparticles can be synthesized by two methods; physical methods and chemical methods. Preparation of hybrid nanoparticles by physical methods is simpler than chemical methods, but the size of the nanoparticles is tough to control. The nanoparticles prepared by physical method, at times remain separate and distinct within the final nanostructure and a direct and robust hybridization between nanoparticles is achievable by this pathway. On the contrary, due to the presence of chemical species like the stabilizing ligands, and polymer shells, nanoparticles prepared by chemical methods can exhibit unwanted properties. The illustration has shown the various processes of the hybrid nanoparticle synthesis in Fig. 7.3.

7.2.1.1 Chemical synthesis methods

Chemical synthesis can be performed either by the reduction of metal precursors or by various processing routes. Reduction of metal precursors can be performed by two ways chemical reduction (CR) and photoreduction (PR). Hydrothermal, thermal decomposition, sol-gel, coprecipitation, electrodeposition, sonochemical, and seeding growth are various processing routes used for fabricating the hybrid nanoparticles.

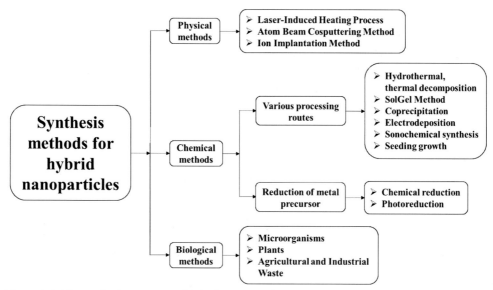

Figure 7.3 The synthesis strategies of hybrid nanoparticles are represented with respective processes.

7.2.1.1.1 Chemical reduction method

This method involves the accumulation of noble metal (NM) nanoparticles on the surface of oxide metal (OM) nanoparticles leading to the NM-decorated OM nanoparticles. The adsorbed NM ions on the surface of OMs are then reduced by chemical-reducing agents. Sometimes the synthesis is assisted by ultrasonication. Examples of chemical reducing agents include diethanolamine, sodium borohydride/ascorbic acid, sodium citrate (Liu et al., 2017), hydrazine (Zhang et al., 2011), N, N-dimethylformamide (Zhang et al., 2006a; Li et al., 2017; Tom et al., 2003), oleylamine (Wang et al., 2010), formaldehyde (Zhang et al., 2011), and glucose (Ebrahimi et al., 2016), ascorbic acid (Khandare and Terdale, 2017).

Synthesis of the $Pd-CeO_2$, $Au-Fe_3O_4$, and $Ag-Mn_3O_4$ nanocomposites reported by Liu and group (Liu et al., 2014). Preparation of Au/TiO_2 hybrid nanoparticles (Damato et al., 2013) and AuNPs decorated ZnO nanohybrids (Chen et al., 2013) is reported by the CR method. Au/TiO_2 hybrid nanoparticles by this method in three main steps:

The drawback of these methods includes the presence of the mixture of both pure NM nanoparticles and hybrid nanoparticles, which three approaches can resolve:

1. Chemical reducing agent is locally immobilized on the surface of OM nanoparticles (Pearson et al., 2011).
2. The redox reaction between metal hydroxide and NM ion (without using the reducing agent) (Liu et al., 2014).
3. Using a low weight ratio of NMs precursors and OMs (like: NMs:OMs <1:30).

7.2.1.1.2 Photoreduction method

In this method, photoelectrons emitted from OMs (e.g., TiO_2 or ZnO) upon light irradiation perform an important the reducing process and act with surface metal ions to form nanoparticles on the surface of hosting nanoparticles (Chen et al., 2010). Light sources of >300 nm are applicable for this purpose. In that, high-pressure mercury arcs (Au/TiO_2 hybrid) (Tanaka et al., 2013), low-pressure mercury lamps (Ag/TiO_2 hybrid) (Albiter et al., 2015), or sunlight (Pd/TiO_2 hybrid) (Leong et al., 2015) are examples.

For biomedical applications like targeted drug delivery, the synthesis of gold/iron (Au/Fe) nanohybrids by photoreduction method has been reported for discriminating and efficient photodynamic therapy (PDT). These nanohybrids were used to deliver methyl aminolevulinate (MAL), which is a prodrug that after metabolism turns into a photosensitizer. For this, they used 300 Watt Cermax xenon lamps as a light source by duration times ranging from 1 to 10 minutes (de Oliveira Gonçalves et al., 2018; Oliveira Gonçalves et al., 2018).

7.2.1.2 Various processing routes
7.2.1.2.1 Hydrothermal-based hybrid nanoparticle synthesis

The hydrothermal-based methods are facile and provide ease in controlling the size and morphology of the nanoparticles. It works at higher temperatures and pressure. In general, this method could/could not involve the use of the ligands, stabilizers, or surfactants in the hydrothermal synthesis of hybrid nanoparticles. Wu et al. have synthesized flower-shaped Au-TiO_2 hybrids (Wu et al., 2010), by using the hydrothermal process with redox procedure and Pt/TiO_2 core-shell NPs (Wu et al., 2009), without ligands or surfactants. The use of microwave irradiation in the hydrothermal reaction at high temperatures was found to be more effective and reduced reaction time. In this direction Song et al. have fabricated Au@TiO_2 core-shell nanoparticles, using the microwave-assisted hydrothermal method (Song et al., 2014). The processes are composed of multiple steps that are represented in Fig. 7.4.

Ag-TiO_2 nanohybrids have been reported by Padmanaban et al. utilizing hexamine as the stabilizer (Padmanaban et al., 2017).

7.2.1.2.2 Sol-Gel method

The size of hybrid nanoparticles is precisely controllable in this method, but the bonding/hybridization between hybrid nanoparticles is relatively weak, as compared to other methods. In this method, the ligand or surfactant was added to the solution containing the NM and/or OM precursors. Depending on the ligand/surfactant/stabilizers, various nanostructures of hybrids can be obtained, such as:

1. Au-TiO_2 core-shell nanoparticle with polyvinyl pyrrolidone as surfactant.

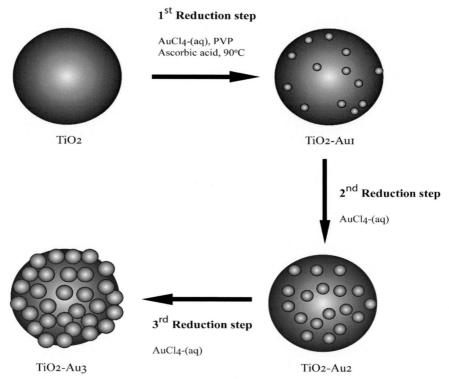

Figure 7.4 The synthesis process has been shown for the preparation of titanium and gold hybrid nanoparticles.

2. Ag/TiO_2 core-shell nanoparticles with cetyltrimethylammonium bromide as a protective agent (Sakai et al., 2006).
3. $Au@SiO_2$ and $SiO_2@Au$ core-shell nanoparticles using a microemulsion-assisted sol-gel method coupled with photoreduction reaction and sodium 3-sulfonatemercaptopropane as the stabilizer (Olteanu et al., 2016).

Coprecipitation method This method is simple and efficient, but might affect the controllability of nanoparticle shape which leads to the broader size distribution with certain aggregations. Also, it is difficult to obtain the purity and stoichiometric phase of nanohybrids by the coprecipitation method (Ma et al., 2015). Coprecipitation synthesis of Au-metal oxide hybrids, such as $Au-Fe_2O_3$, $Au-NiO$, and $Au-Co_3O_4$ have been reported using sodium carbonate, $HAuCl_4$, and metal nitrate (Liu et al., 2017; Wang et al., 2017). In the same way, Donkova and group prepared Au–ZnO nanoparticles using Na_2CO_3, $HAuCl_4$, and $Zn(NO_3)_2$ (Donkova et al., 2011). Ma and the group also reported the synthesis of $Ag-Fe_3O_4$ core-shell nanowires by coprecipitation method using $FeCl_3$, $FeCl_2$, and polyvinylpyrrolidone (PVP) (Ma et al., 2015).

7.2.1.2.3 Sonochemical synthesis

This method is faster, safer, less complicated, and more of an eco-friendly method, as compared to other traditional preparative methods of hybrid nanoparticles. Sivasankaran et al. (2013) demonstrated the sonochemical synthesis of Pd-metal oxide hybrid nanoparticles with the assistance of ultrasound energy (20 and 32 KHz). They have successfully fabricated the Pd-CuO nanohybrids in the sonochemical reactor batch from copper salt in the presence of palladium and water. Ziylan-Yavas and group have synthesized Au-TiO_2 and Pd-TiO_2 nanohybrids by means of high-frequency ultrasound (35 KHz) and UV irradiation (254 nm) both. They used metal salts ($Na_2PdCl_4.3H_2O$, $Na(AuCl_4)0.2H_2O$), commercial TiO_2 powder, and polyethylene-glycol monostearate (Ziylan-Yavas et al., 2015). Ag NP-decorated TiO_2 nanoparticles in the presence of ethylene glycol in an alkaline solution, were also fabricated in this way through the sonochemical route (Jhuang and Cheng, 2016). Likewise, Pol and the group produced the AgNPs decorated SiO_2 with the ultrasound irradiation (20 KHz) in an aqueous solution comprising of silica slurry, silver nitrate, and ammonia (Pol et al., 2002).

7.2.1.2.4 Seeding growth method

To address the problem of lattice mismatch between the two nanoparticles; in the synthesis of hybrid nanoparticles, the seeding growth approach is a very effective method, especially in the case of dumbbell-like hybrid nanoparticles. Fan et al. reasoned that when using the epitaxial growth the lattice mismatch between the two noble nanoparticles was below 5% (Fan et al., 2008). Using the same method, Zhang and group have synthesized the Ag-Fe_3O_4 heterodimeric hybrid nanoparticles in oleylamine and toluene, by utilizing preformed Fe_3O_4 nanoparticles as the seeds (Zhang et al., 2006b).

Due to its high controllability, the seed-mediated growth method has also been effectually used for producing the high-quality NM nanoparticles (Niu et al., 2012). This method involves the use of the shape-directing reagents such as cetyltrimethylammonium bromide and cetylpyridinium chloride (Gao et al., 2003). Similarly, Liu et al. (2015) constructed the dumbbell-like 5−14 nm Au-Fe_3O_4 nanoparticles, expending 5 nm AuNPs as the seeds in the presence of oleic acid and oleylamine. Likewise, the dumbbell-like 3−10 nm Pt-Fe_3O_4NPs were created, in the presence of oleylamine using 3 nm Pt NPs as a seeding agent (Wang et al., 2010).

In addition to the above methods, metal nanoparticles are also synthesized in a gaseous environment for example through flame spray pyrolysis and the selective catalytic reduction method. In the flame spray pyrolysis method, metal nanoparticles are prepared by temperature-mediated reduction, when a metal precursor solution is sprayed (Pisduangdaw et al., 2009). In the selective catalytic reduction technique, the nitrogen oxides are converted into H_2O and N_2 using a gaseous catalyst like ammonia and urea (Sharma et al., 2017; Huynh et al., 2020).

The micro-emulsion is a system consisting of three constituents: an immiscible solvent (continuous phase), a minor droplet (dispersed phase), and a surfactant that covers the droplet. Depending on the properties of all three and the hydrophilic—hydrophobic balance value of the surfactant, there are several types of micro-emulsions, such as water-Triton X-100, water—oil, and oil—water among others. Desired size and composition of the metal nanoparticles, which are synthesized inside the droplets, are achievable. Majorly, microemulsion has been utilized to synthesize bimetallic and trimetallic alloy nanoparticles (Huynh et al., 2020; Zielińska-Jurek et al., 2012).

7.2.1.3 Physical methods of synthesis
7.2.1.3.1 Laser-induced heating process
In order to synthesize NM nanoparticles from their bulk metal targets, the pulsed laser ablation in liquid (PLAL) method has been used most commonly. Nanoparticles synthesized from this method were charged and free of surfactants, thus being very stable, and a pure colloidal solution was obtained (Barcikowski and Compagnini, 2013). Singh and Soni fabricated the rattle-type $Ag@Al_2O_3$ nanohybrids by using the laser (532-nm)-induced heating. In an aqueous solution of PVP, AgNPs and AlNPs were first synthesized by this method from silver and aluminum metallic substrates. Next in the aqueous solution, the As-prepared colloidal solution of Ag-Al nanoparticles was postirradiated by the unfocused laser beam (Singh and Soni, 2015).

Using the same method (PLAL, 248-nm laser), Zhang et al. fabricated the gold nanoparticles (5 nm) on decorated ceria nanotubes (Zhang et al., 2013). Similarly, using the 1064-nm laser, Siuzdak et al. produced TiO_2 nanoparticles decorated with platinum nanoparticles (3—20 nm) (Siuzdak et al., 2014).

7.2.1.4 Ion implantation method
This technique has been extensively applied for optical waveguides and semiconductor chips, which encompasses acceleration and orientation of ionized atoms (guest) into the target (host) substrate. The ion, with several hundred to several million electron volt energies, strikes the host atoms in the host lattice, thus dropping their energy, and finally inserts into the solid matrix. The inserted amount is decided by the ion dose. For silver nanoparticles, the ion doses are in the $1015-1017$ ions/cm^2 range.

Wang and the group, by using high-energy ion implantation, have fabricated Au nanoparticles in TiO_2 single crystal (Wang et al., 2004). Likewise, Chang and group (Chang et al., 2011) have produced the TiO_2 nanoparticles implanted with Ag.

7.2.1.4.1 Radiolytic method
Production of metal nanoparticles by gamma (γ-ray) or electron beam irradiation to reduce metal ions in soluble precursors, to form metal nanoparticles, is called radiolytic synthesis.

The radiolytic method is employed to produce alloy nanoparticles that are not stable when produced by thermal decomposition. The dose of irradiation decides the type of alloy nanoparticle created like a low dose can lead to the creation of core—shell alloy nanoparticles, whereas a higher dose controls the making of mixed alloy nanoparticles (Călinescu et al., 2014; Redjala et al., 2006). The challenge of the radiolytic method lies in directing the shape of the nanoparticles. Though, these techniques are low-cost, environment-friendly, and promising for large applications (Srinoi et al., 2018; Amendola et al., 2013). Examples of the hybrid nanoparticles prepared by radiolytic synthesis are Rh-Pt, Au-Ag, Au-Pt, Rh-Pd, Pt-Ru-Sn, Au-Pt-Ag, Pd-Ru-Ni, and Zr-Ni-Cu alloy nanoparticles (Redjala et al., 2006; Sarker et al., 2013; Sharma et al., 2018).

7.2.1.5 Biological methods

Most of the chemical methods centered on harmful chemicals, massive energy, and high temperature and form nanoparticles with restricted properties. To overcome these shortcomings, green synthesis approaches based on biological sources such as microorganisms, plants, and industrial and agricultural wastes have progressed recently.

7.2.1.5.1 Microorganisms for the production of nanoparticles

Various microorganisms, including yeasts, bacteria, fungi, and viruses, have been deliberated as nanofactories to yield nanoparticles because of their capability to accumulate and purify heavy metals through various reductase enzymes (Gahlawat and Choudhury, 2019). Metal reduction can be performed in the extracellular or intracellular location and various reducing factors involved are proteins, genes, enzymes, and biomolecules of the microorganisms that play roles in reducing factors.

Bacteria, such as *Salmonella typhimurium*, *Escherichia coli*, *Rhodopseudomonas capsulata*, *Listeria monocytogenes*, and *Bacillus subtilis*, have been used to generate Cu-Ag, Pd-Fe, Au-Pd, Pd-Pt, Pd-Ag, Au-Ag, Au-Fe, and Pd-Au-Fe, alloy nanoparticles (Huynh et al., 2020; Deplanche et al., 2012; Han et al., 2019; Jena et al., 2020).

Fungi offer some advantages over bacteria such as easy to culture, high accumulation, high yield, and presence of complex proteins that support in nanoparticle creation. Their exposure to a metal ion environment leads to the production of compounds or biomolecules like anthraquinones, naphthoquinones, or nitrate reductase as reducing agents to create metal particles (Singh et al., 2016; Boroumand Moghaddam et al., 2015). Au-Ag and Cd-S alloy nanoparticles are prepared by fungi, such as *Neurospora crassa*, *Fusarium semitectum*, *Fusarium oxysporum*, *Coriolus versicolor*, *Pleurotus ostreatus*, and yeasts, such as *Saccharomyces cerevisiae*, *Schizosaccharomyces pombe*, *Schizosaccharomyces*, and *Candida glabrata* (Sawle et al., 2008; Feng et al., 2017).

Viruses are also exploited in nanomaterial synthesis. Mostly, plant virus capsids work as a valuable biotemplate in nanoparticle production (Young et al., 2008). And examples include tobacco mosaic virus, cowpea mosaic virus, and red clover necrotic mosaic virus for producing Co-Pt, Fe-Pt, Co-Fe, Cd-Se alloy nanoparticles (Young et al., 2008; Shah et al., 2009).

7.2.1.5.2 Plants for making nanoparticles

The green synthesis of nanomaterials takes into account the utilization of plants, which comprises the use of several plant organs like the stem, root, leaf, seed, fruit peel, and flowers and their extracts to produce nanoparticles. The method is environmentally friendly and stable, and the nanoparticles prepared have prospective use in environmental and biomedical applications. It is suggested that plant constituents, comprising amino acids, protein, organic acid, and polysaccharides, and secondary metabolites such as alkaloids, polyphenols, heterocyclic, flavonoids, and terpenoid compounds act as reducing agents and stabilizing factors (Singh et al., 2016; Parihar et al., 2019). Both the types of nanoparticles monometallic as well as metallic alloy nanoparticles have been prepared using plant-based approaches. For example, Pt-Cu, Ag-Ni, Ag-Cu, Ag-Co, Au-Ag, and Zn-Ag nanoparticles have been created with the leaf extracts of *Azadirachta indica, Canna indica, Moringa oleifera, Alchornea laxiflora, Cacumen Platycladi,* palm, *Mirabilis jalapa* (Akinsiku et al., 2018; Gopiraman et al., 2019; Olajire et al., 2017) and creation of Au-Ag-Sr, and Fe-Ag-Pt nanoparticles were done from the roots of coriander, *Platycodon grandiflorum* (Binod et al., 2018). Algae are also employed for the synthesis of alloy nanoparticles, e.g., *Phaeodactylum tricornutum, Spirulina platensis, Chlamydomonas reinhardtii,* and were utilized to prepare Au-Ag and CdS nanoparticles (Rao and Pennathur, 2017; Govindaraju et al., 2008).

7.2.1.5.3 Agricultural and industrial waste for preparing nanoparticles

Recently, nanoparticles have been prepared largely from industrial and agricultural wastes. Industrial wastes like timber dust, sugar cane bagasse, and wild weeds, including unwanted plants, herbs, or shrubs, which are generally burned, and postharvest wastes such as rice husk, fruit peels, and egg shells, which form about 80% of the biomass on the field, can be used as natural sources for the green synthesis of nanoparticles. These waste materials have benefits counting renewing waste material, reduction of using harmful chemicals, and low-cost and low energy (Adelere and Lateef, 2016; Zamare et al., 2016). By means of banana peels and the else useless weed *Antigonon leptopus*, Au-Ag and CdS alloy nanoparticles were manufactured (Newase and Bankar, 2017; Ganaie et al., 2016).

Without the extra step of attaching to bioactive compounds, the biosynthesized nanoparticles have biocompatible characteristics and can be introduced into biological and pharmacological applications. However, these production methods also have some drawbacks due to the complex parameters or constituents in plant organs; the size and shape of nanoparticles cannot often be controlled well. In some circumstances, the produced nanoparticles are poisonous to the plant and bacteria (Gahlawat and Choudhury, 2019).

7.3 Hybrid nanoparticles and its application in diagnosis

The diagnostic evaluation and treatment of a patient with lung cancer require a different team of specialists, including a pulmonologist, oncologist, pathologist, radiologist, and thoracic surgeon (Latimer and Mott, 2015). Several imaging methods can be used to diagnose patients with lung cancer. In practice combination of several imaging studies is needed to ensure the accuracy of the diagnosis (Park et al., 2020). The traditional methods include chest CT, positron emission tomography PET-CT, brain MRI, and whole body bone scintigraphy to determine the invasion of other organs. The biopsy is an indispensable technique to confirm the metastasis. Various biomarkers are present in different regions in the human body, such as the tumor cells and body fluids, which include urine, blood saliva secretion, sputum, and exhaled breath. Their presence leads to a noninvasive, early detection of the cancer, and precise delivery of drugs to specific target cancer sites (Hassanein et al., 2012; Clark and Mao, 2012). This necessitates finding a better scheme to diagnose lung cancer to refrain from multiple techniques and its high cost. Early identification, apart from detecting primary metastasis, also helps in treating secondary cancer, which demands easily applicable techniques to screen individuals at risk (Table 7.1).

7.3.1 Quantum dots

QDs are emerging and promising tools in the replacement of organic fluorescent dyes with nanoscale physicochemical properties. QDs have several advantages over organic fluorescent dyes like 20 times more brighter and thousands of times better stability to photobleaching than organic dyes (Chan and Nie, 1998). QDs are often used to establish electrochemical luminescence (ECL) sensors due to their high fluorescence intensity, unique size-dependent electrochemical properties, long fluorescence lifetime, strong photostability, and ECL parameter tunability. The detection limit is based on QDs (0.3 pg/mL). A suspension and planar microarray system can be established based on high throughput and low cost. Briefly, the suspension state ground on the target proteins to constitute a sandwich structure between the magnetic beads and the QDs through specific antibody-antigen interactions the modification of lung cancer-specific antibody on the surface of QDs to be done. Single domain antibody (sdAb), a substitution to native antibody can reduce the molecular weight and increase the effect prominently. Though the surface modification of QDs can be used to improve biocompatibility and alleviate cell toxicity, security and targeting specificity are still major obstacles that QDs face (Carrasco-Esteban et al., 2021). Blood-borne metastasis to the lung through HCC is common. In one study, CdSe/ZnS QDs with emission wavelength of 590 nm (QDs 590) linked to alpha fetoprotein (AFP) monoclonal antibody, (AFP protein is the

Table 7.1 Hybrid nanoparticles and their application in diagnosis.

Nanomaterial	Nanohybrid	Application
Quantum dots	• CdSe/ZnS QDs • AgInS$_2$@ZnS core–shell quantum dot • CdSe/ZnS core/shell QDs	• Imaging of HCC • Detection of CYFRA21–1 DNA associated with lung cancer • Detection of AMPB, PRDX2, and PARK7
Gold nanohybrid	• PEG coated • Silica-gold nanoshells • AU NPs based sensor • Hollow gold nanospheres (HGNs) • Thiol-modified aptamer decorated with gold nanoparticles • Graphene quantum dots coated with gold nanoparticles are biofunctionalized with neuron-specific enolase antibody (anti-NSE) • Folic acid-modified dendrimer-entrapped gold nanoprobes (Au DENPs-FA)	• MRI/US fusion imaging of lung cancer • Detection of VOC from lungs • Detection of alpha enolase (ENO1) in lung cancer • Colorimetric detection of lung cancer • Small cell lung cancer detection • Detection of lung adenocarcinoma
Magnetic nanoparticle	• Anti-CD44v6 monoclonal antibody with superparamagnetic iron oxide NPs (SPIONs) conjugated	• Contrast agent in MRI for lung carcinoma
Carbon nanohybrid	• Single-walled carbon nanotubes • Ni II (OTC NPs)-coated pencil graphite electrode	• Detection of markers from VOCs in lung cancer • EGFR exon 21 point mutation in lung cancer
Polymeric nanohybrids	• Gelatin nanoparticle covalently with biotinylated EGF and NeutrAvidin FITC • g-emitting nuclide 99-mTc functionalized, hematoporphyrin conjugated albumin NPs • Cy-5.5 conjugated glycol-chitosan nanoparticle	• Fluorescence imaging of A549 cells • In-vivo and in-vitro detection of murine lung adenocarcinoma detection • In-vivo and in-vitro imaging of lung metastasis
Bio derived nanohybrid	• Cy3 conjugated tailless T4 phage	• A549 cells imaging

biomarker for HCC) as a probe for fluorescence spectral analysis of HCC. The biocompatibility, hemodynamics, and tissue distribution of the QDs-AFP-Ab probes and studied the imaging of HCC and its metastasis in vitro and in vivo (Peng and Li, 2010). Circulating tumor DNA (ctDNA) in vitro has attracted growing attention owing to its potential application in the diagnostics of cancer. A hydrophilic AgInS$_2$@ZnS core-shell

QD nanocrystals and magnetic Fe_3O_4 nanoparticles were used to quantify circulating tumor DNA (ctDNA). The ctDNA-triggered hybridization chain reaction was used to detect the CYFRA21−1 DNA associated with lung cancer. Fe_3O_4 adsorbs and immobilizes the QDs attached to ssDNA. This approach was followed to quantify ctDNA quantification (Yang et al., 2022). Multiplexed analysis of three protein markers associated with lung cancer: α-1-microglobulin/bikunin precursor (AMBP), peroxiredoxin 2 (PRDX2), and Parkinson's disease protein 7 (PARK7). The detection of these lung cancer markers (LCMs) in the human (broncho alveolar lavage fluid) BALF samples was made possible by CdSe/ZnS core/shell QDs with an emission wavelength of 515 nm, coupled with antibodies. This method could provide the multiple detections of biomarkers through fluorescence emission (Bilan et al., 2017).

7.3.2 Gold nanoparticles

Photoimaging, a novel approach in which gold nanoparticles are functionalized, can reach the target organ, thus differentiating the cancerous tissue from the normal tissue, making surgery easy for physicians. Gold nanoparticles come in different shapes and are known to be the best available photoimaging nanoparticles for cancer therapeutics due to their biocompatibility and their ability to provide increased spatial and temporal resolution for imaging (Menon et al., 2013). Silica-gold nanoshells coated with PEG (AuroLase) are under clinical trial for MRI/US fusion imaging of lung cancer and other types of cancer (Singh et al., 2018). Au NPs have been utilized in the development of nanoarray-based sensors for lung cancer diagnosis. It has advantages over the conventional diagnosis methods available for the lung cancer diagnosis, including cost-effectiveness and more accuracy. It works on the principle of differences in volatile organic compounds present in the healthy human as compared to lung cancer patients. 42 various volatile compounds have been screened that are being used to diagnose lung cancer. In a similar way, porous gold nanospheres have been demonstrated to achieve 100 times more sensitive and rapid diagnostic tests for lung cancer than conventional enzyme-linked immunosorbent assay having a limit of detection of 1−10 pg/mL. These HGNs-based surface-enhanced Raman scattering (SERS)-based immunoassay has been represented to diagnose the lung cancer marker, CEA. In that, magnetic beads were utilized as an immunocomplex-supporting substrate. Alpha-enolase (ENO1) conjugated to AuNPs based an electrochemical-immune sensor has been developed to sense and quantify the human lung cancer-associated antigen. Similar electrochemical and contact angle measurements using electrodes made up of GNPs-glass carbon electrodes, which are highly sensitive and rapidly identifying methods have been demonstrated for the detection of different cancer cells, including lung cancer (He et al., 2009). A gold nanoparticle-based colorimetric detection method was developed to detect cancer cells, including lung cancer cells, using a thiol-modified aptamer on the gold nanoparticle surface. There was a visible color change with the minimum detection ability of minimum upto 1000 cells. This method may be useful to distinguish between malignant cells and normal cells in the diagnosis. This was made possible with the help of an aptamer, which gives specific selectivity (Medley et al., 2008).

Further, gold nanoparticle-based sensors have been demonstrated to detect lung cancer through histological examination of voltaic organic compounds (VOCs). It was capable to differentiate between healthy and lung cancer cells, SCLC and NSCLC, and subtypes of NSCLC by VOC (Barash et al., 2012). Aptamer-tagged gold nanoparticles were also used in the detection of cancer cells colorimetrically, which can distinguish the malignant cells from the normal cells (Medley et al., 2008). The combination of gold nanoparticles as an electron acceptor and graphene QDs as an energy donor biofunctionalized with neuron-specific enolase antibody (anti-NSE), which is a biomarker of SCLC. The fluorescent biosensor had a broad linear range from 0.1 pg/mL and 1000 ng/mL (Kalkal et al., 2020). The *in vitro* and *in vivo* CT scan imaging of SPC-A1 cells (human lung adenocarcinoma) treated with folic acid-modified dendrimer-entrapped gold nanoprobes (Au DENPs-FA). Incubation of SPC-A1 cells with a range between 200 and 3000 nm of Au DENPs-FA showed that higher concentrations of Au DENPs-FA could produce brighter CT images. Moreover, the CT intensity was enhanced in the *SPC-A1*-bearing xenograft mouse model (Wang et al., 2013).

7.3.3 Magnetic nanoparticle

Oleic acid and carboxymethyl dextran-coated SPIONs conjugated to mouse anti-CD44v6 monoclonal antibody, a protein marker for metastatic cancer. These nanoparticles can be used as a T2 contrast agent that may improve the detection of lung carcinoma on MRI (Wan et al., 2016).

7.3.4 Carbon nanohybrids

Single-walled carbon nanotubes coated with nonpolymeric organic materials have a high potential for diagnosis, detection, and screening of lung cancer via breath samples. The devices are expected to be relatively inexpensive, portable, and amenable to widespread screening (Peng et al., 2008).

A selective and sensitive electrochemical biosensor to detect EGFR exon 21 point mutation based on two-step electropolymerization of Ni (II)-oxytetracycline conducting metallopolymer nanoparticles (NiOTC NPs) on the surface of pencil graphite electrode modified by reduced graphene oxide/carboxyl functionalized ordered mesoporous carbon (rGO/f-OMC) nanocomposite. It had a wide concentration range and low detection limit (120 nM) (Shoja et al., 2018).

7.3.5 Polymeric nanoparticles

Polymeric NPs are biocompatible, biodegradable site-specific, and increase the bio-availability of the cargo of interest (Castro et al., 2022). Gelatin nanoparticles covalently grafted with biotinylated EGF and NeutrAvidin FITC had a targeted specificity towards A549 lung cancer cells. The 240 nm particle was nontoxic to normal cells (HFL1). The GP—Av—bEGF nanoparticles delivered through inhalation to SCID mice revealed that cancerous lung cells had higher fluorescence accumulation. This paves the way for possible bioimaging techniques to distinguish between normal and malignant lung tissue (Tseng et al., 2007). Due to the role of porphyrin as a potential tumor-imaging marker, albumin NPs (AlNPs) conjugated with hematoporphyrin (HP) functionalized with the g-emitting nuclide 99-mTc. The nanoconstruct has a range between 100 and 200 nm diameters. Results from confocal scanning microscopy and scintigraphic imaging revealed that HP-AlNPs were readily uptaken by murine lung adenocarcinoma cells in both in-vitro and in-vivo studies in contrast to the normal bronchial cells. The scintigraphic imaging of rabbits revealed that 99-mTc conjugated HP-AlNPs exhibit better half-life and tumor distribution in contrast to AlNP unconjugated constructs. Altogether 99-mTc-HP-AlNPs can be employed as promising radiodiagnostic tools for lung cancer diagnosis (Yang et al., 2010). Noninvasive optical imaging method was developed with the help of glycol-chitosan NPs (gCNP) conjugated with near-infrared (NIR) fluorescence dye Cy5.5 for metastatic lung adenocarcinoma in an *in vivo* experiment. The Cy5.5-gCNPs were assessed for in vivo and in-vitro biostability, and accumulation inside metastatic mice. The real-time imaging results accentuated that the Cy5.5-CNPs were freely uptaken by tumor tissue. Consequently, there was excellent metastatic tumor specificity, and these NPs corroborated an immense potential for use in lung cancer imaging (Na et al., 2011).

7.3.6 Bioderived nanohybrids

A tail-less T4 head of cy3 viral nanoparticle was used as a scaffold for the attachment of Cy3 and Alexa 548 was prepared, and uptake was done in A549 cells. The viral particle was able to stay inside the cells for at least 72 hours. The genetically modified tailless T4 virus has a large surface area was able to hold up to 19,000 dyes/virus implies that the surface can be modified with a variety of functional groups by using the available reactive amines over the viral particle (Robertson et al., 2011).

7.4 Hybrid nanoparticles utilized in the lung cancer therapy

The colloidal particles that range between 10 to 1000 nm in size are termed nanoparticles. These nanoparticles are synthesized using many polymers, such as protein, polysaccharides, lipids, and metals. Using this type of polymer will facilitate better targeting of nanoparticles, the good release of the contents of formulations, and decreased cytotoxicity in comparison to conventional therapies (Madni et al., 2017). Nanoparticulate systems with surface modifications via different functional groups, ligands, or targeting agents assist the better distribution of drugs, directing them into the tumor microenvironment through active or passive targeting, which enhances the diagnostic capability and therapeutic efficiency (Table 7.2).

7.4.1 Protein-polymer hybrid nanoparticles

Protein-polymer hybrid nanoparticles comprise protein-polymer conjugates. Protein nanoparticles are already in use for the treatment of many cancers, including lung cancer, but their only limitation is stability and insufficient circulation times. Polymeric nanoparticles are also in use as nanocarriers and are the best suitable drug delivery

Table 7.2 Methods utilized in the synthesis of nanosized hybrid particles.

a	b	c	d
e	f	g	h
i	j	k	l
m	n	o	p
q	r	s	t
u	v	w	x
y	z	aa	ab

[a]Nanoparticle.
[b]Drug used.
[c]Method for synthesis.
[d]Size of the nanoparticle.
[e]HSA nanoparticles.
[f]TRIAL protein/doxorubicin.
[g]Self-assembly.
[h]~340 nm.
[i]Albumin nanoparticles.
[j]Curcumin/doxorubicin.
[k]High-pressure homogenization.
[l]130 nm.
[m]Hydroxyapatite nanoparticles.
[n]Hafnium.
[o]Wet chemical precipitation method.
[p]30−40 nm.
[q]Lipid polymer nanoparticles (LPNs).
[r]Paclitaxel/triptolide.
[s]Nanoprecipitation method.
[t]160 nm.
[u]Tf-LNPs.
[v]Afatinib.
[w]Conjugation technique.
[x]103.5.
[y]Cationic SLNs.
[z]p53.
[aa]Coencapsulation method.
[ab]110 nm.

systems as they have high stability, structural integrity, and sustained release capability. To overcome the limitations of existing protein nanoparticles, they have been modified and conjugated with polymers to enhance the stability and integrity of the particles.

Bovine serum albumin (BSA) has been widely used in the synthesis of nanoparticles and has been popularized in drug delivery systems by encapsulating the selected therapeutic agents. BSA has preferable properties such as nontoxic, nonantigenic, biodegradable, and biocompatible for the formulation of multiple nano and microparticulate drug delivery systems. Li et al. have synthesized the hydroxyapatite nanoparticles and loaded doxorubicin into them and then incubated the HAP/DOX nanoparticles with BSA for the corona formation to obtain BSA/HAP/DOX. BSA/HAP/DOX has shown better tumor-inhibiting ability in lung cancer cell lines than the HAP nanoparticles alone. Due to the high biocompatibility of BSA, the BSA/HAP nanoparticles have shown better biocompatibility than the other cancer drug delivery systems that included HAP nanoparticles (Li et al., 2020).

7.4.2 Inorganic hybrid nanoparticles/metallic hybrid nanoparticles

Over the years, noble metals such as gold and silver nanoparticles have been extensively used as nanoparticle systems for the diagnosis, imaging, classification, and treatment of lung cancers. Gold nanoparticles are best used as drug delivery systems due to their high surface area-to-volume ratio. Having a high affinity to the thiol groups, gold nanoparticles can be surface modified with DNA, RNA, and many ligands to target the specific receptors expressed on lung cancer cells.

Gold nanoparticles release the encapsulated drug in response to light or external stimulus, including irradiation. You et al. synthesized gold nanoparticles and gold nanoshells loading doxorubicin. They found that the payload of gold nanoshells is more than the gold nanoparticles due to the presence of a hollow structure that could entrap more amount of doxorubicin compared with gold nanoparticles. The release of doxorubicin was triggered by NIR irradiation (You et al., 2010).

Gold nanoparticles can also be a good therapeutic gene delivery system. Braun et al. coated 40 nm gold nanoshells with siRNA and Tat peptide. This peptide is a lipid-cell internalizing agent for the facilitation of silencing of gene expression in a particular subset of cells. They have shown that gene silencing can be controlled both temporally and spatially using pulsed NIR light via siRNA release induced by NIR (Braun et al., 2009).

Silver nanoparticles also offer many advantages as drug delivery systems similar to gold nanoparticles, such as adjustable size and shape, surface-bound nucleic acids with enhanced stability, high surface-ligand attachment, easy transmembrane delivery without the use of any harsh transfecting agents, protected delivery of attached therapeutics from degradation and sustained intracellular drug-delivery. Biologically synthesized

Ag-nanoparticles show substantial anticancer activity in comparison to the AgNPs pre-pared using harsh, toxic chemicals. Green synthesis of AgNPs via *Cleome viscosa* plant extract offers a solution for optimizing anticancer activity. Lakshmanan et al. (Lakshmanan et al., 2018) have evaluated the anticancer activity of these AgNPs in human cancer cell lines PA1 (ovarian teratocarcinoma) and A549 (human lung adeno-carcinoma). The results suggested that green synthesized AgNPs could inhibit the cell growth in cancer cell lines and provide a great platform in the treatment of cancers.

7.4.3 Lipid-based hybrid nanoparticles
7.4.3.1 Lipid polymer hybrid nanoparticles
Lipid-polymer hybrid nanoparticles (LPNs) framework comprises of polymer cores and lipid/lipid-PEG shells, which exhibit complementing characteristics of both lipo-somes and polymeric nanoparticles peculiarly in terms of their particle size ranging between 30 and 200 nm, surface functionality, better drug loading, entrapment of multiple therapeutic agents, sustained drug release profile, and good serum and physi-cal stability, biocompatibility. These LNPs attain the characteristics of both polymeric nanoparticles and liposomes, such as (1) a polymeric core that encapsulates the required therapeutic agent, (2) an inner lipid layer that blankets the polymer core to assures biocompatibility to the polymer core, and (3) an outer lipid-PEG layer that provides a coating to the polymer core-shell, PEGylation of the nanoparticles provides the biocompatibility to them (Hadinoto et al., 2013). Lipids can also be coated by PLGA, chitosan, polyacrylic acid, and polyallylamine that facilitate in overcoming the biological obstacles during the drug delivery process (Maurya et al., 2020).

Jia research group (Liu et al., 2018) used LPNs as the DDS to deliver paclitaxel and triptolide to attain a synergistic effect and effective drug resistance in the treatment of NSCLC. They have achieved a particle size of about 160 nm, sustained release, and synergistic effects of the dual drug-loaded LNPs in comparison to the single drug-loaded LNPs in A549 cell lines. Synergetic effects of the dual drugs in LPNs have been shown in-vitro and in-vivo lung cancer models with minimized side effects.

Afatinib is a potent irreversible inhibitor of epidermal growth factor recptor (EGFR) but is limited with low bioavailability and adverse reactions (Wang et al., 2019). Modified redox-sensitive lipid polymer hybrid nanoparticles with transferrin (Tf-SS-Afa-LNPs) so as to increase the bioavailability and sustained drug release. These particles have a size of about 103 ± 4.1 nm and have shown a tremendous *in-vivo* antitumor efficacy by reducing the tumor volume from 919 to 212 mm^3.

7.4.3.2 Solid-lipid nanoparticles
Solid-lipid nanoparticles (SLNs) have emerged in the last decade as an alternative to the present in-use nanocarriers, such as emulsions, liposomes, and polymeric nanopar-ticles. The size of SLNs may range between 50 and 1000 nm and structured with a

physiological solid crystalline lipid core that may include triglycerides, partial glycerides, fatty acids, waxes, and steroids surrounded by interfacial surfactants or emulsifiers (Pink et al., 2019). These SLNs are prepared by different techniques, such as cold homogenization, hot homogenization, high shear homogenization, ultrasonication, or high-speed homogenization (Abdelaziz et al., 2019). These SLNs are used in lung cancer therapy via drug delivery and gene delivery.

S. H. Choi et al. have formulated cationic solid lipid nanoparticles having two positively charged lipid bilayers with a size of 110 nm and a zeta potential of 8–13 mV and have shown the effective targeting of the p53 gene in non-small cell lung carcinoma (Choi et al., 2008). While Han et al. have synthesized surface modified, coencapsulated solid lipid nanoparticles with a particle size of 245 nm and zeta potential of 28.3 mV, containing enhanced green fluorescent protein plasmid (pEGFP) along with doxorubicin in order to create a multifunctional DDS that targets the lung cancer cells (Han et al., 2014) (Table 7.3).

7.4.4 Polymer-based hybrid nanoparticles

7.4.4.1 Chitosan-based nanoparticles

Chitosan is a biodegradable and biocompatible polymer with antimicrobial as well as anticancer properties. Jin Q et al. have synthesized inhalable immunotherapeutic chitosan-antibody conjugated nanoparticles for targeting lung cancer; chitosan was used as a vehicle to assemble with antiprogrammed cell death protein ligand (aPD-L10) to enable efficient transmucosal delivery. However, chitosan exhibits adjuvant properties enhancing the effect of immune response by activating the cyclic-di-GMP-AMP synthase (cGAS)-stimulator of interferon genes (STING) pathway. Inhalation of this complex has effectively activated the immune system and has prolonged the survival of mice for 60 days. In this way, chitosan can be used as a vehicle for the treatment of lung cancer as aerosol inhalation that can be the best cure for respiratory diseases (Table 7.4).

Table 7.3 Solid-lipid nanoparticles utilized in drug delivery.

Drug	Lipid used	Technique used for synthesis of SLN	Consequence
Curcumin	Stearic acid, lecithin	Emulsification and low temperature solidification	SLNs significantly improved the phototoxicity of curcumin
Curcumin	Stearic acid, lecithin	Sol-gel method	SLNs–curcumin ratio (4:1) improved solubility
Sclareol	Precirol	Hot homogenization	Sclareol-SLNs displayed outstanding genocytotoxicity against A549 lung cancer cells

Table 7.4 Solid-lipid nanoparticles utilized in gene delivery.

Gene	Lipid used	Technique used for synthesis of SLNs	Consequence
p53	TC, DC-chol, DOPE	Melt homogenization	SLNs prepared at lipid:DNA 9:1 weight ratio showed higher transfection efficiency than the cationic liposome Lipofectin
DNA	GMS, phospholipids, PE, LHLN	Solvent displacement (nanoprecipitation)	Man-SLN-DNA manifested better transfection efficiency than unmodified SLN-DNA
PTX and siRNA	Cholesteryl oleate, triglyceride, cholesterol, DOPE, DC-chol	Emulsification-solvent evaporation	Optically traceable SLNs using QDs enable in situ fluorescence imaging of lung carcinoma

7.4.4.2 Fibroin-based nanoparticles

Fatemeh et al. (Abdelaziz et al., 2019) have synthesized silk fibroin nanoparticles (SFNPs) loaded with gemcitabine for the treatment of induced lung tumors in the mice model. They have conjugated the SFNPs with SP5—52 peptide forming SP5—52-peptide conjugated SFNPs for the specific delivery of gemcitabine into the lung cancer tissue. The peptide conjugation not only increases the efficiency of specific delivery but also reduces the side effects caused by site-specific drug delivery systems. They have achieved a size of ~105—156 nm after loading of gemcitabine while the conjugation of SP5-52 peptide leads to an increase in the SFNPs size to ~302 nm.

7.5 Conclusions and future perspectives

The hybrid nanoparticles are useful for the diagnosis and therapy or theranostic applications. The hybrid nanoparticles overcome the limitation of the conventional nanoparticle systems, including bioavailability, off-targeting, and insufficient therapeutic efficiency. In the diagnostic aspect, hybrid nanoparticles are also useful for the bioimaging of lung cancer to end up with an accurate diagnosis. However, the physicochemical properties of hybrid nanoparticle systems have limitations of homogeneous particle distribution and reproducibility at a larger scale and the introduction of various functional groups is also challenging. These challenges make hybrid nanoparticles difficult to handle and control in vivo and in clinical setup. The penetration of hybrid nanoparticles to lung tissue through the complex epithelial barriers is also challenging. Thus, the critical examination of developed hybrid nanoparticles should be required before proposing them for clinical translation. Addressing and consideration of all the challenges and concerns are required before designing the hybrid nanoparticles. Therefore, it is warranted to select the best and most promising hybrid nanoparticles with higher reproducibility, cost-effectiveness, and flexibility for the surface functionalization in the future.

References

Abdelaziz, H.M., Freag, M.S., Elzoghby, A.O., 2019. Chapter 5 - Solid lipid nanoparticle-based drug delivery for lung cancer. In: Kesharwani, P. (Ed.), Nanotechnology-Based Targeted Drug Delivery Systems for Lung Cancer. Academic Press, pp. 95–121.

Abera, S.F., Mikolajczyk, R.T., Kantelhardt, E.J., Efremov, L., Bedir, A., Ostheimer, C., et al., 2020. Lung cancer attributed mortality among 316,336 early stage breast cancer cases treated by radiotherapy and/or chemotherapy, 2000–2015: evidence from the SEER database. Front. Oncol. 10, 602397.

Adelere, I.A., Lateef, A., 2016. A novel approach to the green synthesis of metallic nanoparticles: the use of agro-wastes, enzymes, and pigments. J. Nanotechnol. Rev. 5 (6), 567–587.

Ahmad, R., Srivastava, S., Ghosh, S., Khare, S.K., 2021. Phytochemical delivery through nanocarriers: a review. Colloids Surf. B: Biointerfaces 197, 111389.

Akinsiku, A.A., Dare, E.O., Ajanaku, K.O., Ajani, O.O., Olugbuyiro, J.A.O., Siyanbola, T.O., et al., 2018. Modeling and synthesis of Ag and Ag/Ni allied bimetallic nanoparticles by green method: optical and biological properties. Int. J. Biomater. 2018, 9658080.

Albiter, E., Valenzuela, M., Alfaro, S., Valverde-Aguilar, G., Martínez-Pallares, F.J., 2015. Photocatalytic deposition of Ag nanoparticles on TiO2: metal precursor effect on the structural and photoactivity properties. J. Saudi Chem. Soc. 19 (5), 563–573.

Amendola, V., Meneghetti, M., Bakr, O.M., Riello, P., Polizzi, S., Anjum, D.H., et al., 2013. Coexistence of plasmonic and magnetic properties in Au89Fe11 nanoalloys. Nanoscale 5 (12), 5611–5619.

Babu, A., Templeton, A.K., Munshi, A., Ramesh, R., 2013. Nanoparticle-based drug delivery for therapy of lung cancer: progress and challenges. J. Nanomater. 2013, 863951.

Barash, O., Peled, N., Tisch, U., Bunn Jr., P.A., Hirsch, F.R., Haick, H., 2012. Classification of lung cancer histology by gold nanoparticle sensors. Nanomedicine. 8 (5), 580–589.

Barcikowski, S., Compagnini, G., 2013. Advanced nanoparticle generation and excitation by lasers in liquids. Phys. Chem. Chem. Phys. 15 (9), 3022–3026.

Bilan, R., Ametzazurra, A., Brazhnik, K., Escorza, S., Fernández, D., Uríbarri, M., et al., 2017. Quantum-dot-based suspension microarray for multiplex detection of lung cancer markers: preclinical validation and comparison with the Luminex xMAP® system. Sci. Rep. 7 (1), 44668.

Binod, A., Ganachari, S.V., Yaradoddi, J.S., Tapaskar, R.P., Banapurmath, N.R., Shettar, A.S., editors. 2018. Biological synthesis and characterization of tri-metallic alloy (Au Ag, Sr) nanoparticles and its sensing studies. IOP Conference Series: Materials Science and Engineering. IOP Publishing.

Boroumand Moghaddam, A., Namvar, F., Moniri, M., Azizi, S., Mohamad, R., 2015. Nanoparticles biosynthesized by fungi and yeast: a review of their preparation, properties, and medical applications. Molecules 20 (9), 16540–16565.

Brannon-Peppas, L., Blanchette, J.O., 2004. Nanoparticle and targeted systems for cancer therapy. Adv. Drug. Deliv. Rev. 56 (11), 1649–1659.

Braun, G.B., Pallaoro, A., Wu, G., Missirlis, D., Zasadzinski, J.A., Tirrell, M., et al., 2009. Laser-activated gene silencing via gold nanoshell-siRNA conjugates. ACS Nano 3 (7), 2007–2015.

Bębas, E., Borowska, M., Derlatka, M., Oczeretko, E., Hładuński, M., Szumowski, P., et al., 2021. Machine-learning-based classification of the histological subtype of non-small-cell lung cancer using MRI texture analysis. Biomed. Signal. Process. Control. 66, 102446.

Carrasco-Esteban, E., Domínguez-Rullán, J.A., Barrionuevo-Castillo, P., Pelari-Mici, L., Leaman, O., Sastre-Gallego, S., et al., 2021. Current role of nanoparticles in the treatment of lung cancer. J. Clin. Transl. Res. 7 (2), 140–155.

Chan, W.C., Nie, S., 1998. Quantum dot bioconjugates for ultrasensitive nonisotopic detection. Science. 281 (5385), 2016–2018.

Chang, Y.-Y., Shieh, Y.-N., Kao, H.-Y., 2011. Optical properties of TiO2 thin films after Ag ion implantation. Thin Solid Films 519 (20), 6935–6939.

Chen, P., Lee, G., Davies, S., Masten, S., Amutha, R., Wu, J., 2013. Hydrothermal synthesis of coral-like Au/ZnO catalyst and photocatalytic degradation of Orange II dye. Mater. Res. Bull. 48 (6), 2375–2382.

Chen, S.F., Li, J.P., Qian, K., Xu, W.P., Lu, Y., Huang, W.X., et al., 2010. Large scale photochemical synthesis of M@ TiO2 nanocomposites (M = Ag, Pd, Au, Pt) and their optical properties, CO oxidation performance, and antibacterial effect. Nano Res. 3 (4), 244–255.

Chen, Z., Liang, R., Guo, X., Liang, J., Deng, Q., Li, M., et al., 2017. Simultaneous quantitation of cytokeratin-19 fragment and carcinoembryonic antigen in human serum via quantum dot-doped nanoparticles. Biosens. Bioelectron. 91, 60–65.

Choi, S.H., Jin, S.E., Lee, M.K., Lim, S.J., Park, J.S., Kim, B.G., et al., 2008. Novel cationic solid lipid nanoparticles enhanced p53 gene transfer to lung cancer cells. Eur. J. Pharma. Biopharma. 68 (3), 545–554.

Cirne, F., Zhou, S., Kappel, C., El-Kadi, A., Barron, C.C., Ellis, P.M., et al., 2021. ALK inhibitor-induced bradycardia: a systematic-review and meta-analysis. Lung Cancer 161, 9–17.

Clark, D., Mao, L., 2012. Cancer biomarker discovery: lectin-based strategies targeting glycoproteins. Dis. Markers 33 (1), 1–10.

Collins, L.G., Haines, C., Perkel, R., Enck, R.E., 2007. Lung cancer: diagnosis and management. Am. Fam. Physician 75 (1), 56–63.

Cooper, W.A., Lam, D.C.L., O'Toole, S.A., Minna, J.D., 2013. Molecular biology of lung cancer. J. Thorac. Dis. 5 (Suppl 5), S479–S490.

Cryer, A.M., Thorley, A.J., 2019. Nanotechnology in the diagnosis and treatment of lung cancer. Pharmacol. Ther. 198, 189–205.

Călinescu, I., Martin, D., Ighigeanu, D., Gavrila, A., Trifan, A., Patrascu, M., et al., 2014. Nanoparticles synthesis by electron beam radiolysis. Open Chem. J. 12 (7), 774–781.

Castro, K.C.D., Costa, J.M., Campos, M.G.N., 2022. Drug-loaded polymeric nanoparticles: a review. Int. J. Polym. Mater. Polym. Biomater. 71 (1), 1–13.

Damato, T.C., de Oliveira, C.C., Ando, R.A., Camargo, P.H., 2013. A facile approach to TiO2 colloidal spheres decorated with Au nanoparticles displaying well-defined sizes and uniform dispersion. Langmuir 29 (5), 1642–1649.

Danese, A., Leo, S., Rimessi, A., Wieckowski, M.R., Fiorica, F., Giorgi, C., et al., 2021. Cell death as a result of calcium signaling modulation: A cancer-centric prospective. Biochim. Biophys. Acta 1868 (8), 119061.

Deplanche, K., Merroun, M.L., Casadesus, M., Tran, D.T., Mikheenko, I.P., Bennett, J.A., et al., 2012. Microbial synthesis of core/shell gold/palladium nanoparticles for applications in green chemistry. J. R. Soc. Interface. 9 (72), 1705–1712.

Donkova, B., Vasileva, P., Nihtianova, D., Velichkova, N., Stefanov, P., Mehandjiev, D., 2011. Synthesis, characterization, and catalytic application of Au/ZnO nanocomposites prepared by coprecipitation. J. Mater. Sci. 46 (22), 7134–7143.

de Oliveira Gonçalves, K., de Oliveira Silva, F.R., Vieira, D.P., Courrol, L.C., editors. 2018. Synthesis of Hybrid AuFe Nanoparticles by Photoreduction and Methyl Aminoluvinate. 2018 SBFoton International Optics and Photonics Conference (SBFoton IOPC): IEEE.

Ebrahimi, N., Rasoul-Amini, S., Niazi, A., Erfani, N., Moghadam, A., Ebrahiminezhad, A., et al., 2016. Cytotoxic and apoptotic effects of three types of silver-iron oxide binary hybrid nanoparticles. Curr. Pharm. Biotechnol. 17 (12), 1049–1057.

Elshahat, S., Treanor, C., Donnelly, M., 2021. Factors influencing physical activity participation among people living with or beyond cancer: a systematic scoping review. Int. J. Behav. Nutr. Phys. Act. 18 (1), 50.

Fan, F.-R., Liu, D.-Y., Wu, Y.-F., Duan, S., Xie, Z.-X., Jiang, Z.-Y., et al., 2008. Epitaxial growth of heterogeneous metal nanocrystals: from gold nano-octahedra to palladium and silver nanocubes. J. Am. Chem. Soc. 130 (22), 6949–6951.

Feng, H., Liu, S.-Y., Huang, X.-B., Ren, R., Zhou, Y., Song, C.-P., et al., 2017. Green biosynthesis of CdS nanoparticles using yeast cells for fluorescence detection of nucleic acids and electrochemical detection of hydrogen peroxide. Int. J. Electrochem. Sci. 12 (1), 618–628.

Gahlawat, G., Choudhury, A.R., 2019. A review on the biosynthesis of metal and metal salt nanoparticles by microbes. RSC Adv. 9 (23), 12944–12967.

Ganaie, S., Abbasi, T., Abbasi, S., 2016. Rapid and green synthesis of bimetallic Au–Ag nanoparticles using an otherwise worthless weed Antigonon leptopus. J. Exp. Nanosci. 11 (6), 395–417.

Gao, J., Bender, C.M., Murphy, C., 2003. Dependence of the gold nanorod aspect ratio on the nature of the directing surfactant in aqueous solution. Langmuir. 19 (21), 9065–9070.

Gao, Z., Yuan, H., Mao, Y., Ding, L., Effah, C.Y., He, S., et al., 2021. In situ detection of plasma exosomal microRNA for lung cancer diagnosis using duplex-specific nuclease and MoS2 nanosheets. Analyst. 146 (6), 1924–1931.

Gholizadeh, S., Wang, Z., Chen, X., Dana, R., Annabi, N., 2021. Advanced nanodelivery platforms for topical ophthalmic drug delivery. Drug. Discov. Today 26 (6), 1437–1449.

Gopiraman, M., Saravanamoorthy, S., Baskar, R., Ilangovan, A., ILL-Min, C., 2019. Green synthesis of Ag@ Au bimetallic regenerated cellulose nanofibers for catalytic applications. New J. Chem. 43 (43), 17090–17103.

Gould, M.K., Donington, J., Lynch, W.R., Mazzone, P.J., Midthun, D.E., Naidich, D.P., et al., 2013. Evaluation of individuals with pulmonary nodules: when is it lung cancer?: Diagnosis and management of lung cancer, 3rd ed: American College of chest physicians evidence-based clinical practice guidelines. Chest. 143 (5, Supplement), e93S–e120S.

Govindaraju, K., Basha, S.K., Kumar, V.G., Singaravelu, G., 2008. Silver, gold and bimetallic nanoparticles production using single-cell protein (Spirulina platensis) Geitler. J. Mater. Sci. 43 (15), 5115–5122.

Hadinoto, K., Sundaresan, A., Cheow, W.S., 2013. Lipid-polymer hybrid nanoparticles as a new generation therapeutic delivery platform: a review. Eur. J. Pharm. Biopharm. 85 (3 Pt A), 427–443.

Han, R., Song, X., Wang, Q., Qi, Y., Deng, G., Zhang, A., et al., 2019. Microbial synthesis of graphene-supported highly-dispersed Pd-Ag bimetallic nanoparticles and its catalytic activity. J. Chem. Technol. Biotechnol. 94 (10), 3375–3383.

Han, Y., Zhang, P., Chen, Y., Sun, J., Kong, F., 2014. Co-delivery of plasmid DNA and doxorubicin by solid lipid nanoparticles for lung cancer therapy. Int. J. Mol. Med. 34 (1), 191–196.

Hassanein, M., Callison, J.C., Callaway-Lane, C., Aldrich, M.C., Grogan, E.L., Massion, P.P., 2012. The state of molecular biomarkers for the early detection of lung cancer. Cancer Prev. Res. (Philadelphia, Pa.) 5 (8), 992–1006.

He, C., Lin, W., 2015. Hybrid nanoparticles for cancer imaging and therapy. In: Mirkin, C.A., Meade, T.J., Petrosko, S.H., Stegh, A.H. (Eds.), Nanotechnology-Based Precision Tools for the Detection and Treatment of Cancer. Springer International Publishing, Cham, pp. 173–192.

He, F., Shen, Q., Jiang, H., Zhou, J., Cheng, J., Guo, D., et al., 2009. Rapid identification and high sensitive detection of cancer cells on the gold nanoparticle interface by combined contact angle and electrochemical measurements. Talanta. 77 (3), 1009–1014.

Huang, G., Zhang, C., Li, S., Khemtong, C., Yang, S.-G., Tian, R., et al., 2009. A novel strategy for surface modification of superparamagnetic iron oxide nanoparticles for lung cancer imaging. J. Mater. Chem. 19 (35), 6367–6372.

Huynh, K.-H., Pham, X.-H., Kim, J., Lee, S.H., Chang, H., Rho, W.-Y., et al., 2020. Synthesis, properties, and biological applications of metallic alloy nanoparticles. Int. J. Mol. Sci. 21 (14), 5174.

Ihde, D.C., 1992. Chemotherapy of lung cancer. N. Engl. J. Med. 327 (20), 1434–1441.

Jena, P., Bhattacharya, M., Bhattacharjee, G., Satpati, B., Mukherjee, P., Senapati, D., et al., 2020. Bimetallic gold–silver nanoparticles mediate bacterial killing by disrupting the actin cytoskeleton MreB. Nanoscale 12 (6), 3731–3749.

Jhuang, Y.-Y., Cheng, W.-T., 2016. Fabrication and characterization of silver/titanium dioxide composite nanoparticles in ethylene glycol with alkaline solution through sonochemical process. Ultrason. Sonochem. 28, 327–333.

Kalkal, A., Pradhan, R., Kadian, S., Manik, G., Packirisamy, G., 2020. Biofunctionalized graphene quantum dots based fluorescent biosensor toward efficient detection of small cell lung cancer. ACS Appl. Bio Mater. 3 (8), 4922−4932.

Khan, I., Saeed, K., Khan, I., 2019. Nanoparticles: properties, applications and toxicities. Arab. J. Chem. 12 (7), 908−931.

Khandare, L., Terdale, S., 2017. Gold nanoparticles decorated MnO2 nanowires for high performance supercapacitor. Appl. Surf. Sci. 418, 22−29.

Kozower, B.D., Larner, J.M., Detterbeck, F.C., Jones, D.R., 2013. Special treatment issues in non-small cell lung cancer: diagnosis and management of lung cancer, 3rd ed: American College of chest physicians evidence-based clinical practice guidelines. Chest. 143 (5, Supplement), e369S. e99S.

Krebs, M.G., Metcalf, R.L., Carter, L., Brady, G., Blackhall, F.H., Dive, C., 2014. Molecular analysis of circulating tumour cells—biology and biomarkers. Nat. Rev. Clin. Oncol. 11 (3), 129−144.

Lakshmanan, G., Sathiyaseelan, A., Kalaichelvan, P.T., Murugesan, K., 2018. Plant-mediated synthesis of silver nanoparticles using fruit extract of Cleome viscosa L.: assessment of their antibacterial and anticancer activity. Karbala Int. J. Mod. Sci. 4 (1), 61−68.

Larsen, J.E., Minna, J.D., 2011. Molecular biology of lung cancer: clinical implications. JCICM 32 (4), 703−740.

Latimer, K.M., Mott, T.F., 2015. Lung cancer: diagnosis, treatment principles, and screening. Am. Fam. Physician 91 (4), 250−256.

Leong, K.H., Chu, H.Y., Ibrahim, S., Saravanan, P., 2015. Palladium nanoparticles anchored to anatase TiO2 for enhanced surface plasmon resonance-stimulated, visible-light-driven photocatalytic activity. Beilstein J. Nanotechnol. 6 (1), 428−437.

Li, G., Tang, D., Wang, D., Xu, C., Liu, D., 2020. Effective Chemotherapy of Lung Cancer Using Bovine Serum Albumin-Coated Hydroxyapatite Nanoparticles. Med. Sci. Monit. 26, e919716-1-e-8.

Li, H., He, Y., Liu, Z., Jiang, B., Huang, Y.J., 2017. Rapid synthesis of broadband Ag@ TiO2 core−shell nanoparticles for solar energy conversion. Sol. Energy Mater Sol. Cells. 166, 52−60.

Li, J., Zhang, Z., Deng, H., Zheng, Z., 2021b. Cinobufagin-Loaded and Folic Acid-Modified Polydopamine Nanomedicine Combined With Photothermal Therapy for the Treatment of Lung Cancer. 9.

Li, Y., Chen, X., He, W., Xia, S., Jiang, X., Li, X., et al., 2021a. Apigenin enhanced antitumor effect of cisplatin in lung cancer via inhibition of cancer stem cells. Nutr. Cancer 73 (8), 1489−1497.

Liu, J., Wang, W., Shen, T., Zhao, Z., Feng, H., Cui, F., 2014. One-step synthesis of noble metal/oxide nanocomposites with tunable size of noble metal particles and their size-dependent catalytic activity. RSC Adv. 4 (58), 30624−30629.

Liu, J., Cheng, H., Han, L., Qiang, Z., Zhang, X., Gao, W., et al., 2018. Synergistic combination therapy of lung cancer using paclitaxel- and triptolide-coloaded lipid-polymer hybrid nanoparticles. Drug. Des. Devel Ther. 12, 3199−3209.

Liu, P., Morrison, C., Wang, L., Xiong, D., Vedell, P., Cui, P., et al., 2012. Identification of somatic mutations in non-small cell lung carcinomas using whole-exome sequencing. Carcinogenesis. 33 (7), 1270−1276.

Liu, S., Guo, S., Sun, S., You, X.-Z., 2015. Dumbbell-like Au-Fe3O4 nanoparticles: a new nanostructure for supercapacitors. JN 7 (11), 4890−4893.

Liu, Y., Kou, Q., Wang, D., Chen, L., Sun, Y., Lu, Z., et al., 2017. Rational synthesis and tailored optical and magnetic characteristics of Fe3O4−Au composite nanoparticles. 52(17):10163−10174.

Liu, Z., Ma, L., Sun, Y., Yu, W., Wang, X., 2021. Targeting STAT3 signaling overcomes gefitinib resistance in non-small cell lung cancer. Cell Death Dis. 12 (6), 561.

Ma, J., Wang, K., Zhan, M., 2015. Growth mechanism and electrical and magnetic properties of Ag−Fe3O4 core−shell nanowires. ACS Appl. Mater. Interfaces 7 (29), 16027−16039.

Madni, A., Batool, A., Noreen, S., Maqbool, I., Rehman, F., Kashif, P.M., et al., 2017. Novel nanoparticulate systems for lung cancer therapy: an updated review. J. Drug. Target. 25 (6), 499−512.

Malebary, S.J., Khan, R., Khan, Y.D., 2021. ProtoPred: advancing oncological research through identification of proto-oncogene proteins. IEEE Access. 9, 68788−68797.

Martin, T.D., Patel, R.S., Cook, D.R., Choi, M.Y., Patil, A., Liang, A.C., et al., 2021. The adaptive immune system is a major driver of selection for tumor suppressor gene inactivation. Science 373 (6561), 1327–1335.

Maurya, P., Singh, S., Saraf, S.A., 2020. Inhalable hybrid nanocarriers for respiratory disorders. Targeting Chronic Inflammatory Lung Diseases Using Advanced Drug Delivery Systems. Elsevier, pp. 281–302.

Medley, C.D., Smith, J.E., Tang, Z., Wu, Y., Bamrungsap, S., Tan, W., 2008. Gold nanoparticle-based colorimetric assay for the direct detection of cancerous cells. Anal. Chem. 80 (4), 1067–1072.

Menon, J.U., Jadeja, P., Tambe, P., Vu, K., Yuan, B., Nguyen, K.T., 2013. Nanomaterials for photo-based diagnostic and therapeutic applications. Theranostics. 3 (3), 152.

Na, J.H., Koo, H., Lee, S., Min, K.H., Park, K., Yoo, H., et al., 2011. Real-time and non-invasive optical imaging of tumor-targeting glycol chitosan nanoparticles in various tumor models. Biomaterials. 32 (22), 5252–5261.

Nakagawa, K., Nadal, E., Garon, E.B., Nishio, M., Seto, T., Yamamoto, N., et al., 2021. RELAY subgroup analyses by EGFR Ex19del and Ex21L858R mutations for ramucirumab plus erlotinib in metastatic non–small cell lung cancer. Clin. Cancer Res. 27 (19), 5258–5271.

Newase, S., Bankar, A., 2017. Synthesis of bio-inspired Ag–Au nanocomposite and its anti-biofilm efficacy. Bull. Mater. Sci. 40 (1), 157–162.

Nguyen, T., Tran, E., Nguyen, T., Do, P., Huynh, T., Huynh, H., 2004. The role of activated MEK-ERK pathway in quercetin-induced growth inhibition and apoptosis in A549 lung cancer cells. Carcinogenesis. 25 (5), 647–659.

Niu, W., Zhang, L., Xu, G., 2012. Seed-mediated growth method for high-quality noble metal nanocrystals. Sci. China Chem. 55 (11), 2311–2317.

Olajire, A., Kareem, A., Olaleke, A., 2017. Green synthesis of bimetallic Pt@ Cu nanostructures for catalytic oxidative desulfurization of model oil. J. Nanostructure Chem. 7 (2), 159–170.

Oliveira Gonçalves, K., de Oliveira Silva, F.R., Vieira, D.P., Courrol, L.C., editors. 2018. Synthesis of Hybrid AuFe Nanoparticles by Photoreduction and Methyl Aminoluvinate. 2018 SBFoton International Optics and Photonics Conference (SBFoton IOPC): IEEE.

Olteanu, N.L., Lazăr, C.A., Petcu, A.R., Meghea, A., Rogozea, E.A., Mihaly, M., 2016. One-pot synthesis of fluorescent Au@ SiO2 and SiO2@ Au nanoparticles. Arab. J. Chem. 9 (6), 854–864.

Padmanaban, A., Dhanasekaran, T., Kumar, S.P., Gnanamoorthy, G., Munusamy, S., Stephen, A., et al., 2017. Visible light photocatalytic property of Ag/TiO2 composite. Mech. Mater. Sci. Eng. 9 (1).

Parihar, P., Singh, S., Singh, R., Rajasheker, G., Rathnagiri, P., Srivastava, R.K., et al., 2019. An integrated transcriptomic, proteomic, and metabolomic approach to unravel the molecular mechanisms of metal stress tolerance in plants. Plant-Metal Interactions. Springer, pp. 1–28.

Park, H.J., Lee, S.H., Chang, Y.S., 2020. Recent advances in diagnostic technologies in lung cancer. Korean J. Intern. Med. 35 (2), 257–268.

Parvanian, S., Mostafavi, S.M., Aghashiri, M., 2017. Multifunctional nanoparticle developments in cancer diagnosis and treatment. Sens. Bio-Sens. Res. 13, 81–87.

Pearson, A., Bhargava, S.K., Bansal, V., 2011. UV-switchable polyoxometalate sandwiched between TiO2 and metal nanoparticles for enhanced visible and solar light photococatalysis. Langmuir. 27 (15), 9245–9252.

Peng, C.-W., Li, Y., 2010. Application of quantum dots-based biotechnology in cancer diagnosis: current status and future perspectives. J. Nanomater 2010, 676839.

Peng, G., Trock, E., Haick, H., 2008. Detecting simulated patterns of lung cancer biomarkers by random network of single-walled carbon nanotubes coated with nonpolymeric organic materials. Nano Lett. 8 (11), 3631–3635.

Peng, X.-H., Wang, Y., Huang, D., Wang, Y., Shin, H.J., Chen, Z., et al., 2011. Targeted delivery of cisplatin to lung cancer using ScFvEGFR-heparin-cisplatin nanoparticles. ACS Nano 5 (12), 9480–9493.

Pfaff, A., Schallon, A., Ruhland, T.M., Majewski, A.P., Schmalz, H., Freitag, R., et al., 2011. Magnetic and fluorescent glycopolymer hybrid nanoparticles for intranuclear optical imaging. Biomacromolecules. 12 (10), 3805–3811.

Pink, D.L., Loruthai, O., Ziolek, R.M., Wasutrasawat, P., Terry, A.E., Lawrence, M.J., et al., 2019. On the structure of solid lipid nanoparticles. Small. 15 (45), 1903156.

Pisduangdaw, S., Panpranot, J., Methastidsook, C., Chaisuk, C., Faungnawakij, K., Praserthdam, P., et al., 2009. Characteristics and catalytic properties of Pt−Sn/Al$_2$O$_3$ nanoparticles synthesized by one-step flame spray pyrolysis in the dehydrogenation of propane. Appl. Catal. A: Gen. 370 (1−2), 1−6.

Pol, V.G., Srivastava, D., Palchik, O., Palchik, V., Slifkin, M., Weiss, A., et al., 2002. Sonochemical deposition of silver nanoparticles on silica spheres. Langmuir 18 (8), 3352−3357.

Pourrahmat, M.-M., Kim, A., Kansal, A.R., Hux, M., Pushkarna, D., Fazeli, M.S., et al., 2021. Health state utility values by cancer stage: a systematic literature review. Eur. J. Health Econ. 22 (8), 1275−1288.

Rao, M.D., Pennathur, G., 2017. Green synthesis and characterization of cadmium sulphide nanoparticles from Chlamydomonas reinhardtii and their application as photocatalysts. Mater. Res. Bull. 85, 64−73.

Redjala, T., Remita, H., Apostolescu, G., Mostafavi, M., Thomazeau, C., Uzio, D., et al., 2006. Bimetallic Au-Pd and Ag-Pd clusters synthesised by or electron beam radiolysis and study of the reactivity/structure relationships in the selective hydrogenation of Buta-1, 3-Diene. Oil Gas Sci. Technol. 61 (6), 789−797.

Rivera, M.P., Mehta, A.C., Wahidi, M.M., 2013. Establishing the diagnosis of lung cancer: diagnosis and management of lung cancer, 3rd ed: American College of Chest Physicians evidence-based clinical practice guidelines. Chest 143 (5, Supplement), e142S. -e65S.

Rizvi, S.F.A., Mu, S., Zhao, C., Zhang, H., 2022. Fabrication of self-assembled peptide nanoparticles for in vitro assessment of cell apoptosis pathway and in vivo therapeutic efficacy. Microchim. Acta 189 (2), 53.

Robertson, K.L., Soto, C.M., Archer, M.J., Odoemene, O., Liu, J.L., 2011. Engineered T4 viral nano-particles for cellular imaging and flow cytometry. Bioconjugate Chem. 22 (4), 595−604.

Ruiz-Ceja, K.A., Chirino, Y.I., 2017. Current FDA-approved treatments for non-small cell lung cancer and potential biomarkers for its detection. Biomed. Pharmacother. 90, 24−37.

Sachs, E., Sartipy, U., Jackson, V., 2021. Sex and survival after surgery for lung cancer: a Swedish Nationwide Cohort. Chest. 159 (5), 2029−2039.

Sakai, H., Kanda, T., Shibata, H., Ohkubo, T., Abe, M., 2006. Preparation of highly dispersed core/shell-type titania nanocapsules containing a single Ag nanoparticle. J. Am. Chem. Soc. 128 (15), 4944−4945.

Sarker, M., Nakamura, T., Herbani, Y., Sato, S., 2013. Fabrication of Rh based solid-solution bimetallic alloy nanoparticles with fully-tunable composition through femtosecond laser irradiation in aqueous solution. Appl. Phys. A. 110 (1), 145−152.

Sawle, B.D., Salimath, B., Deshpande, R., Bedre, M.D., Prabhakar, B.K., Venkataraman, A., et al., 2008. Biosynthesis and stabilization of Au and Au−Ag alloy nanoparticles by fungus, Fusarium semitectum. Sci. Technol. Adv. Mater. 9 (3), 035012.

Shah, S.N., Steinmetz, N.F., Aljabali, A.A., Lomonossoff, G.P., Evans, D., 2009. Environmentally benign synthesis of virus-templated, monodisperse, iron-platinum nanoparticles. J. Dalton. Trans. 40, 8479−8480.

Sharma, G., Kumar, D., Kumar, A., Ala'a, H., Pathania, D., Naushad, M., et al., 2017. Revolution from monometallic to trimetallic nanoparticle composites, various synthesis methods and their applications: a review. Mater. Sci. Eng. C Mater. Biol. Appl. 71, 1216−1230.

Sharma, G., Kumar, A., Sharma, S., Naushad, M., Ahamad, T., Al-Saeedi, S.I., et al., 2018. Facile fabrication of Zr$_2$Ni$_1$Cu$_7$ trimetallic nano-alloy and its composite with Si$_3$N$_4$ for visible light assisted photodegradation of methylene blue. J. Mol. Liq. 272, 170−179.

Shepard, K.B., Vodak, D.T., Kuehl, P.J., Revelli, D., Zhou, Y., Pluntze, A.M., et al., 2021. Local treatment of non-small cell lung cancer with a spray-dried bevacizumab formulation. AAPS PharmSciTech 22 (7), 230.

Shoja, Y., Kermanpur, A., Karimzadeh, F., 2018. Diagnosis of EGFR exon21 L858R point mutation as lung cancer biomarker by electrochemical DNA biosensor based on reduced graphene oxide /functionalized ordered mesoporous carbon/Ni-oxytetracycline metallopolymer nanoparticles modified pencil graphite electrode. Biosens. Bioelectron. 113, 108−115.

Singh, P., Kim, Y.-J., Zhang, D., Yang, J., et al., 2016. Biological synthesis of nanoparticles from plants and microorganisms. Trends Biotechnol. 34 (7), 588−599.

Singh, P., Pandit, S., Mokkapati, V.R.S.S., Garg, A., Ravikumar, V., Mijakovic, I., 2018. Gold nanoparticles in diagnostics and therapeutics for human cancer. Int. J. Mol. Sci. 19 (7), 1979.

Singh, R., Soni, R., 2015. Synthesis of rattle-type Ag@ Al2O3 nanostructure by laser-induced heating of Ag and Al nanoparticles. Appl. Phys. A. 121 (1), 261–271.

Siuzdak, K., Sawczak, M., Klein, M., Nowaczyk, G., Jurga, S., Cenian, A., 2014. Preparation of platinum modified titanium dioxide nanoparticles with the use of laser ablation in water. Phys. Chem. Chem. Phys. 16 (29), 15199–15206.

Sivasankaran, S., Sankaranarayanan, S., Ramakrishnan, S., 2013. A novel sonochemical synthesis of metal oxides based Bhasmas. Mater. Sci. Forum 754, 87–99. Trans Tech Publ.

Song, M.-K., Rai, P., Ko, K.-J., Jeon, S.-H., Chon, B.-S., Lee, C.-H., et al., 2014. Synthesis of TiO$_2$ hollow spheres by selective etching of Au@ TiO2 core–shell nanoparticles for dye sensitized solar cell applications. RSC Adv. 4, 3529–3535.

Sordella, R., Bell, D.W., Haber, D.A., Settleman, J., 2004. Gefitinib-sensitizing EGFR mutations in lung cancer activate anti-apoptotic pathways. Sciences 305 (5687), 1163–1167.

Srinoi, P., Chen, Y.-T., Vittur, V., Marquez, M.D., Lee, T.R., 2018. Bimetallic nanoparticles: enhanced magnetic and optical properties for emerging biological applications. Appl. Sci. 8 (7), 1106.

Tan, B.-J., Liu, Y., Chang, K.-L., Lim, B.K., Chiu, G.N.J., 2012. Perorally active nanomicellar formulation of quercetin in the treatment of lung cancer. Int. J. Nanomed. 7, 651.

Tanaka, A., Nishino, Y., Sakaguchi, S., Yoshikawa, T., Imamura, K., Hashimoto, K., et al., 2013. Functionalization of a plasmonic Au/TiO2 photocatalyst with an Ag co-catalyst for quantitative reduction of nitrobenzene to aniline in 2-propanol suspensions under irradiation of visible light. Chem. Comm. 49 (25), 2551–2553.

Tao, H., Wu, T., Aldeghi, M., Wu, T.C., Aspuru-Guzik, A., Kumacheva, E., 2021. Nanoparticle synthesis assisted by machine learning. Nat. Rev. Mater. 6 (8), 701–716.

Thangavel, K., Lakshmikuttyamma, A., Thangavel, C., Shoyele, S.A., 2022. CD44-targeted, indocyanine green-paclitaxel-loaded human serum albumin nanoparticles for potential image-guided drug delivery. Colloids Surf. B: Biointerfaces 209, 112162.

Thevenot, J., Troutier, A.-L., David, L., Delair, T., Ladavière, C., 2007. Steric stabilization of lipid/polymer particle assemblies by poly(ethylene glycol)-lipids. Biomacromolecules. 8 (11), 3651–3660.

Tom, R.T., Nair, A.S., Singh, N., Aslam, M., Nagendra, C., Philip, R., et al., 2003. Freely dispersible Au@ TiO2, Au@ ZrO2, Ag@ TiO2, and Ag@ ZrO2 core–shell nanoparticles: one-step synthesis, characterization, spectroscopy, and optical limiting properties. Langmuir 19 (8), 3439–3445.

Tseng, C.-L., Wang, T.-W., Dong, G.-C., Yueh-Hsiu Wu, S., Young, T.-H., Shieh, M.-J., et al., 2007. Development of gelatin nanoparticles with biotinylated EGF conjugation for lung cancer targeting. Biomaterials. 28 (27), 3996–4005.

Ullah, R., Yin, Q., Snell, A.H., Wan, L., 2021. RAF-MEK-ERK pathway in cancer evolution and treatment. Semin. Cancer Biol. 85, 123–154.

Vengurlekar, S., Chaturvedi, S.C., 2021. Chapter 4 - Nanoparticles and lung cancer. In: Yadav, A.K., Gupta, U., Sharma, R. (Eds.), Nano Drug Delivery Strategies for the Treatment of Cancers. Academic Press, pp. 107–118.

Ventola, C.L., 2017. Progress in Nanomedicine: Approved and Investigational Nanodrugs. Pharm. Ther. 42 (12), 742–755.

Verschraegen, C.F., Skubitz, K., Daud, A., Kudelka, A.P., Rabinowitz, I., Allievi, C., et al., 2009. A phase I and pharmacokinetic study of paclitaxel poliglumex and cisplatin in patients with advanced solid tumors. Cancer Chemother. Pharm. 63 (5), 903–910.

Wan, X., Song, Y., Song, N., Li, J., Yang, L., Li, Y., et al., 2016. The preliminary study of immune superparamagnetic iron oxide nanoparticles for the detection of lung cancer in magnetic resonance imaging. Carbohydr. Res. 419, 33–40.

Wang, C., Yin, H., Dai, S., Sun, S., 2010. A general approach to noble metal–metal oxide dumbbell nanoparticles and their catalytic application for CO oxidation. Chem. Mater. 22 (10), 3277–3282.

Wang, C.M., Zhang, Y., Shutthanandan, V., Thevuthasan, S., Duscher, G., 2004. Microstructure of precipitated au nanoclusters in TiO2. J. Appl. Phys. 95 (12), 8185–8193.

Wang, H., Zheng, L., Peng, C., Shen, M., Shi, X., Zhang, G., 2013. Folic acid-modified dendrimer-entrapped gold nanoparticles as nanoprobes for targeted CT imaging of human lung adencarcinoma. Biomaterials. 34 (2), 470−480.

Wang, J., Su, G., Yin, X., Luo, J., Gu, R., Wang, S., et al., 2019. Non-small cell lung cancer-targeted, redox-sensitive lipid-polymer hybrid nanoparticles for the delivery of a second-generation irreversible epidermal growth factor inhibitor—Afatinib: In vitro and in vivo evaluation. Biomed. Pharmacother. 120, 109493.

Wang, Y., Arandiyan, H., Scott, J., Bagheri, A., Dai, H., Amal, R., 2017. Recent advances in ordered meso/macroporous metal oxides for heterogeneous catalysis: a review. J. Mater. Chem. A. 5 (19), 8825−8846.

Wu, X.-F., Song, H.-Y., Yoon, J.-M., Yu, Y.-T., Chen, Y.-F., 2009. Synthesis of core − shell Au@ TiO2 nanoparticles with truncated wedge-shaped morphology and their photocatalytic properties. Langmuir. 25 (11), 6438−6447.

Wu, X.-F., Chen, Y.-F., Yoon, J.-M., Yu, Y.-T., 2010. Fabrication and properties of flower-shaped Pt@ TiO2 core−shell nanoparticles. Mater. Lett. 64 (20), 2208−2210.

Yamamoto, N., Seto, T., Nishio, M., Goto, K., Yamamoto, N., Okamoto, I., et al., 2021. Erlotinib plus bevacizumab vs erlotinib monotherapy as first-line treatment for advanced EGFR mutation-positive non-squamous non-small-cell lung cancer: survival follow-up results of the randomized JO25567 study. Lung Cancer 151, 20−24.

Yang, L., Ma, P.A., Chen, X., et al., 2022. High-sensitivity fluorescence detection for lung cancer CYFRA21-1 DNA based on accumulative hybridization of quantum dots. J. Mater. Chem. B 10 (9), 1386−1392.

Yang, R., Yang, S.-G., Shim, W.-S., Cui, F., Cheng, G., Kim, I.-W., et al., 2009. Lung-specific delivery of paclitaxel by chitosan-modified PLGA nanoparticles via transient formation of microaggregates. J. Pharm. Sci. 98 (3), 970−984.

Yang, S.-G., Chang, J.-E., Shin, B., Park, S., Na, K., Shim, C.-K., 2010. 99mTc-hematoporphyrin linked albumin nanoparticles for lung cancer targeted photodynamic therapy and imaging. J. Mater. Chem. 20 (41), 9042−9046.

Yokoyama, T., Tam, J., Kuroda, S., Scott, A.W., Aaron, J., Larson, T., et al., 2011. EGFR-targeted hybrid plasmonic magnetic nanoparticles synergistically induce autophagy and apoptosis in non-small cell lung cancer cells. PLOS One 6 (11), e25507.

You, J., Zhang, G., Li, C., 2010. Exceptionally high payload of doxorubicin in hollow gold nanospheres for near-infrared light-triggered drug release. ACS Nano 4 (2), 1033−1041.

Young, M., Debbie, W., Uchida, M., Douglas, T., 2008. Plant viruses as biotemplates for materials and their use in nanotechnology. Annu. Rev. Phytopathol. 46, 361−384.

Zamare, D., Vutukuru, S., Babu, R., 2016. Biosynthesis of nanoparticles from agro-waste: a sustainable approach. IJEAST 1 (12), 85−92.

Zeng, D.-Q., Yu, Y.-F., Ou, Q.-Y., Li, X.-Y., Zhong, R.-Z., Xie, C.-M., et al., 2016. Prognostic and predictive value of tumor-infiltrating lymphocytes for clinical therapeutic research in patients with non-small cell lung cancer. Oncotarget. 7 (12), 13765−13781.

Zhai, Z., Wang, C., Sun, Z., Cheng, S., Wang K., editors. 2022. Deep Neural Network Guided by Attention Mechanism for Segmentation of Liver Pathology Image. In Proceedings of 2021 Chinese Intelligent Systems Conference 2022; Singapore: Springer Singapore.

Zhang, J., Chen, G., Chaker, M., Rosei, F., Ma, D., 2013. Gold nanoparticle decorated ceria nanotubes with significantly high catalytic activity for the reduction of nitrophenol and mechanism study. Appl. Catal. B. 132, 107−115.

Zhang, L., Xia, D., Shen, Q.J., 2006a. Synthesis and characterization of Ag@ TiO2 core-shell nanoparticles and TiO2 nanobubbles. J. Nanopart. Res. 8 (1), 23−28.

Zhang, L., Dou, Y.-H., Gu, H.-C., 2006b. Synthesis of Ag−Fe3O4 heterodimeric nanoparticles. J. Colloid. Interface Sci. 297 (2), 660−664.

Zhang, L., Blom, D.A., Wang, H.J., 2011. Au−Cu2O core−shell nanoparticles: a hybrid metal-semiconductor heteronanostructure with geometrically tunable optical properties. Chem. Mater. 23 (20), 4587−4598.

Zhang, R., Meng, Z., Wu, X., Zhang, M., Zhang, S., Jin, T., 2021. Mortalin promotes breast cancer malignancy. Exp. Mol. Pathol. 118, 104593.

Zielińska-Jurek, A., Reszczyńska, J., Grabowska, E., Zaleska, A., 2012. Nanoparticles Preparation Using Microemulsion Systems. InTech, pp. 229—250.

Ziylan-Yavas, A., Mizukoshi, Y., Maeda, Y., Ince, N.H., 2015. Supporting of pristine TiO2 with noble metals to enhance the oxidation and mineralization of paracetamol by sonolysis and sonophotolysis. Appl. Catal. B. 172, 7—17.

CHAPTER 8

Multifunctional nanocrystals for liver cancer

Shalini Shukla, Shalu Singh and Rahul Shukla
Department of Pharmaceutics, National Institute of Pharmaceutical Education and Research-Raebareli, Lucknow, Uttar Pradesh, India

8.1 Introduction

According to the Global Cancer Observatory (GLOBOCAN) 2020 database, liver cancer became the third highest cause of cancer-caused deaths worldwide. Each year, roughly 700,000 new patients with hepatic carcinoma are identified around the world with 600,000 deaths due to liver cancer. Liver cancer can be caused by viral hepatitis B and C infections, diabetes, tobacco smoking, fatty liver disease, also due to other harmful lifestyle practices (Liu et al., 2021). Virus infections are predominant hepatitis cases in East Asia and Africa, despite related daily life-related variables, including alcohol, drug abuse, type-2 diabetes, and obesity, becoming more common in Western, industrialized countries (Ganem et al., 2004).

Only 5%−15% of patients can be candidates for surgical removal, which is only applicable for patients in the initial stages of the illness and due to the lowered regeneration ability of the liver, generally without cirrhosis; right hepatectomy involves a greater risk of postoperative problems than left hepatectomy. During later phases, some potential therapies include: (1) transarterial chemoembolization results in a 23% improvement in survival above that of conservative therapy for patients with intermediate stage HCC and (2) oral dose with the kinase inhibitor sorafenib. However, less than one-third of patients experience therapeutic improvement, and 6 months after the regimen's beginning, resistance sets in (Anwanwan et al., 2020).

A number of gene alterations has been linked to liver cancer, such as apoptosis-related gene dysregulation, tumor suppressor inactivation, and oncogene activation (Man et al., 2021). Detection of liver cancer can be done with ultrasonography or serological testing. A number of emerging nanoformulations are available to treat liver cancer. Nanocrystals are most widely studied because they are well-suited for active and passive targeting with high drug loading (almost 100%). The size of drug particles ranges from a diameter of 10−1000 nm (Ostrowski et al., 2012; Iredale, 2007). They are composed entirely of drugs, with no polymer or lipid as in polymeric or solid lipid nanoparticles (Müller et al., 2011). To stabilize drug nanocrystals, surfactants or

Multifunctional Nanocomposites for Targeted Drug Delivery in Cancer Therapy
DOI: https://doi.org/10.1016/B978-0-323-95303-0.00003-4

213

polymeric steric stabilizers are utilized. Nanocrystals are administered via oral, parenteral, or any other route and possess strong commercial potential. When compared to amorphous pharmaceuticals, drug nanocrystals have less energy and thus stronger structural stability, leading to better dissolution. The rate of dissolution and aqueous solubility of low water-soluble pharmaceuticals saw an increment as the size of drug nanocrystals decreased (Morakul et al., 2014; Cormode et al., 2011). These pharmaceutical nanocrystals are disseminated in the proper aqueous medium like water, non-aqueous or aqueous media, including liquid polyethylene glycol to create nanosuspensions (Junyaprasert and Morakul, 2015). It is anticipated that 40% of pharmacological substances in the development phase would have solubility concerns. Hence, using nanocrystals to improve the dissolution of very less soluble pharmaceuticals was extremely important. Reduction of size to the nanoscale enhances saturation solubility and lowers diffusional routes due to the rise in surface area of nanocrystals, hence increasing bioavailability (Vo et al., 2013; Brough and Williams, 2013). Several studies are undertaken to increase the bioavailability and therapeutic effect of poorly bioavailable anticancer medicines taken orally (Jain et al., 2016; Khadka et al., 2014; Danhier et al., 2014; Patel et al., 2014). A novel drug nanocrystal formulation was developed by Honglei Zhan et al. of camptothecin (CPT), embellished by silver nanoparticles. CPT and gold nanoparticles (Ag NPs) were combined to generate CPT/Ag nanocrystals, which had enhanced drug stability, dispersion characteristics, and cellular absorption rates.

Despite all of these advances, cancer diagnosis and therapy are still challenging issues. In this context, a newer system known as hybrid nanocrystals or multifunctional nanocrystals showed considerable promise. All of the advantages of nanocrystal technology for cancer therapy are combined along with tumor diagnostic properties in hybrid or multifunctional nanocrystals. These devices could perform anticancer therapy and bioimaging at the same time, enticing great interest in theranostics. This chapter focuses on the role of nanocrystals as a diagnostic tool in addition to the therapy of liver cancer.

8.2 Techniques for nanocrystal formulation

8.2.1 Top-down techniques

Top-down techniques decrease the particulate to nanosize through mechanical forces (Van Eerdenbrugh et al., 2008). The production of nanocrystals by utilization of this method has the advantage of being adaptable according to the scale of production (Chen et al., 2011), while the disadvantage is the requirement of high energy, loss of sample crystal nature, and contamination during the process (Möschwitzer, 2013). High-pressure homogenization (HPH) and sample milling are the two conventional methods included in top-down (Van Eerdenbrugh et al., 2008) (Fig. 8.1).

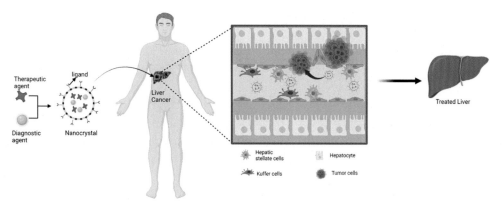

Figure 8.1 Diagrammatic representation of the action of multifunctional nanocrystals in liver cancer.

8.2.1.1 Milling

Milling is a technique that comminutes coarse particles of the drug into nano-sized crystals, by shear, impact, and attrition. The wet milling technique is widely used as it has higher chances of nanosizing (Juhnke et al., 2012). The main cogs of milling are a media milling to pulverize the particles of the media to the nanoscale range, a coolant to regulate the rise in temperature, and a recirculating chamber. Milling of the media commonly contains of spherical pearls consisting of oxides of zircon, glass, derivatives of hard polystyrene, etc. A suitable surfactant that serves as a stabilizer and nonaqueous or aqueous media are added to the unprocessed slurry as it is introduced into the milling chamber. The media for milling particles approximates up ranging of 10%—50% (w/v) of the volume of unrefined slurry carried for grinding, while the slurry volume estimates up to 30% (w/v) of the chamber with a rotating blade. The high kinetic dynamism engendered via the progression of agitation generates impact and shear, thereby lowering the size of the unrefined slurry's particles (Merisko-Liversidge and Liversidge, 2011; Peltonen and Hirvonen, 2010) The milling process can be employed in noncontinuous mode, which means the type of circulation can be modified and conditioned to the final product requirements, allowing the process to be designed to the continuous mode or batch type. Continuous mode is mostly preferred to acquire low-size ranging uniform nanocrystals. The major concern of continuous circulation mode is the upsurge in the temperature in the interiors of the chamber during the process, which may influence the long-term stability of drug particles. A coolant is utilized to circumvent stability issues, and to regulate the temperature elevation inside the milling chamber (Monteiro et al., 2013; George and Ghosh, 2013). The media milling technology was previously designed by Liversidge and coworkers for obtaining nanocrystals. The technique is extensively utilized by Elan Pharma and in several other currently marketed drugs, such as Tricor, Emend, Rapamune, Megace ES, etc. (Zuo et al., 2013). Numerous nanoproducts have been introduced in the market using low-energy milling processes (Pearl Mill) (Pawar et al., 2014).

8.2.1.2 High-pressure homogenization

This involves the diminution of particles to the nanoscale range by forcing particles through the small gap under high pressure causing collision and cavitation. A range of 100−1500 bar can be used by homogenizers (Muller and Keck, 2004). It may be necessary to perform a certain number of homogenization cycles depending on the type and degree of the drug's hardness (Lei et al., 2008). The reduction in size is accomplished by various methods, such as cavitation, collisions among particles, and high-shear forces. The HPH process involves primarily dispersion of the unprocessed powder of drug in media, surfactants, which functions as stabilizers that further undergo size reduction by homogenization or high-speed shearing and low pressure. Consequently, the resultant reduced size dispersion is subjected to HPH with the purpose of obtaining the optimal-sized nanocrystals (Keck and Müller, 2006; Zhang et al., 2007). The HPH techniques can be divided into three categories based on the equipment and media used: microfluidization, aqueous vehicle homogenization, and nonaqueous vehicle homogenization.

8.2.1.3 Aqueous-media based homogenization

This method was established by Muller and coworkers, comprising of piston-gap homogenizers (Möschwitzer, 2013). Particles are firstly dispersed in water with proper stabilizer, which is then flowed via a very narrow homogenization gap with the help of a piston at extremely high pressure (1500−4000 bar). Depending on the dispersion viscosity and ultimate size requirement, homogenization gap width can be accustomed from 5 to 20 µm. Given that the aqueous media is utilized for dispersion, the technique possesses some drawbacks, which involve stability concerns produced by additional steps of drying to eradicate aqueous medium present in large amounts, using high-cost lyophilization methodologies to dry drugs that are sensitive to heat, hydrolysis, and other conditions (Möschwitzer, 2013; Shegokar and Müller, 2010).

8.2.1.4 Nonaqueous media/aqueous admixtures homogenization

This method involves preparation in an organic media, such as polyethylene glycol (PEG) 600, PEG 400, oils (Müller et al., 2011). These may be advantageous in a few instances, such as dispersion in ethanol-water admixtures, which are volatile in nature, reduce the time it takes to produce dry goods, soft gelatin capsules filled with oil-dispersed nanocrystals, aqueous unstable drugs nanosuspension, etc. Fatty acids or oils have very low vapor pressures at room temperature compared to aqueous media, which results in very high boiling points. Thus, the static pressure drops through the process of homogenization is not adequate to generate cavitation. Therefore, the efficiency of the process of particle size diminution is poor to that of aqueous dispersions. Consequently, to have an effective diminution process the nonaqueous process employs high temperature or a deep freeze homogenization process like in "nanopore" where low temperature (−20°C) is maintained (Müller et al., 2011; Möschwitzer, 2013; Bansal and Kumria, 2012).

8.2.1.5 Microfluidization

Microfluidization methodology is centered on the principle of the jet stream. High speed and acceleration are used to move the drug particles through a "Y"- or "Z-shaped" homogenization chamber. The suspension is repeatedly passed in multiples of 10 via these chambers to minimize the size of the particles (Bansal and Kumria, 2012). The main challenges of this methodology for achieving a targeted process of nanocrystal development are the arduous trajectories through chambers and microparticles acquired through the microfluidization procedure (Yang et al., 2012).

8.2.2 Bottom-up techniques

The bottom-up precipitation method includes growing nanocrystals from the solution (Sinha et al., 2013). This process comprises two crucial steps. The first is the process of nucleation, and the second is the development of the crystal. The nucleation process is critical in nanocrystal precipitation because homogeneous and small nanocrystals are required. With an increase in the rate of nucleation, a higher number of nuclei are generated from a supersaturated solution. The result of an increased number of nuclei collectively obtained during the nucleation step is a constricted-sized distribution of nanocrystals (Sinha et al., 2013; Kakran et al., 2012).

Lower energy procedures, simpler instruments, lower costs, and the ability to operate at low temperatures make the bottom-up method ideal for thermolabile pharmaceuticals (Rasenack and Müller, 2004). Precipitation is a bottom-up approach for precipitating drug nanocrystals from a supersaturated solution. There are three forms of precipitation: precipitation in the presence of supercritical fluid, solvent removal, and liquid solvent-antisolvent addition (Chan and Kwok, 2011).

Different techniques of precipitation are the supercritical antisolvent method, multiinlet vortex mixing, sonocrystallisation, liquid jet precipitation, evaporative precipitation in aqueous solvents, high gravity-controlled precipitation, and supercritical solution rapid expansion. These mentioned methods are mountable and employable for the nanocrystals generation (Hu et al., 2011). The antisolvent method is based on the variance in drug solubility in diverse miscible solvents. This involves nanocrystal presence in antisolvent that can be thereby dried by the addition of cryoprotectant or dispersant, then subjected to drying by freeze or spray technique. The resultant nanocrystals are stabilized to a greater extent due to the usage of the stabilizers (such as modified gelatine, sodium n-dodecyl sulfate, poloxamer, and hydroxypropyl methyl cellulose) acting for a small bout of time. Later, the formulation can be rendered unstable due to Ostwald ripening phenomena causing uncontrolled growth of crystal eventually resulting in bigger crystals. Still, the stabilizer addition is essential to evade spontaneous aggregation leading to the formation of microparticles. The patented products available are nanomorph and hydrosol. Disadvantages of the method involve residual content of organic solvent, very poor particle redispersion, stability, and difficulty in scale-up (Patel et al., 2018; Rasenack et al., 2003; Wang et al., 2013).

8.2.3 Combination technique

The process of combining both top-down and bottom-up methods for the generation of nanocrystals is called the combination technique. It is used for crystals of range <100 nm and diminishes the risks associated with both methods used individually. Generally, top-down methods are used as the pretreatment step followed by bottom-up methods. NanoEdge is an amalgamation of precipitation and homogenization (Miao et al., 2018). The Baxter's NanoEdge technique employs a precipitation stage trailed by annealing employing a high-energy method, for instance, HPH. The annealing process stops the nanocrystals from expanding. According to this method, annealing is the method of changing a thermodynamically erratic substance into a more stabilized form by applying energy once or repeatedly, and then thermal relaxation. SmartCrystal, created by Abbott Laboratories, is another combination technology. It integrates various methods that either speed up production by minimizing the number of homogenizer passes or produce extremely tiny nanocrystals that are less than 100 nm in size (Shetea et al., 2014).

8.3 Liver cancer and challenges in drug delivery

8.3.1 Liver cancer

As per World Health Organization predictions, liver cancer will lead to the death of nearly one million people by 2030, presenting it as the fourth most frequent cancer-related death cause globally. The foremost risk factors related to hepatic cancer are infections of hepatitis virus B or C, persistent consumption of alcohol, and, more recently, nonalcoholic fatty liver disease; nevertheless, obesity, iron overload, diabetes, and smoking have also been linked to the development of this illness. The development of liver cancer involves a numerous cellular mechanisms, involving disruption of the apoptosis mechanism and cell cycle, fibrogenesis mechanisms, and inflammatory molecular pathways; all of these constitute significant molecular targets that aid in the creation of new pharmacological therapies (Galicia-Moreno et al., 2021).

Chronic liver disease (CLD), which is marked by ongoing inflammation and hepatocyte regeneration, almost often precedes the development of liver cancer. Pathophysiological changes result from long-term inflammation mechanisms that collaborate to start or promote liver cancer. These procedures involve the development of progenitor cells, the buildup of epigenetic and genetic alterations, and the modification of the microenvironment. Significantly more hepatic progenitor cells are seen in CLDs. The hepatocyte proliferation capacity is thought to be practically unlimited under certain conditions. This capability, however, is compromised in human CLDs, possibly as a result of replicative senescence or infection through the hepatitis virus brought on by prolonged constant regeneration of hepatocytes. The Hering canals, which are canaliculi bordered with cholangiocytes and hepatocytes, are where hepatic stem/progenitor cells originate. The stem cell niche strongly controls stem cell homing, proliferation, and motility. The niche cells in the liver that regulate hepatic stem/progenitors' capacity for self-renewal and division are still unknown. According to research, the intensity of liver fibrosis and inflammation and the HCC risk is correlated with the degree of progenitor cell activation. The initiation and promotion of liver cancer are caused by genetic and epigenetic alterations that accumulate over many years in all hepatic pathways. By causing genomic instability and insertion mutagenesis, hepatitis B virus (HBV) infection leads to HBV genome combination into the host genome and may cause or boost HCC. Additionally, the HBV X gene (HBx) alters NF-B and p53 signaling pathways to support HCC. By altering mitochondrial functioning, hepatitis C virus infection may accelerate the formation of ROS, which causes DNA damage. Genomic instability and HCC are also influenced by telomere shortening driven by increased hepatocyte turnover (Yamashita and Wang, 2013).

8.3.2 Challenges in liver targeting

The liver is the body's greatest abdominal gland and organ, performing over 500 known biological functions, including biochemical synthesis, metabolite detoxification, and glycogen storage (Sanyal et al., 2018). The liver gets blood from two locations: the hepatic artery, which is oxygen-loaded, and the hepatic portal vein, which is rich in nutrients. The liver sinusoids are tiny capillaries that divide these blood vessels into lobules. The triad, which consists of venules, arterioles, and the bile duct, corners the hexagonal lobules, which are made up of plates of hepatocytes (Trefts et al., 2017). The parenchymal hepatocytes contribute 80% of the liver's volume, while nonparenchymal cells such as sinusoidal endothelial cells (SECs), Kupffer cells (KCs), hepatocyte stem cells (HSCs), and comprise 2.8%, 2.1%, and 1.4%, respectively. The space of Disse, which contains HSCs, separates the hepatocyte plates from the hepatic sinusoid. Dynamic endothelial fenestrations spanning $50-200$ nanometers can transport plasma components from the circulation into the space of Disse (Wisse et al., 1985; Zapotoczny et al., 2017). Life-threatening illnesses associated with the liver, like a hepatic failure, hepatic cancer, and liver fibrosis, are usually due to inflammation in the liver called hepatitis (Pan and Zhang, 2005). It induces cirrhosis, along with the formation of hyperplastic nodules having gene mutations, which eventually contribute to hepatic carcinoma (Ganem et al., 2004). Hepatocellular carcinoma (HCC) and liver fibrosis are the key intracellular and extracellular pathophysiological changes affecting the therapeutic delivery (Waller et al., 2015; Giannitrapani et al., 2014).

8.3.2.1 Liver fibrosis

Hepatic fibrosis, an illness that encompasses the production of extracellular matrix, increases highly during the repair process upon injury. The activation of HSC is the major step in the fibrogenesis process, thus aiming for activated HSC (aHSC) can be an appealing approach for managing liver fibrosis, liver tumor metastases, and HCC. Type I and III collagens are the most common cells generated by aHSCs, which are regarded with the myofibroblast-like phenotype (Moreira, 2007). Moreover, chemokines yielded by aHSCs encourage the chemotaxis of tumor and inflammatory cells toward the liver (Zhang et al., 2007). Therefore, hepatic fibrosis is considered a threat aspect for HCC.

IFN-γ, colchicine, pirfenidone, peroxisomal proliferator-activated receptor ligands, and rennin-angiotensin system inhibitors are some of the drug candidates that have been studied for their ability to inhibit HSC proliferation, activation, and/or collagen production (Bataller and Brenner, 2005; Rockey, 2008). Various antioxidants have been proven reduction in fibrogenesis like phosphatidylcholine, silymarin, vitamin E, and S-adenosyl-l-methionine. However, proposed therapies failed in clinical trials, ascribed to an unsatisfactory distribution resulting from pathophysiological differences in fibrotic hepatic condition (Rockey, 2008). The hyperplastic nodules with scarring of fibrogenesis locations and space-consuming ECM dispositions in the space of Disse which in turn demonstrates the growth of intrahepatic connective tissue. Structurally, aHSCs and SECs boost contractile characteristics, resulting in portal hypertension and blocking the portal vein flow. This is one of the foremost impediments to hepatic cirrhosis. Plasma cannot pass in the Disse space because of the loss of fenestrae (Iredale, 2007). These complications reduce the delivery of drugs in fibrosis conditions. In progressive phases, the tissue parts of fibrosis form diseased hepatocytic nodules, ultimately altering the entire liver's structure, and causing the flow of blood to drop. The diseased hepatocytes dissever from the bile ductulus due to damage of their typical microvilli subsequently leading to liver failure (Aubé et al., 2017).

Nanoparticles show decreased drug delivery to the fibrotic hepatocytes owing to the abridged flow of blood. Therefore, the works are focused on increasing the aHSCs' specialized uptake of nanoparticles. The aHSCs upregulate several receptors such as the retinol-binding protein receptor (RBPR), the platelet-derived growth factor receptor-β (PDGFRb), the mannose-6-phosphate receptor, and collagen type VI receptor, which can be actively-targeted by drugs (Giannitrapani et al., 2014). An investigation was conducted on novel theranostic nanomedicine, relaxin-PEGylated superparamagnetic iron-oxide nanoparticles (SPIONs). In 2021, Hu et al. investigated another study on sigma-1 receptor targeting, which was performed by formulating AEAA- pRLN- LPD NPs that deactivated HSCs.

8.3.2.2 Hepatocellular carcinoma

HCC constitutes nearly 90% of predominant cases of hepatic carcinoma in adults and is the fifth most frequent cancer globally, and patients with hepatic cirrhosis are the common mortality cause in patients. HCC develops typically in those who have a history of chronic liver inflammation, including overconsumption of nonalcoholic fatty liver disease, alcohol, and viral hepatitis (El−Serag and Rudolph, 2007; Parkin et al., 2005). Mutations and complex epigenetic changes that activate molecular signaling pathways linked to the avoidance of apoptosis and cellular replication play a role in the development of chronic liver disorders, including HCC (Llovet and Bruix, 2008). The $\sim$80% of drug delivery is hindered by pathophysiological changes. The drug needs to cross the ECM and endothelial barrier before it reaches to the cancer cells, for there is a reduction in the sinusoidal fenestrae (Hu et al., 2019). Blood perfusion in normal liver tissue occurs via the hepatic portal vein, whereas in HCC exclusive perfusion takes place by the hepatic artery. The above factors lead to a reduction in delivery by the portal vein, resulting in decreased drug permeation by systemic administration. However, reports suggest that angiogenesis in the context of HCC tumor conditions is to blame for the rise in microvascular permeability and density. Enhanced permeability and retention effects may cause macromolecules, nanoparticles, and impaired lymphatic drainage to specifically accumulate in the transferrin receptor, asialoglycoprotein receptor (ASGPR), glycyrrhetinic acid receptor, glypican-3, AF-20 antigen somatostatin receptor, and a cluster of differentiation-44. These are examples of active-targeted receptors and proteins that are upregulated on the cellular surface of HCC. Another tumor drug targeting method is based on a reduced pH level at the site of the tumor (pH $\sim$6.5) along with enhanced reductive potential inside of tumor cells (GSH: 2−10 mM) versus to the outside cellular setting (glutathione [GSH]: 2−20 μM). This is triggered by an increase in the generation of GSH and lactic acid, an enhanced rate of glycolysis due to an increase in metabolic rate. These redox and pH variations can be applicable for pH-sensitive and redox-triggered delivery to aid with tumor-specific delivery (Böttger et al., 2020).

8.3.3 Routes of administration

The flexibility of the nanocrystals to fit diverse administration routes is one of its significant benefits. Contrary to many other accepted dose forms, they can be delivered in several ways, including oral, parenteral, cutaneous, ophthalmic, nasal, pulmonary, and vaginal. Table 8.1 highlights various routes of administration of nanocrystals along with some examples and their significance.

Oral administration of drug nanocrystals such as curcumin, itraconazole, amphotericin B, and fenofibrate to increase the dissolution properties of low-water-soluble drugs results in a significant improvement in bioavailability (Junyaprasert and Morakul, 2015; Patel et al., 2014). Absolute bioavailability (100%) was achieved after administering nanocrystal compositions intravenously, which could aid in the pharmacological screening of new chemical substances regardless of the solubility problem (Danhier et al., 2014; Christodoulou et al., 2014). The topical application of nanocrystal formulations

Table 8.1 Highlights of various nanocrystals available in the market with their routes of administration and significance.

S. No.	ROA	Nanocrystals	Significance
1.	Oral	Curcumin, itraconazole, amphoterecin B, fenofibrate	Useful for poorly soluble drugs to improve their bioavailability
2.	Intravenous	Curcumin, paclitaxel, asulacrine, oridonin	Provides 100% bioavailability
3.	Dermal	Hesperetin, tretinoin, apigenin, leutein, resveratrol	Increase in thermodynamic activity, thereby enhancing the efficacy
4.	Ophthalmic	Meloxicam, dexamethasone acetate, mycophenolate mofetil, hydrocortisone, brinzolamide	Enhanced drug saturation solubility and resident time in the eye, resulting in increased bioavailability (Miao et al., 2018)
5.	Ocular	Forskolin, moxifloxacin	Show increased absorption rates, longer duration time, and greater intensity (Miao et al., 2018)
6.	Pulmonary	Budesonide, cinaciguat, curcumin acetate, salbutamol sulfate, budesonide	Enhanced bioavailability (Miao et al., 2018)
7.	Targeted delivery (tumor targeting)	Paclitaxel, docetaxel paclitaxel combination, camptothecin	Targeted therapy without affecting normal cells and providing high drug loading to the target site

ROA, Route of administration.

causes supersaturated conditions with higher thermodynamic activity, leading to the improvement in the efficacy of the drug under study (Vidlářová et al., 2016; Pireddu et al., 2016). The ophthalmic approach for nanocrystal delivery is being investigated to get a longer retention effect, hence promoting therapeutic effectiveness (Romero et al., 2016; Tuomela et al., 2014). The free drug does not last as long as the ocular administration. The bioavailability of nanocrystals administered through the pulmonary route is higher. Targeted delivery of drug nanocrystals promotes high drug loading to the target site and also prevents normal cells from being affected (Pardhi et al., 2018).

8.4 Drug targeting

Drug targeting in the liver can be accomplished using passive and active methods. The passive techniques depend on the hepatic build-up of nanoparticles in order to attain enhanced drug concentrations in the immediate area. Nontargeted delivery to additional organs is limited at the same time, reducing the negative effects. This is commonly done by altering physicochemical properties like size and making surface changes to minimize binding to nontargeted sites or employing a locoregional approach. Consequently, certain anatomic or pathologic characteristics that complement the nanoparticle attributes are required for passive nanoparticle accumulation at a specific body region. Active targeting, on the other hand, includes decorating the cell surface with a cell-specific ligand, such as protein-carbohydrate, peptide, or antibody, and binding to the specific receptor present in the cell membrane. This method possesses the benefit of concentrating on a specific type of liver cell that is important to a condition, at the same time, minimizing the effects on other liver cells (Santos-Magalhães and Mosqueira, 2010).

8.4.1 Passive targeting

The liver, unlike many other tissues, does not have an impervious basal lamina resulting in the lack of intervening processes such as protein interaction or aggregation Hence, these nanoparticles show fast passive hepatic accumulation on systemic administration (Jacobs et al., 2010).

The liver sinusoidal fenestrae has a diameter, which allows selectivity for KCs and SECs (>100 nm) and HSCs and hepatocytes (100 nm) determining passive targeting of liver cells. Besides these ways, it is predicted that in some cases of vigorous extrusion, bigger deformable nanocarriers (400 nm) can flow out into the Disse region, probably facilitated by temporary contacts with SECs (Romero et al., 1999). Because of their position in the liver sinusoid, the sinusoidal endothelium's nonparenchymal cells were primarily targeted in earlier used passive targeting techniques (i.e., KCs). A well-known function of KCs is the endocytosis of particles by scavenger receptors (Alving, 1983; Moghimi and Hunter, 2001). Additionally, SECs help to remove liposomes with negative charge through the scavenger receptor stabilizing (Campbell et al., 2018; Rothkopf et al., 2005).

Nanoparticles aggregate passively on inflamed or malignant tissues, including HCC liver metastases, due to the EPR effect (Matsumura and Maeda, 1986). It is induced by a leaky tumor vasculature along with increased penetrability of nanoparticles as well as macromolecules as a consequence of fast and partial tumor angiogenesis to receive more nutrients and oxygen.

Additionally, tumors have poor lymphatic outflow, which causes nanoparticles to be retained in the tumor tissue (Maeda et al., 2000). Endothelial cells in tumors have gap junctions that are 400−600 nm in width, facilitating nanoparticles present in the tumor vasculature to effectively extravasate into the tumor (Yuan et al., 1995; Iyer et al., 2006). In addition to particle properties, the intravenous method affects intraliver dispersion and uptake.

8.4.2 Active targeting

After passive hepatic transport, the ligand connects to a receptor on a particular cell type, and then endocytosis takes place (Mishra et al., 2013). Several receptors located in various liver cell types were identified as potential targets. ASGPR has been particularly targeted for drug delivery to hepatocytes by several ligands (D'Souza and Devarajan, 2015). In general, cellular targets or receptors on liver cells recognize specific surface ligands on nanoparticles, and then the gene or drug is delivered into the cells. Nanoparticles have been altered to actively target various liver cells types such as hepatocytes, HSCs, HCC cells, KCs, and endothelial cells. There are nine active targeting techniques to choose from, to target liver cancer cells (Wang et al., 2015).

Various opsonins identify foreign particles and encourage phagocytosis and clearance through the reticuloendothelial system (RES) (Li and Huang, 2008). A range of proteins found in the blood can coat nanoparticles, which may be extracellular receptor ligands. A better knowledge of nanoparticle protein coronas in the past few years has developed ways for regulating the proteins that are adsorbed and, as a result, employing them to target actively to specific receptors of cells, thereby utilizing the endogenous system delivery of drugs (Cagliani et al., 2019).

Several foreign chemicals, including nanoparticles, are predominantly picked up by the liver due to the first-pass effect and the crucial role of the liver in metabolism, even when no targeted methods are applied. Nanoparticles accumulate faster in the liver than in every other organ due to this unique physiological function. One key difficulty is that the nanoparticles may not aggregate in the targeted liver cells. The liver (KCs) contains about 80% of all the macrophages in the human body, and these cells trap xenobiotics, especially particles larger than 150 nm in size. Hepatocytes have a massive number of transporters and endocytic receptors on their cell membrane, which takes up a significant amount of xenobiotics. For liver cell-specific delivery, it is now crucial to continue introducing innovative nanoparticles and targeting ligands.

8.5 Recent advancements in liver cancer targeting and future prospects

Diagnostic probes and anticancer medications can be delivered together via nanotechnology-based devices. The cancer theranostics systems result in cancer treatment while simultaneously accomplishing tumor recognition, evaluation, and transmission stages (Li et al., 2016; Tan and Wu, 2016). Polymeric nanoparticles, liposomes, micelles, polymersomes, and other nanotechnology-based delivery methods are used for tumor theranostics. Imaging probes that are either directly adhered to the surface, enclosed inside the core, or maybe chemically attached to the drug that is encapsulated, are used in these approaches (Mhaske et al., 2023).

Multifunctional nanocrystals, also referred to as hybrid nanocrystals, are a form of theranostic nanocrystals that combine drug nanocrystals and diagnostic probes to improve tumor targeting. As multifunctional nanocrystals include fewer excipients than most other nano-based formulations, including solid lipid nanoparticles, liposomes, polymeric nanoparticles, and so on, they can avoid the negative effects of multiple excipients in all these nano-based formulations.

Furthermore, because multifunctional nanocrystal formulations have a larger percent drug content in comparison to other formulations, the amount necessary to attain an effective treatment response is less. Multifunctional nanocrystals have several other benefits of nanoformulations, including improved pharmacokinetics as well as chemotherapeutic drug biodistribution (Liang et al., 2020).

It could also be due to nanocrystals' physically stable crystalline nature, in comparison to numerous amorphous drug substances. The interactions between nanocrystals and plasma proteins are reduced due to the steady nature provided by these crystalline substances, improving the effectiveness of anticancer agents. Numerous studies were conducted on this subject and showed remarkable results due to the multifunctional nanocrystals' great potential (Joseph and Singhvi, 2019).

In 2008, Park et al. developed a quantum dot delivery system for doxorubicin, a small molecule anticancer agent. Wang et al. showed that a composite gold nanoparticle-iron oxide system may be used to image cancer cells as well as to photothermally ablate them. Concerning changes in PEG density, the iron oxide nanoparticle coating can be adjusted, which prevents aggregation and Kupffer cell uptake and changes charge, allowing complexation with the nucleic acid. In addition, nanoparticle tracking through magnetic resonance imaging (MRI) and imaging of fluorescence can be done owing to the presence of an iron oxide core and a fluorescent dye. The iron oxides concede subcellular nanoparticle distribution using transmission electron microscopy (Cormode et al., 2011). With the use of doxorubicin-functionalized SPIONs, Mouli et al. developed a novel image-guided local administration strategy that resulted in dramatically increased intratumoral medication absorption and negligible off-target effects (El-Safty and Shenashen, 2020). To image therapeutic administration, the anticancer drug doxorubicin was used with the superparamagnetic iron oxide (SPIO) platform as MRI contrast agent.

For hepatic cancer therapy, Shen and coworkers developed SMCC-7721 liver membrane loaded nanocrystal platform. The prepared nanocrystals, functionalized with folic acid (FA) for ligand specific targeting (folate receptor) and site directed therapy. These receptors are overexpressed in hepatoma and therefore possess strong affinity towards folate receptor. FA was adsorbed onto the SMMC-7721 CM surface to optimize the drug delivery system's targeting, leading to folate-functionalized SMMC-7721 liver cancer CM-cloaked PTX nanocrystals (FCPN) (Shen et al., 2021).

In 2020, Pan Liang et al. prepared nanocrystals of parthenolide (PTL), to be administered with sorafenib, enhancing therapeutic effects against advanced HCC. Sorafenib (Sora), an oral multikinase inhibitor, reduces tumor angiogenesis and inhibits the vascular endothelial growth factor, which prompts apoptosis of tumor cells. However, HCC demonstrated that single antiangiogenic therapy showed drug resistance. Overexpression of nuclear factor kappa B, a key factor in HepG2 cell proliferation and invasion, and also the expression of invasion-related molecules, causes this.

Hence, combination therapy came into consideration (Liang et al., 2020). PTL can be used for additional therapeutic effects. It induces autophagy and apoptosis and inhibits angiogenesis along with tumor cell proliferation, specifically the HepG2 cell line. It has poor aqueous solubility, low bioavailability, and gastrointestinal side effects on oral administration. These limitations were resolved by using a HPH process to make PTL nanocrystals using lecithin and poloxamer 188 (Chang et al., 2015).

A huge number of anticancer medications are likely to be required in the future to formulate into smart delivery of drugs with diagnostic technologies like multifunctional nanocrystal systems. A large number of multifunctional nanocrystal-based delivery systems would be developed on the market if there was a higher demand for providing anticancer therapy together with diagnostics with enhanced efficacy and fewer adverse effects.

This could result in the creation of a far less expensive method of generating multifunctional nanocrystals without affecting the quality of established systems, thus lowering the cost of anticancer detection and treatment (Schumacher et al., 2015; Barderas et al., 2015; Schwarzenbach et al., 2011). A long-term study would also look into the safety and efficacy of newly built multimodal imaging nanoprobes and multifunctional nanoparticles. Image-guided drug delivery systems, in particular, are more useful for screening for early medication effects and choosing patients who are suitable for experimental treatment in clinical trials. The multifunctional nanoparticles will also highlight the move toward "personalized treatment" in which the individuals who show more drug uptake via damaged liver cells get the treatment (Fateminia et al., 2017).

For intravenous treatment, KCs, are specialized macrophages in the liver, quickly absorb SPIOs, which causes a susceptibility effect that reduces the magnetic resonance signal strength and results in hypointense images. As KCs are solely found in the healthy liver parenchyma, SPIOs help to distinguish between healthy and sick tissue. Tumors, which are mainly devoid of macrophages, show a sustained decline in signal strength after injecting iron oxide. It is possible to identify tumors or metastases in the liver as tiny as 2−3 mm. In comparison to nonenhanced imaging, the use of SPIOs increases both lesion conspicuity and identification (Corot et al., 2006). Hence the multifunctional crystals can be further explored in the future to incorporate therapeutic moiety in the crystals so that they can also provide treatment along with the diagnosis.

8.6 Conclusion

Multifunctional nanocrystals of a drug are an efficient drug delivery system for moieties that have a poor affinity toward water, and due to their low dimensions and high loading capacity, they resolve solubility, structural stability, and bioavailability issues.

They act as a promising diagnostic and therapeutic tool because of their size, which helps determine effective retention and permeation in tumor cells. Hence, it gained popularity in oncogenic therapy, and various routes of administration can be utilized to target different organs. The preparative method includes top-down, bottom-up, and their combination. Here, a review of the targeting of multifunctional nanocrystals in hepatic cancer was done. Targeting can be active or passive targeting. Active targeting use receptors on the cell membrane, while passive targeting involves passive accumulation due to the absence of basal lamina. Diseases of the liver like fibrosis and hepatocellular cancer, leading to the formation of nodules and alteration in the perfusion of particles targeting nanocrystals, can be a challenge. The multifunctional nanocrystal is a promising method that helps in drug delivery of small molecules like doxorubicin and PTX at the targeted site, imaging of the liver to analyze the tumor cells with the help of iron oxide and fluorescent dyes, improves antiangiogenic properties of sorafenib with simultaneous administration of PTL NC. Future research on the cellular effects of multifunctional nanocrystals has to be carried out to obtain precise knowledge concerning cellular toxicity, internalization inside the cell, internalization mechanism, etc.

References

Alving, C.R., 1983. Delivery of liposome-encapsulated drugs to macrophages. Pharmacol. Ther. 22 (3), 407–424. Available from: https://www.sciencedirect.com/science/article/pii/0163725883900104.

Anwanwan, D., Singh, S.K., Singh, S., Saikam, V., Singh, R., 2020. Challenges in liver cancer and possible treatment approaches. Biochim. Biophys. Acta. Rev. Cancer 1873 (1), 188314. Available from: https://www.sciencedirect.com/science/article/pii/S0304419X19301283.

Aubé, C., Bazeries, P., Lebigot, J., Cartier, V., Boursier, J., 2017. Liver fibrosis, cirrhosis, and cirrhosis-related nodules: imaging diagnosis and surveillance. Diagn. Interv. Imaging 98 (6), 455–468. Available from: https://www.sciencedirect.com/science/article/pii/S2211568417300694.

Bansal, S., Kumria, R., 2012. Nanocrystals: current strategies and trends. Int. J. Res. Pharm. Biomed. Sci. 3, 407–419.

Barderas, R., Villar-Vázquez, R., Casal, J.I., 2015. In: Preedy, V.R., Patel, V.B. (Eds.), Colorectal Cancer Circulating Biomarkers BT - Biomarkers in Cancer. Springer, Dordrecht, Netherlands, pp. 573–599. Available from: https://doi.org/10.1007/978-94-007-7681-4_29.

Bataller, R., Brenner, D., 2005. Liver fibrosis. J. Clin. Investig. 115, 209–218.

Böttger, R., Pauli, G., Chao, P.-H., Al-Fayez, N., Hohenwarter, L., Li, S.-D., 2020. Lipid-based nanoparticle technologies for liver targeting. Adv. Drug Deliv. Rev. 154–155.

Brough, C., Williams, R.O., 2013. Amorphous solid dispersions and nano-crystal technologies for poorly water-soluble drug delivery. Int. J. Pharm. 453 (1), 157–166. Available from: https://www.sciencedirect.com/science/article/pii/S0378517313004882.

Cagliani, R., Gatto, F., Bardi, G., 2019. Protein adsorption: a feasible method for nanoparticle functionalization? Materials 12, 1991.

Campbell, F., Bos, F.L., Sieber, S., Arias-Alpizar, G., Koch, B.E., Huwyler, J., et al., 2018. Directing nanoparticle biodistribution through evasion and exploitation of Stab2-dependent nanoparticle uptake. ACS Nano 12 (3), 2138–2150. Available from: https://doi.org/10.1021/acsnano.7b06995.

Chan, H.-K., Kwok, P.C.L., 2011. Production methods for nanodrug particles using the bottom-up approach. Adv. Drug Deliv. Rev. 63 (6), 406–416. Available from: https://www.sciencedirect.com/science/article/pii/S0169409X11000627.

Chang, T.-L., Zhan, H., Liang, D., Liang, J.F., 2015. Nanocrystal technology for drug formulation and delivery. Front. Chem. Sci. Eng. 9 (1), 1–14. Available from: https://doi.org/10.1007/s11705-015-1509-3.

Chen, H., Khemtong, C., Yang, X., Chang, X., Gao, J., 2011. Nanonization strategies for poorly water-soluble drugs. Drug Discov. Today 16 (7), 354–360. Available from: https://www.sciencedirect.com/science/article/pii/S1359644610000723.

Christodoulou, S., Vaccaro, G., Pinchetti, V., De Donato, F., Grim, J.Q., Casu, A., et al., 2014. Synthesis of highly luminescent wurtzite CdSe/CdS giant-shell nanocrystals using a fast continuous injection route. J. Mater. Chem. C 2 (17), 3439–3447. Available from: https://doi.org/10.1039/C4TC00280F.

Cormode, D.P., Skajaa, G.O., Delshad, A., Parker, N., Jarzyna, P.A., Calcagno, C., et al., 2011. A versatile and tunable coating strategy allows control of nanocrystal delivery to cell types in the liver. Bioconjug. Chem. 22 (3), 353–361.

Corot, C., Robert, P., Idée, J.M., Port, M., 2006. Recent advances in iron oxide nanocrystal technology for medical imaging. Adv. Drug Deliv. Rev. 58 (14), 1471–1504.

D'Souza, A.A., Devarajan, P.V., 2015. Asialoglycoprotein receptor mediated hepatocyte targeting—Strategies and applications. J. Control. Release 203, 126–139. Available from: https://www.sciencedirect.com/science/article/pii/S0168365915001224.

Danhier, F., Ucakar, B., Vanderhaegen, M.-L., Brewster, M.E., Arien, T., Préat, V., 2014. Nanosuspension for the delivery of a poorly soluble anti-cancer kinase inhibitor. Eur. J. Pharm. Biopharm. 88 (1), 252–260. Available from: https://www.sciencedirect.com/science/article/pii/S0939641114001635.

El-Safty, S.A., Shenashen, M.A., 2020. Nanoscale dynamic chemical, biological sensor material designs for control monitoring and early detection of advanced diseases. Mater. Today Bio. 5, 100044. Available from: https://www.sciencedirect.com/science/article/pii/S2590006420300041.

El-Serag, H.B., Rudolph, K.L., 2007. Hepatocellular carcinoma: epidemiology and molecular carcinogenesis. Gastroenterology 132 (7), 2557–2576. Available from: https://www.sciencedirect.com/science/article/pii/S0016508507007998.

Fateminia, S.M.A., Wang, Z., Liu, B., 2017. Nanocrystallization: an effective approach to enhance the performance of organic molecules. Small. Methods (San Diego, Calif.) 1 (3), 1600023. Available from: https://doi.org/10.1002/smtd.201600023.

Galicia-Moreno, M., Silva-Gomez, J.A., Lucano-Landeros, S., Santos, A., Monroy-Ramirez, H.C., Armendariz-Borunda, J., 2021. Liver cancer: therapeutic challenges and the importance of experimental models, Fan Y-C, editor. Can. J. Gastroenterol. Hepatol. 2021, 8837811. Available from: https://doi.org/10.1155/2021/8837811.

Ganem, D., Prince, A.M., Hepatitis, B., 2004. Virus infection—natural history and clinical consequences. N. Engl. J. Med. 350 (11), 1118–1129. Available from: https://doi.org/10.1056/NEJMra031087.

George, M., Ghosh, I., 2013. Identifying the correlation between drug/stabilizer properties and critical quality attributes (CQAs) of nanosuspension formulation prepared by wet media milling technology. Eur. J. Pharm. Sci. 48 (1), 142–152. Available from: https://www.sciencedirect.com/science/article/pii/S0928098712003867.

Giannitrapani, L., Soresi, M., Bondì, M., Montalto, G., Cervello, M., 2014. Nanotechnology applications for the therapy of liver fibrosis. World J. Gastroenterol. 20, 7242–7251.

Hu, J., Ng, W.K., Dong, Y., Shen, S., Tan, R.B.H., 2011. Continuous and scalable process for water-redispersible nanoformulation of poorly aqueous soluble APIs by antisolvent precipitation and spray-drying. Int. J. Pharma. 404 (1), 198–204. Available from: https://www.sciencedirect.com/science/article/pii/S0378517310008318.

Hu, M., Wang, Y., Xu, L., An, S., Tang, Y., Zhou, X., et al., 2019. Relaxin gene delivery mitigates liver metastasis and synergizes with check point therapy. Nat. Commun. 10 (1), 2993. Available from: https://doi.org/10.1038/s41467-019-10893-8.

Iredale, J.P., 2007. Models of liver fibrosis: exploring the dynamic nature of inflammation and repair in a solid organ. J. Clin. Investig. 117 (3), 539–548. Available from: https://doi.org/10.1172/JCI30542.

Iyer, A.K., Khaled, G., Fang, J., Maeda, H., 2006. Exploiting the enhanced permeability and retention effect for tumor targeting. Drug Discov. Today 11 (17), 812–818. Available from: https://www.sciencedirect.com/science/article/pii/S1359644606002716.

Jacobs, F., Wisse, E., De Geest, B., 2010. The role of liver sinusoidal cells in hepatocyte-directed gene transfer. Am. J. Pathol. 176 (1), 14—21. Available from: https://www.sciencedirect.com/science/article/pii/S0002944010603185.

Jain, S., Reddy, V.A., Arora, S., Patel, K., 2016. Development of surface stabilized candesartan cilexetil nanocrystals with enhanced dissolution rate, permeation rate across CaCo-2, and oral bioavailability. Drug Deliv. Transl. Res. 6 (5), 498—510. Available from: https://doi.org/10.1007/s13346-016-0297-8.

Joseph, E., Singhvi, G., 2019. Multifunctional nanocrystals for cancer therapy: a potential nanocarrier. Nanomaterials for Drug Delivery and Therapy. Elsevier Inc pp. 91—116. Available from: http://doi.org/10.1016/B978-0-12-816505-8.00007-2.

Juhnke, M., Märtin, D., John, E., 2012. Generation of wear during the production of drug nanosuspensions by wet media milling. Eur. J. Pharm. Biopharm. 81 (1), 214—222. Available from: https://www.sciencedirect.com/science/article/pii/S0939641112000069.

Junyaprasert, V.B., Morakul, B., 2015. Nanocrystals for enhancement of oral bioavailability of poorly water-soluble drugs. Asian J. Pharm. Sci. 10 (1), 13—23. Available from: https://www.sciencedirect.com/science/article/pii/S1818087614000555.

Kakran, M., Shegokar, R., Sahoo, N.G., Al Shaal, L., Li, L., Müller, R.H., 2012. Fabrication of quercetin nanocrystals: comparison of different methods. Eur. J. Pharm. Biopharm. 80 (1), 113—121. Available from: https://www.sciencedirect.com/science/article/pii/S0939641111002438.

Keck, C.M., Müller, R.H., 2006. Drug nanocrystals of poorly soluble drugs produced by high pressure homogenisation. Eur. J. Pharm. Biopharm. 62 (1), 3—16. Available from: https://www.sciencedirect.com/science/article/pii/S0939641105001797.

Khadka, P., Ro, J., Kim, H., Kim, I., Kim, J.T., Kim, H., et al., 2014. Pharmaceutical particle technologies: an approach to improve drug solubility, dissolution and bioavailability. Asian J. Pharm. Sci. 9 (6), 304—316. Available from: https://www.sciencedirect.com/science/article/pii/S1818087614000348.

Lei, G., Dianrui, Z., Minghui, C., 2008. Drug nanocrystals for the formulation of poorly soluble drugs and its application as a potential drug delivery system. J. Nanopart. Res. 10 (5), 845—862. Available from: http://inis.iaea.org/search/search.aspx?orig_q = RN:39092005.

Li, S.-D., Huang, L., 2008. Pharmacokinetics and biodistribution of nanoparticles. Mol. Pharma. 5 (4), 496—504. Available from: https://doi.org/10.1021/mp800049w.

Li, S.-Y., Cheng, H., Xie, B.-R., Qiu, W.-X., Song, L.-L., Zhuo, R.-X., et al., 2016. A ratiometric theranostic probe for tumor targeting therapy and self-therapeutic monitoring. Biomaterials 104, 297—309. Available from: https://www.sciencedirect.com/science/article/pii/S0142961216303556.

Liang, P., Wu, H., Zhang, Z., Jiang, S., Lv, H., 2020. Preparation and characterization of parthenolide nanocrystals for enhancing therapeutic effects of sorafenib against advanced hepatocellular carcinoma. Int. J. Pharma. 583, 119375. Available from: https://doi.org/10.1016/j.ijpharm.2020.119375.

Liu, X., Dong, S., Dong, M., Li, Y., Sun, Z., Zhang, X., et al., 2021. Transferrin-conjugated liposomes loaded with carnosic acid inhibit liver cancer growth by inducing mitochondria-mediated apoptosis. Int. J. Pharma. 607, 121034. Available from: https://doi.org/10.1016/j.ijpharm.2021.121034.

Llovet, J.M., Bruix, J., 2008. Molecular targeted therapies in hepatocellular carcinoma. Hepatology (Baltimore, Md.) 48 (4), 1312—1327. Available from: https://doi.org/10.1002/hep.22506.

Maeda, H., Wu, J., Sawa, T., Matsumura, Y., Hori, K., 2000. Tumor vascular permeability and the EPR effect in macromolecular therapeutics: a review. J. Control. Release 65 (1), 271—284. Available from: https://www.sciencedirect.com/science/article/pii/S0168365999002485.

Man, S., Luo, C., Yan, M., Zhao, G., Ma, L., Gao, W., 2021. Treatment for liver cancer: from sorafenib to natural products. Eur. J. Med. Chem. 224, 113690. Available from: https://doi.org/10.1016/j.ejmech.2021.113690.

Matsumura, Y., Maeda, H., 1986. A new concept for macromolecular therapeutics in cancer chemotherapy: mechanism of tumoritropic accumulation of proteins and the antitumor agent smancs. Cancer Res. 46 (12 Part 1), 6387LP — 6392. Available from: http://cancerres.aacrjournals.org/content/46/12_Part_1/6387.abstract.

Merisko-Liversidge, E., Liversidge, G.G., 2011. Nanosizing for oral and parenteral drug delivery: a perspective on formulating poorly-water soluble compounds using wet media milling technology. Adv. Drug Deliv. Rev. 63 (6), 427—440. Available from: https://www.sciencedirect.com/science/article/pii/S0169409X11000044.

Mhaske, A., Sharma, S., Shukla, R., 2023. Nanotheranostic: the futuristic therapy for copper mediated neurological sequelae. J. Drug Deliv. Sci. Technol. 80, 104193. Available from: https://doi.org/10.1016/j.jddst.2023.104193.

Miao, X., Yang, W., Feng, T., Lin, J., Huang, P., 2018. Drug nanocrystals for cancer therapy. Wiley Interdiscip. Rev. Nanomed. Nanobiotechnol. 10 (3), 1–22.

Mishra, N., Yadav, N.P., Rai, V.K., Sinha, P., Yadav, K.S., Jain, S., et al., 2013. Efficient hepatic delivery of drugs: novel strategies and their significance, Gupta U, editor. Biomed. Res. Int. 2013, 382184. Available from: https://doi.org/10.1155/2013/382184.

Moghimi, S., Hunter, A., 2001. Recognition by macrophages and liver cells of opsonized phospholipid vesicles and phospholipid headgroups. Pharma. Res. 18, 1–8.

Monteiro, A., Afolabi, A., Bilgili, E., 2013. Continuous production of drug nanoparticle suspensions via wet stirred media milling: a fresh look at the Rehbinder effect. Drug Dev. Ind. Pharm. 39 (2), 266–283. Available from: https://doi.org/10.3109/03639045.2012.676048.

Morakul, B., Suksiriworapong, J., Chomnawang, M.T., Langguth, P., Junyaprasert, V.B., 2014. Dissolution enhancement and in vitro performance of clarithromycin nanocrystals produced by precipitation-lyophilization-homogenization method. Eur. J. Pharm. Biopharm. 88 (3), 886–896.

Moreira, R.K., 2007. Hepatic stellate cells and liver fibrosis. Arch. Pathol. Lab. Med. 131 (11), 1728–1734. Available from: https://doi.org/10.5858/2007-131-1728-HSCALF.

Möschwitzer, J.P., 2013. Drug nanocrystals in the commercial pharmaceutical development process. Int. J. Pharma. 453 (1), 142–156. Available from: https://www.sciencedirect.com/science/article/pii/S0378517312009088.

Muller, R., Keck, C., 2004. Challenges and solutions for the delivery of biotech drugs — A review of drug nanocrystal technology and lipid nanoparticles. J. Biotechnol. 113, 151–170.

Müller, R.H., Gohla, S., Keck, C.M., 2011. State of the art of nanocrystals — Special features, production, nanotoxicology aspects and intracellular delivery. Eur. J. Pharm. Biopharm. 78 (1), 1–9. Available from: https://www.sciencedirect.com/science/article/pii/S0939641111000142.

Ostrowski, A.D., Chan, E.M., Gargas, D.J., Katz, E.M., Han, G., Schuck, P.J., et al., 2012. Controlled synthesis and single-particle imaging of bright, Sub-10 nm lanthanide-doped upconverting nanocrystals. ACS Nano 6 (3), 2686–2692. Available from: https://doi.org/10.1021/nn3000737.

Pan, C.Q., Zhang, J.X., 2005. Natural history and clinical consequences of hepatitis B virus infection. Int. J. Med. Sci. 2 (1), 36–40. Available from: https://www.medsci.org/v02p0036.htm.

Pardhi, V., Lanke, T.V., Flora, S., Chandasana, H., Shukla, R., 2018. Nanocrystals: an overview of fabrication, characterization and therapeutic applications in drug delivery. Curr. Pharma. Des. 24 (43), 5129–5146.

Parkin, D.M., Bray, F., Ferlay, J., Pisani, P., 2005. Global cancer statistics, 2002. CA: Cancer J. Clin. 55 (2), 74–108. Available from: https://doi.org/10.3322/canjclin.55.2.74.

Patel, K., Patil, A., Mehta, M., Gota, V., Vavia, P., 2014. Oral delivery of paclitaxel nanocrystal (PNC) with a dual Pgp-CYP3A4 inhibitor: preparation, characterization and antitumor activity. Int. J. Pharma. 472 (1), 214–223. Available from: https://www.sciencedirect.com/science/article/pii/S0378517314004517.

Patel, V., Sharma, O.P., Mehta, T., 2018. Nanocrystal: a novel approach to overcome skin barriers for improved topical drug delivery. Expert Opin. Drug Deliv. 15 (4), 351–368. Available from: https://doi.org/10.1080/17425247.2018.1444025.

Pawar, V., Singh, Y., Meher, J., Gupta, S., Chourasia, M., 2014. Engineered nanocrystal technology: in-vivo fate, targeting and applications in drug delivery. J. Control. Release 183.

Peltonen, L., Hirvonen, J., 2010. Pharmaceutical nanocrystals by nanomilling: critical process parameters, particle fracturing and stabilization methods. J. Pharm. Pharmacol. 62 (11), 1569–1579. Available from: https://doi.org/10.1111/j.2042-7158.2010.01022.x.

Pireddu, R., Caddeo, C., Valenti, D., Marongiu, F., Scano, A., Ennas, G., et al., 2016. Diclofenac acid nanocrystals as an effective strategy to reduce in vivo skin inflammation by improving dermal drug bioavailability. Colloids Surf. B: Biointerfaces 143, 64–70. Available from: https://www.sciencedirect.com/science/article/pii/S0927776516301813.

Rasenack, N., Hartenhauer, H., Müller, B.W., 2003. Microcrystals for dissolution rate enhancement of poorly water-soluble drugs. Int. J. Pharma. 254 (2), 137–145. Available from: https://www.sciencedirect.com/science/article/pii/S037851730300005X.

Rasenack, N., Müller, B., 2004. Micron-size drug particles: common and novel micronization techniques. Pharm. Dev. Technol. 9, 1−13.

Rockey, D.C., 2008. Current and future anti-fibrotic therapies for chronic liver disease. Clin. Liver Dis. 12 (4), 939−962. Available from: https://doi.org/10.1016/j.cld.2008.07.011.

Romero, E.L., Morilla, M.-J., Regts, J., Koning, G.A., Scherphof, G.L., 1999. On the mechanism of hepatic transendothelial passage of large liposomes. FEBS Lett. 448 (1), 193−196. Available from: https://www.sciencedirect.com/science/article/pii/S0014579399003646.

Romero, G.B., Keck, C.M., Müller, R.H., Bou-Chacra, N.A., 2016. Development of cationic nanocrystals for ocular delivery. Eur. J. Pharm. Biopharm. 107, 215−222. Available from: https://www.sciencedirect.com/science/article/pii/S0939641116302685.

Rothkopf, C., Fahr, A., Fricker, G., Scherphof, G.L., Kamps, J.A.A.M., 2005. Uptake of phosphatidylserine-containing liposomes by liver sinusoidal endothelial cells in the serum-free perfused rat liver. Biochim. Biophys. Acta Biomembr. 1668 (1), 10−16. Available from: https://www.sciencedirect.com/science/article/pii/S0005273604002834.

Santos-Magalhães, N.S., Mosqueira, V.C.F., 2010. Nanotechnology applied to the treatment of malaria. Adv. Drug Deliv. Rev. 62 (4), 560−575. Available from: https://www.sciencedirect.com/science/article/pii/S0169409X09003652.

Sanyal, A.J., Boyer, T.D., Lindor, K.D., 2018. Front Matter. In: Seventh, E. (Ed.), Terrault NABT-Z and BH. Elsevier, Philadelphia, pp. i−ii. Available from: https://www.sciencedirect.com/science/article/pii/B9780323375917000665.

Schumacher, T.N., Kesmir, C., van Buuren, M.M., 2015. Biomarkers in cancer immunotherapy. Cancer Cell 27 (1), 12−14. Available from: https://www.sciencedirect.com/science/article/pii/S1535610814005133.

Schwarzenbach, H., Hoon, D.S.B., Pantel, K., 2011. Cell-free nucleic acids as biomarkers in cancer patients. Nat. Rev. Cancer 11 (6), 426−437. Available from: https://doi.org/10.1038/nrc3066.

Shegokar, R., Müller, R.H., 2010. Nanocrystals: industrially feasible multifunctional formulation technology for poorly soluble actives. Int. J. Pharma. 399 (1), 129−139. Available from: https://www.sciencedirect.com/science/article/pii/S0378517310005715.

Shen, W., Ge, S., Liu, X., Yu, Q., Jiang, X., Wu, Q., et al., 2021. Folate-functionalized SMMC-7721 liver cancer cell membrane-cloaked paclitaxel nanocrystals for targeted chemotherapy of hepatoma. Drug Deliv. 29 (1), 31−42. Available from: https://doi.org/10.1080/10717544.2021.2015481.

Shetea, G., Jaina, H., Punja, D., Prajapata, H., Akotiyaa, P., Bansala, A.K., 2014. Stabilizers used in nano-crystal based drug delivery systems. J. Excip. Food Chem. 5 (4), 184−209.

Sinha, B., Müller, R.H., Möschwitzer, J.P., 2013. Bottom-up approaches for preparing drug nanocrystals: formulations and factors affecting particle size. Int. J. Pharma. 453 (1), 126−141. Available from: https://www.sciencedirect.com/science/article/pii/S0378517313000355.

Tan, M., Wu, A., 2016. Nanomaterials for Tumor Targeting Theranostics. World Scientific Publishing Co Pte Ltd.

Trefts, E., Gannon, M., Wasserman, D.H., 2017. The liver. Curr. Biol. 27 (21), R1147−R1151. Available from: https://www.sciencedirect.com/science/article/pii/S0960982217311831.

Tuomela, A., Liu, P., Puranen, J., Rönkkö, S., Laaksonen, T., Kalesnykas, G., et al., 2014. Brinzolamide nanocrystal formulations for ophthalmic delivery: reduction of elevated intraocular pressure in vivo. Int. J. Pharma. 467 (1), 34−41. Available from: https://www.sciencedirect.com/science/article/pii/S0378517314002038.

Van Eerdenbrugh, B., Van den Mooter, G., Augustijns, P., 2008. Top-down production of drug nanocrystals: nanosuspension stabilization, miniaturization and transformation into solid products. Int. J. Pharma. 364 (1), 64−75. Available from: https://www.sciencedirect.com/science/article/pii/S0378517308005280.

Vidlářová, L., Romero, G.B., Hanuš, J., Štěpánek, F., Müller, R.H., 2016. Nanocrystals for dermal penetration enhancement − Effect of concentration and underlying mechanisms using curcumin as model. Eur. J. Pharm. Biopharm. 104, 216−225. Available from: https://www.sciencedirect.com/science/article/pii/S0939641116301679.

Vo, C.L.-N., Park, C., Lee, B.-J., 2013. Current trends and future perspectives of solid dispersions containing poorly water-soluble drugs. Eur. J. Pharm. Biopharm. 85 (3, Part B), 799−813. Available from: https://www.sciencedirect.com/science/article/pii/S0939641113003007.

Waller, L.P., Deshpande, V., Pyrsopoulos, N., 2015. Hepatocellular carcinoma: a comprehensive review. World J. Hepatol. 7, 2648–2663.

Wang, H., Thorling, C.A., Liang, X., Bridle, K.R., Grice, J.E., Zhu, Y., et al., 2015. Diagnostic imaging and therapeutic application of nanoparticles targeting the liver. J. Mater. Chem. B 3 (6), 939–958. Available from: https://doi.org/10.1039/C4TB01611D.

Wang, Y., Zheng, Y., Zhang, L., Wang, Q., Zhang, D., 2013. Stability of nanosuspensions in drug delivery. J. Control. Release 172 (3), 1126–1141. Available from: https://www.sciencedirect.com/science/article/pii/S016836591300463X.

Wisse, E., de Zanger, R.B., Charels, K., van der Smissen, P., McCuskey, R.S., 1985. The liver sieve: considerations concerning the structure and function of endothelial fenestrae, the sinusoidal wall and the space of disse. Hepatology (Baltimore, Md.) 5 (4), 683–692. Available from: https://doi.org/10.1002/hep.1840050427.

Yamashita, T., Wang, X.W., 2013. Cancer stem cells in the development of liver cancer. J. Clin. Investig. 123 (5), 1911–1918. Available from: https://doi.org/10.1172/JCI66024.

Yang, Y., Marshall-Breton, C., Leser, M.E., Sher, A.A., McClements, D.J., 2012. Fabrication of ultrafine edible emulsions: comparison of high-energy and low-energy homogenization methods. Food Hydrocoll. 29 (2), 398–406. Available from: https://www.sciencedirect.com/science/article/pii/S0268005X12000847.

Yuan, F., Dellian, M., Fukumura, D., Leunig, M., Berk, D.A., Torchilin, V.P., et al., 1995. Vascular permeability in a human tumor xenograft: molecular size dependence and cutoff size. Cancer Res. 55 (17), 3752–3756. Available from: http://cancerres.aacrjournals.org/content/55/17/3752.abstract.

Zapotoczny, B., Szafrańska, K., Owczarczyk, K., Kus, E., Chlopicki, S., Szymonski, M., 2017. Atomic force microscopy reveals the dynamic morphology of fenestrations in live liver sinusoidal endothelial cells. Sci. Rep. 7.

Zhang, D., Tan, T., Gao, L., Zhao, W., Wang, P., 2007. Preparation of azithromycin nanosuspensions by high pressure homogenization and its physicochemical characteristics studies. Drug Dev. Ind. Pharm. 33 (5), 569–575. Available from: https://doi.org/10.1080/03639040600975147.

Zuo, B., Sun, Y., Li, H., Liu, X., Zhai, Y., Sun, J., et al., 2013. Preparation and in vitro/in vivo evaluation of fenofibrate nanocrystals. Int. J. Pharm. 455 (1), 267–275. Available from: https://www.sciencedirect.com/science/article/pii/S0378517313006261.

CHAPTER 9

Nanocarrier-mediated delivery targeting for pancreatic cancer

Ankit Kumar and Awanish Mishra
Department of Pharmacology and Toxicology, National Institute of Pharmaceutical Education and Research (NIPER) —
Guwahati, Kamrup, Assam, India

9.1 Introduction

Pancreatic cancer (PC) is one of the malignant cancers that have higher fatality rates. Pancreatic tumors can develop in the pancreas exocrine or endocrine portion. The prevalence of exocrine tumors predominates in the occurrence of endocrine tumors and contributes to 93% of all pancreatic tumors. The most common form of PC is pancreatic ductal adenocarcinoma (PDAC), which is associated with higher prevalence, mortality, and poor diagnosis. PDAC is the third leading cause of cancer death in the United States (Principe et al., 2021). The overall five-year survival rate is approximately 10% (Puik et al., 2022). In India, the PC ranks 24th with 10,860 new cases (1.03%) and 18th in mortality (Rawla et al., 2019).

Treatment for PC depends on the stage and location of the cancer as well as on overall health and personal preferences. Treatment may include surgery, radiation, chemotherapy, or a combination of these. Radiation therapy can be coupled with chemotherapy (chemoradiation). Gemcitabine and nab-paclitaxel, or 5-fluorouracil, leucovorin, irinotecan, and oxaliplatin (OXA), are the two frontline treatments now being used to treat PDAC patients with positive performance status (Diab et al., 2019).

PC is difficult to diagnose at early stage, with most cancers found to be already metastatic at the time of initial diagnosis. PDAC may show weight loss, jaundice, malabsorption, pain, dyspepsia, and nausea; however, many patients are asymptomatic and no early warning signs of PC have been established (Zhang et al., 2018). The blood group antigen CA19−9, which distinguishes benign from malignant pancreatic diseases, is the most widely used marker for PC (Corbo et al., 2012).

Though understanding has advanced significantly over the years, treatment for PC is still difficult using conventional method. Numerous nanocarrier-based formulations have been created because of recent advancements in nanotechnology, which improve PC immunotherapy methods as well as drug delivery (Liu et al., 2022). Recent research has also concentrated on using nanocarriers to target the stroma in PCs to increase immune infiltration and reactivate immune effector activities (Liu et al., 2020).

Multifunctional Nanocomposites for Targeted Drug Delivery in Cancer Therapy
DOI: https://doi.org/10.1016/B978-0-323-95303-0.00004-6

9.2 Pancreatic cancer

When pancreatic cells undergo alterations, they grow uncontrollably and form malignant tumors. Tumors develop either in exocrine or endocrine portion of pancreas, but exocrine tumors are seen in most cases. PDAC is the most prevalent type of PC that develops in the exocrine part of the pancreas.

9.2.1 Risk factors

Several risk factors of PCs have been identified and can be divided into two categories: modifiable and nonmodifiable risk factors. Modifiable risk factors include smoking, alcohol, obesity, dietary factors, and exposure to toxic substances, whereas nonmodifiable risk factors are gender, age, ethnicity, diabetes mellitus, family history of PC, genetic factors, chronic infections, and chronic pancreatitis (McGuigan et al., 2018).

9.2.2 Pathology

The neoplastic cells that make up PC are a complex and heterogeneous entity. Pancreatic intraepithelial neoplasia (PaIN), intraductal papillary mucinous neoplasm, and mucinous cystic neoplasm are three recognized precursor lesions that lead to the development of PC. The most typical lesion that precedes PDAC is PaIN (Noë and Brosens, 2016). PanIN is a microscopic, noninvasive flat or papillary epithelial neoplasia that is too small to be detected by radiological methods (Kim and Hong, 2018). The macroscopic mass-forming lesions mucinous cystic neoplasm and intraductal papillary mucinous neoplasm can be found using imaging modalities (Scarlett et al., 2011).

Key genes mutated in the majority of PDAC include *KRAS, TP53, SMAD4, CDKN2A (*Waddell et al., 2015*)*. KRAS gene mutation is a type of point mutation that is seen in greater than 90% of the PC patients. KRAS is a 21 kDa small GTPase that activates MAPK−ERK signaling, mutation leads to overactivation of GTPase activity, which leads to overactivation of various intracellular signaling pathways that provoke PC development (Hayashi et al., 2021). CDKN2A is a tumor suppressor gene whose product p16 arrests the cell cycle in the G1 phase (Witkiewicz et al., 2015). TP53 is a tumor suppressor gene whose protein product serves as a major guardian of genome integrity by modulating transcription, DNA repair, genomic stability, cell cycle control, and apoptosis (Vogelstein et al., 2000). SMAD4, also a tumor suppressor gene involved in TGFβ signaling pathway that controls tissue homeostasis within the pancreatic epithelium and other tissue types, has been seen switched off in 50% of PDAC cases, which provokes the migratory behavior, immune evasion, and autocrine activation (Massagué, 2008).

9.2.3 Drug resistance in pancreatic cancer

Drug resistance is divided into two groups: acquired resistance and intrinsic resistance. Patients who have innate medication resistance are not responsive to treatment. Acquired resistance only appears after tumor cells are exposed to anticancer medications. Although the medications may at first cause the cancer cells to respond, ongoing treatment ultimately leads to tumor recurrence and metastasis (Yokoi et al., 2013). Chemoresistance can arise from a variety of molecular and cellular alterations, including those that affect the apoptosis pathway, drug efflux pumps, cancer stem cells, or the epithelial-to-mesenchymal transition (EMT) pathway, as well as the up or downregulated expression of microRNAs (Grasso et al., 2017).

The production of energy-demanding transporters (which expel chemotherapeutic medicines from cancer cells), insensitivity to drug-induced apoptosis, and stimulation of drug-detoxification pathways are the three most frequent causes of the development of drug resistance. Moreover, cancer stem cells and the epithelial-mesenchymal transition (EMT) phenotype may play important roles in treatment resistance. In addition, aberrant miRNA expression has been linked to both the emergence of cancer stem cells and the acquisition of an EMT phenotype (Wang et al., 2011).

There are solid tumor masses within pancreatic tumors that have an intense desmoplastic response but inadequate vascular. A variety of mechanisms, including aberrant gene expression, mutations, deregulation of important signaling pathways (like NF-kB, Akt, and apoptosis pathways), EMT, and the presence of stroma cells, highly resistant cells, and stem cells, contribute to drug resistance in PC (Long et al., 2011).

Lowered glucose concentrations, oxidative stress, poor vascularization, low oxygen partial pressures, and reduced intratumor perfusion are the difficulties that tumor growth and the tumor microenvironment provide to neoplastic cells. This lack of nutrients and oxygen creates a selection pressure that encourages the formation of the most competitive and fit PDAC cells, which induces activation of hypoxia-inducible factors HIFs (like HIF-1α, PIM1, CAIX, PDK1, CCND1), responsible for apoptosis, cellular senescence, cellular metabolism, DNA repair, drug resistance, and oxidative stress. Additionally, HIF-1 has been directly connected to PDA hypoxia chemoresistance (Chand et al., 2016).

Multiple processes, including embryonic development, cell polarity, proliferation, migration, survival, and maintenance of somatic stem cells are regulated by the Wnt/-catenin signaling system. Drug resistance in PC has been linked to dysregulated Wnt/-catenin signaling system (Ram Makena et al., 2019).

Exosomes are a heterogeneous population of extracellular membranous vesicles with a diameter ranging from 40 to 100 nm that carries various cargos such as lipids, proteins, and nucleic acids that are important for cell-to-cell communication. The modulation of drug efflux and targets, cell cycle, survival pathways, and/or apoptotic response are a few miRNAs that have been shown to modify cellular response to anti-cancer drugs, with a critical role for PDAC. After prolonged gemcitabine treatment, miR-155 is in fact overexpressed in PDAC and creates a positive feedback loop that increases gemcitabine resistance by increasing exosomal release and activating antiapoptotic pathways (Qian et al., 2019). miR-210, miR-146a, miR-21 are some of other exosomal miRNA involved in resistance to gemcitabine (Yang et al., 2020; Qiu et al., 2018; Giovannetti et al., 2010). BCL-2, BCL-XL, and MCL-1, members of the BCL-2 family of antiapoptotic proteins, contribute to the development of cancer and its resistance to chemotherapy and radiation. BCL-XL degradation caused by DT2216, and concurrent gemcitabine MCL-1 suppression are responsible for the synergistic anticancer action (Comandatore et al., 2022).

It is important to comprehend the molecular pathways behind the development of PC and to create potent anticancer therapies. Gemcitabine received FDA approval in 1997 for the management of patients with locally progressed or metastatic PC. The degree of resistance to gemcitabine is escalating; however, it is unknown what is causing it to happen. Gemcitabine chemoresistance is mostly attributed to a variety of transcription factors, including enzymes and signaling pathways involved in nucleoside metabolism (Zeng et al., 2019). Gemcitabine plus nanoparticle (NP) albumin-bound nab-paclitaxel is one of the standards of care in advanced PDAC therapy and is suitable for a larger spectrum of patients as compared to alternate schedules, such as the more toxic FOLFIRINOX regimen (McBride et al., 2017). Even though gemcitabine plus nab-paclitaxel is more effective than gemcitabine alone in terms of overall survival and progression-free survival, chemoresistance severely reduces the effectiveness of this combination (Comandatore et al., 2022). Changes in hENT1, deoxycytidine kinase, and ribonucleotide reductase affect gemcitabine's activity. P-glycoprotein, also known as multidrug resistance protein 1 or ATP-binding cassette subfamily B member 1 or breast cancer resistance protein, is an essential part of multidrug resistance and is involved in promoting resistance to all taxanes (Maloney and Hoover, 2020).

9.3 Current approaches for the treatment of pancreatic cancer

Chemotherapy, radiation therapy, and surgery are used to treat PC. Targeted therapy and immunotherapy, especially using nanocarriers, are currently being used for the better treatment of PC.

Surgery: Because most PCs are discovered after the disease has progressed, only 20% of cases are diagnosed with anatomically resectable disease (Casolino et al., 2021). Depending on the location and size of the pancreatic tumor, surgery for PC may involve removing all or part of the pancreas. It is also common practise to remove some of the healthy tissue surrounding the tumor. We refer to this as a margin. Having "clean margins" or "negative margins," which indicates there are no cancer cells in the boundaries of the healthy tissue removed, is one of the surgical goals (McCain, 2014).

Radiation therapy: Surgery and/or chemotherapy are frequently combined with radiation therapies. High-energy X-rays or other types of radiation are used in radiation treatment to kill cancer cells. PC is commonly treated with external beam therapy, stereotactic body radiotherapy, and proton therapy. External beam therapy painlessly delivers precise radiation doses to a tumor while minimizing the dose to surrounding normal tissue. Proton therapy and stereotactic body radiation are treatments that are highly targeted, high dose, and have fewer adverse effects (https://www.radiologyinfo.org/en/info/pancreatic-cancer-treatment).

Chemotherapy: After curative resection, adjuvant chemotherapy can significantly improve disease-free survival and overall survival. The two current gold standard first-line treatment regimens for advanced PC are FOLFIRINOX and gemcitabine/nab-paclitaxel (Saung and Zheng, 2017).

9.4 Advantages of nanocarriers over conventional drug delivery system

The two most common drug delivery methods are intravenous injection and oral administration. The drugs circulate throughout the body and have an influence on diseased cells as well as some negative effects on healthy cells. Additionally, substantial doses are required for conventional medication delivery to achieve the required bioavailability (Zhang et al., 2008). Some side effects of conventional drug delivery systems (DDSs) for chemotherapy are nausea, vomiting, fatigue, hair loss, and even death in extreme cases (Edis et al., 2021). Establishing a DDS that maximizes the drug's effectiveness while minimizing it's in vivo side effects is important because most of a dose of a medicine is dispersed to the rest of the body and only a tiny portion reaches the site of therapeutic action (Sci et al., 2011).

As a new tool for cancer treatment, nanocarriers have been developed and are being used to overcome the various limitations of conventional DDSs. Nanocarrier-mediated drug targeting has made it possible to deliver chemotherapy agents directly to tumors (Patra et al., 2018; Dai, 2021).

Entrapment within nanocarriers alleviate several of the limitations of conventional drug administration, including poor water solubility, unfavorable pharmacokinetics, unacceptable toxicity, and limited stability due to metabolic or enzymatic destruction (Greene et al., 2021a). Nanocarriers have several advantages over free medicines, such as they do not allow the drug to deteriorate too quickly, increase drug absorption into a specific tissue, the medication's pharmacokinetics and tissue distribution are under control, improve cellular penetration, minimize drugs from getting affected by the biological environment too rapidly, reduce the body's toxic levels. Utilizing different nanocarrier systems has increased drug accumulation in the tumor and decreased side effects (Mozafari et al., 2009). Polymeric, lipidic, inorganic, carbon-based, and other vesicular nanocarriers are revolutionizing the way that different diseases are treated today.

9.5 Role of nanocarriers in the treatment of pancreatic cancer

Nanocarriers are colloidal drug carrier systems having submicron particle sizes typically <500 nm (Din et al., 2017). The field of targeted drug delivery, particularly in the treatment of cancer, has shown significant potential for nanocarriers made of liposomes, micelles, polymeric NPs, and other like inorganic materials such as carbon, silica, and metals, including gold, silver, and iron oxide (Manju and Sreenivasan, 2010). Due to the enhanced permeability and retention (EPR) and effectiveness of NPs between 10 and 100 nm in size, they preferably aggregate at tumor locations in cancer disease. Nanocarriers have the potential to drastically improve cancer diagnostics for early tumor detection and act as adaptable therapeutic devices for integrated imaging and therapy of various cancer types (Huang et al., 2011). Most PC treatment choices are limited to traditional chemotherapy, which often involves the use of two or more drugs in combination, but only slight and temporary improvements are experienced by patients along with the side effects of these drug regimens (Greene et al., 2021b). Nanocarriers have become the best tool for overcoming the challenges that traditional medication delivery systems confront. For treating and diagnosing diseases such as cancers with increased selectivity and specificity, nanocarriers are the ideal choice.

9.5.1 Types of nanocarriers

Based on the materials, nanocarriers can be classified into lipid-based nanocarriers, polymeric-based nanocarriers, inorganic-based nanocarriers, carbon-based NPs, and vesicular NPs. The different types of nanocarriers with their advantages and disadvantages have been enlisted in Table 9.1.

9.5.1.1 Lipid-based nanocarriers

In addition to biocompatibility, biodegradability, and the capacity to entrap both hydrophobic and hydrophilic medicines, lipid-based DDSs have appealing qualities (Fig. 9.1). Liposomes, nanoemulsions, solid lipid NPs (SLNPs), and phospholipid micelles are lipid-based nanocarriers (Rocha et al., 2017). One of the most potential colloidal carriers for bioactive organic compounds is lipid-based NP systems. SLNPs have some disadvantages like low drug loading capacity and the possibility of drug expulsion during storage conditions (Ghasemiyeh and Mohammadi-Samani, 2018). Because of their modern use in oncology, some chemotherapeutic drugs now have improved antitumor activity, improving the way that cancer is treated. Great temporal and thermal stability, high loading capacity, simplicity of preparation, low production

Table 9.1 Types of nanocarriers with their advantages and limitations.

Nanocarriers	Types	Advantages	Limitations
Lipid-based nanocarriers	Liposomes, solid lipid nanoparticles, nanoemulsions, nanostructured lipid carriers	High bioavailability, amphiphilic, longer circulation time, biocompatible, biodegradable	Low drug loading efficiency, drug expulsion
Polymeric-based nanocarriers	Nanospheres, nanocapsules	Biocompatible, biodegradable, easy to fabricate, nontoxic, nonimmunogenic, and site-specific targeting to organs or tissues	Nonbiodegradability, brittle, costly production, and toxic solvent residuals
Inorganic-based nanocarriers	Metals – gold, iron Silver metal oxide – iron oxide	Facile preparation, excellent biocompatibility, and wide surface conjugation chemistry	Toxicity to normal cells
Carbon-based nanoparticles	Fullerenes, graphene, carbon nanotubes, carbon nanofibers	Higher drug-loading capacity, low immunogenicity, increased biocompatibility	Impurity, heterogeneity, high surface area, hydrophobicity, and insolubility
Vesicular nanoparticles	Exosomes, microvesicles, apoptotic bodies, and gigantic oncosome	Specificity, safety, and stability	Lack of standardized isolation and purification methods, limited drug loading efficiency

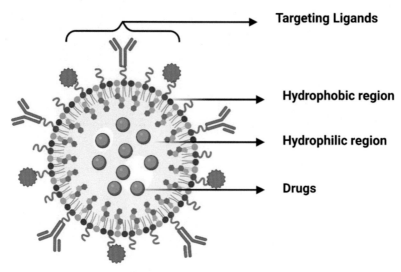

Figure 9.1 Representative image of liposome with drugs and targeting ligands. *Image created with BioRender.org.*

costs, and large-scale industrial production are some benefits of lipid-based nanocarriers (García-Pinel et al., 2019).

The first nanocarriers were liposomes, which Bangham originally reported in 1965, and the first to have chemotherapeutic medications. Clinically authorized by the Food and Drug Administration (FDA) in 1996 (Forssen' and Ross, 1994). Phospholipids, which make up many of these NPs, are arranged in a bilayer form because of their amphipathic characteristics. They develop vesicles when there is water present, which increases the solubility and stability of anticancer medications once they are loaded into their structure. They can encapsulate hydrophobic or hydrophilic medications. Other substances, such as cholesterol, can be added to their formulations in addition to phospholipids, which improves the stability of these NPs in blood by reducing the fluidity of the NP and increasing the penetration of hydrophobic medicines through the bilayer membrane (Yingchoncharoen et al., 2016).

Lipidic NPs are less toxic and more biocompatible than some polymeric NPs because their structural elements resemble those of plasma membrane lipids and human cholesterol (Liu et al., 2022). To shield hydrophilic payloads from oxidation and metabolism, liposomes have the unique ability to load hydrophobic drug moieties into the shell layer while encasing them in the watery core (Liu et al., 2022). A change in temperature or pH can cause medications to leak into cells and increase the therapeutic effectiveness of lipidic nanomedicines (Abri Aghdam et al., 2019). Numerous ongoing initiatives are being made to create possible cancer nanotherapeutics, and as a result, several liposomal medicinal products are readily available on the market (Greene et al., 2021b).

Like liposomal features, SLNPs have desirable physicochemical characteristics, good biocompatibility, and the capacity to carry hydrophobic chemicals. By inducing either a humoral or cellular immune response against cancer cells, SLNPs effectively harness immune responses, provide precise immune reagent release, and reduce off-target cytotoxic T lymphocyte (CTL) response (Yuba, 2018).

9.5.1.2 Polymeric-based nanocarrier

Colloidal systems, which typically range in size from about 5—10 nm to a maximum of 1000 nm, although the range typically attained is 100—500 nm, can be used to define polymer NPs. Most natural polymers are typically biodegradable; however, certain synthetic polymers are not. A variety of metal ions, small molecules, surfactants, or polymers can be used to functionalize the surface of polymeric NPs to improve specific binding to ligands, reduction in dose, and modulation of immune. Most delivery methods, such as intravenous or intramuscular injections, dermal or nasal absorptions, oral administration, etc., are suitable for polymer NPs. Beginning in 2005, clinics could purchase the first commercially available polymer NP DDS called Abraxane, which was composed of human serum albumin NPs carrying paclitaxel (Lu et al., 2011).

Polymer nanospheres and nanocapsules are referred to as polymer NPs (Fig. 9.2). Polymer nanospheres are matrix particles, that is, particles whose entire mass is solid. They can also act as carriers for other biologically active compounds that are either enclosed within the particles or adsorbed at the surface of the sphere (Rao and Geckeler, 2011). In nanocapsules, which function as a type of reservoir, the entrapped materials are contained in a hollow with a liquid core (either oil or water) and a solid material shell around it. When made from biopolymers that are biocompatible or biodegradable, polymer NPs have several benefits over other particulate DDSs, including high drug encapsulation efficiency, higher intracellular uptake, higher stability of encapsulating active substances, and biocompatibility with tissue and cells (Kreuter, 2007).

Polymer NP disadvantages include potential nonbiodegradability, brittle, more costly production, and toxic solvent residuals, among others. Other polymeric NP

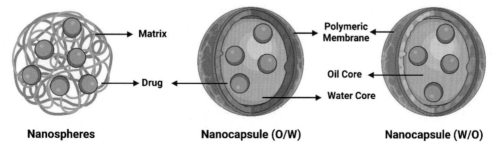

Figure 9.2 Different types of polymer nanoparticles, including nanospheres and nanocapsules, containing oil or water core. *Image created with BioRender.org.*

includes micelles, hydrogels, and dendrimers. Emulsification and solvent evaporation/extraction, nanoprecipitation, supercritical antisolvent approach, and salting out are some of the popular techniques for creating polymeric NPs (Masood, 2016).

Several commercially available biodegradable synthetic polymer types, such as polyethylene glycol (PEG), polyesters (such as polylactic-co-glycolic acid), and polyanhydride, have been researched as platforms for nanocarriers (George et al., 2019; Banerjee et al., 2019). PEG makes hydrophobic small molecule medications more soluble than the drug alone, making it possible to administer them. PEGylation is the process of attaching PEG to a different medication or chemical. When administering chemotherapeutics, PEGylation prolongs the circulatory half-lives of tiny molecules by reducing unfavorable immune recognition. For instance, PEGylation helped Genexol and Doxil to be successful (Cao et al., 2020).

Polymeric micelles are self-assembled amphiphilic core-shell particles suitable to deliver hydrophobic drugs (when drugs are trapped in a hydrophobic core) as well as hydrophilic drugs (when drugs are integrated with the outer portion of the micelles). To transport small interfering ribonucleic acid (siRNA) to PC, PEGylated calcium phosphate hybrid micelles have been developed (Pittella et al., 2014). A pancreatic tumor model called BxPC-3, which shares histological characteristics with human PC, was used to demonstrate the therapeutic value of the micelles containing the mRNA encoding the antiangiogenic protein sFlt-1 (Uchida et al., 2016). Polymeric nanogels are crosslinked networks with high-water content that serve as carriers for therapeutic payloads. They can improve stability, lengthen retention, and increase loading capacity (Kousalová and Etrych, 2018). Dendrimers are desirable delivery systems for payloads because of their globular structure, which has an accessible internal cavity (central core), and adaptable surface functioning (Zhang et al., 2013).

9.5.1.3 Inorganic-based nanoparticles

Numerous inorganic NPs have been used in nanotherapeutic applications (Li and Liu, 2017). Due to their great functionalities (such as imaging, targeted delivery, and controlled drug release) and superior physicochemical features (including magnetic, thermal, optical, and catalytic performance), inorganic NPs have found widespread use in the detection and treatment of malignancies (Zhou et al., 2020). Inorganic NP formulations offer the benefits of easy manufacturing, great biocompatibility, and a variety of surface conjugation chemistry over other NP formulations (Wang et al., 2016). One of the disadvantages of inorganic NPs is their cytotoxicity to normal cells (Lamberti et al., 2014).

Inorganic NPs are typically classified as those made of metal or metal oxide. Metal-based NPs are produced at nanometric scales from metals using either destructive or constructive techniques. The NPs stand out due to their unique characteristics, which include sizes between 10 and 100 nm, high surface area to volume ratios, pore sizes, surface charge densities, crystalline and amorphous structures, spherical and cylindrical

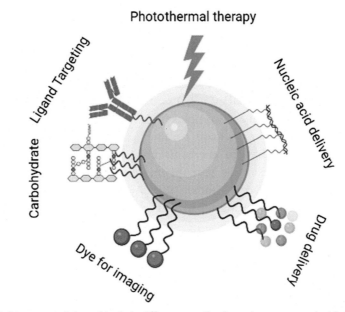

Figure 9.3 Gold nanoparticles with their different applications. *Image created with BioRender.org.*

shapes, color, reactivity, and sensitivity to environmental factors like air, moisture, heat, and sunlight, among others. Iron, silver copper, gold, cobalt, and zinc are the most often employed metals for the creation of NPs (Ealias and Saravanakumar, 2017).

One of these is the use of gold NPs (Fig. 9.3), which have antiangiogenic and anti-cancer capabilities and can be utilized as active agents to directly interfere with cellular processes (Mukherjee et al., 2005). By employing light with longer wavelengths for tissue penetration, gold NPs' capacity to adjust the size and form of the particles and their surface conjugation with antibodies enable selective imaging and photothermal death of cancer cells (Liong et al., 2008). Recently, an orthotopic model of PC showed a substantial suppression of tumor development following the targeted delivery of a modest dose of gemcitabine employing cetuximab (CTX) as a targeting agent and gold NPs as a delivery vehicle (Patra et al., 2008). PEGylated Au (III) NPs have been shown to deliver doxorubicin (DOX) to PDAC cells in vitro and to be pH dependent in their release of DOX (Moustaoui et al., 2016). Metal oxide NPs are created primarily because of their improved efficiency and reactivity (Tai et al., 2007). Examples include iron oxide and aluminum oxide, both of which have been produced to exhibit superior properties to their metal equivalents.

9.5.1.4 Carbon-based nanoparticles

Carbon-based NPs are those made entirely of carbon. They fall within the categories of fullerenes, graphene, carbon nanotubes (CNTs), carbon nanofibers, carbon black, and occasionally nanoscale activated carbon (Ealias and Saravanakumar, 2017; Bhaviripudi et al., 2007). Biodegradable charged polyester vectors (BCPVs) and graphene quantum dots (GQD/DOX/BCPV/siRNA nano complexes) have been synthesized to coload DOX and siRNA for PC. It showed excellent K-ras downregulation activity, robust stability in media that simulated physiological settings, and effective bioactivity inhibition for MiaPaCa-2 cells. More crucially, laser light was used to harm the cells by heating the nano complexes via the photothermal effect. The nano complexes then released their payloads because of this heat. This triggered release mechanism dramatically enhanced the anticancer activity of the nano complexes (Yang et al., 2019). These materials have shown increased biocompatibility, decreased immunogenicity, and higher drug-loading capacity (Debnath and Srivastava, 2021). The presence of impurity, morphological and structural heterogeneity, high surface area, hydrophobicity, and insolubility are some factors that limit the applications of CNTs (Porwal, 2017).

9.5.1.5 Vesicular nanoparticles

Extracellular vesicles (EVs) are tiny, membrane-containing vesicles that develop inside cells. EVs are divided into four subgroups: exosomes, microvesicles, apoptotic bodies, and gigantic oncosome (Huyan et al., 2020). An exosome-based delivery system has benefits such as specificity, safety, and stability (Bunggulawa et al., 2018). Although EVs' characteristics make them ideal for drug delivery, EV-based drug delivery remains challenging due to lack of standardized isolation and purification methods, limited drug loading efficiency, and insufficient clinical grade production (Meng et al., 2020). Exosomes are the most widely used EVs in cancer theragnostic among these membrane-derived vesicles (Fig. 9.4) because of their remarkable adaptability (He et al., 2018). Exosomes, which can be obtained from body fluids or cell culture,

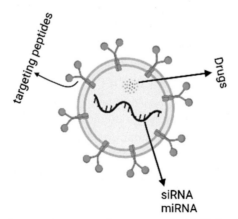

Figure 9.4 Exosome with therapeutic cargoes. *Image created with BioRender.org.*

are specialized membranous EVs that are 30–150 nm in size and are released when several cells fuse (Xu et al., 2020). Exosomes have advantages over liposomes in that they are less toxic, circulate more readily in circulation, and act as carriers for molecules that can block oncogenes, activate tumor suppressor genes, trigger immunological responses, and regulate cell proliferation (Oliveira et al., 2021).

Exosomes have been loaded with therapeutic cargoes, such as chemotherapeutic medicines and siRNA, for delivery to PC cells. These therapeutic cargoes have come from a variety of biological sources, such as tumor cells, fibroblasts, macrophages, and mesenchymal stem cells. Circulating monocytes' ability to remove exosomes is controlled by CD47 on the exosome. It has been demonstrated that exosomes with deletion CD47 can suppress KRAS by targeting PC cells with siRNA or short hairpin RNA, which reduces tumor development and metastasis (Liu et al., 2022; Kamerkar et al., 2017). For targeted chemotherapy of PC, GEM was loaded into autologous exosomes to create ExoGEM, which demonstrated decreased tumor development (Li et al., 2020).

Upon disruption of the galectin-9/dectin 1 axis, an exosome-based dual delivery biosystem for improving PDAC immunotherapy and reversing tumor immunosuppression of M2-like tumor-associated macrophages is developed. Exosomes from bone marrow mesenchymal stem cells, galectin-9 siRNA that has been electroporated, and the prodrug OXA, which acts as an immunogenic cell death trigger, are used to create the delivery system (Zhou et al., 2021). In syngeneic subcutaneous and orthotopic models of PC, exosomes carrying the CRISPR/Cas9 gene editing tool can target the mutant KrasG12D oncogenic allele in PC cells to reduce proliferation and restrain tumor growth (McAndrews et al., 2021). By reducing cancer cell proliferation, attachment, migration, and chemoresistance to GEM, the M1Exo nanoformulations combining GEM and Deferasirox considerably improved the therapeutic efficacy of the GEM-resistant PANC-1/GEM cells and 3D tumor spheroids (Zhao et al., 2021).

9.5.2 Nanocarrier-mediated delivery of nucleic acids

Short regulatory RNAs are used in RNAi, a regulatory mechanism, to halt the translation of mRNA and regulate the levels of protein synthesis. RNAi is made up of the two main RNA molecules siRNA and miRNA, which are produced via actions that both include the dicer protein. Both siRNA and miRNA are endogenous noncoding RNAs that can selectively silence the target mRNA. SiRNA is 20–25 base pairs in length, whereas miRNA is 19–25 nucleotides. The negative charge of siRNA, immediate breakdown by serum proteins, the dense fibrotic stroma, PC vascular barriers, and quick clearance from the reticuloendothelial system are some of the difficulties. While siRNA makes an activated RNA-induced silencing complex to facilitate matching with a target mRNA of complementary sequence, resulting in cleavage and degradation, miRNA binds to the mRNA strand to prevent the synthesis of certain proteins (Kim et al., 2021).

The straight injection of naked, unmodified siRNA was not shown to be successful because of the challenges it would face. As a result, nanocarrier-mediated (in the range of 10–200 nm) techniques that operate as a protective delivery vehicle for siRNA have become useful therapeutic tools (Rosenblum et al., 2018). Several therapeutically used passively directed nanomedicines, such as Abraxane and onyvede, demonstrate that the EPR effect can influence therapeutic results (Shi et al., 2017). Exosomes, naturally occurring extracellular vesicles, have attracted interest as a potential RNAi delivery mechanism in addition to the active targeting of NPs with ligands (Attia et al., 2019). A lipid NP formulation (LNPK15) was created to deliver KRAS-targeting siRNA to MIA PaCa-2 cells in vitro and in tumors in vivo, suggesting anticancer effectiveness (Sasayama et al., 2019). siRNA targeting III-tubulin was administered to orthotopic pancreatic tumors in the form of star-shaped polymeric NPs, which resulted in decreased expression of III-tubulin and slowed tumor growth (Teo et al., 2016). Using an innovative branched PEGylated poly-L-ornithine-based intravenous drug delivery method, mice were given PRDM14-specific chimeric siRNA, which significantly decreased breast and pancreatic tumor growth and metastasis in vivo (Taniguchi et al., 2021). Recent developments in PC drug delivery include siRNA administration of traditional anticancer medicines using a variety of nonviral delivery vehicles (Aghamiri et al., 2021).

9.5.3 Targeted drug delivery systems using nanocarriers

Many application programming interfaces (APIs) frequently exhibit poor water solubility, biological degradation, inadequate bioavailability, and unintended inherent adverse effects. The development of innovative drug carrier systems is necessary to address these issues. Targeted delivery systems using nanocarriers that carry genes or medications to tissues or cells have been extensively researched to meet these objectives (Attia et al., 2019). Targeted DDS using nanocarriers should be designed in such a way that the drug should accumulate in the cancer cells, should not be recognized by the mononuclear phagocyte system, remain stable and circulate in the blood for a long time, and should have very low clearance by the reticuloendothelial system (Barar and Omidi, 2013). Targeted DDSs protect healthy cells from cytotoxic substances, reduce dose-limiting side effects, and fight drug-resistant malignant cells, among other benefits.

9.5.3.1 Passive targeting

PDA's hypovascularity and extensive fibrosis cause tumor cells to become hypoxic, which causes them to die and release growth factors that cause angiogenesis, which causes nearby capillaries to sprout new blood vessels, increasing their permeability.

These newly formed leaky vessels allow selectively enhanced permeation of macromolecules larger than 40 kDa and nanosystems to the tumor stroma through the EPR effect (Rocha et al., 2017; Attia et al., 2019; Khare et al., 2014). PEGylated liposomes, also known as stealth liposomes, have steady circulation periods, a very low likelihood of captivating macrophages, selectively aggregate at target areas via the EPR effect, and have higher therapeutic efficiency (Yang et al., 2011). Albumin-Gem NPs and Gem-loaded PEGylated liposomes have been used to deliver Gem to PCs utilizing passive and active targeting, and they have demonstrated a significantly stronger antitumor impact than free Gem (Li et al., 2009; Cosco et al., 2009). Passive drug targeting is, however, constrained by high interstitial fluid pressure in the PC tissue microenvironment (TME).

9.5.3.2 *Active targeting*

Due to the limited effectiveness of passive targeting strategies, great efforts have been made to create active strategies by conjugating target-specific ligand molecules to nanocarriers that provide preferential accumulation in tumor-bearing organs. The interaction of ligand-specific nanocarriers with cells enables active targeting due to the presence of receptors on the membranes of malignant cells. By enhancing interactions between NPs and cells, ligand-mediated targeting of nanocarriers enhances drug accumulation in tumor cells (Fig. 9.5). These interactions between ligands and receptors

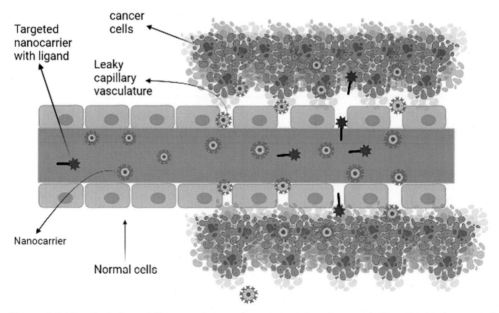

Figure 9.5 Targeted drug delivery systems using nanocarriers to pancreatic cells. *Image created with BioRender.org.*

Table 9.2 Targeted drug delivery systems in the pancreatic cancer.

Nanocarriers	Targeting ligand	Therapeutic agent	Receptor	Approach	References
Liposome	Lysine	Gemcitabine	$ATB^{0,+}$	Therapy	Kou et al. (2020)
Polymeric nanoparticles	Cetuximab	Camptothecin (CPT)	EGFR	Therapy	McDaid et al. (2019)
Chitosan nanoparticles	Anti-HER2 mAb	Gemcitabine	HER2	Therapy	Arya et al. (2011)
PLGA NPs	MUC1 antibody	Paclitaxel	MUC1	Therapy	Wu et al. (2018)
Iron oxide	CD44 Ab	Hyaluronic acid	CD44	Imaging	Luo et al. (2019)
Graphene oxide (GO)	Poly-L-lysine hydrobromide	siRNA, doxorubicin	VEGF	Therapy	Sun et al. (2018)
APTA-12	—	Gemcitabine	Nucleolin	Therapy	Park et al. (2018)
Liposome	Single-chain antibody	p53 gene	Transferrin	Therapy	Camp et al. (2013)
Albumin	HA & GQD	Gemcitabine	CD44	Therapy/ Imaging	Nigam et al. (2014)
Lipid-polymer	Anti-CEA hAb	Paclitaxel	CEA	Therapy	Hu et al. (2010)
Gold	Cetuximab	Gemcitabine	EGFR	Therapy	Patra et al. (2008)
Exosome (M1Exo)	—	Gemcitabine, Deferasirox	—	Therapy	Zhao et al. (2021)

$ATB^{0,+}$, amino acid transporter $B^{0,+}$; CD44, cluster of differentiation 44; CEA, Ccarcinoembryonic antigen; EGFR, epidermal growth factor receptor; HER2, human epidermal growth factor receptor 2; MUC1, mucin 1; siRNA; small interfering ribonucleic acid; VEGF, vascular endothelial growth factor.

increase drug uptake without changing biodistribution and lessen nonspecific toxicity (Manju and Sreenivasan, 2010; Malam et al., 2009).

Utilizing the cellular aberrations of PC for cell-specific delivery is the principle behind ligand-targeted NPs. The development of cancer-targeted nanocarriers currently makes considerable use of a wide variety of targeting ligands, such as proteins (antibodies), peptides, vitamins (folic acid), nucleic acids, fucose, epidermal growth factor, and transferrin, as nanocarrier surface modifiers (Liu et al., 2022; Khare et al., 2014). Some of the targeted delivery systems have been highlighted in Table 9.2.

A new method for improving PC treatment uses lysine-conjugated liposomes for amino acid transporter $B^{0,+}$ ($ATB^{0,+}$)-targeted liposomal medication delivery (Kou et al., 2020). Researchers created the proteolysis-targeting chimeric induced PDEδ degrader, which demonstrated improved antitumor effectiveness against KRAS mutant malignancies (Dong and Li). Hyaluronic acid, the primary cluster of differentiation 44 (CD44) binding molecule, has proved a significant ally in developing nanocarriers that demonstrate preferential tumor accumulation and increased cell uptake (Mattheolabakis et al., 2015). To lessen the cytotoxicity of systemic treatment, ADAM9-responsive mesoporous silica NPs for targeted drug delivery in PC have demonstrated promise (Slapak et al., 2021).

The antiepidermal growth factor receptor (EGFR) antibody CTX as a targeting agent, conjugated with camptothecin (CPT)-loaded polymeric NPs directed against

KRAS mutant CTX-resistant PC cells enhanced NP binding and CPT administration to CTX-resistant cancer cell lines slowed the development of the tumor (McDaid et al., 2019). For the treatment of PC, Herceptin-conjugated gemcitabine-loaded chitosan nanoparticles (HER2-Gem-CS-NPs) demonstrated greater antiproliferative activity as well as an improved S-phase arrest, resulting in PC cell death (Arya et al., 2011). In PC, mucin 4 (MUC4), a high molecular weight glycoprotein, is differentially overexpressed and functionally aids in the development of the disease. Dendritic cells were activated by purified recombinant human MUC4-beta protein in polyanhydride NPs, which led to the induction of adaptive immunity (Banerjee et al., 2019).

PLGA NPs loaded with paclitaxel and conjugated with MUC1 antibody have demonstrated therapeutic efficacy against PC because MUC1 is a membrane-tethered glycoprotein that is aberrantly overexpressed in more than 80% of PD (Wu et al., 2018). Iron oxide conjugated with CD44 Ab and loaded with hyaluronic acid has been developed for PC cells imaging purposes (Luo et al., 2019) Graphene oxide could deliver siRNA into PC cells and downregulate the expression of the desired gene, which leads to an antitumor effect (Sun et al., 2018).

9.6 Future prospectives

Though understanding has advanced significantly over the years, treatment for PC is still difficult. The specific characteristics of PDAC and its surrounding milieu that prevent effective penetration and tumor killing by chemotherapeutic and immunotherapy agents have been better understood, but the clinical outcomes remain steady. Currently, combined cytotoxic chemotherapy (FOLFIRINOX, nab-paclitaxel) is the main treatment for metastatic PDAC. Future work on PC treatments using nanocarriers targeting gene mutation (KRAS, CDKN2A, SMAD4, BRCA1/2and TP53), pancreatic tumor stroma, immune system modulators, has great promise for improving patient survival rates.

KRAS mutation (seen in 90% of PC cases) leads to PC formation and growth through multiple pathways. Hence, KRAS or their signaling pathways (RAS−MAPK pathway) inhibition using nanocarriers could be a great clinical outcome. Cancer-associated fibroblasts produce a dense fibrous stroma, a characteristic feature of PC, which limits the penetration of therapeutic agents due to increased interstitial fluid pressure. Normalizing PC's stroma and vasculature have great promise for improved immunotherapy as well as drug delivery. Antistroma therapy along with immune checkpoint blockade agents can enhance the delivery of therapeutic agents and sensitivity of the immunotherapeutic agents by enhancing the T-cells response.

Nanocarriers like exosomes have shown great therapeutic value by delivery of gene silencing agents, which inhibits the expression of mRNA of PC cells. If stability, off-target effects, and the conventional method of isolation are solved, using nanocarriers to transport miRNA and siRNA for gene expression and silencing could have excellent therapeutic results.

In the coming years, innovative agents should concentrate on combination therapies using appropriate nanocarriers. Future therapies for PDAC should address pathological signaling networks, genetic abnormalities caused by gene mutations, improved immunotherapy, more specific targeted drug delivery using better nanocarriers, vaccine development, minimal side effects, and low cost.

References

Abri Aghdam, M., Bagheri, R., Mosafer, J., Baradaran, B., Hashemzaei, M., Baghbanzadeh, A., et al., 2019. Recent advances on thermosensitive and pH-sensitive liposomes employed in controlled release. J. Control. Release 315, 1−22.

Aghamiri, S., Raee, P., Talaei, S., Mohammadi-Yeganeh, S., Bayat, S., Rezaee, D., et al., 2021. Nonviral siRNA delivery systems for pancreatic cancer therapy. Biotechnol. Bioeng. 118 (10), 3669−3690.

Arya, G., Vandana, M., Acharya, S., Sahoo, S.K., 2011. Enhanced antiproliferative activity of Herceptin (HER2)-conjugated gemcitabine-loaded chitosan nanoparticle in pancreatic cancer therapy. Nanomedicine. 7 (6), 859−870.

Attia, M.F., Anton, N., Wallyn, J., Omran, Z., Vandamme, T.F., 2019. An overview of active and passive targeting strategies to improve the nanocarriers efficiency to tumour sites. J. Pharm. Pharmacol 71 (8), 1185−1198.

Banerjee, K., Gautam, S.K., Kshirsagar, P., Ross, K.A., Spagnol, G., Sorgen, P., et al., 2019. Amphiphilic polyanhydride-based recombinant MUC4β-nanovaccine activates dendritic cells. Genes. Cancer 10 (3−4), 52−62.

Barar, J., Omidi, Y., 2013. Dysregulated pH in tumor microenvironment checkmates cancer therapy. BioImpacts. 3:, 149−162.

Bhaviripudi, S., Mile, E., Steiner, S.A., Zare, A.T., Dresselhaus, M.S., Belcher, A.M., et al., 2007. CVD synthesis of single-walled carbon nanotubes from gold nanoparticle catalysts. J. Am. Chem. Soc. 129 (6), 1516−1517.

Bunggulawa, E.J., Wang, W., Yin, T., Wang, N., Durkan, C., Wang, Y., et al., 2018. Recent advancements in the use of exosomes as drug delivery systems. J. Nanobiotechnol 16 (1), 81.

Camp, E.R., Wang, C., Little, E.C., Watson, P.M., Pirollo, K.F., Rait, A., et al., 2013. Transferrin receptor targeting nanomedicine delivering wild-type p53 gene sensitizes pancreatic cancer to gemcitabine therapy. Cancer Gene Ther. 20 (4), 222−228.

Cao, J., Huang, D., Peppas, N.A., 2020. Advanced engineered nanoparticulate platforms to address key biological barriers for delivering chemotherapeutic agents to target sites, Adv. Drug Deliv. Rev, 167:. Elsevier B.V, pp. 170−188.

Casolino, R., Braconi, C., Malleo, G., Paiella, S., Bassi, C., Milella, M., et al., 2021. Reshaping preoperative treatment of pancreatic cancer in the era of precision medicine. Ann. Oncol. 32 (2), 183−196.

Chand, S., O'Hayer, K., Blanco, F.F., Winter, J.M., Brody, J.R., 2016. The landscape of pancreatic cancer therapeutic resistance mechanisms. Int. J. Biol. Sci. 12:, 273−283.

Comandatore, A., Immordino, B., Balsano, R., Capula, M., Garajovà, I., Ciccolini, J., et al., 2022. Potential role of exosomes in the chemoresistance to gemcitabine and nab-paclitaxel in pancreatic cancer. Diagnostics. 12 (2), 286.

Corbo, V., Tortora, G., Scarpa, A., 2012. Molecular pathology of pancreatic cancer: from bench-to-bedside translation. Curr. Drug. Targets 13 (6), 744−752.

Cosco, D., Bulotta, A., Ventura, M., Celia, C., Calimeri, T., Perri, G., et al., 2009. In vivo activity of gemcitabine-loaded PEGylated small unilamellar liposomes against pancreatic cancer. Cancer Chemother. Pharmacol. 64 (5), 1009−1020.

Dai, S., 2021. Nanocarriers-types and uses. Res. Rev. J. Pharm. Nanotechnol. 9.

Debnath, S.K., Srivastava, R., 2021. Drug delivery with carbon-based nanomaterials as versatile nanocarriers: progress and prospects. Front. Nanotechnol. 3.

Diab, M., Azmi, A., Mohammad, R., Philip, P.A., 2019. Pharmacotherapeutic strategies for treating pancreatic cancer: advances and challenges. Expert. Opin. Pharmacother. 20 (5), 535−546.

Din, F.ud, Aman, W., Ullah, I., Qureshi, O.S., Mustapha, O., Shafique, S., et al., 2017. Effective use of nanocarriers as drug delivery systems for the treatment of selected tumors. Int. J. Nanomed. 12, 7291−7309.

Dong G., Li H. Targeted delivery of a PROTAC induced PDEδ degrader by a biomimetic drug delivery system for enhanced cytotoxicity against pancreatic cancer cells Amino acid derivatives of pyropheophorbide-a ethers as photosensitizer: Synthesis and photodynamic activity View project CD20 Ccrosslink View project [Internet]. Available from: http://www.ajcr.us.

Ealias A.M., Saravanakumar M.P. A review on the classification, characterisation, synthesis of nanoparticles and their application. In: IOP Conference Series: Materials Science and Engineering. Institute of Physics Publishing; 2017.

Edis, Z., Wang, J., Waqas, M.K., Ijaz, M., Ijaz, M., 2021. Nanocarriers-mediated drug delivery systems for anticancer agents: an overview and perspectives. Int. J. Nanomed. 16, 1313−1330.

Forssen', E.A., Ross, M.E., 1994. DAUNOXOME@ Treatment of solid tumors: preclinical and clinical investigations forssen and ross. J. Liposome Res. 4.

García-Pinel, B., Porras-Alcalá, C., Ortega-Rodríguez, A., Sarabia, F., Prados, J., Melguizo, C., et al., 2019. Lipid-based nanoparticles: application and recent advances in cancer treatment. Nanomaterials. 9 (4).

George, A., Shah, P.A., Shrivastav, P.S., 2019. Natural biodegradable polymers based nano-formulations for drug delivery: a review, Int. J. Pharm., 561. pp. 244−264.

Ghasemiyeh, P., Mohammadi-Samani, S., 2018. Solid lipid nanoparticles and nanostructured lipid carriers as novel drug delivery systems: applications, advantages and disadvantages. Res. Pharm. Sci. 13 (4), 288.

Giovannetti, E., Funel, N., Peters, G.J., del Chiaro, M., Erozenci, L.A., Vasile, E., et al., 2010. MicroRNA-21 in pancreatic cancer: correlation with clinical outcome and pharmacologic aspects underlying its role in the modulation of gemcitabine activity. Cancer Res. 70 (11), 4528−4538.

Grasso, C., Jansen, G., Giovannetti, E., 2017. Drug resistance in pancreatic cancer: impact of altered energy metabolism. Crit. Rev. Oncol. Hematol. 114, 139−152.

Greene, M.K., Johnston, M.C., Scott, C.J., 2021a. Nanomedicine in pancreatic cancer: current status and future opportunities for overcoming therapy resistance. Cancers (Basel) 13 (24), 6175.

Greene, M.K., Johnston, M.C., Scott, C.J., 2021b. Nanomedicine in pancreatic cancer: current status and future opportunities for overcoming therapy resistance. Cancers. MDPI 13.

Hayashi, A., Hong, J., Iacobuzio-Donahue, C.A., 2021. The pancreatic cancer genome revisited. Nat. Rev. Gastroenterol. Hepatol. 18 (7), 469−481.

He, C., Zheng, S., Luo, Y., Wang, B., 2018. Exosome theranostics: biology and translational medicine. Theranostics. 8 (1), 237−255.

Hu, C.M.J., Kaushal, S., Cao, H.S.T., Aryal, S., Sartor, M., Esener, S., et al., 2010. Half-antibody functionalized lipid − polymer hybrid nanoparticles for targeted drug delivery to carcinoembryonic antigen presenting pancreatic cancer cells. Mol. Pharm. 7 (3), 914−920.

Huang, H.C., Barua, S., Sharma, G., Dey, S.K., Rege, K., 2011. Inorganic nanoparticles for cancer imaging and therapy. J. Control. Release 155:, 344−357.

Huyan, T., Li, H., Peng, H., Chen, J., Yang, R., Zhang, W., et al., 2020. Extracellular vesicles − advanced nanocarriers in cancer therapy: progress and achievements. Int. J. Nanomed. 15, 6485−6502.

Kamerkar, S., LeBleu, V.S., Sugimoto, H., Yang, S., Ruivo, C.F., Melo, S.A., et al., 2017. Exosomes facilitate therapeutic targeting of oncogenic KRAS in pancreatic cancer. Nature. 546 (7659), 498−503.

Khare, V., Alam, N., Saneja, A., Dubey, R.D., Gupta, P.N., 2014. Targeted drug delivery systems for pancreatic cancer. J. Biomed. Nanotechnol. 10 (12), 3462−3482.

Kim, J.Y., Hong, S.M., 2018. Precursor lesions of pancreatic cancer. Oncol. Res. Treat. 41 (10), 603−610.

Kim, M.J., Chang, H., Nam, G., Ko, Y., Kim, S.H., Roberts, T.M., et al., 2021. RNAi-based approaches for pancreatic cancer therapy, Pharmaceutics, 13. MDPI.

Kou, L., Huang, H., Lin, X., Jiang, X., Wang, Y., Luo, Q., et al., 2020. Endocytosis of ATB$^{0,+}$ (SLC6A14)-targeted liposomes for drug delivery and its therapeutic application for pancreatic cancer. Expert. Opin. Drug. Deliv. 17 (3), 395−405.

Kousalová, J., Etrych, T., 2018. Polymeric nanogels as drug delivery systems. Physiol. Res. 67, S305−S317.

Kreuter, J., 2007. Nanoparticles-a historical perspective. Int. J. Pharm 331, 1−10.

Lamberti, M., Zappavigna, S., Sannolo, N., Porto, S., Caraglia, M., 2014. Advantages and risks of nano-technologies in cancer patients and occupationally exposed workers. Expert. Opin. Drug. Deliv. 11 (7), 1087−1101.

Li, L., Liu, H., 2017. Biodegradable inorganic nanoparticles: an opportunity for improved cancer therapy? Nanomedicine. 12 (9), 959−961.

Li, J.ming, Chen, W., Wang, H., Jin, C., Yu, X.jun, Lu, W.yue, et al., 2009. Preparation of albumin nanospheres loaded with gemcitabine and their cytotoxicity against BXPC-3 cells in vitro. Acta Pharmacol. Sin. 30 (9), 1337−1343.

Li, Y.J., Wu, J.Y., Wang, J.M., Hu, X.B., Cai, J.X., Xiang, D.X., 2020. Gemcitabine loaded autologous exosomes for effective and safe chemotherapy of pancreatic cancer. Acta Biomater. 101, 519−530.

Liong, M., Lu, J., Kovochich, M., Xia, T., Ruehm, S.G., Nel, A.E., et al., 2008. Multifunctional inorganic nanoparticles for imaging, targeting, and drug delivery. ACS Nano 2 (5), 889−896.

Liu, Y., Guo, J., Huang, L., 2020. Modulation of tumor microenvironment for immunotherapy: focus on nanomaterial-based strategies, Theranostics, 10:. pp. 3099−3117.

Liu, L., Kshirsagar, P.G., Gautam, S.K., Gulati, M., Wafa, E.I., Christiansen, J.C., et al., 2022. Nanocarriers for pancreatic cancer imaging, treatments, and immunotherapies, Theranostics, 12:. pp. 1030−1060.

Long, J., Zhang, Y., Yu, X., Yang, J., Lebrun, D.G., Chen, C., et al., 2011. Overcoming drug resistance in pancreatic cancer. Expert. Opin. Ther. Targets 15:, 817−828.

Lu, X.Y., Wu, D.C., Li, Z.J., Chen, G.Q., 2011. Polymer nanoparticles. Progress in Molecular Biology and Translational Science. Elsevier B.V, pp. 299−323.

Luo, Y., Li, Y., Li, J., Fu, C., Yu, X., Wu, L., 2019. Hyaluronic acid-mediated multifunctional iron oxide-based MRI nanoprobes for dynamic monitoring of pancreatic cancer. RSC Adv. 9 (19), 10486−10493.

Malam, Y., Loizidou, M., Seifalian, A.M., 2009. Liposomes and nanoparticles: nanosized vehicles for drug delivery in cancer. Trends Pharmacol. Sci. 30 (11), 592−599.

Maloney, S.M., Hoover, C.A., Morejon-Lasso, L.v, Prosperi, J.R., 2020. Mechanisms of taxane resistance. Cancers (Basel) 12 (11), 3323.

Manju, S., Sreenivasan, K., 2010. Functionalised nanoparticles for targeted drug delivery. Biointegration of Medical Implant Materials: Science and Design. Elsevier Ltd, pp. 267−297.

Masood, F., 2016. Polymeric nanoparticles for targeted drug delivery system for cancer therapy. Mater. Sci. Eng: C. 60, 569−578.

Massagué, J., 2008. TGFβ in cancer. Cell. 134 (2), 215−230.

Mattheolabakis, G., Milane, L., Singh, A., Amiji, M.M., 2015. Hyaluronic acid targeting of CD44 for cancer therapy: from receptor biology to nanomedicine. J. Drug. Target. 23 (7−8), 605−618.

McAndrews, K.M., Xiao, F., Chronopoulos, A., LeBleu, V.S., Kugeratski, F.G., Kalluri, R., 2021. Exosome-mediated delivery of CRISPR/Cas9 for targeting of oncogenic Kras [G12D] in pancreatic cancer. Life Sci. Alliance 4 (9), e202000875.

McBride, A., Bonafede, M., Cai, Q., Princic, N., Tran, O., Pelletier, C., et al., 2017. Comparison of treatment patterns and economic outcomes among metastatic pancreatic cancer patients initiated on *nab*-paclitaxel plus gemcitabine versus FOLFIRINOX. Expert. Rev. Clin. Pharmacol. 10 (10), 1153−1160.

McCain, J., 2014. Carlos Fernández-del Castillo confronts the challenge of pancreatic cancer: although progress has been slow, a renowned expert on the disease sees reasons for hope. P T 39 (4), 281−289.

McDaid, W.J., Greene, M.K., Johnston, M.C., Pollheimer, E., Smyth, P., McLaughlin, K., et al., 2019. Repurposing of Cetuximab in antibody-directed chemotherapy-loaded nanoparticles in EGFR therapy-resistant pancreatic tumours. Nanoscale. 11 (42), 20261−20273.

McGuigan, A., Kelly, P., Turkington, R.C., Jones, C., Coleman, H.G., McCain, R.S., 2018. Pancreatic cancer: a review of clinical diagnosis, epidemiology, treatment and outcomes. World J. Gastroenterol. 24 (43), 4846−4861.

Meng, W., He, C., Hao, Y., Wang, L., Li, L., Zhu, G., 2020. Prospects and challenges of extracellular vesicle-based drug delivery system: considering cell source. Drug. Deliv. 27 (1), 585−598.

Moustaoui, H., Movia, D., Dupont, N., Bouchemal, N., Casale, S., Djaker, N., et al., 2016. Tunable design of Gold(III)−doxorubicin complex−PEGylated nanocarrier. the golden doxorubicin for oncological applications. ACS Appl. Mater. Interfaces 8 (31), 19946−19957.

Mozafari, M.R., Pardakhty, A., Azarmi, S., Jazayeri, J.A., Nokhodchi, A., Omri, A., 2009. Role of nano-carrier systems in cancer nanotherapy. J. Liposome Res. 19, 310−321.

Mukherjee, P., Bhattacharya, R., Wang, P., Wang, L., Basu, S., Nagy, J.A., et al., 2005. Antiangiogenic Properties of gold nanoparticles. Clin. Cancer Res. 11 (9), 3530−3534.

Nigam, P., Waghmode, S., Louis, M., Wangnoo, S., Chavan, P., Sarkar, D., 2014. Graphene quantum dots conjugated albumin nanoparticles for targeted drug delivery and imaging of pancreatic cancer. J. Mater. Chem. B. 2 (21), 3190−3195.

Noë, M., Brosens, L.A.A., 2016. Pathology of pancreatic cancer precursor lesions. Surg. Pathol. Clin. 9 (4), 561−580.

Oliveira, C., Calmeiro, J., Carrascal, M.A., Falcão, A., Gomes, C., Miguel Neves, B., et al., 2021. Exosomes as new therapeutic vectors for pancreatic cancer treatment. Eur. J. Pharm. Biopharm. 161, 4−14.

Park, J.Y., Cho, Y.L., Chae, J.R., Moon, S.H., Cho, W.G., Choi, Y.J., et al., 2018. Gemcitabine-incorporated G-Quadruplex aptamer for targeted drug delivery into pancreas cancer. Mol. Ther. Nucleic Acids 12, 543−553.

Patra, C.R., Bhattacharya, R., Wang, E., Katarya, A., Lau, J.S., Dutta, S., et al., 2008. Targeted delivery of gemcitabine to pancreatic adenocarcinoma using cetuximab as a targeting agent. Cancer Res. 68 (6), 1970−1978.

Patra, J.K., Das, G., Fraceto, L.F., Campos, E.V.R., Rodriguez-Torres, M.del P., Acosta-Torres, L.S., et al., 2018. Nano based drug delivery systems: recent developments and future prospects. J. Nanobiotechnol. 16 (1), 71.

Pittella, F., Cabral, H., Maeda, Y., Mi, P., Watanabe, S., Takemoto, H., et al., 2014. Systemic siRNA delivery to a spontaneous pancreatic tumor model in transgenic mice by PEGylated calcium phosphate hybrid micelles. J. Control. Release 178, 18−24.

Porwal, M., 2017. An overview on carbon nanotubes. MOJ Bioequiv. Bioavailab. 3 (5).

Principe, D.R., Underwood, P.W., Korc, M., Trevino, J.G., Munshi, H.G., Rana, A., 2021. The current treatment paradigm for pancreatic ductal adenocarcinoma and barriers to therapeutic efficacy. Front. Oncol. 11.

Puik, J.R., Swijnenburg, R.J., Kazemier, G., Giovannetti, E., 2022. Novel strategies to address critical challenges in pancreatic cancer. Cancers (Basel) 14 (17), 4115.

Qian, L., Yu, S., Chen, Z., Meng, Z., Huang, S., Wang, P., 2019. Functions and clinical implications of exosomes in pancreatic cancer, Biochim. Biophys. Acta − Rev. Cancer, 1871. pp. 75−84.

Qiu, J., Yang, G., Feng, M., Zheng, S., Cao, Z., You, L., et al., 2018. Extracellular vesicles as mediators of the progression and chemoresistance of pancreatic cancer and their potential clinical applications, Molecular Cancer, 17.

Ram Makena, M., Gatla, H., Verlekar, D., Sukhavasi, S., K. Pandey, M., C. Pramanik, K., 2019. Wnt/β-catenin signaling: the culprit in pancreatic carcinogenesis and therapeutic resistance. Int. J. Mol. Sci. 20 (17), 4242.

Rao, J.P., Geckeler, K.E., 2011. Polymer nanoparticles: preparation techniques and size-control parameters, Prog. Polym. Sci., 36:. pp. 887−913.

Rawla, P., Sunkara, T., Gaduputi, V., 2019. Epidemiology of pancreatic cancer: global trends, etiology and risk factors. World J. Oncol. 10 (1), 10−27.

Rocha, M., Chaves, N., Bao, S., 2017. Nanobiotechnology for breast cancer treatment. Breast Cancer - From Biology to Medicine. InTech.

Rosenblum, D., Joshi, N., Tao, W., Karp, J.M., Peer, D., 2018. Progress and challenges towards targeted delivery of cancer therapeutics. Nat. Commun. 9 (1), 1410.

Sasayama, Y., Hasegawa, M., Taguchi, E., Kubota, K., Kuboyama, T., Naoi, T., et al., 2019. In vivo activation of PEGylated long circulating lipid nanoparticle to achieve efficient siRNA delivery and target gene knock down in solid tumors. J. Control. Release 311–312, 245–256.

Saung, M.T., Zheng, L., 2017. Current standards of chemotherapy for pancreatic cancer. Clin. Ther. 39 (11), 2125–2134.

Scarlett, C.J., Salisbury, E.L., Biankin, A.v, Kench, J., 2011. Precursor lesions in pancreatic cancer: morphological and molecular pathology. Pathology. 43 (3), 183–200.

Sci, I.J.T., Singh, S., Pandey, V.K., Prakash Tewari, R., Agarwal, V., 2011. Nanoparticle based drug delivery system: advantages and applications. Indian. J. Sci. Technol. [Internet] 4 (3), 25–29. Available from: http://www.indjst.org.

Shi, J., Kantoff, P.W., Wooster, R., Farokhzad, O.C., 2017. Cancer nanomedicine: progress, challenges and opportunities. Nat. Rev. Cancer 17 (1), 20–37.

Slapak, E.J., Kong, L., el Mandili, M., Nieuwland, R., Kros, A., Bijlsma, M.F., et al., 2021. ADAM9-responsive mesoporous silica nanoparticles for targeted drug delivery in pancreatic cancer. Cancers (Basel) 13 (13), 3321.

Sun, Q., Wang, X., Cui, C., Li, J., Wang, Y., 2018. Doxorubicin and anti-VEGF siRNA co-delivery via nano-graphene oxide for enhanced cancer therapy in vitro and in vivo. Int. J. Nanomed. 13, 3713–3728.

Tai, C.Y., Tai, C.T., Chang, M.H., Liu, H.S., 2007. Synthesis of magnesium hydroxide and oxide nanoparticles using a spinning disk reactor. Ind. Eng. Chem. Res. 46 (17), 5536–5541.

Taniguchi, H., Natori, Y., Miyagi, Y., Hayashi, K., Nagamura, F., Kataoka, K., et al., 2021. Treatment of primary and metastatic breast and pancreatic tumors upon intravenous delivery of a <scp> PRDM14 </scp> -specific chimeric <scp> siRNA </scp> /nanocarrier complex. Int. J. Cancer 149 (3), 646–656.

Teo, J., McCarroll, J.A., Boyer, C., Youkhana, J., Sagnella, S.M., Duong, H.T.T., et al., 2016. A rationally optimized nanoparticle system for the delivery of RNA interference therapeutics into pancreatic tumors in vivo. Biomacromolecules. 17 (7), 2337–2351.

Uchida, S., Kinoh, H., Ishii, T., Matsui, A., Tockary, T.A., Takeda, K.M., et al., 2016. Systemic delivery of messenger RNA for the treatment of pancreatic cancer using polyplex nanomicelles with a cholesterol moiety. Biomaterials. 82, 221–228.

Vogelstein, B., Lane, D., Levine, A.J., 2000. Surfing the p53 network. Nature. 408 (6810), 307–310.

Waddell, N., Pajic, M., Patch, A.M., Chang, D.K., Kassahn, K.S., Bailey, P., et al., 2015. Whole genomes redefine the mutational landscape of pancreatic cancer. Nature. 518 (7540), 495–501.

Wang, Z., Li, Y., Ahmad, A., Banerjee, S., Azmi, A.S., Kong, D., et al., 2011. Pancreatic cancer: understanding and overcoming chemoresistance. Nat. Rev. Gastroenterol. Hepatol 8, 27–33.

Wang, F., Li, C., Cheng, J., Yuan, Z., 2016. Recent advances on inorganic nanoparticle-based cancer therapeutic agents. Int. J. Env. Res. Public. Health 13 (12), 1182.

Witkiewicz, A.K., McMillan, E.A., Balaji, U., Baek, G., Lin, W.C., Mansour, J., et al., 2015. Whole-exome sequencing of pancreatic cancer defines genetic diversity and therapeutic targets. Nat. Commun. 6 (1), 6744.

Wu, S.ta, Fowler, A.J., Garmon, C.B., Fessler, A.B., Ogle, J.D., Grover, K.R., et al., 2018. Treatment of pancreatic ductal adenocarcinoma with tumor antigen specific-targeted delivery of paclitaxel loaded PLGA nanoparticles. BMC Cancer 18 (1), 457.

Xu, M., Yang, Q., Sun, X., Wang, Y., 2020. Recent advancements in the loading and modification of therapeutic exosomes. Front. Bioeng. Biotechnol. 8.

Yang, F., Jin, C., Jiang, Y., Li, J., Di, Y., Ni, Q., et al., 2011. Liposome based delivery systems in pancreatic cancer treatment: from bench to bedside. Cancer Treat. Rev. 37 (8), 633–642.

Yang, C., Chan, K.K., Xu, G., Yin, M., Lin, G., Wang, X., et al., 2019. Biodegradable polymer-coated multifunctional graphene quantum dots for light-triggered synergetic therapy of pancreatic cancer. ACS Appl. Mater. Interfaces 11 (3), 2768—2781.

Yang, Z., Zhao, N., Cui, J., Wu, H., Xiong, J., Peng, T., 2020. Exosomes derived from cancer stem cells of gemcitabine-resistant pancreatic cancer cells enhance drug resistance by delivering miR-210. Cell. Oncol. 43 (1), 123—136.

Yingchoncharoen, P., Kalinowski, D.S., Richardson, D.R., 2016. Lipid-based drug delivery systems in cancer therapy: what is available and what is yet to come. Pharmacol. Rev. 68 (3), 701—787.

Yokoi, K., Godin, B., Oborn, C.J., Alexander, J.F., Liu, X., Fidler, I.J., et al., 2013. Porous silicon nano-carriers for dual targeting tumor associated endothelial cells and macrophages in stroma of orthotopic human pancreatic cancers. Cancer Lett. 334 (2), 319—327.

Yuba, E., 2018. Liposome-based immunity-inducing systems for cancer immunotherapy. Mol. Immunol. 98, 8—12.

Zeng, Pöttler, Lan, Grützmann, Pilarsky, Yang, 2019. Chemoresistance in pancreatic cancer. Int. J. Mol. Sci. 20 (18), 4504.

Zhang, L., Gu, F., Chan, J., Wang, A., Langer, R., Farokhzad, O., 2008. Nanoparticles in medicine: therapeutic applications and developments. Clin. Pharmacol. Ther. 83 (5), 761—769.

Zhang, X., Zhao, J., Wen, Y., Zhu, C., Yang, J., Yao, F., 2013. Carboxymethyl chitosan-poly(amidoa-mine) dendrimer core—shell nanoparticles for intracellular lysozyme delivery. Carbohydr. Polym. 98 (2), 1326—1334.

Zhang, L., Sanagapalli, S., Stoita, A., 2018. Challenges in diagnosis of pancreatic cancer. World J. Gastroenterol. 24 (19), 2047—2060.

Zhao, Y., Zheng, Y., Zhu, Y., Zhang, Y., Zhu, H., Liu, T., 2021. M1 macrophage-derived exosomes loaded with gemcitabine and deferasirox against chemoresistant pancreatic cancer. Pharmaceutics. 13 (9), 1493.

Zhou, H., Ge, J., Miao, Q., Zhu, R., Wen, L., Zeng, J., et al., 2020. Biodegradable inorganic nanoparti-cles for cancer theranostics: insights into the degradation behavior. Bioconjug Chem. 31 (2), 315—331.

Zhou, W., Zhou, Y., Chen, X., Ning, T., Chen, H., Guo, Q., et al., 2021. Pancreatic cancer-targeting exosomes for enhancing immunotherapy and reprogramming tumor microenvironment. Biomaterials. 268, 120546.

CHAPTER 10

Nanocarrier-mediated delivery for targeting stomach cancer

Mohd Aman Mohd Ateeq, Mayur Aalhate, Srushti Mahajan, Ujala Gupta, Indrani Maji, Kedar Khaparkhuntikar, Anish Dhuri, Namitha Mohan C., Saurabh Srivastava and Pankaj Kumar Singh
Department of Pharmaceutics, National Institute of Pharmaceutical Education and Research (NIPER), Hyderabad, Telangana, India

10.1 Introduction

Gastric cancer stands sixth and third in the number of new cancer cases and new death as per GLOBOCAN estimates of year 2020. Males are twofold highly prone to stomach cancer than females. Though the number of stomach cancer incidents are getting low in the European countries from the past few years, but still it remains high in Eastern Asian countries (Sung et al., 2021).

Dyspepsia, stomach pain, weight loss, and palpable abdominal mass are the most common signs of gastric cancer. Ascites, jaundice, and gastrointestinal obstruction are all signs that the disease has spread. The accumulation of these symptoms is linked to a larger probability of mortality. Metastasis is defined as the spread of cancer beyond the localized lymph nodes to other organs. Ovarian metastases, hematogenous metastases, peritoneal metastases (that extend to the lungs and bone), liver metastases, and metastases to distant lymph nodes (such as mesenteric, mediastinal, paraaortic, or neck lymph nodes) are the most common locations of distant metastases from gastric cancer (Maconi et al., 2008; Thrumurthy et al., 2013; Catalano et al., 2009).

In one of the research projects, 611 individuals were investigated to determine the rate and pattern of recurrence after gastric cancer after a surgery that was expected to be curative. The remaining stomach, lymph nodes, peritoneal, local, and hematogenous spread were all documented as recurrence patterns in this investigation. According to the findings, 80% of relapses occurred during the first 2 years. Recurrence of disease was recorded in 40.1% of patients, with 50% of patients having a single recurrence (Wu et al., 2003). Peritoneal spread is the most common pattern of failure after curative resection, according to numerous investigations. Positive cytology is classified as a stage IV disease in the TNM classification for gastric cancer (Axon, 2006; Sano et al., 2017).

Multifunctional Nanocomposites for Targeted Drug Delivery in Cancer Therapy
DOI: https://doi.org/10.1016/B978-0-323-95303-0.00006-X

10.2 Types of gastric cancer

Generally, all gastric cancers are adenocarcinomas, and as per Lauren's classification, they can be classified into intestinal or diffuse. In high incidence areas, intestinal cancers are the ones that are more common in a large proportion. Exposure to diffuse gastric cancer depends upon race and geography (Lauren, 1965). Intestinal gastric cancer is significantly more common than diffuse gastric cancer. Over the last few decades, epidemiologic investigations have revealed another type of gastric cancer: gastric cardia/gastroesophageal junction (GEJ) tumors (Van Cutsem et al., 2016; Asaka et al., 2001). A summary of generally identified risk factors for the development of stomach cancer are included in the Table 10.1 and Fig. 10.1.

10.2.1 Noncardia gastric cancer

Intestinal noncardia gastric cancer has a multistep pathophysiology that is most likely triggered by persistent inflammation (e.g., as a result of *Helicobacter pylori* infection, autoimmune gastritis, or chronic gastritis) (Hansen et al., 1999; Uemura et al., 2001). Chronic gastritis, dysplasia, and intestinal metaplasia are all symptoms of the condition. Tobacco, high salt intake, and alcohol usage are all environmental factors that enhance the incidence of noncardia gastric cancer (Yusefi et al., 2018). Prospective studies have found a strong dose-dependent link between smoking and the incidence of gastric cancer (Colquhoun et al., 2015; Praud et al., 2018).

Table 10.1 Types of gastric cancer and associated risk factors (Gomceli et al., 2012).

Gastric cancer types	Epidemiology	Prevalent risk factor	
Noncardia gastric cancer	Significant morphological variances, more common in high-risk areas	Environmental clinical	High salt intake, tobacco age, *Helicobacter pylori* infection
Diffuse gastric cancer	Worldwide distributed rising incidences Established genetic predeposition syndrome	Environmental clinical Genetic	Not identified *H. pylori* infection CDH1 mutation
Proximal gastric cancer	Coupled with gastroesophageal junction and distal esophageal adenocarcinoma cases increasing in industrial states/nations	Environmental, clinical Genetic	Tobacco, alcohol, GERD, obesity not identified

GERD, Gastroesophageal reflux disease.

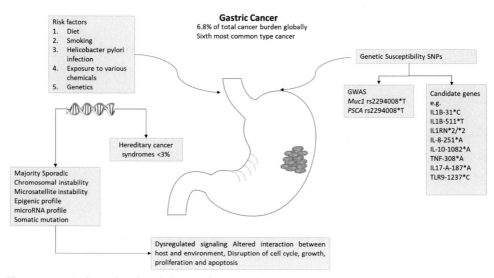

Figure 10.1 Etiological and pathological features of gastric cancer.

10.2.2 Diffuse gastric cancer

Although the E-cadherin gene mutation or epigenetic silencing appears to be a significant carcinogenic factor in diffuse gastric cancer, there is no reported precursor lesion (Pharoah et al., 2001; Huntsman et al., 2001). Immunohistochemistry detects E-cadherin loss in about half of patients with sporadic diffuse gastric cancer. The genome sequencing also confirms the same implying that this pathway may be a common precursor event in the development of diffuse gastric cancer, distinct from the chronic inflammation and gastric atrophy that characterize intestinal noncardia gastric cancer (Blair et al., 2006).

The International Gastric Cancer Linkage Consortium (IGCLC) classified hereditary diffuse gastric cancer (HDGC) as a genetic risk condition in 1999. Loss of function, mutations in the E-cadherin (CDH1) gene cause HDGC. Patients with a CDH1 mutation are currently advised to undergo preventive gastrectomy, which is thought to significantly lower the chance of developing gastric cancer (Pharoah et al., 2001; Hansford et al., 2015). Notably, HDGC accounts for over 30% of all family gastric malignancies. The genetic origins of the remaining individuals are unknown (Hamilton and Meltzer, 2006).

10.2.3 Proximal gastric cancer (gastric cardia and gastroesophageal junction)

GEJ and distal esophageal adenocarcinoma are sometimes lumped together with proximal gastric cancer (Inomata et al., 2003). Perhaps the most compelling epidemiologic evidence favoring proximal gastric cancer over noncardia gastric cancer is the differential influence of *H. pylori* infection on the development of these illnesses. In certain case-control cohort studies, *H. pylori* infection appears to protect against the formation of more proximal tumors, despite the fact that it is linked to an elevated risk of noncardia gastric adenocarcinoma (Kikuchi et al., 2000; Kuipers, 1997).

10.3 Risk factors associated with gastric cancer

Risk factor and various symptoms associated with gastric cancer are summarized in Fig. 10.2.

10.3.1 Diet

Diet influences the gastric cancer either worsening or inhibiting the condition. Vegetables, fruits, and dietary fibers decrease the risk of gastric cancer, whereas the frying cooking habit and use of pickled food resulted in a higher incidence of gastric cancer. Meat cooked with high heat release certain carcinogenic polycyclic aromatic hydrocarbon and heterocyclic amines (Huang et al., 2020). Pickled food contains nitrites and nitrates that react to form N-Nitroso compounds, which are carcinogenic. Studies also showed that excess intake of salted foods increase the cancer risk (Wu et al., 2021a). In a study, it was reported that subgroups that are positive to *H. pylori* and those who never smoked showed less risk due to higher consumption of lycopene, which is a dietary carotenoid. Hence it is understood that carotenoids like lycopene containing vegetables are safe to add in diet (Kim et al., 2018). The common spice in Indian food is turmeric, contains curcumin, which is antineoplastic nature. It can activate P553 and inhibit the PI3K signaling pathway of cancer, thus inhibiting proliferation and causing programmed cell death in gastric cancerous cells (Fu et al., 2018).

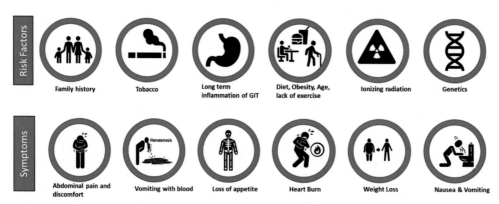

Figure 10.2 Risk factors and symptoms of gastric cancer.

10.3.2 Ionizing radiation

Long term exposure of ionizing radiation leads to genetic mutations. A prospective study of effect of ionizing radiation in survivors from atomic bombing among Japan population indicated that ionizing radiation increased the risk of gastric cancer (Sauvaget et al., 2005). Patients suffering from Hodgkin's lymphoma under sub-diaphragmatic radiotherapy showed dose-dependent risk of gastric cancer. In such cases, the recurrence rate is more, and survivors should be screened for gastric cancer (Morton et al., 2013).

10.3.3 Infections

H. pylori carries cytotoxic elements that cause gastric cancer, as well as a vulnerability toward gastric cancer. The virulent factors in *H. pylori* can activate signaling pathways in cancer, such as PI3K/m-TOR/AKT pathway, JAK/STAT pathway, which control cell proliferation (Alipour, 2021). Such factors include cytotoxin associated gene-A (Cag A) and vacuolating cytotoxin A. Infection with the Epstein-Barr virus increases the risk of gastric cancer by 18 times, and males are more susceptible than females (Tavakoli et al., 2020).

10.3.4 Economic status

Higher mortality rate of gastric cancer is due to the late detection. People with high socioeconomic background and age lesser than 65 years getting good income often have more survival rate. Elderly who are illiterate fails to understand the early symptoms of gastric cancer, which are closely related to gastric acidity and ulcer. Medication without knowing the exact cause also results in gastric cancer (Wu et al., 2014).

10.3.5 Family history

Familial clustering of diseases is common, especially in case of cancers. A family with history of gastric cancer is three times highly prone to get affected, and its incidence depends on the subtype of the gastric cancer and gastric atrophy. In a large prospective study, it was found that family history of gastric cancer was associated with low level of biomarker pepsinogen. Family history is significant in noncardia gastric cancer and insignificant in cardia type (Song et al., 2018).

10.3.6 Genetic variations

Human epidermal growth factor receptor 2 (HER2) is a prototype oncogene that is found on the 17q21 region of chromosome and belongs to the human epidermal growth factor receptor (EGFR) family. This gene encodes for a transmembrane tyrosine kinase receptor protein that controls signaling in cell survival, proliferation, and differentiation (Iqbal and Iqbal, 2014; Mitri et al., 2012). Amplification of the HER2 gene was originally detected in breast cancer and later in gastric carcinoma (Akiyama, 1986; Tai et al., 2010). In one of the findings, the rate of HER2 overexpression in gastric cancer is 12%, while in recent investigations, the rate is around 22.1% using immunohistochemical strain. HER2 overexpression is commonly seen in carcinomas of the cardiac or poximal gastric and GEJ (24%–35%), as well as in intestinal type carcinoma (Albarello et al., 2011). The humanized monoclonal antibody against HER2, trastuzumab (Herceptin), when combined with chemotherapeutic agent, such as cisplatin, capecitabine, or 5-fluorouracil, effectively prolong overall survival and progression-free survival, and increases the response rate in HER2 positive advanced gastric carcinoma, according to a large scale phase III international clinical trial called ToGA (Boku, 2014; Chua and Merrett, 2012). Trastuzumab was given regulatory approval in the United States for patients with HER2 positive metastatic adenocarcinoma of the gastric or GEJ based on these findings. All patients with gastric malignancies should now be regularly screened for the presence of HER2 at the time of diagnosis (Van Cutsem et al., 2009).

10.4 Treatment

Long-term treatment with proton pump inhibitors should be based on a risk-benefit analysis of the individual, as well as a risk factor analysis. This risk is due to the hypergastrinemia as a result of negative feedback mechanism (Cheung and Leung, 2019). In a cohort study, it was reported that patients who received radiotherapy for testicular cancer showed 5.9-fold increased risk of gastric cancer (Hauptmann et al., 2015).

10.4.1 Surgery and chemotherapy

Since then, surgery has been an important part of the therapy of gastric cancer. Endoscopic resection and minimally invasive access are two major technological developments that have altered treatment practise in the previous two decades (Orditura et al., 2014). Early endoscopic resection was basically used for the treatment of gastric cancer few years ago, without the need for substantial abdominal manipulation. However, in order to avoid severe oncological disasters, horizontal and vertical margin invasion, as well as the possibility of nodal involvement, had to be quickly recognized (Hartgrink et al., 2009). For differentiated-type adenocarcinoma without ulcerative signs, endoscopic mucosal resection was first recommended as standard therapy (Sanomura et al., 2012).

Laparoscopic gastric surgery was developed for benign esophagogastric disorders and is now the primary treatment for hiatal hernias and achalasia. Used of laparoscopic treatment was initially limited to the treatment of distal-sided early gastric cancer that did not need total gastrectomy (Kodera et al., 2010). The laparoscopic method has increasingly been expanded to include advanced gastric cancer patients who require complete gastrectomy and radical lymphadenectomy. Despite the fact that evidence is still inconclusive, a number of experiments have demonstrated that laparoscopic therapy of advanced gastric cancer is possible, safe, and oncologically sufficient (Azagra et al., 1999; Ohgami et al., 1999).

Early gastric cancer was treated with minimally invasive treatments, including endoscopic treatment and laparoscopic surgery; however, advanced cancer requires multimodality treatment that includes radiation, chemotherapy, and surgery (Sastre et al., 2006). Due to the findings of wide clinical trials data, surgery with prolonged lymphadenectomy is not been recommended as a conventional treatment for advanced gastric cancer. Adjuvant chemotherapy after curative resection has been proven to improve survival in recent clinical trials when compared to surgery alone. Furthermore, new improvements in targeted drug delivery agents might be useful as one of the treatment options for advanced gastric cancer (Takahashi et al., 2013; Wicki et al., 2015).

10.5 Nanomedicine

Nanomedicine includes the application of nanotechnology for the medical research and intervention. Nanomedicine is currently used for the targeted delivery of several drugs. Nano-based formulations are capable of passive targeting to the tumor tissue (Fig. 10.3). Certain pathophysiological characteristics of the tumor tissue, such as

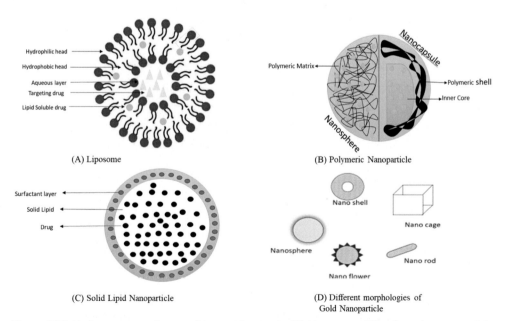

Figure 10.3 Various nanocarriers used in gastric cancer. (A) Liposomes, (B) polymeric nanoparticle, (C) solid lipid carrier, and (D) different morphologies of gold nanoparticle.

enhanced permeability and retention (EPR), make it possible (Ogawara et al., 2013). Delivery of certain monoclonal antibodies is made successful in the form nanoparticles to target micro RNAs, which are overexpressed in gastric cancer. These molecules are well absorbed by the process of receptor-mediated endocytosis with enhanced cellular uptake (Wu et al., 2017). Radiolabeled nanomedicines can be used to study the drug delivery, predicting the therapeutic potential of targeted nanomedicine. Imaging drug release and efficacy is also done by theranostic nanomedicines (Lammers et al., 2011). Targeted detection of gastric cancer cells can be done by a biosensing system and peptide coupled with metal nanoparticles. This distinguishes the targeted and nontargeted cells (Chen et al., 2011).

10.6 Nanocarriers for drug delivery in gastric cancer

10.6.1 Liposomes

Liposomes are spherical vesicles of lipid where the aqueous phase can be entrapped within its bilayer (Fig. 10.3A). Its size ranges from 100−500 nm; functionally, liposomes are of two types. Immunoliposomes are having antibody attached to it, and this can target the antigen, whereas longcirculating liposomes are capable of remaining in the blood for longer period of time (Akbarzadeh et al., 2013). Antineoplastic drug-loaded liposomes are used in first-line chemotherapy for gastric cancer with good clinical efficacy and less adverse events (Han et al., 2019). Salvage therapy of cancer includes combination of two different classes of antineoplastic agents in order to avoid cross resistance. When a combined version of a medication is integrated into a liposome, it also has therapeutic advantages. Combination of PEGylated liposomal doxorubicin and oxaliplatin are used as a second-line therapy for metastatic gastric cancer is one such example. In comparison to their parent molecule, both medicines are effective and have low toxicity. It was found that this treatment is well tolerated among the patients under study (Recchia et al., 2010). Liposome can be used to target certain marker proteins, which are overexpressed in gastric cancer and can be used a therapeutic target. When antineoplastic drugs and small interfering RNA (siRNA) are delivered together, gene silencing occurs, resulting in a synergistic antitumor effect. One such example is SATB1 that is therapeutic target in gastric cancer treatment. Its activity can be suppressed by using gene silencing to inhibit proliferation and promote apoptosis (Peng et al., 2014). Other than drugs, photosensitizers used in photodynamic and radiation therapy can also be liposomalized. Main objective of this less invasive technique is to increase the therapeutic efficacy by targeting the tumor tissues alone. Apoptotic index and tumor accumulation was higher in such in vivo models (Igarashi et al., 2003). Liposomes are used in advanced gastric cancer due to low incidence of adverse effects compared to conventional delivery Paclitaxel is insoluble in water, and its formulation contains cremophore, which exhibits certain toxicities. Liposomal paclitaxel showed high histocompatibility and cellular affinity, stability, and low toxicity (Xu et al., 2013).

Liposomes are currently one of the most widely utilized delivery vehicles, both as an experimental model and as a commercially available drug delivery system. Due to its unique features, i.e., target-specific nature, low toxicity, biodegradability, and biocompatibility, along with its ability to entrap both hydrophilic and lipophilic drugs (Torchilin, 2005). Antitumor activity of the drugs, which are poorly soluble, can be enhanced by formulating liposomes. Peptides-functionalized liposomes tagged within imaging agent are used for the diagnostic and therapeutic purpose (Zheng et al., 2018). As peptides are degraded by various enzymes, which reduce their bioavailability, they are encapsulated in liposomes. PEGylation of such liposomes prevents the degradation of attached targeting proteins (Sonju et al., 2020). Tetraspanin 1 (TSPAN1) is a protein that is significantly produced in cancer, immune cells, and cytoplasm. Tetraspanin contains four lipophilic domains that mediate multiple signal transductions, which regulates and activates the cancer cell development (Hemler, 2014). IL-17 content in gastric cancer correlates TSPAN1 expression positively. Thus it is believed that reducing TSPAN1 expression in Th17 cells can inhibit tumor metastasis by reversing the polarization of Th17 cells which decrease the secretions of IL-17 (Liu et al., 2012). Surface modification of Si-RNA loaded liposomes with Th17 antibody, which has an excellent ability to target Th-17 cells and silencing TSPAN1 mRNA expression. The formed liposomal spheres of cholesterol delivered TSPAN1 Si-RNA to Th17-cells to improve the targeting ratio. As cationic liposomes are cystine-rich, they are readily removed by the reticuloendothelial system (RES) and their short half-life limits their wide applicability. To avoid this, cationic liposomes are PEGylated, which increases their half-life in the body by shielding the charge on the surface of the body (Kim et al., 2010).

PEG-coated liposomes are long-circulating and stable drug carrier, which can be useful for the delivery of the doxorubicin. When PEGylated liposomes are compared with conventional liposomes, PEGylated liposomes last longer in the circulation and are taken up less by the RES (Lukyanov et al., 2004; Duggan and Keating, 2011). Due to long circulation and having the ability to extravasculate through tumor cells, it results in the localization of doxorubicin in the tumor tissue due to EPR effect (Solomon and Gabizon, 2008). Most of the studies showed that PEGylated doxorubicin liposomes had higher intratumor drug concentration with excellent therapeutic response (Gabizon, 2001). Doxorubicin (MCC-465), which is chemically attached to PEG, and the F(ab')2 fragment of monoclonal antibody GAH, which primarily recognizes cell surface molecules in diverse cancer types, were encapsulated in a newly created immunoliposome (Hamaguchi et al., 2004). The antitumor activity of MCC-465 was then compared to GAH nonconjugated PEG-liposomal doxorubicin against GAH positive gastric cancer B37 cells. The findings revealed that MCC-465 was more effective against B37 cells than GAH nonconjugated PEG-liposomal doxorubicin. GAH-tagged liposomes were widely internalized, while GAH-non tagged liposomes were not, according to florescence labeled liposomes. After analyzing all of the clinical data, it was determined that GAH-conjugated immunoliposomes were extremely effective for targeting, particularly in the case of human gastric cancers (Matsumura et al., 2004).

Ginsenosides were coupled with paclitaxel, which was found to suppress human gastric cancer cell growth in a synergistic manner (Jin et al., 2018). In this work, multifunctional liposomal system was developed in which ginsenosides served as a membrane stabilizer and chemotherapy adjuvant. These have benefits such as a long blood circulation duration and the capacity to target actively (Yu et al., 2013) Ginsenoside liposomes were compared to conventional liposomes and PEGylated liposomes in order to investigate long blood circulation. The result showed slower elimination of Ginsenoside loaded liposomes comparable to PEGylated liposomes (Hong et al., 2019). Epirubicin is an anthracycline medication that has anticancer properties against a wide range of cancers. In patients with early gastric cancer and metastatic cancer, it is administered alone or in conjunction with other medicines (Taghdisi et al., 2016). Epirubicin has major side effects that include myelosuppression and cardiotoxicity, which are caused by its poor targeting effect (Bonadonna et al., 1993). Tetrandrine is an analgesic, antiinflammatory, and hypotensive isoquinoline alkaloid. It's been utilized in the clinic to treat cardiovascular disorders, including hypertension and arrhythmia. Tetrandrine acts by reducing tumor metastasis and reversing multidrug resistance in recent years (Yu-Jen, 2002). Jing et al. fabricated R8GD modified epirubicin with tetrandrine liposomes. Epirubicin was utilized as an anticancer drug in these liposomes to constrain tumor cells, and tetrandrine was used as a regulatory agent to stop tumors from spreading. R8GD acted as a targeted ligand for enhancing gastric tumor cell intracellular uptake. Targeted liposomes improved antitumor effectiveness by preventing tumor cell metastasis and obstructing tumor cell energy supply. Targeting liposomes may increase anticancer efficacy by killing tumor cells and eradicating tumors, blocking tumor cell energy supply and inhibiting tumor cell metastasis (Li et al., 2021a).

In one of the study, gastric cancer was effectively treated with R8-modified vinorelbine with schisandrin B liposomes. R8 was integrated into liposomes to increase intracellular absorption, schisandrin B was encapsulated into liposomes to prevent tumor cell metastasis, and vinorelbine was enclosed into liposomes as an anticancer medication. The experiments were carried out in vitro on BGC-823 cells and confirmed in vivo on BGC-823 cell xenografts mice. In vitro results showed that the targeted liposome caused apoptosis in BGC-823 cells, limit tumor cell metastasis and improve tumor cell targeting. As a result, R8 modified vinorelbine combined with schisandrin B liposomes might be a safe and effective treatment for gastric cancer (Li et al., 2021b) (Table 10.2).

Table 10.2 Compilation of liposomal formulations for gastric cancer.

S. No.	Phospholipid/ligand	Method of synthesis	In vitro and in vivo efficacy	Conclusion	References
1.	Egg-phosphatidylcholine & cholesterol	Thin film dispersion and ammonium sulfate method	**In vitro:** BGC-823 cell loaded epirubicin plus tetrandrine liposome IC_{50} for epirubicin liposome was 9.89 ± 0.98 μM, for epirubicin plus tetrandrine liposomes 5.45 ± 0.4 μM, for R_8GD modified epirubicin plus tetrandrine liposomes was 1.9 ± 0.4 μM	Enhanced liposomal stability, active targeting, and low toxicity.	Li et al. (2021a)
2.	Polyethylene glycol-distearoyl phosphatidylethanolamine, cholesterol, egg-phosphatidylcholine & DSPE-PEG2000-R8	Thin film dispersion and ammonium sulfate method	**In vitro:** BGC-823 cell loaded vinorelbine plus schisandrin-B liposomes. The IC50 value of R8 modified vinorelbine with schisandrin-B liposomes was the lowest	Vinorelbine inhibits proliferation of tumor cells, and Schisandrin-B promotes apopotosis and low cytotoxicity	Li et al. (2021b)
3.	Lipid (1,2-dioleoyl-3-trimethyl ammonium–propane) DOTAP, & cholesterol (1:1) molar ratio	Lipid-film hydration method	**In vitro:** Th17-LPDT therapy, CD4 + T cells' polarization to Th17 cells decreased **In vivo:** Treatment with Th17-LPDT substantially reduces the occurrence of gastric cancers	Th17-LPDT prevents gastric cancer growth by lowering TSPAN 1 gene and protein expression in Th17 cells	Lu et al. (2020)
4.	Egg-yolk lecithin & cholesterol	Thin-film hydration	**In vitro:** BGC-823 cell loaded paclitaxel liposome. Ginsenoside liposomes had much lower IC_{50} values than free paclitaxel	Ginsenoside liposomes had a greater inhibitory impact on the BGC-823 cell line, as well as a membrane stabilizer and chemotherapy adjuvant	Hong et al. (2019)

(Continued)

Table 10.2 (Continued)

S. No.	Phospholipid/ligand	Method of synthesis	In vitro and in vivo efficacy	Conclusion	References
5.	3b-[N-(N′,N′ dimethyl amino ethane) carbamoyl] cholesterol (DCChol) Ligand– Doxorubicin and SATB1 shRNA	Thin film hydration	**In vitro**: apoptosis rate was 22.3% in cells treated with free drug and 32.4% in cells treated with shSATB1 and drug loaded liposome **In vivo**: In MKN-28 murine xenograft models, the median time for tumor volume of 2 cm^3 was 30 days for drug loaded liposome	Magnetically targeted and showing thermosenstive release	Peng et al. (2014)
6.	Dipalmitoylphosphatidylcholine, maleimidated cipalmitoylphosphatidyletahnolamine, & cholesterol	—	**In vitro**: GAH nonconjugated PEG liposomal Doxorubicin was considerably less effective against B37 cells than MCC-465	MCC-465 was tolerated well	Matsumura et al. (2004)
7.	Dimyristoyl phosphatidyl choline (DMPC) and dimyristoyl phosphatidyl glycerol (DMPG)	Thin film hydration method	**In vivo**: 69.6% increase in the necrotic area compared to that of free photofrin, which is 39.6%. The apoptotic index was 6.9 ± 0.4 in the liposomal photofrin group and 2.1 ± 0.4 in the free photofrin group	Photofrin level in tumor tissue in the liposomal photofrin group was increase by 2.4–fold of that in the free photofrin group. The apoptotic index of the tumor was also significantly higher	Igarashi et al. (2003)

10.6.2 Polymeric nanoparticles

Polymeric nanoparticles are colloidal system made up of polymers of natural or synthetic in origin. They are of two types: nanoshells and nanocapsule as shown in Fig. 10.3B (Gagliardi et al., 2021). By ligand targeting, polymeric nanoparticles are employed to actively target malignant cells. Tumor cells are characterized by overexpression of certain receptors, which act as biomarker, as this can be used to conjugate polymeric nanoparticles with ligands of such receptors. This results in targeting toward the specific tumor cells of interest. Polymerosome, nanogels, nanoshells, stealth nanoparticles are few examples of such nanocarriers (Zhong et al., 2014). Both natural and synthetic polymers can be used in fabrication of NPs. Biodegradable polymers are more beneficial, e.g., mPEG-PCLco-polymer. Paclitaxel and tetrandrine were encapsulated in core shell type of polymeric NP for the gastric cancer treatment. Formulation provided an oxidation therapy where tetrandrine produced ROS species and activated the programmed death of tumor cells, i.e., apoptosis. This resulted in increased cytotoxicity than free form of drug (Mehnert and Mäder, 2012). Polymeric nanoparticles coated with natural albumin by physical adsorption and interfacial embedding provides enhanced drug delivery to solid tumors (Hyun et al., 2018). Many such albumin conjugated anticancer drugs are under clinical study. They improve the solubility of the anticancer drugs; best example is paclitaxel, which is commercially available (Roviello et al., 2019). Docetaxel is a hydrophobic drug that is effectively used in chemotherapy. It is formulated as nanoparticles using chitosan derivative and also conjugated with peptide, which acts as targeting ligand. It is quite useful to have a pH-dependent accelerated release of active drug in the gastrointestinal environment (Zhang et al., 2019). pH sensitive release of drugs can be achieved by using polymers such as complex of hyaluronic acid with gelatin conjugate polyethylene glycol. Such polymeric structure used in codelivery of doxorubicin in low dose along with natural anticancer agents like epigallocatechin gallate in the treatment of gastric cancer. It also showed surface overexpressed CD44 receptor-mediated tumor recognition. The in vivo study on mouse showed good clinical efficacy of drugs (Mi et al., 2018). Small interfering RNA is used efficiently in gastric cancer where the cause is overexpression of certain genes. Short sequence of RNA can be incorporated into copolymer structure, which gives promised result in treatment of gastric cancer. Copolymers provide low cytotoxicity, flexibility, and low cost (Wu et al., 2010). The biodegradable polymers itself are nontoxic, but the stabilizers used along with it may exhibit toxicity (Grabowski et al., 2015) (Table 10.3).

10.6.3 Solid lipid nanoparticle

Solid lipid nanoparticles (SLN) are the colloidal particles, which are made up of biodegradable physiological lipids that are solid at the room temperature and are safe for use (Mehnert and Mäder, 2012; Pathak and Raghuvanshi, 2015). SLNs are spherical

Table 10.3 Compilation of polymeric nanoparticles reported for gastric cancer.

S. No.	Phospholipid/ligand	Method of synthesis	In vitro and in vivo results	Conclusion	References
1.	N-deoxycholic acid glycol chitosan (DGC), docetaxel	Nanoprecipitation	**In vitro**: Stronger cytotoxicity against cocultured gastric cancer cells and human umbilical vein endothelial cells (co-HUVEC) than free drug within 100 μM **In vivo**: 67.05% inhibition rate	Diffusion & swelling controlled release of docetaxel in the acid environment with stronger cytotoxicity	Zhang et al. (2019)
2.	PEG-conjugated gelatin, picatechin-3-gallate and Doxorubicin	Nanoprecipitation	**In vitro**: 70.89% and 68% accumulative release of drugs at pH 5.0 **In vivo**: tumor volume ratio 1.2 in case of loaded polymeric nanoparticle and 1.8 in case of normal drug solution	Active targeting resulted in great antitumor activity than free drug at the same concentration in a mouse gastric tumor model	Mi et al. (2018)
3.	Methoxy PEG-PCL block copolymer. Paclitaxel and cepharanthine	Nanoprecipitation	**In vivo**: tumor inhibitory rates of the free and drug-loaded polymeric nanoparticle groups on the 12th day were 39.8% and 73.2%, respectively	Improved antitumor efficacy and survival	Zhong et al. (2014)
4.	mPEG-PCL block copolymer, tetrandrin and paclitaxel	Nanoprecipitation	**In vitro**: In first 5 h, less than 50% of tetrandrin was released at a pH of 7.4 while more than 80% was detected in the release medium at a pH of 4.0 **In vivo**: An inhibition rate of 50% in drug-loaded nanoparticle and less than 20% in same dose of free drug	Novel therapeutic strategy based on "oxidation therapy" against gastric cancer shows synergistic and better stability	Mehnert and Mäder (2012)

colloids composed of phospholipids and size ranged from 5−1000 nm as shown in Fig. 10.3C (Duan et al., 2020). SLNs are used in targeted delivery of several anticancer drugs by utilizing active and passive targeting mechanisms (Bayón-Cordero et al., 2019). Particle size reduction is an important step for the oral performance of the low-soluble drugs (Kamiya et al., 2006). Lipophilic drugs like paclitaxel can be successfully incorporated into SLNs. In order to prevent toxic effects and resistance, such drugs are coadministered with another class of antineoplastic agent. Such codelivery of drugs into SLN provides synergistic action and sustained release (Ma et al., 2018). Encapsulating such drugs with SLN increases the surface area as particle size decreases and increases the solubility. SLN of paclitaxel with hydroxypropyl-β-cyclodextrin found to enhance the solubility of paclitaxel by 12−15 folds compared to paclitaxel solution (Baek et al., 2012). Both in vitro and in vivo study of etoposide loaded nanostructures lipid carriers showed enhanced cytotoxicity (Jiang et al., 2016). Enhanced cellular uptake was observed by solid lipid encapsulated drug compared to free form of etoposide in SGC7901 gastric cells. SLNs show enhanced penetration into the mucus membrane due to nanosize of particles and due to EPR affect it endocytosed into the tumor cells, there it follows mitochondria-mediated apoptosis (Wang et al., 2014a). Certain tumor suppressant gene specific to gastric cancer can also be formulated as SLNs (Li et al., 2017). In vitro and in vivo advantages of SLN was shown in Fig. 10.4.

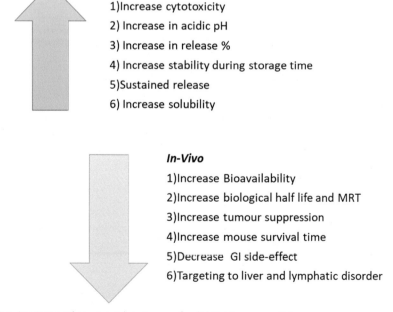

In-Vitro
1) Increase cytotoxicity
2) Increase in acidic pH
3) Increase in release %
4) Increase stability during storage time
5) Sustained release
6) Increase solubility

In-Vivo
1) Increase Bioavailability
2) Increase biological half life and MRT
3) Increase tumour suppression
4) Increase mouse survival time
5) Decrease GI side-effect
6) Targeting to liver and lymphatic disorder

Figure 10.4 In vitro and in vivo advantages of solid lipid nanoparticles.

SLNs and nanostructured lipid carriers (NLC) have several advantages such as they can be prepared without using an organic solvent and can be constructed by using biocompatible and biodegradable ingredients, encapsulating drugs and reducing their adverse effects on the GI tract, having low sensitivity toward the acidic environment and have the ability to encapsulate hydrophobic drugs easily. Fig. 10.5 shows the use of SLN as a promising nanocarrier in hydrophobic drug delivery (Naseri et al., 2015; Ghasemiyeh and Mohammadi-Samani, 2018). SLNs also show few disadvantages such as an expulsion of the encapsulated drug at the time of storage and low drug loading. This leads to the formation of a NLC which is a mixture of solids and liquids lipids to produce NP that remain solid at room and body temperature (Lingayat et al., 2017). Compare to SLNs, NLCs have more drug loading capacity and less loss during storage. SLNs are prepared by using solid fats, surfactants, and drugs (Poonia et al., 2016). The selection of appropriate lipids and surfactants combination is an important step in the formulation of lipid nanoparticles. To prevent aggregation and stabilize the dispersed lipid system in the aqueous phase of the NP surfactants are used (Nasirizadeh and Malaekeh-Nikouei, 2020). In the preparation of SLNs, the lipids used should be physiologically biocompatible and biodegradable with low toxicity, as this lipid should have the ability to promote oral absorption of the encapsulated drugs through selective lymphatic uptake (Jenning et al., 2000). NPs prepared by using such lipids show high solubility and strong mucosal adhesion with increased GI-residence time (Radomska-Soukharev, 2007). By promoting drug permeation across the GI tract and improving

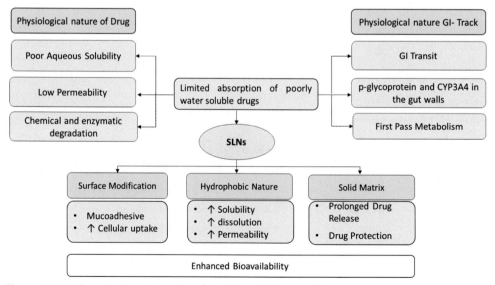

Figure 10.5 Schematic representation of oral drug delivery and SLNs as promising nanocarriers in hydrophobic drug delivery. *SLNs*, Solid lipid nanoparticles.

cellular uptake, the SLN enhanced drug absorption. Lipid NPs are prepared by multiple methods such as high-pressure homogenization, which includes hot and cold homogenization, sonication, high-shear homogenization, microemulsion method, solvent evaporation method, lyophilization, spray drying, solvent injection method (Mukherjee et al., 2009). They protect sensitive drugs from degradation in an acidic environment, and they have some impacts on stability during storage. As a consequence, the drug is released at the targeted site (Nasirizadeh and Malaekeh-Nikouei, 2020). Encapsulating cytotoxic drugs in SLN may reduce their exposure to GI tract and reduce their adverse effect. For the achievement of oral bioavailability suitable solubility of the drug is necessary. Some anticancer drugs are lipophilic, possess low solubility, and have a low absorption rate, encapsulating such drugs in SLN can overcome the solubility problem (Bummer, 2004). PEGylation of the NP is also used as a method for improvement of the mucus penetration. In one of the studies, SLN was formulated using 10% PEG, which allows for the most drug penetration across the cellular layer. SLN showed excellent potential to enhance the bioavailability and GI absorption of various drugs, e.g., all-trans retinoic acid (ATRA) absorption was increased significantly by formulating SLNs. As the particle size reduction is an important step for the oral performance of the low soluble drugs (Kamiya et al., 2006). Encapsulating such drugs with SLN increases the surface area as particle size decreases and increases the solubility. SLN of paclitaxel with hydroxypropyl-β-cyclodextrin enhanced solubility of paclitaxel by 12–15 folds compared to paclitaxel solution (Baek et al., 2012).

Epirubicin-loaded lysine SLNs were formulated and assessed as an effective targeted delivery system. Amino acid-coupled SLNs were synthesized and analyzed in terms of shape, cytotoxicity, drug loading, and release pattern. From lysine SLNs, 50% of epirubicin was released in 1 h, compared to unchanged or modified SLNs, which showed 68% of drug release in 48 hr. According to toxicity investigation, the epirubicin loaded lysin-SLN has an antiproliferative impact on the cell-lines MCF-7BC, with an 3 μm IC50 value. The manufactured targeted drug delivery system may be a promising option for cancer targeted therapy after in vivo investigations (Bayat et al., 2021) (Table 10.4).

Curcumin is naturally occurring constituent from "Curcuma longa," which possess antibacterial, anticancer, antiviral, antimicrobial, antiinflammatory properties. Curcumin has been used in anticancer drugs (repressing IL-10 and 18). Curcumin has anticancer potential which acts by lowering high levels of cyclin D1 and CDK4 (proteins which are involved in cell cycle proliferation) and therefore blocking the cell cycle in the G1 phase and induce apoptosis. Curcumin used with standard anticancer medicines, such as doxorubicin, 5-fluorouracil, cisplatin, and paclitaxel, has been explored to improve the chemotherapy impact. Due to its poor aqueous solubility, poor bioavailability, physiological instability, and rapid metabolism, its clinical application is limited. To overcome

Table 10.4 Compilation of solid lipid nanoparticles reported for gastric cancer.

S. No.	Formulation	Lipid type/emulsifier	Method	In vitro and in vivo efficacy	Conclusion	References
1.	Chrysin loaded SLNs	—	High shear homogenizer	**In vitro**: studies show that compared to pure chrysin and C-SLN, MC-SLN is less hemolytic but more cytotoxic and preferred to be taken up by ACG tumor cells	Targeting efficiency and bioavailability was better	Pandey et al. (2021)
2.	Curcumin–SLN	Glyceryl monostearate, Tween 80, PEG–600, phospholipon 90G	High pressure hot homogenization technique	—	Enhanced bioavailability and solubility	Gupta et al. (2020)
3.	Lysine decorated SLN	Tripalmitin glyceride and steric acid	Solvent diffusion method	Epirubicin—loaded lysin-SLNs had an anti-proliferative impact on MCF-7 BC cells with an IC$_{50}$ value of 3µM, according to a toxicity investigation	Remarkable effect on breast cancer cell lines	Bayat et al. (2021)
4.	Etoposide–NLC	Glycerol monostearate, soya bean phosphatidylcholine	Solvent injection method	Etoposide–NLCs improved in vitro and in vivo antitumor activity against SGC7901 cells	Achieve sustained behavior and improve cytotoxicity	Jiang et al. (2016)
5.	Hydroxypropyl-β–CD-SLN	Stearic acid, poloxamer 188	Hot sonication Method	**In vitro**: Caco-2 lines loaded with Paclitaxel-SLN, Paclitaxel solutions shows 90% of paclitaxel release in 1 h, the smPSH shows $89.70 \pm 3.99\%$ controlled release of paclitaxel for 24 h and burst release of $36.54\% \pm 4.81\%$ in 1 h	Cellular uptake increased by 5.3 fold, Solubility enhanced by 12- to 15-fold	Baek et al. (2012)

these barriers, the curcumin-encapsulated lipidic nanoconstructed SLNs using glyceryl monostearate, tween 80, PEG-600 prepared by high-pressure hot homogenization method, where results revealed enhanced the bioavailability, solubility and reduced the chemical degradation of the curcumin (Gupta et al., 2020). Also, paclitaxel-loaded tri-myristin SLN with the egg L-α-phosphatidylcholine (PC) and DSPE−methyl polyethylene glycol-2000 as emulsifier showed an increase in intracellular uptake of paclitaxel in MCF/ADR by caveola-mediated endocytosis (Xu et al., 2018) PEGylation of the NP is also used as a method for improvement of the mucus penetrating properties. In one of the studies, SLN was formulated using 10% PEG that provides the highest level of drug permeation across the cellular layer (Salah et al., 2020). Morin hydrate is a natural bioflavonoid used in food and traditional medicine on a large scale. According to numerous research reports, Morin hydrate has shown antiinflammatory, antioxidant, and antiproliferative effects (Baek et al., 2012). This bioflavonoid is reported to increase apoptosis in various cancers (Sivaramakrishnan et al., 2008). When Morin hydrate SLNs were formulated, they showed excellent results because of their outstanding biocompatibility, control of drug release, high drug loading, avoiding the use of organic solvents, high stability, and increased oral bioavailability (Ensign et al., 2012). Cell culture experiments revealed three times higher cytotoxicity to the cancerous cells via Morin hydrate-loaded SLN, which indicates its high efficacy compared to conventional Morin hydrate (Karamchedu et al., 2020).

10.6.4 Gold nanoparticles

Gold nanoparticles are of different morphologies and can range from 1 to 100 nm (Fig. 10.3D). Gold nanoparticles can be prepared by mechanical and chemical methods. Mechanical methods include top-down and bottom-up approaches. Top-down approach involves slicing of bulk materials into simple units, whereas bottom-up includes simple addition of individual units. Chemical methods include aqueous reduction of $HAuCl_4$ by sodium citrate (Hu et al., 2020). The surface of gold nanoparticles is conjugated with ligands and can be used for drug delivery. Noncovalent conjugation of ligands can be used for gene delivery. Larger biomolecules can be successfully delivered by gold nanoparticles. Photothermal destruction of tumor tissue made possible using gold nanoparticles (Ghosh, 2008). Being inorganic or metal in origin also possesses certain toxicity issues. Toxicity of gold nanoparticles is influenced by many factors. Increase in the particle size prevents the ease of endocytosis and increase the toxicity at cellular level. It also results in accumulation in certain organs like kidney and liver. Surface modification with anionic groups is safer as the cationic group shows interaction with the negatively charged cell structures. It also interacts with the immune system. Hence all such factors have to be optimized to avoid such toxicities (Jia et al., 2017). To overcome toxicity issues, chitosan-modified gold nanoparticles

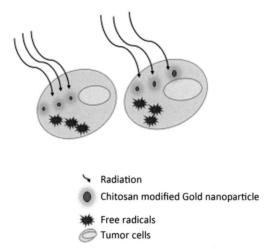

↘ Radiation
⬤ Chitosan modified Gold nanoparticle
✳ Free radicals
🥚 Tumor cells

Figure 10.6 Mechanism of chitosan modified gold nanoparticle with enhanced tumor damage capacity.

are beneficial. It gave them a better biocompatibility. This can be used for radiotherapy as it showed increased gastric cell radiation sensitivity (Zhang et al., 2011). Mechanism of chitosan-modified gold nanoparticle demonstrated in Fig. 10.6.

Aptamers for gene therapy in gastric cancer can be delivered by gold nanoparticles. They provide targeted delivery into the gastric tumor tissue. The drug release and uptake can be estimated with the help of fluorescence spectroscopy (Zhang et al., 2020). Herbal drugs can also be incorporated into gold nanoparticles. One such example is "*Cardiospermum halicacabum,*" which has good antitumor activity. The in vivo study in AGS gastric carcinoma cells showed apoptotic activity by inhibiting inducing antiapoptotic proteins (Li et al., 2019). "*Vitex negundo*"-loaded gold nanoparticles showed higher cytotoxicity in tumor tissue due to their ability to induce the caspases and other proapoptotic proteins (Yun et al., 2020). Resistance is the major drawback that comes in view of long-term use of anticancer drugs. Trastuzumab, which is a monoclonal antibody and extensively used in cancer therapy, shows resistance. This may be due to the upregulation of m-TOR, loss of phosphatase activity, and expression of certain proteins. In order to overcome resistance, human epidermal growth factor 2 targeted gold nanoparticles were prepared by conjugating Trastuzumab. In vitro and in vivo studies showed positive results in overcoming the resistance, but systemic delivery of these drugs has to be further studied (Kubota et al., 2018). Early detection of gastric cancer can decrease the mortality rate. One such example is detection of gastric cancer biomarkers, which are volatile in nature by breath or exhaled air. It involves the transport of sensors with the help of gold nanoparticles (Chen et al., 2016) (Table 10.5).

Table 10.5 Compilation of gold nanoparticles reported for gastric cancer treatment.

S. No.	Polymer/ligand	In vitro and in vivo efficacy	Conclusion	References
1.	Chitosan-modified gold nanoparticle	**In vivo**: Survival fraction was 56.3%,	Gold nanoparticles can enhance the cell radiation therapeutic sensitivity	Barzegar Behrooz et al. (2017)
2.	Gold nanoparticle conjugated with AS1411 aptamer	**In vitro**: Low IC_{50} of NPs when exposed to the laser at 2 or 2.5 W/cm^2 compared to the free drug **In vivo**: Developed formulation showed higher activity (about 22%) with laser exposure at 2.5 W/cm^2 in comparision to free drug (about 30%)	Appropriate size, stability, and safety, Specifically targeting ability, and potent antitumor effect	Zhang et al. (2020)
3.	Cardiospermum halicacabum gold nanoparticle	**In vitro**: IC50 25 µg/mol	Potent anticancer in vitro activity	Li et al. (2019)
4.	Trastuzumab gold nanoparticle	**In vivo**: IC50 dose of T-AuNPs on NCI-N87 cells was 4.6×109 particles/mL and a dose of Tmab included in this concentration of T-AuNPs was 1.3 µg/mL	Overcome resistance to trastuzumab-induced resistance	Kubota et al. (2018)

10.6.5 Dendrimers

Dendrimers are radially symmetric, branched with monodisperse structure in nanosize range (Sampathkumar and Yarema, 2007). The nanocarrier dendrimer is derived from the Greek word "dendron" that means "tress" and "Meros," which means "part." In 1978, dendrimers were discovered as unimolecular, artificial polymeric systems with their unique structural properties created an excellent interest and attracted many researchers. Vogtle and his team by using Michael reactions of amines and acetonitrile formulates high branded molecules, which cause a reduction of nitriles to amines (Liu and Fréchet, 1999; Kesharwani et al., 2014). In 1980, first family of dendritic polyami-done (PAMAM) was synthesized (Chauhan and Kaul, 2018). The structure of dendrimers consists of three components: (1) core that may be one or more than one reactive group. (2) repeating branched units also known as generation monomers, which bonds to initiator core and it is referred to as generations. (3) peripheral surface group that is used to determine the nature of dendrimers and bonds in branch unit of each generation (Wang et al., 2018). Adding two or four branched units to the core of dendrimers produces the first generation, and adding branched units to monomers of the first generation produces the second generation. The three structural components of dendrimers, core, interior, and periphery, determine the physical and chemical characteristics of dendrimers. The molecular weight and number of tertiary amine groups are determined by the core multiplicity and branch cell multiplicity of dendrimers (Najafi et al., 2020). The size of dendrimers also depends upon the generation, and it can be controlled by the method of preparation (Abbasi et al., 2014). Dendrimer shape also play a role in determining the particular binding of a functional group on its surface. Dendrimers have two types of shapes: (1) a spherical shape and (2) an ellipsoid shape (Nanjwade et al., 2009). Another feature of dendrimers is low viscosity, which is highest with 4-generation and diminishes as generation rises. Dendrimers have a high degree of monodispersibility, which makes them a nanosize tool in bioavailability and distribution, along with that the reactivity and solubility depend upon the nature of the end group on the dendrimer surface (Tripathy and Das, 2013). For example, if the dendrimer surface consists of the lipophobic terminal groups, it develops a highly soluble structure in the aqueous solvent, and the insolubility of the lipophilic end group on the dendrimers increases. Dendrimers, on the other hand, have a lipophilic inner and a lipophobic outside, indicating their unimolecular origin, which led to their use as a solubility booster (Baig et al., 2015). Nanostructure within the size of 1−10 nm can easily cross the cell membrane of the tumor cell. Dendrimers are also known as artificial proteins as they possess similarities in size with other cellular components (Chen et al., 2003). For example, 2-generation dendrimers have the same size as insulin, 7- and 10-generation dendrimers mimic histone clusters, and cytochromic protein's shape and size are mimiced by 3-generation dendrimers. Compare to traditional molecules, dendrimer provides an exactly controlled molecular surface (Yang and Kao, 2006). Several biodegradable polymers are extensively used for the preparation of dendrimer (Jain et al., 2010).

PAMAM is extensively used as dendrimer in chemotherapy of cancer. PAMAM can be conjugated with aptamer, which is single strand of oligonucleotides capable of binding to target molecule without eliciting immunogenicity. Antineoplastic agents like 5-fluorouracil can be successfully incorporated into dendrimer providing targeted delivery for gastric cancer (Barzegar Behrooz et al., 2017). Capecitabine used in neoadjuvant therapy of cancer can also be complexed with PAMAM dendrimer. *In vivo* results were successful against target delivery to gastric cancer in mice (Li et al., 2018). Dendrimer can also be used for gene therapy. Certain gene can be targeted toward gastric cancerous cells by entrapping nanoparticles of interest into a dendrimer

(Nabavizadeh, 2019). Certain functional group can be conjugated with dendrimer using cross linkers as a carrier for delivering micro RNA specific to gastric cancer with antitumor efficacy (Song et al., 2019). Labeling the dendrimer with radionuclide is used to reduce the dose of radiopharmaceutical by delivering it on the target site (Liko et al., 2016). Surface of the dendrimer is modified with pH sensitive polymer and conjugated with doxorubicin to form stimuli responsive vesicle to treat gastric cancer (Nie et al., 2016).

Most of the anticancer drugs show poor water solubility and required various solvents for their miscibility, but these solvents show carcinogenic properties. So there is a need to fabricate a delivery system that increases solubility, pharmacokinetic behaviors, and controlled-released properties, selection of carrier based on which lacks the unwanted interaction between drug molecule and other components (Guljar and Patel, 2013). Dendrimers are considered suitable carriers for different drug molecules as they show versatile features such as high aqueous solubility, controlled releas, and monodispersibility that enhance cellular uptake, biodistribution, an increased therapeutic index, and low toxicity of anticancer medication, as well as increased drug accumulation in the tumor location due to the EPR effect (Wolinsky and Grinstaff, 2008; Yang, 2016). Sugar compounds, such as galactose and mannose, can be utilized as targeting moieties on the surface of the ligand to improve cellular absorption at specific locations for targeted treatment (Woller and Cloninger, 2001).

Dendrimers have complex structural characteristics, such as toxicity owing to the presence of amine groups on the surface, and its application in cancer therapy is limited due to its high actual clearance rate from the body during cancer chemotherapy. Dendrimers create a compound with metals, and their extended usage causes cytotoxicity, hemolytic toxicity, and hematological toxicity, to name a few (Madaan et al., 2014). Dendrimers have the size 1−10 nm can easily mimic biological components, this results in the interaction of dendrimers with biological components such as vitamins, nucleic acids, ions, metals, and plasma membrane (Tomalia, 2005). In comparison to anionic and neutral dendrimers, cationic dendrimers are more hazardous (Bodewein et al., 2016). Hemolytic toxicity occurs when cationic charges on the surface of dendrimers interact with negative charges on the surface of the cell membrane of RBCs, resulting in a drop in RBC counts and an increase in WBC counts (Ziemba et al., 2012). Researcher proves that the toxicity of dendrimers is mostly determined by their generation (size), concentration, type of terminal ends, and incubation period (Yellepeddi et al., 2009). Types and benefits of dendrimer surface functionalization with different targeting moiety are shown in Fig. 10.7.

The most complicated barrier for dendrimers is the interaction with the cell membrane, which enhances the permeability of dendrimers across the cell membrane but causes various side effects, such as membrane thinning, membrane disruption, formation of nanoholes, which causes leakage of cytosolic proteins and ends with cell lysis.

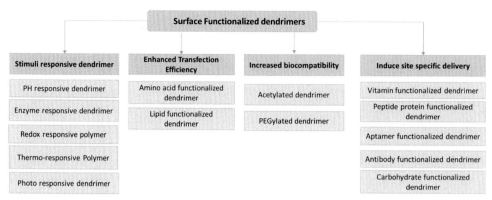

Figure 10.7 Benefits of dendrimer surface functionalization with various targeting moiety in terms of medication distribution.

Membrane disruption is caused by high concentrations and densities of cationic charges, and large molecular size dendrimers impact nanohole creation and membrane rupture (Jain et al., 2010; Mecke et al., 2004). Another barrier for dendrimers is their high renal clearance and accumulation in the liver and kidneys, which is associated with a positive charge and small size of dendrimers (Wijagkanalan et al., 2011). Accumulation in various organs depends upon the size (generation) generally with size less than 5 nm accumulates in the kidneys, and large size dendrimers are recognized by RES and get accumulated in the liver, which results in serious injuries. To overcome such barriers was a great challenge in front of scientists. Therefore, functionalization of dendrimers with various targeted moieties such as antibodies, amino acids, vitamins, and PEG chain enhance bioavailability, efficacy of transfection, involves site-specific administration, improved therapeutic efficiency, and toxicity reduction of two or more targeted moieties can be connected to the surface of dendrimers at the same time, resulting in a multifunctional system (He et al., 2011). Fabrication of dendrimers with biocompatible moieties also increases biocompatibility, and the circulation time of dendrimers is also a method of functionalization (Lesniak et al., 2005). Cationic dendrimers are more toxic as compared to other dendrimers; therefore, the capping of cationic charges in dendrimers and the decrease in electrostatic interaction between the cell membrane and the cationic surface are important for lowering the toxicity. Functionalization of dendrimers with PEG is most suitable. PEGylation of dendrimers improves pharmacokinetics behaviors, biodistribution, stability and also enhance drug loading capacity (Guillaudeu et al., 2008). Researcher shows that encapsulation of anticancer drugs with PEGylation dendrimers shows high drug loading capacity (Luong et al., 2016). Another way to reduce the toxicity of dendrimers is acetylation by conjugating to the terminal surface group, which neutralized the positive charges on dendrimers surface. Compared to PEGylation, acetylation has several advantages, which include (1) PEG chain has high steric hindrance compare to acetylation. (2) High efficiency and simplicity. (3) Required low amount of acetylation. (4) Acetylated dendrimers have more permeability than PEGylated one (Majoros et al., 2003; Kolhatkar et al., 2007). Other moieties, including peptides, amino acids, and carbohydrates, are also used to decrease toxicity through neutralization of positive charge. In cancer therapy, lack of target specificity is the major barrier, as compared to healthy cells special receptors utilized to deliver extra nutrients to cells were overexpressed in malignant cells, ligands with affinity for these receptors might be utilized as targeting moieties for dendrimer surface functionalization, resulting in drug accumulation at the tumor location by suppressing RES and increasing EPR effect. Ligands used are folic acid, transferrin, and biotin (Gupta et al., 2010). High transfection efficiency is shown by higher generation dendrimers but also results in severe toxicities. Besides, low generation shows low toxicity with low transfection efficiency. Therefore, to reduce such toxicities, surfaces of dendrimers are conjugated with acetyl and PEG group moieties, which results in a decrease in positive charge on the surface by neutralizing them. Transfection efficiency can also be increased by functionalization of dendrimers with lipids, amino acids (arginine), fluorination, β-CD, etc. (Abedi-Gaballu et al., 2018) (Table 10.6).

10.6.6 Quantum dots

Quantum dots are nanocarriers made up of semiconductor materials containing core and a shell. There are three types of quantum dots mainly graphene quantum dots, carbon nanodots, and polymer dots. Based on the composition, classification is shown in Table 10.7 Core type of QD consists of single materials, such as metals. Core shell QD is composed of core and shell with a semiconductor core encapsulated by another semiconductor. Alloyed type of QD is homogenous mixture of semiconductors (Alami and Faraj, 2022).

Quantum dots are particularly used in the imaging of cells, both plant and animal cells. Multicolor and multiplexing potentialities of quantum dots are used for the detection of biomarkers in cancer (Valizadeh et al., 2012). Clinicopathologic data of gastric cancer patients show elevated levels of carbohydrate antigen 72.4 in the gastric juice, which could be treated as an important biomarker (Virgilio et al., 2020). Labeling the monoclonal antibodies against CA 72.4, conjugating with CdSe/ZnSe quantum dots and combining charge coupled device for fluorescence detection could be successfully utilized for the diagnosis of gastric cancer. These strips are more accurate and sensitive compared to traditional flow strips used for biomarker detection (Yan et al., 2016a). Carbon dots are more advantageous than semiconductor dots in terms of biocompatibility. Intrinsic potential hazards of heavy metal elements can be avoided using carbon dots. Fluorescent carbon dots can be used for delivering siRNA to the tumor tissue to arrest the tumor growth. This methodology could be used for

Table 10.6 Compilation of dendrimers reported for gastric cancer treatment.

S. No.	Polymer/ligand	In vitro and in vivo efficacy	Conclusion	References
1.	PEG, PAMAM with boron-dipyrrome-thene followed by labeling with APTAS1411 aptamer	**In vitro**: IC50 of PAMAM-PEG and PAMAM-PEG-APTAS1411 was more than 1 µg /mL **In vivo**: In HEK293 (healthy) cells, there was 64.38% cellular uptake of the free drug, whereas in MKN45 cancer-positive cells, cellular uptake was rise to 98.78%	Increased PAMAM-PEG-5-FU uptake by MKN45 gastric cancer cells	Barzegar Behrooz et al. (2017)
2.	HA-G5 PAMAM and plasmid METase	Tumor volume became half when compared with free drug	Significantly suppressed tumor growth	Li et al. (2018)
3.	h-PAMAM, PEG, cis-aconityl-doxorubicin	**In vitro**: As pH decreases drug release increases. DOX release increased from 49.5%—93.0% and 30%—73.9% in 72 h as the pH decreased from 7.4 to 5.0 in PPCD conjugate and vesicles respectively **In vivo**: 90% of cell viability was observed	Safe and effective drug delivery system for the therapy of gastric cancer	Li et al. (2018)

Table 10.7 Types of quantum dots (Alami and Faraj, 2022).

Quantum dot	Examples
Single core structure	Cds, CdSe, ZnSe, CdTe
Core/shell structure	CdSe, ZnTe, CdTe
Alloy	CuXZn1-XS HgXCd1-XTe ZnXCd1-XSe

imaging and treatment hence a theranostic (Wang et al., 2014b). Layered double hydroxides (LDHs) are biocompatible and biodegradable 2D nanomaterial used as carrier for drug delivery. They show a pH dependent release. Graphene, which has good optical properties, can be used to develop quantum dots for the imaging of gastric tumors. Both in vitro and in vivo fluorescence imaging capability of graphene dots has been demonstrated (Wu et al., 2021b).

Quantum dots consist of inorganic nanomaterials with immanent fluorescent, electronic and optical properties, which also can be modified to attain water solubility and can be fabricated to a small size as 2—5 nm. The physicochemical properties of QDs depend on the synthesis technique; they can be prepared by two methods: (1) biosynthetically (using bacteria) or (2) synthetically (using homogenization, microwave production, etc.) (Mi et al., 2011). In one of the studies, both methods are been compared to check their nature of toxicity, QDs prepared by using *E. coli* and by microwave production, and it is concluded as QDs generated using microwave technique are more highly toxic compare to E. coli. PEGylation techniques also are used to increase biodistribution, stability and to reduce the toxicity of Quantum dots (Kominkova et al., 2017). Traditional QDs are made out of a multilayer structures of a metallic core material. Most frequently cadmium selenide or cadmium sulfide, which emit fluorescence were included into the system. A coating substance is usually applied to the core to prevent it from leaking and to offer protection. Physicochemical characterization of QDs is done to a large extent determining their size, morphology, stability, toxicity, biocompatibility, and photoluminance (Kim et al., 2015). The performance of the QDs can be strengthen by coating the surface with a biocompatible material such as PEG or antibodies (Zhang et al., 2008).

Apoptosis is a mechanism that regulates cell death, but in cancer, the mechanism gets dysregulated. Furthermore, apoptosis can be employed to treat a variety of cancers (Singh et al., 2012). An experiment is performed in vivo to image apoptotic cells in zebrafish. In this experiment, the graphene QDs are conjugated using annexin antibodies and then introduced. Later, it was observed that apoptotic cells in fish show red color distinguishable from the cells which did not (Garcia-Calvo et al., 2021). Further studies evaluate that at low doses there are low toxicity, and this method can be used as an investigation tool for various diseases and Cancers (Roy et al., 2015). RNase A is used as a template to synthesize cadmium telluride QDs, which show inhibition of tumor cells. Here QDs are prepared by using RNase-A-Cdteqds with HER2 monoclonal antibody and investigates to check the ability of targeted diagnosis in the therapy of gastric cancer and concluded as HER2ase QD nanoprobes can be used in imaging and treating gastric cancer (Ruan et al., 2012) (Table 10.8).

10.6.7 Carbon nanotubes

Carbon nanotubes (CNTs) are commonly known as buckytubes, with diameters ranging from roughly 1 to 10 nm and lengths up to mm. The cylindrical carbon molecules have high aspect ratios (length-to-diameter values), often exceeding 10^3 (Sheikhpour et al., 2017). Multiwall (MWCNTs), single-wall (SWCNTs) and double

Table 10.8 Summary table of quantum dots.

Sr. No.	Formulation	In vitro and in vivo efficacy	Conclusion	References
1.	CdSe/ZnS quantum dot-labeled lateral flow strips	**In vitro**: sensitivity of 2 IU/mL and 10 min detection time	Quick biomarker detection of gastric cancer	Yan et al. (2016)
2.	Fluorescent carbon dot containing siRNA-PEI	**In vivo**: significant increase in cellular delivery of siRNA, inducing efficient knockdown for survivin protein to 6.1%	Carbon dot can be used as imaging agent and siRNA nanocarrier	Wang et al. (2014b)
3.	Layered hydroxide — sulfur doped — QD conjugated with etoposide	**In vivo**: cell proliferation was the lowest, at 35%, and apoptosis was 35% higher than with free etoposide	Multifunctional agent for visualization therapy	Wu et al. (2021b)

-wall (DWCNTs) are the three important types of CNTs (Baughman et al., 2002). Yang et al. described that CNTs can be used in both diagnosis and therapy of cancers owing to its unique properties like drug encapsulation, high surface area, and conjugation ability. CNTs have been hailed as promising agents for cancer diagnostics and treatment. CNTs have the capacity to choose molecules by being functionalized with different types of molecules, making them suitable for medication delivery systems (Sheikhpour et al., 2017; Yang et al., 2007). Many scientists reviewed the use of CNTs for in vivo delivery and concluded that well-functionalized nanotubes had no appreciable toxicity. For manufacturing of CNTs, different techniques are used such as chemical, physical, and some miscellaneous methods. Arc discharge and laser ablation are two physical techniques that may be utilized to make SWCNTs and MWCNTs of various sizes (Mylvaganam and Zhang, 2007). Chemical schemes such as high-pressure carbon monoxide reaction, cobalt molybdenum, and vapor deposition, procedure is also frequently employed to make various types of CNTs. Electrolysis, flame synthesis, and helium arc discharges are used as the miscellaneous methods, which are rarely used for the fabrication of CNTs (Kingston and Simard, 2003; Fu and Yu, 2014). In which the helium arc discharge technique appears to have commercial uses (Hutchison et al., 2001). The most significant limitations in regard to CNTs are their hydrophobicity and cytotoxicity. Although several studies have determined that CNTs have no cytotoxicity, but various degrees of cytotoxicity on different cells are mentioned in certain research. To overcome these limitations, modifications of CNTs can be done (Shao et al., 2013). The toxicity and the hydrophobicity of the drug can be decreased by functionalization of CNTs by various chemical groups. CNTs have benefits such as cell permeability, chemical accessibility, and photothermal characteristics (Sanginario et al., 2017). Sh-MWCNT-amide was made by adding isatin derivatives to carboxylated short MWCNTs (Sh-MWCNTs-COOH), and Sh-MWCNT-amide was made by adding hydrazine to carboxylated short MWCNTs (Sh-MWCNTs-COOH). The harmful effects of nanotubes on MKN-45 cell-line, cells were next investigated. The findings revealed that ShMWCNT-amide has a high toxicity and might be used in chemotropic techniques. MWCNT-quino was created by combining MWCNT-amide with 2-aminobenzophenone to create another form of functionalized MWCNT. In comparison to earlier studies of CNTs, the effects of MWCNT-quino on the multiplication of MKN-45 cells were examined, and the findings revealed that MWCNT-quino had more harmful effects. Sh-MWCNT-imidazole was produced by modifying the Sh-MWCNTs by aromatic aldehyde (Tahermansouri and Ghobadinejad, 2013). MKN-45 cells were then tested to see if the modified MWCNT had any inhibitory effects on their multiplication. Sh-MWCNT-imidazole has a significant toxicity against gastric cancer cells (71%—77%), according to the findings. An investigation was conducted, CNTs were used to target stem cells of gastric cancer (Tahermansouri and Chitgar, 2013). The SWCNTs were fabricated using chitosan and hyaluronic acid as coating agents and functionalization agents, respectively, and loaded with salinomycin. The mammosphere and colon production skills of gastric cancer stem cells were evaluated utilizing the stated CNTs, and the findings revealed a substantial reduction in these cells' capacities, which explains that the hyaluronic acid is a component of the structure that is required for its function. Because free hyaluronic acid inhibits cellular absorption of SAL-SWCNT-CHI-HA, an endocytosis mechanism for hyaluronic acid entrance into the structure is likely. It was also reported that SAL-SWCNT-CHI-antitumor HA's effects were achieved by triggering apoptosis in gastric cancer stem cells and reaching to the mammospheres of cancer stem cells (Yao et al., 2014).

According to Nia et al. research, to act as a vehicle for shRNA delivery, a modified branching polyethylenimine (PEI) was grafted to carboxylated (SWCNT) through a polyethylene glycol (PEG) linker. Because the nucleolin receptor was overexpressed on the surface of the cancer cells, the SWCNT-PEG-PEI was coupled to the AS1411 aptamer enabling codelivery of the drug to the tumor cells. In a cell survival testing, the demonstrated targeted delivery technique reduced the development of nucleolin-abundant gastric cancer cells with remarkable cell selectivity in a GFP expression and transfection experiment against L929 and AGS cells. Following that, it was shown that pairing the selected shRNAs with DOX had a powerful tumoricidal effect (Taghavi et al., 2017). For Photoacoustic imaging of in vivo gastric cancer cells, RGD coupled gold nanorods coated with silica on the surface of MWCNTs were used. The effects of RGD-attached sGNR/MWNT (Silica coated Gold nanorods) probes on the viability of MGC8o3 and GES-1 cells were examined after RGD peptides were coupled with the sGNR/MWNT nanostructure. The nude mice's gastric cell lines were injected with RGD-conjugated sGNR/MWNT probes. According to the findings, the RGD-coupled sGNR/MWNT probes exhibited high Hydrophilicity and negligible cytotoxicity were capable of targeting in vivo gastric cancer cells, and had strong photoacoustic imaging in the nude model and these RG-D conjugated MWCNTs demonstrate outstanding photothermal treatment and photoacoustic imaging applications (Wang et al., 2014c) (Table 10.9).

10.7 Gene therapy in gastric cancer

Techniques for directly altering a cell's genetic information have substantially increased hopes for genetic manipulations in therapeutics. These breakthroughs have sparked optimism that diseases which appeared to be incurable may be healed in the near future (Verma et al., 2000). Gene therapy has emerged as a unique therapeutic and even preventative intervention against cancer at the level of cellular gene expression (Cavazzana-Calvo et al., 2004). Gene therapy is the therapeutic introduction and expression of an exogenous gene into human cells and it is frequently confined to human disorders with single-gene defects (Khalighinejad et al., 2008). Oncological studies define it as the introduction of DNA into cells (either neoplastic or normal) in order to shrink or eliminate a malignant tumor (Roth and Cristiano, 1997). This can be accomplished by causing malignant cells to die directly, modifying the immune response to tumors, or reversing the malignant process by correcting genetic defects. It may also be able to improve a tumor's response to therapies like chemotherapy and radiation while simultaneously protecting normal tissue by introducing genetic elements that confer resistance to the treatment's damaging effects (Amer, 2014; Gutierrez et al., 1992). To achieve cancer gene therapy, a variety of ways have been devised. Cytotoxic gene therapy, immunotherapy, and antisense treatment were among the methods used (Rochlitz, 2001; Sorrentino, 2002).

One of the most difficult aspects of gene therapy is getting the right nucleic acid sequences to the right cells. Various techniques have emerged, which may be grouped into two categories. Viral vectors include adenoviruses and retroviruses, with adenoviruses being the most well-studied viral vector (Seth, 2005; Pahle and Walther, 2016). Non-viral vectors include liposomes, which is extensively explored nonviral vector (Schatzlein, 2001) while other methods include direct injection of plasmid DNA (Hickman et al., 1994).

Table 10.9 Compilation of carbon nanotubes reported for gastric cancer treatment.

Formulation	Functionalizing agent	In vitro efficacy	Conclusion	References
SWCNT–PEG–PEI	Polyethyleneimine	**In vitro**: SWCNT–PEG–PEI complexed with or without AS1411 aptamer at C/P ratio of 6 evaluated in AGS, L929 cell lines	Improvement in results	Taghavi et al. (2017)
SAL–SWCNT–CHI–HA	Chitosan, hyaluronic acid	**In vitro**: Release of SAL from SAL–SWCNT–CHI & SAL–SWCNT–CHI–HA was 60% in 24 h. Percent apoptosis in cancer stem cells of free SAL, SAL–SWCNT–CHI & SAL–SWCNT–CHI–HA was 34.4%, 39.4%, 47.8%	Inhibit metastasis of gastric cancer and improvement in treatment	Yao et al. (2014)
RGD-Conjugated silica-coated gold nanorods MWCNT	Silica, gold nanorods	**In vitro**: RGD–GNR–MWNT probes with a concentration of 50 µg/mL in the medium exhibited no cellular toxicity **In vivo**: enhance in photoacoustic imaging of cells	Improved solubility, Low cellular toxicity, used as photoacoustic imaging and photothermal therapy	Wang et al. (2014c)
Short(sh-MWCNT–amide), (sh-MWCNT– Spiro)	Isatin and its derivatives, hydralazine	**In vitro**: MKN-45, SW-742 cell lines treated with sh-MWCNT–amide/Spiro diffused into cancerous cells. Toxicity of amide was 79.6% in MKN-45, and 74% in SW-742	High toxicity of sh-MWCNT–amide compared to others	Tahermansouri and Chitgar (2013)

10.8 Cytotoxic gene therapy

One of the most promising approaches for gene therapy against many forms of cancer is the introduction of a suicide gene, which is the transduction of a gene that converts a nontoxic "prodrug" into a damaging molecule (Seidl et al., 2010). In vitro antitumor activity of suicide gene therapy employing the herpes simplex virus type 1 thymidine kinase (HSV-TK) gene has been reported in a range of cancer types. To improve the effectiveness of transfection of HSV-tk into carcinoembryonic antigen (CEA)-expressing cells, a modification of this technique was developed by inserting the CEA promoter into the viral vector (Zhang et al., 2004). CEA was shown to be expressed in roughly 40% of gastric cancers and CEA-producing gastric cancer cell lines were responsive to this therapy (Zhang et al., 2004; Zhang and Liu, 2003). Okino et al. described that N-methyl-N'-nitro-N-nitrosoguanidine (MNNG)-induced gastric cancer in rats can be treated by suicide gene therapy. In situ gene transfer with a recombinant adenovirus vector expressing the HSV-TK gene driven by the CAG promoter in the gastric tumor was used in the suicide gene therapy group, followed by the antiviral medication ganciclovir (GCV). Apoptosis in gastric cancers was observed after the mice were sacrificed. The 30-day therapy group had considerably more histological alterations, cancer tissue degradation, fibrosis after necrosis and apoptosis. PCR detection of the HSV-TK gene in peripheral blood was possible until 30 days after gene transfer (Okino et al., 2001; Lan et al., 1996).

10.9 Antisense therapy

When oligonucleotides bond to their corresponding RNA or DNA, translation or transcription is inhibited. This "antisense" strategy of inactivating oncogenes that are overexpressed in tumors is a conceptually appealing method (Tong et al., 2005). The gastric cancer cell line was treated by antisense therapy. Proliferating cell nuclear antigen (PCNA) has been demonstrated to accelerate DNA synthesis by DNA polymerase delta and to be highly expressed by gastric cancer cells with significant proliferative activity. All gastric cancer cell lines studied were inhibited by antisense oligonucleotides specific for PCNA mRNA, but random sequence oligonucleotides had no impact (Miki, 1999; Lee et al., 2003).

10.10 p53 gene

The p53 gene has point mutations in around 60% of human gastric cancers and because of its central location, this nuclear protein is assumed to have a role in the modulation of the cellular response to DNA damage. In this situation, wild-type p53 replacement therapy is a viable option (Ohashi et al., 1999). In vitro and in vivo responses of human gastric cancer cell lines to recombinant adenovirus expressing wild-type p53 gene were studied. Growth suppression was seen in cell lines that express p53 mutations, but not in cells expressing wild-type p53. Apoptosis was also discovered to be the process of cell death. As a result, p53 replacement therapy appears to be promising in the treatment for human gastric cancer (Khalighinejad et al., 2008; Sutter and Fechner, 2006).

The primary objective of genetic immunotherapy is to strengthen the host's immune response to a particular tumor. One way is to infuse DNA encoding a tumor-associated antigen like CEA into the muscle, either directly or via a viral vaccination. In one of the research, they discovered a new method for improving nucleic acid vaccine efficiency by binding VP22, a herpes simplex virus type 1 (HSV-1) tegument protein, to a model antigen (Matsueda and Graham, 2014; Yu et al., 2002).

10.11 Natural phytochemicals in gastric cancer

Alkaloids, saponins, glycosides, and other natural phytochemicals have long been employed in traditional medicine therapy. Furthermore, investigations have shown that these medicines have a variety of therapeutic effects. Benefits such as simplicity of availability, high efficacy, low toxicity, and convenience of administration point to a promising treatment strategy for gastric cancer alone or in combination (Qi et al., 2015). Several in vitro and in vivo investigations have revealed that phytochemicals such as flavonoids and polyphenols have promising results in gastric cancer. Curcumin is a polyphenolic chemical derived from the "Curcuma longa" plant species (Sharma et al., 2005). Traditional Chinese and Indian medicines are also based on this concept. In vitro and in vivo, curcumin exhibits antioxidant, anti-inflammatory, antibacterial, chemopreventive, antiproliferative, and anticarcinogenic properties in a variety of tumor cells (Barati et al., 2019; Giordano and Tommonaro, 2019). Curcumin is also being explored for the prevention of gastric cancer because to its remarkable anticancer effects and low toxicity (Shanmugam et al., 2015). The technique, according to Sintara et al., can minimize the cancer incidence of N-methyl-N-nitrosourea-induced gastric cancer in rats with benign tumors. Repression of NF-B and a considerable decrease in oxidative DNA damage were responsible for the result (Sintara et al., 2012). Curcumin prevents NF-B activation and promotes apoptosis via inhibiting the IB kinase (IKK) signaling pathway, which phosphorylates IB (Foryst-Ludwig et al., 2004).

Doxorubicin is a commonly used chemotherapeutic drug for gastric cancer patients because it is well tolerated (Arcamone, 2012). When doxorubicin is used alone, it has insufficient clinical effects, such as minimal patient improvement; however, these drawbacks can be avoided by combining it with cisplatin and an epoxide chemotherapy drug (Preusser et al., 1989). Their therapeutic effectiveness is reduced owing to chemoresistance, and drug resistance is controlled by NF-kB and NF-kB regulated genes. These cytotoxic drugs inhibit cell proliferation and promote apoptosis in SGC-7901 cells while also causing IB- phosphorylation. When IB-phosphorylation is lost, NF-B is activated. When curcumin is combined with these chemotherapeutic drugs, it suppresses IB-phosphorylation and significantly boosts drug cytotoxicity, according to Yu et al. (2011).

Panahi et al. investigated the effect of combining docetaxel and cisplatin-5 fluorouracil treatment with extracts from Curcumin longa. When compared to a placebo, the authors found that this strategy enhanced quality of life evaluation. This was accompanied by a decrease in pro-inflammatory markers such IL-6, TNF-, TGF-, and hs-CRP in the blood (Panahi et al., 2014).

Curcumin inhibits cancer cell proliferation, angiogenesis, invasion, and metastasis by suppressing numerous signaling pathways (Zhen et al., 2014). Curcumin can inhibit gastric cancer through a variety of mechanisms, such as, antiproliferative effect, apoptosis, and inhibiting chemoresistance in gastric cancer cells, according to the studies. Curcumin's methods of action in gastric cancer cell growth suppression are explored, as well as treatment techniques for gastric cancer management. As a result, curcumin might be considered a therapy option for decreasing the development of gastric cancer cells (Hassanalilou et al., 2019).

Because of its antiproliferative and proapoptotic effects on cancer cells, as well as its potential to limit tumor formation in animals, dietary phytoalexin resveratrol has evolved as a viable chemo-preventive drug (Savouret and Quesne, 2002). Resveratrol therapy causes DNA synthesis to be suppressed, nitric oxide synthase to be activated, apoptosis to be induced, and total PKC and PKC activity to be inhibited in gastric cancer cells. Treatment of gastric cancer SNU-1 cells with resveratrol resulted in accumulation of tumor suppressor p21 and p53, which is preceded by loss of membrane-associated PKC protein and a simultaneous rise in cytosolic PKC, according to Mary Jo Atten et al. At the transition from the S to the G2/M phases, the cell cycle comes to a halt. Both Fas and Fas-L proteins are upregulated in SNU-1 cells in response to resveratrol therapy. Overall, the data suggest that resveratrol activates PKC and signals in gastric cancer SNU-1 cells prior to antiproliferative and pro-apoptotic signals being upregulated. Resveratrol's unique cell death signals appear to be cell type-specific, implying that it retains chemopreventive potential even after mutational alterations have occurred (Atten et al., 2005).

Isothiocyanates are plant phytochemicals that contain significant anticarcinogenic agents and their consumption has been related to a lower risk of cancer in numerous body sites (Bianchini and Vainio, 2004). When mice were administered sulforaphane (SFN), studies on the chemopreventive impact of isothiocyanates on gastric cancer caused by benzo[a]pyrene revealed a substantial decrease in tumors size. These observations are consistent with previous studies from their research of phenyl-ethyl-iso-thiocyanates' chemopreventive effect on N-methyl-N-nitrosourea-induced cancer in mice. When coupled, isothiocyanate has the capacity to suppress gastric cancer cells in vitro, prevent chemically induced cancer in vivo, and decrease inflammation caused by *H. Pylori* infection in the stomach (Øverby et al., 2014).

Alejandra et al. investigated the antioxidant effect of blueberry leaf extract treated with methyl jasmonate on gastric cancer. Methyl jasmonate treated plants showed a significant reduction in cancer cell migration and expression of gastric cancer-related proteins, primarily related to the mitogen-activated protein kinase (MAPK) pathway. Methyl jasmonate boosted antioxidant molecules, according to their results. AGS cells' viability and migratory potential were both reduced by anthocyanins. Furthermore, leaf extracts from methyl jasmonate treated plants were able to reduce the expression of proteins linked to gastric cancer (Ribera-Fonseca et al., 2020).

You-Cheng Hseu and colleagues investigated the synergistic effects of combining a natural anticancer medication flavokawain B (FKB) with doxorubicin on human gastric cancer cells. Small doses of FKB plus doxorubicin inhibited AGS cell growth when compared to individual treatments. FKB increased doxorubicin-mediated mitochondrial and death receptor pathways, which potentiated doxorubicin-induced DNA fragmentation and apoptotic cell death (Hseu et al., 2020).

Jawed et al. formulated a curcumin-loaded PLGA-NP by solvent evaporation method to increase bioavailability and anticancer activity. When gastric cells were treated with curcumin, the inhibition of gastric cancer was increased to 67% in 24 h from 6%. As in the case of nanocurcumin, the inhibition rate was increased from 7%−69%. Nanocurcumin had a more apoptotic effect on gastric cells when compared with free curcumin. Hence, curcumin-loaded PLGA-NP can be used in treatment of gastric cancer as well as *H. Pylori* (Alam et al., 2022).

Weihong and coworkers formulated vitamin B12-sericin-PBLG poly(γ-benzyl-L-glutamate)-PTX loaded micelles and explored its antitumor property and cellular uptake mechanism. This nanoformulation showed a potential apoptosis effect and it was able to reverse the drug resistance. Thus, formulation can be a promising alternative for gastric cancer (Guo et al., 2019).

10.12 Marketed formulation for gastric cancer treatment

Various marketed nanoformulations as well as traditional pills, capsules, and injectables are summarized in Table 10.10. Clinical investigations have showed that nanoformulations had a great deal of success in past couple of years. They are not only found to increase the effectiveness but also decreased toxicities of traditional dose regimens. Given the complexities of gastric cancer, there is still a long way to go for accurate, effective and long-term treatment.

Table 10.10 Marketed approved formulations are summarized below.

Marketed formulation	Drug approved for the treatment of gastric cancer	Company	Type of formulation	Approval year
CYRAMZA	Ramucirumab	Eli-Lilly & Co.	IV Injection	21 April, 2014
TAXOTERE	Docetaxel	Sanofi & Aventis	IV injection	31 March, 2006
ADRIYAMYCIN	Doxorubicin HCl	Pfizer	IV injection	7 September, 1993
ENHERTUR	Fam–Trastuzumab Deruxtecan-nxki	Daiichi-Sankyo & Astra-Zeneca	IV injection	15 January, 2021
ADRUCIL	5-Fluorouracil injection	Pharmacia & Upjohn Co.	IV injection	25 February, 2000
FLURACIL	Fluorouracil injection	Zydus	IV injection	13 April, 2007
HERCEPTIN	Trastuzumab	Genentech.inc	IV injection	20 October, 2010
KEYTRUDA	Pembrolizumab	Merck	IV injection	22 September, 2017
LONSURF	Trifluridine and Tipiracil HCl		Film-coated tablet	22 September, 2015
JELMYTO	Mitomycin	UroGen Pharma Ltd.	IV injection	15 April, 2020
OPDIVO	Nivolumab	Bristol-Myers Squibb Co	IV injection	22 December, 2014
PLATINOL	Cisplatin	Cadila Pharmaceuticals	IV injection	19 December, 1978

10.13 Conclusion and future perspectives

Higher incidence and mortality rate of gastric cancer pave the way for researchers to develop best therapy and palliation for this malignancy. Advanced nanomedicines are providing better strategy for improving the drawbacks of the current methods. Due to the small size of nanomedicine, they are capable of penetrating into the barriers and adequately control the drug response at cellular level. Use of biodegradable polymers in developing nanoformulations is more beneficial. Biosafety of these nanocarriers is to be studied broadly further. Early detection of gastric cancer is necessary for avoiding mortality, which could be made possible by adopting nanotechnology to the imaging techniques. Gene therapy via gene silencing could be used in advance gastric cancer for targeted delivery of anticancer drugs by nanocarriers. Considering the complexities involved gastric cancer, there is still long way to go for effective and long-term treatment.

References

Abbasi, E., et al., 2014. Dendrimers: synthesis, applications, and properties. Nanoscale Res. Lett. 9 (1), 1−10.

Abedi-Gaballu, F., et al., 2018. PAMAM dendrimers as efficient drug and gene delivery nanosystems for cancer therapy. Appl. Mater. Today 12, 177−190.

Akbarzadeh, A., et al., 2013. Liposome: classification, preparation, and applications. Nanoscale Res. Lett. 8 (1), 1−9.

Akiyama, T., 1986. The product of the human c-erbB-2 gene: a 185-kilodalton glycoprotein with tyrosine kinase activity. Science 232, 1644−1646. 10.1126/science.3012781.

Alam, J., Dilnawaz, F., Sahoo, S.K., Singh, D.V., Mukhopadhyay, A.K., Hussain, T., Pati, S., 2022. Curcumin encapsulated into biocompatible co-polymer PLGA nanoparticle enhanced anti-gastric cancer and anti-Helicobacter Pylori effect. Asian Pac. J Cancer Prev. 23 (1), 61.

Alami, A.H., Faraj, M., 2022. Quantum Dots: Types and Characteristics, in Encyclopedia of Smart Materials. Elsevier, Oxford, pp. 183−191.

Albarello, L., Pecciarini, L., Doglioni, C., 2011. HER2 testing in gastric cancer. Adv. Anat. Pathol. 18 (1), 53−59.

Alipour, M., 2021. Molecular mechanism of helicobacter pylori-induced gastric cancer. J. Gastrointest. Cancer 52 (1), 23−30.

Amer, M.H., 2014. Gene therapy for cancer: present status and future perspective. Mol. Cell Ther. 2 (1), 1−19.

Arcamone, F., 2012. Doxorubicin: Anticancer Antibiotics. Elsevier.

Asaka, M., et al., 2001. Gastric cancer. Helicobacter Pylori: Physiology and Genetics. ASM Press, pp. 481−498.

Atten, M.J., Godoy-Romero, E., Attar, B.M., Milson, T., Zopel, M., Holian, O., 2005. Resveratrol regulates cellular PKC α and δ to inhibit growth and induce apoptosis in gastric cancer cells. Invest. New Drugs. 23, 111−119.

Axon, A.J., 2006. Symptoms and diagnosis of gastric cancer at early curable stage. Best Pract. Res. Clin. Gastroenterol. 20 (4), 697−708.

Azagra, J.S., Goergen, M., De Simone, P., Ibanez-Aguirre, J., 1999. Minimally invasive surgery for gastric cancer. Surgical endoscopy 13, 351−357.

Baek, J.-S., et al., 2012. Solid lipid nanoparticles of paclitaxel strengthened by hydroxypropyl-β-cyclodextrin as an oral delivery system. Int. J. Mol. Med. 30 (4), 953−959.

Baig, T., et al., 2015. A review about dendrimers: synthesis, types, characterization and applications. Int. J. Adv. Pharmacy, Biol. Chem. 4 (1), 44−59.

Barati, N., Momtazi-Borojeni, A.A., Majeed, M., Sahebkar, A., 2019. Potential therapeutic effects of curcumin in gastric cancer. J Cell Physiol. 234 (3), 2317−2328.

Barzegar Behrooz, A., et al., 2017. Smart bomb AS 1411 aptamer-functionalized/PAMAM dendrimer nanocarriers for targeted drug delivery in the treatment of gastric cancer. Clin. Exp. Pharmacol. Physiol. 44 (1), 41−51.

Baughman, R.H., Zakhidov, A.A., De Heer, W.A., 2002. Carbon nanotubes—the route toward applications. Science 297 (5582), 787−792.

Bayat, P., Pakravan, P., Salouti, M., Dolatabadi, J.E., 2021. Lysine decorated solid lipid nanoparticles of epirubicin for cancer targeting and therapy. Adv. Pharm. Bull. 11 (1), 96.

Bayón-Cordero, L., Alkorta, I., Arana, L., 2019. Application of solid lipid nanoparticles to improve the efficiency of anticancer drugs. Nanomaterials 9 (3), 474.

Bianchini, F., Vainio, H., 2004. Isothiocyanates in cancer prevention. Drug. Metab. Rev. 36 (3−4), 655−667.

Blair, V., Martin, I., Shaw, D., Winship, I., Kerr, D., Arnold, J., et al., 2006. Hereditary diffuse gastric cancer: diagnosis and management. Clin Gastroenterol Hepatol. 4 (3), 262−275.

Bodewein, L., et al., 2016. Differences in toxicity of anionic and cationic PAMAM and PPI dendrimers in zebrafish embryos and cancer cell lines. Toxicol. Appl. Pharmacol. 305, 83−92.

Boku, N., 2014. HER2-positive gastric cancer. Gastric Cancer 17 (1), 1−12.

Bonadonna, G., et al., 1993. Drugs ten years later: epirubicin. 4(5), 359−369.

Bummer, P.M., 2004. Physical chemical considerations of lipid-based oral drug delivery—solid lipid nanoparticles. Crit. Rev. Ther. Drug. Carr. Syst. 21 (1), 1−20.

Catalano, V., et al., 2009. Gastric cancer. Crit. Rev. Oncol. Hematol 71 (2), 127−164.

Cavazzana-Calvo, M., Thrasher, A., Mavilio, F., 2004. The future of gene therapy. Nature 427 (6977), 779−781.

Chauhan, A.S., Kaul, M., 2018. Engineering of "critical nanoscale design parameters"(CNDPs) in PAMAM dendrimer nanoparticles for drug delivery applications. J. Nanopart. Res. 20 (9), 1−11.

Chen, H., et al., 2003. Interaction of dendrimers (artificial proteins) with biological hydroxyapatite crystals. J. Dental Res. 82 (6), 443−448.

Chen, L., et al., 2011. A prototype of giant magnetoimpedance-based biosensing system for targeted detection of gastric cancer cells. Biosens. Bioelectron. 26 (7), 3246−3253.

Chen Y., Zhang Y., Pan F., Liu J., Wang K., Zhang C., et al., 2016. Breath analysis based on surface-enhanced Raman scattering sensors distinguishes early and advanced gastric cancer patients from healthy persons. ACS nano. 10(9):8169−8179.

Cheung, K.S., Leung, W.K., 2019. Long-term use of proton-pump inhibitors and risk of gastric cancer: a review of the current evidence. Ther. Adv. Gastroenterol. 12:1756284819834511.

Chua, T.C., Merrett, N.D., 2012. Clinicopathologic factors associated with HER2-positive gastric cancer and its impact on survival outcomes—A systematic review. Int. J. Cancer 130 (12), 2845−2856.

Colquhoun, A., Arnold, M., Ferlay, J., Goodman, K.J., Forman, D., Soerjomataram, I., 2015. Global patterns of cardia and non-cardia gastric cancer incidence in 2012. Gut 64 (12), 1881−1888.

Duan, Y., et al., 2020. A brief review on solid lipid nanoparticles: part and parcel of contemporary drug delivery systems. RSC Adv. 10 (45), 26777−26791.

Duggan, S.T., Keating, G.M., 2011. Pegylated liposomal doxorubicin. Drugs 71 (18), 2531−2558.

Ensign, L.M., Cone, R., Hanes, J., 2012. Oral drug delivery with polymeric nanoparticles: the gastrointestinal mucus barriers. Adv. Drug. Deliv. Rev. 64 (6), 557−570.

Foryst-Ludwig, A., Neumann, M., Schneider-Brachert, W., Naumann, M., 2004. Curcumin blocks NF-κB and the motogenic response in Helicobacter pylori-infected epithelial cells. Biochem. Biophys. Res. Commun. 316 (4), 1065−1072.

Fu, H., Wang, C., Yang, D., Wei, Z., Xu, J., Hu, Z., et al., 2018. Curcumin regulates proliferation, autophagy, and apoptosis in gastric cancer cells by affecting PI3K and P53 signaling. J Cell Physiol. 233 (6), 4634−4642.

Fu, L., Yu, A., 2014. Carbon nanotubes based thin films: fabrication, characterization and applications. Rev. Adv. Mater. Sci. 36 (1), 40−61.

Gabizon, A.A., 2001. Pegylated liposomal doxorubicin: metamorphosis of an old drug into a new form of chemotherapy. Cancer Investig. 19 (4), 424−436.

Gagliardi, A., et al., 2021. Biodegradable polymeric nanoparticles for drug delivery to solid tumors. Front. Pharmacol. 12, 17.

Garcia-Calvo, E., Cabezas-Sanchez, P., Luque-Garcia, J., 2021. In-vitro and in-vivo evaluation of the molecular mechanisms involved in the toxicity associated to CdSe/ZnS quantum dots exposure. Chemosphere 263, 128170.

Ghasemiyeh, P., Mohammadi-Samani, S., 2018. Solid lipid nanoparticles and nanostructured lipid carriers as novel drug delivery systems: applications, advantages and disadvantages. Res. Pharm. Sci. 13 (4), 288.

Ghosh, P., et al., 2008. Gold nanoparticles in delivery applications 60 (11), 1307−1315.

Giordano, A., Tommonaro, G., 2019. Curcumin and cancer. Nutrients 11 (10), 2376.

Gomceli, I., Demiriz, B., Tez, M., 2012. Gastric carcinogenesis. World J. Gastroenterol. 18 (37), 5164.

Grabowski, N., et al., 2015. Surface coating mediates the toxicity of polymeric nanoparticles towards human-like macrophages. Int. J. Pharma. 482 (1−2), 75−83.

Guillaudeu, S.J., et al., 2008. PEGylated dendrimers with core functionality for biological applications. Bioconjug. Chem. 19 (2), 461−469.

Guljar, D., Patel, P.M., 2013. Dendrimers: synthesis, types, and application: a review. Glob. ChemXpress 2 (3), 136−147.

Guo, W., et al., 2019. Vitamin B12-conjugated sericin micelles for targeting CD320-overexpressed gastric cancer and reversing drug resistance. 14(3), 353−370.

Gupta, T., et al., 2020. Enhancing bioavailability and stability of curcumin using solid lipid nanoparticles (CLEN): a covenant for its effectiveness. 8, 879.

Gupta, U., et al., 2010. Ligand anchored dendrimers based nanoconstructs for effective targeting to cancer cells. Int. J. Pharma. 393 (1−2), 186−197.

Gutierrez, A.A., Lemoine, N.R., Sikora, K.J.T.L., 1992. Gene therapy for cancer. 339(8795), 715−721.

Hamaguchi, T., et al., 2004. Antitumor effect of MCC-465, pegylated liposomal doxorubicin tagged with newly developed monoclonal antibody GAH, in colorectal cancer xenografts. Cancer Sci. 95 (7), 608−613.

Hamilton, J.P., Meltzer, S.J., 2006. A review of the genomics of gastric cancer. Clin. Gastroenterol. Hepatol. 4 (4), 416−425.

Han, G., et al., 2019. Clinical efficacy and safety of paclitaxel liposomes as first-line chemotherapy in advanced gastric cancer. Future Oncol. 15 (14), 1617−1627.

Hansen, S., et al., 1999. Helicobacter pylori infection and risk of cardia cancer and non-cardia gastric cancer: a nested case-control study. 34(4), 353−360.

Hansford, S., et al., 2015. Hereditary diffuse gastric cancer syndrome: CDH1 mutations and beyond. 1(1), 23−32.

Hartgrink, H.H., et al., 2009. Gastric cancer. Lancet 374 (9688), 477−490.

Hassanalilou, T., Ghavamzadeh, S., Khalili, L., 2019. Curcumin and gastric cancer: a review on mechanisms of action. J. Gastrointest. Cancer 50 (2), 185−192.

Hauptmann, M., et al., 2015. Increased stomach cancer risk following radiotherapy for testicular cancer. 112(1), 44−51.

He, H., et al., 2011. PEGylated poly (amidoamine) dendrimer-based dual-targeting carrier for treating brain tumors. Biomaterials 32 (2), 478−487.

Hemler, M.E., 2014. Tetraspanin proteins promote multiple cancer stages. Nat. Rev. Cancer 14 (1), 49−60.

Hickman, M.A., et al., 1994. Gene expression following direct injection of DNA into liver. Hum Gene Ther 5 (12), 1477−1483.

Hong, C., et al., 2019. Novel ginsenoside-based multifunctional liposomal delivery system for combination therapy of gastric cancer. 9(15), 4437.

Hseu, Y.-C., et al., 2020. Flavokawain B and doxorubicin work synergistically to impede the propagation of gastric cancer cells via ROS-mediated apoptosis and autophagy pathways. 12(9), 2475.

Hu, X., et al., 2020. Multifunctional gold nanoparticles: a novel nanomaterial for various medical applications and biological activities. 8, 990.

Huang, L., et al., 2020. Preventable lifestyle and eating habits associated with gastric adenocarcinoma: a case-control study. J. Cancer 11 (5), 1231.

Huntsman, D.G., et al., 2001. Early gastric cancer in young, asymptomatic carriers of germ-line E-cadherin mutations. 344(25), 1904−1909.

Hutchison, J., et al., 2001. Double-walled carbon nanotubes fabricated by a hydrogen arc discharge method. 39(5), 761−770.

Hyun, H., et al., 2018. Surface modification of polymer nanoparticles with native albumin for enhancing drug delivery to solid tumors. Biomaterials 180, 206−224.

Igarashi, A., et al., 2003. Liposomal photofrin enhances therapeutic efficacy of photodynamic therapy against the human gastric cancer. Toxicol. Lett. 145 (2), 133−141.

Inomata, M., et al., 2003. Gastric remnant cancer compared with primary proximal gastric cancer. Hepatogastroenterology 50 (50), 587−591.

Iqbal, N., Iqbal, N., 2014. Human epidermal growth factor receptor 2 (HER2) in cancers: overexpression and therapeutic implications. Mol. Biol. Int. 2014.

Jain, K., et al., 2010. Dendrimer toxicity: let's meet the challenge. Int. J. Pharm. 394 (1−2), 122−142.

Jenning, V., Thünemann, A.F., Gohla, S.H., 2000. Characterisation of a novel solid lipid nanoparticle carrier system based on binary mixtures of liquid and solid lipids. Int. J. Pharma. 199 (2), 167−177.

Jia, Y.-P., et al., 2017. The in vitro and in vivo toxicity of gold nanoparticles. 28(4), 691−702.

Jiang, H., et al., 2016. Etoposide-loaded nanostructured lipid carriers for gastric cancer therapy. Drug. Deliv. 23 (4), 1379−1382.

Jin, X., et al., 2018. The combined administration of parthenolide and ginsenoside CK in long circulation liposomes with targeted tLyp-1 ligand induce mitochondria-mediated lung cancer apoptosis. 46 (sup3), S931−S942.

Kamiya, S., et al., 2006. Physical characteristics of freeze-dried griseofulvin-lipids nanoparticles. Chem. Pharm. Bull. 54 (2), 181−184.

Karamchedu, S., et al., 2020. Morin hydrate loaded solid lipid nanoparticles: characterization, stability, anticancer activity, and bioavailability. 233, 104988.

Kesharwani, P., Jain, K., Jain, N.K., 2014. Dendrimer as nanocarrier for drug delivery. Prog. Polym. Sci. 39 (2), 268−307.

Khalighinejad, N., et al., 2008. Adenoviral gene therapy in gastric cancer: a review. 14(2), 180.

Kikuchi, S., et al., 2000. Effect of age on the relationship between gastric cancer and Helicobacter pylori. Tokyo Research Group of Prevention for Gastric Cancer. Jpn. J. Cancer Res 91 (8), 774−779.

Kim, H.-K., et al., 2010. Enhanced siRNA delivery using cationic liposomes with new polyarginine-conjugated PEG-lipid. Int. J. Pharm. 392 (1−2), 141−147.

Kim, J., et al., 2015. Highly fluorescent CdTe quantum dots with reduced cytotoxicity-A Robust biomarker. Sens. Bio-Sensing Res. 3, 46−52.

Kim, J.H., et al., 2018. Dietary carotenoids intake and the risk of gastric cancer: a case—control study in Korea. 10(8), 1031.

Kingston, C.T., Simard, B., 2003. Fabrication of carbon nanotubes. Anal. Lett. 36 (15), 3119−3145.

Kodera, Y., et al., 2010. Laparoscopic surgery for gastric cancer: a collective review with meta-analysis of randomized trials. 211(5), 677−686.

Kolhatkar, R.B., et al., 2007. Surface acetylation of polyamidoamine (PAMAM) dendrimers decreases cytotoxicity while maintaining membrane permeability. Bioconjug. Chem. 18 (6), 2054−2060.

Kominkova, M., et al., 2017. Comparative study on toxicity of extracellularly biosynthesized and laboratory synthesized CdTe quantum dots. J. Biotechnol. 241, 193−200.

Kubota, T., Kuroda, S., Kanaya, N., Morihiro, T., Aoyama, K., Kakiuchi, Y., et al., 2018. HER2-targeted gold nanoparticles potentially overcome resistance to trastuzumab in gastric cancer. Nanomedicine. 14(6):1919−1929.

Kuipers, E.J., 1997. Helicobacter pylori and the risk and management of associated diseases: gastritis, ulcer disease, atrophic gastritis and gastric cancer. Aliment Pharmacol. Ther. 11 (S1), 71–88.

Lammers, T., et al., 2011. Theranostic nanomedicine. Acc. Chem. Res. 44 (10), 1029–1038.

Lan, K.H., et al., 1996. Tumor-specific gene expression in carcinoembryonic antigen–producing gastric cancer cells using adenovirus vectors. 111(5), 1241–1251.

Lauren, P., 1965. The two histological main types of gastric carcinoma: diffuse and so-called intestinal-type carcinoma: an attempt at a histo-clinical classification. Acta Pathol. Microbiol. Scand. 64 (1), 31–49.

Lee, K.E., Lee. H.J., Kim, Y.H., Yu, H.J., Yang, H.K., Kim, W.H., et al., 2003. Prognostic significance of p53, nm23, PCNA and c-erbB-2 in gastric cancer. Jpn J Clin Oncol. 33 (4), 173–179.

Lesniak, W., et al., 2005. Silver/dendrimer nanocomposites as biomarkers: fabrication, characterization, in vitro toxicity, and intracellular detection. Nano Lett. 5 (11), 2123–2130.

Li, C., et al., 2019. An investigation on the cytotoxicity and caspase-mediated apoptotic effect of biologically synthesized gold nanoparticles using Cardiospermum halicacabum on AGS gastric carcinoma cells. 14, 951.

Li, T., et al., 2017. MiR-542-3p appended sorafenib/all-trans retinoic acid (ATRA)-loaded lipid nanoparticles to enhance the anticancer efficacy in gastric cancers. Pharm. Res. 34 (12), 2710–2719.

Li, X.-T., et al., 2021a. Enhanced antitumour efficiency of R8GD-modified epirubicin plus tetrandrine liposomes in treatment of gastric cancer via inhibiting tumour metastasis. 31(2), 145–157.

Li, X.-Y., et al., 2021b. Functional vinorelbine plus schisandrin B liposomes destroying tumor metastasis in treatment of gastric cancer. 47(1), 100–112.

Li, Y.-F., Zhang, H.-T., Xin, L., 2018. Hyaluronic acid-modified polyamidoamine dendrimer G5-entrapped gold nanoparticles delivering METase gene inhibits gastric tumor growth via targeting CD44 + gastric cancer cells. J. Cancer Res. Clin. Oncol. 144 (8), 1463–1473.

Liko, F., Hindre, F., Fernandez-Megia, E., 2016. Dendrimers as innovative radiopharmaceuticals in cancer radionanotherapy. Biomacromolecules 17 (10), 3103–3114.

Lingayat, V.J., Zarekar, N.S., Shendge, R.S., 2017. Solid lipid nanoparticles: a review. Nanosci. Nanotechnol. Res. 2, 67–72.

Liu, M., Fréchet, J.M., 1999. Designing dendrimers for drug delivery. Pharm. Sci. Technol. Today 2 (10), 393–401.

Liu, T., et al., 2012. Increased circulating Th22 and Th17 cells are associated with tumor progression and patient survival in human gastric cancer. J. Clin. Immunol. 32 (6), 1332–1339.

Lu, Z., et al., 2020. Delivery of TSPAN1 siRNA by novel Th17 targeted cationic liposomes for gastric cancer intervention. 109(9), 2854–2860.

Lukyanov, A.N., et al., 2004. Tumor-targeted liposomes: doxorubicin-loaded long-circulating liposomes modified with anti-cancer antibody. J. Control. Release 100 (1), 135–144.

Luong, D., et al., 2016. PEGylated PAMAM dendrimers: enhancing efficacy and mitigating toxicity for effective anticancer drug and gene delivery. Acta Biomater. 43, 14–29.

Ma, L., et al., 2018. Co-delivery of paclitaxel and tanespimycin in lipid nanoparticles enhanced anti-gastric-tumor effect in vitro and in vivo. Artif. Cells Nanomed. Biotechnol. 46 (sup2), 904–911.

Maconi, G., Manes, G., Porro, G.B., 2008. Role of symptoms in diagnosis and outcome of gastric cancer. World J. Gastroenterol. 14 (8), 1149.

Madaan, K., et al., 2014. Dendrimers in drug delivery and targeting: drug-dendrimer interactions and toxicity issues. J. Pharm. Bioallied Sci. 6 (3), 139.

Majoros, I.J., et al., 2003. Acetylation of poly (amidoamine) dendrimers. Macromolecules 36 (15), 5526–5529.

Matsueda, S., Graham, D.Y., 2014. Immunotherapy in gastric cancer. World J. Gastroenterol. 20 (7), 1657.

Matsumura, Y., et al., 2004. Phase I and pharmacokinetic study of MCC-465, a doxorubicin (DXR) encapsulated in PEG immunoliposome, in patients with metastatic stomach cancer. Ann. Oncol. 15 (3), 517 525.

Mecke, A., et al., 2004. Direct observation of lipid bilayer disruption by poly (amidoamine) dendrimers. Chem. Phys. Lipids 132 (1), 3–14.

Mehnert, W., Mäder, K., 2012. Solid lipid nanoparticles: production, characterization and applications. Adv. Drug. Deliv. Rev. 64, 83–101.

Mi, C., et al., 2011. Biosynthesis and characterization of CdS quantum dots in genetically engineered *Escherichia coli*. J. Biotechnol. 153 (3–4), 125–132.

Mi, F.-L., et al., 2018. Active tumor-targeted co-delivery of epigallocatechin gallate and doxorubicin in nanoparticles for combination gastric cancer therapy. ACS Biomater. Sci. Eng. 4 (8), 2847–2859.

Miki, Y., 1999. Future perspectives of gene therapy for gastric cancer. Multimodality Therapy for Gastric Cancer. Springer, pp. 187–193.

Mitri, Z., et al., 2012. The HER2 receptor in breast cancer: pathophysiology, clinical use, and new advances in therapy. 2012.

Morton, L.M., et al., 2013. Stomach cancer risk after treatment for Hodgkin lymphoma. 31(27), 3369.

Mukherjee, S., Ray, S., Thakur, R., 2009. Solid lipid nanoparticles: a modern formulation approach in drug delivery system. Indian J. Pharm. Sci. 71 (4), 349.

Mylvaganam, K., Zhang, L.C., 2007. Fabrication and application of polymer composites comprising carbon nanotubes. Recent. Pat. Nanotechnol. 1 (1), 59–65.

Nabavizadeh, F., 2019. Targeted drug delivery of capecitabine to mice xenograft gastric cancer by PAMAM dendrimer nanocarrier.

Najafi, F., Salami-Kalajahi, M., Roghani-Mamaqani, H., 2020. Synthesis of amphiphilic Janus dendrimer and its application in improvement of hydrophobic drugs solubility in aqueous media. Eur. Polym. J. 134, 109804.

Nanjwade, B.K., et al., 2009. Dendrimers: emerging polymers for drug-delivery systems. Eur. J. Pharm. Sci. 38 (3), 185–196.

Naseri, N., Valizadeh, H., Zakeri-Milani, P., 2015. Solid lipid nanoparticles and nanostructured lipid carriers: structure, preparation and application. Adv. Pharm. Bull. 5 (3), 305.

Nasirizadeh, S., Malaekeh-Nikouei, B., 2020. Solid lipid nanoparticles and nanostructured lipid carriers in oral cancer drug delivery. J. Drug. Deliv. Sci. Technol. 55, 101458.

Nie, J., Wang, Y., Wang, W., 2016. In vitro and in vivo evaluation of stimuli-responsive vesicle from PEGylated hyperbranched PAMAM-doxorubicin conjugate for gastric cancer therapy. Int. J. Pharm. 509 (1–2), 168–177.

Ogawara, K.-i., et al., 2013. Nanoparticle-based passive drug targeting to tumors: considerations and implications for optimization. Biol. Pharm. Bull. 36 (5), 698–702.

Ohashi, M., et al., 1999. Adenovirus mediated p53 tumour suppressor gene therapy for human gastric cancer cells in vitro and in vivo. 44(3), 366–371.

Ohgami, M., et al., 1999. Curative laparoscopic surgery for early gastric cancer: five years experience. 23 (2), 187.

Okino, T., et al., 2001. Sequential histopathological changes in vivo after suicide gene therapy of gastric cancer induced by N-methyl-N′-nitro-N-nitrosoguanidine in rats. 92(6), 673–679.

Orditura, M., et al., 2014. Treatment of gastric cancer. World J. Gastroenterol. 20 (7), 1635.

Øverby, A., Zhao, C.-M., Chen, D., 2014. Plant phytochemicals: potential anticancer agents against gastric cancer. Curr. Opin. Pharmacol. 19, 6–10.

Pahle, J., Walther, W., 2016. Vectors and strategies for nonviral cancer gene therapy. Expert. Opin. Biol. Ther. 16 (4), 443–461.

Panahi, Y., et al., 2014. Adjuvant therapy with bioavailability-boosted curcuminoids suppresses systemic inflammation and improves quality of life in patients with solid tumors: a randomized double-blind placebo-controlled trial. 28(10), 1461–1467.

Pandey, S.S., et al., 2021. Mannosylated solid lipid nanocarriers of chrysin to target gastric cancer: optimization and cell line study. Curr. Drug Deliv 18 (10), 1574–1584.

Pathak, K., Raghuvanshi, S., 2015. Oral bioavailability: issues and solutions via nanoformulations. Clin. Pharmacokinet. 54 (4), 325–357.

Peng, Z., et al., 2014. Co-delivery of doxorubicin and SATB1 shRNA by thermosensitive magnetic cationic liposomes for gastric cancer therapy. PLoS One 9 (3), e92924.

Pharoah, P.D., et al., 2001. Incidence of gastric cancer and breast cancer in CDH1 (E-cadherin) mutation carriers from hereditary diffuse gastric cancer families. 121(6), 1348–1353.

Poonia, N., et al., 2016. Nanostructured lipid carriers: versatile oral delivery vehicle. Future Sci. OA 2 (3), FSO135.

Praud, D., et al., 2018. Cigarette smoking and gastric cancer in the Stomach Cancer Pooling (StoP) Project. 27(2), 124–133.

Preusser, P., et al., 1989. Phase II study with the combination etoposide, doxorubicin, and cisplatin in advanced measurable gastric cancer. 7(9), 1310–1317.

Qi, F., et al., 2015. The advantages of using traditional Chinese medicine as an adjunctive therapy in the whole course of cancer treatment instead of only terminal stage of cancer. 9(1), 16–34.

Radomska-Soukharev, A., 2007. Stability of lipid excipients in solid lipid nanoparticles. Adv. Drug Deliv. Rev. 59 (6), 411–418.

Recchia, F., et al., 2010. Liposomal pegylated doxorubicin and oxaliplatin as salvage chemotherapy in patients with metastatic gastric cancer treated earlier. Anti-Cancer Drugs 21 (5), 559–564.

Ribera-Fonseca, A., et al., 2020. The anti-proliferative and anti-invasive effect of leaf extracts of blueberry plants treated with methyl jasmonate on human gastric cancer in vitro is related to their antioxidant properties. 9(1), 45.

Rochlitz, C.J.S.M.W., 2001. Gene therapy of cancer. 131(0102).

Roth, J.A., Cristiano, R.J., 1997. Gene therapy for cancer: what have we done and where are we going? J. Natl Cancer Inst. 89 (1), 21–39.

Roviello, G., et al., 2019. Nanoparticle albumin-bound paclitaxel: a big nano for the treatment of gastric cancer. Cancer Chemother. Pharmacol. 84 (4), 669–677.

Roy, P., et al., 2015. Photoluminescent graphene quantum dots for in vivo imaging of apoptotic cells. Nanoscale 7 (6), 2504–2510.

Ruan, J., et al., 2012. HER2 monoclonal antibody conjugated RNase-A-associated CdTe quantum dots for targeted imaging and therapy of gastric cancer. 33(29), 7093–7102.

Salah, E., et al., 2020. Solid lipid nanoparticles for enhanced oral absorption: a review. p. 111305.

Sampathkumar, S.G., Yarema, K.J., 2007. Dendrimers in cancer treatment and diagnosis. Nanotechnologies Life Sciences: Online. Wiley.

Sanginario, A., Miccoli, B., Demarchi, D., 2017. Carbon nanotubes as an effective opportunity for cancer diagnosis and treatment. Biosensors (Basel) 7 (1), 9.

Sano, T., et al., 2017. Proposal of a new stage grouping of gastric cancer for TNM classification: International Gastric Cancer Association staging project. 20(2), 217–225.

Sanomura, Y., et al., 2012. Clinical validity of endoscopic submucosal dissection for submucosal invasive gastric cancer: a single-center study. 15(1), 97–105.

Sastre, J., García-Saenz, J.A., Díaz-Rubio, E., 2006. Chemotherapy for gastric cancer. World J. Gastroenterol. 12 (2), 204.

Sauvaget, C., et al., 2005. Lifestyle factors, radiation and gastric cancer in atomic-bomb survivors (Japan). Cancer Causes Control. 16 (7), 773–780.

Savouret, J.F., Quesne, M., 2002. Resveratrol and cancer: a review. Biomed. Pharmacother. 56 (2), 84–87.

Schatzlein, A.G., 2001. Non-viral vectors in cancer gene therapy: principles and progress. Anticancer. Drugs 12 (4), 275–304.

Seidl, C., et al., 2010. Differential gene expression triggered by highly cytotoxic α-emitter-immunoconjugates in gastric cancer cells. 28(1), 49–60.

Seth, P., 2005. Vector-mediated cancer gene therapy: an overview. Cancer Biol. Ther. 4 (5), 512–517.

Shanmugam, M.K., et al., 2015. The multifaceted role of curcumin in cancer prevention and treatment. 20(2), 2728–2769.

Shao, W., et al., 2013. Carbon nanotubes for use in medicine: potentials and limitations. 13, 285–311.

Sharma, R.A., Gescher, A.J., Steward, W.P., 2005. Curcumin: the story so far. Eur. J. Cancer 41 (13), 1955–1968.

Shcikhpour, M., et al., 2017. Carbon nanotubes: a review of novel strategies for cancer diagnosis and treatment. 76, 1289–1304.

Singh, B.R., et al., 2012. ROS-mediated apoptotic cell death in prostate cancer LNCaP cells induced by biosurfactant stabilized CdS quantum dots. Biomaterials 33 (23), 5753–5767.

Sintara, K., Thong-Ngam, D., Patumraj, S., Klaikeaw, N. 2012. Curcumin attenuates gastric cancer induced by N-methyl-N-nitrosourea and saturated sodium chloride in rats. J Biomed Biotechnol. 2012, 915380.

Sivaramakrishnan, V., Shilpa, P.N., Kumar, V.R., Devaraj, S.N. 2008. Attenuation of N-nitrosodiethylamine-induced hepatocellular carcinogenesis by a novel flavonol—Morin. Chem Biol Interact. 171(1), 79–88

Solomon, R., Gabizon, A.A., 2008. Clinical pharmacology of liposomal anthracyclines: focus on pegy-lated liposomal doxorubicin. Clin. Lymphoma Myeloma 8 (1), 21–32.

Song, M., et al., 2018. Family history of cancer in first-degree relatives and risk of gastric cancer and its precursors in a Western population. Gastric Cancer 21 (5), 729–737.

Song, Z., et al., 2019. Phenylboronic acid-functionalized polyamidoamine-mediated miR-34a delivery for the treatment of gastric cancer. Biomater. Sci. 7 (4), 1632–1642.

Sonju, J.J., et al., 2020. Peptide-functionalized liposomes as therapeutic and diagnostic tools for cancer treatment. J. Control. Release 329, 624–644.

Sorrentino, B.P., 2002. Gene therapy to protect haematopoietic cells from cytotoxic cancer drugs. Nat. Rev. Cancer 2 (6), 431–441.

Sung, H., Ferlay, J., Siegel, R.L., Laversanne, M., Bray, F., Soerjomataram, I., et al., 2021. Global cancer statistics 2020: GLOBOCAN estimates of incidence and mortality worldwide for 36 cancers in 185 countries. CA Cancer J. Clin. 71 (3), 2019–2249.

Sutter, A.P., Fechner, H., 2006. Gene therapy for gastric cancer: is it promising? World J. Gastroenterol. 12 (3), 380.

Taghavi, S., et al., 2017. Polyethylenimine-functionalized carbon nanotubes tagged with AS1411 aptamer for combination gene and drug delivery into human gastric cancer cells. 516(1–2), 301–312.

Taghdisi, S.M., et al., 2016. Double targeting and aptamer-assisted controlled release delivery of epirubi-cin to cancer cells by aptamers-based dendrimer in vitro and in vivo. 102, 152–158.

Tahermansouri, H., Chitgar, F., 2013. Synthesis of isatin derivative on the short multiwalled carbon nanotubes and their effect on the mkn-45 and sw742 cancer cells. J. Chem. 2013.

Tahermansouri, H., Ghobadinejad, H., 2013. Functionalization of short multi-walled carbon nanotubes with creatinine and aromatic aldehydes via microwave and thermal methods and their influence on the MKN45 and MCF7 cancer cells. Comptes Rendus Chimie 16 (9), 838–844.

Tai, W., Mahato, R., Cheng, K., 2010. The role of HER2 in cancer therapy and targeted drug delivery. J. Control. Release. 146 (3), 264–275.

Takahashi, T., Saikawa, Y., Kitagawa, Y., 2013. Gastric cancer: current status of diagnosis and treatment. Cancers (Basel) 5 (1), 48–63.

Tavakoli, A., et al., 2020. Association between Epstein-Barr virus infection and gastric cancer: a systematic review and meta-analysis. BMC Cancer 20, 1–14.

Thrumurthy, S.G., Chaudry, M.A., Hochhauser, D., Mughal, M., 2013. The diagnosis and management of gastric cancer. BMJ 347.

Tomalia, D.A., 2005. Birth of a new macromolecular architecture: dendrimers as quantized building blocks for nanoscale synthetic polymer chemistry. Prog. Polym. Sci. 30 (3–4), 294–324.

Tong, Q.S., Zheng, L.D., Chen, F.M., Zeng, F.Q., Wang, L., Dong, J.H., Lu, G.C. Selection of optimal antisense accessible sites of survivin and its application in treatment of gastric cancer. World J Gastroenterol. 11(5), 634–640.

Torchilin, V.P., 2005. Recent advances with liposomes as pharmaceutical carriers. Nat. Rev. Drug. Discov. 4 (2), 145–160.

Tripathy, S., Das, M.K., 2013. Dendrimers and their applications as novel drug delivery carriers. J. Appl. Pharm. Sci. 3 (9), 142–149.

Uemura, N., Okamoto, S., Yamamoto, S., Matsumura, N., Yamaguchi, S., Yamakido, M., et al., 2001. Helicobacter pylori infection and the development of gastric cancer. N Engl J Med. 345 (11), 784–789.

Valizadeh, A., et al., 2012. Quantum dots: synthesis, bioapplications, and toxicity. Nanoscale Res. Lett. 7 (1), 1–14.

Van Cutsem, E., Kang, Y., Chung, H., Shen, L., Sawaki, A., Lordick, F., et al., 2009. Efficacy results from the ToGA trial: a phase III study of trastuzumab added to standard chemotherapy in first-line HER2-positive advanced gastric cancer. J clin oncol 27 (18), LBA4509.

Van Cutsem, E., et al., 2016. Gastric cancer. Lancet 388 (10060), 2654–2664.

Verma, I.M., et al., 2000. Gene therapy: promises, problems and prospects. Genes and Resistance to Disease. Springer, pp. 147–157.

Virgilio, E., et al., 2020. Elevated gastric juice carbohydrate antigen 72.4 (Ca 72.4) is an independent prognostic factor of poor survival for gastric cancer patients. Anticancer. Res. 40 (3), 1691–1695.

Wang, C., Bao, C., Liang, S., Fu, H., Wang, K., Deng, M., et al., 2014. RGD-conjugated silica-coated gold nanorods on the surface of carbon nanotubes for targeted photoacoustic imaging of gastric cancer. Nanoscale Res Lett. 9 (1), 264.

Wang, J., et al., 2014a. Intracellular uptake of etoposide-loaded solid lipid nanoparticles induces an enhancing inhibitory effect on gastric cancer through mitochondria-mediated apoptosis pathway. Int. J. Nanomed. 9, 3987.

Wang, Q., et al., 2014b. Fluorescent carbon dots as an efficient siRNA nanocarrier for its interference therapy in gastric cancer cells. J. Nanobiotechnol. 12 (1), 1–12.

Wang, J., et al., 2018. Polyamidoamine dendrimer microgels: hierarchical arrangement of dendrimers into micrometer domains with expanded structural features for programmable drug delivery and release. Macromolecules 51 (15), 6111–6118.

Wicki, A., Witzigmann, D., Balasubramanian, V., Huwyler, J. 2015. Nanomedicine in cancer therapy: challenges, opportunities, and clinical applications. Journal of controlled release. 200, 138–157

Wijagkanalan, W., Kawakami, S., Hashida, M., 2011. Designing dendrimers for drug delivery and imaging: pharmacokinetic considerations. Pharm. Res. 28 (7), 1500–1519.

Wolinsky, J.B., Grinstaff, M.W., 2008. Therapeutic and diagnostic applications of dendrimers for cancer treatment. Adv. Drug. Deliv. Rev. 60 (9), 1037–1055.

Woller, E.K., Cloninger, M.J., 2001. Mannose functionalization of a sixth generation dendrimer. Biomacromolecules 2 (3), 1052–1054.

Wu, B., et al., 2021a. Dietary salt intake and gastric cancer risk: a systematic review and meta-analysis ietary salt intake and gastric cancer. Front. Nutr 8.

Wu, B., et al., 2021b. Trifunctional graphene quantum Dot@ LDH integrated nanoprobes for visualization therapy of gastric cancer. Adv. Healthc. Mater. 2100512.

Wu, C.-C., et al., 2014. The effect of individual and neighborhood socioeconomic status on gastric cancer survival. PLoS One 9 (2), e89655.

Wu, C.W., Lo, S.S., Shen, K.H., Hsieh, M.C., Chen, J.H., Chiang, J.H., Lin, H.J., Li, A.F., Lui, W.Y., 2003. Incidence and factors associated with recurrence patterns after intended curative surgery for gastric cancer. World Journal of Surgery 27 (2), 153–158.

Wu, F.-L., et al., 2017. Enhanced antiproliferative activity of antibody-functionalized polymeric nanoparticles for targeted delivery of anti-miR-21 to HER2 positive gastric cancer. Oncotarget 8 (40), 67189.

Wu, Y., et al., 2010. The investigation of polymer-siRNA nanoparticle for gene therapy of gastric cancer in vitro. Int. J. Nanomed. 5, 129.

Xu, W., Bae, E.J., Lee, M.-K., 2018. Enhanced anticancer activity and intracellular uptake of paclitaxel-containing solid lipid nanoparticles in multidrug-resistant breast cancer cells. Int. J. Nanomed. 13, 7549.

Xu, X., et al., 2013. Clinical comparison between paclitaxel liposome (Lipusu®) and paclitaxel for treatment of patients with metastatic gastric cancer. Asian Pac. J. Cancer Prev. 14 (4), 2591–2594.

Yan, X., Wang, K., Lu, W., Qin, W., Cui, D., He, J., 2016. CdSe/ZnS quantum dot-labeled lateral flow strips for rapid and quantitative detection of gastric cancer carbohydrate antigen 72-4. Nanoscale Res. Lett. 11 (1), 1–8.

Yang, H., Kao, W.J., 2006. Dendrimers for pharmaceutical and biomedical applications. J. Biomater. Sci. Polym. Ed. 17 (1–2), 3–19.

Yang, H., 2016. Targeted nanosystems: advances in targeted dendrimers for cancer therapy. Nanomed.: Nanotechnol. Biol. Med. 12 (2), 309–316.

Yang, W., Thordarson, P., Gooding, J.J., Ringer, S.P., Braet, F. 2007. Carbon nanotubes for biological and biomedical applications. Nanotechnology. 18 (41), 412001.

Yao, H.J., Zhang, Y.G., Sun, L., Liu, Y. 2014. The effect of hyaluronic acid functionalized carbon nanotubes loaded with salinomycin on gastric cancer stem cells. Biomaterials. 35(33), 9208–9223.

Yellepeddi, V.K., Kumar, A., Palakurthi, S., 2009. Surface modified poly (amido) amine dendrimers as diverse nanomolecules for biomedical applications. Expert. Opin. Drug. Deliv. 6 (8), 835−850.

Yu, H., Teng, L., Meng, Q., et al. 2013. Development of liposomal Ginsenoside Rg3: formulation optimization and evaluation of its anticancer effects. International journal of pharmaceutics. 450 (1-2), 250-258.

Yu, L.L., Wu, J.G., Dai, N., Yu, H.G., Si, J.M. 2011 Curcumin reverses chemoresistance of human gastric cancer cells by downregulating the NF-κB transcription factor. Oncology Reports. 26 (5), 1197-1203.

Yu, Z.C., Ding, J., Pan, B.R., Fan, D.M., Zhang, X.Y. 2002. Expression and bioactivity identification of soluble MG7 scFv. World J. Gastroenterol. 8 (1), 99.

Yu-Jen, CH., 2002. Potential role of tetrandrine in cancer therapy. Acta Pharmacol. Sin. 23, 1102−1106.

Yun, Z., Chinnathambi, A., Alharbi, S.A., Jin, Z. 2020. Biosynthesis of gold nanoparticles using Vetex negundo and evaluation of pro-apoptotic effect on human gastric cancer cell lines. J. Photochem. Photobiol. B, Biol. 203, 111749.

Yusefi, A.R., Lankarani, K.B., Bastani, P., Radinmanesh, M., Kavosi, Z., 2018. Risk factors for gastric cancer: a systematic review. Asian Pacific Journal of Cancer Prevention 19 (3), 591.

Zhang, C., Liu, Z.-K., 2003. Gene therapy for gastric cancer: a review. World J. Gastroenterol. 9 (11), 2390.

Zhang, C., Huang, P., Bao, L., He, M., Luo, T., Gao, G., Cui, D. 2011. Enhancement of gastric cell radiation sensitivity by chitosan-modified gold nanoparticles. J. Nanosci. Nanotechnol. 11(11), 9528−9535.

Zhang, E., et al., 2019. Vascular targeted chitosan-derived nanoparticles as docetaxel carriers for gastric cancer therapy. Int. J. Biol. Macromol. 126, 662−672.

Zhang, H., Yee, D., & Wang, C. (2008). Quantum dots for cancer diagnosis and therapy: biological and clinical perspectives.

Zhang, J.H, Wan, M.X., Pan, B.R., Yu, B. 2004. Cytotoxicity of HSV tk and hrTNF-alpha fusion genes with IRES in treatment of gastric cancer. Cancer Biol. Ther. 3 (11), 1075−1080.

Zhang, Y., Tan, J., Zhou, L., Shan, X., Liu, J., Ma, Y., 2020. Synthesis and application of AS1411-functionalized gold nanoparticles for targeted therapy of gastric cancer. ACS Omega 5 (48), 31227−31233.

Zhen, L., Fan, D., Yi, X., Cao, X., Chen, D., Wang, L., 2014. Curcumin inhibits oral squamous cell carcinoma proliferation and invasion via EGFR signaling pathways. Int. J. Clin. Exp. Pathol. 7 (10), 6438.

Zheng, X.-C., et al., 2018. The theranostic efficiency of tumor-specific, pH-responsive, peptide-modified, liposome-containing paclitaxel and superparamagnetic iron oxide nanoparticles. Int. J. Nanomed. 13, 1495.

Zhong, Y., et al., 2014. Ligand-directed active tumor-targeting polymeric nanoparticles for cancer chemotherapy. Biomacromolecules 15 (6), 1955−1969.

Ziemba, B., et al., 2012. Influence of dendrimers on red blood cells. Cell. Mol. Biol. Lett. 17 (1), 21−35.

CHAPTER 11

Nanocarrier-mediated delivery for targeting colon cancer

Rajesh Singh Pawar[1], Shweta Kumar[2] and Sulakshana Pawar[3]
[1]Truba Institute of Pharmacy, Bhopal, Madhya Pradesh, India
[2]Department of General Medicine, All India Institute of Medical Sciences, Bhopal, Madhya Pradesh, India
[3]Institute of Pharmacy, Bundelkhand University, Jhansi, Uttar Pradesh, India

11.1 Introduction

Cancer is a multistep, multigene disease in which a group of cells show uncontrolled growth and does not follow the normal rule of cell division. In case of normal cell division, they are continuously subjected to signals that give the information whether the cell should divide and proliferate into another cell or die; this is not possible in case of cancerous cells (Fig. 11.1). The cancer cells not only proliferate continuously but may also spread to other body parts (metastasize) (Yahya and Alqadhi, 2021; Stewart and Kleihues, 2003). Currently, cancer is the main reason for mortality in most of the developed and developing countries, and among them colon cancer is the third most frequently diagnosed carcinoma globally. It mainly affects old persons, but it has been reported to be more common in younger population these days. The rise in incidence of colonic cancer cases demand effective treatment strategies (Malki et al., 2021; Stoffel and Murphy, 2020).

A cancer of the colon typically develops in the form of adenomatous (precancerous) polyps at the innermost wall of the large intestine (Fig. 11.2). Progression with time, some polyps gets converted into cancerous forms. Such abnormal growth of cells is responsible for the development of colon cancer (Labianca et al., 2010; Rajamanickam and Agarwal, 2008).

11.2 Symptoms and causes

Colon cancer may cause signs and symptoms such as:
- Alteration in frequency of bowel movements, such as diarrhea or constipation or a feeling of incomplete emptying.
- Rectal bleeding or blood in stool (bright or dark red).
- Abdominal pain/discomfort.
- Bloated stomach.
- Weakness or tiredness.
- Unexplained weight loss.

Multifunctional Nanocomposites for Targeted Drug Delivery in Cancer Therapy
DOI: https://doi.org/10.1016/B978-0-323-95303-0.00001-0

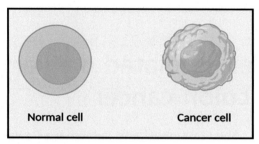

Figure 11.1 Representation of normal cell vs cancer cell.

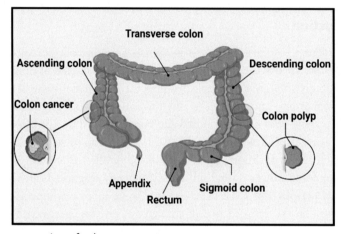

Figure 11.2 Representation of colon cancer.

The various factors that can increase the risk of colon cancer include the following (Terzić et al., 2010):

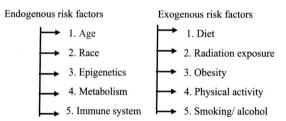

Unfortunately, this type of cancer sometimes does not exhibit any signs or symptoms. So, the undetected and untreated colon carcinoma extends through the layer of the colon and invades to the adjacent lymphoid tissue and organs. Eventually, it may be metastasized to the distant organs such as the brain, lungs, liver, and bones (Engstrom et al., 2009).

The screening can be done by fecal immunochemical tests, colonoscopy, X-rays, CT scans, etc. Various diagnostic tools are available to confirm colon cancer. In case of suspicion of colon cancer, laboratory tests such as blood tests and urine analysis will be done. In order to confirm the diagnosis, a biopsy may be performed during colonoscopy (Burt, 2000).

11.2.1 Different stages of colon cancer

Colon remains a key part of the gastrointestinal (GI) tract, and the development of colon cancer is described clinically by the stages, including stage I, stage II, stage III, and stage IV (Fig. 11.3):

Stage 0: This is known as carcinoma in situ. Disease remains within the innermost lining or mucosa of colon.

Stage I: The tumor has grown through the mucosa.

Stage II: The tumor has begun to spread to the muscular layer of colon into the adjacent tissue.

Stage III: It has spread to one or more lymph nodes beyond the wall of colon to other organs in the abdomen.

Stage IV: It is a malignant form of colon cancer and results in metastasis. It has metastasized to distant body parts, such as the liver, lungs, ovaries, or bones (Ulanja et al., 2019).

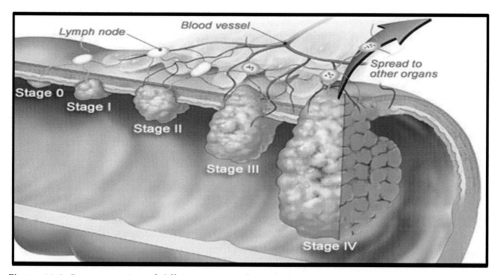

Figure 11.3 Representation of different stages of colon cancer.

11.2.2 Therapeutic management strategies for colon cancer

For the effective management of colon cancer, different conventional strategies include surgery polypectomy, targeted therapy, chemotherapy, and radiation therapy. Advanced therapies used to treat cancer include gene therapy, immunotherapy, etc. But still chemotherapy is the most widely used for the removal of cancerous cells. Metastatic colon cancer is conventionally treated with first-line chemotherapeutic agents like 5-fluorouracil, leucovorin, irinotecan, and oxaliplatin (Banerjee et al., 2017).

Epidermal growth factor receptor (EGFR) is one of the key molecular target for colon cancer management using several therapeutics and monoclonal antibodies. It is among the tyrosine kinase family and also associated with angiogenesis. Hence, tyrosine kinase inhibitors are the most promising therapeutics to tackle colon cancer, and recent drug development focus on new analogs of drug molecules that precisely target tyrosine kinase (Yarom and Jonker, 2011). Vascular endothelium growth factors (VEGFs) are another important molecular target for colon cancer management, where therapeutics downregulate the activity of VEGF and limit the supply of blood and nutrients to the growing tumor. Cancer cells primarily bypass immune surveillance, resulting in the rapid growth of tissue. Immune stimulators are new generation therapeutics to tackle colon cancer effectively where PD-1 receptor and CTLA4 is a key target to boost immune response and activates cytotoxic T cells (Malki et al., 2020). Table 11.1 summarizes FDA-approved immunotherapeutic drugs for the management of colon cancer.

Table 11.1 A summary of food and drug administration-approved therapeutics for the management of colon cancer and their mechanisms of action.

Sl. No.	Drug	Mechanism of action	References
1.	Cetuximab	Cetuximab action is to inhibit the growth and survival of epidermal growth factor receptor (EGFR)-expressing tumor cells with high specificity and higher affinity than epidermal growth factor (EGF) and transforming growth factor–alpha (TGF-α)	Harding and Burtness (2005)
2.	Bevacizumab	Bevacizumab, is antiangiogenic drug molecule sold as Avastin, is an effective therapeutic for colon and other types of cancer. Drug selectively targets circulating vascular endothelial growth factor (VEGF) and inhibits the binding of VEGF to its cell surface receptors. Tumors lack nutrient supply due to inhibition of VEGF receptor and are deprived of oxygen and nutrients	Ellis (2006)

(Continued)

Table 11.1 (Continued)

Sl. No.	Drug	Mechanism of action	References
3.	Panitumumab	Colon cancer remains associated with overexpression of EGFR, and Panitumumab is a monoclonal antibody against EGFR, binds selectively to receptor and changes downsignaling cascade	Dubois and Cohen (2009)
4.	Ziv-Aflibercept	Ziv-Aflibercept regulates angiogenesis by targeting human VEGF. As a result, decreased neovascularization and vascular permeability result in shortage of oxygen and nutrient supply to the tumor tissue	Patel and Sun (2014)
5.	Regorafenib	Regorafenib is a tyrosine kinases inhibitor that restricts the activity of enzyme associated in angiogenesis. Regorafenib alters the tumor tissue microenvironment where supply of nutrients, including oxygen, gets impaired	Grothey et al. (2019)
6.	Ramucirumab	Ramucirumab is a monoclonal antibody and VEGFR2 antagonist. Drug possesses a high affinity to the extracellular domain of VEGFR2 and stops the binding of natural VEGFR ligands (VEGF-A, VEGF-C, and VEGF-D). As a result, tumor tissue fails in angiogenesis and supply of nutrient to growing tumor	Verdaguer et al. (2016)
7.	Pembrolizumab	Pembrolizumab is a humanized monoclonal IgG4 isotype antibody, which selectively targets the programmed cell death protein-1 (PD-1) receptor on the surface of lymphocytes. The blocking of PD-1 receptor prevents the interaction and activation with immune-supressing ligands, PD-L1/PD-L2. This helps to restore the immune response by triggering the T cells to find and kill tumor cells	Kwok et al. (2016)
8.	Nivolumab	Nivolumab is the first-in-human immunoglobulin G4 (IgG4) anti-PD-1 monoclonal antibody (mAb) that disrupts its binding with its ligands PD-L1 and PD-L2. By inhibiting PD-1 pathway, allowing T-cells to kill the cancer cells	Guo et al. (2017)
9.	Ipilimumab	Ipilimumab is a humanized monoclonal IgG1 monoclonal antibody that blocks cytotoxic T lymphocyte antigen-4 (CTLA-4) interaction with CD80/CD86 allowing the t-cells to fully activate. Thus, they can recognize and attack cancer cells	Camacho (2015)

A schematic diagram is shown below where therapeutics has been developed based on these three key molecular targets (EGFR, VEGF, and inhibitors of PD1 and CTLA 4) (Figs. 11.4 and 11.5).

These immunotherapy strategies are quite effective, but they are used as second- and third-line treatment options because of their high cost and side effects. The various conventional drug delivery systems available for the treatment of colon cancer are not effective as the drug does not reach at the location in sufficient concentration (Anderson et al., 2016). Moreover, some of the therapeutic moieties are sensitive to the upper GI tract environment because of the presence of bile salts, proteolytic enzymes, and gastric pH, which could deteriorate the active moiety. This results in an unacceptable variation in bioavailability of drugs to the target site, which stops it to achieve effective therapeutic level. So, to reduce the drug absorption in nontarget sites or to achieve targeted drug delivery of the drug toward the colon, we focused on nanotechnology-based targeted drug delivery system. In recent decades nanotechnology has immense potential in the management of cancer. A voluminous amount of research has been done in the field of novel nanocarrier-based targeted drug delivery systems that will possibly benefit clinical cancer care (Edis et al., 2021; Lee et al., 2020).

The approach of targeted drug delivery systems has helped in enhancing clinical efficacy by improving bioavailability and reducing systemic toxicity of chemotherapeutics. However, nanomedicines often face several challenges in their clinical translation owing to the vast heterogeneity within and between tumors, which affect its efficiency (De et al., 2021). So, to mitigate such challenges, researchers are investigating various carrier systems to deliver chemotherapeutic agents at the site of action without

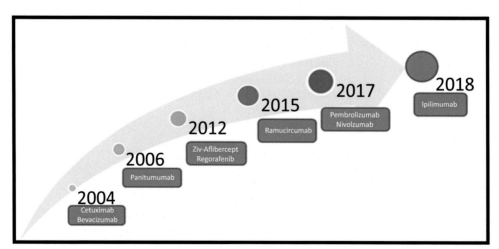

Figure 11.4 Schematic representation of therapeutic development targeting EGFR, VEGF, and PD1, CTLA4 inhibitors. *EGFR*, Epidermal growth factor receptor; *VEGFs*, Vascular endothelium growth factors; *CTLA-4*, cytotoxic T lymphocyte antigen-4.

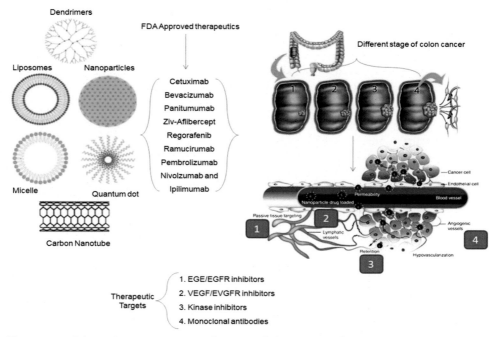

Figure 11.5 Schematic representation of approved therapeutics for the management of colon cancer and their therapeutic targets.

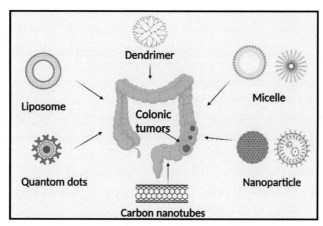

Figure 11.6 Different types of nanocarriers for drug delivery in colon cancer.

affecting the healthy cells. With further advancement in nanomedicine, different types of nanocarriers have been successfully deisgned and developed in the form of nanomedicine liposomes, micelles, and polymeric nanoparticles (NPs) have been investigated (Yu et al., 2010) (Fig. 11.6).

11.3 Nanocarrier-based targeted drug delivery strategies in colon cancer

In order to improve anticancer therapy, a range of novel nanocarrier-mediated drug delivery systems are tailored to deliver the drugs at targeted sites. The different types of nanocarriers-based delivery systems are illustrated in the figure below. Some of the popular nanocarriers include dendrimers, chitosan, liposomes, polymeric NPs, micelles, carbon nanotubes (CNTs), solid lipid NPs, magnetic NPs, and quantum dots (QDs). These nanocarriers are discussed in the following subsections.

1. **Nanoparticles**: NPs could offer the possibility to encapsulate various drugs, protect therapeutic molecules, and provide many advantages over their bulk counterparts. NPs consist of a solid sphere structure, which is produced via a self-assembly process. They include nanospheres and nanocapsules due to the different modes of formation of the NPs. In nanospheres, the loading agents are dissolved and dispersed throughout the polymer matrix, while the drugs encapsulated in nanocapsules are confined in a shell-like wall made by a single polymer membrane (Truong et al., 2015).

   NPs show a lot of advantages as a delivery system due to their biocompatibility, low toxicity, and controlled release properties. However, one of the most important properties is that they can be modified to specifically deliver drugs to targeted tumor tissues, surface modification can be possible in two manner such as by using targeting ligands or by using enteric polymer, which enhances the efficient navigation of the in vivo environment and sustained release of anticancer drugs along with significantly improve the therapeutic efficacy of the anticancer drugs and minimize the side effects (You et al., 2016). Tumor tissues classically present an acidic microenvironment as well as a leaky vasculature with impaired lymphatic drainage. The treatment of colon cancer commonly depends on the tumor size, the local microenvironment, and the range of cancer metastasis (Anitha et al., 2016). Considering these physiological features, encapsulating the anticancer drugs in polymer-based NPs can be a desirable method to overcome biologic barriers. When treating a certain cancer, the NPs encapsulating anticancer drugs must penetrate diverse biological barriers and specifically reach the tumor sites at a precise concentration. In addition, the active agents should selectively kill cancer cells, increasing the therapeutic efficacy and decreasing side effects simultaneously (Egusquiaguirre et al., 2012; Schroeder et al., 2012).

2. **Liposomes**: Liposomes are the most popular nanocarriers for targeted drug delivery. These consists vesicles that are spherical in shape and are made up of phospholipid bilayers. They act as a good drug delivery system for drugs with various physicochemical properties (Akbarzadeh et al., 2013). As drug delivery, liposomes offer certain benefits like the capacity to enclose both hydrophilic and lipophilic drugs biodegradability, biocompatibility, and other nontoxic properties (Pereira et al., 2016). In order to

improve liposomal drug delivery to the tumor site, targeting approaches with the conjugation of ligands to the surface of liposomes have been extensively studied (Kaur et al., 2020). Handali et al. described optimization of the preparation conditions for obtaining 5FU targeted liposomes with high encapsulation value and proper particle size for the management of colon cancer (Handali et al., 2018).

3. **Dendrimers**: Dendrimers are highly ordered, branched polymeric molecules; they have a very different structure from classical polymers, which make them unique. They consist of globular molecules made out of branched layers (generations). Such a precise synthesis leads to obtaining monodisperse molecules (Carvalho et al., 2020). On their outer surface, dendrimers can be engineered to have various functional groups such as COOH, COONa, NH2, or OH (Singh et al., 2016). Therefore, after very simple surface modification, dendrimers render intelligent NPs, transporting drugs into specific areas, and at the same time, they can be used for monitoring the state of organs attacked by cancer cells as well as the progress of the curing process. They can help to limit the anticancer drug delivery to designed goals only, eliminating many side effects of chemotherapy (Stanczyk et al., 2012).

4. **Carbon nanotubes**: The application of CNTs as versatile tools for cancer treatment is progressing at a very fast pace. They are rolled up by graphene sheets so that both ends are open, forming hollow cylindrical structures. Based on the layer formation, CNTs are named as single-walled carbon nanotubes (SWCNTs) and multi-walled carbon nanotubes (MWCNTs), each showing a variation in properties. SWCNTs possess unique physicochemical properties that improve their quality as nanocarriers and have a wide variety of applications (Sajid et al., 2016). SWCNTs often enter the cells by direct penetration but MWCNTs enter via the endocytosis pathway (Mu et al., 2009). SWCNTs improve the loading of drugs, DNA, proteins, antibodies, polymers, and photodrugs and facilitate both covalent and noncovalent functionalization of targeting moieties that make them unique nanocarriers in drug delivery systems (Tuncel, 2011). Sundaram et al. synthesized a nanobiocomposite consisting of hyaluronic acid-coupled SWCNTs coated with Ce6 for efficient PDT of colon cancer cells (Sundaram and Abrahamse, 2020).

5. **Quantum dots**: Due to the unique physical and chemical properties, such as great biocompatibility, superb electrical conductivity, and few layered atomic structure, QDs have attracted obvious attention nowadays (Matea et al., 2017). They are spherical semiconductor NPs with versatile surface chemistry, which can be modulated. They have high potential in various biological applications, including bioimaging and drug delivery systems (Matysiak-Brynda et al., 2018). Furthermore, QDs have much superiority compared to other drug carriers, such as larger specific surface area, smaller size, and stronger adsorption capacity. QD-based drug delivery provides a promising area for improving the efficacy of drugs and developing new therapies (Probst et al., 2013). Plich et al. formulate QDs as good carriers of

unsymmetrical bisacridines for modulating cellular uptake and the biological response in lung and colon cancer cells (Pilch et al., 2021).

6. **Micelles**: They are nanostructures of amphiphilic block copolymers that gather by itself in certain solvents above concentrations called critical micelle concentration. A typical micelle in water forms an aggregate with the hydrophilic "head" regions in contact with surrounding solvent, sequestering the hydrophobic single-tail regions in the micelle center (Zhang et al., 2014). They have demonstrated a variety of shapes such as spheres, rods, vesicles, tubules, and lamellae depending on the relative length of hydrophobic/hydrophilic blocks as well as the solvent environment (Shen et al., 1999). These nanosized delivery systems have been under the spotlight in recent years with new achievements in terms of their in vivo stability, ability to protect entrapped drugs, release kinetics, ease of cellular penetration, and thereby increased therapeutic efficacy. Gang Ma et al. designed azo polymeric micelles for colon-targeted dimethyl fumarate delivery for colon cancer therapy (Ma et al., 2016) (Table 11.2).

Table 11.2 Table summarizes key targets for anticancer therapy in colon cancer management and limitations of nanocarriers (Cerrito and Grassilli, 2021; Prados et al., 2013).

Sl. No.	Nanocarriers for colon cancer	Key targets	Limitations
1.	Nanoparticles	EGE/EGFR	Inorganic nanoparticles often remain associated with potential toxicity due to varying tissue distribution
2.	Dendrimers	VEGF/EVGFR	Dendrimers remain associated with complex preparation and drug loading events. They are poor in biological barrier transport and immunogenic in nature
3.	Carbon nanotubes	Wnt/β-catenin	CNTs cause potential toxicity, and surface modification is required to tackle CNTs-mediated toxicity
4.	Quantum dots	IGF/IGF1R	Nonbiodegradable, higher cost in production, and creating drug conjugates
5.	Micelles	Kinase inhibitors	Micelles are associated with a undefined microstructure unclear tissue distribution
6.	Liposomes	HGF/c-MET	Liposomes-based nanocarriers are associated with rapid renal clearance. Additionally, high low volume of distribution may lead to tissues specific toxicity

11.4 Approaches for nanocarrier-mediated colon-specific drug delivery

1. **pH-responsive drug delivery system**: The higher pH of the colon as compared to the upper GI tract can be used as a targeting strategy for colonic drug delivery. So, pH-dependent polymers such as cellulose acetate phthalates, polyacrylamide-modified hydroxypropyl methyl-cellulose phthalate, copolymers of methacrylic acid, and methyl methacrylate (e.g., Eudragit S 100, Eudragit L, Eudragit FS, and Eudragit P4135 F) can be used to deliver drug in the colon (Rashid et al., 2016). Particularly, Eudragit polymers are the most commonly used synthetic copolymers for drug delivery into the colon due to its pH-responsive and adhesive property with mucosa (Naik and Waghulde, 2018). As a result, drug delivery systems coated with pH-dependent polymers having a dissolution threshold of pH 5.5−7.5 possibly decrease the solubility of drug and selectively release the drug in the colon (Zhang et al., 2012). The dynamic variation in pH by many internal and external factors may affect the efficiency of pH-responsive controlled drug release systems. For instance, patients with ulcerative colitis, have more acidic colonic pH in contrast to healthy humans. This results in incomplete drug release from enteric coated systems at the target site. Other factors, such as the nature of food, fluid intake, and metabolism of microbes, may cause poorly site-selective drug release (Lee et al., 2020).

2. **Polymer-based drug delivery system**: A successful delivery of a drug to the colon requires protection of the drug from degradation or release in the stomach and then controlled release of drug in colon (Vyas and Khar, 2002). The desired properties of colon-targeted drug delivery systems can be achieved by using some polymers either alone or in a combination because it is now recognized that polymers can potentially influence the rate of release and absorption of drugs and play an important role in formulating colon-targeted drug delivery systems (Sureshkumar et al., 2014). Natural polysaccharides, such as guar gum, pectin, chitosan, chondroitin sulfate (CS), cyclodextrin, and amylose, are extensively used for the development of solid oral dosage forms for colonic delivery of drugs. These are biodegradable polymers and generally hydrophilic in nature and have limited swelling characteristic in acidic pH. Along with that, these polymers are inexpensive and available in a variety of structures. Linear polysaccharides remain intact in the stomach and small intestine, but the bacteria of human colon degrade them and thus make them potentially useful in colon-targeted drug delivery systems (Rajpurohit et al., 2010).

3. **Lipid-based formulation**: For the successful delivery of protein and peptide lipid-based delivery system could be designed. Lipid-based formulations are particularly promising because of their wide diversity, favorable biocompatibility, and specific functionality. Various lipoidal delivery systems for colon targeting, such as liposome, NP, nanocapsule, and emulsion, can be formulated by using different lipid excipients, including fatty acids, fatty alcohols, long- and medium-chain monoglycerides,

diglycerides, triglycerides, and phospholipids. Structurally, these amphiphillic molecules possess a hydrophobic region and hydrophilic core (Niu et al., 2016).

4. **Ligand/receptor-mediated drug delivery system**: In order to treat colonic diseases with reduced toxic side effects, ligand/receptor-mediated systems have been explored that increase target specificity via the interaction between targeting ligands on the carrier surface and specific receptors expressed at disease sites. Ligand/receptor-mediated system can be designed using various ligands (e.g., antibodies, peptides, folic acid, and hyaluronic acids) and selected based on the functional expression profiles of specific receptors/proteins at the target cells/organs. It can be also combined with pH-dependent systems to maximize its GI stability and site specificity, if needed (Si et al., 2016).

5. **Magnetically-driven drug delivery system:** Magnetic micro/nanocarriers, including magnetic microspheres, magnetic NPs, magnetic liposomes, and magnetic emulsions, are emerging novel formulations for controlled and targeted drug delivery (Luo and He, 2020). To improve the targeted treatment of colorectal cancer by mAb198.3 (a FAT1-specificmonoclonal antibody), Grifantini et al. (2018) developed two different novel drug delivery systems that have magnetic properties to improve the targeted treatment of colorectal cancer by mAb198.3 (a FAT1-specific monoclonal antibody), where mAb198.3 was directly bound to superparamagnetic NPs or embedded into human erythrocyte-based magnetized carriers. They observed that both systems were very effective at targeting colon cancer cells and inhibiting cancer growth at significantly lower antibody doses. This study demonstrated the potential of magnetically-driven drug delivery systems at improving the bioavailability and target specificity of anti-FAT mAb198.3, opening a new avenue for colon-targeted drug delivery (Grifantini et al., 2018). The various stages and approaches for nanocarrier-mediated colon-specific drug delivery are schematically represented in Fig. 11.7.

11.5 Phyto-nanocarrier-based strategies for targeting colon cancer

Recent studies have revealed that the anticarcinogenic potential of phytochemicals is widely utilized. Regardless of their exceptional anticancer potential, their low water solubility, limited bioavailability, low cell permeation, low therapeutic indices, liver disposition, and quick uptake by normal tissues impede their pharmacological activity. In this context, novel nanotechnological approaches have potentiated the utility of phytochemicals in cancer treatment. The various phytodrug conjugated nanocarriers investigated for colon cancer are discussed as below.

To overcome the bioavailability issue of poorly water soluble drugs, such as silymarin, its biocompatable nanosized carrier system (100–150 nm) was prepared from poly (hydroxybutyrate-co-hydroxyvalerate) using nanoprecipitation method. The prepared nanocarrier system was further characterized using scanning electron microscopy and atomic force microscopy

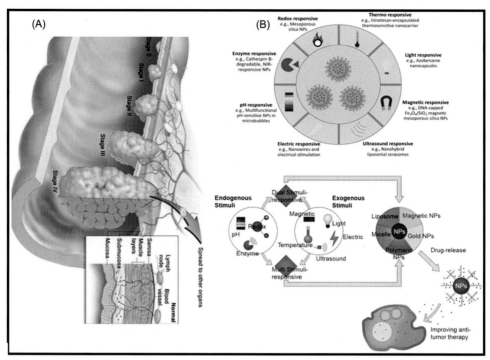

Figure 11.7 Schematic overview of (A) stages of colon cancer and (B) eight different types of stimuli applied in the design of stimuli-responsive nanocarriers for drug delivery: magneto responsive, thermo responsive, photo responsive, ultrasound responsive, electro responsive, pH responsive, enzyme responsive, and redox responsive. *NIR*, Near infrared; *NP*, nanoparticle.

analysis to confirm the size distribution of prepared NPs. The nanocarrier system of silymarin at 100 ug/mL has shown cytotoxic potential in both HT 29 cancer cells in monolayer culture systems and in 3D microtumor systems (spheroids) of the same cells (Radu et al., 2017).

Niosomes as a nanocarrier system for curcumin and methotrexate was developed, and further developed carrier systems were evaluated for its potential of growth inhibition and induction of apoptosis in HCT 116 cells of colorectal cancer origin (Mousazadeh et al., 2022).

Phlebotonic flavonoid–loaded phytosomes (diosmin) were prepared to improve drug dissolution and intestinal permeability. Prepared phytosomal nanocarriers have the lowest particle size (316 nm). Prepared phytosomes have shown promising drug loading (99.12% ± 0.09%). Furthermore, prepared nanocarriers have shown enhanced dissolution rate, intestinal permeability in both in vitro and ex vivo experiments (Freag et al., 2013).

Magnetic nanocarrier (mean size 70 nm), iron oxide NPs combined with silibinin were prepared using coprecipitation procedure and evaluated for its potential against human colon cancer using HT-29 cell line (Ramya et al., 2021).

Hydrophobicity-related limitation of curcumin was addressed by encapsulating curcumin into monomethoxy poly(ethylene glycol)-poly(ε-caprolactone) (MPEG-PCL) micelles via a single-step nanoprecipitation method. Prepared micelles were monodispersed, having mean particle size of 27.3 ± 1.3 nm and drug loading of $12.95\% \pm 0.15\%$. Intravenous administration of prepared formulation at dose 25 mg/kg curcumin have shown inhibition of subcutaneous C-26 colon carcinoma and enhanced anticancer effect via inhibiting angiogenesis and directly killing of cancer cells than that of free curcumin (Gou et al., 2011).

Poor water solubility of natural flavonoid fisetin was addressed by preparing its micelles using MPEG-PCL. Prepared nanocarrier system has mean particle size $(22 \pm 3$ nm) and drug loading $(9.88\% \pm 0.14\%)$. Prepared micelles have shown sustained and prolonged in vitro release and enhanced cytotoxicity and fisetin triggered apoptosis in CT26 cells. In vitro cytotoxicity research have revealed that fisetin micelles have $(IC50 = 7.968$ μg/mL) in contrast to free drugs $(IC50 = 28.513$ μg/mL). Furthermore, fisetin micelles have shown effective tumor suppression in CT26 subcutaneous tumor models (Chen et al., 2015).

Berry-derived anthocyanidins were encapsulated in bovine milk derived exosomes as a nanocarrier for the chemoprevention of bacteria driven colon tumor development. Anthocyanidins encapsulated in exosomes have shown four to 16-fold decrease in IC50 values compared to free anthocyandins in HCT-116, HT-29 in colon cancer cell lines and CCD-18Co in normal colon cells. Anthocyanidins exosomes at dose 8.6 mg/kg/day have shown significant reduction in colon tumor when compared to exosomes vehicle control group (Mudd et al., 2020).

Colon targeted delivery of pelargonidin-3-O-glucoside (P3G) utilizing pectin (P)/chitosan (CH)-functionalized nanoliposome (NL) was evaluated. Results of the study indicate that polymer-coated nanoliposomes have improved temperature and food stimulant stability in addition to enhanced retention of P3G. Simulated intestinal fluid digestion, ABTS antioxidant activity of pectin/chitosan functionalized nanoliposomes (P-CH-P3G-NL) is higher when compared to P3G-NL and CH-P3G-NL (Shishir et al., 2020).

Reactive oxygen species (ROS)-sensitive nanocomplexes (NCs) were developed using CS and anthocyanins (ATC) from black soya beans (CS-ATC). Doxorubicin (DOX) was entrapped in a CS-ATC NC by intermolecular stacking interaction. 1.67 times higher DOX was released from CS-ATC-DOX compared to the CS-DOX complex. HCT-116 human colon cancer cells treated with CS-ATC-DOX showed ROS-dependent cytotoxicity of the NC. Further, in vivo tumor inhibition effect of CS-ATC-DOX is higher compared to CS-DOX (Jeong et al., 2016). In another similar study, ATC and sulfuric hyaluronic acid (sHA) were explored to develop ROS sensitive NC. DOX was loaded into sHA-ATC NCs. Developed NC has shown improved apoptosis of CD44 + colon cancer HT29 cells. Further, results of the study indicate sHA-ATC NCs could optimize biodistribution of DOX and also reduce myelosuppression of DOX (Xiong et al., 2021). The various phytodrug conjugated nanocarriers investigated for colon cancer are summarized in Table 11.3.

To improve the therapeutic delivery of anticancer drugs to the colon, it is essential to consider the physiological and pathophysiological properties of the colon and the microenvironment surrounding disease site(s). The various novel nanocarriers developed using a triggered release mechanism (pH responsive, enzyme responsive, magnetic responsive, redox responsive) and phyto-nanocarriers discussed above have improved the local therapeutic outcome in colonic diseases, especially colon cancers. It has several advantages compared to conventional nontargeted therapy in terms of reducing off-target toxicity. Therefore, colon-targeted controlled delivery systems have gained wide acceptance as an effective tool for the treatment of colon cancer.

Table 11.3 The various phytodrug conjugated nanocarriers investigated for colon cancer.

Natural products	Carrier system	Study type	References
Silymarin	Poly(hydroxybutyrate-co-hydroxyvalerate)	Colon cancer cell line (HT-29)	Radu et al. (2017)
Curcumin (CUR) and methotrexate	Niosomes	HTT-116	Mousazadeh et al. (2022)
Diosmin	Phytosomal nanocarreir	Based on available data of diosmin (colon cancer treatmnet)	Freag et al. (2013)
silibinin	Magnetic nanocarrier	Colon cancer cell lines (HT-29)	Ramya et al. (2021)
Curcumin	Monomethoxy poly (ethylene glycol)- poly (ε-caprolactone) micelles	C-26 colon carcinoma	Gou et al. (2011)
Fisetin	Monomethyl poly(ethylene glycol)—poly (ε-caprolactone)	CT26 cell lines	Chen et al. (2015)
Berry-derived anthocyanidins	Bovine milk–derived exosomes	Colon cancer cell lines HCT-116 and HT-29	Mudd et al. (2020)
Pelargonidin-3-O-glucoside (P3G)	Pectin/chitosan-functionalized nanoliposome	Ex vivo (simulated fluid)	Shishir et al. (2020)
Black soya bean anthocyanin	Doxorubicin-chondroitin sulfate-anthocyanin-based nanocomplex	HCT-116 cell lines	Jeong et al. (2016)
Anthocyanin	Sulfuric hyaluronic acid-anthocyanin	HT 29 cell lines	Xiong et al. (2021)

References

Akbarzadeh, A., Rezaei-Sadabady, R., Davaran, S., Joo, S.W., Zarghami, N., Hanifehpour, Y., et al., 2013. Liposome: classification, preparation, and applications. Nanoscale Res. Lett. 8 (1), 1–9.

Anderson, D.S., Sydor, M.J., Fletcher, P., Holian, A., 2016. Nanotechnology: the risks and benefits for medical diagnosis and treatment. J. Nanomed. Nanotechnol. 7 (4), 143–153.

Anitha, A., Maya, S., Sivaram, A.J., Mony, U., Jayakumar, R., 2016. Combinatorial nanomedicines for colon cancer therapy. Wiley Interdiscip. Rev.: Nanomed. Nanobiotechnol. 8 (1), 151–159.

Banerjee, A., Pathak, S., Subramanium, V.D., Dharanivasan, G., Murugesan, R., Verma, R.S., 2017. Strategies for targeted drug delivery in treatment of colon cancer: current trends and future perspectives. Drug Discov. Today 22 (8), 1224–1232.

Burt, R.W., 2000. Colon cancer screening. Gastroenterology 119 (3), 837–853.

Camacho, L.H., 2015. CTLA-4 blockade with ipilimumab: biology, safety, efficacy, and future considerations. Cancer Med. 4 (5), 661–672. Available from: https://doi.org/10.1002/cam4.371.

Carvalho, M.R., Reis, R.L., Oliveira, J.M., 2020. Dendrimer nanoparticles for colorectal cancer applications. J. Mater. Chem. B 8 (6), 1128–1138.

Cerrito, M.G., Grassilli, E., 2021. Identifying novel actionable targets in colon cancer. Biomedicines 9 (5), 579. Available from: https://doi.org/10.3390/biomedicines9050579. Published 2021 May 20.

Chen, Y., Wu, Q., Song, L., He, T., Li, Y., Li, L., et al., 2015. Polymeric micelles encapsulating fisetin improve the therapeutic effect in colon cancer. ACS Appl. Mater. Interfaces 7 (1), 534–542.

De, C., Oliveira, S.L., Schomann, A.L., de Geus-Oei, T., Kapiteijn, L.F., Cruz, E., et al., 2021. Nanocarriers as a tool for the treatment of colorectal cancer. Pharmaceutics 13 (8), 1321.

Dubois, E.A., Cohen, A.F., 2009. Panitumumab. Br. J. Clin. Pharmacol. 68 (4), 482–483. Available from: https://doi.org/10.1111/j.1365-2125.2009.03492.x.

Edis, Z., Wang, J., Waqas, M.K., Ijaz, M., Ijaz, M., 2021. Nanocarriers-mediated drug delivery systems for anticancer agents: an overview and perspectives. Int. J. Nanomed. 16, 1313.

Egusquiaguirre, S.P., Igartua, M., Hernández, R.M., Pedraz, J.L., 2012. Nanoparticle delivery systems for cancer therapy: advances in clinical and preclinical research. Clin. Transl. Oncol. 14 (2), 83–93.

Ellis, L.M., 2006. Mechanisms of action of bevacizumab as a component of therapy for metastatic colorectal cancer. Semin. Oncol. 33 (5 Suppl. 10), S1–S7. Available from: https://doi.org/10.1053/j.seminoncol.2006.08.002. PMID: 17145519.

Engstrom, P.F., Arnoletti, J.P., Benson, A.B., Chen, Y.J., Choti, M.A., Cooper, H.S., et al., 2009. Colon cancer. J. Natl. Compr. Cancer Netw. 7 (8), 778–831.

Freag, M.S., Elnaggar, Y.S., Abdallah, O.Y., 2013. Lyophilized phytosomal nanocarriers as platforms for enhanced diosmin delivery: optimization and ex vivo permeation. Int. J. Nanomed. 8, 2385.

Gou, M., Men, K., Shi, H., Xiang, M., Zhang, J., Song, J., et al., 2011. Curcumin-loaded biodegradable polymeric micelles for colon cancer therapy in vitro and in vivo. Nanoscale 3 (4), 1558–1567.

Grifantini, R., Taranta, M., Gherardini, L., Naldi, I., Parri, M., Grandi, A., et al., 2018. Magnetically driven drug delivery systems improving targeted immunotherapy for colon-rectal cancer. J. Control. Release 280, 76–86.

Grothey, A., Prager, G., Yoshino, T., 2019. The mechanism of action of regorafenib in colorectal cancer: a guide for the community physician. Clin. Adv. Hematol. Oncol. 17 (Suppl 12(8)), 1–19. PMID: 32720931.

Guo, L., Zhang, H., Chen, B., 2017. Nivolumab as programmed death-1 (PD-1) inhibitor for targeted immunotherapy in tumor. J. Cancer 8 (3), 410–416. Available from: https://doi.org/10.7150/jca.17144. Published 2017 Feb 10.

Handali, S., Moghimipour, E., Rezaei, M., Ramezani, Z., Kouchak, M., Amini, M., et al., 2018. A novel 5-FLuorouracil targeted delivery to colon cancer using folic acid conjugated liposomes. Biomed. Pharmacother. 108, 1259–1273.

Harding, J., Burtness, B., 2005. Cetuximab: an epidermal growth factor receptor chemeric human-murine monoclonal antibody. Drugs Today (Barc) 41 (2), 107–127. Available from: https://doi.org/10.1358/dot.2005.41.2.882662. PMID: 15821783.

Jeong, D., Bae, B.C., Park, S.J., Na, K., 2016. Reactive oxygen species responsive drug releasing nano-particle based on chondroitin sulfate—anthocyanin nanocomplex for efficient tumor therapy. J. Control. Release 222, 78—85.

Kaur, V., Singh, A.S., Kaur, K., Rath, G., 2020. Targeted based drug delivery system for colon cancer. J. Drug Deliv. Ther. 10 (1), 111—122.

Kwok, G., Yau, T.C., Chiu, J.W., Tse, E., Kwong, Y.L., 2016. Pembrolizumab (Keytruda). Hum. Vaccin Immunother. 12 (11), 2777—2789. Available from: https://doi.org/10.1080/21645515.2016.1199310.

Labianca, R., Beretta, G.D., Kildani, B., Milesi, L., Merlin, F., Mosconi, S., et al., 2010. Colon cancer. J. Crit. Rev. Oncol./Hematol. 74 (2), 106—133.

Lee, S.H., Bajracharya, R., Min, J.Y., Han, J.W., Park, B.J., Han, H.K., 2020. Strategic approaches for colon targeted drug delivery: an overview of recent advancements. J. Pharm. 12 (1), 68—87.

Luo, L., He, Y., 2020. Magnetically driven microfluidics for isolation of circulating tumor cells. Cancer Med. 9 (12), 4207—4231.

Ma, Z.G., Ma, R., Xiao, X.L., Zhang, Y.H., Zhang, X.Z., Hu, N., et al., 2016. Azo polymeric micelles designed for colon-targeted dimethyl fumarate delivery for colon cancer therapy. Acta Biomater. 44, 323—331.

Malki, A., ElRuz, R.A., Gupta, I., Allouch, A., Vranic, S., Al Moustafa, A.E., et al., 2021. Molecular mechanisms of colon cancer progression and metastasis: recent insights and advancements. Int. J. Mol. Sci. 22 (1), 130.

Malki, A., ElRuz, R.A., Gupta, I., Allouch, A., Vranic, S., Al Moustafa, A.E., et al., 2020. Molecular mechanisms of colon cancer progression and metastasis: recent insights and advancements. Int. J. Mol. Sci. 22 (1), 130.

Matea, C.T., Mocan, T., Tabaran, F., Pop, T., Mosteanu, O., Puia, C., et al., 2017. Quantum dots in imaging, drug delivery and sensor applications. Int. J. Nanomed. 12, 5421.

Matysiak-Brynda, E., Bujak, P., Augustin, E., Kowalczyk, A., Mazerska, Z., Pron, A., et al., 2018. Stable nanoconjugates of transferrin with alloyed quaternary nanocrystals Ag—In—Zn—S as a biologi-cal entity for tumor recognition. Nanoscale 10 (3), 1286—1296.

Mousazadeh, N., Gharbavi, M., Rashidzadeh, H., Nosrati, H., Danafar, H., Johari, B., 2022. Anticancer evaluation of methotrexate and curcumin-coencapsulated niosomes against colorectal cancer cell lines. Nanomedicine 17 (4), 201—217.

Mu, Q., Broughton, D.L., Yan, B., 2009. Endosomal leakage and nuclear translocation of multiwalled carbon nanotubes: developing a model for cell uptake. Nano Lett. 9 (12), 4370—4375.

Mudd, A.M., Gu, T., Munagala, R., Jeyabalan, J., Egilmez, N.K., Gupta, R.C., 2020. Chemoprevention of colorectal cancer by anthocyanidins and mitigation of metabolic shifts induced by dysbiosis of the gut microbiome. Cancer Prev. Res. 13 (1), 41—52.

Naik, J.B., Waghulde, M.R., 2018. Development of vildagliptin loaded Eudragit® microspheres by screening design: in vitro evaluation. J. Pharm. Investig. 48 (6), 627—637.

Niu, Z., Conejos-Sánchez, I., Griffin, B.T., O'Driscoll, C.M., Alonso, M.J., 2016. Lipid-based nanocar-riers for oral peptide delivery. Adv. Drug Deliv. Rev. 106, 337—354.

Patel, A., Sun, W., 2014. Ziv-aflibercept in metastatic colorectal cancer. Biologics 8, 13—25. Available from: https://doi.org/10.2147/BTT.S39360.

Pereira, S., Egbu, R., Jannati, G., 2016. Docetaxel-loaded liposomes: the effect of lipid composition and purification on drug encapsulation and in vitro toxicity. Int. J. Pharm. 514 (1), 150—159.

Pilch, J., Kowalik, P., Bujak, P., Nowicka, A.M., Augustin, E., 2021. Quantum dots as a good carriers of unsymmetrical bisacridines for modulating cellular uptake and the biological response in lung and colon cancer cells. Nanomaterials 11 (2), 462.

Prados, J., Melguizo, C., Ortiz, R., Perazzoli, G., Cabeza, L., Alvarez, P.J., et al., 2013. Colon cancer therapy: recent developments in nanomedicine to improve the efficacy of conventional chemothera-peutic drugs. Anti-Cancer Agents Med. Chem. 13 (8), 1204—1216. Available from: https://doi.org/10.2174/18715206113139990325.

Probst, C.E., Zrazhevskiy, P., Bagalkot, V., Gao, X., 2013. Quantum dots as a platform for nanoparticle drug delivery vehicle design. Adv. Drug Deliv. Rev. 65 (5), 703—718.

Radu, I.C., Hudita, A., Zaharia, C., Stanescu, P.O., Vasile, E., Iovu, H., et al., 2017. Poly (hydroxybuty-rate-co-hydroxyvalerate)(PHBHV) nanocarriers for silymarin release as adjuvant therapy in colo-rectal cancer. Front. Pharmacol. 8, 508.

Rajamanickam, S., Agarwal, R., 2008. Natural products and colon cancer: current status and future prospects. J. Drug Dev. Res. 69 (7), 460−471.

Rajpurohit, H., Sharma, P., Sharma, S., Bhandari, A., 2010. Polymers for colon targeted drug delivery. Indian J. Pharm. Sci. 72 (6), 689.

Ramya, S., Thiruvenkataswamy, S., Kavithaa, K., Preethi, S., Winster, H., Balachander, V., et al., 2021. pH dependent drug release of Silibinin, a polyphenol conjugated with magnetic nanoparticle against the human colon cancer cell. J. Clust. Sci. 32 (2), 305−317.

Rashid, M., Kaur, V., Hallan, S.S., Sharma, S., Mishra, N., 2016. Microparticles as controlled drug delivery carrier for the treatment of ulcerative colitis: a brief review. Saudi Pharm. J. 24 (4), 458−472.

Sajid, M.I., Jamshaid, U., Jamshaid, T., Zafar, N., Fessi, H., Elaissari, A., 2016. Carbon nanotubes from synthesis to in vivo biomedical applications. Int. J. Pharm. 501 (1-2), 278−299.

Schroeder, A., Heller, D.A., Winslow, M.M., Dahlman, J.E., Pratt, G.W., Langer, R., et al., 2012. Treating metastatic cancer with nanotechnology. Nat. Rev. Cancer 12 (1), 39−50.

Shen, H., Zhang, L., Eisenberg, A., 1999. Multiple pH-induced morphological changes in aggregates of polystyrene-block-poly (4-vinylpyridine) in DMF/H2O mixtures. J. Am. Chem. Soc. 121 (12), 2728−2740.

Shishir, M.R., Karim, N., Xie, J., Rashwan, A.K., Chen, W., 2020. Colonic delivery of pelargonidin-3-O-glucoside using pectin-chitosan-nanoliposome: transport mechanism and bioactivity retention. Int. J. Biol. Macromol. 159, 341−355.

Si, X.Y., Merlin, D., Xiao, B., 2016. Recent advances in orally administered cell-specific nanotherapeutics for inflammatory bowel disease. World J. Gastroenterol. 22 (34), 7718.

Singh, J., Jain, K., Mehra, N.K., Jain, N.K., 2016. Dendrimers in anticancer drug delivery: mechanism of interaction of drug and dendrimers. Artif. Cells Nanomed. Biotechnol. 2;44 (7), 1626−1634.

Stanczyk, M., Dziki, A., Morawiec, Z., 2012. Dendrimers in therapy for breast and colorectal cancer. Curr. Med. Chem. 19 (29), 4896−4902.

Stewart, B.W., Kleihues, P. (Eds.), 2003. World Cancer Report. IARC Press, Lyon.

Stoffel, E.M., Murphy, C.C., 2020. Epidemiology and mechanisms of the increasing incidence of colon and rectal cancers in young adults. J. Gastroenterol. 158 (2), 341−353.

Sundaram, P., Abrahamse, H., 2020. Effective photodynamic therapy for colon cancer cells using chlorin e6 coated hyaluronic acid-based carbon nanotubes. Int. J. Mol. Sci. 21 (13), 4745.

Sureshkumar, R., Munikumar, M., Ganesh, G.N., Jawahar, N., Nagasamyvenkatesh, D., Senthil, V., et al., 2014. Formulation and evaluation of pectin-hydroxypropyl methylcellulose coated curcumin pellets for colon delivery. Asian J. Pharm. 3 (2).

Terzić, J., Grivennikov, S., Karin, E., Karin, M., 2010. Inflammation and colon cancer. J. Gastroenterol. 138 (6), 2101−2114.

Truong, N.P., Whittaker, M.R., Mak, C.W., Davis, T.P., 2015. The importance of nanoparticle shape in cancer drug delivery. Expert. Opin. Drug Deliv. 12 (1), 129−142.

Tuncel, D., 2011. Non-covalent interactions between carbon nanotubes and conjugated polymers. Nanoscale 3 (9), 3545−3554.

Ulanja, M.B., Rishi, M., Beutler, B.D., Sharma, M., Patterson, D.R., Gullapalli, N., et al., 2019. Colon cancer sidedness, presentation, and survival at different stages. J. Oncol. 2019.

Verdaguer, H., Tabernero, J., Macarulla, T., 2016. Ramucirumab in metastatic colorectal cancer: evidence to date and place in therapy. Ther. Adv. Med. Oncol. 8 (3), 230−242. Available from: https://doi.org/10.1177/1758834016635888.

Vyas, S.P., Khar, R.K., 2002. Controlled Drug Delivery Concepts and Advances, 1. Vallabh Prakashan, pp. 411−417.

Xiong, Y., Yang, G., Zhou, H., Li, W., Sun, J., Tao, T., et al., 2021. A ROS-responsive self-assembly driven by multiple intermolecular interaction enhances tumor-targeted chemotherapy. J. Pharm. Sci. 110 (4), 1668−1675.

Yahya, E.B., Alqadhi, A.M., 2021. Recent trends in cancer therapy: a review on the current state of gene delivery. Life Sci. 269, 119087.

Yarom, N., Jonker, D.J., 2011. The role of the epidermal growth factor receptor in the mechanism and treatment of colorectal cancer. Discov. Med. 11 (57), 95–105.

You, X., Kang, Y., Hollett, G., Chen, X., Zhao, W., Gu, Z., et al., 2016. Polymeric nanoparticles for colon cancer therapy: overview and perspectives. J. Mater. Chem. B 4 (48), 7779–7792.

Yu, B.O., Tai, H.C., Xue, W., Lee, L.J., Lee, R.J., 2010. Receptor-targeted nanocarriers for therapeutic delivery to cancer. Mol. Membr. Biol. 27 (7), 286–298.

Zhang, L., Zhu, W., Yang, C., Guo, H., Yu, A., Ji, J., et al., 2012. A novel folate-modified self-microemulsifying drug delivery system of curcumin for colon targeting. Int. J. Nanomed. 7, 151.

Zhang, Y., Huang, Y., Li, S., 2014. Polymeric micelles: nanocarriers for cancer-targeted drug delivery. AAPS PharmSciTech 15 (4), 862–871.

CHAPTER 12

Multifunctional nanocomposites for blood cancer

Monika Targhotra and Meenakshi Kanwar Chauhan
Department of Pharmaceutics, Delhi Institute of Pharmaceutical Sciences and Research, DPSR-University, New Delhi, India

12.1 Introduction

Leukemia is among the most challenging diseases to cure, and several sufferers' lives are at risk. Early detection and systemic treatment for cancer are essential for lowering cancer-related death rates and morbidity. Cancer-based chemotherapy cure performance is calculated not just by the anticancer medication itself but by how well the medication reagent is transported toward its target (Alexiou et al., 2000). Despite the great attempt to overcome the relevant challenges, developing a new technique to mark and monitor the target cancerous cells for timely treatment and diagnosis of tumors remains a major difficulty. Furthermore, antibiotic resistance is a global challenge in the treatment of related diseases, and the development of multidrug resistance is among the biggest roadblocks toward the efficacy of tumor chemotherapy (Paul et al., 1996; Litman et al., 1997). It should be remembered that the underlying mechanisms of cancerous cell treatment resistance are multifactor activities. Furthermore, the intracellular absorption of certain medicines by altered tumor cells could be low. Drug-resistance proteins can transport active ingredients out of mutant tumor cells, lowering the concentration of drugs within the cells (Song et al., 2008). As a result, effective medication distribution targeted at appropriate cancerous cells may provide a novel technique for successful therapy of localized tumors (Ping et al., 2009; Wu et al., 2005).

Leukemia is a type of hematological malignancy that involves the bone marrow, lymph vessels, and blood platelets, and it is most prevalent in adults (Siegel et al., 2016). This is clonal hematopoiesis, which is detected by the unregulated development of poorly differentiated white blood cells in the bone marrow. Therapy for this condition is determined by various criteria, including the kind of leukemia, age, the severity of illness, and the patient history. Target-based therapy (chemotherapy), radiation therapy, and bone marrow transplants are standard treatments for people with leukemia (Greaves, 2016). Acute lymphocytic leukemia (ALL), chronic myeloid leukemia (CML), chronic lymphocytic leukemia (CLL), and acute myeloid leukemia (AML) are the four primary types of leukemia disease, depending on the extent of cell generation (acute or chronic) and the kind of cell damaged (myeloid or lymphoid). AML leukemia is by far the most frequent kind in adults, while ALL is much more prevalent in childhood. The distinction between CML and CLL is determined by the number of cancerous white blood cells. CLL develops defective cells from lymphocytic blood stem cells (B cells), whereas CML develops faulty cells from myeloid blood stem cells (Jabbour and Kantarjian, 2014; Wierda et al., 2019). Conventional cancer treatments, like surgeries, chemo and radiotherapy, can result in inadequate cancer elimination or even the destruction of healthy cells. Nanomaterials overcome the shortcomings of conventional approaches by acting as a lead in tumor surgical removal, specifically attacking chemotherapeutics, and being selective to malignant cells. The innovative technology helps patients live longer by lowering their risk and increasing their likelihood of living. The capacity to selectively direct nanostructure carriers to tumor locations is a big advantage of employing them. Chemotherapeutic medications are cytotoxic, meaning they destroy cancerous cells that are constantly proliferating, and they can also equally harm normal tissue that are growing. The larger surface ratio and composition of particles allow cancer-specific compounds to be attached to the surface of nanocarriers, where they can attach to specific receptors on those cancerous cells. Internalization of nanoparticles (NPs) into cell results in increased drug agent intracellular absorption and antitumor efficacy. Delivering drugs limits the medicine's action to only the cancerous cells carrying the specific molecule, reducing the systemic toxic side effects of a drug, some of which might be fatal.

Nanoscale particulates have played a key role with in the identification of cancer biomarkers, which would be critical for customized evaluation that underpins precision medicine. The nanocarrier's flexible functional and structural features open the door to quick, specialized, and accurate diagnostics as well as decentralized evaluation and/or peripheral follow-up. In terms of treatments, the nanoconstructs' average size enables particles to much more efficiently traverse biological membranes, which could be further enhanced by surface functionalization of nanoconstructs' surface with targeting ligands for precision distribution to a cancer's focal point. Furthermore, these can act as standalone bioactive molecules or as transporters for several compounds with specialized functions such as targeted therapy, cancerous cell ablation, and real-time surveillance of cancerous cell expansion or degradation. Adaptability is critical for theranostics or even the concurrent identification and treatment of diseases. The majority of methods have been targeted at solid tumors, but nonsolid cancers, including lymphoma and leukemia, have gotten less attention. Less selectivity challenges traditional chemotherapeutics in hematological malignancies, leading to limited treatment efficacy and significant undesirable effects. Novel nanomaterial techniques could be able to solve these problems. Nanotechnology breakthroughs that aid in the diagnosis and treatment of leukemia and lymphoma biomarkers. Because the molecular mechanisms of each class of individuals are well characterized by frequent genetic translocations, an associated mutation in oncogenes, gene expression patterns, and immunological phenotypes, hematological illnesses are ideal candidates for these kinds of targeting. Furthermore, a single blood sample (liquid biopsy) gives access to a patient's entire tumor profile, allowing for more targeted therapy regimens. Liquid tumors are dispersed throughout the circulation, like solid tumors, which need NPs to reach the site of action. Because circulating tumor cells are widely accessible to these compounds, almost all of the hurdles that NPs experience in reaching solid tumors are not quite as significant in liquid tumors.

12.2 Leukemia

One of its three blood types of cancer is leukemia, which is also known as myeloma and lymphoma. Leukemia patients create an abnormally high amount of immature white blood cells that compress the bone marrow and prevent the production of the remainder of critical red blood cells required for a healthy immune response and plasma. Leukemia is divided into two main categories, each of which has two distinct parts.

Acute leukemia arises quickly and progresses rapidly, necessitating prompt medical attention.

- AML is by far the most prevalent type of leukemia in people over the age of 70, but it can affect older adults. The growth and deposition of immature hematopoietic cells in the bone marrow and blood define the malignancy, which is a diverse collection of neoplastic illnesses. Several genetic variables that predispose toward the formation of AML have already been found. In this respect, genetic predisposition as well as the presence of preceding hematological diseases have already been linked to a higher risk of AML (Crooke, 2022).
- The most frequent leukemia in kids is ALL. Adults account for around half of the instances, while children account for the other half. ALL is another very diverse illness with immature lymphoid cells in the peripheral blood and bone marrow exhibiting poor proliferation and differentiation. But, in recent years, the outlook of such individuals has changed, particularly in youngsters, with treatment outcomes reaching 80%—90% because of therapy intensification, individual categorization regarding clinical risk variables, and minimal residual disease surveillance (Paul et al., 2016).

Chronic leukemia manifests itself more gradually, taking months or years to manifest.

- CML is a rare cancer, affecting approximately 700 individuals each year. CML, also known as clonal myeloproliferative disease, was the first adult cancer to be linked to a specific chromosomal defect and is marked by the existence of a BCR-ABL fusion oncogene. Anemia, hypercellular bone marrow, platelet failure, and a growth in the number of leukocytes, particularly immature myeloid cell and neutrophils, are all clinical indications of this condition (Melo and Barnes, 2007).

- CLL is much more prevalent in those above 60 and extremely rare in anyone under 40. The steady buildup of clonally enlarged CD5$^+$ B cells in peripheral lymphoid tissues, secondary lymphoid organs, and bone marrow defines CLL, a frequent B-cell malignancy. It can also be a genetically and biologically complicated disease, with the gene mutation state of a variable part of the chromosome 17p deletion, the immunoglobulin gene, and TP53 gene alterations being the most often used variables to categorize CLL individuals (Haseeb et al., 2018).

It is among the most frequent cancers that affect people all over the world. Leukemia was the 15th highest commonly diagnosed malignancy worldwide in 2018, with 437,033 instances and 309,006 deaths, making it the 11th major cause of mortality due to carcinogenic conditions (Bray et al., 2018). Leukemia has a global distribution pattern, with high incidence and mortality risk in much more industrialized nations. In developing nations, although, the death rate was much higher. A detailed pattern of the incidence of cancer rates in total, and leukemia prevalence in specific, accessible. According to the American Cancer Society's and Cancer Statistics and Facts, 178,520 people in the US are expected to be diagnosed with leukemia and myeloma by 2020. It reflects 9.9% of the total of 1,806,590 newly diagnosed cancers diagnosed during that year. Although both males and females are impacted, males are much more likely to develop leukemia. In the US in the year 2018, the age-standardized prevalence rate for leukemia in men and women was 6.1 and 4.3 per 100,000, respectively. Males had a death rate of 4.2 per 100,000 population, while females had a mortality of 2.8 per 100,000.

The occurrence of leukemia is influenced by variables such as race and age. In the United Kingdom, for instance, 42.8% of all leukemia's affect those above the age 65 (Deschler and Lübbert, 2006). According to a study conducted in the United States, the total age-adjusted leukemia prevalence is 15 per 100,000 in the White population, 11 over 100,000 in the Black population, and 10.6 per 100,000 within the Hispanic population. The frequency was 7.8 per 100,000 in Asian/Pacific Islanders and 8.3 per 100,000 in American Indian Natives. Age-adjusted mortality rates per 100,000 population displayed comparable ethnic and racial trends, with 4.8 for Hispanics, 5.6 for Blacks, 3.3 for Indians, and 3.8 for Pacific Islanders natives (Bispo et al., 2019). Although leukemia impacts people of all ages, the spread of a disease differs depending on the type of disease. From 2012 to 2016, the age-adjusted higher incidence of leukemia in kids, adults, and early adulthood younger than 20 years in the United States was predicted to be around 4.6 per 100,000. Individuals less than 20 years old accounted for about 4.8% of all leukemia and lymphoma occurrences. As a result, it accounted for roughly 20%–30% of all malignancies in this age category. ALL is by far the most frequent kind of leukemia in children and adolescents, accounting for about 75% of all leukemia cases in those under the age of 20 and one-quarter of all pediatric malignancies.

Morphological, clinical, and immunophenotypic assessment are the foundations of blood diagnosis of cancer followed by molecular characterization. In this case, genetics is crucial for classification methods and frequently aids risk stratification, ranging from poor to fair outlook. The kind of leukemia/lymphoma, stage of the disease, previous treatment record, age, general condition, and genetic profile all influence therapy. Chemotherapeutics is used to treat the majority of patients; however, one might additionally require radiotherapy, bone marrow transplantation, or targeted therapy (Keeney et al., 2017).

AML occurs in two stages: childhood development and later in adulthood. The average age of clinically diagnosed patients with AML is 66 years old, whereas the condition can strike at any age; it is unlikely to be diagnosed even before age 40. According to information collected in the U.S. between 2000 and 2004, the prevalence is 1.7 per 100,000 in those under the age of 65 and 16.8 per 100,000 in those 65 and older. Whereas the condition can strike at any age, it is unlikely to be diagnosed even before age 40. According to information collected in the U.S. between 2000 and 2004, the prevalence is 1.7 per 100,000 in that are under the age of 65, and 16.8 per 100,000 in those 65 and above. AML is three times greater in White children in their first few years than in Black children, although Black children do seem to have increased rates of the condition after such an age. AML was much more frequent in Whites in the U.S. between 2000 and 2004, with a prevalence of 3.7 per 100,000 population, than in Blacks, with a frequency of 3.2 per 100,000 (Ries et al., 2007). The development of myelodysplastic syndromes (MDS) to AML is believed to be involved with higher occurrence by age. MDS-based AML is characterized by chromosomal abnormalities that are prevalent in both AML and MDS, as well as an elevated risk of poor outcomes. From 2005 and 2009, the prevalence of acute myeloblastic leukemia in children aged 0–14 years was predicted to be 7.7 occurrences per million. The greatest relative risk in the pediatric population comes during the first year of life, resulting in a gradual drop till the age of 4 years. The prevalence is 18.4 per million in newborns under the age of 1 year (Xie et al., 2003). Excluding a slight increase in the older group, the prevalence of AML has remained relatively stable among adults and children. For most situations, the genesis of AML is unknown, with the exception of MDS. There has been a substantial deal of information and knowledge acquired about leukemogenic medications, particularly chemotherapy regimens used this to treat a number of malignant disorders. Various molecular pathologies, like the t (8;21) translocation and chromosomal 16 inversions, have already been linked to AML. In association with genetic modifications, epigenetic changes have now been identified in the pathophysiology of AML, such as promoter suppression by hypermethylation of other and p15/INK4b genes. Certain hereditary variables, such as genetic abnormalities, have been linked to AML, particularly in youngsters. As previously stated, individuals with a range of genetic diseases, like down's syndrome, have a significantly increased risk of developing malignant conditions, like AML. Trisomy 21 patients, for instance, have a 10−20-fold greater risk of having acute leukemia, most commonly AML (Fong and Brodeur, 1987).

ALL is by far the most common cancer in children and adolescents, accounting for 25%−30% of all carcinogenic malignancies in this age category. Between the ages of 0 and 14, the incidence rate of ALL in the U.S. is around 4.6 cases per 100,000, with the highest prevalence at 2−5 years. Women have a somewhat higher incidence of ALL in the first year of life than men. Different environmental variables, such as parental preconception, in postnatal and uteroionizing exposure to radiation, have already been investigated. Nonionizing rays, toxins, diseases, hydrocarbons, and insecticides have also been assessed for their hazards. The impacts of alcohol, tobacco, and illegal drug usage on offspring's formation of ALL were investigated. As in the formation of leukemia in ALL, in particular, genetics plays a significant influence. Concordance investigations on identical twins with leukemia demonstrate the impact of heredity. By integrating 23 subcategories characterized by chromosomal reconfigurations, sequence alterations, or diverse genetic changes, a modified classification of B-ALL underscores the cancer's genetic complexity (Gu et al., 2019). The majority of such molecular alterations are received rather than inherited. This has been postulated that epigenetic priming may play a role in pediatric ALL. For the development of ALL, the latest two-hit scenario mixes mutated genes and susceptibility with one or even more viruses. The updated two-hit theory for the formation of B-cell precursor ALL proposes a two-step procedure for the condition's onset. A predisposed gene mutation is an initial step. Phase 2 implies that you have been exposed to one or even more diseases (Greaves, 2018). As a result, the hypothesis proposes that the process of creating ALL begins in utero with the production of fusion genes or hyperdiploidy and the creation of a preleukemic clone.

12.3 Nanocomposites

NPs comprise atomic aggregates with an amorphous or crystalline structure, which have different physicochemical properties and vary in diameter from 1 to 100 nm. Several important biomolecules, like antibodies, membrane transporters, nucleotides, and peptides, have nanosized sizes comparable to NPs. Nanotechnology is a significant feature of modern nanomedicine because of its size-imitating properties and high surface-to-volume proportion. Engineering solutions for a range of nanosystems in many application areas, like cellular imaging, point-of-care diagnosis, and localized therapeutics, have been significantly boosted by the growing need for medical applications and the growth of nanotechnology. It appears fair to assume that NPs' remarkable properties have resulted in an overall rise in molecular and cellular interaction. Designing multifunctional NPs may drastically enhance current expertise to tackle these issues. Monofunctional NPs only have one function. A nanoliposome, for instance, may carry medications in tissues and cells but cannot differentiate between normal and infected cellular components. Multifunctional-based NPs, on the other hand, integrate multiple functions in a unified encapsulated nanocomposite. A NP, for instance, might be designed and synthesized with a compound that has a localized targeting activity and identifies the distinctive surface characteristic of its target cells. Similarly, the very same particle could be altered with an imaging compound to track the phase transition and assess specific clinical characteristics. Lastly, it could be coupled to a moiety in order to assess a medication's clinical efficiency and prevent complications. Theranostics can be used to describe such multifunctional-based NPs (diagnostics and therapeutics combination). Since these NPs make contact with cells and fluids, particles are subjected to a variety of self-assembled alterations in regards to pH, ionic strength, the concentration of protein, and compositions, all of which affect NP characteristics and interaction with cells. The distinctive features of NPs in terms of cellular transcytosis, endocytosis, circulatory, and neuronal distribution and translocation, which make them attractive for both diagnostic and therapeutic uses, can potentially be linked to toxic potential.

The mixture of multiple therapies in the treatment of cancer, as well as the negative consequences of destroying normal tissue in chemotherapeutics, has sparked a lot of interest in developing controlled drug delivery. Several researchers have been drawn to the creation of nanocomposite materials for the treatment of cancer due to their superior anticancer activity. Nanocomposites are made up of many nanoscaled substances that include both soft and hard materials. It increases the flexibility of the drug carrier when conjugating pharmaceuticals to soft materials, such as polymeric nanogels, or mixing medicines with harder materials like metals. The below are the most essential functions of nanocomposite to highlight its involvement in the cancer-targeted delivery of drugs.

- Nanomaterial-based chemotherapy could be designed and synthesized to distribute medicines specifically toward the location of the tumor.
- Nanocomposites having a longer half-life ($t_{1/2}$) of encapsulated medication could be produced.
- These could be induced to circulate for a prolonged period of time inside the vascular system.
- Because nanocomposites contain over one nanosized polymer or metal, they may achieve a variety of physical and chemical characteristics by combining incompatible components.
- Further alterations like the derivatization of fluorinated graphene with Fe_3O_4 for cancer treatment (Jiuyao et al., 2017) are feasible.

- Nanocomposite surface and size chemistry can be changed to adjust their cytotoxic action.
- Nanocomposites-based photothermal treatment is less invasive and effective in removing cancerous cells.
- Nanocomposites with an increase in surface area are better for the biomolecular load.
- Because nanocomposites have a lot of functional groups, they can be bioconjugated, designed, especially for the treatment of cancer.
- For multiresponses, nanocomposites feature specialized structures with strong interaction moiety.
- After intravenous infusion or oral application, pluronic-loaded polymeric-based nanocomposites could be employed for in vivo bioimaging (Chu et al., 2014).
- Quantum dots (QDs) could be used to enclose nanomaterials for cell imaging and cancer detection.
- Nanocomposites having magnetic core-shell nanomaterials and two photothermal chemicals for diagnostic imaging and directed photothermal cancer treatment allow for concurrent detection of cancer and therapy (Han et al., 2017).
- Nanocomposites could be coupled with ligands like folic acid (FA) to specifically target cancerous cells and improve therapeutic potential through effective internalization (Park et al., 2015).

Two-dimensional (2D)-based NPs are a type of independent sheet-like NPs with a large lateral size-to-thickness ratio. Ever since the development of exfoliated graphene, 2D NPs have received much interest as a new type of NPs. Graphene-based nanomaterials, palladium nanosheets, transition metal dichalcogenides, transition metal carbides, black phosphorus, nitrides, and carbonitrides (MXenes), and 2D clays like layered double hydroxides, and other 2D NPs have all been published previously. Solvothermal/hydrothermal/synthesis, chemical vapor deposition, liquid-phase exfoliation, and mechanical exfoliation are only a few of the methodologies that were explored thus far to design and fabricate diverse types of 2D nanomaterials. Bottom-up and top-down methodologies could have been used to classify such strategies. Due to unique physical and chemical properties, flexible features, enormous diversity of species, and broad application possibilities in catalysis, electronics, optoelectronics, solar cells, and other fields, 2D NPs have definitely been one of the research hotspots of research scientists in a broad variety of fields. The benefit of 2D nanostructured materials is that, in comparison to certain other particles, these have a quite large surface area, allowing them to effectively bind a range of substances such as stimulants, nucleic acids, fluorescent probes, proteins, as well as other molecules via noncovalent or covalent interactions, and obtain greater controlled drug release via external stimulation. Similarly, a variety of function-based NPs, like TiO_2 NPs, Fe_3O_4 NPs, and AuNPs, as well as some inorganic QDs, might be successfully attached to the surface of 2D nanomaterials, conferring extra functionality like magnetic, radiological, and imaging properties, and so on.

The self-assembly of a poly (ethylene oxide)-b-poly (n-butyl acrylate)-b-poly (acrylic acid) triblock terpolymer (PEO-b-PnBA-b-PAA) was used to create functional multiple-layer micelles that was then used as a framework for nAg confined by a PAA block. The water-insoluble PnBA micellar part was packed with CUR. The combined effect of two anticancer agents announced from the effect of micelles on AML (HL-60), its multidrug-resistant subline HL60/DOX, and human urinary bladder carcinoma (Ej) cells was studied. The in vitro tests demonstrated that the cytotoxic effect of nAg and CUR NPs was effective (Petrov et al., 2016). The efficacious distribution of daunorubicin-loaded PLA nanocomposite scaffolds with multi-walled carbon nanotubes (MWCNTs) and iron oxide (PLA/MWCNT/Fe_3O_4) was examined in terms of a proliferation inhibitor influence on leukemia K562 cell lines. The impact of nanofiber concentration on the delivery of drugs was also investigated in the absence and presence of an externally applied magnetic field. The findings suggested that incorporating daunorubicin into primed nanofiber scaffolds in the presence of magnetic fields may have synergistic cytotoxic activity on leukemia cancer cells (Hosseini et al., 2016).

12.4 Polymeric-based nanocomposites

Effective chemotherapeutic drug distribution toward the desired target or cell lines for a prolonged period of time will provide therapeutic outcomes over time. Polymeric-based NPs could be effectively customized to produce an intended therapeutic dose toward the site in a sustained manner. Biodegradable-based nanocomposites containing anticancer drugs are helpful for targeted and controlled delivery as they could raise the concentration of drugs in carcinoma cells, thereby improving the antitumor effect.

Rajan et al. created chitosan-loaded poly oxalate-based nanocarriers that maintained the discharge of cisplatin upon the deterioration of nanocomposites developed in complexation with ethylene glycol (Rajan et al., 2016). The release of the drug was affected both by erosion and diffusion of a composite. Confocal microscopy was used to study uptake in MCF-7 cell lines with all preparations developed. All nanocomposites were ascertained to enter cancerous cells. The nanocomposites were found both in the nucleus and cytoplasm, implying uptake. As a result, all four nanocomposites as cisplatin carriers do have the possibility to attack the entire cell cytosol with no cellular interference. These nanocomposites could be used as transmitters for targeted and controlled drug delivery in cancer treatment.

Prabhu et al. created a polymeric superparamagnetic iron oxide-based nanocomposite loaded with geldanamycin (GDM) that demonstrated passive targeting of tumor cells (Prabhu et al., 2017). The significant observation is that the established GDM-based nanocomposites eliminated or lowered cellular toxicity that is highly relevant during medication. Second, the designed nanocomposite was less damaging to the liver. The polymeric-based GDM nanocomposite was reported to exhibit a significant delay in tumor growth, and thus the researchers deduced that such a preparation is a viable target for diagnostic use in the treatment of cancer.

The doxorubicin (DOX) in a carboxymethyl cellulose/graphene oxide (CMC/GO)-based nanocomposite hydrogel for controlled release (Rasoulzadeh and Namazi, 2017). The above nanocomposite is not only able to regulate the discharge of an encapsulated drug but also release it at the required physiological pH. The preparation in vitro cytotoxicity analysis on human colon cancer cells (SW480) revealed that the GO-CMC/DOX does have the possibility to preferentially kill cancerous cells in vitro.

Dhivya et al. created a curcumin-based PMMA-PEG/ZnO bionanocomposite for the purpose of targeting gastrointestinal cancerous cells (Dhivya et al., 2017). This was proposed that nanomaterials access the cytosol, in which the polymer deteriorates and the encapsulated curcumin is released at lower pH levels. The nanocomposite established had not only the benefits of improved drug loading due to the higher concentration of curcumin but also the benefits of improved absorption of the drug at action site. The studies show that tumor cell growth was inhibited by apoptotic cell death in this study. Total cell growth analysis was carried out to fully understand the cell death route. Curcumin enhances G1 cells and yet reduces S-cells, and decreased expression of cyclin D1 interpretation causes damage to DNA, according to the findings. Cell death is triggered by the occurrence of a cell cycle halt and damage to DNA. According to the report's promising findings, the curcumin-based PMMA-PEG/ZnO-loaded bionanocomposite is an active composite for stacking water-insoluble drugs with improved absorption.

12.5 Aptamer-loaded nanocomposites

Different drug delivery technologies have been created to provide better cancerous cells positioning. Many scientists have been using antibodies to target cancerous cells, and enticing outcomes have been observed. Antibodies, on the other hand, show lengthy blood residence time, which creates in vivo imaging problems because of higher background signals. As a result, a new nanomaterial, an oligonucleotide such as an aptamer, was investigated for glioblastoma-based cell targeting effectiveness (Li et al., 2010). The aptamer binds directly to tenascin-C, an extracellular protein involved in tumor cell proliferation and migration. The nanocomposite-based material was created by combining dendrimers with QDs, which aids in cancerous cells imaging. Dendrimers are basically branched globular particles with numerous locations of complexation with other particles. Polyamidoamine, a polymer with a thiol functional group, was used to make a dendrimer toward which cadmium selenide QDs solution was introduced. The aptamer was added to the dendrimer-QDs NPs to improve targeting effectiveness. Agarose gel electrophoresis with agarose gel (2%) smeared with ethidium bromide dye was used to categorize the complexation of the aptamer. On U251 glioblastoma cells culture, the cell binding and targeting efficiency of Apt-dQDs was assessed. According to the findings, Apt-dQDs specifically bind to glioblastoma cells. As a result, these nanocomposites have excellent cancer-attacking and bioimaging capabilities.

For the planning and aiming of cancerous cells, alternative techniques were used. The use of siRNA to silence genetic traits is a massive breakthrough in the treatment of cancer, with promising outcomes both in vitro and in vivo. The infected gene feature is impeded by this technique, and cancerous cells cannot sustain as a result. However, efficient implementation and aiming are essential for the success of such a method, and several nanocomposite delivery methods that might deliver effective siRNA have already been intended. Magnetic mesoporous silica particles (M-MSNs) were chosen as the choice material to create nanocomposite for their low cytotoxic effects, improved biocompatibility, ability to accept huge quantities of the drug, and control release of drug attributes. To create the nanocomposite, siRNA was encased within M-MSN and then coated with polyethyleneimine (PEI). The attacking capacity of these nanocomposites was enhanced by the addition of the fusogenic peptide system KALA. In vivo anticancer activity recommended that nanocomposite treatment reduced the expression of epidermal growth factor that is responsible for tumor metastasis (Li et al., 2013).

12.6 Hyaluronic acid-loaded nanocomposites

To reach a stable and efficient nanosystem, a nanocomposite layout necessitates a stronger insight into attacking moiety and the suitable preparation methods. The presence of hyaluronic acid (HA) inside the extracellular environment of epithelial, connective, and neural tissues aids in cell migration and proliferation. HA transports vehicles of cancerous cells to a nonmalignant location, causing tumor progression and cell growth. As a result, HA serves as one of the indicators of cancer progression. The HA receptors like cluster determinant 44 (CD44) are upregulated. The connections of CD44 to HA result in CD44 integration. As a result, the HA-CD44 conducting site may be utilized for the specifically aimed anticancer drug delivery to tumor cells. As a result, the HA-CD44 interaction mechanism is used to produce anticancer drugs for tumor cells via nanocomposites containing HA as a polymer. Lately, a therapeutic and diagnostic nanosystem predicated on HA matrix was established for delivering of resveratrol (RSV). RSV is just an estrogen diethylstilbestrol that is lipid soluble. The nanocomposite has been created by electrospraying HA-ceramide (HACE) and soluplus (SP). Methanol was employed to disintegrate the SP and HACE matrix. The arising solution was contained in a needle with a stainless steel needle and started spraying over a sheet using a syringe pump at a rate of 1 mL/h. The preparation was then eliminated from the sheet and characterized. On MDA–MB-231 cells, uptake research findings of HACE-SP-RSV nanocomposite revealed great promise. The *in vivo* distribution research was carried out on the MB-231 tumor-xenografted animal model using a near-infrared fluorescence imaging strategy that also recommended improved tumor targetability (Lee et al., 2016). Thus, the manufacturing of nanocomposites is dependent on two factors: (1) the choice of a target for better delivery of drugs to cancer cells and (2) an improved technique of preparing nanocomposites. MSNs had also emerged as an appealing bearer for regulation and focused drug delivery since the last decade.

12.7 Folic acid-targeted nanocomposites

FA, also referred to as vitamin Bc or B9, is a vital bioactive compound involved in the biosynthesis of DNA. FA reaches the cell through three multiple routes: (1) reduced folate carrier, (2) proton-coupled folate transporter, and (3) folate receptor (FAR). FAR is a cellular glycosyl phosphatidyl inositol anchored glycopeptide that creates FA to be internalized into cells in the shape of vesicles via the endocytotic route. FARs are abundantly expressed in types of cancer of the mammary gland, ovary, prostate, nose, and throat, brain, among others. As a result, FA may act as the targeting substrate capable of delivering the drug through direct interactions with cells expressing FARs. As a result, nanocomposites with folate are possible. Lately, aminated starch/ZnO encased iron oxide nanocomposite with FA as an attacking compound was evolved for delivering curcumin, an organic drug (Saikia et al., 2017). The starch first was aminated throughout this research, and then the aminated mixture of starch and preswelled, in addition to the sonicated solution of ZnO, was encased in an iron oxide center. The drug then was loaded into the composite aqueous suspension. Eventually, FA adhesion with NPs was carried out. According to the viability analysis on human lymphocytes, these are biocompatible. Cell growth and absorption studies were also conducted on two carcinoma cell lines, MCF7 and HepG2 cells, which both demonstrated successful outcomes in FA aimed nanocomposites.

12.8 Magnetic nanocomposites

Radiation therapy and chemotherapy have long been employed in the cancer treatment process. The idea of "hyperthermia," wherein cancerous cells are exposed to a temperature of about 41°C–45°C, has now been discovered to enhance the efficacy of such treatments. A few techniques have been created to heat cancerous cells locally or via invasive techniques and heat exchange probes. However, such methodologies are unpleasant and may even harm nonmalignant cells. Inside the shape of a medication delivery system, nanocomposite science has established nanocarriers that cause hyperthermia in the cancer cells. A hydrogel nanocomposite of poly (ethylene glycol) methyl ether methacrylate and dimethacrylate was developed and designed with Fe_3O_4 NPs dispersed as magnetite (Samantha et al., 2010). Glioblastoma cell culture was employed to test the nanocomposite. The hydrogel was warmed from a distance and governed by an alternating electromagnetic wave. Based on the magnitude of the magnetic field, the hydrogel could be warmed to hyperthermic temperatures of $41°C-44°C$ or thermoablative temperatures of $61°C-64°C$. Under cultured cells environments, the malignant cell has died at thermablative temperature. The hydrogel may be used in conjunction with radiation therapy or chemotherapy and can be warmed to hyperthermic temperatures for efficient treating cancer. Magnetic nanocomposite hydrogel could also achieve pulsating release of the drug. The implementation of an alternating magnetic field increases the temperature, causing the hydrogel polymer to implode and discharge imbibed liquid as well as the drug. Many nanomaterials have already been created by investigating the magnetic NP by warming when subjected to a magnetic wave. Lately, CSPEG-polyvinylpyrrolidone (PVP) polymeric nanocomposites (CS-PEG-PVP) were developed for the active targeting of curcumin as well as the conjugation of NPs with Fe_3O_4. The antitumor activity of the delivery system was evaluated in HCT-116 and Caco-2 cell lines, and the findings show that activity improved significantly as compared to the NPs, which are nonmagnetic in nature (Prabha and Raj, 2016).

12.9 Clay-based nanocomposites

Distinct nanocarrier components have been used to create nanocomposites for carcinoma targeting. Clay has also become a preferred candidate for several scientists due to its nontoxicity, natural occurrence, biocompatibility, and low price. Halloysite (Hal) seems to be a naturally occurring clay composed of aluminosilicate that is accessible in the nanotube framework. A nanocomposite-based hydrogel was created by combining Hal-sodium sodium hyaluronate and poly (hydroxyethyl methacrylate) (HEMA) for delivering the 5-FU drug, which is used to cure colon cancer (Rao et al., 2014). The drug could be encased in both hydrogel and the shell of Hal nanotubes, which is an additional benefit of the nanostructure. The drug (5-FU) was integrated into hydrogel and Hal nanotubes by vacuuming the nanocomposite and afterward dragging and busting the vacuum as needed. One such system for delivering drugs is pH sensitive, when it comes into contact with the colon of pH, quick release of the drug occurs, and it is suitable for the dosage form of 5-FU. Clays of various types have been recognized for the creation of new nanocomposites. Palygorskite (Pal) is a type of hydrated magnesium aluminum silicate that is broadly used to prepare nanocomposite for melanoma attack and image analysis due to its own nanostructure, low cost, fibrous form, and significant surface area. Pal was inserted using the pairing grafting method with PEI.

The nanocomposite also was combined with FA for cancerous cells attacking and fluorescein isothiocyanate (FI) for cancerous cell imaging. The Pal-PEI-FA-FI nanocarrier was also tested for uptake effectiveness in HeLa cells expressing upregulation FARs.

12.10 Graphene nanocomposites

Due to their excellent near-infrared absorption, high surface area, and abundance of integrals for effective biomolecular loading capacity, bioconjugation, and aiming, graphene-based materials (like GO and lowered GO) have already shown potential for the treatment of cancer. Graphene nanocomposites have demonstrated significant medicinal uses in anticancer therapy, particularly in subcellular attacking, cellular image analysis, and drug carriers. Graphene composites are frequently designed and synthesized with polymeric materials like PEG, PEI, gelatin, or CS to boost uptake. One benefit of packing substances on graphene is that the resulting nanostructure is much more stable and lowers the risk of discharge outside the cell surface. A biofunctionalized limited GO may be used for nuclear anticancer drug delivery. To particularly distribute doxorubicin toward the nucleus of HER2 constitutively active breast carcinoma cells, this was covalently linked to GO, lowered to form poly-L-lysine designed and synthesized reduced GOs, and afterward labeled with anti-HER2 antibodies (Hosseini et al., 2016). Interleukin-6 (IL-6) plays a role in inflammatory and immune response regulation. Liu et al. created an electrochemiluminescence (ECL) immunosensor for detecting IL-6 using a GO/PANi nanocomposite and CdSe QDs (Liu et al., 2013). The ECL immunosensor was highly sensitive, reproducible, stable, and offered a wide range. Indeed, the ECL immunosensor has affected the level of IL-6 in a sequential range of 0.0005−10 ng/mL, which has considerable therapeutic potential (Table 12.1).

Table 12.1 Applications of nanocomposites in blood cancer.

Nanocomposite/drug	Size	Loading technique	Delivery
Zeolite	60−80 nm	"Direct" targeting with the application of external magnetic field	Hyperthermia (Zheng et al., 2020)
COF nanocomposites	150 ± 8 nm	Self-assembly approach	Renal cancer (Zhang et al., 2020)
CuO-TiO$_2$-chitosan-berbamine nanocomposites	57 nm	Encapsulate	Human chronic myelogenous leukemia (K562) (Elderdery et al., 2022)
Daunorubicin	30 nm	EDOC method	Leukemia (Lv et al., 2008)

References

Alexiou, C., Arnold, W., Klein, R.J., Parak, F.G., et al., 2000. Locoregional cancer treatment with magnetic drug targeting. Cancer Res. 60 (23), 6641—6648.

Bispo, J.A.B., Pinheiro, P.S., Kobetz, E.K., 2019. Epidemiology and etiology of leukemia and lymphoma. Cold Spring Harb. Perspect. Med. 10 (6), a034819. Available from: https://doi.org/10.1101/cshperspect.a034819.

Bray, F., Ferlay, J., Soerjomataram, I., Siegel, R.L., Torre, L.A., Jemal, A., 2018. Global cancer statistics 2018: GLOBOCAN estimates of incidence and mortality worldwide for 36 cancers in 185 countries. CA: A Cancer J. Clin. 68 (6), 394—424. Available from: https://doi.org/10.3322/caac.21492.

Chu, M., Li, H., Wu, Q., Wo, F., Shi, D., 2014. Pluronic-encapsulated natural chlorophyll nanocomposites for in vivo cancer imaging and photothermal/photodynamic therapies. Biomaterials 35 (29), 8357—8373. Available from: https://doi.org/10.1016/j.biomaterials.2014.05.049.

Crooke, S.T., 2022. Progress in molecular biology and translational science addressing the needs of nano-rare patients. Prog. Mol. Biol. Transl. Sci. 190 (1), 127—146. Available from: https://doi.org/10.1016/bs.pmbts.2022.04.002.

Deschler, B., Lübbert, M., 2006. Acute myeloid leukemia: epidemiology and etiology. Cancer 107 (9), 2099—2107. Available from: https://doi.org/10.1002/cncr.22233.

Dhivya, R., Ranjani, J., Bowen, P.K., Rajendhran, J., Mayandi, J., Annaraj, J., 2017. Biocompatible curcumin loaded PMMA-PEG/ZnO nanocomposite induce apoptosis and cytotoxicity in human gastric cancer cells. Mater. Sci. Eng. C 80, 59—68. Available from: https://doi.org/10.1016/j.msec.2017.05.128. S0928493117308585.

Elderdery, A.Y., Alzahrani, B., Hamza, S.M.A., Mostafa-Hedeab, G., Mok, P.L., Subbiah, S.K., 2022. CuO-TiO$_2$-chitosan-berbamine nanocomposites induce apoptosis through the mitochondrial pathway with the expression of P53, BAX, and BCL-2 in the human K562 cancer cell line. Bioinorg. Chem. Appl. 2022, 9602725. Available from: https://doi.org/10.1155/2022/9602725.

Fong, C.T., Brodeur, G.M., 1987. Down's syndrome and leukemia: epidemiology, genetics, cytogenetics and mechanisms of leukemogenesis. Cancer Genet. Cytogenet. 28, 55—76. Available from: https://doi.org/10.1016/0165-4608(87)90354-2.

Greaves, M., 2016. Leukaemia 'firsts' in cancer research and treatment. Nat. Rev. Cancer 16 (3), 163—172. Available from: https://doi.org/10.1038/nrc.2016.3.

Greaves, M., 2018. Author Correction: a causal mechanism for childhood acute lymphoblastic leukaemia. Nat. Rev. Cancer 18, 526.

Gu, Z., Churchman, M.L., Roberts, K.G., Moore, I., Zhou, X., Nakitandwe, J., et al., 2019. PAX5-driven subtypes of B-progenitor acute lymphoblastic leukemia. Nat. Genet. 51 (2), 296. Available from: https://doi.org/10.1038/s41588-018-0315-5.

Han, L., Zhang, Y., Zhang, Y., Shu, Y., Chen, X.W., Wang, J.H., 2017. A magnetic polypyrrole/iron oxide core/gold shell nanocomposite for multimodal imaging and photothermal cancer therapy. Talanta 171, 32—38. Available from: https://doi.org/10.1016/j.talanta.2017.04.056.

Haseeb, M., Anwar, M.A., Choi, S., 2018. Molecular interactions between innate and adaptive immune cells in chronic lymphocytic leukemia and their therapeutic implications. Front. Immunol. 9, 2720. Available from: https://doi.org/10.3389/fimmu.2018.02720.

Hosseini, L., Mahboobnia, K., Irani, M., 2016. Fabrication of PLA/MWCNT/Fe$_3$O$_4$ composite nanofibers for leukemia cancer cells. Int. J. Polym. Mater. Polym. Biomater. 65 (4), 176—182. Available from: https://doi.org/10.1080/00914037.2015.1074912.

Jabbour, E., Kantarjian, H., 2014. Chronic myeloid leukemia: 2014 update on diagnosis, monitoring, and management. Am. J. Hematol. 89 (5), 547—556. Available from: https://doi.org/10.1002/ajh.23691.

Jiuyao, D., Liu, J., Gong, P., Tian, M., et al., 2017. Construction of a novel fluorinated graphene-based magnetic nanocomposite and its application in cancer photochemotherapy. Mater. Lett. 196 (2017), 165—167.

Keeney, M., Hedley, B.D., Chin-Yee, I.H., 2017. Flow cytometry-recognizing unusual populations in leukemia and lymphoma diagnosis. Int. J. Lab. Hematol. 39, 86—92. Available from: https://doi.org/10.1111/ijlh.12666.

Lee, S.Y., Lee, J.J., Park, J.H., Lee, J.Y., Ko, S.H., Shim, J.S., et al., 2016. Electrosprayed nanocomposites based on hyaluronic acid derivative and Soluplus for tumor-targeted drug delivery. Colloids Surf. B: Biointerfaces 145, 267–274. Available from: https://doi.org/10.1016/j.colsurfb.2016.05.009.

Li, X., Chen, Y., Wang, M., Ma, Y., Xia, W., Gu, H., 2013. A mesoporous silica nanoparticle – PEI – Fusogenic peptide system for siRNA delivery in cancer therapy. Biomaterials 34 (4), 1391–1401. Available from: https://doi.org/10.1016/j.biomaterials.2012.10.072.

Li, Z., Huang, P., He, R., Lin, J., Yang, S., Zhang, X., et al., 2010. Aptamer-conjugated dendrimer-modified quantum dots for cancer cell targeting and imaging. J. Nanosci. Nanotechnol. 64 (3), 375–378. Available from: https://doi.org/10.1016/j.matlet.2009.11.022.

Litman, T., Nielsen, D., Skovsgaard, T., Zeuthen, T., Stein, W.D., 1997. ATPase activity of P-glycoprotein related to emergence of drug resistance in Ehrlich ascites tumor cell lines. Biochim. Biophys. Acta 1361 (2), 147–158. Available from: https://doi.org/10.1016/s0925-4439(97)00025-2.

Liu, P.Z., Hu, X.W., Mao, C.J., Niu, H.L., Song, J.M., Jin, B.K., et al., 2013. Electrochemiluminescence immunosensor based on graphene oxide nanosheets/polyaniline nano-wires/CdSe quantum dots nanocomposites for ultrasensitive determination of human interleukin-6. Electrochim. Acta 113, 176–180. Available from: https://doi.org/10.1016/j.electacta.2013.09.074.

Lv, G., He, F., Wang, X., Gao, F., Zhang, G., Wang, T., et al., 2008. Novel nanocomposite of nano Fe$_3$O$_4$ and polylactide nanofibers for application in drug uptake and induction of cell death of leukemia cancer cells. Langmuir 24 (5), 2151–2156. Available from: https://doi.org/10.1021/la702845s.

Melo, J.V., Barnes, D.J., 2007. Chronic myeloid leukaemia as a model of disease evolution in human cancer. Nat. Rev. Cancer 7 (6), 441–453. Available from: 10.1038/nrc2147.

Park, Y.H., Park, S.Y., In, I., 2015. Direct noncovalent conjugation of folic acid on reduced graphene oxide as anticancer drug carrier. J. Ind. Eng. Chem. 30, 190–196. Available from: https://doi.org/10.1016/j.jiec.2015.05.021. S1226086X15002580.

Paul, S., Breuninger, L.M., Tew, K.D., Shen, H., Kruh, G.D., 1996. ATP-dependent uptake of natural product cytotoxic drugs by membrane vesicles establishes MRP as a broad specificity transporter. Proc. Natl. Acad. Sci. 93 (14), 6929–6934. Available from: https://doi.org/10.1073/pnas.93.14.6929.

Paul, S., Kantarjian, H., Jabbour, E.J., 2016. Adult acute lymphoblastic leukemia. Mayo Clin. Proc. 91 (11), 1645–1666. Available from: https://doi.org/10.1016/j.mayocp.2016.09.010.

Petrov, P.D., Yoncheva, K., Gancheva, V., Konstantinov, S., Trzebicka, B., 2016. Multifunctional block copolymer nanocarriers for co-delivery of silver nanoparticles and curcumin: synthesis and enhanced efficacy against tumor cells. Eur. Polym. J. 81, 24–33. Available from: https://doi.org/10.1016/j.eurpolymj.2016.05.010.

Ping, G., Xin-Xia, L., Ping, X., Ji-Shan, H., 2009. Local magnetic nanoparticle delivery in microvasculature. Chin. Phys. Lett. 26 (1), 018703. Available from: https://doi.org/10.1088/0256-307X/26/1/018703.

Prabha, G., Raj, V., 2016. Preparation and characterization of polymer nanocomposites coated magnetic nanoparticles for drug delivery applications. J. Magnetism Magnetic Mater. 408, 26. Available from: https://doi.org/10.1016/j.jmmm.2016.01.070. S0304885316300737.

Prabhu, S., Ananthanarayanan, P., Aziz, S.K., Rai, S., Mutalik, S., Sadashiva, S.R.B., 2017. Enhanced effect of geldanamycin nanocomposite against breast cancer cells growing in vitro and as xenograft with vanquished normal cell toxicity. Toxicol. Appl. Pharmacol. 320, 60–72. Available from: https://doi.org/10.1016/j.taap.2017.02.012.

Rajan, M., Murugan, M., Ponnamma, D., Sadasivuni, K.K., Munusamy, M.A., 2016. Poly-carboxylic acids functionalized chitosan nanocarriers for controlled and targeted anti-cancer drug delivery. Biomed. Pharmacother. 83, 201–211. Available from: https://doi.org/10.1016/j.biopha.2016.06.026.

Rao, K.M., Nagappan, S., Seo, D.J., Ha, C.S., 2014. pH sensitive halloysite-sodium hyaluronate/poly (hydroxyethyl methacrylate) nanocomposites for colon cancer drug delivery. Appl. Clay Sci. 97–98, 33–42. Available from: https://doi.org/10.1016/j.clay.2014.06.002.

Rasoulzadeh, M., Namazi, H., 2017. Carboxymethyl cellulose/graphene oxide bio-nanocomposite hydrogel beads as anticancer drug carrier agent. Carbohydr. Polym. 168, 320–326. Available from: https://doi.org/10.1016/j.carbpol.2017.03.014.

Ries, L.A.G., Melbert, D., Krapcho, M., Mariotto, A., Miller, B.A., Feuer, E.J., et al., (Eds.), 2007. SEER Cancer Statistics Review, 1975−2004. National Cancer Institute, Bethesda, MD. Available from: https://seer.cancer.gov/csr/1975_2004/.

Saikia, C., Das, M.K., Ramteke, A., Maji, T.K., 2017. Evaluation of folic acid tagged aminated starch/ZnO coated iron oxide nanoparticles as targeted curcumin delivery system. Carbohydr. Polym. 157, 391−399. Available from: https://doi.org/10.1016/j.carbpol.2016.09.087.

Samantha, A., Meenach, J., Zach, H., Kimberly, W.A., 2010. Poly(ethylene glycol)-based magnetic hydrogel nanocomposites for hyperthermia cancer therapy. Acta Biomater. 6, 1039−1046. Available from: https://doi.org/10.1016/j.actbio.2009.10.017.

Siegel, R.L., Miller, K.D., Jemal, A., 2016. Cancer statistics. CA: A Cancer J. Clin. 66 (1), 7−30. Available from: https://doi.org/10.3322/caac.21332.

Song, M., Guo, D., Pan, C., Jiang, H., Chen, C., Zhang, R., et al., 2008. The application of poly(N-isopropylacrylamide)-co-polystyrene nanofibers as an additive agent to facilitate the cellular uptake of an anticancer drug. Nanotechnology 19 (16), 165102. Available from: https://doi.org/10.1088/0957-4484/19/16/165102.

Wierda, W.G., Byrd, J.C., Abramson, J.S., et al., 2019. NCCN guidelines insights: chronic lymphocytic leukemia/small lymphocytic lymphoma, version 2.2019. J. Natl. Compr. Cancer Netw. 17 (1), 12−20. Available from: https://doi.org/10.6004/jnccn.2019.0002.

Wu, W., Wieckowski, S., Pastorin, G., Benincasa, M., Klumpp, C., Briand, J.P., et al., 2005. Targeted delivery of amphotericin B to cells by using functionalized carbon nanotubes. Angew. Chem. Int. Ed. Engl. 44 (39), 6358−6362. Available from: https://doi.org/10.1002/anie.200501613.

Xie, Y., Davies, S.M., Xiang, Y., Robison, L.L., Ross, J.A., 2003. Trends in leukemia incidence and survival in the United States (1973−1998). Cancer 97 (9), 2229−2235. Available from: 10.1002/cncr.11316.

Zhang, G., Jiang, B., Wu, C., Liu, Y., He, Y., Huang, X., et al., 2020. Thin platelet-like COF nanocomposites for blood brain barrier transport and inhibition of brain metastasis from renal cancer. J. Mater. Chem. B 8 (20), 4475−4488. Available from: https://doi.org/10.1039.D0TB00724B.

Zheng, L., Zhang, Y., Lin, H., Kang, S., Li, Y., Sun, D., et al., 2020. Ultrasound and near infrared light dual-triggered upconversion zeolite-based nanocomposite for hyperthermia enhanced multi-modal melanoma therapy via a precise apoptotic mechanism. ACS Appl. Mater. Interfaces 12 (29), 32420−32431. Available from: https://doi.org/10.1021/acsami.0c07297.

CHAPTER 13

Multifunctional nanocarrier-mediated codelivery for targeting and treatment of mouth and throat cancer

Akansha Bhatt[1] and Munindra Ruwali[2]
[1]Biocon Limited, Bengaluru, Karnataka, India
[2]Amity Institute of Biotechnology, Amity University Haryana, Gurgaon, Haryana, India

13.1 Introduction

The head and neck squamous cell carcinoma (HNSCC) are collectively defined as the cancers of oral cavity, pharynx, and larynx, which mainly arises from the squamous lining of the mucosal epithelial surfaces of mouth and throat (Gandini et al., 2008). The major cause for the development of mucosal dysplasia and neoplasia in the mouth and throat cancer is the high consumption of tobacco and alcohol, or could be the synergistic effect of both (Gandini et al., 2008), whereas human papillomavirus (HPV), primarily HPV-16 infection, is the cause of significant increase in pharynx cancer cases (Glastonbury et al., 2020). Nasopharyngeal carcinoma (NPC) is associated with Epstein—Barr virus infection histopathological subtype, which is a significantly different neoplasm. Globally, oral cancer is a prevalent cancer and the limitations in conventional treatments can be overcomed by developing the novel therapeutic and prognostic strategies (Irimie et al., 2017).

Nanotechnology could be used as an alternative to traditional therapy as they are more efficient and less toxic drug delivery system. From several years, the clinicians and researchers are facing some of the serious challenges for the development of new therapeutic agents for oral cancer treatment. Over the years, different types of nanoparticle carrier systems, such as metallic, polymeric and lipid vesicles-based formulations, further incorporated with siRNA, natural compounds, and chemotherapeutics, have been successfully developed to solve the problem of multidrug resistance (Jin et al., 2019). For the site-specific targeted delivery of therapeutic agents or drugs, single nanoparticles have been extensively explored since a long time. This further minimized the exposure to the healthy cells/tissues. Nanoparticles possess some unique properties such as their size is small and have large surface area to volume ratio, which allows them to carry various drugs, therapeutics, and imaging agents with high efficiency to the target region (Irimie et al., 2017; Shi et al., 2019). Over the decades, various nanoparticle-mediated delivery systems such as liposomes, dendrimers, nanostructured lipids, nanoemulsions,

Multifunctional Nanocomposites for Targeted Drug Delivery in Cancer Therapy
DOI: https://doi.org/10.1016/B978-0-323-95303-0.00012-5
341

polymeric nanoparticles, quantum dots, mesoporous silica, magnetic nanoparticles, etc., have been extensively developed for site-specific targeted therapeutic delivery usages (Taratula et al., 2009; Alibakhshi et al., 2017; Majumdar et al., 2022). Besides the fact that single-functional nanoparticles are capable of addressing issues such as stability, ease-of-availability, control release, etc. of many drugs, the need for multifunctional nanoparticles arises as the demand for more specific targeting and simultaneous imaging of the tissue and cells is required to identify diseases of different morphologies.

Multifunctional nanoparticles can efficiently perform multiple functions such as delivery of chemotherapeutic agents, drugs, nucleic acids and peptides along with the simultaneous function of optical imaging (Majumdar et al., 2022). Fig. 13.1 illustrates the different types of multifunctional nanoparticles and their important applications in targeting, diagnostics, and therapeutics, while Table 13.1 lists the major multifunctional nanomaterials and their major advantages. Many different strategies are now available to develop targeted multifunctional nanoparticles, although the very simplest way includes the modification of the parent nanoparticle's surface by attaching affinity ligands using physical or covalent bond via s a polymeric linker such as polyethylene glycol (PEG), citric acid, etc. (Garbuzenko et al., 2019; Majumdar et al., 2022). The specificity of these ligands is only for certain receptors, which are present on the target cell, cell-penetrating, and imaging agents as well as on stimuli-sensitive components. For instance, the luteinizing hormone-releasing hormone (LHRH) receptors are

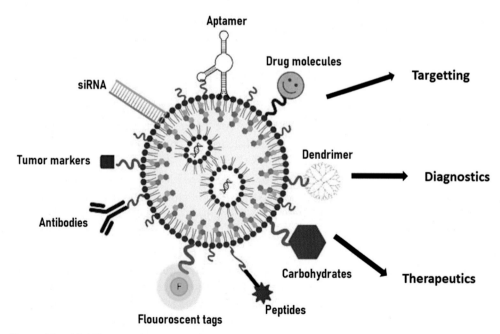

Figure 13.1 Multifunctional nanoparticles and their applications.

Table 13.1 The major multifunctional nanomaterials and their major advantages.

S. No.	Multifunctional nanomaterial	Major advantages	References
1.	Lipid vesicle-based nanoconjugation with siRNA	Significantly increased antitumor and apoptotic effects, tumor regression, increased cell death, controlled release at target specific site	Kampel et al. (2021), Xu et al. (2017), Chen et al. (2015a)
2.	Metal with combination of siRNA	Can successfully overcome chemoresistance, and allow bioimaging both in vitro and in vivo, suppressed the proliferation and migration of cancer cells, high gene silencing efficiencies	Jin et al. (2019), Teng et al. (2017), Cao et al. (2013)
3.	Dendrimer-based conjugation multifunctional nanoparticles	A thermo-chemotherapy strategy, high triggered response as cytotoxic effect and apoptosis, effective transfection, "smart" cancer targeting, and a promising siRNA nanocarrier	Shukla et al. (2019), Han et al. (2020), Montazerabadi et al. (2019), Yuan et al. (2019), Li et al. (2013)
4.	Photodynamic therapy	Decreased cell viability, generating of reactive oxygen species, enhanced cellular internalization, and induced gene silencing efficiency, the tumor growth is almost negligible, personalized treatment of advanced malignancies	Wang et al. (2021), Yeh et al. (2021), Liu et al. (2016), Ali et al. (2014), Cho et al. (2011), de Martimprey et al. (2010)
5.	Mesosporous silica nanoparticles	Controlling the drug release and cellular internalization, enhanced cytotoxicity and apoptosis by inhibiting the MDR1 function, enhanced the therapeutic effects, more transfection efficiency	Wang et al. (2020), Qi et al. (2016)

overexpressed on the plasma membrane of different cancer cells, causing the preferential accumulation of targeted multifunctional nanoparticles by attaching to the specific peptide in the tumor. This complex further enhances the efficiency of the treatment and hence limits the adverse side effects. One type of spacer-nanocarrier combination was conjugated by the nondegradable bond (e.g., amide) or via biodegradable bond (e.g., ester). Another type of combination is by using electrostatic interaction. The active components, such as negatively charged nucleic acids or drugs, can be coupled with the charged carrier, such as cationic liposomes. This can be done by the incorporation into the outer lipid membrane or lipid inner core (for lipophilic drugs) or can be dissolved in water-based inner core for hydrophilic nanoparticles or the encapsulation into inner pores of transporters or ion channels (Chandna et al., 2010; Bhaskar et al., 2010; Trapani et al., 2012; Deshpande et al., 2013).

An emerging technology of nanocrystals has gained impetus for the successful delivery of drugs to provide as a tool for the different types of cancers. Features like great physicochemical and pharmacokinetic properties, such as tailored dissolution, high stability, and more retention time for circulation in the body, made them a promising formulation for the treatment of cancers. A large number of cancer-specific drugs, such as cyclosporin, paclitaxel, and busulfan, are coupled with nanocrystals to be implemented as a therapeutic approach for the treatment of cancer (Khairnar et al., 2022). Ray et al. (2020) developed a cocrystallization method to overcome the issue of different drug-resistant cancers. They evaluated the formulation of cocrystals of niclosamaide-nicotinamide and its effects on A549 human lung adenomas by spray drying method. The maximum amount of cytotoxicity was observed as compared to pure drug as well as confocal microscopy revealed the similar kind of results when the autophagy-mediated cell death was analyzed. Autophagy-mediated pathway causing inhibition of cancer cell death can be mediated by colocalization of nanocarriers in the endoplasmic reticulum and mitochondria (Singh et al., 2021). A new strategy of self-assembling nanoparticles has a great significance for developing future treatments of various cancers (Varma et al., 2020).

Although the vast majority of systems are available but the basic need for all the drug delivery mechanisms is that all the nanocarriers should be released inside the targeted cells. For the continuous release of the drugs inside the targeted cells or specific tissues, it is necessary that either the disruption of spacers or complete degradation of whole nanoparticles should be accomplished. In addition, suppression of cellular defense mechanisms could give rise to desired therapeutic effect. A variety of complex multifunctional nanocarriers have been developed in recent years for the therapeutic and diagnostic usage. Rationally designed multifunctional nanostructured materials can produce improved drug carriers that play an increasingly important role in mouth and throat cancer treatment. As a result, in comparison with conventional drug combination approaches, code-livery systems of multiple drugs achieve sophisticated targeting strategies, and multifunctionality for a better and effective mouth and throat cancer treatment.

13.2 Lipid vesicle based nanoconjugation

In the study done by Xu et al. (2017), the dual therapeutic-loaded EGFR-targeting ligand, GE11 peptide-conjugated liposome-encapsulated docetaxel DTX/ABCG2-siRNA molecules were developed to enhance the therapeutic efficacies for the cancer of larynx. The highlight of this study was a combined treatment against the ABCG2 gene, major regulator of multidrug resistance in many tumors. For the regulation of ambient release of DTX and the specific identification of squamous epithelial, the GE11 peptides were conjugated with the nanosized drug-infused liposomes. As a result, it was found that the GE11 peptides increased the number of uptakes of liposomal constructs by Hep-2 laryngeal cancer cells, as well as there was increase in cytotoxicity against Hep-2 laryngeal cancer cells as compared to the cells treated with free DTX. Additionally, the complex had impacted by increasing antitumor and apoptotic effects as well.

Kampel et al. (2021) worked on human papillomavirus (HPV), which is one of the major causes for larynx cancers. The efficient and systematic transportation and delivery of siRNA at specific site by using the lipid-based nanocarriers (LNPs) has tremendous potential that could be used for the therapeutic manipulation of HPV E6/E7 oncoproteins. The recombinant protein linker that enables uniform conjugation of targeting antibodies to the LNPs can be used for the therapeutic efficacy of a xenograft HPV-positive tumor model. This study showed that the targeted antiepidermal growth factor receptor (EGFR) antibodies, when ligated to the LNPs, will mitigate the tumor activity as well as facilitate the specific target delivery at the site. Moreover, the treated siE6 via tLNPs had shown 50% greater reduction of tumor volume as compared to treatment with control, siRNA coated with isotype control antibodies on LNPs. The study demonstrated that in both in vitro and in vivo systems, there was high suppression of HPV oncogenes as well as induced apoptosis by the tLNPs. Besides this, the complex of inhibitory siE6 with anti-EGFR antibodies elicited antitumor effects and successfully restricted tumor progression. Overall, this combination has the potential to be used as a therapeutic tool against other cancer models.

Combination therapy has a potential to serve as a major tool in oral cancer treatment. Chen et al. (2015b) developed a combinatorial approach for the treatment of oral squamous cell carcinoma by using the anisamide-targeted lipid-calcium-phosphate (LCP) nanoparticles in combination of photodynamic therapy (PDT) for the effective transfer of HIF1α siRNA to the cytoplasm of sigma receptor-expressing SCC4 and SAS cells. They observed that HIF1α siRNA nanoparticles successfully reduced the HIF1α expression, soared cell death, and hindered cell growth when combined with photosan-mediated photodynamic therapy in cultured cells.

13.3 Metal in combination with siRNA

Silencing of eukaryotic translation initiation factor eIF4E, a valuable marker in cancer prognostics, via delivery of siRNA may be able to overcome chemoresistance. Cisplatin has been widely accepted as a first line cancer drug for its great applicability in clinical area. Although, there are some limitations such as peripheral neuropathy, nephrotoxicity, and hearing loss. Moreover, the major obstacle for its application is the drug resistance from platinum. So, to reduce the platinum resistance, platinum (IV) prodrugs can be reduced to Pt(II) by mercaptan and glutathione, which act as reducing agents. The advantage is that it is chemically inert and very less toxic. Moreover, combinational therapies with Pt-coupled drugs are gaining attention all around the world. Teng et al. (2017) reported the approach, which causes the upconversion of eukaryotic translation initiation factor (eIF)-4E siRNA and Pt(IV). This therapeutic tool has the capability of sensitizing the laryngeal cancer cells to cisplatin-based chemotherapy and, subsequently, allowing bioimaging processes both in vitro and in vivo.

Cao et al. (2013) reported an innovative approach for miRNA-203 delivery in esophageal cancer cells by using protamine sulfate (PS)-nanodiamond (ND) nanoparticles. This method exhibited the high potential in miRNA-based cancer therapies. It was found that on successful delivery of miR-203, which targets the Ran and ΔNp63 genes, there is significant reduction in the proliferation and migration of esophageal cancer cells. In another study, for the target specific delivery of therapeutic siRNAs into Ca9−22 oral cancer cells, the novel ferric ion–based combination of siRNA with the polyethyleneimine (PEI)-modified magnetic Fe_3O_4 was formed. This was further used to target B-cell lymphoma-2 (BCL2) and baculoviral IAP repeat-containing 5 (BIRC5), generating high gene silencing efficiencies. Furthermore, this system had efficiently inhibited the cell survival and migration of Ca9−22 cells.

13.4 Dendrimer-based conjugated multifunctional nanoparticles

Montazerabadi et al. (2019) defined a novel multifunctional nanoplatform, which is constructed from generation III dendrimers, named as, methoxy-PEGylated poly(amidoamine) (PAMAM), and it is further encapsulated with superparamagnetic iron oxide nanoparticles (SPIONs) in its core (Fig. 13.2). The payload drug, curcumin acting on the folate, i.e., the targeting ligand and this entire multifunctional combinatorial is abbreviated as FA-mPEG-PAMAM G3-CUR@SPIONs. The role of SPIONs is to act as a hyperthermia agent, as when they get excited by an alternating magnetic field (AMF), they generate localized heat, and hence, work as a thermo-chemotherapeutic agent for cancer treatment. The obtained results showed that, as compared to control, the KB nasopharyngeal cancer cell death was higher as the triggered response can be confirmed by the overexpressing folate receptors, which caused the cytotoxicity. Therefore, functionalizing the nanocomplex with folate can subsequently shift the cell death pathways toward apoptosis and could be used as the modulator for the thermo-chemotherapeutic responses.

Another similar study done by Han et al. (2020) investigated the usage and inhibitory effects of nanomaterial PAMAM on the human nasopharyngeal cancerous cell line, CNE-2. They demonstrated the possible effects of TNF-α gene transfection into

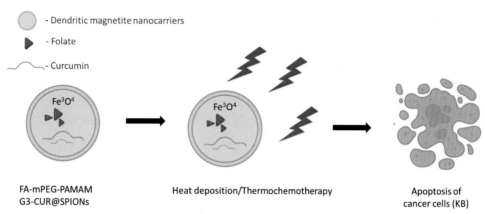

- Dendritic magnetite nanocarriers

- Folate

- Curcumin

FA-mPEG-PAMAM
G3-CUR@SPIONs

Heat deposition/Thermochemotherapy

Apoptosis of
cancer cells (KB)

Figure 13.2 Targeted thermo-chemotherapy of cancer cells using folate-modified and curcumin-loaded dendritic magnetite nanocarriers.

CIK (cytokine-induced killer) cells. Firstly, to measure the transfection efficiency, the pEGFP-N1-TNF-α recombinant plasmid was prepared and further by using the nanomaterial PAMAM, the transfection was performed on the CIK cells. The results showed the clear indication of CIK cells can significantly inhibit CNE-2 cell growth ($P < 0005$) as the TNF-α secretion was increased. Yuan et al. (2019) in their study suggested the receptor-mediated delivery by the development of polyamidoamine dendrimers coupled with epidermal growth factor (EGF) as therapeutics to cancer cells. They demonstrated the key regulator, EPS8, responsible for the squamous carcinoma growth and migration, can be modulated. The results showed that there was remarkable inhibition of cell growth as well as more reduction in cell movement. With the repeated exposure to the targeting reagent, it was proved to cause more repression.

Li et al. (2013) developed a siRNA-based delivery that was a triblock dendritic nanocarrier containing the three ligands-polyamidoamine-polyethylene glycol-cyclic RGD (PAMAM-PEG-cRGD). This multifunctional nanoplatform was studied on the human anaplastic thyroid carcinoma cell lines for the deletion of human ether-à-go-go-related gene (hERG). For the confirmation of successful synthesis of siRNA coupled with triblock components, different parameters such as zeta potential, particle size, structure characterization, and gel retardation assay were performed. Results suggest that in thyroid carcinoma cells, the gene knockdown of hERG elicited growth suppression and apoptosis by triggering the caspase-3 cascade, and there was a significant abolishment of vascular endothelial growth factor secretion. This study demonstrated that this triblock polymer, PAMAM-PEG-cRGD, has negligible toxicity to cell, effective transfection, "smart" cancer targeting, and therefore can be used as a promising siRNA nanocarrier. The study performed by Liu et al. (2011) used a novel and attractive target for oral cancer, the human telomerase reverse transcriptase (hTERT), the catalytic subunit of telomerase complex. They studied the polyamidoamine (PAMAM) dendrimer-mediated short hairpin RNA (shRNA) anticancer effects against hTERT. The efficient complex is effectively able to efficiently silence the hTERT gene in vitro as well as the suppression in cell growth and induced cell death was also found in a xenograft model. These studies suggest that as the hTERT is overexpressed in the oral cancer cells, the complex approach of dendrimer delivery with the RNAi-mediated gene silencing might be promising for the treatment of oral cancer.

13.5 Photodynamic therapy

A recent advancement in treatment of head and neck cancer was reported by Yeh et al. (2021). They used the combinatorial approach by firstly modulating entrapped EGFR siRNA into lipid-calcium phosphate nanoparticles (LCP Pyro PA NPs), with the novel photodynamic therapy photosensitizer, pyropheophorbide phosphatydic acids (Pyro PA), and finally conjugated with aminoethylanisamide. In qPCR and western blotting results, the treated cancerous cells with EGFR siRNA with PDT had shown decreased expression in EGFR levels and reduced EGFR protein expression, respectively, as compared to control siRNA or PDT alone. Along with that, the in vitro studies showed EGFR gene knockdown after inhibiting optimum growth and reduced tumor volume in treated ones.

Wang et al. (2021) developed a novel nanocomposite, chitosan nanoparticles entrapped in 5-aminolevulinic acid (ALA) photosensitizer with shRNA (CS-ALA-shGBAS) to investigate the oral squamous cell carcinoma (OSCC) cells. This nanoparticle had good spherical structure, low toxicity, and high dispersion capability. Interestingly, the orthotopic animal model of HNSCC for in-vivo experiments as well as in vitro results showed that this combination had shown extensive mitochondrial targeted killing on OSCC as well as good transfection efficiency. The efficiency and efficacy of codelivery system of CS-TPP-(shMTHFD1L-ALA)-PDT was evaluated by the gene expression studies. The induced apoptosis and further formation of reactive oxygen species (ROS) were subsequently confirmed by Annexin V-PI and DCFH-DA assays, respectively. They reported that CS TPP, around 145 nm in size, conjugated ALA-PDT showed an increased cell death of OSCC cells when compared to control. Additionally, this combined therapy was able to produce distinguished effects such as pro-apoptotic, antitumorigeniss with generation of ROS, both in vitro and in vivo. These observations indicate that CS-TPP-(shMTHFD1L-ALA) NPs may be an ideal candidate for gene/photosensitizer delivery.

Another photodynamic therapy by conjugation with novel organic photosensitive ITIC-th nanoparticles for oral leukoplakia was developed by Lin et al. (2022). This was the first promising interdisciplinary multimodal therapy. The major specifications of this complex were an excellent photothermal conversion efficiency with suitable ability to generate ROS when irradiated with laser of 660 nm. The multifunctional nanoplatform when used against the induced oral cancerous animal model by 4-nitroquinoline, resulted in suppression in OLK's with very low systemic toxicity. In order to treat head and neck cancer, poly-L-arginine (PLR) and dextran sulfate (DEX) based nanosized polyelectrolyte complex (nanocomplex) was created, which deliver epidermal growth factor receptor (EGFR) siRNA (Cho et al., 2011). The nanocomplex includes EGFR siRNA that has in vitro cellular uptake efficiency as well as silencing effect of EGFR gene, which occurs in Hep-2 and FaDu cells. In Hep-2 and FaDu cells, PLR-DEX complex showed the best uptake of cellular efficiency of EGFR siRNA, which were analyzed by flow cytometry and confocal laser scanning microscopy (CLSM). The PLR-DEX complex is the highest EGFR gene in terms of silencing efficiency in both of the cell lines.

Liu et al. (2016) developed a theranostic nanoparticle platform for the treatment of anaplastic thyroid tumors (ATC), which includes a near-infrared (NIR) fluorescent polymer, which efficiently delivers in vivo siRNA. This technique can be used for tracking accumulation of tumor by noninvasive NIR imaging. The NIR polymeric NPs are tiny particles of approximately 50 nm in length. It shows long blood circulation and high tumor accumulation and also facilities the tumor imaging. This study explains that the systemic siRNA delivery done using NPs can efficiently silence the V-Raf murine sarcoma viral oncogene homolog B (BRAF) expression in the tumor tissues. It also suppresses metastasis and the tumor growth in an orthotopic mouse model of ATC.

A study conducted by de Martimprey et al. (2010) utilized multifunctional nanoparticles by polymerization of isobutylcyanoacrylate and isohexycyanoacey-late with chocolate in an attempt to elaborate on a major challenge involved in efficient in-vivo delivery nanodevices. The nanoparticles were loaded with siRNA by adsorption, following which their biological activity was assessed in mice with papillary thyroid carcinoma after intratumoral and intravenous administration. Thus, the resulting strong antitumoral activity was due to the antisense siRNA associated with nanoparticles. Following the intravenous injection of antisense siRNA-loaded nanoparticles, compared to control, the tumor growth in test subjects were negligible. Thus, it was concluded that poly (alkylcyanoacrylate) nanoparticle-coated chitosan are appropriate carriers to attain in-vivo delivery of active siRNA to tumor, including after systemic administration. A noncationic nanosystem for treatment of papillary thyroid carcinoma was developed by Ali et al. (2014), which targets the squalenoyl nanostructures having a combinatorial peptide consisting of GALA cholestrol and squalene nanoparticles. In vitro studies suggest enhanced cellular internalization and decreased cell viability. Increase in gene silencing efficiency was seen in both human PTC cell lines. In vivo results for siRNA RET /PTC1 -SQ GALA- chol NPs did not show efficiency in controlling gene silencing or inhibiting the tumor growth as compared to PTC1 -SQ NPs.

13.6 Mesosporous silica nanoparticles

Qi et al. (2016) demonstrated that the small molecule, TH287 was successfully loaded and delivered with the MDR1 siRNA in oral squamous cell carcinoma. The results showed that the HA-assembled mesoporous silica nanoparticles were quite promising for effective controlling of the drug release and internalization in CAL27 cancer cells. The combination of TH287 + MDR1 siRNA was more effective in reducing the cytotoxicity and apoptosis, compared to that of TH287 (MTH1 inhibitor) alone. SiTMSN and HA-siTMSN significantly reduced the tumor burden when compared to untreated control and free TH287. Altogether, the HA-siTMSN platform was studied to have been the promising vector for the systemic delivery of MDR1 siRNA/ TH287 for treatment of cancer of oral cavity.

Wang et al. (2020) explored the inhibitory and synergistic actions of 5-fluorouracil and curcumin on Hep-2 laryngeal cancer cells and explored the effect of mesoporous silica nanoparticles as drug carriers. The inhibitory effects of 5-fluorouracil and curcumin on Hep-2 cells were detected and the growth of subcutaneous tumors in BALB/c nude after the intraperitoneal injection with drug-loaded mesoporous silica nanoparticles was recorded. The research indicated that 5-fluorouracil and curcumin synergistically induced apoptosis and cell cycle arrest in Hep-2 cells. In addition to this, it was also observed that the combination of mesoporous silica nanoparticles as drug carriers further enhanced the therapeutic effects of 5-fluorouracil and curcumin.

13.7 Other studies

One of the promising approaches using multifunctional nanoparticles was done by Li et al. (2016), which could be used as a strategic application for radiotherapy. The siRNa with HIF-1 was conjugated with encapsulated hypercin (HyHPPNP), and its combined effects have been studied by transfecting into hypoxic NPC cells. The results shown the nanocomplex can accumulate in the tumor necrosis area with increased retention time, which leads to uptake upto 50% of siRNA and more permeability. Similar kind of study performed by Chen et al. (2015b) that used a novel biodegradable D-α-tocopheryl PEG 1000 succinate-b-poly(ε-caprolactone-ran-glycolide) (TPGS-b-(PCL-ran-PGA)) nanoparticle (NP) as a cargo to deliver siRNA, which targets HIF alpha to treat NPC. The same results were obtained as the treated ones showed less expression of HIF alpha, which further caused the significant increase in cytotoxicity of CNE 2 cells, when compared with the control.

The protein-free RNA nanoparticle exhibits minimal antigenicity, making it an ideal candidate for reducing the need for frequent, long-term administrations, thus unlocking its vast potential in treating NPC. Guo et al. (2006) developed such nanoparticle combination that targets human folate receptors, highly expressed in case of NPC. As the folate binding to HFR gives rise to an endocytosis response, the folate is coupled with 5′ AMP, which is again ligated to 5′ end of the bacteriophage phi29 motor pRNA. The pRNA 5′ overhang increases the accessibility of receptor binding of folate. The protein-free RNA construct was prepared carrying pRNA nanoparticles for HFR, a detection marker, and a siRNA.

13.8 Conclusions

Cancer therapy suffers from several drawbacks following the administration of anticancer drugs. These drugs spread throughout the body instead of preferentially accumulating within the tumor leading to normal tissue toxicity and several complications for cancer patients. In recent times, nanocarriers-based approaches have gained a lot of importance in drug delivery of chemotherapeutics as they overcome conventional chemotherapy's limitations and reduce the toxicity. Many different strategies are present to develop targeted multifunctional nanoparticles. Over the years, different types of nanosystems have been developed for the treatment of oral cancer, including polymeric, metallic, and lipid-based formulations that incorporate chemotherapeutics, natural compounds, siRNA, or other molecules for overcoming the multidrug resistance. The results are promising, and better and more effective mouth and throat cancer treatment is now becoming a possibility with the development of multifunctional nanocarrier-mediated codelivery for targeting and treating mouth and throat cancer.

References

Ali, H.M., Maksimenko, A., Urbinati, G., Chapuis, H., Raouane, M., Desmaële, D., et al., 2014. Effects of silencing the RET/PTC1 oncogene in papillary thyroid carcinoma by siRNA-squalene nanoparticles with and without fusogenic companion GALA-cholesterol. Thyroid. 24 (2), 327–338. Available from: https://doi.org/10.1089/thy.2012.0544. Epub 2014 Jan 9. PMID: 23885719.
Alibakhshi, A., Kahaki, A.F., Ahangarzadeh, S., et al., 2017. Targeted cancer therapy through antibody fragments-decorated nanomedicines. J. Control. Rel. 28 (268), 323–334. 12.
Bhaskar, S., Tian, F., Stoeger, T., et al., 2010. Multifunctional nanocarriers for diagnostics, drug delivery and targeted treatment across blood-brain barrier: perspectives on tracking and neuroimaging. Part. Fibre Toxicol. 7 (3), 3.
Cao, M., Deng, X., Su, S., Zhang, F., Xiao, X., Hu, Q., et al., 2013. Protamine sulfate-nanodiamond hybrid nanoparticles as a vector for MiR-203 restoration in esophageal carcinoma cells. Nanoscale. 5 (24), 12120–12125. Available from: https://doi.org/10.1039/c3nr04056a. PMID: 24154605.
Chandna, P., Khandare, J.J., Ber, E., et al., 2010. Multifunctional tumor-targeted polymer-peptide-drug delivery system for treatment of primary and metastatic cancers. Pharm. Res. 27 (11), 2296–2306 [PubMed: 20700631].

Chen, W.H., Lecaros, R.L., Tseng, Y.C., Huang, L., Hsu, Y.C., 2015a. Nanoparticle delivery of HIF1α siRNA combined with photodynamic therapy as a potential treatment strategy for head-and-neck cancer. Cancer Lett. 359 (1), 65−74. Available from: https://doi.org/10.1016/j.canlet.2014.12.052. Epub 2015 Jan 14. PMID: 25596376; PMCID: PMC5010227.

Chen, Y., Xu, G., Zheng, Y., Yan, M., Li, Z., Zhou, Y., et al., 2015b. Nanoformulation of D-α-tocopheryl polyethylene glycol 1000 succinate-b-poly(ε-caprolactone-ran-glycolide) diblock copolymer for siRNA targeting HIF-1α for nasopharyngeal carcinoma therapy. Int. J. Nanomed. 10, 1375−1386. Available from: https://doi.org/10.2147/IJN.S76092. PMID: 25733830; PMCID: PMC4337506.

Cho, H.J., Chong, S., Chung, S.J., Shim, C.K., Kim, D.D., 2011. Poly-L-arginine and dextran sulfate-based nanocomplex for epidermal growth factor receptor (EGFR) siRNA delivery: its application for head and neck cancer treatment. Pharm. Res. 29 (4), 1007−1019. Available from: https://doi.org/10.1007/s11095-011-0642-z. Epub 2011 Dec 15. PMID: 22169985.

de Martimprey, H., Bertrand, J.R., Malvy, C., Couvreur, P., Vauthier, C., 2010. New core-shell nanoparticles for the intravenous delivery of siRNA to experimental thyroid papillary carcinoma. Pharm. Res. 27 (3), 498−509. Available from: https://doi.org/10.1007/s11095-009-0043-8. Epub 2010 Jan 20. PMID: 20087631.

Deshpande, P.P., Biswas, S., Torchilin, V.P., 2013. Current trends in the use of liposomes for tumor targeting. Nanomedicine 8 (9), 1509−1528 [PubMed: 23914966]. An excellent and important manuscript that highlights advances in liposome research in tumor targeting and pH-triggered drug delivery.

Gandini, S., Botteri, E., Iodice, S., Boniol, M., Lowenfels, A.B., Maisonneuve, P., et al., 2008. Tobacco smoking and cancer: a meta-analysis. Int. J. Cancer 122 (1), 155−164. Available from: https://doi.org/10.1002/ijc.23033. PMID: 17893872.

Garbuzenko, O.B., Kuzmov, A., Taratula, O., et al., 2019. Strategy to enhance lung cancer treatment by five essential elements: inhalation delivery, nanotechnology, tumor-receptor targeting, chemo-and gene therapy. Theranostics. 9 (26), 8362−8376 [PubMed: 31754402]. An extreamly important manuscript that demonstrates advantages of complex multifunctional targeted delivery systems for treatment of cancer.

Guo, S., Huang, F., Guo, P., 2006. Construction of folate-conjugated pRNA of bacteriophage phi29 DNA packaging motor for delivery of chimeric siRNA to nasopharyngeal carcinoma cells. Gene Ther. 13 (10), 814−820. Available from: https://doi.org/10.1038/sj.gt.3302716. Erratum in: Gene Ther. 2006 Nov;13(21):1553. PMID: 16482206; PMCID: PMC2840388.

Glastonbury, C.M., 2020. Head and neck squamous cell cancer: approach to staging and surveillance. In: Hodler, J., Kubik-Huch, R.A., von Schulthess, G.K. (Eds.), Diseases of the Brain, Head and Neck, Spine 2020−2023: Diagnostic Imaging [Internet]. Springer, Cham, 2020. Chapter 17. PMID: 32119254.

Han, X., Wang, X., Wang, L., Yao, X., Zhao, G., Cui, Z., 2020. Inhibition human nasopharyngeal carcinoma cells TNF-α gene transfected cytokine-induced killer cells based on nanomaterial polyphthalamide monoamine dendrimer nanomaterial. J. Nanosci. Nanotechnol. 20 (10), 6133−6139. Available from: https://doi.org/10.1166/jnn.2020.18557. PMID: 32384962.

Irimie, A.I., Sonea, L., Jurj, A., Mehterov, N., Zimta, A.A., Budisan, L., et al., 2017. Future trends and emerging issues for nanodelivery systems in oral and oropharyngeal cancer. Int. J. Nanomed. 12, 4593−4606. Available from: https://doi.org/10.2147/IJN.S133219. PMID: 28721037; PMCID: PMC5500515.

Jin, L., Wang, Q., Chen, J., Wang, Z., Xin, H., Zhang, D., 2019. Efficient delivery of therapeutic siRNA by Fe3O4 magnetic nanoparticles into oral cancer cells. Pharmaceutics 11 (11), 615. Available from: https://doi.org/10.3390/pharmaceutics11110615. PMID: 31744202; PMCID: PMC6921101.

Kampel, L., Goldsmith, M., Ramishetti, S., Veiga, N., Rosenblum, D., Gutkin, A., et al., 2021. Therapeutic inhibitory RNA in head and neck cancer via functional targeted lipid nanoparticles. J. Control. Rel. 337, 378−389. Available from: https://doi.org/10.1016/j.jconrel.2021.07.034. Epub 2021 Jul 23. PMID: 34303750.

Khairnar, P., Handa, M., Shukla, R., 2022. Nanocrystals: an approachable delivery system for anticancer therapeutics. Curr. Drug. Metab. 23 (8), 603.

Li, G., Hu, Z., Yin, H., Zhang, Y., Huang, X., Wang, S., et al., 2013. A novel dendritic nanocarrier of polyamidoamine-polyethylene glycol-cyclic RGD for "smart" small interfering RNA delivery and in vitro antitumor effects by human ether-à-go-go-related gene silencing in anaplastic thyroid carcinoma cells. Int. J. Nanomed. 8, 1293–1306. Available from: https://doi.org/10.2147/IJN.S41555. Epub 2013 Mar 27. PMID: 23569377; PMCID: PMC3615931.

Li, Y., Zhang, J., Wang, B., Shen, Y., Ouahab, A., 2016. Co-delivery of siRNA and hypericin into cancer cells by hyaluronic acid modified PLGA-PEI nanoparticles. Drug. Dev. Ind. Pharm. 42 (5), 737–746. Available from: https://doi.org/10.3109/03639045.2015.1091469. Epub 2015 Oct 16. PMID: 26472259.

Lin, L., Song, C., Wei, Z., Zou, H., Han, S., Cao, Z., et al., 2022. Multifunctional photodynamic/photothermal nano-agents for the treatment of oral leukoplakia. J. Nanobiotechnol. 20 (1), 106. Available from: https://doi.org/10.1186/s12951-022-01310-2. PMID: 35246146; PMCID: PMC8895861.

Liu, X., Huang, H., Wang, J., Wang, C., Wang, M., Zhang, B., et al., 2011. Dendrimers-delivered short hairpin RNA targeting hTERT inhibits oral cancer cell growth in vitro and in vivo. Biochem. Pharmacol. 82 (1), 17–23. Available from: https://doi.org/10.1016/j.bcp.2011.03.017. Epub 2011 Mar 29. PMID: 21453684.

Liu, Y., Gunda, V., Zhu, X., Xu, X., Wu, J., Askhatova, D., et al., 2016. Theranostic near-infrared fluorescent nanoplatform for imaging and systemic siRNA delivery to metastatic anaplastic thyroid cancer. Proc. Natl Acad. Sci. U S A. 113 (28), 7750–7755. Available from: https://doi.org/10.1073/pnas.1605841113. Epub 2016 Jun 24. PMID: 27342857; PMCID: PMC4948349.

Majumdar, D., Jana, S., Kumar Ray, S., 2022. Gold nanoparticles decorated 2D-WSe$_2$ as a SERS substrate. Spectrochim. Acta A. Mol. Biomol. Spectrosc. 278, 121349. Available from: https://doi.org/10.1016/j.saa.2022.121349.

Montazerabadi, A., Beik, J., Irajirad, R., Attaran, N., Khaledi, S., Ghaznavi, H., et al., 2019. Folate-modified and curcumin-loaded dendritic magnetite nanocarriers for the targeted thermo-chemotherapy of cancer cells. Artif. Cell Nanomed. Biotechnol. 47 (1), 330–340. Available from: https://doi.org/10.1080/21691401.2018.1557670. PMID: 30688084.

Qi, X., Yu, D., Jia, B., Jin, C., Liu, X., Zhao, X., et al., 2016. Targeting CD133(+) laryngeal carcinoma cells with chemotherapeutic drugs and siRNA against ABCG2 mediated by thermo/pH-sensitive mesoporous silica nanoparticles. Tumour Biol. 37 (2), 2209–2217. Available from: https://doi.org/10.1007/s13277-015-4007-9. Epub 2015 Sep 9. PMID: 26353857.

Ray, E., Vaghasiya, K., Sharma, A., Shukla, R., Khan, R., Kumar, A., et al., 2020. Autophagy-inducing inhalable co-crystal formulation of niclosamide-nicotinamide for lung cancer therapy. AAPS PharmSciTech 21 (7), 1–14.

Shi, X.L., Li, Y., Zhao, L.M., Su, L.W., Ding, G., 2019. Delivery of MTH1 inhibitor (TH287) and MDR1 siRNA via hyaluronic acid-based mesoporous silica nanoparticles for oral cancers treatment. Colloids Surf. B Biointerfaces 173, 599–606. Available from: https://doi.org/10.1016/j.colsurfb.2018.09.076. Epub 2018 Sep 29. PMID: 30352381.

Shukla, R., Singh, A., Pardhi, V., Kashyap, K., Dubey, S.K., Dandela, R., et al., 2019. Dendrimer-based nanoparticulate delivery system for cancer therapy. Polymeric Nanoparticles as a Promising Tool for Anti-cancer Therapeutics. Elsevier, pp. 233–255.

Singh, A., Handa, M., Ruwali, M., Flora, S.J.S., Shukla, R., Kesharwani, P., 2021. Nanocarrier mediated autophagy: an emerging trend for cancer therapy. Process. Biochem. 109, 198–206.

Taratula, O., Garbuzenko, O.B., Kirkpatrick, P., et al., 2009. Surface-engineered targeted PPI dendrimer for efficient intracellular and intratumoral siRNA delivery. J. Control. Release 140 (3), 284–293 [PubMed: 19567257].

Teng, B., Ma, P., Yu, C., Zhang, X., Feng, Q., Wen, L., et al., 2017. Upconversion nanoparticles loaded with eIF4E siRNA and platinum(iv) prodrug to sensitize platinum based chemotherapy for laryngeal cancer and bioimaging. J. Mater. Chem. B. 5 (2), 307–317. Available from: https://doi.org/10.1039/c6tb02360f. Epub 2016 Dec 9. PMID: 32263549.

Trapani, G., Denora, N., Trapani, A., et al., 2012. Recent advances in ligand targeted therapy. J. Drug. Target. 20 (1), 1–22 [PubMed: 21942529].

Varma, L.T., Singh, N., Gorain, B., Choudhury, H., Tambuwala, M.M., Kesharwani, P., et al., 2020. Recent advances in self-assembled nanoparticles for drug delivery. Curr. Drug. Deliv. 17 (4), 279–291.

Wang, D., Yu, D., Liu, X., Wang, Q., Chen, X., Hu, X., et al., 2020. Targeting laryngeal cancer cells with 5-fluorouracil and curcumin using mesoporous silica nanoparticles. Technol. Cancer Res. Treat. Available from: https://doi.org/10.1177/1533033820962114. Jan-Dec;19:1533033820962114. PMID: 33267716; PMCID: PMC7720313.

Wang, J., Wang, K., Liang, J., Jin, J., Wang, X., Yan, S., 2021. Chitosan-tripolyphosphate nanoparticles-mediated co-delivery of MTHFD1L shRNA and 5-aminolevulinic acid for combination photodynamic-gene therapy in oral cancer. Photodiagnosis Photodyn. Ther. 36, 102581. Available from: https://doi.org/10.1016/j.pdpdt.2021.102581. Epub 2021 Oct 12. PMID: 34648994.

Xu, W.W., Liu, D.Y., Cao, Y.C., Wang, X.Y., 2017. GE11 peptide-conjugated nanoliposomes to enhance the combinational therapeutic efficacy of docetaxel and siRNA in laryngeal cancers. Int. J. Nanomed. 12, 6461−6470. Available from: https://doi.org/10.2147/IJN.S129946. PMID: 28919747; PMCID: PMC5592908.

Yeh, C.H., Chen, J., Zheng, G., Huang, L., Hsu, Y.C., 2021. Novel pyropheophorbide phosphatydic acids photosensitizer combined EGFR siRNA gene therapy for head and neck cancer treatment. Pharmaceutics 13 (9), 1435. Available from: https://doi.org/10.3390/pharmaceutics13091435. PMID: 34575510; PMCID: PMC8470636.

Yuan, Q., Yeudall, W.A., Lee, E., Yang, H., 2019. Targeted inactivation of EPS8 using dendrimer-mediated delivery of RNA interference. Int. J. Pharm. 557, 178−181. Available from: https://doi.org/10.1016/j.ijpharm.2018.12.060. Epub 2018 Dec 28. PMID: 30597261.

CHAPTER 14

Nanocarrier-mediated delivery for targeting for prostate cancer

Sumel Ashique[1,2], Prathap Madeswara Guptha[3], Satish Shilpi[3,4], Saurabh Sharma[5,6], Shubneesh Kumar[1,7], Mohammad A. Altamimi[8], Afzal Hussain[8], Sandhya Chouhan[9] and Neeraj Mishra[3]

[1]Department of Pharmaceutics, Bharat Institute of Technology (BIT), School of Pharmacy, Meerut, Uttar Pradesh, India
[2]Department of Pharmaceutics, Pandaveswar School of Pharmacy, Pandaveswar, West Bengal, India
[3]Amity Institute of Pharmacy, Amity University Madhya Pradesh, Gwalior, Madhya Pradesh, India
[4]Department of Pharmacy, DIT University, Dehradun, Uttarakhand, India
[5]School of Pharmaceutical Sciences, CT University, Sidhwan Khurd, Punjab, India
[6]Chandigarh College of Pharmacy, Chandigarh Group of Colleges, Landran, Greater Mohali, Punjab, India
[7]Department of Life Sciences, School of Basic Sciences and Research, Sharda University, Greater Noida, Uttar Pradesh, India
[8]Department of Pharmaceutics, College of Pharmacy, King Saud University, Riyadh, Emirate of the Riyadh Province, Saudi Arabia
[9]Noida Institute of Engineering and Technology (Pharmacy Institute), Greater Noida, Uttar Pradesh, India

14.1 Introduction

Prostate cancer is a very common and frequently diagnosed cancer in the male population, and it is the third leading cause of malignancy deaths. The major challenge behind this is the metastatic nature of prostate malignant tumors. Although various therapeutic strategies have been applied for the management of overall survival (Siegel et al., 2017), current management options for prostate cancer in the advanced stage often become unsuccessful due to relapse. The main barrier to therapeutic efficacy in prostate cancer stem cells (PCSCs), which is responsible for resistance to maximum advanced therapies is considered to be the main mechanism of cancer metastasis and recurrence. Diagnosis of prostate cancer has several limitations such as the vast existence of gaps accompanying over testing, nonspecificity, and heterogeneous nature of prostate cancer (Kasivisvanathan et al., 2018). Interestingly, PCSCs employ various signaling pathways (Hurt et al., 2008) to help their peculiar features like Hedgehog (Chang et al., 2011), Wnt/β-catenin (Bisson and Prowse, 2009), and TGF-β (Chen et al., 2015), which would be a promising therapeutic target. Although, the transportation of drugs to the target site with better specificity and low cytotoxicity indicates the advancement of novel drug delivery systems for targeted PC management and thus nanomedicine has been utilized in the field of medicine and diagnosis for avoiding conventional treatment challenges mainly in various cancers (Espinoza et al., 2019). Nanotechnology-based therapies in prostate cancer results in the advancement of stealthing that shows the enhanced

Multifunctional Nanocomposites for Targeted Drug Delivery in Cancer Therapy
DOI: https://doi.org/10.1016/B978-0-323-95303-0.00008-3

accumulation of nanotherapeutics into the tumor site with greater retention time in the bloodstream, and these are achieved via coating the nanocarrier with hydrophilic polymers, which leads to the induction of better stealth functions (Cui et al., 2018). Several kinds of nanocarriers are being used, such as liposomes, niosomes, lipid hybrid nanoparticles (NPs), polymer-drug conjugates, polymeric nanospheres, nanomicelles, metallic NPs, and immune-conjugates, for the successful delivery of nanotherapeutics to the targeted cancer cells (Adjei et al., 2018). Nanotechnology provides various advantages like tumor targeting, minimal macrophage phagocytic system, increased retention time, improved bioavailability, and decreased cytotoxicity (Pearce et al., 2017; Wicki et al., 2015). The application of nanomaterials in the field of biomedicines has had a great impact on the delivery of antineoplastics. Efficient strategies regarding active targeting are either improved or under clinical evaluation.

14.2 Pathophysiology of the prostate gland and prostate cancer

The prostate is a male sex glandular tissue composed of various secretory units (acini) and ducts with lined epithelial cells, and this gland is highly prone to malignant progression than other organs in the urogenital tract. Various studies reported that the diagnosis of prostatic carcinogenesis is closely associated with organogenesis embryologically, including hormone signaling like testosterone and other signaling pathways like Sonic Hedgehog expression (Shh), leading to stromal tumor development and progression (Karhadkar et al., 2004; Fan et al., 2004). Prostate cancer starts primarily from the epithelium and is therefore known as carcinoma; additionally, there are other subtypes like sarcomas and lymphomas (Humphrey, 2017). Neoplastic alteration mainly initiates from the peripheral glandular tissue and the prostatic epithelium consists of luminal, basal, and rare neuroendocrine (NE) cells (Lee and Shen, 2015). The epithelial luminal shields the internal surface of the prostatic ducts and releases prostatic fluid. They are covered by basal cells, which develop proteins utilized for fluid production and the formation of the acinar basement membrane. Both basal and NE cell types are deficient in ARs and therefore are not testosterone or androstenedione dependent (Blagoev et al., 2021). The focus of scientists is to recognize the key responsible factor for oncogenic transformation in prostate cancer (Wang and Shen, 2011). Findings revealed that about 90%–95% of prostate cancers initiate from the peripheral prostatic gland (Alizadeh and Alizadeh, 2014) and transformation of benign epithelial cells into malignant phenotype. The most frequent approach to cancer progression in the prostate is known as prostatic intraepithelial neoplasia (Murray, 2021; Kim and Yang, 2002). Prostate cancer proliferation initially depends on AR activation, via testosterone and dihydrotestosterone, leading to nuclear translocation of the receptor and subsequent binding to androgen response elements, initiating transcription of genes that regulate cellular differentiation, proliferation, and apoptosis (Nelson, 2014).

The tumor microenvironment (TME) delineates several types of supporting cells, such as immune cells, fibroblasts, adipose cells, and microvasculature, and constituents of the extracellular matrix (ECM) that creates a tight network around the tumor cells, which can play a promising role in pathogenicity, mainly responsible for the transformation of normal cells into progressive cancer cells. Various reports have revealed that tumors can "hijack" the immune cells and help them for metastatic potential (Thienger and Rubin, 2021, Gevaert et al., 2020). CD8-T cells can convey PSA in the invasive state of prostate cancer, which probably increases the chances of the cancer cell metastasizing from lymphatic tissue, bone, and other organs. Thus, it is clear that TME can assist such an environment where alternative cells can modulate into progressive cancer cells and results in the invasiveness of local and systemic structures (Ganguly et al., 2014). Downregulation in the programmed cell death system is also responsible for the pathogenesis of prostate cancer (McKenzie and Kyprianou, 2006). Mainly two distinct pathways are involved: the first is extrinsic mechanisms that are linked to the intracellular binding of apoptosis-inducing ligands, and the second is the intrinsic pathway that is associated with the initiation of mitochondria via intracellular injury like DNA damage through chemoradiotherapy. Bcl-2 categories like Bax, Bid, and Bad are proapoptotic factors that target the mitochondrial membrane and the upstream of Bcl-2 associated receptors, which are also responsible for malignant prostate cancer pathogenesis (Navone et al., 1993).

14.3 Advantages and implications of targeted nanocarrier for prostate cancer

Due to collateral side effects and indefinite dispensation of PC therapeutic approaches, created from traditional delivery strategies, which provide poor efficiency, thus researchers have considered an alternative approach to avoid the limitations. A nanotechnology is a novel approach with numerous beneficial advantages such as safety, less toxicity, prolonged retention time, and targeted drug delivery to prostate cancer cells using suitable nanocarriers (various generations) (Tables 14.1 and 14.2). Not only in PC but also nanomedicine has opened a new advanced era of therapeutic options to overcome such limitations faced by conventional treatment strategies against various types of cancers and intracellular disorders (Espinoza et al., 2022). Advanced transmembrane crossing provide a payload delivery of bioactive, increased retention time, enhanced solubility profile, and site-specific delivery of therapeutics obtained from nanotechnology. For example, the modified nanocarriers can improve the pharmacokinetics and pharmacodynamics of bioactive, which help to transfer the therapeutic to the definite site at a ratiometric dose. Drug-loaded nanocarriers can aggregate to the targeted cancer cells by following active and passive targeting mechanisms (Fig. 14.1). The surface of NPs is modified by utilizing specific ligands, allowing the therapeutics

Table 14.1 List of nanoparticle-based formulations used to treat prostate cancer.

S. No.	NPs type	Drug	Cell culture/animal model	Findings	References
1.	Poly (lactic-co-glycolic acid)-CUR nanoparticles (PLGA CurNPs)	Curcumin	Lymph node carcinoma of the prostate, C4—2 DU-145 and PC-3/C4-2-xenograft	In both pancreatic cells and tumor xenograft tissues, PLGA-Cur NPs inhibited nuclear –catenin expression. Inhibition of key Mcl-1, Bcl-xL, and induced poly ADP ribose polymerase (PARP) cleavage was also observed, leading to apoptosis by inhibiting STAT3 and AKT phosphorylation	Azandeh et al. (2017)
2.	Peptide–based NPs	Docetaxel and curcumin codelivery and imaging	Prostate cancer cells and xenografts	Using epidermal growth factor receptor (EGFR) peptide targeting and the enhanced permeability and retention (EPR) effect of NPs, docetaxel and curcumin could be delivered into prostate tumor cells at the same time. NPs that are based on peptides can also be used for imaging	Yeh et al. (2016)
3.	PLGA NPs	Cell penetrating peptide and 8-dibenzothiophen-4-yl-2-morpholin-4-yl-chromen-4-one (a radio-sensitizer), encapsulate bicalutamide	human prostatic carcinoma cell line	The formulations released encapsulated radiosensitizer in two phases and were actively taken up by PC-3 cells in a dose and magnetic field-dependent manner. In vitro, the NPs were effective at radiation sensitizing prostate cancer cell lines. Bicalutamide has also been encapsulated with PLGA-NPs	Guo et al. (2015)

No.	Nanoparticle	Drug	Cell line	Findings	Reference
4.	Solid lipid nanoparticles	Retinoic acid	Lymph Node Carcinoma of the Prostate– LNCap cells	With increasing drug concentrations, NPs showed a decrease in cell viability. The cellular uptake of NPs revealed that they were localized within the cytoplasm of cells, and flow cytometry analysis revealed that the fraction of cells expressing early apoptotic markers had increased	De Jesus et al. (2010)
5.	Superparamagnetic iron oxide nanoparticle	Prostate-specific membrane antigen and docetaxel	c4–2(CaP cell line derived from LNCaP cells) and pc-3(a human prostate cancer cell line used in prostate cancer)	In prostate cancer cells, NPs were efficiently incorporated and showed potent anticancer efficacy through induction of apoptosis-associated proteins, downregulation of antiapoptotic proteins, and inhibition of chemoresistance associated protein	Wang et al. (2008)

Table 14.2 List of nanoparticles that are currently being used to treat prostate cancer, as well as their bioactive ingredients and targets.

S. No.	Generation	Nanocarriers	Target	Entrapped drug	References
1.	First	Liposome (egg PC:L-α-phosphatidylcholine/DPPE-PEG-2000)	Enhanced permeability and retention (EPR)	Celecoxib/genistein	Tian et al. (2019)
2.	Second	Polymeric [1]/nanobubble	Enhanced permeability and retention (EPR)	Curcumin	Bessone et al. (2019)
3.		Liposome	Enhanced permeability and retention (EPR)	PEG (avoid uptake of reticuloendothelial system)	Milla et al. (2012)
4.		Liposome (PLGA: poly(lactic–co–glycolic acid))	Apatamer (nucleic acid molecules that mimic antibodies)	Triple-forming oligonucleotide	Jiao et al. (2016)
5.	Third	Liposome (PEGylated lipid, cholesterol)	Peptide	Doxorubicin/vinorebline	Yeh et al. (2016)
6.		Liposome (soybean phosphatidylcholine [SPC])	Antibody (simvastatin)	Doxorubicin	Li et al. (2019b)
7.		DNA nanostructure	Apatamer	Doxorubicin	Taghdisi et al. (2018)
8.	Fourth	PMB (planetary ball milled nanoparticles)	Small molecule (folic acid)	Reservatrol/docetaxel	Singh et al. (2018)
9.		Liposome	RGD	siRNA (GRP 78 siRNA)/docetaxel	Zhang et al. (2019)
10.		Gold nanoparticle	Small molecule (folic acid)	siRNA	Rahme et al. (2019)

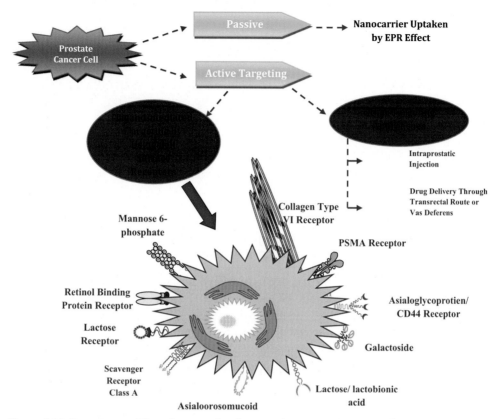

Figure 14.1 Receptors and ligand approaches for targeting prostate cancer cells.

for the development of multimodal, multifunctional nanocomponents (Wu et al., 2020). Nanocarrier-based therapy for PC also results in progressed stealthing that leads to enhanced accumulation of nanomedicine at the specific tumor sites with prolonged retention time in the systemic circulation when the surface is modified by coating with hydrophilic polymers (Cui et al., 2018, Rosenblum et al., 2018). Nanotechnology also helps to identify the associated biomarkers in PC with marked sensitivity as equated to the traditional enzyme-linked immunosorbent assay (ELISA) technique (Nicolosi et al., 2019). The greater sensitivity of the nanocarrier fabricated pointer is involved with low cost because only traces of biomarkers are needed to identify prostate cancer (Koo et al., 2019). Definite nano-based detectors are able to decrease the overdiagnosis and underdiagnosis of cell progression because of great specificity and sensitivity, respectively, and could recognize the risk of further occurrence after recovery (Yoon et al., 2014). The major limitation of most of the carrier systems is the inadequate transfer of therapeutics at high concentrations because of cytotoxicity at the specific site. The surface-functionalized nanoparticles with one or more ligands help to increase the targeting affinity; thus, advanced PC therapy considers the application of drug-loaded nanocarriers. nanoparticles also have several advantages like being small and having great surface-to-volume ratios that help numerous molecules to attach like therapeutics and antibodies, which provides efficient therapeutic approaches (Whitesides et al., 1991). Due to the small size, NPs influence the uptake of bioactive in an intracellular way, and by entrapping the drugs, NPs also enhance the solubility profile, release drugs in a controlled manner (Chrastina et al., 2011), offer decreased cytotoxicity, and improved the pharmacokinetics of drugs (Davis et al., 2008; Pettitt et al., 2013). Despite having various beneficial effects, nanocarriers also show few limitations such as off-targeting effects, face-first pass metabolism, and often immunogenicity.

14.4 Various synthetic and biological nanotechnology-based outlooks for targeting prostate cancer follow several routes

Nanocarrier-based drug delivery has been considered a significant approach for efficient delivery of anticancer therapeutics (Weissleder, 2001) for enhancing pharmacokinetic profile along with bioavailability, circulation time, increased therapeutic index, and solubility profile (Shenoy and Amiji, 2005; Schroeder et al., 1998). For the systemic nano-drug delivery method, the main limitation of prostate cancer diagnosis is the application of nonphysiological animal models, which cannot imitate the human disease state. The main consideration is to improve the retention time of NPs at the desired site, which can be successfully obtained by the modification of cancer cell-targeted ligands by using nanoparticles (Friedman et al., 2013). For nanomedicine delivery through localized methods, tumors are basically blocked to the particular local area at the beginning of diseased initiation, and at the middle phase, enclose even the lymph nodes, and additionally, tumors in the later phase move from the primary site to another organ site of progression (Fig. 14.2) (Martin et al., 2013). On the basis of tumor nature and their definite prevailing phases, localized prostate cancer therapy is most considerable (Van Hemelrijck et al., 2014). In the case of PC management, localized therapy has become the most efficient approach for physiological purposes (Denmeade et al., 2014). By following the intraprostatic injection route, a high concentration of therapeutic can be transported, which results in less exposure to the blood circulation, and eventually shows decreased toxicities and associated adverse events (Linxweiler et al., 2018). The limitations of the intraprostatic injection route for the localized treatment of prostate cancer are the limited amount of drugs that would be transported and the backflow of injectables because uncontrolled injectant leaks from the prostate capsule can damage tissues, and to avoid this limitation, there is a need for designing a site-specific nanomedicine delivery that offers potent encapsulation and high specificity of therapeutics (Wolinsky et al., 2012). However, the limitation of localized nanodrug delivery for PC management can be overcome by introducing a transrectal route or vas deferens. In the case of nanodrug delivery through the

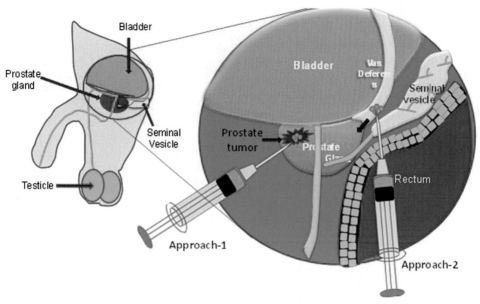

Approach-1: Intra-prostate Injection of anticancer drug
Drawback: Serious tissue injury and may chances of spreading cancer cells

Approach-2: Intra-Vas Deferens injection of anticancer drug loaded nanoformulation.
Benefit: No tissue injury and no chances of spreading cancer cells. Drug formulation injected via intra rectal into Vas deferens. Vas Deferens deliver drug loaded nanocarrier to prostate glands directly.

Figure 14.2 Approaches to deliver drug and novel formulations directly to prostate glands.

transrectal route, the rectum is a proximally placed site for the prostate, which influences the measuring of prostate-involved disorders by following digital rectal evaluation and transrectal ultrasound-guided prostate biopsies. Along with the application of ultrasound for diagnosis purposes, site-specific nanomedicine is also transported into the prostate cancer cell (Krishnan et al., 2010; Wu et al., 2014). Additionally, in humans, the rectal route offers a more easy way to reach the prostate cancer site without any invasion. Thus, the rectal route offers a new window for localized nanodrug delivery. The vas deferens route is a passage through which spermatozoa move from the urethra to the epididymis, and the transportation of nanotherapeutics by using this route is significant for targeting PC. The research was conducted where styrene-maleic anhydride (SMA) was used as a reference drug model, and the results showed controlled drug transportation at the prostate cancer cell site (Guha et al., 2011).

14.5 Current prostate cancer treatment approaches with their limitations

Over the past decades several strategies have been available for managing PC treatment, although combination chemotherapies have been more beneficial than monotherapies (Galsky and Vogelzang, 2010). Therefore, currently, researchers are focusing on various FDA-allowed chemotherapeutic strategies, and the efficacy of the approaches is very significant. In spite of several advantages, there are some certain limitations that influence the clinical efficacy of drugs on their pharmacodynamics and pharmacokinetic properties. The presence of biological barriers inhibits the absorption and delivery of chemotherapeutics, and their nonspecific distribution into the various tissue compartments also limits their wide application. These barriers could range from delivery of cellular membranes, humoral attacks, and efflux pump-based removal to endosomal involvement (Sriraman et al., 2014). Only about 1 in 10,000 drug moieties could be able to make it to a specific site, resulting in poor efficiency (Zhou et al., 2019). To improve the bioavailability and for adequate drug accumulation to the targeted site, higher doses are given, which causes collateral toxicity and multidrug resistance (Gillet and Gottesman, 2010). Recently, combination therapy of cytotoxic bioactives and antiandrogen regimens are used widely against castration-resistant prostate cancer, for example docetaxel (DTX) with Prednisone, which showed enhanced clinical results (Price et al., 2004). Common adverse events associated with anticancer drugs such as neutropenia, allergic reactions, stomatitis, peripheral neuropathy, and fluid retention (Elmhadi et al., 2016). The codelivery approach mainly depends on the independent pharmacokinetics, biodistribution, and clearance rate of the respective actives, which leads to challenging individual effectiveness, thus upturning the nature of synergism. Due to the above-mentioned limitations, it is needed to take an approach where the drug would be pharmacologically stable, with greater solubility, safety, and specificity of numerous anticancer agents. Therefore, to overcome these challenges, the only advanced approach is nanomedicine (Webster, 2006; Sakamoto et al., 2010).

14.6 Nanotechnology awaiting possibilities in prostate cancer management

To overcome various limitations, researchers have considered alternative approaches to face these challenges, and nanotechnology is such a design that guarantees the safety, specificity, and therapeutic efficiency for prostate cancer treatment. Nanocarriers compose of biodevices and agents with numerous functional and structural features like polymers, lipids, inorganic vectors, and biological scaffolds to design nanomedicine (NPs) for targeted delivery of anticancer bioactive (Nagpal et al., 2020). Advancement of nanocarriers for targeted prostate cancer management has allowed for entrapping a high dose of antineoplastic drugs or a combination of one or more active moieties in a single nanocarrier, payload transport of active agents, decreased cytotoxicity, and overall enhance the therapeutic efficacy (Blankfield, 2012; Miao et al., 2014; Pan et al., 2019). Furthermore, several findings have currently described the chance for codelivery of a chemogene (chemo-and-gene dependent treatment) in a single nano-carrier to synergize gene silencing and cytotoxicity for prostate cancer treatment (Senapati et al., 2018), which showed improved site-specific drug delivery with reduced drug toxicity and also protected the anticancer moieties from humoral attacks (Shetty et al., 2019).

14.7 Nanotheranostics for managing prostate cancer

"Theranostics" means the combination of therapeutics (thera) and diagnostics (nostics) for specific disease therapy. Currently, the advancement of nanotechnology has given a wide multimodal nanotheranostics way, which influences the diagnostics, therapeutics, and real-time diagnosis of tissue response. This design approach offers numerous characteristics like imaging, specific targeting, and enhancing therapeutic outcomes. To design theranostic nanoplatforms, various components are needed (de Barros et al., 2012), thus NPs for radionuclide imaging and therapy promoting various functionalities are under investigation (Kennel et al., 2017; Xie et al., 2010; Su and Hu, 2018). Theranostic nanotechnology is developed to increase the therapeutic output, decrease toxicity, enhance tumor penetration, and increase the aggregation of drug-encapsulated nanocar-rier at the targeted cancer cell (Sun et al., 2017). For better enhancement of tumor pen-etration, various approaches have been taken like specific targeting, intratumorally drug transportation, or maintaining the TME and vasculature, which result in improved tumor penetration and enhanced therapeutic potency (Singh et al., 2019).

14.8 Various types of nanocarriers used in prostate cancer treatment

Currently, nanocarriers are broadly applied in several biomedical fields due to their numerous beneficial effects, mainly for the management of targeted disease condi-tions. Prostate cancer is a very commonly diagnosed cancer that requires site-specific targeted drug delivery. In terms of targeting purpose, nanocarriers (nanoemulsions, liposomes, polymeric nanocapsule, carbon nanotubes, gold NPs, magnetic NPs, silica mesoporous NPs, and quantum dots [QDs]) are the best-suited approach for the management of tumor-associated tissues with enhanced outcomes in PC management (Tables 14.2 and 14.3). The following drug-loaded nanocarriers can accumulate at the targeted site by following active and passive targeting (Zhang et al., 2019). siRNAs represent an emerging strategy for cancer therapy. However, one of the diffi-culties is the limitation of targeted delivery to the site of cancer, including PCa. To date, various carriers were designed for the delivery of siRNA for PCa, such as poly-meric NPs, lipid NPs, nanobubbles, and cyclodextrins (Tables 14.4 and 14.5) (Mishra et al., 2022).

Table 14.3 List of nanosystems that has been used in prostate cancer research.

S. No.	Nanoparticle	Drug	Research model	Impact	References
1.	HPMA– HPMA, N-(2-hydroxypropyl) methacrylamide	Cyclopamine	RC-92a/hTERT and PC3 (prostate carcinoma) cell lines	In vitro: sphere-forming capacity decrease decrease percentage of CD133[+] population decrease	Zhou et al. (2012)
2.	HPMA– HPMA, N-(2-hydroxypropyl) methacrylamide	Apitolisib– GDC–0980	PC3 cell line PC3 tumor xenograft nude mice	In vitro, the percentage of CD133 + population decreases as sphere-forming capacity decreases.In vivo, the survival rate of mice improves	Zhou et al. (2015)
	Mesoporous silica nanoparticles	Ga-Au@mSiO$_2$–gallium –gold	LNCap and DU145	Significant antitumor effect in vitro cell line study	Liu et al. (2019)
	Quantum dots (QDs)	Doxorubicin	Enhanced permeability and retention effect	Capable of binding toward prostate cancer cells in all in vivo and in vitro studies	Barani et al. (2020)
	HA – hyaluronic acid	CDDP, cis-dichloro diammino platinum (II)	DU145(prostate carcinoma), and PC3 cell lines (adenocarcinoma)	Sphere-forming capacity decreases in vitro, while colony-forming capacity decreases.	Malek et al. (2014)
	Graphene oxide	Doxorubicin, camptothecin, and paclitaxel	PC3 cell line	In vitro: sphere-forming capacity decreases	Fiorillo et al. (2015)

Table 14.4 List of nanoparticle-based formulations used to treat prostate cancer (Tian et al., 2017).

S. No.	Nanoparticle type	Drug	Cell culture/animal model	Findings	References
1.	Poly (lactic-co-glycolic acid)–CUR nanoparticles (PLGA CurNPs)	Curcumin	Lymph node carcinoma of the prostate, C4–2 DU-145 and PC–3/C4–2-xenograft	In both pancreatic cells and tumor xenograft tissues, PLGA-Cur NPs inhibited nuclear catenin expression. Inhibition of key Mcl-1, Bcl-xL, and induced poly ADP ribose polymerase (PARP) cleavage was also observed, leading to apoptosis by inhibiting STAT3 and AKT phosphorylation.	Azandeh et al. (2017)
2.	Peptide–based NPs	Docetaxel and curcumin	Prostate cancer cells and xenografts	Using the epidermal growth factor receptor (EGFR), peptide targeting and enhanced EPR effect of NPs, docetaxel, and curcumin could be delivered into PC cells at the same time	Yeh et al. (2016)
3.	PLGA NPs	Bicalutamide	Human prostatic carcinoma cell line	The formulations released encapsulated radiosensitizer in two phases and were actively taken up by PC-3 cells in a dose and magnetic field dependent manner. Bicalutamide has been encapsulated with PLGA-NPs	Guo et al. (2015)

(Continued)

Table 14.4 (Continued)

S. No.	Nanoparticle type	Drug	Cell culture/animal model	Findings	References
4.	Solid lipid nanoparticles	Retinoic acid	Lymph node carcinoma of the prostate – LNCap cells	With increasing drug concentrations, NPs showed a decrease in cell viability. The cellular uptake of NPs revealed that they were localized within the cytoplasm of cells, and flow cytometry analysis revealed that the fraction of cells expressing early apoptotic markers had increased	De Jesus. et al. (2010)
5.	Superparamagnetic iron oxide nanoparticle	Prostate-specific membrane antigen and docetaxel	c4–2 (CaP cell line derived from LNCaP cells) and pc–3 (a human prostate cancer cell line used in prostate cancer)	In PC cells, NPs were efficiently incorporated and showed potent anticancer efficacy through induced apoptosis-associated proteins, downregulation of antiapoptotic proteins, and inhibition of chemoresistance-associated protein	Wang et al. (2008)

Table 14.5 List of the nanosystems that have been used in prostate cancer research.

S. No.	Nanoparticle	Drug	Research model	Impact	References
1.	HPMA- *HPMA, N-(2-hydroxypropyl) methacrylamide*	Cyclopamine	RC-92a/hTERT and PC3 (Prostate carcinoma) cell lines	In vitro: sphere-forming capacity decrease percentage of CD133$^+$ population	Zhou et al. (2012)
2.	HPMA- *HPMA, N-(2-hydroxypropyl) methacrylamide*	Apitolisib- GDC-0980	PC3 cell line PC3 tumor xenograft nude mice	In vitro, the percentage of CD133$^+$ population decreases as sphere-forming capacity decreases. In vivo, the survival rate of mice improved	Zhou et al. (2015)
3.	Mesoporous silica NPs	Ga-Au@mSiO$_2$-Gallium -gold	LNCap and DU145	Significant antitumor effect in vitro cell line study	Liu et al. (2019)
4.	Quantum dots (QD)	Doxorubicin	Enhanced permeability and retention effect	Capable of binding toward prostate cancer cells in all in vivo and in vitro studies	Barani et al. (2020)
5.	HA (hyaluronic acid)	*CDDP, cis*-dichloro diammino platinum (II)	DU145(prostate carcinoma) and PC3 cellslines (adenocarcinoma)	Sphere-forming capacity decreases in vitro, while colony-forming capacity decreases.	Malek et al. (2014)
6.	Graphene oxide	Doxorubicin, camptothecin and paclitaxel	PC3 cell line	In vitro: sphere-forming capacity decreases	Fiorillo et al. (2015)

14.8.1 Liposomes

Liposomes are widely acceptable lipid carriers for novel drug delivery systems in various diseases because of tissue targeting ability by following active and passive targeting methods. Thangapazhem et al. synthesized novel NPs to target prostate cancer for effective delivery of curcumin in the core of liposomes fabricated with PSMA-specific antibodies, and the result showed a significant reduction of cell proliferation without any cell viability (Bode et al., 2009; Narayanan et al., 2009). Narayanan et al. also utilized a combination of resveratrol and curcumin-loaded liposomal formulation against prostate cancer management in male B6C3F1 and PTEN mice. In-vitro assays utilized PEN-CAP8 cancer cells were conducted to check the synergistic action of curcumin with resveratrol on activated p-Akt cyclin D1, cell progression, cell cycle, apoptosis, and androgen receptor proteins responsible for cancer cell progression, and curcumin and resveratrol-loaded liposomal formulation showed a significant improvement in inhibiting prostatic adenocarcinoma. The results of the following study considered the acceptance of photochemical against prostate cancer imaging as well as management purposes by following active and passive mechanisms (Kroon et al., 2014; Park et al., 2014; Kroon et al., 2014). In maximum preclinical prostate cancer research, passive liposomal targeting of antineoplastic therapeutics (through EPR) results in improved anticancer effectivity and reduced adverse effects than nontargeted bioactives, thus the total efficient dose of anticancer therapeutics is significantly reduced. Active (ligand-mediated) liposomal targeting of tumor cells or tumor-involved stromal cells shows a useful response, but few preclinical studies were revealed. Till now, clinical research for prostate cancer was conducted with liposomal doxorubicin only, which resulted in greater retention, PEGylated, liposomal doxorubicin basically conquers traditional short-retaining liposomal doxorubicin, stressing the significance of passive tumor targeting for this bioactive in prostate cancer (Wang et al., 2010). PEGylated liposome-based delivery systems show various advantages like biocompatibility, improved in vivo stability, loading efficiency, increased circulation lifetime (surface functionalized vesicle bypassing phagosomal clearance), and low toxicity (Fig. 14.3). Indeed, serum proteins react with liposomes, causing destabilization of the membrane and leading to rapid clearance.

14.8.2 Nanoemulsion

A novel approach has been designed to coentrap paclitaxel and Herceptin to treat prostate cancer progression (Tsai and Chen, 2016). The HER2 receptors are mainly exposed on the surface of some prostate cells, thus Herceptin is being used as a targeting tool for prostate cancer cells. The research was conducted where Herceptin molecules were fabricated to the surface, which was successfully able to target the HER2 overexpressing prostate cells (Panda et al., 2019). A formulation containing trastuzumab and paclitaxel palmitate-loaded nanoemulsion was evaluated on prostate cells of transgenic mice (Guan et al., 2017) and the result showed no allergic reaction during the study and found more effective outcomes than other

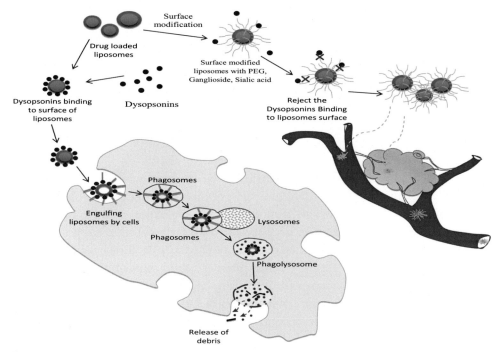

Figure 14.3 Stealthening of nanocarriers by PEGylation.

reported approaches for inhibiting prostate cancer cell progression. The remarkable property-performance relationships of oleosomes have generated a lot of interest to incorporate them into oil-in-water emulsions and take advantage of their sophisticated membrane. It offers emoliency, self-emulsification, an antioxidant, and film-forming properties, which lead to controlled and sustained releases of encapsulated bioactives. Taken together, the fabricated lipophilic drug-loaded magnetic oleosome can be a powerful tool for oil-based drug delivery agents for cancer therapy.

14.8.3 Niosomes

Niosomes are a lipid–based bilayer system that is used for numerous drug delivery purposes. Akbarzadeh et al. prepared a doxycycline-encapsulated niosomal delivery system for site-specific delivery in prostate cancer cells, and the in-vitro, in-vivo results were found to be increased chemotherapeutic response against prostate cancer cells (Akbarzadeh et al., 2020). The enhanced anticancer action involved the genes in the cell cycle of PC3 cells after introducing liposomal formulation (Thakor and Gambhir, 2013). The antitumor efficacy of niosomes on PC3 (prostate cancer cell lines) was evaluated by using MTT assay, gene expression, and flow cytometry. Therefore, various reported cases revealed that this nanocarrier system can be a promising drug transporting tool in prostate cancer cells.

14.8.4 Polymeric nanoparticles

They are a group of nanosized particles, although specifically, they are referred to as nanospheres and nanocapsules (Prabhu et al., 2015). Nanospheres, spheric and solid molecules, are attached or adsorbed to their surface. Various polymers are used to modify the surface of the particles for passive and ligand-targeted transportation of active compounds (Sanna and Sechi, 2012). These polymeric drug-loaded NPs are widely used in the treatment of PC management as they increase the pharmacokinetics and bioavailability features of selected anticancer drugs (Makadia and Siegel, 2011). The natural polymers used are chitosan (CHT), poly(D, L-lactic-co-glycolic acid) (PLGA), poly(D, L-lactic acid), and poly(caprolactone), which can be modified with PEG units shaping pegylated copolymers, are the widely accepted polymers for drug delivery (Riley et al., 2001; Mondal et al., 2020). A study demonstrated the application of polymeric NPs for targeting a DT-A (diphtheria toxin gene) acquired from prostate-specific promoters to cells. The injection of DT-A gene identification resulted in a significant reduction of the size of prostate tumors and glands, whereas direct injection showed zero or less effect. The effectivity of these polymeric NPs was evaluated with in-vitro and in-vivo studies for cellular uptake and site-specific transportation of Dtx by PCa cells. More advanced nanotechnological systems are needed to target the PCa and many cancer conditions that combine both therapeutic and diagnostic agents (Dhar et al., 2008). Dhar et al. designed an advanced method to transport cisplatin to the targeted prostate cancer cell by developing Pt (IV) loaded with prostate-specific membrane antigen (PSMA) of PLGA poly(ethylene glycol) (PEG)-poly(d,l-lactic-co-glycolic acid) modified controlled polymers. By utilizing PLGA-b-PEG NPs with PSMA targeting aptamers (apt) on the surface as a mediator for the platinum agent, a remarkably lethal dose of cisplatin was targeted specifically to prostate cancer cells (Nanjwade et al., 2009).

14.8.5 Dendrimers

They are one kind of polymeric particle (Wu et al., 2015) having several distinct characteristics that make them considerable in various targeted drug delivery systems (Ashique et al., 2021). The higher generations are more globular and dense than the lower generations. Lee and Kantoff (2019) developed a camptothecin-modified dendrimersome (redox-responsive) to transport gene and active chemotherapeutics to prostate cancer cells and the result found better accumulation by prostate cancer cells than unmodified dendrimer. Lim et al. (2019) developed triazine-loaded dendrimers fabricated with 4, 16, and 64 PSMA-targeted ligands for better prostate cancer cell uptake. Lesniak et al. (2019) prepared a PAMAM dendrimeric nanocarrier system and concluded that this delivery system can be considered a fit for imaging and therapeutic agents. Chlorambucil combined Ugi dendrimers with a PAMAM-NH core system was designed by Seixas et al. (2019) and revealed that the system improved targeting efficiency toward the prostate cancer cell. Another study was conducted by Sanchez-Milla et al. (2019) who positively showed better antitumor effectivity of dendrimer-based systems (dendriplexes) against proliferative prostate cancer.

14.8.6 Mesoporous silica nanoparticles

Currently, mesoporous silica nanoparticles (MSNs) are widely considered in research fields due to their composition of cationic quaternary ammonium surfactants, uniform structures, greater surface volume ratio, modulated pore size, and ability to immobilize enzymes. Surface decorated Ga-Au loaded mesoporous silica is a widely accepted NP to manage and diagnose prostate cancer (Chaudhary et al., 2019). "Chuanlam Gu and coworkers" utilized Ga-Au-encapsulated MSNs to apply photothermal therapy against prostate cancer cell lines. In-vitro measuring data revealed that these NPs effectively block the development of PC cells (Gu et al., 2020) and also destroyed the cancer cells. Other findings found that surface-modified Ga-Au-loaded MSNs could effectively block the proliferation of PC cells and resulted in an important antitumor impact in in-vitro cell line study (Liu et al., 2019). "Huan wang and coworkers" utilized MSNs for the management of tumors. PSA is the most advanced approach for prostate malignancy, and many researchers designed a label-free electrochemical immunosensor for prostate-definite antigens dependent on silver hybridized mesoporous silica NPs to target prostate tumors (Wang et al., 2013).

14.8.7 Gold nanoparticles

They are broadly utilized in several drug delivery systems, including neurodegenerative diseases, cancer therapy, because of numerous advantages like low toxicity, good optical features for detection and imaging purposes, the ability to reduce oxidative stress, inflammation, a greater surface-to-volume ratio, and excellent biocompatibility (Ashique et al., 2022). Additional properties like increased radiative features include absorption, scattering, and a plasmonic field for surface-improved Raman of adjacent molecules considering Au NPs widely acceptable for molecular cancer diagnostics. A study was conducted where surface modification of gold NPs was done with an RNA aptamer, which allowed binding to PSMA and provided a targeted molecular computed tomography (CT) imaging approach. The resulting PSMA aptamer-conjugated Au-NPs resulted in fourfold greater CT intensity for specific prostate cancer cells than nontargeted prostate epithelial cells (Kim et al., 2010). AuNPs also provide significant flexibility in the medical field such as diagnostic imaging, drug delivery, radiation, and phototherapy (Miao et al., 2018). Advanced development in nanotechnology has accepted the wide application of Au NPs as nanobiosensors (Sharifi et al., 2020). Au NPs fabricated with specific hydrophilic polymers showed greater in-vivo retention time and better aggregation to the targeted site by the enhanced permeability and retention effect (EPR) (Chen et al., 2016). Lue et al. combined PSMA-1 (PCa targeting antigen) to Au NPs for X-ray radiotherapy enhancement and found that the target-specific ligand increased Au absorption by PSMA-expressing PC3 pip cells compared to PC3flu cells which are insufficient to PSMA receptors.

14.8.8 Iron oxide-based nanoparticles

The core of these NPs is composed of iron oxide, and the stability can be increased by using a hydrophilic surface coat of dextran or other biocompatible polymers (Daniel and Astruc, 2004). These metallic NPs show size-dependent superparamagnetism, which can be applied under any magnetic-based treatment strategy, but the major challenge is that without a magnetic field it will not show the effect. Superparamagnetic iron oxide nanoparticles (SPIONs) were efficiently used as T2-weighted Mr contrast components to monitor cancer cells (Bulte and Kraitchman, 2004). These metallic NPs provide more beneficial effects over gadolinium-based contrast compounds, such as slower renal clearance and greater imaging sensitivity and specificity (Talelli et al., 2009). Ultra-small SPIONs are used in MRI for effective diagnosis of primary prostate cancer stage (Li et al., 2008) where these ultra-small superparamagnetic NPs can describe a better reduction in the signal-to-noise ratio of the prostate gland.

14.8.9 Carbon-based nanoparticles

They are cylindrical, hollow compounds with a hexagonal structure of linked carbons, single or multiple walls, and a nanometer size (Ahmed et al., 2018) They are considered advanced nanovectors for serum samples and human tissue for electrochemical identification of PSA biomarkers (Quintero-Jaime et al., 2019) and also as fluorescent bioimaging tools (Bhunia et al., 2013; Kumar et al., 2013). Carbon nanotubes (CNTs) for influencing hyperthermia have been evaluated in prostate malignancy xenografts in bare mice, with a tumor reaction being described. The specific prostate cancer antigen 3 (PCA3) was revealed more specifically as a prominent biomarker for prostate cancer. Soares et al. revealed the first limitation and electrochemically-based nanosensors, which can identify PCA3 as low as 0.128 nmol/L. The nanosensors are made up of PCA3-complementary single-stranded DNA probe, immobilized on CHT, and muti-walled CNTs (MWCNT) layer-by-layer film (Soares et al., 2019). Apt-conjugated MWCNTs were set up by Gu et al. (2018), and both in-vitro and in-vivo ultrasound imaging showed that the novel nano-ultrasound component provided improvement, accuracy, and can prove to be a targeted ultrasound tool, basically for prostate tumors. Another research group suggested a fluorescent CNT sensor for the recognition of metastatic prostate tumor cells (Williams et al., 2018). Xia et al., in 2018, demonstrated modified MWCNTs that showed that H3R6 polypeptide (MHR-CpG) was significant multifunctional nanotechnology for prostate malignancy immunotherapy designed carbon NPs that sensitize prostate cancer cells while combined with DTX and mitomycin C.

14.8.10 Quantum dots

Quantum dots (QDs) are used for targeting drugs in prostate cancer cells due to their unique optical properties, nanometric crystalline structure, and quantum controlling utility. An in-vivo study revealed that QD can be entered into the tumor cells actively and passively. The active targeting can be achieved by conjugating antibodies with QDs and can be employed to target PSMA. The retention time and binding of antibody PSMA to the target cells depend on the targeting efficiency for PCa (Wang et al., 2020; Garcia-Cortes et al., 2016). Ehzari et al. (2020) designed an enzyme-free immunosensitive nickel-cadmium QD for detecting PSA biomarkers, and surface-engineered QDs are being considered for fast diagnosing the PC and fast delivery of drugs (Gao et al., 2005). Cai and Chen (2007) labeled prostate tumor cells with antibodies conjugated QDs for PSMA. In another study, Jigyasu et al. (2020) prepared CdTe that showed the antiproliferative response against prostate cancer. A binary-color magnetic-QD-nanobead system was prepared to diagnose prostate cancer (Rong et al., 2019). A paper-based fluorometric immune responsive QDs were developed, which were capable to detect carcinoembryonic antigens and PSAs continuously (Chen et al., 2019).

14.8.11 Graphene-based system

Graphene is a crucial component in the biosensors research area having extraordinary electrochemical, electrical, magnetic, and optical characteristics (Justino et al., 2017). Given its many benefits, including functionalization, increased flexibility, and optical transmittance, it has been thought to be widely utilized in nanosensors (Palys, 2019; Li et al., 2019a). Several findings have reported the probability for sensitive identification of PCa biomarkers (Wang et al., 2019), which can result in early diagnosis and identification of PCa diagnosis. Pothipor et al. (2019) prepared graphene-modified porous-gold-silver NPs electrode for signal amplification of PSA. It was found the system sensed efficiently by 120 times in comparison to gold NPs (Jeong et al., 2019; Pothipor et al., 2019; Littrup et al., 2005; Wallace et al., 2003).

14.8.12 Albumin-complex system

Human serum albumin (HSA) has been thought of as a major drug transporter due to having many benefits like nontoxic, endogenous, and nonimmunogenic characteristics (Hawkins et al., 2008). Albumin is capable to carry hydrophobic molecules that approve the delivery of these therapeutic molecules in the body and their release at the cell surface (Elzoghby et al., 2012). A sol of Nab-paclitaxel mixed with human albumin was thought of for the loading of conventional concentration of drug than a regular formulation and resulted in lesser adverse effects, short infusion time, and no pretreatment (Cucinotto et al., 2013). The utilization of HSA in prostate tumors was rumored to be experimental; though, a similar strategy may be used to boost the transportation of inhibitors to prostatic adenocarcinoma cells (Shepard et al., 2009). HSA has been considered a significant drug transporter because of several advantages like it is nontoxic and nonimmunogenic (Hawkins et al., 2008). Albumin can carry both hydrophilic and hydrophobic therapeutic molecules that approve its delivery to the specific organ or tissue of the body (Elzoghby et al., 2012). A colloidal suspension of paclitaxel with HSA was utilized for the higher drug loading and resulted in lesser adverse effects (Cucinotto et al., 2013). The HSA was utilized to improve the transportation of some enzyme inhibitors to prostate cancer cells (Shepard et al., 2009).

14.8.13 Aptamer-based nanodelivery in prostate cancer therapy

Aptamers are single-strand oligonucleotides that are able to bind with definite molecules in the body and offer substitutes to antibodies. It is easy to develop, low price (Lakhin et al., 2013), and have distinctive features. Ranges of an aptamer-based nanocarrier are being utilized to deliver chemotherapeutically active substances for site-specific delivery. It can control the medicine to accumulate in the tumor by acting as a molecular probe to recognize and fuse with conformist receptors. Like antigen-antibody interaction, an aptamer can alter its three-dimensional moiety automatically and bind with the receptor (Zhu et al., 2014). The PSMA aptamer/polo-like kinase 1 (Plk1)-siRNA (A10-Plk1) chimera was designed to prevent prostate tumor progression (McNamara et al., 2006). The advanced PSMA-Plk1 chimeras were designed to extend the site-specificity and gene-silencing in case of cancer treatment. Considerably, the second-generation chimeras were utilized to inhibit the progression of prostate cancer cells at a minimum amount when compared with the first-generation aptamers chimeras (Dassie et al., 2009).

14.8.14 Extracellular vesicles-based nanodelivery in prostate cancer therapy

These nanosized vesicles are discharged essentially from all kinds of cells in their extracellular fluids like plasma, urine, saliva, cerebrospinal fluid. They conciliate intercellular interference by transporting subatomic details between cells (Thakur et al., 2020). Extracellular vesicles (EVs) are classified on the basis of their size, surface markers, and their biogenic pathways like exosomes (40−100 nm), microvesicles (MVs) (50−1000 nm), and apoptotic bodies (800−5000 nm) (Crescitelli et al., 2013). Currently, the researchers discovered that the acceptableness of two distinct forms of EVs (exosomes and MVs), as a delivery system of paclitaxel to prostatic adenocarcinoma cells significantly. It had been found that the assembly of paclitaxel to autologous prostate cancer cells by utilizing EVs showed improved cytotoxic impact while the without drug-loaded EVs multiplied the neoplastic cell viability, the general impact of enhanced toxicity persists in each EVs. Both types of delivered paclitaxel to the recipient cells through endocytosis, up the reaching of medicine to the targeted tissue. The removal of surface proteins showed no impact on exosomes, whereas the transportation of the medicine by utilizing MVs was blocked midway, which resulted that cancer cell-specific EVs may be used as viable delivery systems of paclitaxel to the targeted cells together with therapeutic efficaciousness, exosomes also are prostatic adenocarcinoma glandular cancer designation (like identification of extended PSA expression on PC-derived exosomes, both in-vitro and clinical trials) (Logozzi et al., 2017). Moreover, various exosomal microRNAs have shown enhanced therapeutic efficaciousness in prostate cancer actinotherapy (Malla et al., 2017). For instance, Che et al. studied that exosomes derived from miR-143 overexpressing mesenchymal stem cells (MSCs) can block the cell metastasis and invasion of PCs via TFF3 downregulation (Che et al., 2019). In another study, microRNA-205-loaded exosomes derived from human bone marrow, MSCs showed a reduction of neoplastic cell proliferation of PCs by RHPN2 inhibition (Jiang et al., 2019). The exosomal vaccine was additionally developed to treat PCs by the alteration of the interferon-γ (Shi et al., 2020). Tables 14.6 and 14.7 summarized various miscellaneous nanocarriers and surface functionalized NPs to control PC, respectively.

14.8.15 Computational modeling and artificial intelligence in nanomedicine for prostate cancer

Computational modeling techniques with information technology are widely utilized in applied science for the treatment of different disease conditions like cancer. This technology is an efficient strategy for recognizing biomarkers for targeted nanodrug delivery to get an optimum therapeutic response without toxicity (Gaurav et al., 2020). Currently, RNA aptamers are a widely accepted element that may be used for accuracy and effectiveness in cancer therapy. Because of insufficient knowledge regarding their secondary and tertiary structure, the clinical application has become restricted (Xu et al., 2016). Current analysis has explored that an entire homeobox-B13 (HOXB13) macromolecule was designed by utilizing an advanced model for characterization of the functional response of single-nucleotide-polymorphisms (SNPs) in the treatment of diseases. HOXB13 suppressed the progression of prostate cancer cells through the negative response of T-cell factor-4. This study would support the forthcoming genome-wide association studies and clinical studies connected to the role of SNPs in hereditary prostate cancer and additionally target tools for prostate cancer biomarkers (Chandrasekaran et al., 2017). In addition, the utilization of artificial intelligence (AI) is wide growing in nanomedicine for the treatment of different together of prostate cancer (Mishra et al., 2022). Another study discovered the alteration of BET bromodomain, ZEN-3694, and Enzalutamide integrated dosing during a patient affected by metastatic prostate cancer by introducing AI Platform (CURATE.AI), resulting in improved treatment potential and tolerance (Pantuck et al., 2018).

Table 14.6 Various miscellaneous nanocarriers and specific cancer biomarkers.

S. No.	NPs	Biomarker	Detection medium	Attribute	References
1.	Magnetic NPs	Prostate-specific antigen (PSA)	Human plasma	Appropriate linear range between 0.001 and 1 μg/L (via SWV method) with a 0.001 μg/L LLOQ	Farshchi et al. (2020)
2.	Gold NPs	Prostate-specific antigen (PSA)	Serums of healthy and prostate patients	Linear range 0∼0.8 ng/mL for PSA measurement with a detection maximum of 0.02 ng/mL	Xia et al. (2018)
3.	Lab-on-a-chip systems	Prostate specific membrane antigen (PSMA), and platelet factor-4 (PF-4)	Serum	Detection limits for the three proteins in undiluted calf serum was 300−500 fg/mL	Kadimisetty et al. (2016)
4.	Micro-cantilever	Prostate-specific antigen (PSA)	Human serum albumin (HSA), human plasminogen (HP)	With high-throughput label-free analyses, provide a strong platform for DNA-protein, protein-protein binding, and DNA hybridization interactions	Wu et al. (2001)

Table 14.7 Surface functionalized nanodelivery systems developed for the prostate cancer therapy.

S. No.	Method of delivery	Feature	References
1.	Elastin-like polypeptide (ELP)–fused gastrin-releasing peptide–based genetically modified self-assembling nanoparticle (GRP)	When GRP receptor positive PC cells were added, intracellular calcium concentrations increased, indicating specific receptor activation	Zhang et al. (2016)
2.	Bombesin (BN)–polyethylene glycol-1,2-Distearoyl-sn-glycero-3-phosphoethanolamine (BN-PEG-DSPE)	Cabazitaxel (CAB)-loaded, BN-PEG-DSPE-containing LPNs (BN–CAB-LPNs) were created, and in vitro and in vivo, they demonstrated increased antitumor ability in PC	Chen et al. (2016)
3.	Silver-decorated gold nanorods (AuNR\Ag)	Antibodies against the epithelial cell adhesion molecule (anti-EpCAM) and doxorubicin are covalently attached to the thiolated polyethylene glycol coated AuNR\Ag	Nima et al. (2017)
4.	Polyethylene glycol hyper-branched polymers	It's made by polymerizing RAFT and assigning glutamate urea targeting ligands for prostate-specific membrane antigen (PSMA) in the periphery	Pearce et al. (2017)
5.	G protein-coupled receptors (GPCRs) based nano delivery system	It's made by combining elastin-like polypeptide (ELP)–dependent self-assembling NP with gastrin–releasing peptide via genetic engineering (GRP)	Zhang et al. (2016)
6.	Photodynamic therapy (PDT) based multifunctional nano-platform	For dualmodal photothermal and photodynamic treatment, a delivery device that can create efficient heat and ROS simultaneously with light activation at the tumor area is needed	Lin et al. (2016)
7.	Cabazitaxel (CAB) loaded, BN-PEGDSPE contained LPNs (BN-CAB-LPNs)	Bombesin (BN) used lipid polymer hybrid nanoparticles (LPNs) to attack GRP-overexpressed prostate cancer	Chen et al. (2016)
8.	Engineered sub-50 nm diameter (oiuytwq; UTRWQ copolymer NPs)	In comparison to the administration of individual medications, NPs containing both Wtmn and Dtxl discharge the pharmaceuticals in an optimal serial manner to maximize therapeutic effectiveness	Au et al. (2015)

(Continued)

Table 14.7 (Continued)

S. No.	Method of delivery	Feature	References
9.	RNAi using dendrimer nano vector based targeted delivery	It entails a siRNA/dendrimer combination that is coupled with a peptide for dual targeting as well as cell penetration properties, resulting in enhanced anticancer and gene silencing action	Liu et al. (2014)
10.	Glutathione-stabilized (Au@GSH) gold NPs	The neuropilin-1 (Nrp-1) receptor is used to deliver a platinum (IV) medication	Kumar et al. (2014)
11.	Folic acid conjugated-poly(lactide-coglycolide) (PLGA) polymer	This is directed at folate-enhanced cancer cells that have selective absorption as well as folic acid cytotoxicity	El-Gogary et al. (2014)
12.	Dual-targeted delivery platform for paclitaxel (PTX)	This entails combining PTX with nanocarriers with high magnetization, which might be used for dual active targeting	Yang et al. (2012)
13.	Expression of neuropilin-1 epitope by means of gold nano shells	When NPs are exposed to a pulsed near-infrared laser, siRNA is released, resulting in efficient endosomal secretion inside the cell	Huang et al. (2014)
14.	Cell-uptake assortment approach to segregate PCa-specific internalizing 20-O-methyl RNA aptamers (Apts) for NP integration	Internalizing aptamers generated through cell-uptake selection are useful for cancer therapy.	Xiao et al. (2012)
15.	Targeted chemo Immuno drug delivery system	A dendrimer and a single-strand hybrid of DNA-A9 PSMA and RNA aptamer are required	Lee et al. (2011)
16.	Anti-PSMA-conjugated nanocarrier	Poly (lactic-co-glycolic acid) is used to load paclitaxel -PTX on the surface of nanocarriers (PLGA)	Cho et al. (2010)
17.	Quantum dot (QD)-aptamer (Apt)-doxorubicin (Dox) conjugate [QD-Apt (Dox)]	The A10 RNA aptamer, which recognizes the region extracellular to the PSMA, is functionalized on the surface of fluorescent QD	Bagalkot et al. (2007)
18.	PSMA aptamer-conjugated GNP-prostate-specific membrane antigen	The surface of gold nanoparticles (GNPs) is functionalized with a PSMA RNA aptamer, which binds to PSMA	Kim et al. (2010)
19.	Targeted chemo immuno drug delivery system	A dendrimer and a single-strand hybrid of DNA-A9 PSMA and RNA aptamer are required for this	Lee et al. (2011)
20.	RGDfK surface-modified gold nanorods (GNRs)	Endothelial cells use selective binding and uptake	Gormley et al. (2011)

14.8.16 Natural products in nanoparticles for prostate cancer treatment

Various findings revealed that natural therapeutic molecules have been used for effective management of prostatic carcinoma in a preclinical animal model and also clinically. The previous reports represented that epigallocatechin-3-gallate-loaded nanocarriers like polylactic acid-poly-ethylene-glycol nanocarrier offer proapoptotic action and reduction of growth (Siddiqui et al., 2009). In another study, bovine serum albumin NPs showed higher cellular uptake and increased cytotoxicity (Zu et al., 2009). The saccharide matrix of gum and maltodextrin NPs showed a long circulation time and higher cytotoxicity in the biological system (Rocha et al., 2011). Similarly, EGCG decorated radiolabelled Au NPs improved biological stability and cell targeting affinity (Nune et al., 2009), and AU-198 gold NPs showed high retention of phytoconstituents in the tumor (Shukla et al., 2012). Curcumin-loaded PGLA nanospheres (Mukerjee and Vishwanatha, 2009), liposomes made up of PSMA antibody (Hawkins et al., 2008), hydroxypropyl methylcellulose-coated NPs (Yallapu et al., 2012), and fibrinogen containing NPs (Rejinold et al., 2011) shown significant stability and therapeutic effect in-vitro and in-vivo. Resveratrol taxanes-loaded liposome (Narayanan et al., 2009), transferrin conjugated polymeric RNA A10-aptamer (Sahoo et al., 2004; Gu et al., 2008), polymeric specific nanomedicines (Chandran et al., 2008), and poly(lactide-co-caprolactone) and poly (lactide-coglycolide-co-caprolactone) NPs for targeted prostate cancer. The most commonly used cytotoxic drug like taxol (Sanna et al., 2011), DTX has been used with or without nanocarriers for the management of prostate cancer (Weaver, 2014).

14.8.17 Clinical trials of nanoparticle delivery system for prostate cancer therapy

The promising outcomes of NP-based drug delivery have been found in animal studies to manage PCs. Thus, a study was carried out on 45 subjects with intravenous administration of drug-loaded auro-shell particles followed by ultrasound-guided laser irradiation. (https://clinicaltrials.gov/ct2/show/NCT02680535 (Accessed 5 Sept 2020)). A clinical trial was carried out by Nanology, LLC, using NanoPac focal therapy on prostate cancer patients. It absolutely was an n-label, dose rising, phases IIa trial of NanoPac injected intratumorally at the dose of 6, 10, or 15 mg/mL in subjects with PCs regular for prostatectomy (Table 14.8).

14.9 Conclusion

Research is going on the structure-activity relationship of NPs for the advancement in drug transport systems. The application of targeted NPs leads designing of new classes of remedies. A multifunctional delivery system with different drug substance halves could be an efficacious tool for PC therapy (Kang et al., 2015). Advancements in nanotechnology

Table 14.8 Clinical Trials of nanomedicines for prostate cancer.

Study title	Nanomedicine/device for prostate cancer	Status
Magnetic nanoparticle-based therapy for prostate cancer (phase 0)	Magnetic nanoparticle injection	Completed
Nanoparticle loaded with camptothecin and enzalutamide delivery in progressive metastatic prostate cancer	Enzalutamide	Completed
A phase 2 study with docetaxel-loaded nanoparticles in case of metastatic advanced prostate cancer	Docetaxel	Completed
Nanoparticle-based focal therapy for ablation of prostate cancer cells	AuroShell	Completed
Focal ablation with NanoTherm therapy in case of prostate cancer	NanoTherm	Recruiting
Nanoparticles-based diagnosis for surgical operation of prostate cancer	(64Cu)-labeled PSMA	Recruiting
Paclitaxel-loaded albumin nanoparticle with advanced tumors	Paclitaxel	Withdrawn
NanoPac focal therapy for prostate cancer	Paclitaxel	Terminated
NBTXR3 nanoparticles in prostate adenocarcinoma	NBTXR3 activated by IMRT	Terminated

https://www.clinicaltrials.gov/ct2/results?cond = Prostate + Cancer&term = Nanoparticles (Accessed 5 September 2020).

science and nanotechnology have offered nanomedicine-based drug delivery systems in medical science, arising as promising strategies for cancer treatment. To advance the development of a library of nanomaterials, accurate monitoring of their physicochemical characteristics and a simple approach of surface engineering to enhance the target capability are needed for the administration of cancer nanotherapeutics. Nano-biointerfacial interactions and targeting of NPs to the cancer cells are critical for cancer therapy. The strategy of nanocarrier-dependent drug delivery systems has advanced in the medicinal and biomedical fields. The design and development of modified medicine-loaded NPs are extensively used in different cancer-targeted drug deliveries. Nanotechnology-based effective transport nanovehicles have influenced primary success in prostate cancer diagnosis, imaging, and regulation. Though having different advancements, the debate about the dragonizing of PC and localized therapeutic modalities still persists a limitation. Thus, different explored strategies lead to positive results in in-vitro and in-vivo experimental models of PC but were ineffective in clinical phase studies. Therefore, further genetic investigation-dependent identification approaches are needed to estimate individualities at high PC hazards. For cancer treatment, including PC regulation, overall nanodrug delivery has been extensively considered for various advantages. Nanotechnology-dependent studies have given an important pathway to the biomedical field, substantially point-of-care devices and personalized cancer therapies.

References

Adjei, I.M., Temples, M.N., Brown, S.B., Sharma, B., 2018. Targeted nanomedicine to treat bone metastasis. Pharmaceutics 10, 205.

Ahmed, W., Elhissi, A., Dhanak, V., Subramani, K., 2018. Carbon nanotubes: applications in cancer therapy and drug delivery research. Emerging Nanotechnologies in Dentistry. Elsevier, Amsterdam, The Netherlands, pp. 371–389.

Akbarzadeh, I., Yaraki, M.T., Bourbour, M., Noorbazargan, H., Lajevardi, A., Shilsar, S.M., et al., 2020. Optimized doxycycline-loaded niosomal formulation for treatment of infection-associated prostate cancer: an in-vitro investigation. J. Drug. Deliv. Sci. Technol. 57, 101715.

Alizadeh, M., Alizadeh, S., 2014. Survey of clinical and pathological characteristics and outcomes of patients with prostate cancer. Glob. J. Health Sci. 6 (7), 49.

Ashique, S., Sandhu, N.K., Chawla, V., Chawla, P.A., 2021. Targeted drug delivery: trends and perspectives. Curr. Drug. Deliv 18 (10), 1435–1455.

Ashique, S., Upadhyay, A., Kumar, N., Chauhan, S., Mishra, N., 2022. Metabolic syndromes responsible for cervical cancer and advancement of nanocarriers for efficient targeted drug delivery-A review. Adv. Cancer Biology-Metastasis 14, 100041.

Au, K.M., Min, Y., Tian, X., Zhang, L., Perello, V., Caster, J.M., et al., 2015. Improving cancer chemoradiotherapy treatment by dual controlled release of wortmannin and docetaxel in polymeric nanoparticles. ACS Nano. 9 (9), 8976–8996.

Azandeh, S.S., et al., 2017. Anticancer activity of curcumin-loaded PLGA nanoparticles on PC3 prostate cancer cells. Iran. J. Pharm. Res. 16, 868–879.

Bagalkot, V., Zhang, L., Levy-Nissenbaum, E., Jon, S., Kantoff, P.W., Langer, R., et al., 2007. Quantum dot − aptamer conjugates for synchronous cancer imaging, therapy, and sensing of drug delivery based on bi-fluorescence resonance energy transfer. Nano Lett. 7 (10), 3065–3070.

Barani, M., Sabir, F., Rahdar, A., Arshad, R., Kyzas, G.Z., 2020. Nanotreatment and nanodiagnosis of prostate cancer: recent updates. Nanomaterials. 10 (9), 1696.

Bessone, F., Argenziano, M., Grillo, G., Ferrara, B., Pizzimenti, S., Barrera, G., et al., 2019. Low-dose curcuminoid-loaded in dextran nanobubbles can prevent metastatic spreading in prostate cancer cells. Nanotechnology 30 (21), 214004.

Bhunia, S.K., Saha, A., Maity, A.R., Ray, S.C., Jana, N.R., 2013. Carbon nanoparticle-based fluorescent bioimaging probes. Sci. Rep 3 (1), 1–7.

Bisson, I., Prowse, D.M., 2009. WNT signaling regulates self-renewal and differentiation of prostate cancer cells with stem cell characteristics. Cell Res. 19 (6), 683–697.

Blagoev, K.B., Iordanov, R., Zhou, M., Fojo, T., Bates, S.E., 2021. Drug-resistant cells with very large proliferative potential grow exponentially in metastatic prostate cancer. Oncotarget. 12 (1), 15.

Blankfield, R.P., 2012. Androgen deprivation therapy for prostate cancer and cardiovascular death. JAMA. 307 (12), 1252–1253.

Bode, C., Trojan, L., Weiss, C., Kraenzlin, B., Michaelis, U., Teifel, M., et al., 2009. Paclitaxel encapsulated in cationic liposomes: a new option for neovascular targeting for the treatment of prostate cancer. Oncol. Rep. 22 (2), 321–326.

Bulte, J.W., Kraitchman, D.L., 2004. Iron oxide MR contrast agents for molecular and cellular imaging. NMR Biomed. 17, 484–499.

Cai, W., Chen, X., 2007. Nanoplatforms for targeted molecular imaging in living subjects. Small 3 (11), 1840–1854.

Chandran, S.-S., Banerjee, S.R., Mease, R.C., Pomper, M.G., Denmeade, S.R., 2008. Characterization of a targeted nanoparticle functionalized with a urea-based inhibitor of prostate-specific membrane antigen (PSMA). Canc. Biol. Ther. 7, 974–982.

Chandrasekaran, G., Hwang, E.C., Kang, T.W., Kwon, D.D., Park, K., Lee, J.-J., et al., 2017. Computational Modeling of complete HOXB13 protein for predicting the functional effect of SNPs and the associated role in hereditary prostate cancer. Sci. Rep. 7, 43830.

Chang, H.H., Chen, B.Y., Wu, C.Y., Tsao, Z.J., Chen, Y.Y., Chang, C.P., et al., 2011. Hedgehog overexpression leads to the formation of prostate cancer stem cells with metastatic property irrespective of androgen receptor expression in the mouse model. J. Biomed. Sci. 18 (1), 6.

Chaudhary, Z., Subramaniam, S., Khan, G.M., Abeer, M.M., Qu, Z., Janjua, T., et al., 2019. Encapsulation and controlled release of resveratrol within functionalized mesoporous silica nanoparticles for prostate cancer therapy. Front. Bioeng. Biotechnol. 7, 225.

Che, Y., Shi, X., Shi, Y., Jiang, X., Ai, Q., Shi, Y., et al., 2019. Exosomes derived from miR143-overexpressing MSCs inhibit cell migration and invasion in human prostate cancer by downregulating TFF3. Mol. Ther. Nucleic Acids 18, 232–244.

Chen, Q., Cai, Z., Chen, Y., et al., 2015. Poly r(C) binding protein-1 is central to maintenance of cancer stem cells in prostate cancer cells. Cell. Physiol. Biochem. 35, 1052–1061.

Chen, W., Guo, M., Wang, S., 2016. Anti prostate cancer using PEGylated bombesin containing, cabazitaxel loading nano-sized drug delivery system. Drug. Dev. Ind. Pharm. 42 (12), 1968–1976.

Chen, Y., Xu, Z., Zhu, D., Tao, X., Gao, Y., Zhu, H., et al., 2016. Gold nanoparticles coated with polysarcosine brushes to enhance their colloidal stability and circulation time in vivo. J. Colloid Interface Sci. 1 (483), 201–210.

Chen, Y., Guo, X., Liu, W., Zhang, L., 2019. based fluorometric immunodevice with quantum-dot labeled antibodies for simultaneous detection of carcinoembryonic antigen and prostate specific antigen. Microchim. Acta 186 (2), 1–9.

Cho, H.S., Dong, Z., Pauletti, G.M., Zhang, J., Xu, H., Gu, H., et al., 2010. Fluorescent, superparamagnetic nanospheres for drug storage, targeting, and imaging: a multifunctional nanocarrier system for cancer diagnosis and treatment. ACS Nano 4 (9), 5398–5404.

Chrastina, A., Massey, K.A., Schnitzer, J.E., 2011. Overcoming in vivo barriers to targeted nanodelivery. Wiley Interdiscip. Rev. Nanomed. Nanobiotechnol. 3 (4), 421–437.

Crescitelli, R., Lässer, C., Szabo, T.G., Kittel, A., Eldh, M., Dianzani, I., et al., 2013. Distinct RNA profiles in subpopulations of extracellular vesicles: apoptotic bodies, microvesicles and exosomes. J. Extracell. Vesicles 2, 20677.

Cucinotto, I., Fiorillo, L., Gualtieri, S., Arbitrio, M., Ciliberto, D., Staropoli, N., et al., 2013. Nanoparticle albumin bound Paclitaxel in the treatment of human cancer: nanodelivery reaches prime-time. J. Drug. Delivery 2013.

Cui, J., Björnmalm, M., Ju, Y., Caruso, F., 2018. Nanoengineering of poly (ethylene glycol) particles for stealth and targeting. Langmuir 34 (37), 10817–10827.

Daniel, M.C., Astruc, D., 2004. Gold nanoparticles: assembly, supramolecular chemistry, quantum-size-related properties, and applications toward biology, catalysis, and nanotechnology. Chem. Rev. 104, 293–346.

Dassie, J.P., Liu, X., Thomas, G.S., Whitaker, R.M., Thiel, K.W., Stockdale, K.R., et al., 2009. Systemic administration of optimized aptamer-siRNA chimeras promotes regression of PSMA-expressing tumors. Nat. Biotechnol. 27, 839–846.

Davis, M.E., Zhuo, C., Dong, M.S., 2008. Nanoparticle therapeutics: an emerging treatment modality for cancer. Nature. 7, 771.

de Barros, A.B., Tsourkas, A., Saboury, B., Cardoso, V.N., Alavi, A., 2012. Emerging role of radiolabeled nanoparticles as an effective diagnostic technique. EJNMMI Res. 2 (1), 1–5.

De Jesus., M.B., Ferreira, C.V., de Paula, E., Hoekstra, D., Zuhorn, I.S., 2010. Design of solid lipid nanoparticles for gene delivery into prostate cancer. J. Control. Release 148 (1), e89–90.

Denmeade, S.R., Isaacs, J.T., Denmeade, S.R., Isaacs, J.T., Comprehensive, K., 2014. A history of prostate cancer treatment. Nat. Rev. Cancer 2, 389–396.

Dhar, S., Gu, F.X., Langer, R., Farokhzad, O.C., Lippard, S.J., 2008. Targeted delivery of cisplatin to prostate cancer cells by aptamer functionalized Pt (IV) prodrug-PLGA–PEG nanoparticles. Proc. Natl Acad. Sci. 105 (45), 17356–17361.

Ehzari, H., Amiri, M., Safari, M., 2020. Enzyme-free sandwich-type electrochemical immunosensor for highly sensitive prostate specific antigen based on conjugation of quantum dots and antibody on surface of modified glassy carbon electrode with core–shell magnetic metal-organic frameworks. Talanta. 1 (210), 120641.

El-Gogary, R.I., Rubio, N., Wang, J.T., Al-Jamal, W.T., Bourgognon, M., Kafa, H., et al., 2014. Polyethylene glycol conjugated polymeric nanocapsules for targeted delivery of quercetin to folate-expressing cancer cells in vitro and in vivo. ACS Nano. 8 (2), 1384–1401.

Elmhadi, C., Tanz, R., Khmamouche, M.R., Toreis, M., Mahfoud, T., Slimani, K.A., et al., 2016. Toxicities of docetaxel: original drug versus generics—a comparative study about 81 cases. Springerplus. 5 (1), 1–7.

Elzoghby, A.O., Samy, W.M., Elgindy, N.A., 2012. Albumin-based nanoparticles as potential controlled release drug delivery systems. J. Control. Release 157 (2), 168.

Espinoza, S.M., Patil, H.I., Martinez, E.S.M., Pimentel, R.C., Ige, P.P., 2019. Poly-ε-caprolactone (PCL), a promising polymer for pharmaceutical and biomedical applications: focus on nanomedicine in cancer. Int. J. Polym. Mater. 69, 85–126.

Espinoza, S.M., Patil, H.I., San Martin, M.E., Casañas, P.R., Ige, P.P., 2022. Poly-ε-caprolactone (PCL), a promising polymer for pharmaceutical and biomedical applications: focus on nanomedicine in cancer. Int. J. Polymeric Mater. Polymeric Biomater. 69 (2), 85–126.

Fan, L., Pepicelli, C.V., Dibble, C.C., Catbagan, W., Zarycki, J.L., Laciak, R., et al., 2004. Hedgehog signaling promotes prostate xenograft tumor growth. Endocrinology 145 (8), 3961–3970.

Farshchi, F., Hasanzadeh, M., Mokhtarzadeh, A., 2020. A novel electroconductive interface based on Fe3O4 magnetic nanoparticle and cysteamine functionalized AuNPs: preparation and application as signal amplification element to minoring of antigen-antibody immunocomplex and biosensing of prostate cancer. J. Mol. Recognit. 33 (4), e2825.

Fiorillo, M., Verre, A.F., Iliut, M., Peiris-Pagés, M., Ozsvari, B., Gandara, R., et al., 2015. Graphene oxide selectively targets cancer stem cells, across multiple tumor types: implications for non-toxic cancer treatment, via "differentiation-based nano-therapy.". Oncotarget 6 (6), 3553.

Friedman, A.D., Claypool, S.E., Liu, R., 2013. The smart targeting of nanoparticles. Curr. Pharm. Des. 19 (35), 6315–6329.

Galsky, M.D., Vogelzang, N.J., 2010. Docetaxel-based combination therapy for castration-resistant prostate cancer. Ann. Oncol. 21 (11), 2135–2144.

Ganguly, S.S., Li, X., Miranti, C.K., 2014. The host microenvironment influences prostate cancer invasion, systemic spread, bone colonization, and osteoblastic metastasis. Front. Oncol. 15 (4), 364.

Gao, X., Yang, L., Petros, J.A., Marshall, F.F., Simons, J.W., Nie, S., 2005. In vivo molecular and cellular imaging with quantum dots. Curr. Opin. Biotechnol. 16 (1), 63–72.

Garcia-Cortes, M., Encinar, J.R., Costa-Fernandez, J.M., Sanz-Medel, A., 2016. Highly sensitive nanoparticle-based immunoassays with elemental detection: application to prostate-specific antigen quantification. Biosens. Bioelectron. 15 (85), 128–134.

Gaurav, I., Singh, T., Thakur, A., Kumar, G., Rathee, P., Kumari, P., et al., 2020. Synthesis, in-vitro and in-silico evaluation of silver nanoparticles with root extract of Withania somnifera for antibacterial activity via binding of penicillin-binding protein-4. Curr. Pharm. Biotechnol. 21, 1674–1687.

Gevaert, T., Van Eycke, Y.R., Vanden, B.T., Van, P.H., Salmon, I., Rorive, S., et al., 2020. The potential of tumour microenvironment markers to stratify the risk of recurrence in prostate cancer patients. PLoS One 15 (12), e0244663.

Gillet, J.P., Gottesman, M.M., 2010. Mechanisms of multidrug resistance in cancer. Multi-drug Resistance in Cancer. Humana Press, pp. 47–76.

Gormley, A.J., Malugin, A., Ray, A., Robinson, R., Ghandehari, H., 2011. Biological evaluation of RGDfK-gold nanorod conjugates for prostate cancer treatment. J. Drug. Target. 9 (10), 915–924.

Gu, F., Zhang, L., Teply, B.A., Mann, N.A., Wang, A.F., Radovic, M., et al., 2008. Precise engineering of targeted nanoparticles by using self-assembled biointegrated block copolymers. Proc. Natl. Acad. Sci. U. S. A. 105, 2586–2591.

Gu, F., Hu, C., Xia, Q., Gong, C., Gao, S., Chen, Z., 2018. Aptamer-conjugated multi-walled carbon nanotubes as a new targeted ultrasound contrast agent for the diagnosis of prostate cancer. J. Nanopart. Res. 20 (11), 303.

Gu, C., Li, C., Zhang, J., Li, X., Wang, L., Ju, Y., et al., 2020. Ultra-effective near-infrared Photothermal therapy for the prostate cancer nursing care through novel intended and surface tailored photo-responsive Ga-Au@ MPS nanovesicles. J. Photochem. Photobiol. B: Biol. 202, 111685.

Guha, S.K., Chauhan, V., Banerjee, S., 2011. Designed self-assembly of nanoliposomes in the male reproductive tract for model drug delivery to the prostate. Open. Nanosci. J. 5 (1), 4.

Guan, Y.B., Zhou, S.Y., Zhang, Y.Q., Wang, J.L., Tian, Y.D., Jia, Y.Y., et al., 2017. Therapeutic effects of curcumin nanoemulsions on prostate cancer. J. Huazhong Univ. Sci. Technol. [Med. Sci.] 37 (3), 371–378.

Guo, J.U., Wu, S.H., Ren, W.G., Wang, X.L., Yang, A.Q., 2015. Anticancer activity of bicalutamide-loaded PLGA nanoparticles in prostate cancers. Exp. Ther. Med. 10 (6), 2305–2310.

Hawkins, M.J., Soon-Shiong, P., Desai, N., 2008. Protein nanoparticles as drug carriers in clinical medicine. Adv. Drug. Deliv. Rev. 60 (8), 876–885.

Huang, X., Pallaoro, A., Braun, G.B., Morales, D.P., Ogunyankin, M.O., Zasadzinski, J., et al., 2014. Modular plasmonic nanocarriers for efficient and targeted delivery of cancer-therapeutic siRNA. Nano Lett. 14 (4), 2046–2051.

Humphrey, P.A., 2017. Histopathology of prostate cancer. Cold Spring Harb. Perspect. Med. 7 (10), a030411.

Hurt, E.M., Kawasaki, B.T., Klarmann, G.J., Thomas, S.B., Farrar, W.L., 2008. CD44 + CD24 − prostate cells are early cancer progenitor/stem cells that provide a model for patients with poor prognosis. Br. J. Cancer 98 (4), 756–765.

Jeong, B., Kim, Y.J., Jeong, J.Y., Kim, Y.J., 2019. Label-free electrochemical quantification of microRNA-375 in prostate cancer cells. J. Electroanalytical Chem. 1 (846), 113127.

Jiang, S., Mo, C., Guo, S., Zhuang, J., Huang, B., Mao, X., 2019. Human bone marrow mesenchymal stem cells-derived microRNA-205-containing exosomes impede the progression of prostate cancer through suppression of RHPN2. J. Exp. Clin. Canc Res. 38, 495.

Jiao, J., Zou, Q., Zou, M.H., Guo, R.M., Zhu, S., Zhang, Y., 2016. Aptamer-modified PLGA nanoparticle delivery of triplex forming oligonucleotide for targeted prostate cancer therapy. Neoplasma. 63 (4), 569–575.

Jigyasu, A.K., Siddiqui, S., Jafri, A., Arshad, M., Lohani, M., Khan, I.A., 2020. Biological synthesis of CdTe quantum dots and their anti-proliferative assessment against prostate cancer cell line. J. Nanosci. Nanotechnol. 20 (6), 3398–3403.

Justino, C.I., Gomes, A.R., Freitas, A.C., Duarte, A.C., Rocha-Santos, T.A., 2017. Graphene based sensors and biosensors. TrAC. Trends Anal. Chem. 91, 53–66.

Kadimisetty, K., Mosa, I.M., Malla, S., Satterwhite-Warden, J.E., Kuhns, T.M., Faria, R.C., et al., 2016. 3D-printed supercapacitor-powered electrochemiluminescent protein immunoarray. Biosens. Bioelectron. 15 (77), 188–193.

Kang, L., Gao, Z., Huang, W., Jin, M., Wang, Q., 2015. Nanocarriermediated co-delivery of chemotherapeutic drugs and gene agents for cancer treatment. Acta Pharma. Sin. B (APSB) 5 (3), 169–175.

Karhadkar, S.S., Bova, G.S., Abdallah, N., Dhara, S., Gardner, D., Maitra, A., et al., 2004. Hedgehog signalling in prostate regeneration, neoplasia, and metastasis. Nature 431 (7009), 707–712.

Kasivisvanathan, V., Rannikko, A.S., Borghi, M., Panebianco, V., Mynderse, L.A., Vaarala, M.H., et al., 2018. MRI-targeted or standard biopsy for prostate-cancer diagnosis. N. Engl. J. Med. 378 (19), 1767–1777.

Kennel, S., Appavoo, A., Schulz, J., Barthélémy, P., 2017. Nanoparticles for radionuclide imaging and therapy: principles. Diagnostic and Therapeutic Nuclear Medicine for Neuroendocrine Tumors. Humana Press, Cham, pp. 447–471.

Kim, D., Jeong, Y.-Y., Jon, S., 2010. A drug-loaded aptamer − gold nanoparticle bioconjugate for combined CT imaging and therapy of prostate cancer. ACS Nano 4 (7), 3689–3696.

Kim, H.L., Yang, X.J., 2002. Prevalence of high-grade prostatic intraepithelial neoplasia and its relationship to serum prostate-specific antigen. Int. Braz. J. Urol. 28 (5), 413–416.

Koo, K.M., Mainwaring, P.N., Tomlins, S.A., Trau, M., 2019. Merging new-age biomarkers and nanodiagnostics for precision prostate cancer management. Nat. Rev. Urol. 16 (5), 302–317.

Krishnan, S., Diagaradjane, P., Cho, S.H., 2010. Nanoparticle-mediated thermal therapy: evolving strategies for prostate cancer therapy. Int. J. Hyperth. 26 (8), 775–789.

Kroon, J., Metselaar, J.M., Storm, G., van der Pluijm, G., 2014. Liposomal nanomedicines in the treatment of prostate cancer. Cancer Treat. Rev. 40 (4), 578–584.

Kumar, A., Huo, S., Zhang, X., Liu, J., Tan, A., Li, S., et al., 2014. Neuropilin-1-targeted gold nanoparticles enhance therapeutic efficacy of platinum (IV) drug for prostate cancer treatment. ACS Nano 8 (5), 4205–4220.

Kumar, V., Toffoli, G., Rizzolio, F., 2013. Fluorescent carbon nanoparticles in medicine for cancer therapy. ACS Med. Chem. Lett. 4 (11), 1012–1013.

Lakhin, A.V., Tarantul, V.Z., Gening, L.V., 2013. Aptamers: problems, solutions, and prospects. Acta Nat. 5, 34–43.

Lee, C.H., Kantoff, P., 2019. Treatment of metastatic prostate cancer in 2018. JAMA Oncol. 5 (2), 263–264.

Lee, I.H., An, S., Yu, M.K., Kwon, H.K., Im, S.H., Jon, S., 2011. Targeted chemoimmunotherapy using drug-loaded aptamer–dendrimer bioconjugates. J. Control. Release. 155 (3), 435–441.

Lee, S.H., Shen, M.M., 2015. Cell types of origin for prostate cancer. Curr. Opin. Cell Biol. 1 (37), 35–41.

Lesniak, W.G., Boinapally, S., Banerjee, S.R., Azad, B.B., Foss, C.A., Shen, C., et al., 2019. Evaluation of PSMA-targeted PAMAM dendrimer nanoparticles in a murine model of prostate cancer. Mol. Pharm. 16 (6), 2590–2604.

Li, C.S., Harisinghani, M.G., Lin, W.C., Braschi, M., Hahn, P.F., Mueller, P.R., 2008. Enhancement characteristics of ultrasmall superparamagnetic iron oxide particle within the prostate gland in patients with primary prostate cancer. J. Comput. Assist. Tomogr. 32, 523–552.

Li, N., Xie, X., Hu, Y., He, H., Fu, X., Fang, T., et al., 2019a. Herceptin-conjugated liposomes co-loaded with doxorubicin and simvastatin in targeted prostate cancer therapy. Am. J. Transl. Res. 11 (3), 1255.

Li, Z., Zhang, W., Xing, F., 2019b. Graphene optical biosensors. Int. J. Mol. Sci. 20 (10), 2461.

Lim, J., Guan, B., Nham, K., Hao, G., Sun, X., Simanek, E.E., 2019. Tumor uptake of triazine dendri-mers decorated with four, sixteen, and sixty-four PSMA-targeted ligands: passive versus active tumor targeting. Biomolecules. 9 (9), 421.

Lin, T.Y., Guo, W., Long, Q., Ma, A., Liu, Q., Zhang, H., et al., 2016. HSP90 inhibitor encapsulated photo-theranostic nanoparticles for synergistic combination cancer therapy. Theranostics 6 (9), 1324.

Linxweiler, J., Körbel, C., Müller, A., Hammer, M., Veith, C., Bohle, R.M., et al., 2018. A novel mouse model of human prostate cancer to study intraprostatic tumor growth and the development of lymph node metastases. Prostate 78 (9), 664–675.

Littrup, P.J., Freeman-Gibb, L., Andea, A., White, M., Amerikia, K.C., Bouwman, D., et al., 2005. Cryotherapy for breast fibroadenomas. Radiology 234 (1), 63–72.

Liu, C.M., Chen, G.B., Chen, H.H., Zhang, J.B., Li, H.Z., Sheng, M.X., et al., 2019. Cancer cell membrane-cloaked mesoporous silica nanoparticles with a pH-sensitive gatekeeper for cancer treat-ment. Colloids Surf. B: Biointerfaces 1 (175), 477–486.

Liu, X., Liu, C., Chen, C., Bentobji, M., Cheillan, F.A., Piana, J.T., et al., 2014. Targeted delivery of Dicer-substrate siRNAs using a dual targeting peptide decorated dendrimer delivery system. Nanomed. Nanotechnol. Biol. Med. 10 (8), 1627–1636.

Logozzi, M., Angelini, D.F., Iessi, E., Mizzoni, D., Di Raimo, R., Federici, C., et al., 2017. Increased PSA expression on prostate cancer exosomes in in vitro condition and in cancer patients. Canc. Lett. 403, 318–329.

Makadia, H.K., Siegel, S.J., 2011. Poly lactic-co-glycolic acid (PLGA) as biodegradable controlled drug delivery carrier. Polymers 3 (3), 1377–1397.

Malek, S.J., Khoshchehreh, R., Goodarzi, N., Khoshayand, M.R., Amini, M., Atyabi, F., et al., 2014. cis-Dichlorodiamminoplatinum (II) glyconanoparticles by drug-induced ionic gelation technique tar-geted to prostate cancer: preparation, optimization and in vitro characterization. Colloids Surf. B: Biointerfaces 1 (122), 350–358.

Malla, B., Zaugg, K., Vassella, E., Aebersold, D.M., Dal Pra, A., 2017. Exosomes and exosomal MicroRNAs in prostate cancer radiation therapy. Int. J. Radiat. Oncol. 98, 982–995.

Martin, T.A., Ye, L., Sanders, A.J., Lane, J., Jiang, W.G., 2013. Cancer invasion and metastasis: molecular and cellular perspective. Madame Curie Bioscience Database [Internet]. Landes Bioscience.

McKenzie, S., Kyprianou, N., 2006. Apoptosis evasion: the role of survival pathways in prostate cancer progression and therapeutic resistance. J. Cell. Biochem. 97 (1), 18–32.

McNamara, J.O., Andrechek, E.R., Wang, Y., Viles, K.D., Rempel, R.E., Gilboa, E., et al., 2006. Cell type–specific delivery of siRNAs with aptamer-siRNA chimeras. Nat. Biotechnol. 24, 1005–1015.

Miao, L., Guo, S., Zhang, J., Kim, W.Y., Huang, L., 2014. Nanoparticles with precise ratiometric co-loading and co-delivery of gemcitabine monophosphate and cisplatin for treatment of bladder cancer. Adv. Funct. Mater. 24 (42), 6601–6611.

Miao, Z., Gao, Z., Chen, R., Yu, X., Su, Z., Wei, G., 2018. Surface-bioengineered gold nanoparticles for biomedical applications. Curr. Med. Chem. 25 (16), 1920−1944.

Milla, P., Dosio, F., Cattel, L., 2012. PEGylation of proteins and liposomes: a powerful and flexible strategy to improve the drug delivery. Curr. Drug Metab. 13 (1), 105−119.

Mishra, N., Ashique, S., Garg, A., Rai, V.K., Dua, K., Goyal, A., et al., 2022. Role of siRNA-based nanocarriers for the treatment of neurodegenerative diseases. Drug. Discov. Today 27 (5), 1431−1440.

Mondal, S., Adhikari, N., Banerjee, S., Amin, S.A., Jha, T., 2020. Matrix metalloproteinase-9 (MMP-9) and its inhibitors in cancer: a minireview. Eur. J. Med. Chem. 194, 112260.

Mukerjee, A., Vishwanatha, J.K., 2009. Formulation, characterization and evaluation of curcumin-loaded PLGA nanospheres for cancer therapy. Anticancer. Res. 29, 3867−3875.

Murray, T.B., 2021. The pathogenesis of prostate cancer. Exon Publ. 27, 29−41.

Nagpal, K., Foote, D., Tan, F., Liu, Y., Chen, P.H., Steiner, D.F., et al., 2020. Development and validation of a deep learning algorithm for Gleason grading of prostate cancer from biopsy specimens. JAMA Oncol. 6 (9), 1372−1380.

Nanjwade, B.K., Bechra, H.M., Derkar, G.K., Manvi, F.V., Nanjwade, V.K., 2009. Dendrimers: emerging polymers for drug-delivery systems. Eur. J. Pharm. Sci. 38 (3), 185−196.

Narayanan, N.K., Nargi, D., Randolph, C., Narayanan, B.A., 2009. Liposome encapsulation of curcumin and resveratrol in combination reduces prostate cancer incidence in PTEN knockout mice. Int. J. Cancer 125, 1−8.

Navone, N.M., Troncoso, P., Pisters, L.L., Goodrow, T.L., Palmer, J.L., Nichols, W.W., et al., 1993. p53 protein accumulation and gene mutation in the progression of human prostate carcinoma. JNCI: J. Natl Cancer Inst. 85 (20), 1657−1669.

Nelson, P.S., 2014. Targeting the androgen receptor in prostate cancer—a resilient foe. N. Engl. J. Med. 371 (11), 1067−1069.

Nicolosi, P., Ledet, E., Yang, S., Michalski, S., Freschi, B., O'Leary, E., et al., 2019. Prevalence of germline variants in prostate cancer and implications for current genetic testing guidelines. JAMA Oncol. 5 (4), 523−528.

Nima, Z.A., Alwbari, A.M., Dantuluri, V., Hamzah, R.N., Sra, N., Motwani, P., et al., 2017. Targeting nano drug delivery to cancer cells using tunable, multi-layer, silver-decorated gold nanorods. J. Appl. Toxicol. 37 (12), 1370−1378.

Nune, S.K., Chanda, N., Shukla, R., Katti, K., Kulkarni, R.R., Thilakavathy, S., et al., 2009. Green nanotechnology from tea: phytochemicals in tea as building blocks for production of biocompatible gold nanoparticles. J. Mater. Chem. 19, 2912.

Palys, B. (Ed.), 2019. Handbook of Graphene, Volume 6, Biosensors and Advanced Sensors, 12. John Wiley & Sons.

Pan, Q., Nie, C., Hu, Y., Yi, J., Liu, C., Zhang, J., et al., 2019. Aptamer-functionalized DNA origami for targeted codelivery of antisense oligonucleotides and doxorubicin to enhance therapy in drug-resistant cancer cells. ACS Appl. Mater. Interfaces 12 (1), 400−409.

Panda, P.K., Saraf, S., Tiwari, A., Verma, A., Raikwar, S., Jain, A., et al., 2019. Novel strategies for targeting prostate cancer. Curr. Drug. Deliv. 16 (8), 712−727.

Pantuck, A.J., Lee, D.-K., Kee, T., Wang, P., Lakhotia, S., Silverman, M.H., et al., 2018. Modulating BET bromodomain inhibitor ZEN-3694 and enzalutamide combination dosing in a metastatic prostate cancer patient using CURATE.AI, an artificial intelligence Platform. Adv. Ther. 1, 1800104.

Park, J.H., Cho, H.J., Yoon, H.Y., Yoon, I.S., Ko, S.H., Shim, J.S., et al., 2014. Hyaluronic acid derivative-coated nanohybrid liposomes for cancer imaging and drug delivery. J. Control. Release. 174, 98−108.

Pearce, A.K., Simpson, J.D., Fletcher, N.L., Houston, Z.H., Fuchs, A.V., Russell, P.J., et al., 2017. Localised delivery of doxorubicin to prostate cancer cells through a PSMA targeted hyper branched polymer theranostic. Biomaterials 141, 330−339.

Pettitt, J., Zeitlin, L., Kim, D.H., Working, C., Johnson, J.C., Bohorov, O., et al., 2013. Therapeutic intervention of Ebola virus infection in rhesus macaques with the MB-003 monoclonal antibody cocktail. Sci. Transl. Med. 5 (199).

Pothipor, C., Wiriyakun, N., Putnin, T., Ngamaroonchote, A., Jakmunee, J., Ounnunkad, K., et al., 2019. Highly sensitive biosensor based on graphene—poly (3-aminobenzoic acid) modified electrodes and porous-hollowed-silver-gold nanoparticle labelling for prostate cancer detection. Sens. Actuators B: Chem. 1 (296), 126657.

Prabhu, R.H., Patravale, V.B., Joshi, M.D., 2015. Polymeric nanoparticles for targeted treatment in oncology: current insights. Int. J. Nanomed. 10, 1001.

Price, N., Jain, V.K., Sartor, O., 2004. Docetaxel improves survival in metastatic androgen-independent prostate cancer. Clin. Prostate Cancer 3 (1), 18—20.

Quintero-Jaime, A.F., Berenguer-Murcia, Á., Cazorla-Amorós, D., Morallón, E., 2019. Carbon nanotubes modified with Au for electrochemical detection of prostate specific antigen: effect of Au nanoparticle size distribution. Front. Chem. 7, 147.

Rahme, K., Guo, J., Holmes, J.D., 2019. Bioconjugated gold nanoparticles enhance siRNA delivery in prostate cancer cells. Rna Interference and Cancer Therapy. Humana, New York, NY, pp. 291—301.

Rejinold, N.S., Muthunarayanan, M., Chennazhi, K.P., Nair, S.V., Jayakumar, R., 2011. Curcumin loaded fibrinogen nanoparticles for cancer drug delivery. J. Biomed. Nanotechnol. 7, 521—534.

Riley, T., Stolnik, S., Heald, C.R., Xiong, C.D., Garnett, M.C., Illum, L., et al., 2001. Physicochemical evaluation of nanoparticles assembled from Poly (lactic acid) − Poly (ethylene glycol)(PLA − PEG) block copolymers as drug delivery vehicles. Langmuir 17 (11), 3168—3174.

Rocha, S., Generalov, R., Pereira, M., Do, C., Peres, I., Juzenas, P., et al., 2011. Epigallocatechin gallate-loaded polysaccharide nanoparticles for prostate cancer chemoprevention. Nanomedicine 6, 79—87.

Rong, Z., Bai, Z., Li, J., Tang, H., Shen, T., Wang, Q., et al., 2019. Dual-color magnetic-quantum dot nanobeads as versatile fluorescent probes in test strip for simultaneous point-of-care detection of free and complexed prostate-specific antigen. Biosens. Bioelectron. 145, 11719.

Rosenblum, D., Joshi, N., Tao, W., Karp, J.M., Peer, D., 2018. Progress and challenges towards targeted delivery of cancer therapeutics. Nat. Commun. 9 (1), 1—2.

Sahoo, S.K., Labhasetwar, W., Ma, V., 2004. Efficacy of transferrin-conjugated paclitaxelloaded nanoparticles in a murine model of prostate cancer. Int. J. Cancer 112, 335—340.

Sakamoto, J.H., van de Ven, A.L., Godin, B., Blanco, E., Serda, R.E., Grattoni, A., et al., 2010. Enabling individualized therapy through nanotechnology. Pharmacol. Res. 62 (2), 57—89.

Sanchez-Milla, M., Munoz-Moreno, L., Sanchez-Nieves, J., Maly, M., Gomez, R., Carmena, M.J., et al., 2019. Anticancer activity of dendriplexes against advanced prostate cancer from protumoral peptides and cationic carbosilane dendrimers. Biomacromolecules 20 (3), 1224—1234.

Sanna, V., Roggio, A.M., Posadino, A.M., Cossu, A., Marceddu, S., Mariani, A., et al., 2011. Novel docetaxel-loaded nanoparticles based on poly(lactide-co-caprolactone) and poly(lactide-co-glycolide-co-caprolactone) for prostate cancer treatment: formulation, characterization, and cytotoxicity studies. Nanoscale Res. Lett. 6, 260.

Sanna, V., Sechi, M., 2012. Nanoparticle therapeutics for prostate cancer treatment. Maturitas. 73 (1), 27—32.

Schroeder, U., Sommerfeld, P., Ulrich, S., Sabel, B.A., 1998. Nanoparticle technology for delivery of drugs across the blood-brain barrier. J. Pharm. Sci. 87 (11), 1305—1307.

Seixas, N., Ravanello, B.B., Morgan, I., Kaluđerović, G.N., Wessjohann, L.A., 2019. Chlorambucil conjugated Ugi dendrimers with PAMAM-NH2 core and evaluation of their anticancer activity. Pharmaceutics. 11 (2), 59.

Senapati, S., Mahanta, A.K., Kumar, S., Maiti, P., 2018. Controlled drug delivery vehicles for cancer treatment and their performance. Signal. Transduct. Target. Ther. 3 (1), 1—9.

Sharifi, M., Hosseinali, S.H., Alizadeh, R.H., Hasan, A., Attar, F., Salihl, A., et al., 2020. Plasmonic and chiroplasmonic nanobiosensors based on gold nanoparticles. Talanta. 15 (212), 120782.

Shenoy, D.B., Amiji, M.M., 2005. Poly (ethylene oxide)-modified poly (ε-caprolactone) nanoparticles for targeted delivery of tamoxifen in breast cancer. Int. J. Pharm. 293 (1—2), 261—270.

Shepard, D.R., Dreicer, R., Garcia, J., Elson, P., Magi-Galluzzi, C., Raghavan, D., et al., 2009. Phase II trial of neoadjuvant nab-paclitaxel in high-risk patients with prostate cancer undergoing radical prostatectomy. J. Urol. 181 (4), 1672—1677.

Shetty, Y., Prabhu, P., Prabhakar, B., 2019. Emerging vistas in theranostic medicine. Int. J. Pharma. 558, 29—42.

Shi, X., Sun, J., Li, H., Lin, H., Xie, W., Li, J., et al., 2020. Antitumor efficacy of interferon-γ-modified exosomal vaccine in prostate cancer. Prostate 80, 811−823.

Shukla, R., Chanda, N., Zambre, A., Upendran, A., Katti, K., Kulkarni, R.-R., et al., 2012. Laminin receptor specific therapeutic gold nanoparticles (198AuNP-EGCg) show efficacy in treating prostate cancer. Proc. Natl Acad. Sci. U. S. A. 109, 12426−12431.

Siddiqui, I.A., Adhami, V.M., Bharali, D.J., Hafeez, B.B., Asim, M., Khwaja, S.I., et al., 2009. Introducing nanochemoprevention as a novel approach for cancer control: proof of principle with green tea polyphenol epigallocatechin-3-gallate. Cancer Res. 69, 1712−1716.

Siegel, R.L., Miller, K.D., Fedewa, S.A., Ahnen, D.J., Meester, R.G., Barzi, A., et al., 2017. Colorectal cancer statistics, 2017. CA: A Cancer J. Clin 67 (3), 177−193.

Singh, S., Gill, A.A., Nlooto, M., Karpoormath, R., 2019. Prostate cancer biomarkers detection using nanoparticles based electrochemical biosensors. Biosens. Bioelectron. 137, 213−221.

Singh, S.K., Lillard Jr, J.W., Singh, R., 2018. Reversal of drug resistance by planetary ball milled (PBM) nanoparticle loaded with resveratrol and docetaxel in prostate cancer. Cancer Lett. 28 (427), 49−62.

Soares, J.C., Soares, A.C., Rodrigues, V.C., Melendez, M.E., Santos, A.C., Faria, E.F., et al., 2019. Detection of the prostate cancer biomarker PCA3 with electrochemical and impedance-based biosensors. ACS Appl, Mater. Interfaces 11, 46645−46650.

Sriraman, S.K., Aryasomayajula, B., Torchilin, V.P., 2014. Barriers to drug delivery in solid tumors. Tissue Barriers 2 (3), e29528.

Su, Y.L., Hu, S.H., 2018. Functional nanoparticles for tumor penetration of therapeutics. Pharmaceutics 10 (4), 193.

Sun, Q., Ojha, T., Kiessling, F., Lammers, T., Shi, Y., 2017. Enhancing tumor penetration of nanomedicines. Biomacromolecules. 18 (5), 1449−1459.

Taghdisi, S.M., Danesh, N.M., Ramezani, M., Yazdian-Robati, R., Abnous, K., 2018. A novel AS1411 aptamer-based three-way junction pocket DNA nanostructure loaded with doxorubicin for targeting cancer cells in vitro and in vivo. Mol. Pharm. 15 (5), 1972−1978.

Talelli, M., Rijcken, C.J., Lammers, T., et al., 2009. Superparamagnetic iron oxide nanoparticles encapsulated in biodegradable thermosensitive polymeric micelles: toward a targeted nanomedicine suitable for image-guided drug delivery. Langmuir 25, 2060−2067.

Thakor, A.S., Gambhir, S.S., 2013. Nanooncology: the future of cancer diagnosis and therapy. CA: A Cancer J. Clin 63 (6), 395−418.

Thakur, A., Mishra, A.P., Panda, B., Rodríguez, D.C.S., Gaurav, I., Majhi, B., 2020. Application of artificial intelligence in pharmaceutical and biomedical studies. Curr. Pharm. Des. 26, 3569−3578.

Thienger, P., Rubin, M.A., 2021. Prostate cancer hijacks the microenvironment. Nat. Cell Biol. 23 (1), 3−5. 2021.

Tian, J., Guo, F., Chen, Y., Li, Y., Yu, B., Li, Y., 2019. Nanoliposomal formulation encapsulating celecoxib and genistein inhibiting COX-2 pathway and Glut-1 receptors to prevent prostate cancer cell proliferation. Cancer Lett. 28 (448), 1−10.

Tian, J.-Y., Guo, F.-J., Zheng, G.-Y., Ahmad, A., 2017. Prostate cancer: updates on current strategies for screening, diagnosis and clinical implications of treatment modalities. Carcinogenesis 39 (3), 307−317.

Tsai, Y.J., Chen, B.H., 2016. Preparation of catechin extracts and nanoemulsions from green tea leaf waste and their inhibition effect on prostate cancer cell PC-3. Int. J. Nanomed. 11, 1907.

Van Hemelrijck, M., Feller, A., Garmo, H., Valeri, F., Korol, D., Dehler, S., et al., 2014. Is there an increased risk of second primary malignancy after diagnosis of thyroid cancer? PLoS One e102596.

Wallace, A.M., Hoh, C.K., Vera, D.R., Darrah, D.D., Schulteis, G., 2003. Lymphoseek: a molecular radiopharmaceutical for sentinel node detection. Ann. Surg. Oncol. 10 (5), 531−538.

Wang, A.Z., Bagalkot, V., Vasilliou, C.C., Gu, F., Alexis, F., Zhang, L., et al., 2008. Superparamagnetic iron oxide nanoparticle−aptamer bioconjugates for combined prostate cancer imaging and therapy. ChemMedChem 3 (9), 1311−1315.

Wang, H., Zhang, Y., Yu, H., Wu, D., Ma, H., Li, H., et al., 2013. Label-free electrochemical immunosensor for prostate-specific antigen based on silver hybridized mesoporous silica nanoparticles. Anal. Biochem. 434 (1), 123−127.

Wang, H.M., Huang, X.Q., Wang, A.J., Luo, X., Liu, W.D., Yuan, P.X., et al., 2020. Construction of efficient "on-off-on" fluorescence aptasensor for ultrasensitive detection of prostate specific antigen via covalent energy transfer between g-C3N4 quantum dots and palladium triangular plates. Analytica Chim. Acta 1 (1104), 53–59.

Wang, J., Sui, M., Fan, W., 2010. Nanoparticles for tumor-targeted therapies and their pharmacokinetics. Curr. Drug. Metab. 11 (2), 129–141.

Wang, Z., Hao, Z., Yu, S., Moraes, D., Suh, C.G., Zhao, L.H., et al., 2019. An ultraflexible and stretchable aptameric graphene nanosensor for biomarker detection and monitoring. Adv. Funct. Mater. 29 (44), 1905202.

Wang, Z.A., Shen, M.M., 2011. Revisiting the concept of cancer stem cells in prostate cancer. Oncogene 30 (11), 1261–1271.

Weaver, B.A., 2014. How taxol/paclitaxel kills cancer cells. Mol. Biol. Cell. 25, 2677–2681.

Webster, T.J., 2006. Nanomedicine: what's in a definition? Int. J. Nanomed. 1 (2), 115.

Weissleder, R., 2001. A clearer vision for in vivo imaging. Nat. Biotech. 19, 316–317.

Whitesides, G.M., Mathias, J.P., Seto, C.T., 1991. Molecular self-assembly and nanochemistry: a chemical strategy for the synthesis of nanostructures. Science 254 (5036), 1312–1319.

Wicki, A., Witzigmann, D., Balasubramanian, V., Huwyler, J., 2015. Nanomedicine in cancer therapy: challenges, opportunities, and clinical applications. J. Control. Release. 200, 138–157.

Williams, R.M., Lee, C., Heller, D.A., 2018. A fluorescent carbon nanotube sensor detects the metastatic prostate cancer biomarker uPA. Acs Sens. 3 (9), 1838–1845.

Wolinsky, J.B., Colson, Y.L., Grinstaff, M.W., 2012. Local drug delivery strategies for cancer treatment: gels, nanoparticles, polymeric films, rods, and wafers. J. Control. Release. 159 (1), 14–26.

Wu, G., Datar, R.H., Hansen, K.M., Thundat, T., Cote, R.J., Majumdar, A., 2001. Bioassay of prostate-specific antigen (PSA) using microcantilevers. Nat. Biotechnol. 19 (9), 856–860.

Wu, L.P., Ficker, M., Christensen, J.B., Trohopoulos, P.N., Moghimi, S.M., 2015. Dendrimers in medicine: therapeutic concepts and pharmaceutical challenges. Bioconjug. Chem. 26 (7), 1198–1211.

Wu, L.P., Wang, D., Li, Z., 2020. Grand challenges in nanomedicine. Mater. Sci. Eng.: C. 1 (106), 110302.

Wu, X., Zhang, F., Chen, R., Zheng, W., Yang, X., 2014. Recent advances in imaging-guided interventions for prostate cancers. Cancer Lett. 349 (2), 114–119.

Xia, Q., Gong, C., Gu, F., Wang, Z., Hu, C., Zhang, L., et al., 2018. Functionalized multi-walled carbon nanotubes for targeting delivery of immunostimulatory CpG oligonucleotides against prostate cancer. J. Biomed. Nanotechnol. 14 (9), 1613–1626.

Xiao, Z., Levy-Nissenbaum, E., Alexis, F., Lupták, A., Teply, B.A., Chan, J.M., et al., 2012. Engineering of targeted nanoparticles for cancer therapy using internalizing aptamers isolated by cell-uptake selection. ACS Nano 6 (1), 696–704.

Xie, J., Lee, S., Chen, X., 2010. Nanoparticle-based theranostic agents. Adv. Drug Deliv. Rev. 62 (11), 1064–1079.

Xu, X., Dickey, D.D., Chen, S.-J., Giangrande, P.H., 2016. Structural computational modeling of RNA aptamers. Methods 103, 175–179.

Yallapu, M.M., Dobberpuhl, M.R., Maher, D.M., Jaggi, M., Chauhan, S.C., 2012. Design of curcumin loaded cellulose nanoparticles for prostate cancer. Curr. Drug Metabol. 13, 120–128.

Yang, H.W., Hua, M.Y., Liu, H.L., Tsai, R.Y., Chuang, C.K., Chu, P.C., et al., 2012. Cooperative dual-activity targeted nanomedicine for specific and effective prostate cancer therapy. ACS Nano. 6 (2), 1795–1805.

Yeh, C.Y., Hsiao, J.K., Wang, Y.P., Lan, C.H., Wu, H.C., 2016. Peptide-conjugated nanoparticles for targeted imaging and therapy of prostate cancer. Biomaterials 1 (99), 1–5.

Yoon, H.J., Kozminsky, M., Nagrath, S., 2014. Emerging role of nanomaterials in circulating tumor cell isolation and analysis. ACS Nano 8 (3), 1995–2017.

Zhang, J., Wang, L., You, X., Xian, T., Wu, J., Pang, J., 2019. Nanoparticle therapy for prostate cancer: overview and perspectives. Curr. Top. Med. Chem. 19 (1), 57–73.

Zhang, W., Garg, S., Eldi, P., Zhou, F.H., Johnson, I.R., Brooks, D.A., et al., 2016. Targeting prostate cancer cells with genetically engineered polypeptide-based micelles displaying gastrin-releasing peptide. Int. J. Pharm. 513 (1–2), 270–279.

Zhou, M., Li, L., Li, L., Lin, X., Wang, F., Li, Q., et al., 2019. Overcoming chemotherapy resistance via simultaneous drug-efflux circumvention and mitochondrial targeting. Acta Pharm. Sin. B 9 (3), 615–625.

Zhou, Y., Yang, J., Kopeček, J., 2012. Selective inhibitory effect of HPMA copolymer-cyclopamine conjugate on prostate cancer stem cells. Biomaterials 33 (6), 1863–1872.

Zhou, Y., Yang, J., Zhang, R., Kopeček, J., 2015. Combination therapy of prostate cancer with HPMA copolymer conjugates containing PI3K/mTOR inhibitor and docetaxel. Eur. J. Pharm. Biopharm. 1 (89), 107–115.

Zhu, J., Huang, H., Dong, S., Ge, L., Zhang, Y., 2014. Progress in aptamer-mediated drug delivery vehicles for cancer targeting and its implications in addressing chemotherapeutic challenges. Theranostics 4, 931–944.

Zu, Y., Yuan, S., Zhao, X., Zhang, Y., Zhang, X., Jiang, R., 2009. Preparation, activity and targeting ability evaluation in vitro on folate mediated epigallocatechin-3-gallate albumin nanoparticles. Yao Xue Xue Bao 44, 525–531.

Index

Note: Page numbers followed by "*f*" and "*t*" refer to figures and tables, respectively.

Printed in the United States
by Baker & Taylor Publisher Services